Lecture Notes in Information Systems and Organisation

Volume 2

For further volumes:
http://www.springer.com/series/11237

Lecture Notes in Information Systems and Organisation

Volume 2

Series Editors

Richard Baskerville
Marco De Marco
Nancy Pouloudi
Paolo Spagnoletti
Dov Te'eni
Jan vom Brocke
Robert Winter

For further volumes:
http://www.springer.com/series/11237

Paolo Spagnoletti
Editor

Organizational Change and Information Systems

Working and Living Together in New Ways

Springer

Editor
Paolo Spagnoletti
The Research Center on Information
Systems (CeRSI)
LUISS Guido Carli
Rome
Italy

ISSN 2195-4968 ISSN 2195-4976 (electronic)
ISBN 978-3-642-37227-8 ISBN 978-3-642-37228-5 (eBook)
DOI 10.1007/978-3-642-37228-5
Springer Heidelberg New York Dordrecht London

Library of Congress Control Number: 2013935768

Printed on acid-free paper

Springer is part of Springer Science+Business Media (www.springer.com)

Program Committee

Rocco Agrifoglio	University of Naples Parthenope
Daniela Baglieri	University of Messina
Peter Bednar	University of Portsmouth
Alessio Maria Braccini	University of Tuscia
Roberto Candiotto	University of Piemonte Orientale
Paolo Depaoli	University of Urbino
Massimo Magni	University of Milan Bocconi
Daniela Mancini	University of Naples Parthenope
Marcello Martinez	Second University of Naples
Daniele Mascia	Catholic University of the Sacred Heart
Concetta Metallo	University of Naples Parthenope
Michele Missikoff	IASI-CNR
Lapo Mola	University of Verona
Daniel Muzio	University of Manchester
Andrea Resca	LUISS Guido Carli University
Cecilia Rossignoli	University of Verona
Laura Tarantino	University of L'Aquila
Francesco Virili	University of Cassino
Robert Winter	University of St. Gallen
Stefano Za	LUISS Guido Carli University

Foreword

The IX Conference of the Italian chapter of AIS was held in Roma at the Università Cattolica del Sacro Cuore on 28–29 September 2012. The conference presented a number of interesting research works around the conference topic, Organization change and Information Systems: Working and living together in new ways. This book contains a selection of the best papers presented at the conference.

While in other countries scholars often refer to their research area as "management of information systems", in Italy we tend to use the phrase "organization of information systems." It is a clear recognition of how studies of ICT in organizations are a core part of the organizational studies discipline in our country. In fact, such phenomenon remarks the originality of the Italian experience in terms of integration between two communities that abroad are, quite often, separate. In this respect, therefore, Italy is in a sense "ahead" if compared to other countries, and shows a significant strength and a distinctive feature of our joint endeavor.

If we go back to the mid-1990s, the Italian way to the study of information systems started to be closely related to the organizational studies domain. In fact, with the entry of leading figures such as Marco De Marco, Alessandro D'Atri, Gianni Jacucci, and Claudio Ciborra the community of organizational scholars has recognized studies on information systems as part of the core content of the organizational discipline. Alessandro and Claudio are no longer among us and our thoughts go to their memory as leading and passionate academics.

In the past 15 years, a number of changes affected both the academia and the practitioners arenas. The advent of Internet and ERP technologies, the continuous innovation in ICT (Wi-Fi, RFID, social networks), the availability of wide amount of data of corporate interest, new organizational forms driven by technology (virtual enterprises, network organizations,...) are only a few drivers that have been greatly affecting the business landscape and the way of working in organizations. New teaching opportunities and training courses have therefore been developed to meet such changes. New professional figures were needed to create interfaces between technology vendors and organizational designers. University courses were established in order to respond to such an increasing demand.

All of these novelties gave rise to new research approaches capable of shedding light on the variety and richness of the phenomena taking place in the business world. For too many years technology-oriented scholars had underestimated the importance of the organizational consequences of technology, leading to implementation failures and to poor business results. In fact, on the research side, the rapidity of technological progress was a powerful driver of change and a matter of concern for organizational scholars. It has been an important element that kept organizational studies updated and aligned with the evolution of the business world.

A number of theories and research paradigms have therefore been launched to interpret this evolving reality. Organizational versus technological imperative, transaction cost economics applied to information systems, knowledge-based theories of organization, social constructivism, critical management studies, are only a few of the research approaches of the past two decades.

The Italian community has greatly contributed to the scientific debate by hosting a number of international conferences, such as ECIS 2003 in Napoli, ECIS 2009 in Verona, the annual ItAIS meetings (the first ItAIS was held at University of Napoli Federico II in 2004), ALPIS, MCIS 2007, and the forthcoming ICIS 2013 in Milano. On these occasions significant advancements have been brought about in the scientific debate and have explored established research practices and institutional arrangements in new and often radical ways.

Many Workshops of the Italian scholars of Organizational studies (WOA) have included in their programs sections and tracks on information systems, and a growing number of Italian scholars have participated in outstanding committees and scientific committees of international conferences, journal special issues, and edited book collections.

I firmly believe that the ItAIS community represents a stimulating environment where to debate controversial topics within organizational studies. I am very glad that we have managed to establish a sound and fertile relationship among organizational and information systems scholars, two cultures that draw on an ultimate common goal: letting organizations of the twenty-first century work in a better way.

R. Mercurio
Università di Napoli Federico II

Contents

Contributors

Rocco Agrifoglio Department of Management, Parthenope University, Naples, Italy, e-mail: agrifoglio@uniparthenope.it

Enrico Angioni University of Cagilari, Cagilari, Italy

Pasquale Ardimento Department of Informatics, University of Bari Aldo Moro, Bari, Italy; SER and Practices, Spin-off of the University of Bari Aldo Moro, Bari, Italy, e-mail: ardimento@di.uniba.it

Fabrizio D'Ascenzo Department of Management, University of Rome La Sapienza, Rome, Italy, e-mail: fabrizio.dascenzo@uniroma1.it

Alessandro Avenali Department of Computer, Control and Management Engineering "Antonio Ruberti", Sapienza University of Rome, Rome, Italy, e-mail: alessandro.avenali@uniroma1.it

Daniela Baglieri University of Messina, Messina, Italy, e-mail: dbaglieri@unime.it

Gustavo Barresi University of Messina, Piazza Pugliatti I, Messina, Italy, e-mail: barresig@unime.it

Peter M. Bednar School of Computing, University of Portsmouth, Portsmouth, UK, e-mail: peter.bednar@port.ac.uk

Francesco Bellini Department of Management, University of Rome La Sapienza, Rome, Italy, e-mail: francesco.bellini@uniroma1.it

Massimo Bianchi Forlì Faculty of Economics, Bologna University, Forlì, Italy, e-mail: massimo.bianchi@unibo.it

Devis Bianchini Dipartimento di Ingegneria dell'Informazione, Università di Brescia, via Branze 38, 25123 Brescia, Italy

Guido Boella Università di Torino, Torino, Italy, e-mail: guido@di.unito.it

Nicola Boffoli Department of Informatics, University of Bari, Bari, Italy; Software Engineering Research and Practices (SER and Practices), Spin-off of the University of Bari, Bari, Italy

Francesco Bolici DIAM-Orgalb, IESEG Business School, Università degli Studi di Cassino e del Lazio Meridionale, Paris-Lille, Italy

Riccardo Bonazzi HEC, Information Systems Institute, University of Lausanne, Lausanne, Switzerland, e-mail: riccardo.bonazzi@unil.ch

Alessio Maria Braccini Dipartimento di Economia e Impresa, Università degli Studi della Tuscia, Viterbo, Italy, e-mail: abraccini@unitus.it

Giovanni Bronzetti University of Calabria, Calabria, Italy, e-mail: bronzetti@exnet.it

Francesca Cabiddu University of Cagilari, Cagilari, Italy

Roberto Candiotto University of Eastern Piedmont, Novara, Italy, e-mail: roberto. candiotto@eco.unipmn.it

Paolo Canonico Department of Management, University of Naples Federico II, Naples, Italy, e-mail: pcanonic@unina.it

Franca Cantoni Università Cattolica del Sacro Cuore, Piacenza, Italy, e-mail: franca.cantoni@unicatt.it

Leonardo Caporarello SDA Bocconi School of Management, Learning Lab, Milan, Italy, e-mail: leonardo.caporarello@unibocconi.it

Andrea Carugati Aarhus University, Business and Social Sciences, Aarhus, Denmark, e-mail: andreac@asb.dk

Rosanna Cassino Università di Salerno, Salerno, Italy, e-mail: rcassino@unisa.it

Cristiano Castelfranchi ISTC-CNR, Rome, Italy

Daniela Castelluccia Department of Informatics, University of Bari, Bari, Italy, e-mail: daniela.castelluccia@uniba.it

Maurizio Cavallari Università cattolica, Milano, Italy, e-mail: maurizio. cavallari@unicatt.it

Fabrizio Cesaroni Department of Business Administration, Carlos III University, Madrid, Spain, e-mail: fabrizio.cesaroni@uc3m.es

Domenico Consoli Department of Economics, Society and Politics, University of Urbino, Urbino, Italy, e-mail: domenico.consoli@uniurb.it

Vito Nicola Convertini Department of Informatics, University of Bari Aldo Moro, Bari, Italy, e-mail: convertini@di.uniba.it

Michela Cortini Università di Chieti, Pescara, Italy

Renata Paola Dameri Department of Business Administration, University of Genova, Via Vivaldi 2, 16126 Genoa, Italy, e-mail: dameri@economia.unige.it

Valeria De Antonellis Dipartimento di Ingegneria dell'Informazione, Università di Brescia, via Branze 38, 25123 Brescia, Italy

Ernesto De Nito Department of Scienze Giuridiche, Storiche, Economiche e Sociali, University Magna Græcia of Catanzaro, Catanzaro, Italy, e-mail: denito@unicz.it

Lasanthi De Silva University of Colombo, Colombo, Sri Lanka, e-mail: lnc@ucsc.lk

Capucine Defert IESEG School of Management, 3 Rue de la Digue, 59000 Lille, France, e-mail: capucine.defert@ieseg.fr

Walter Del Prete E-leva s.r.l., Pesaro, Italy, e-mail: walter@e-leva.com

Paolo Depaoli Università degli Studi di Urbino "Carlo Bo", Urbino, Italy

Angela Dettori University of Cagliari, Cagliari, Italy, e-mail: angela.dettori@libero.it

Pasquale Di Giovanni Università di Salerno, Salerno, Italy, e-mail: pdigiovanni@unisa.it

Maria Chiara Di Guardo University of Cagliari, Cagliari, Italy

Claudia Dossena Faculty of Economics, University of Pavia, Pavia, Italy, e-mail: claudia.dossena@eco.unipv.it

Gianfranco Ennas University of Cagliari, Cagliari, Italy

Tommaso Federici Dipartimento di Economia e Impresa, Università degli Studi della Tuscia, Viterbo, Italy, e-mail: tfederici@unitus.it

Daniela Fogli Dipartimento di Ingegneria dell'Informazione, Università degli Studi di Brescia, Brescia, Italy, e-mail: fogli@ing.unibs.it

Alberto Francesconi Faculty of Economics, University of Pavia, Pavia, Italy, e-mail: afrancesconi@eco.unipv.it

Mariagrazia Fugini DEI and DIG Departments, Politecnico di Milano, Milan, Italy, e-mail: fugini@elet.polimi.it

Silvia Gandini Department "Studi per l'Economia e l'Impresa", University of Eastern Piedmont, Novara, Italy, e-mail: silvia.gandini@eco.unipmn.it

Alessandra Ghi Department of Management, University of Rome La Sapienza, Rome, Italy, e-mail: alessandra.ghi@uniroma1.it

Antonio Giangreco IESEG School of Management (LEM–CNRS), Lille, France, e-mail: a.giangreco@ieseg.fr

Athula Ginige University of Western Sydney, Sydney, Australia, e-mail: a.ginige@uws.edu.au

Tamara Ginige Australian Catholic University, North Sydney, Australia, e-mail: Tamara.Ginige@acu.edu.au

Ernestina Giudici Department of Business Economics, University of Cagliari, Cagliari, Italy, e-mail: giudici@unica.it

Luca Giustiniano DIM, Luiss Guido Carli University, Rome, Italy

Frank Goethals IESEG School of Management, 3 Rue de la Digue, 59000 Lille, France, e-mail: f.goethals@ieseg.fr

Jeevani Goonethilaka University of Colombo, Colombo, Sri Lanka, e-mail: jsg@ucsc.lk

Pier Luigi Guida Rete Ferroviaria Italiana, Rome, Italy, e-mail: pl.guida@rfi.it

Camilla Guttormsen University of Agder, Agder, Norway, e-mail: milla_g_88@hotmail.com

Amaury Hocquet IESEG School of Management, 3 Rue de la Digue, 59000 Lille, France, e-mail: amaury.hocquet@ieseg.fr

Llio Humphreys Università di Torino, Torino, Italy; University of Luxembourg, Luxembourg, Luxembourg, e-mail: humphreys@di.unito.it

Mario Pezzillo Iacono Department of Economics, Second University of Naples, Capua, Italy, e-mail: mario.pezzilloiacono@unina2.it

Stefania Laudonia Dipartimento di Entomologia e Zoologia Agraria "Filippo Silvestri", University of Naples "Federico II", Portici, Naples, Italy, e-mail: laudonia@unina.it

Luigi Lepore Department of Management, Parthenope University, Naples, Italy, e-mail: lepore@uniparthenope.it

Paul Leroy IESEG School of Management, 3 Rue de la Digue, 59000 Lille, France, e-mail: paul.leroy@ieseg.fr

Johan Maes IESEG School of Management, 3 Rue de la Digue, 59000 Lille, France, e-mail: j.maes@ieseg.fr

Piercarlo Maggiolini DEI and DIG Departments, Politecnico di Milano, Milan, Italy, e-mail: piercarlo.maggiolini@polimi.it

Gianluigi Mangia Department of Management, University of Naples Federico II, Naples, Italy, e-mail: mangia@unina.it

Marina Margiotta Dipartimento di Entomologia e Zoologia Agraria "Filippo Silvestri", University of Naples "Federico II", Portici, Naples, Italy, e-mail: ma.margiotta@studenti.unina.it

Marcello Martinez Department of Economics, Second University of Naples, Capua, Italy, e-mail: marcello.martinez@unina2.it

Francesca Marzo ISTC-CNR, Rome, Italy; CeRSI LUISS Guido Carli, Rome, Italy

Giorgio Matteucci Department of Computer, Control and Management Engineering "Antonio Ruberti", Sapienza University of Rome, Rome, Italy, e-mail: giorgio.matteucci@uniroma1.it

Romilda Mazzotta University of Calabria, Calabria, Italy, e-mail: romilda.mazzotta@unical.it

Michele Melchiori Dipartimento di Ingegneria dell'Informazione, Università di Brescia, via Branze 38, 25123 Brescia, Italy

Claudia Melis University of Cagliari, Cagliari, Italy, e-mail: cmclaudiamelis@gmail.com

Concetta Metallo Department of Management, Parthenope University, Naples, Italy, e-mail: metallo@uniparthenope.it

Enrico Maria Mosconi Dipartimento di Economia e Impresa, Università degli Studi della Tuscia, Viterbo, Italy, e-mail: enrico.mosconi@unitus.it

Gianmario Motta Dipartimento di Ingegneria Industriale e dell'Informazione, University of Pavia, Via Ferrata 1, Pavia, Italy, e-mail: motta05@unipv.it

Hanne Westh Nicolajsen Roskilde University & Aalborg University, Copenhagen, Denmark, e-mail: westh@hum.aau.dk

Fabio Nonino Department of Computer, Control and Management Engineering "Antonio Ruberti", Sapienza University of Rome, Rome, Italy, e-mail: fabio.nonino@uniroma1.it

Luigi Orsi Department of Economics, Management and Quantitative Methods and TTO "UNIMITT", University of Milan, Milan, Italy, e-mail: luigi.orsi@unimi.it.

Michela Piccarozzi Dipartimento Economia e Impresa (D.E.Im), University of Tuscia, Viterbo, Italy, e-mail: piccarozzi@unitus.it

Antonio Piccinno Dipartimento di Informatica, Università degli Studi di Bari, Bari, Italy, e-mail: piccinno@di.uniba.it

Stefano Poponi Dipartimento di Economia e Impresa, Università degli Studi della Tuscia, Viterbo, Italy, e-mail: poponi@unitus.it

Walter Del Prete E-leva s.r.l., Pesaro, Italy, e-mail: walter@e-leva.com

Marco Romano Università di Salerno, Salerno, Italy, e-mail: marromano@unisa.it

Cecilia Rossignoli Business Administration Department, University of Verona, Verona, Italy, e-mail: cecilia.rossignoli@univr.it

Daniele Sacco Dipartimento di Ingegneria Industriale e dell'Informazione, University of Pavia, Via Ferrata 1, Pavia, Italy, e-mail: daniele.sacco01@ateneopv.it

Øystein Sæbø University of Agder, Agder, Norway, e-mail: Oystein.Sabo@uia.no

Giacomo Sarchioni SDA Bocconi School of Management, Learning Lab, Milan, Italy, e-mail: giacomo.sarchioni@gmail.com

Giuseppe Scaratti Università Cattolica del Sacro Cuore, Milan, Italy

Ada Scupola Roskilde University & Aalborg University, Copenhagen, Denmark, e-mail: ada@ruc.dk

Antonio Sebastiano Università Carlo Cattaneo- LIUC, Castellanza, Italy, e-mail: asebastiano@liuc.it

Monica Sebillo Università di Salerno, Salerno, Italy, e-mail: msebillo@unisa.it

Cecilia Silvestri Dipartimento di Economia e Impresa, Università degli Studi della Tuscia, Viterbo, Italy, e-mail: c.silvestri@unitus.it

Paolo Spagnoletti The Research Center on Information Systems (CeRSI), LUISS Guido Carli, Rome, Italy, e-mail: pspagnoletti@luiss.it

Francesca Spagnoli Department of Management, University of Rome La Sapienza, Rome, Italy, e-mail: francesca.s@uniroma1.it

Laura Tampieri Forlì Faculty of Economics, Bologna University, Forlì, Italy, e-mail: laura.tampieri@unibo.it

Laura Tarantino University of L'Aquila, L'Aquila, Italy, e-mail: laura.tarantino@univaq.it

Genoveffa Tortora Università di Salerno, Salerno, Italy, e-mail: tortora@unisa.it

Valeria Traversi Department of Management, University of Rome La Sapienza, Rome, Italy, e-mail: valeria.traversi@uniroma1.it

Maurizio Tucci University of Salerno, Fisciano, SA, Italy, e-mail: mtucci@unisa.it

Ramon Salvador Vallès ETSEIB, Universitat Politècnica de Catalunya, Barcelona, Spain, e-mail: ramon.salvador@upc.edu

Leendert Van der Torre University of Luxembourg, Luxembourg, Luxembourg, e-mail: leon.vandertorre@uni.lu

Luisa Varriale Department of Management, Parthenope University, Naples, Italy, e-mail: Luisa.varriale@uniparthenope.it

Massimo Villari University of Messina, Piazza Pugliatti I, Messina, Italy, e-mail: mvillari@unime.it

Giuseppe Visaggio Department of Informatics, University of Bari Aldo Moro, Bari, Italy; Software Engineering Research and Practices (SER and Practices), Spin-off of the University of Bari, Bari, Italy, e-mail: visaggio@uniba.it

Giuliana Vitiello Università di Salerno, Salerno, Italy, e-mail: gvitiello@unisa.it

Christine Welch Portsmouth Business School, University of Portsmouth, Portsmouth, UK, e-mail: christine.welch@port.ac.uk

Gihan Wikramanayake University of Colombo, Colombo, Sri Lanka, e-mail: gnw@ucsc.lk

Stefano Za CeRSI, LUISS Guido Carli University, Rome, Italy

Introduction

Paolo Spagnoletti

The 2012 ItAIS[1] ninth conference, from which this book is titled, attracted contributions far beyond the Italian IS community. In fact, the 202 authors—whose 86 papers were selected for presentation at the conference by means of a double-blind review process—include researchers from Italy and from more than 16 countries of 5 continents (i.e. Australia, France, South Africa, Sri Lanka, etc.). Moreover, the 17 tracks of the conference addressed many aspects of the relationship between "Organizational Change and Information Systems" and the contributions included in this book are signed by researchers working in different disciplines: organization, management, accounting, human-computer interaction, knowledge management, IS design, IS development, and IT governance studies. Authors have considered ItAIS as a suitable and stimulating arena for sharing and enriching their research endeavors within, and often beyond, their primary areas of interest. The outcome of the conference was consistent with its subtitle: "working and living together in new ways" since different backgrounds and perspectives shed light on the multi-faceted relationship between organizations and information systems.

Almost two decades after the establishment of the majority of IS basket journals[2] and one decade after the establishment of ItAIS, the IX edition of the Italian conference has been an opportunity to comment on the achievements of the community and to discuss the challenges ahead within the international debate. The closing plenary session was devoted to consider the main trends emerging

[1] ItAIS is the Italian Chapter of the Association for Information Systems, www.aisnet.org.

[2] AIS has identified a "basket" of 8 journals that are recognized as top journals in the field. These are listed below in chronological order starting from to the oldest (in parenthesis the starting year): *MIS Quarterly* (1977), *Journal of MIS* (1984), *Journal of Information Technology* (1986), *Information Systems Journal* and *Information Systems Research* (1990), *European Journal of Information Systems* and *Journal of Strategic Information Systems* (1991), *Journal of AIS* (2000).

P. Spagnoletti (✉)
Center for Research on Information Systems (CeRSI), Luiss Guido Carli University, Rome, Italy
e-mail: pspagnoletti@luiss.it

P. Spagnoletti (ed.), *Organizational Change and Information Systems*, Lecture Notes in Information Systems and Organisation 2, DOI: 10.1007/978-3-642-37228-5_1,

from the analysis of the papers that have been presented at ItAIS in the last three years. First, there is an increasing presence of contributions from the managerial disciplines as opposed to the engineering and computer science papers. Second, in most of the contributions there is a strong focus on organizational aspects. Third, change in the track list shows the evolutionary character of the conference: for example, the track on "e-Business, Communities, and Social Networks" replaced "e-Service", a track that was introduced in 2010.

Other interesting comments can be made if the papers are positioned on the map of 'theories-in-use' by IS researchers described in a recent essay [1] published in the 25th anniversary special issue of the Journal of Information Technology. Allen Lee[3] makes a retrospective and prospective examination of five foundational concepts: 'information', 'systems', 'theory', 'organization', and 'relevance'. The result of this exercise is designing the contour of a discipline where 'information' includes syntax, representation, and adaptation besides the traditional data view. A 'systems' discipline that focuses on ties and interfaces instead of single organizational or technical subsystems. A research area where the notion of 'relevance' is not only referred to scientific knowledge (*epistêmê*) but takes also into account the *technê* and *pronêsis* of IS professionals, managers, executives, and consultants. A field whose theories go beyond the explaining and predicting goals by including also design and action as final objectives. Finally, a discipline in which the term 'organizational' is not used interchangeably with 'social', 'group', 'behavioral', and 'human' and monolithically referred to any and all people-related issues but that recognizes the importance of a meso-level of analysis.

Although a thorough examination of theories-in-use by ItAIS authors is beyond the scope of this introduction, the results of a preliminary analysis, is depicted in Fig. 1 and is built on the abstracts of the five tracks that attracted more papers in the last three years. Among the five foundational concepts mentioned above, the meso-level and design orientation have been adopted as dimensions for evaluating the theories-in-use with respect to 'organization' and 'theory' respectively. Abstracts of papers selected in these tracks have been attributed a score between −5 and +5 according to the extent to which they correspond to the ideal typical theories-in-use in the Lee's classification. Results are shown in the two-dimensional map in the figure.

Contributions from the human-computer interaction and from the more organizational[4] tracks are intuitively positioned in the right/lower corner and in the left/upper corner respectively. This result reflects both the explanatory and predictive nature of organization studies and the design orientation of human-computer interaction studies in which the individual lens prevails over the collective one. On the contrary, both management and accounting contributions show a better balance

[3] Allen S. Lee is former Editor-in-Chief of MIS Quarterly and founding Editor of MIS Quarterly Executive.

[4] Tracks titled "Organizational change and impact of ICT" and "New ways to work and interact via the internet" attract most of the traditional organizational works.

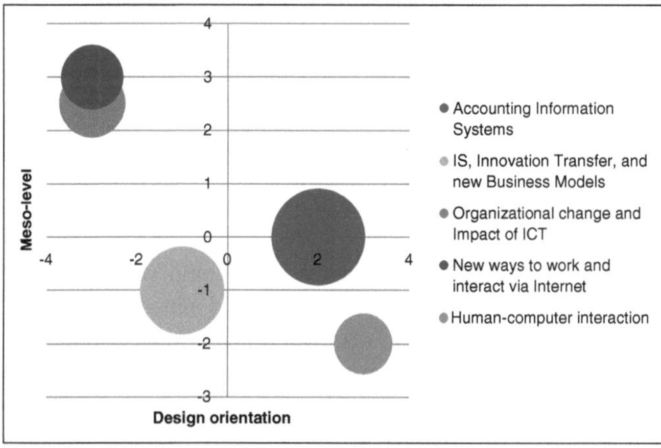

Fig. 1 Positioning of ItAIS 2012 contributions

of theories-in-use and therefore their position is closer to the center of the map. Since none of the tracks is positioned in the left/lower corner, the community shows a behavior similar to the one envisaged by Allen Lee.

This achievement is coherent with the research path that was outlined by Professor Alessandro (Sandro) D'Atri when he co-founded ItAIS.[5] Prof D'Atri has always promoted a design orientation of IS research and stressed the importance of addressing multiple and interconnected levels within a systemic approach. His contribution to organization and IS studies [2] has been recently commemorated in a book edited by Richard Baskerville, Marco De Marco, and myself that started the new Springer series Lecture Notes in Information Systems and Organisations (LNISO). From now on the best papers presented at the ItAIS conferences will be further revised and then collected in the issues of the LNISO series with the intent of advancing towards the research goals that Sandro was pursuing.

This book collects 45 chapters that are based on a selection of the best contributions submitted at the conference in Roma. Chapters are grouped in 8 parts that are briefly introduced in the following sections. They contain the topics that where conceived by the Track Chairs.

This volume is the outcome of the joint effort of a community of people that have offered their valuable contribution to collate, review, and organize the chapters. I am grateful to all the members of the Editorial Board and of course to all the authors. I am also grateful to Marco De Marco, the VP and co-founder of ItAIS, to Cecilia Rossignoli and Americo Cicchetti, the ItAIS 2012 Conference Chairs, and to Daniele Mascia and Lapo Mola who shared with me the responsibility of chairing the Programme Committee. Finally, a particular thanks must go to the members of CeRSI "Alessandro D'Atri", the Research Centre on

[5] Prof. D'Atri passed away in 2011.

Information Systems at LUISS Guido Carli University, for their unique contribution in organizing the conference.

1 Part I: Organizational Change and Impact of ICT in Public and Private Sector

ICTs are part of corporate transformations in today competitive environments. The vast majority of change projects imply redesign and adaptation of ICT solutions, and in many cases they are entirely centered around these technologies. Organizations expect to use the new ICT to run new processes, innovate products and services, gain higher responsiveness, and implement new corporate environments aimed at transforming their internal structures into better achieving organizations. To date, both practice and literature have widely shown that the effective implementation of new ICT is one of the most challenging tasks faced by managers, since it requires people to understand, absorb and adapt to the new requirements. The capacity to absorb and to fully implement the adoption of new ICTs is a key factor to gain extra competitive abilities, because the ultimate impact of ICT is mediated by a number of factors many of which require an in-depth understanding of the organizational context and human behavior. Despite the many change strategies and tactics applied so far and the fact that many research findings have associated successful tactics with organizational contexts, it is proving difficult to develop a comprehensive theory of change management and change implementation. Empirical investigation must be conducted hand-in-hand with theory building if we want to better interpret today's corporate environments.

2 Part II: New Ways to Work and Interact Via Internet

Internet has created new ways of working and interacting, reduced the geographic, temporal, and organizational distance between individuals. Internet facilitates dispersed interaction across time and/or space, allowing at individuals, groups or organizations, to communicate and collaborate sharing knowledge and information. In particular, new Internet applications, such as Web 2.0 applications, allow a strong level of interaction among users and provide new work arrangements supporting both work activities and social relationships such as: remote work, telecommuting, telework, telecommunity, global and virtual teams, mobile offices, web community, social network, microblogging, etc. Recently, social networks have been growing significantly in the private and leisure sphere of people, while a similar diffusion has not been achieved in the business world. However, there is a great expectation that this will happen in the near future. The expected benefits will be very relevant, starting from the improved cooperation opportunity to the possibility of unleashing new forms of collective intelligence and open innovation. In this direction, there is the emerging idea of Enterprise 2.0, where new forms of collaboration and knowledge sharing will be achieved. In general, scholars have mainly focused on the role of technology in supporting communication and coordination processes among employees, investigating some constructs such as autonomy, job performance, motivation, worklife balance, conflict, socialization processes, quality communication, etc.

The chapters presented in this part contribute to the ongoing debate on the role of Internet facilitating new ways to work and interact and its social and behavioral consequences on individual employees.

3 Part III: E-Business, Communities and Social Networks

Since the introduction of pioneering strategic information systems at the end of the 1970s, a dual perspective has emerged within the discipline of information systems: the business strategy perspective focused on the role of the organization itself, whereas the industrial economic perspective privileged the role of the competitive environment. Chapters presented in this part aim to overcome this dualism as a sustainable competitive advantage requires considering what actually takes place both within the walls of an organization and in the market. Information technology gives chance to reconfigure entire businesses due to the possibility to, first, unbundle sets of economic activities and, second, reallocate them in an innovative way. Production, finance, marketing, research and development, distribution channels all are subject to ongoing revaluation and improvement via new solutions. Solutions that take shape as businesses consider customers, providers, and competitors as potential partners for co-designing and co-producing. External actors and new competences are mobilized, old business borders are overcome and actors roles are reshuffled. If this reconfiguration involves not only products or services but a whole business system, an ecogenesis occurs. The rules of the game transform, leading to a new infrastructure and new business ideas that influence strategies, actions and networks of other actors within the system. Nevertheless, the spread of the internet has affected not only the business world but also the society at large. The proliferation of virtual communities is a recent but relevant event. All over the world individuals exchange information and share knowledge. Distance, time, culture, and organizational membership are no more an obstacle to collaboration and interaction. A new environment for free discussion about different topics is at hand and the literature agrees that virtual communities exist and play a key role in fostering the socialization process as well as learning. Phenomena such as peer production, user-generated content and crowdsourcing can be seen as the combination of the spread of ICT and the internet in the business world and in society. For instance, virtual communities do not only represent a virtual place to socialize and interact, but also an opportunity for marketing strategies.

4 Part IV: Information Systems, Innovation Transfer, and New Business Models

Chapters presented in this part examine how new ICT tools may support firms rejuvenating activities by providing support on reorganization, and promote new business models by rethinking firms R&D strategies. Consistent with open innovation approach, firms can profit of their R&D activity by transferring the results of their innovation processes to external organizations aiming at further adopting and applying that knowledge. In ICT fields, a great opportunity is given by co-operative projects focused on research and development technologies and innovation transfer, provided that technology-based innovation processes be adapted to deep changes in organisational contexts. Advanced ICT tools offer a set of new possibilities to facilitate the use of open cooperative and decentralised models where different entities asynchronously cooperate by adapting transfer/diffusion processes and roles to specific cases, situations, countries and cultures. This part of the volume provides insights on how information systems enable and facilitate the leverage of technological knowledge supporting (open) innovation by handling ICT based innovation. Moreover it addresses new theories and tools and best practices in cooperative and network-based ICT transfer and diffusion.

5 Part V: Information Systems Management: A Critical Perspective

Approaching the research on information systems adopting a critical view seems to be challenging, since it remains poorly adopted, mainly in the Mediterranean area. The aim of this stream is to stem from this marginalization of the critical approach within the IS and IT research. This part of the book is dedicated to understanding of the concept of value for business. Theoretical reflections on the concept of value are deemed central to any understanding of market exchange and the recent financial crisis has contributed to engage in a rethinking of market exchange relations pulling towards a re-conceptualization of the idea of value, including the perspective of ethical economy. The widespread diffusion of internet-platform related based upon forms of social production has represented the field for a new analysis of the concept of ethical value, stimulating new insights on the emancipator potential of new social media and any future infrastructure. Chapters in this part give the audience critical insights on the current challenges and new perspectives for the future of critical IS research, taking into account the implications on the concept of value.

6 Part VI: Professional Skills, Certification of Curricula, On-line Education

The research stream on IS professional skills includes issues pertaining to education and training as well as with and through information technologies. The education and development of Information Systems professionals in the emerging technological and economic world of the 21st century will require innovative methods and approaches. Both formal education programmes and assessment/certification frameworks are affected by continuous developments in digital technologies whilst the new possibilities and challenges of IS and IT have implications for both IT specialists and non-specialists within organizations. The cognitive ICT chain could use the independent standards of process and governance (like ITIL, COBIT, etc.) and the competence and profile standards like EUCIP and e-CF as habilitation technologies to enhance the value of learning outcomes. Furthermore, IT has led to the enhancement of the educational experience across disciplines and to the proliferation of online groups and communities both within and across organizations. Many, originally off-line activities (such as quality circles, task forces, and communities of practice) now take place online whilst IT enables knowledge creation and diffusion, co-production, mentoring, networking, and learning processes within organizational contexts. These groups, communities and activities can be highly heterogeneous in their structural configurations and span temporal and spatial boundaries; something which requires a diverse range of technological and organizational support systems and solutions. However, the necessary management competencies and support structures are often lacking whilst conflict and negative dynamics may also surface and undermine group outcomes. Furthermore, there is limited understanding of how group success is achieved in different work practices and industry contexts. Companies also find it challenging to design business models to leverage the potential of these communities.

This part of the book aims to contribute to the current debate on professional skills, certification of curricula, on-line education and communities.

7 Part VII: Human-Computer Interaction

Human-computer interaction (HCI) is an interdisciplinary research and practice field that deals with the design, evaluation, and use of interactive technologies. The field has gained increasing attention in the last decades due to the pervasiveness of Information Technology in our lives. Traditional HCI topics, such as user-centred system design, usability engineering, accessibility, and information visualization are important to Management Information Systems (MIS) as they influence technology usage in business, managerial, organizational, and cultural contexts. As the user base of business interactive systems is expanding from IT experts to consumers of different types, including elderly, young and special needs people, who access services and information via Web, new and exciting HCI research topics have emerged dealing with broader aspects of the interaction, such as designing for improving the overall user experience, favouring social connections and supporting collaboration. Moreover, the introduction of advanced interactive devices and technology is dragging researchers attention towards innovative methods and processes for interaction design, modeling and evaluation, which take fully into account the potential of modern multimodal user interfaces.

Chapters in this part of the book discuss theories, practices, methodologies, techniques and applications about the interaction among humans, information and technology.

8 Part VIII: Information and Knowledge Management

In the recent years, with the emergence of multiple Webs, like Web 2.0, the Social Web, and the Semantic Web, the variety of available web resources has been growing significantly, from unstructured messages or posts to structured data and ontology specifications. In this scenario, modern organizations require new advanced methods and tools to support effective and pervasive information and knowledge sharing, on and across the different Webs. Integrated exploitation of available web resources can allow people in organizations to achieve a number of aims: to improve business processes; to extend business knowledge; to collaborate with potential partners; and to develop, share and access huge quantities of available resources from different sources. This part of the book presents research contributions on information and knowledge management and collaboration in modern organizations. Such contributions provide insights on the ways in which new technologies and systemic tools and techniques may contribute to "extract", represent, and organize "knowledge" and provide effective support for collaboration, communication and sharing of information and knowledge.

References

1. Lee, A. S. (2010). Retrospect and prospect: Information systems research in the last and next 25 years. *Journal of Information Technology, 25*, 336–348.
2. Spagnoletti, P., Baskerville, R., & De Marco, M. (2013). The contributions of Alessandro D'Atri to organization and information systems studies. In R. Baskerville, M. De Marco, & P. Spagnoletti (Eds.), *Designing organizational systems, LNISO* (Vol. 1, pp. 1–18). Heidelberg: Springer. Available for free download at www.itais.org.

Part I
Organizational Change and Impact of ICT in Public and Private Sector

Does ICT Influence Organizational Behaviour? An Investigation of Digital Natives Leadership Potential

Alessio Maria Braccini

Abstract It was stated that intense use of ICTs since birth stimulated the development of new skills in a cohort of persons called digital natives. Such skills shall allow them to more easily interact with ICTs compared to the digital immigrants, the cohort of persons that entered in contact with the technologies later in their life. Taking this point of view this paper represents an exploratory study in the investigation of the potential influence of the use of ICTs by digital natives on their organizational behavior. On the basis of a dataset of interest for such purpose, this paper investigates the potential cause/effect relationship between the fact of being digital native and the emotional intelligence, a necessary prerequisite to wield good leadership.

Keywords Emotional intelligence · Digital natives · Leadership · Fs/QCA

1 Introduction

It was stated that intense interaction with ICTs since the early phases of a persons' life makes him a savvy with respect to technology use [1, 2]. A cohort of persons called *digital natives* [2, 3], or *net generation* [1], or *millennials* [4] was then identified. Such cohort is characterized by the fact that its members entered massively in contact with ICTs during the early ages of their lives and, as a consequence, they had probably developed peculiar multi-tasking, networking, and interacting skills with the technology, that differ from the skills possessed by individuals who started to use ICTs later during their lives, the *digital immigrants*.

A. M. Braccini (✉)
Dipartimento di Economia e Impresa, Università degli Studi della Tuscia, Viterbo, Italy
e-mail: abraccini@unitus.it

P. Spagnoletti (ed.), *Organizational Change and Information Systems*, Lecture Notes in Information Systems and Organisation 2, DOI: 10.1007/978-3-642-37228-5_2,

Several studies support the claim that digital natives show peculiar physical and behavioral capabilities in the use of ICTs. For example, a study using magnetic resonance imaging on a group of Facebook users indicated that people with a denser network of friends possess more gray matter in their brain [5]. Moreover a study on college students' behavior showed that they are more accustomed to PCs instead of textbooks, and that they developed a sort of ICT usage addiction [6]. The phenomenon of digital natives and ICT was thence particularly studied in the context of education [7].

This paper proposes to investigate the phenomenon under an organizational behavior perspective. Assumed that digital natives share a common chronological trait (they are born in a world with ICTs), and significant life events (they interacted heavily with ICTs from their birth), they form a generation following Kupperschmidt [8], or a cohort following Rhodes [9]. This paper then investigates whether there are cause/effect relationships between digital nativity and emotional intelligence [10], being emotional intelligence a prerequisite to wield a good leadership [11].

The paper unfolds as follows. In Sect. 2, literature on digital natives and emotional intelligence is discussed. In Sect. 3 the research question and the methodology followed to answer to it will be described. Section 4 will present and discuss the result of data analysis. Some final considerations on the findings, the limitation of the work, and the directions for future research efforts will be drawn in Sect. 5.

2 Theoretical Framework

This section describes the relevant literature for the problem investigated in this paper. This section is divided into two sub-sections. In the first one the characteristics of digital natives will be described. In the second one the relevance of these characteristics in terms of organizational behavior, and specifically in terms of emotional intelligence, will be discussed.

2.1 Digital Natives and Digital Immigrants

According to Tapscot [1], people born after the year 1980 are characterized by the fact of being born in a world already permeated by ICTs. They had then the opportunity to access digital and networked technologies since the early years in their lives. As a consequence they developed specific skills on how to use ICTs in their personal and professional lives. Tapscot names this group of persons the *net generation* [1].

Prensky extends the concept of *net generation* distinguishing between two different cohorts called respectively *digital natives* and *digital immigrants* [2, 3].

Digital natives are those for which ICTs were part of their lives since their birth. In line with Tapscot, Prensky states that digital natives grew up in an already digital world, and developed a deep familiarity with ICTs, living surrounded by any kind of digital toys [2, 3]. Digital immigrants on the other side are people who started to use ICTs later in their adult age. According to Prensky not only the usage patterns of ICTs differ between digital natives and digital immigrants, but also the former acquire, think, and process information in a deeply different manner. According to Palfrey and Gassser [12] and Palfrey et al. [13] digital natives are a subset of the millennial generation that grew up in an intense networked world, with access to ubiquitous digital technologies, who develop deep abilities to use them in a fluent and sophisticated way.

Even though the names used for this generation vary, the traits used by different authors to describe it, show high degree of coherence. This generation is described as: constantly immersed in ICTs; depending on Internet based technologies; using them to access and process information, and to interact with others; adopting an experiential approach which leaded to the acquisition of peculiar skills in ICTs use, including multi-tasking skills [1–3, 14, 15]. For digital natives the digital world has always been a part of their daily lives and, besides these skills, they also developed a sort of dependence on ICTs on using them to carry out personal, social, and professional activities [16]. Regarding the experience of digital natives with technology, Valkenburg and Peter [17] reports that, by the age of 20, they will have spent 20,000 hours online using different transaction and decision support systems, for information retrieval, entertainment, and collaboration, both for personal and professional purposes.

Summarizing the salient digital natives traits are:

- Digitally literate, highly connected, experiential, social, and in need of immediate gratification [18];
- More comfortable with extensive peer to peer collaboration, and less reluctant to disclose personal data [19];
- Optimistic, team-oriented achievers, talented with technology [4, 20].

2.2 *Organizational Behavior and Emotional Intelligence*

The previous section highlights that a generation called digital native shows specific characteristics regarding the perception and the use of technology, and that these characteristics affect the behaviors of its members under many perspectives (information processing, learning, collaboration, gratification). As mentioned in the introduction what this paper investigates is if these characteristics affect their organizational behavior at the workplace. This is particularly relevant as digital natives entered the job market, and are also part of different organization, and managers have to deal with generational differences that appear to exist among workers [21].

Table 1 The five components of *emotional intelligence* [11]

Dimension	Definition	Traits
Self-awareness	Ability to recognize and understand own moods, emotions, and drivers, as well as their effects on others	Self-confidence, realistic self-assessment, self-deprecating sense of humor
Self-regulation	Ability to control or redirect disruptive impulses and moods, propensity to suspend judgment and to think before acting	Trustworthiness and integrity, comfort with ambiguity, openness to change
Motivation	Passion to work for reasons that go beyond money or status, propensity to pursue goals with energy and persistence	Strong drive to achieve, optimism, even in the face of failure, organizational commitment
Empathy	Ability to understand the emotional makeup of other people, skill in treating people according to their emotional reactions	Expertise in building and retaining talent, cross-cultural sensitivity, service to clients and customers
Social skill	Proficiency in managing relationships and building networks, ability to find common ground and build rapport	Effectiveness in leading change, persuasiveness, expertise in building and leading teams

The presence of similarities in terms of shared experiences and values is recognized to influence a person's feelings, attitudes, interests, and beliefs towards an organization [9]. In literature there is a high attention towards generational differences, attitudes, and behaviors in the workplace [8, 21–23], and many organizational related phenomena were proven to be generations dependent [24].

The specific behavioral characteristic investigated in this paper is emotional intelligence. Goleman [10, 11] describes emotional intelligence as the "sine qua non of leadership", and as the more effective characteristic for a potential leader. Emotional intelligence is the ability to manage emotions of oneself, of others, and of groups. According to Goleman [11], emotional intelligence covers five dimensions. These dimensions along with their description and the main traits associated to each one are listed in Table 1.

3 Research Design

This paper investigates digital nativity in relation with emotional intelligence. The research question to be answered is: are there cause/effect relationships between digital nativity and emotional intelligence? To answer this research question a dataset of interest for this analysis, formed by a sample with observations from 20 graduated students with a (sometimes ongoing) professional experience in an organization, was used. The data were collected with a face-to-face administered survey on a different research project, but are also of relevance for this research paper.

Given the exploratory nature of this study, and the small dimension of the sample, the fuzzy set Qualitative Comparative Analysis (fs/QCA) technique was used to analyze data [25, 26]. The fs/QCA is an extension of a Boolean data analysis technique called Qualitative Comparative Analysis (QCA). QCA allows a systematical analysis of small samples, ensuring quantitative rigor. QCA is based on the assumption that multiple combinations of certain characteristics of a phenomenon affect an outcome of the same phenomenon [25], but only allows researchers to focus on the presence or absence of these characteristics and outcomes. The fs/QCA overpasses these limitations introducing the use of fuzzy sets, allowing the researcher to focus on different degrees of presence/absence of the phenomenon. Since these kinds of techniques are designed to identify, within a phenomenon, the combinations of elements that are necessary and sufficient for obtaining a specific outcome [27, 28], it was reputed a suitable methodology given the aim of this paper to identify cause/effect relationships between digital nativity and emotional intelligence.

3.1 Variables and Analysis

The sample used for the analysis covers the dimensions described in Table 2. For each of them a fuzzy score was identified in a scale as follows: 0.05 (absent), 0.25 (almost absent), 0.75 (almost present), 0.95 (present). The column type indicates whether the factors are used in the analysis as causal conditions (C) or as outcomes (O).

To answer the research question, analysis were made to investigate the cause/effect relationship between digital natives traits and potential leadership, and between digital natives traits and each dimension of emotional intelligence.

The research model investigated is represented by the following set of equations:

Table 2 Description of investigated variables

Causal factors	Type	Description
TECH_USE	C	Intense technology user
NET_TIME	C	Intense internet user (in terms of hour used browsing the internet)
SOCIAL_NET	C	Intense social network user
MULTITASK	C	User of multiple ICTs/Media at the same time
SECURE	O	Self secure individual
MOTIV_FUTURE	O	Individual seeking delayed motivation
MEDIATOR	O	Individual capable of mediation in work groups
INFLUENCER	O	Individual capable of influencing others' decisions
EMPATHIC	O	Empathic individual
POT_LEADER	O	Potential leader

$$POT\_LEADER = f(TECH\_USE, NET\_TIME, SOCIAL\_NET, MULTITASK) \quad (1)$$

$$SECURE = f(TECH\_USE, NET\_TIME, SOCIAL\_NET, MULTITASK) \quad (2)$$

$$MOTIV\_FUTURE = f(TECH\_USE, NET\_TIME, SOCIAL\_NET, MULTITASK) \quad (3)$$

$$MEDIATOR = f(TECH\_USE, NET\_TIME, SOCIAL\_NET, MULTITASK) \quad (4)$$

$$INFLUENCER = f(TECH\_USE, NET\_TIME, SOCIAL\_NET, MULTITASK) \quad (5)$$

$$EMPATHIC = f(TECH\_USE, NET\_TIME, SOCIAL\_NET, MULTITASK) \quad (6)$$

Given the small dimension of the investigated sample, frequency and consistency cutoffs were fixed, respectively, at 1 and 0.85 for all fs/QCA analysis.

4 Data Analysis and Discussion

The results of the analysis are shown in Table 3. All the results were produced through the Quine-McClusky algorithm with the parameters to produce the most parsimonious solution. The table contains the results of only 5 analyses, which refer to Eqs. (1)–(5). It was not possible to investigate equation number (6) since none of the configurations of the observed phenomena satisfied the consistency threshold used for this study.

Table 3 Results of the analysis of data

Equation	Solutions	Raw coverage	Unique coverage	Consistency
(1)	~Multitask	0.267123	0.036986	0.951219
	~Social_net	0.356164	0.075343	1.000000
	~Tech_use	0.291781	0.082192	1.000000
	Solution coverage: 0.500000–Solution consistency: 0.973333			
(2)	~Social_net	0.361111	0.361111	1.000000
	Solution coverage: 0.361111–Solution consistency: 1.000000			
(3)	~Tech_use	0.304286	0.304286	1.000000
	Solution coverage: 0.304286–Solution consistency: 1.000000			
(4)	~Multitask	0.264516	0.047742	1.000000
	~Social_net	0.335484	0.070968	1.000000
	~Tech_use	0.274839	0.077419	1.000000
	Solution coverage: 0.483871–Solution consistency: 1.000000			
(5)	~Multitask	0.290780	0.151773	1.000000
	~Tech_use*social_net	0.252482	0.113475	0.946809
	Solution coverage: 0.404255–Solution consistency: 0.966102			

* OR

The solution identified by the analysis to Eq. (1) tells us that to be a potential leader a digital native has not to be: an intense technology user, or an intense social networks user, or an individual which makes use of several media at the same time. Further considerations can be formulated looking at the solutions generated by the analysis for the other dimensions of emotional intelligence.

The solution for Eq. (2) suggests that the characteristics of a self-secure individual are compatible with the absence of intense usage of social networks. The absence of intense technology usage is coherent with the presence of an individual that seeks delayed rather then immediate motivation according to the solution for Eq. (3). Moreover, the solution for Eq. (4) shows that the absence of intense usage of technology, or the absence of intense usage of social networks, or the lack of multitasking (intended as the usage of multiple media at the same time) are compatible with an individual with deep mediating skills. A more complex solution, similar to the one for Eq. (1), was instead found for the presence of an individual capable of influencing others' decisions. In this case, following the solution found for Eq. (5), a digital native has to: either not use several media at the same time, or not to be an intense technology user and be an intense user of social networks together.

To formulate general conclusions regarding these results, it can be noticed that almost all the causal conditions included in the solutions identified by the analysis are negated. It is therefore not the presence of the causal conditions that is linked with a cause/effect relationship to the outcomes, but rather it is the absence that influences it. In general it can be noticed that not having the habits to use several media at the same time (multitask), not being an intense user of social networks, and not being an intense user of technology are indicated as causes of several dimensions of emotional intelligence, with a reflection on potential leadership. The only causal condition whose presence counts is the intense usage of social networks in relationship with the capability of influencing others' decisions, but it is combined with the absence of intense technology usage. Since the intense usage of social networks was measured considering the size of the social network of individuals in Facebook, it can be argued that to be an influencer a digital native shall have a large social network but potentially managing the relations with it via traditional (i.e. face to face) contacts.

Finally, a general consideration concerning the data analyzed has to be formulated. At first it must be stated that all the 20 individuals observed are digital natives. A consequence is that several, when not all, individuals in the sample possessed the characteristics of digital natives. Secondly, the examination of the truth tables during the analysis, not reported here due to lack of space, showed that large part of the observation felt below the consistency threshold. In general, out of 20 observations, only 2–5 observations satisfied the consistency threshold for the analysis.

5 Conclusion

The analysis of the data suggests that no specific characteristic of digital natives is linked with a cause/effect relationship with emotional intelligence. The analysis showed that the absence of three characteristics of digital natives, multitasking, intense technology usage, and intense social network usage, is linked with the traits of potential leader, and with some of the emotional intelligence dimensions. Given that many digital natives, and the sample used here confirm such statement, possess these characteristics, it can be argued that, since none of the characteristics of digital natives is beneficial for possessing the traits of potential leadership, but the absence of some of them is, digital natives could probably not possess intrinsic leadership potential.

The current study is an exploratory analysis, which aimed at investigating the phenomenon of digital natives under an organizational behavior perspective. This work possesses several limitations that shall be discussed. First of all the analysis is based on a sample of data that is of relevance for the research question of this paper, but that was collected for a different research project. The analysis has therefore to be repeated on data collected specifically for the need of the research question, possibly directly using fuzzy scales to measure both digital nativity and emotional intelligence. Moreover, given that many observations felt below the consistency threshold, it could be necessary to increase both sample size and diversity in future analysis. It would probably be beneficial also to include in the sample digital immigrants for a comparison. Finally given that many scales for measuring emotional intelligence are available in literature future research could use SEM or PLS to test a theoretical model which relates digital nativity to emotional intelligence. In this case the development of specific scales to measure digital nativity is necessary.

Acknowledgments This paper stems from an idea originally discussed with Prof. Alessandro D'Atri, who sadly passed away before he could see it put in practice. The paper awarded the Alessandro D'Atri prize at the ItAIS 2012 conference. The author is thankful for this praise, and wishes to thank Prof. D'Atri for his precious mentoring and support during four years of joint work.

References

1. Tapscott, D. (1998). *Growing up digital: The rise of the net generation.* New York: McGraw-Hill.
2. Prensky, M. (2001). Digital natives, digital immigrants. *On the Horizon, 9*, 1–6.
3. Prensky, M. (2001). Digital natives, digital immigrants, part II: Do they really think differently? *On the Horizon, 9*, 1–9.
4. Howe, N., & Strauss, W. (2000). *Millennials rising: The next great generation.* New York: Vintage.

5. Kanai, R., Bahrami, B., Roylance, R., & Rees, G. (2012). Online social network size is reflected in human brain structure. *Proceedings of the Biological Sciences/The Royal Society, 279*, 1327–1334.
6. MarketWatch. College students boost digital adoption, according to course smart survey, http://www.marketwatch.com/story/college-students-boost-digital-adoption-according-to-coursesmart-survey-2012-05-23.
7. Bennet, S., Maton, K., & Kervin, L. (2008). The "digital natives" debate: A critical review of the evidence. *British Journal of Educational Technology, 39*, 775–786.
8. Kupperschmidt, B. R. (2000). Multigeneration employees: Strategies for effective management. *The Health Care Manager, 19*, 65–76.
9. Rhodes, S. (1983). Age-related differences in work attitudes and behavior: A review and conceptual analysis. *Psychological Bulletin, 93*, 328–367.
10. Goleman, D. (1998). *Working with emotional intelligence*. New York: Bantam Books.
11. Goleman, D. (2004). What makes a leader? *Harvard Business Review, 82*, 82–91.
12. Palfrey, J., & Gasser, U. (2008). *Born digital*. New York: Basic Books.
13. Palfrey, J., Gasser, U., Simun, M., & Barnes, R. (2009). Youth, creativity, and copyright in the digital age. *International Journal of Learning, 1*, 79–97.
14. Frand, J. L. (2000). The information-age mindset: Changes in students and implications for higher education. *Educause Review, 35*, 14–24.
15. Oblinger, D. T., & Oblinger, J. L. (2005). Is it age or IT: First steps toward understanding the net generation. In D. G. Oblinger & J. L. Oblinger (Eds.), *Educating the net generation* (pp. 2.1–2.20). North Carolina State University.
16. Vodanovich, S., Sundaram, D., & Myers, M. (2010). Digital natives and ubiquitous information systems. *Information Systems Research, 21*, 711–723.
17. Valkenburg, P. M., & Peter, J. (2008). Adolescents' identity experiments on the internet: Consequences for social competence and self-concept unity. *Communication Research, 35*, 208–231.
18. McMahon, M., Pospisil, R. (2005) Laptops for a digital lifestyle: Millennial students and wireless mobile technologies. *Proceedings of Ascilite Conference*, 421–431. Australia: Brisbane.
19. Leung, L. (2003). Impacts of net-generation attributes, seductive properties of the internet, and gratifications obtained on internet use. *Telematics Informatics, 20*, 107–129.
20. Howe, N., Strauss, W. (2003). Millennials go to College. Washington, DC.
21. Smola, K. W., & Sutton, C. D. (2002). Generational differences: Revisiting generational work values for the new millennium. *Journal of Organizational Behavior, 23*, 363–382.
22. Jurkiewicz, C. E. (2000). Generation X and the public employee. *Public Personnel Management, 29*, 55–74.
23. Parry, E., & Urwin, P. (2010). Generational difference in work values: A review of theory and evidence. *Journal of Management Reviews, 13*, 79–96.
24. Joshi, A., Dencker, J. C., & Franz, G. (2011). Generations in organizations. *Research in Organizational Behavior, 31*, 177–205.
25. Ragin, C. (1987). *The comparative method: Moving beyond qualitative and quantitative strategies*. Berkeley: University of California Press.
26. Ragin, C. (2000). *No fuzzy-set social science*. Chicago: University of Chicago Press.
27. Braumoeller, B. F., & Goertz, G. (2000). The methodology of necessary conditions. *American Journal of Political Science, 44*, 844–858.
28. Fiss, P. (2007). A set-theoretic approach to organizational configurations. *Academy of Management Review, 32*, 1180–1198.

In the Face of Customers' Changing Behaviour, Should Italian Banks' Approach to Online Trading Remain the Same?

Franca Cantoni and Cecilia Rossignoli

Abstract What drives the behaviors of banks and their customers in times of profound changes? The modern crisis affecting economic and social systems has significantly diminished customers' willingness to invest, and this trend, together with improved information about financial services, has made them more price sensitive, more rational in their decision making, and thus more challenging for banks to attract. Therefore, banks have invested in projects to improve their internal processes and online services, in particular by deploying web 2.0–based mobile banking and payment opportunities. In the Italian banking sector, 12 years after the publication of "New Distribution Models for Financial Services: The Italian Banks' Approach to the On Line Trading Development," this article considers how general and structural changes in customer behavior and the banking sector have affected the strategy banks use to provide online trading services, including the use of outsourcing and new managerial practices.

Keywords On line trading · Banks · Outsourcing · Web 2.0 technology · Social trading

1 Introduction

This article consists of four main sections. The first briefly reviews business models adopted by Italian banks to meet customers' evolving needs, with a particular focus on the novelties that have arisen since 2000, the year that Cantoni and

F. Cantoni (✉)
Università Cattolica del Sacro Cuore, Piacenza, Italy
e-mail: franca.cantoni@unicatt.it

C. Rossignoli
Business Administration Department, University of Verona, Verona, Italy
e-mail: cecilia.rossignoli@univr.it

P. Spagnoletti (ed.), *Organizational Change and Information Systems*, Lecture Notes in Information Systems and Organisation 2, DOI: 10.1007/978-3-642-37228-5_3,

Rossignoli published "New Distribution Models for Financial Services: The Italian Banks' Approach to the On Line Trading Development." Then we describe customers' demands for financial services, as well as how they have changed and the peculiarities of new, integrated services offered by web 2.0–based technology.

In the third section, we argue that to overcome their lack of specific competencies and technology, banks do not need to outsource anymore but instead can turn to smart sourcing. Banks should focus their precious resources on what they do best and innovate on their core competencies, but they also need partners that can innovate in non-core processes. Smart sourcing entails the use of partners that can help the bank do so, as well as balance risk and opportunity, lower costs, increase innovation across all processes, and put in place attitudes to optimize these factors, both socially and politically. Outsourcing and offshoring (which were common when e-banking was still trying to enter the market) are essential components only if they pave the way for banks to free up resources to focus on their core competencies and generate greater innovations. Finally, this article concludes by summarizing the main differences in the online trading scenario between 2000 (the year the foundational article for this research was published) and today.

2 The Italian Banking System: Is the Search for New Business Models Still in Progress?

The deregulation process adopted by the Banca d'Italia aimed to ensure the Italian banking system met EU market demands, as well as match evolution of customer demands and diversified needs and deal with the consolidation in the market, which produced aggressive competition in offers of new financial products. These signals paralleled the massive restructuring of the Italian banking system, in which more than a decade ago, Italian banks started to adopt new business models and redesign their strategies [1]. Their competition was no longer based on the product or price but rather on customer loyalty and indirectly customer satisfaction [2]. In this setting, to gain a stable competitive advantage, banks also must improve their customer lifetime value. To do so, banks might focus on:

- A multichannel strategy that integrates innovative, electronic banking services with traditional ones and supports interactive management of relationships with customers across all channels.
- Guarantees of transparency and reduced information asymmetry between banks and customers, together with constantly upgraded online training and interactive opportunities.
- Offers of a vast amount of consumer choices to compose and manage their portfolios.

2.1 Multichannel Strategy

With a multichannel strategy, every customer can use the devices he or she prefers (telephone, e-mail, web), and the bank can adopt different policies according to channel choices, thus maximizing the benefits of every contact with the customer with higher added value services. On the basis of two main features—accessibility and level of coordination—we define four multichannel strategy models, as we show in Table 1, that reflect their intersection [3].

Model A is a basic multichannel strategy: The newly introduced channel appears side-by-side with the old one, with no integration between them. The customer simply chooses one; the bank thus avoids integration, cannibalism, and reward and pricing problems. Model A is most appropriate for banks that can create neat distinctions among customers on the basis of their channel preferences. As the new channel gets consolidated into the system, Model A evolves into Model B, a parallel multichannel strategy. For example, the manager of the new channel might ask for more decision control, in which case that channel starts to compete with the existing channel, instead of working in parallel. Some brokers even rely on e-banking services managed by a parallel company or another brand. Model A instead morphs into Model D if the bank offers the customer the option of simultaneously using different channels. In this case, the bank likely is interested in achieving global profitability. Finally, Model C is difficult to implement, because it requires coordination across channels and shared information, which is not possible if there is any competition across channels.

The most common models are B and D; Model B in particular arises from the constitution of an autonomous division. However, it is not always possible to identify the most convenient strategy or a perfect model to apply in each economic situation or by every specific bank. Each bank, according to its market, the profile of its customers, and its surrounding context, must determine the most suitable model.

Compared with 2000, the multichannel model is no longer a novelty; instead, it has become the norm in financial services [4]. It also features a greater focus on the customer, with the goal of optimizing the integration across different distribution channels and the range of products offered, which means a substantial change to the traditional market approach. Furthermore, banks today can exploit collaborative tools through web 2.0, not only to reach customers but also to invest in their loyalty. This approach transforms the Internet into a unique platform that provides services shared by various customers, generates value through the creative use of distributed and collectively integrated technologies, and allows for the distribution of new services and the improvement of those already in place [5].

Table 1 Multichannel strategy models [3]

	Competitive channels	Complementary channels
Multi-accessibility	Model C: cross-eyed	Model D: integrated
Mono-accessibility	Model B: parallel	Model A: base

2.2 Transparency and Information Flow

Transparency implies less *asymmetric information* and the provision of the best available information about the market and services. To improve transparency, Italian banks have formed the "Patti Chiari" consortium, with information available both on site and online. People consulting the Patti Chiari website find offers from different banking institutes and collect all the information needed to make a transaction. This improved information availability for customers has encouraged their mobility across banking institutes; the bank receiving the new customer even closes the old bank account and initiates the transfer process. Thus customers' average duration with any one bank is only eight or nine years.

The consortium also offers online training, meetings, forums, and seminars, including debates and discussions with traders and professionals, technical analysis conferences, descriptions of the use of platforms, and tips on investment techniques. Unencumbered access to information has premium importance in financial trading, such that the free exchange of information is of interest to small-scale and individual investors. The facilities provided on the platform help customers reach the best conditions for making their choice.

2.3 Diversified Portfolio

Banks offer modern customers a vast amount of investment portfolio choices. In contrast, in the 1990s, the limited availability of information and investment products, together with the advantage granted to an intermediary that sold one specific product instead of another, meant proposals were limited. Today customers can take advantage of unlimited proposals, ranging from those composed of intermediary products (e.g., funds managed by an SGR) to direct purchases of actions and obligations on the market. An intermediary might propose existing products available on the market or specialize by itself in a specific field. Moreover, traders can work together in trading teams, which can pool funds, divide research responsibilities, or share information.

Therefore the survival of any bank depends critically on its ability to maintain its faithful customers. In recognizing the importance of existing customers, the identity of banks has shifted, from the "agency that produces a service" to an "agency whose final scope is to understand and satisfy customers' needs" [5]. In turn, these faithful customers lead to higher profit margins for the firm.

3 Is this the Social Trading Era?

From the user's point of view, the Internet offers a steady distribution channel for a multitude of banking products and financial trade services. Prior to the emergence of the Internet, financial trading centered on the relationship between customers and brokers, requiring physical locations such as exchanges. As the Internet gathered momentum, electronic trading grew into a major focus for trades of financial assets among individual investors. The emergence of the web 2.0, as well as social networking functions through Facebook and Twitter, affected the financial trading industry significantly. Financial traders were among the earliest adopters of knowledge-sharing capacities. They perceived these services as new sources of information, whether financial, economical, or technical in their essence. Online financial trading companies have exploited the popularity of social networking channels; fully fledged social trading networks even have emerged, using online social networks as their model. The assimilation of web 2.0 properties into almost every trading platform has pushed financial traders to pursue information through these services, which is more social than financial. This information extraction is either explicit (intentionally following trading activities by one or more selected traders, manually or automatically) or implicit, such as when one person's trading decisions are unintentionally influenced by the trading activities of others.

Web 2.0 technology also offers banks a chance to obtain advantages over their competitors in terms of improved operative efficiency, competitive cost structures, and scale economies and flexibility [6]. Thus web 2.0 technology assumes a fundamental role in the new competitive scenario, where financial brokers act aggressively and represent innovative, dynamic resources for banks, as well as catalysts of new techniques and new and customized services.

3.1 Social Trading

The pervasiveness of web 2.0 technology and tools is so evident that it has prompted a named trend: "social trading." This label refers to the process in which financial investors rely heavily on user-generated financial content gathered from various web 2.0 applications, such that it becomes the major information source in their trading decisions. Social trading also suggests a new way to analyze financial data. Until recently, investors and traders relied on fundamental technical analyses to form investment decisions. Now the investment decision process integrates social indicators, fuelled by transparent, real-time trading data that is available to all users of the social trading network. This trend suggests a new term, "social financial analysis."

3.2 *Questions of Image and Gist*

Web 2.0 technology can support strategies based on the differentiation and expansion of services offered; it aims to give banks a precise image, recognized by the sector more widely [7]. Integrated technology reflects the accuracy and rapidity of processes and communication forms in the market, which supports wider adaptability of the services offered to specific customers' needs. It also promotes integrated offers of the wide range of services, such that it can contribute to sustainable advantages over competitors. Such technology offers a real strategic lever, able to manage changes by redefining banks' distributive model. In particular, through online technologies, banks can meet their customers' individual needs and induce significant changes in the nature of their competition. Customer satisfaction demands more than prompt, courteous service; it also requires designing products and services to meet individual customer needs [6]. Thus, the exploitation of web 2.0 technologies represents a critical success factor.

In such a scenario, a set of question naturally arises, not necessarily confined to the Italian experience: How should banks react to technological changes? Should they regard this potential new role as Internet brokers as a strategic opportunity or an unnecessary burden that distracts them from their core business? How can the Italian banks leverage the positive aspects to gain a competitive advantage and improve their competitive position in the financial sector? We address these questions and offer some related insights in the following section.

4 Smart Sourcing

The continuous growth of new products and services whose diffusion takes place through the Internet provides Italian banks with an opportunity to reassess which activities should remain in house and which should be sourced externally, whether through purchase or cooperative agreements [8, 9]. Quinn and Hilmer [10] suggest that banks should concentrate their resources on a set of "core competencies" that grant them definable pre-eminence and provide unique value to customers [11] but strategically outsource other activities [12]. If we apply the recommendation to a typical Italian bank that offers online services, it appears immediately clear that such trading is becoming a core service. Although it represents a critical strategic need, the bank does not always have the capabilities needed to offer this kind of service, nor is it necessarily in a position of technology leadership.

The bank's decision to outsource its online service stems from multiple drivers, both tactical (e.g., cost reductions, unavailability of internal resources) and strategic (e.g., improved bank focus, acceleration of reengineering benefits, access to world-class capabilities, risk monitoring) [13]. Swamidass [14] proposes a three-stage evolutionary process of sourcing decisions: cost minimization, competitive advantage, and strategic asset. With customer satisfaction as a lever of business tactics, competitive advantages of Italian banks stem from their ability to create value for customer in terms of quality, service, and product innovation. We argue that all three stages combine, because a bank that brings its trading online services in-house can simultaneously minimize costs, gain and sustain competitive advantages, and exploit its strategic assets by reverting to smart sourcing instead of outsourcing.

4.1 Reconciling the Seemingly Contradictory Mandates of Cost Cutting and Innovation

As a business decision, smart sourcing leverages the competencies of service providers (internal and external) to achieve significant increases in total innovative capacity. It requires the bank to be able to combine in-house solutions with outsourcing and thereby achieve greater synchronization and coordination of processes that may reside across multiple internal and external partners. Furthermore, they must recognize that driving down costs is not an episodic phenomenon. Instead, continuing and accelerating pressures to drive costs down will persist. The answer to this ever-rising challenge of attaining productivity with lower costs lies in a new approach that features:

- A global view of managing work and its movements through tightly orchestrated business processes.
- A new smart sourcing model for partnering with service providers that creates high accountability, innovation, and trust.
- A sustained focus on shedding non-core activities to invest profitability in core competencies.

Our analysis shows that smart sourcing—using partners so that the bank can focus on its core capabilities—balances risk and opportunity, lowers costs, increases innovation across processes, and establishes appropriate attitudes to optimize these factors. Outsourcing and offshoring are essential components of this solution, though only if they help organizations free up resources so they can focus on core competencies that lead to greater innovation.

For example, ABILab, observing IT banking architectures in 2010, found that 27.7 % of banks use in-sourcing, whereas 51.7 % outsource. Small and medium-sized banks (fewer than 500 branches in the national territory) tend to use total outsourcing as a managerial practice. Cedacri [15] also shows that global outsourcing allows them to access more specific competencies and more flexibility in the operational area. The outsourcing decision thus ultimately depends on the bank's size. The three largest groups—Intesa Sanpaolo, Unicredit, and Monte Paschi Siena—all prefer in-house solutions (in-sourcing) and create specific intergroup societies or define specific internal functions. Medium-sized banks (e.g., Banco Popolare, UBI Bank, BPER, BNL, BNP Paribas, BPM, Credem,

Pop. VI Bank, Veneto Banca) use mixed systems, such that they retain most application solutions in-house and externalize other functions, such as facility management. According to Cedacri [15] some small- to medium-sized banks instead adopt full outsourcing of applications and infrastructure which is much more frequent than outsourcing of processes. Currently 95 % of operators entrust, totally or partially, their informative system to an outside source.

To estimate the convenience of outsourcing, banks must consider their positions and whether they belong to a larger group. It may be appropriate to outsource when ICT costs are substantial as a proportion of total assets. From this point of view, banks in groups likely perceive a weaker relationship between costs and assets, compared with other, non-group banks, and thus may gain an advantage from outsourcing [16].

4.2 The Outsourcers

In an uncertain, competitive environment, banks seek economic efficiency and prefer to share business and technology risks [17]. Table 2 contains a list of the main outsourcers operating in Italy and their descriptions, in an attempt to reveal how banks behave when they create *ad hoc* companies.

In Italy, "co-sourcing" relationships (see Fig. 1) describe many-to-one alliances in which several clients contract with a single IT vendor for services, and these are the most diffused structures.

Table 2 List of outsourcers (authors' elaboration)

Outsourcer	Typology	Members/stockholders/main banks
SIA SSB	Consortium	Intesa San Paolo, Unicredit, Monte dei Paschi di Siena, Banca Nazionale del Lavoro, Telecom Italia, UBI Banca, ICBPI, Deutsche Bank, Banco Popolare, Banca Popolare di Milano
CEDACRI	Consortium	Banca Mediolanum, Gruppo Credem, Banco Desio, Gruppo UGF, Barclays, Banca Etruria, IW Bank
CSE	Consortium	ING Direct, Unibanca
UBI SISTEMI E SERVIZI	Consortium	–
SGS BP	–	Company belonging to the Banco Popolare group; it provides the technological infrastructure, information services, and application software to the group
SEC	Consortium	Provides Banca Popolare di Vicenza, Veneto Banca, Che Banca, and Allianz bank, which are also partners.
ISIDE	Consortium (cooperative banks)	Born to provide services to cooperative banks ICCREA, but also includes non-cooperative members
BASSILICHI SPA	–	Participated by Monte Paschi Siena and Banca Popolare dell'Emilia Romagna

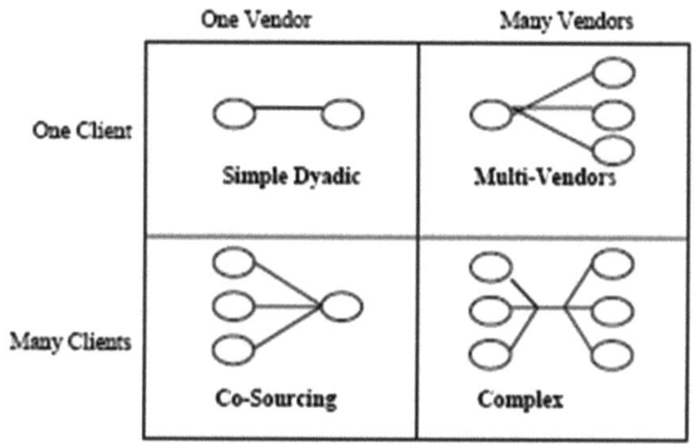

Fig. 1 Taxonomy of *four classes* of outsourcing relationships [16]

For example, Monte Paschi Siena and many other large banks participate in the stock capital of more than one outsourcer. These large Italian banks appear particularly committed to developing their own "insourcers," dedicated companies internal to the group. Other banks, mostly smaller ones, rely on consortia that they create so that they may share the costs of information systems or combine their efforts to create a dedicated insourcer company. Yet another choice evident in a few banks is to turn to a multinational with extensive experience, as when Fineco Bank, Banca Popolare del'Emilia Romagna, and BancoPosta rely on, respectively, Sistemi Informativi Spa (Gruppo I.B.M.), Oracle Italia, and SAP Italia.

5 Conclusions

Twelve years after the publication of "New Distribution Models for Financial Services: The Italian Banks' Approach to the On Line Trading Development," [18] we argue that the Italian market is now assisting in the explosion of online trading and bank branches are not unique or preferred channels for customers to perform transactions. Italian banks are well aware of these trends and recognizing the enormity of the changes, which is increasing the urgency with which they develop new and adequate strategies. Furthermore, research into new business models has expanded in the past 12 years: the idea that there is no one universal model, but rather situational and contingent preferences that fit each unique situation, has emerged and become consolidated. The "social trading era" also is affecting these situational models, and web 2.0 technology is assuming a fundamental role in the new competitive scenario [19–21]. In this sense, the development of adequate information systems to support changing customers' needs constitutes a truly important opportunity for retaining customers and developing their loyalty.

Smart sourcing might help banks combine in—and outsourcing solutions, decrease costs, and substantially enhance business process excellence and innovation through collaborative partnerships. Such co-sourcing as a business practice allows a service to be performed by staff within the organization, as well as by an external service provider. For banks engaged in offering online trading services, co-sourcing provides an advantage over total outsourcing, in that it minimises sourcing risks, enhances transparency and clarity, and offers better control over processes.

Research limitations/implications. In this initial attempt to address the focal research question, the focus is on a literature review and in-depth investigation of banks' websites, along with documentation from Italian economic and financial journals and data gathered from ABI. Some subjectivity is involved in interpreting the results, as is the case for any study that adopts a real-life approach.

References

1. Padovan, F. (2011). *Come investono le banche nel* 2011. Bancaforte.
2. Merola, B. (2002). Una proposta di qualificazione delle dinamiche concorrenziali in ottica sistemico vitale, Atti AIDEA, Giuffré, Milano.
3. Nieri, L. (2002). La distribuzione dei servizi bancari e finanziari, i principi della Marketing Channels Theory per la costituzione di un sistema distributivo efficace ed efficiente, Banche e banchieri, 5.
4. Frei, F.X., et al. (1990). *Performance in consumer financial services organizations: Framework and results from the pilot study*. Philadelphia: The Wharton School, University of Pennsylvania.
5. Caleca, M., Gatelli, P., & Patrignani, N. (2008) CRM 2000 Cetif technology outlook. http://www.onbanca.com/docs/Banca-Online-CeTIF-crm.pdf.
6. Rockart, J. F., et al. (2006). *The new IT organization: Eight imperatives*. Cambridge: MIT Press.
7. Pole, A., Puschmann, T., Fischbach, M., & Alt, R. (2011) Web 2.0 applications in private banking: Classification, potentials, and application fields. *ECIS Proceedings, Paper* 266.
8. Currie, W. (1995). *Outsourcing: The new IT strategy, management strategy for IT, financial times* (pp. 131–153). London: Pitman Publishing.
9. Jennings, D. (1996). Outsourcing opportunities for financial services. *Long Range Planning, 29*(3), 393–404.
10. Quinn, J. B., & Hilmer, F. G. (1994). Strategic outsourcing. *Sloan Management Review, 35*(4), 43–55. Summer.
11. Quinn, J. B., Doorley, T. L., & Paquette, P. C. (1990). Technology in services: Rethinking strategic focus. *Sloan Management Review, 31*(2), 79–87. Winter.
12. Quinn, J. B. (1992). *Leveraging knowledge and service based strategies through outsourcing, intelligent enterprise*. New York: Free Press.
13. Heng, S., Meyer, T., & Stobbe, A. (2007). Implications of Web 2.0 for financial institutions: Be a driver, not a passenger. *Deutsche Bank Research.*
14. Swamidass, P. (1993). Import sourcing dynamics: An integrative perspective. *Journal of International Business Studies*, 672–690.
15. Cedacri, (2000). White Paper.
16. Corigliano, R., & Torluccio, G. (2006). ICT e sistema bancario italiano: spesa, impatto sui processi e sulle performance, Banche e Banchieri, pp. 456–475.
17. Gallivan, M.J., & Wonseok, O. (1999). Analyzing IT outsourcing relationships as alliances among multiple clients and vendors, system sciences. *Proceedings of the* 32*nd Annual Hawaii International Conference on IS* (*HICSS*-32).

18. Cantoni, F., & Rossignoli, C. (2000). New distribution models for financial services: The Italian banks' approach to the on line trading development. *Journal of Electronic Commerce Research, 1*(2), 60–66.
19. Celent, (2008). Web 2.0 and retail banking: Less hype equals opportunity. Press release, 14 Nov 2008.
20. Kim, D. J., Yue, K. B., Hall, S. P., & Gates, T. (2009). Global diffusion of the internet XV: Web 2.0 technologies, principles, and applications: A conceptual framework from technology push and demand pull perspective. *Communications of AIS, 24*(1), 657–672.
21. van Zyl, A. S. (2009). The impact of social networking 2.0 on organisations. *The Electronic Library, 27*(6), 906–918.

From IT Governance to IT Service Delivery. Implementing a Comprehensive Framework at Ansaldo STS

Renata Paola Dameri

Abstract IT governance is crucial for information systems, as it defines guidelines and policies to be applied to manage and control IT in business. IT governance promotes, encourages, discourages or bans different management behaviors regarding IT, aiming to achieve business goals and requirements and to manage IT risks. However, IT is more and more a service activity. Users, process owners and the business itself demand efficient and effective IT services. Therefore, it is necessary to design and implement a comprehensive IT governance and service framework, able to link the two aspects: both to define "decision rights and accountabilities to encourage desirable behaviors in the use of IT" (Weill, MIS Q Executive 3:1–17, 2004) and to deliver the required IT services. In this chapter, an IT governance and service comprehensive framework is defined, supported by the empirical implementation of this theoretical model in a large industrial company.

Keywords IT governance · IT service · Flexibility · Service management

1 Introduction

IT governance is one of the more important topics relating information systems [1–5]. It has been becoming more and more interesting, because of two reasons: the need to manage complex information systems in large and global corporations, aiming to reach the best results; and the concurrent obligation to assure the security and affordability of information systems and the integrity of databases.

R. P. Dameri (✉)
Department of Business Administration, University of Genova,
Via Vivaldi 2, 16126 Genova, Italy
e-mail: dameri@economia.unige.it

P. Spagnoletti (ed.), *Organizational Change and Information Systems*, Lecture Notes in Information Systems and Organisation 2, DOI: 10.1007/978-3-642-37228-5_4,

2 The Business Case: Ansaldo STS and its Own IT Governance Model

Ansaldo STS is a large, global industrial company producing transportation solutions. During the latest ten years, Ansaldo had a fast growth, especially pursued by M&A both in Italy and in foreign countries. In 2008 Ansaldo started a large reorganisation, for facing global increasing competition, for integrating its several subsidiaries and for responding to requirements for IPO at Milano Stock Exchange. Main strategic goals of this reorganisation have been: to uniform the enterprise organisation, by formalising business processes and standardising the product offer; to improve the strategic positioning, by focusing on core business and becoming a pure player in transportation solutions; and strengthening of financial capabilities pursuing financial leverage and synergies across the corporation.

Also information system has been involved in this reengineering of the company, by the so called Transformation Program. The aim of this program was initially to define the Functional Operative Model (FOM), which standardises the processes in the main subsidiaries and departments of the Group, to efficiently support company's global growth. The FOM defined a comprehensive model supporting both common business processes and the definition of specific business needs in terms of IT support. The global FOM deriving from the Transformation Program has been the basis for the implementation of the corporate ERP [6, 7].

To support the rapid globalisation and growth of the company and the strong focusing on its core business, Ansaldo STS defined some common IT strategic goals and consequent IT management instruments. The password in this phase were "centralisation" and the following IT organisational structures have been settle [8].

- a central IT Department, to support the IT requirements of the Group and manage the shared IT platform;
- local IT structures to support the IT requirements of the single business units;
- the standardization/homogenization of common IT tools (SAP, Hyperion, Primavera, etc.) to support business improvement activities within the different subsidiaries of the Group, also through cross-companies projects, and to improve the efficiency and effectiveness of IT operations.

In the same period, Ansaldo STS started its IPO program, to become listed at the Milano Stock Exchange. This required to write down and to communicate the IT Governance model within the Corporate Governance of the Group [9]. Ansaldo STS Management decided to started an IT Governance project in order to extend the Corporate Governance concepts to IT operations.

According with its strategic goals, Ansaldo defined a transformation roadmap for its information system, aligning business and IT as explained in the following (Table 1) [10].

To achieve all the complex strategic goals regarding both corporate strategies and information system redesign, Ansaldo STS drove its action towards

Table 1 Business strategy and IT strategy

Business strategy	IT strategy
Global increasing competition	Centralisation and new organisational structures
Integration	Functional operative model (FOM)
Listing	IT governance and compliance model

formalisation. All the efforts have been spent in standardisation of processes, control of operations, accountability and governance by the holding [11]. A strong focus regarded information system affordability; indeed, the Ansaldo STS governance model is based on COBIT, but two additional dimensions are included: *Business continuity* and *Information security.*

At the end of the transformation roadmap, Ansaldo STS reached the goals stated at the beginning. However, the obtained results have not been completely satisfactory. The main reasons are: too much rigidity of the IT governance model, that prevents information system evolution; too much standardisation, applied to different cultures and IT maturity in different subsidiaries and geographical areas; too much process orientation, instead of IT service orientation, that reduces the effectiveness and fit between IT and business.

For these reasons, Ansaldo STS decided to start a new phase, conceived for building on IT governance continual improvement. The new model should maintain the results obtained from the first phase, especially integration of subsidiaries, savings in information system thanks to standardisation, and compliance with law. But the focus of the new project has been to define IT like service delivery, underlining that business requires results, that is, value added IT services, and not mere IT processes, or controls, or governance guidelines [12].

To address the new IT governance model, several aspects have bee taken into main consideration:

- to continue working on IT Governance, defining a flexible framework, to support company changes and IT maturity improves;
- continual improvement, without rigid processes difficult to modify;
- quality of IT services, based on best practices and performance indicators, aiming to measure not only the quality of the process itself but the adequacy of IT services delivered to the business.

3 The IT Governance and Service Model: Basic Principles

To drive the second phase of IT governance redesign at Ansaldo STS, aiming to realise a service management framework to support value delivery from IT to the business, the Board decided for the first to set some general principles and values. In the second phase, the password has been "flexibility", to grant to the company the required agility to face an ever changing, global economic landscape [13].

To orient the IT governance and service model, flexibility has been defined along to three dimensions: horizontal, vertical and time flexibility (Fig. 1).

Horizontal flexibility in IT governance should take into consideration the cultural, geographical and economic differences between subsidiaries. In the first phase, Ansaldo STS especially aimed to standardisation and integration. At that time, it was necessary, because Ansaldo STS Corporation was the result of a series of mergers, acquisitions and settlements of different companies and subsidiaries. Moreover, a strong formalisation of IT processes was required by the compliance to the listing rules. However, different subsidiaries show different IT cultures, different IT organisations (for example, different IT support to engineering in certain countries) and different economic scenarios: rapid growth in Asia Pacific, positioning consolidation and further industrialisation in USA and Europe. It requires a different way in defining priorities for IT investments and in designing IT services for business. It implies also different IT budget and spending. Too much rigidity in applying IT procedures could create difficulties to observe these rules, and IT governance becomes an obstacle instead of helping IT to produce desired results. However, too much freedom means difficulties in managing the integrity of information systems and the risk to be not compliant to governance rules for security and affordability of IT, and finally a concrete risk to loose the control of the information system [14].

Ansaldo STS answered to this need defining three different levels of governance and control instruments:

- IT guidelines, flexible and aiming to align IT and business: they are the same all over the corporation, but give the freedom to maintain the general values applying them in accordance with the specificity of each subsidiary and its own specific economic and IT landscape;

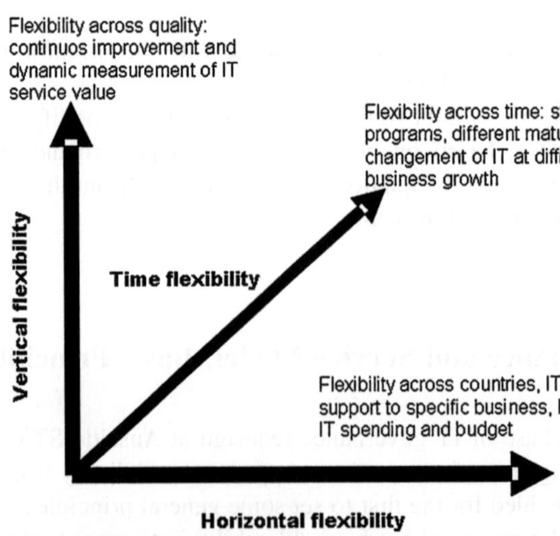

Fig. 1 IT flexibility and its dimensions

- IT global procedures: formal rules and processes to be applied all over the world to assure the integrity, affordability and control of information system at the holding level;
- IT local procedures: formal rules defined by the subsidiaries, respecting the common guidelines and the perimeter of the IT global procedures, but setting specific IT management processes for local needs.

The solution adopted, Guidelines + Global and Local Procedures, allowed for a strong customizing of the content for local needs, while remaining synchronized with the high-level directives.

Time flexibility addresses the need to consider IT governance and service delivery not the goal, but the path [15]. It means that there is not a definitive way to define optimal IT governance or completely satisfactory service delivery, because the correct way to see IT service management is the continuous alignment with the changing economic landscape and company strategic goals. It required by Ansaldo STS to redefine its programs regarding IT, for the first conceiving them not like a unique work-to-do, but like a step-by-step process. This is the only way to support the company changes over time and pursue an ever increasing IT maturity level.

Vertical flexibility regards the need to define the quality of IT governance and service delivery activities [16]. Whereas Time flexibility links the evolution of IT with the changes over time, Vertical flexibility addresses the improvement of IT by the continuous increasing of value delivered by high quality, well addressed IT services. It requires the use of IT service performance indicators standardised at worldwide level, even if aligned with the specific goals of each subsidiary. The right basis to apply the same measurement instruments, is an homogeneous and standardised IT content, as defined by FOM in the first phase of information system reengineering. IT performance measurements have been defined especially based on people and services: internal team efficiency measurement, business process owner satisfaction, user satisfaction, best practices.

Basic IT principles based on flexibility and IT service delivery are summarised in Table 2.

4 Lessons Learned

The business case here studied is very useful to analyse some lessons learned after several years of IT governance implementations in large companies all over the world. This could be the first step to address a new wave in IT governance best practices, more suitable respect to a changing economic landscape and an ever more complex IT environment.

1. IT governance models are generally too rigid. Born to respond to control requirements, these models—especially standards like COBIT—forced companies to adapt their IT management process to rigid schemas, thought for

Table 2 IT flexibility dimensions

Dimension	Goals	Instruments
Horizontal flexibility	Flexibility across countries, IT cultures, IT support to specific business, IT maturity, IT spending and budget	Common IT guidelines and procedures + Local IT procedures. Customising for local IT service need
Time flexibility	Flexibility across time to accomplish with the evolution of business and economic landscape	Step by step programs, different maturity models
Vertical flexibility	Flexibility across quality: continuos improvement of IT services	Standardised performance indicators, based on service levels and stakeholder satisfaction

abstract firms not easy to find in the real world. This criticism is similar to the one presented by Davenport in his famous paper "Putting Enterprise into the Enterprise Systems"; in that case, the ERP were the source of constraints for companies, nowadays IT governance processes are the constraint. Moreover, IT governance frameworks are too much process oriented; they give higher priority to the correctness of the process, instead of to the business quality of the IT services. However, the economic landscape requires more flexibility and more appropriateness of IT respect to specific business needs, also to obtain better returns from IT spending [17].

2. The traditional IT governance frameworks try to involve top managers, but don't involve users in the IT governance definition. But IT users are the real stakeholders of IT services; they are also the personable to know in details what really each business process needs. They don't ask for IT for itself, but for IT services adequate to their activities. It means to involve them in the process mapping and in the service catalog definition. It requires not to use IT governance standards, but to define firm-specific IT governance frameworks, based on IT services. (IT governance and IT service management standards remain the starting point for IT governance and service frameworks design) The involvement of users is able to realise a high responsibility respect to the adequacy and alignment between IT and business and to achieve the "desirable behaviors in the use of IT" [18].
3. The quality of IT especially depends on the quality of IT service management. IT governance standards generally measure the success of information systems in terms of correctness and formal effectiveness of their activities. However, correctness, security and efficiency are the "must have" of an information system [19, 20]. The real added value derives from the alignment between IT services and business requirements. The IT infrastructure is more and more only a facility; the more it is transparent for he users, the better it is. In traditional IT governance and management models, KPI are focused on IT

processes; therefore they are not able to measure the IT actual role for the business. Also the evaluation framework should be rethought and designed on IT service levels; it should take in high consideration flexibility, user satisfaction and IT service appropriateness for the business.

References

1. Weill, P., & Ross, J. (2004). *IT governance: How top performers manage IT decision rights for superior results*. Boston: Harvard Business School Press.
2. Sambamurthy, V., & Zmud, R. (1999). Arrangements for information technology governance: A theory of multiple contingiencies. *MIS Quarterly, 23*(2), 261–290.
3. van Grembergen, W. (2002). Introduction to the Mini track IT governance and mechanisms. *Proceedings of the* 35*th Hawaii International Conference on System Science.*
4. van Grembergen, W. (2004). *Strategies for information technologies governance* (2a ed.). Hershey: Idea Group.
5. IT Governance Institute, (2005). CobiT 4.0. control objectives for information and related technology.
6. Feetke, P., & Loos, P. (2006). Business process reference models: survey and classification. *Lecture Notes in Computer Science, 3812*, 469–483.
7. Curran, T. A., & Keller, G. (1999). *SAP R/3 business blueprint: Business engineering mit den R/3-Referenzprozessen*. Reading, MA: Addison Wesley.
8. van Grembergen, W., de Haes, S., & Guldentops, E. (2004). Structures, processes and relational mechanism for IT governance. In W. van Grembergen (Ed.), *strategies for information technologies governance* (2a ed.). Hershey: Idea Group.
9. Dameri, R.P. (2008). Using an enterprise information management system to enhance IT compliance and information value. *Second European Conference on Information Management and Evaluation* (*ECIME*), London.
10. Earl, M. (2003). Integrating business and IT strategy: Reframing the applications development Portfolio. In J. Luftman (Ed.), *Competing in the information age: Align in the sand*. New York: Oxford University Press.
11. Damianides, M. (2005). Sarbanes-Oxley and IT governance: New guidance on IT control and compliance. *Information Systems Management, 22*(1), 77–85.
12. Brown, A., & Grant, G. (2005). Framing the frameworks: a review of IT governance research. *Communications of the Association for Information Systems, 15*, 696–712. September.
13. Reevles, M., & Deimler, M. (2011). Adaptability: The new competitive advantage. *Harvard Business Review, 89*(7/8), 134–141. Jul–Aug.
14. Rai, A., et al. (2010). Transitioning to a modular enterprise architecture: Drivers, constraints, and actions. *MIS Quarterly Executive, 9*(2), 83–94. June.
15. Goodhue, D. L., et al. (2009). Addressing business agility challenges with enterprise systems. *MIS Quarterly Executive, 8*(2), 73–87. June.
16. Mitra, S., & Sambamurthy, V. (2011). Measuring IT performance and communicating value. *MIS Quarterly Executive, 10*(1), 47–59. March.
17. de Haes, S., van Grembergen, W. (2005) IT governance structures, processes and relational mechanisms: Achieving IT/business alignment in major Belgian financial group. *Proceedings of the* 38*th Hawaii International Conference on System Sciences.*
18. Weill, P. (2004). Don't just lead, govern: How top-performing firms govern IT. *MIS Quarterly Executive, 3*(1), 1–17.

19. Agarwal, R., & Sambamurthy, V. (2002). Principles and model for organizing the IT function. *MIS Quarterly Executive, 1*(1), 1–16.
20. Duffy, J. (2002). IT governance and business value—Part I and II. IDC documents #27291 e #27807.

Public Innovative ICT Based Employment Services Success Factors

Test Cases in Lombardy and Catalonia

Mariagrazia Fugini, Piercarlo Maggiolini and Ramon Salvador Vallès

Abstract This chapter discusses two systems in the employment services in Lombardy and in Catalonia aimed at providing a relevant eGovernment function to citizens and companies. The cases are the *Borsa Lavoro Lombardia* (BLL) Portal and the Catalan Services to Employment (SOC) Portal. By analyzing their features we show the differences in the use of ICT (Information and Communication Technologies) and in the employment policies. Although ICT in its innovative forms (service technologies, communications means, etc.) can provide enhanced functions, these are far from being a true improvement of government activities in both Countries. Our experience in National and in EU Projects allows us to outline a comparison between the Italian and the Catalan systems, which operate on very similar economic and social areas.

Keywords e-Employment · Job marketplaces · Web portals · Federative collaboration · Social impacts · eGovernment

1 Introduction

As countries develop increasingly sophisticated eGovernment infrastructures, there is growing concern about how to ensure the success of these projects. Research underway try to identify factors affecting adoption for the different

M. Fugini (✉) · P. Maggiolini
DEI and DIG Departments, Politecnico di Milano, Milan, Italy
e-mail: fugini@elet.polimi.it

P. Maggiolini
e-mail: piercarlo.maggiolini@polimi.it

R. S. Vallès
ETSEIB, Universitat Politècnica de Catalunya, Barcelona, Spain
e-mail: ramon.salvador@upc.edu

P. Spagnoletti (ed.), *Organizational Change and Information Systems*, Lecture Notes in Information Systems and Organisation 2, DOI: 10.1007/978-3-642-37228-5_5,

maturity levels and relates these to the skills of the user and the digital divide. Categories of factors considered are technical, political, organizational, legal and financial capabilities [1–4]. Suggestions from different bodies and authors regarding the evaluation or benchmarking of eGovernment projects exist. Different levels such as political/strategic, economic, technical/operational and social are included within the evaluation, involving maturity levels, stakeholders and assessment levels [5–7]. Successful information system models for eCommerce are verified for eGovernment [8, 9]. However, there is still a need to better understand how to develop eGovernment in specific areas.

The objective of this chapter is to illustrate two cases, namely the BLL and the SOC, which help to understand some aspects of eGovernment. The proposed cases are eGovernment applications and identify the main commonalities and diversities of ICT-based systems supporting employment, as a paradigmatic example of eGovernment functions. The two systems operate in Lombardy and Catalonia, which are very similar Regions from a social/cultural and economic viewpoint. The chapter discusses the approach and features of each system and outlines the main difficulties in developing true systems of eGovernment in both Regions.

The results of our research will help to highlight the importance of factors related to the socio-cultural environment. In particular, the conditions of use of the innovative services and the cultural factors are analysed with a bearing on skills for using public employment services based on ICT. These factors seem to markedly affect the success of eGovernment projects for the labour market and match those identified in recent studies of other applications [3, 4].

The crucial point, in our opinion, is that the job market, in order to work properly and to be well governed, needs a federation of adequately supported and coordinated initiatives. As a consequence, their support information systems should be based on federations of information systems (cooperative information systems), such that local autonomies are preserved while a loosely-coupled cooperation is created to support knowledge sharing. The adopted technological solutions can provide only the enabling features; these need to be coupled to suitable organizational, political, and cultural measures. In order to achieve actual performing and fruitful solutions, all these measures have to be harmonized. To this purpose, the chapter tries a comparison between the Employment Systems in Lombardy and in Catalonia and draws some conclusions.

2 Employment Services as a Paradigmatic Example

2.1 eGovernment and the Job Marketplace

In the variety of organizational forms in Europe, models and experiences cannot be easily compared and address different ideas of welfare but, straight for this reason, are relevant. At the macro level, the most interesting cases regard the Danish,

English, Irish, and Dutch systems. These Countries are considered, as "top of the form" and, even with great differences in their strategies, have successfully leaded renovation policies of their information systems, of flexibility of the job market, of support of investments, of competitiveness development, and of reductions of fiscal charges on employment. Denmark and the United Kingdom, although in different measures, have tried to activate the job market by limiting the passive policies and by making people in search of an employment more responsible. Ireland has intensively counted upon the continuous economical support and upon the re-balancing of the internal differences. The Netherlands have targeted the increase of job flexibility.

This short presentation shows that if traditionally the job market has been a prerogative of specialized organizations (private/public employment agencies, head-hunting and job search companies), its social implications and enormous impact on the political/strategic decisions of governments have seen an increasing implication of National and Local Public Administrations, with the goal of using ICT to improve the effectiveness and efficiency of the relationship of government with citizens, private companies and employment agencies.

2.2 Relevance of Services to Employment

Currently the job market is changing significantly and rapidly in short-term issues but also in structure; public employment services try to assimilate these dramatic changes, mainly in southern Europe, and react properly. One of the most worrying effects of the economic slowdown is the great increase in the number of unemployed, especially among young people entering the labor market.

Among the causes of changes in the labor market we have the market unpredictable trends and the high variability of demand, which have mined the firm's stability in recent years. Firms in turn have reorganized their activities to improve competitive capabilities by focusing on innovation and flexibility. Such phenomena had a strong impact on the job market place and on the occupational dynamics, originating high job mobility dynamics, unforeseeable in the past years [10]. The request for labour and work is becoming more frequent, due to less stability in the employment relationship, dynamic changes in traditional and new sectors, diversification of career development and labour mobility. In reaction to the market need to receive help in recruitment, the employment mediation industry has experienced fast expansion. It is in fact one of the fastest growing sectors. On the European scene, the further pressure for data sharing and exchanges across system and organisational boundaries arises from labour mobility, regional horizontal collaboration in the wake of decentralisation in labour market regulations, and eGovernment programs (such as IDABC). On the other hand, due to the poor visibility of labor supply and demand, the problem of unsatisfied demands is highly felt. The root cause of these problems is the de-fragmentation of the employment market.

3 Methodological Approach

The regional level is considered appropriate for the provision of public employment services and implementation of policies, and therefore for the development of systems to provide these services. The methodological approach adopted in this chapter, based on the comparison between the two systems, takes this fact into consideration. Lombardy (Italy) and Catalonia (Spain) are analyzed and if they were similar from the standpoint of social and economic, they would enable the identification of critical success factors (CSF) for the performance of ICT-based services. The basic conceptual scheme guiding our proposal to identify the success factors for the social-economic level, by determining the skills, and also for the technological level considers questions raised regarding eGovernment evaluation [5–9].

Thus, the basic research question deriving from this approach is that various different sets of ICT-based services in similar contexts would have to produce significantly different results for these services. Otherwise, why not? Would it be because the influence of the ICTs is irrelevant? Or would it be because the innovative services require conditions of use that are not available in those contexts? What are these conditions? Are cultural factors, perhaps, more important than technological ones?

4 The Lombard and the Catalan Cases

4.1 Employment Services in Lombardy

The BLL supports both the intermediaries of the job market place (e.g. provincial public offices as well as temporary work agencies, or job placement agencies) and the end users, namely the job seekers and the employers (people and companies looking for people to hire). Although in this chapter we focus on the job-related services, BLL is not only a job market place creator or a service/web system for unemployed people, but rather addresses several aspects of human capital growth as well (e.g. vocational training, information provision, continuous education). The laws require all the actors playing an intermediation role in the job market place (e.g. temporary work agencies, job placement agencies, head hunters …) to share some digest information about the curriculums vitae (CVs) and the Job Offers (JOs) they collect. Not all the CVs and JOs are shared, as well as not all the content of a single CV or JO, since the information to be shared was designed to foster *coopetition* (cooperation and collaboration on different activities). Out of information represented by the set of shared CVs and JOs digests, some services are built, e.g. an actor can query for available CVs and JOs matching specific criteria (skill, residence, spoken language, etc.) or can ask to be notified when a suitable CV or JO gets available.

BLL is a web portal that can be used by the job intermediaries, by the job seekers, and by the employers to match job request and offer through a job matching engine. Job seekers and employers can submit CVs and JOs directly with no intermediation. Public and private job intermediaries benefit from information sharing, especially when local unmatched job offers or requests find a match somewhere else (local with respect to the single intermediary boundaries). However, private intermediaries make business from data and they don't like to share their source of business. In this scenario, a *coopetitive model* is used in the BLL to address the conflict among the usefulness of data sharing (for matching local unmatched requests) and the business protection. The solution comes out by observing that, given a CV or a JO, the information subset used for business is different from the information subset used to match CVs and JOs. The matching operations are performed over skills descriptions, while business is performed on trading the "contact information". The public profile is shared among the actors. It contains no personal or contact information but its content is enough to perform an initial CVs/JOs match. The private profile can be identified as the whole information content of a CV (or of a Job Offer description). Private profiles are shared according to some business rules: the employer has to pay a fee to the involved intermediaries in case the proposed job seeker is hired. Private profiles sharing has to be acknowledged by the data owner (the job seekers), in order to prevent privacy-relevant situations.

4.1.1 Performance and Success Factors

BLL is on line since 2004. Its performance can be considered as medium or low. The average of the percentage of persons who seek employment through the BLL above unemployed population seeking employment ranges from 10 to 11 % [11]. It has been observed that the low use of the BLL can be related to several factors such as: (a) the poor habit of end users to interact with a (web) system and to a scarce habit of the employment offices (both public and private) in advertising the potentialities of an interconnected system; (b) people might distrust the information sharing features provided by BLL since a potential threat to privacy is felt; (c) the not exciting performances of BLL can be a further reason of scarce use; and (d) the BLL user interface towards the final users can be ameliorated in terms of usability (customer interfaces), content organization, and simplification of the used vocabulary (for professions, skills, and so on).

4.2 Employment Services in Catalonia

In the case of the Catalan system, named SOC, ICT is used both to provide public services and to inform the Spanish government a list of the unemployed to compute the unemployment contributions. In this sense, the SOC has been used for long as the management and control tool of unemployment within the Catalan Autonomous Community. In any case, the SOC has evolved since 2007 onwards and has undergone a deep renewal. Currently, the SOC, which is attached to the Catalan Department of Labour, integrates and manages active employment policies. It provides services for job seekers and recruiting companies to improve the labour market's efficiency and to increase employment level and quality. The SOC has a network of 73 public employment offices and uses technological channels such as the Internet, a call centre (number 012), a network of self-service interactive units (providing access to some Internet services) and a telephone line to each office.

The SOC website (http://www.oficinadetreball.cat) provides services for job seekers, employers and the general public. Citizens—job seekers mainly—are provided with information on the labour market such as the skills required for particular jobs, training courses, professional help, counselling, grants, etc. Selected information on job offers—including a description of the post, the skills required and the deadline for submitting an application—is provided through a link to a portal called Feina Activa (https://www.feinaactiva.gencat.cat), where job seekers can apply for job offers. Nonetheless, job seekers must personally visit the company, public institution or private agency and to the employment office to carry out any employment-related procedures. A limited number of online procedures such as controls regarding benefits, checking the CV saved with the SOC and obtaining official certificates are offered to those who have registered at a public agency in advance.

The SOC website also features services for companies, private agencies and training organizations, providing information on training programmes in companies, guidance regarding employment contracts and information on finance and employment promotion activities. The website allows firms, public institutions and private agencies to upload publish and manage job offers and to furnish the SOC with data on employment contracts, provided the firms have already registered at a public agency. It offers information on regulations and registration to private agencies and training centres and provides services to citizens such as information about the SOC, news and events, links to other labour market websites and a suggestions box.

4.2.1 Performance and Success Factors

Similar to that of the BLL system, the performance of the SOC system can be considered as medium or low, nevertheless improvements are made successively introducing ICTs in some processes. For example, in 2010–2011 70 % of the renewal of labor demand, were conducted over the Internet (website and self-service points), with great staff savings. On the opposite side we would have little effect on the placement. The rate of registered job seekers on the total unemployed population varies between 20 and 25 %, including mandatory enrollees to perceive the unemployment benefits [12].

Analysing different factors that could be involved in the performance of the system, we have: (a) many of the procedures are not available on the web; (b) the low level of collaboration and integration of information systems among the various interested parties because of the fragmentation of the labour market and legal regulations; (c) the web site doesn't provide complete information about job positions (influences the quality of information); (d) the web site is seen as a complementary channel to the network of SOC offices; (e) the web site is not well known to wider public, people are not accustomed to using it, and employment office staff have skills built up over the years, and now it is proving difficult to change their mindset in order to encourage them to use the web; and (f) users have the perception that the public system offers only administrative benefits rather than providing real job opportunities.

5 A Comparison

Lombardy and Catalonia are very similar from both the economic and the cultural viewpoint, and within their respective countries. It has been observed that the structures of the labor market, the employment rates by sex and age, and employment by full-time/part-time and sex are similar [13]. The margin is narrow enough to be perceived to support this point. Thus, it is considered that the skills to use innovative services and cultural-social factors are similar too.

The analysis of the two service systems is showing that both largely exploit advanced ICT models and infrastructures to achieve their goals. However, the service provisioning models are quite different. In both Regions, outstanding and expensive efforts have been made to develop and implement new information systems in a complex area such as public service supply (eGovernment). BLL connects public and private operators on a federation providing services to job seekers and employers. BLL leverages web technologies through which final users can post job offers and demands with no need for physical a presence in front of operators or mediators (agencies). On the other hand, the SOC Catalan system is based on a network of public offices which do not yet fully collaborate with private agencies of recruitment for instance via a fully fledged database sharing. ICT is used in such a context to provide some services and is also useful to communicate to the central Spanish Government the lists of unemployed to trigger unemployment contributions.

Both the Lombard and Catalan system do not show exciting performances about the user exploitation. Both websites are scarcely popular among citizens and the users' perception is that the public systems offer only administrative advantages rather than increasing the number of contracts. BLL and SOC present apparently the same level of popularity in their regional areas, as testified by statistics reported [14].

6 Discussion

Coming to the features of Lombardy and Catalonia, we can affirm that the two Regions have various similarities from the demographic, economic, and cultural point of view. In such similar contexts, the comparison of the two quite different service provisioning systems stimulates some interesting considerations about the impact of the ICT based employment services on the local employment market and in general about the employment context. First, there exist significant differences in providing public innovative ICT-based services to the employment between the two Regions, and in the technical infrastructure, organization, and management. Nevertheless the systems performance is similar, and because of that it would it appear that the ICT "influence" is irrelevant. Second, according to the above reasons, the irrelevance is perceived of the institutional system—in terms of infrastructure, organization and management of ICT—against the predominant weight of socio-economic factors. The potential of personal networks, combined with social networks (LinkedIn, Facebook, etc.) as ways to expand personal networks contribute to sharpen this situation. Third, the CSFs found in both Regions show that office staff, citizen groups and business organizations are not used to web systems in the employment area and distrust using the Internet; they also have the perception that the system does not provide real benefits and job opportunities. It seems that innovative services require conditions of use for the ICT-based public employment services that are not yet realized in the context of the employment marketplace. These conditions, together with cultural factors are quite similar in the two Regions and have a bearing on skills in using ICT. The limited success obtained by both systems lies, in our opinion, in a cultural deficit, both from the citizens' side and the companies' side in the two Regions, which negatively influences the user's trust in public ICT systems, irrespective of whether they are service-based, accessible via web or technologically advanced. The fact that people still prefer to use personal social networks to find a job could be a reason and time and efforts are needed to unhinge such mind-set.

7 Conclusions

It seems that the main factors influencing the performance of public employment systems are those related to the socio-cultural environment. For this reason the development and use of ICT-based public employment systems at the regional level should consider the identified success factors in order to reduce the risk of not achieving the desired results. While this is not a conclusive result, and other systems and Regions should be analysed, it highlights the influence of the user environment and mentality over systems design. Stakeholders will use the means at their disposal to meet their objectives in the most efficient and effective way. For this reason they will choose, from among the options available to them at any time, those most advantageous for them, public or not.

Acknowledgments We thank M. Cesarini and M. Mezzanzanica for ideas in this chapter.

References

1. Coursey, D., & Norris, D. F. (2008). Models of e-government: Are they correct? An empirical assessment. *Public Administration Review, 68*(3), 523–536.
2. Lee, J. (2010). 10 year retrospect on stage models of e-government: A qualitative meta-synthesis. *Government Information Quarterly, 27*, 220–230.
3. Gauld, R., Goldfinch, S., & Horsburgh, S. (2010). Do they want it? Do they use it? The "Demand-Side" of e-government in Australia and New Zealand. *Government Information Quarterly, 27*, 177–186.
4. Shareef, M. A., Kumar, V., Kumar, U., & Dwivedi, Y. K. (2011). e-government adoption model (GAM): Differencing service maturity levels. *Government Information Quarterly, 28*, 17–35.
5. Irani, Z., Love, P. E. D., & Jones, S. (2008). Learning lessons from evaluating e-government: Reflexive case experiences that support transformational government. *Journal of Strategic Information Systems, 17*, 155–164.
6. Liu, J., Derzsi, Z., Raus, M., & Kipp, A. (2008). e-government project evaluation: An integrated framework. In M. A. Wimmer, H. J. Scholl, & E. Ferro (Eds.), *Electronic government, LNCS 5184* (pp. 85–97). Heidelberg: Springer.
7. Esteves, J., & Joseph, R. C. (2008). A comprehensive framework for the assessment of e-government projects. *Government Information Quarterly, 25*, 118–132.
8. Wang, I. S., & Liao, Y. (2008). Assessing e-government systems success: A validation of the DeLone and McLean model of information systems success. *Government Information Quarterly, 25*, 717–733.
9. Teo, T. S. H., Srivastava, S. C., & Jiang, L. (2009). Trust and electronic government success: An empirical study. *Journal of Management Information Systems, 25*(3), 99–131.
10. Mezzanzanica, M., Lovaglio, P. (2008) Numeri al lavoro. Il sistema statistico del mercato del lavoro: metodologie e modelli di analisi. Quaderni dell'Osservatorio Mercato Del Lavoro 3, Franco Angeli.
11. Cesarini, M., Fugini, M., Maggiolini, P., Mezzanzanica, M., Salvador Vallès, R. (2009) The neglected problem: How to really Benchmark the effectiveness of ICT based services? A case study. *Proceedings of* 14*th Conference Association Information and Management*, (pp. 1–9). Marrakech.
12. Servei d'Ocupació de Catalunya (2011) Employment service report 2010. Generalitat de Catalunya.
13. Eurostat 2012, General and regional statistics. Regional labour market statistics. Employment by full-time/part-time and sex, at NUTS levels 1 and 2, Statistical Office of the European Communities. http://epp.eurostat.ec.europa.eu/statistics_explained/index.php/Unemployment_statistics.
14. Celino, I., Cerizza, D., Cesarini, M., Della Valle, E., de Paoli, F., Estublier, J., Fugini, M.G., Gómez Pérez, A., Kerrigan, M., Guarrera, P., Mezzanzanica, M., Ramìrez, J., Villazon, B., Zhao, G. (2010). SEEMP: A networked marketplace for employment services, semantic technologies for e-government: A European perspective, Part 2 (pp. 151–183). Springer, Heidelberg.

The Pursuit of Happiness: The Virtuous Circle of an IT Tool for its Users and Beneficiaries

Antonio Sebastiano, Andrea Carugati and Antonio Giangreco

Abstract This study analyzes the modernization process of an Italian nursing home driven by the development and usage of software developed in-house. To clarify contradictory results regarding information technology performance in healthcare settings, this study points at the benefits gained by both the users of the software and the guests of the nursing home. This is done collecting both qualitative and descriptive quantitative data regarding the quality of life of the guests and the way operators are affected as result of the new tool adopted. Our study shows that bottom-up participatory design with autonomy, user friendliness and job simplification, and orientation toward guests, were the elements that concurrently generated a virtuous circle for the guests, the users and therefore the organization as a whole.

Keywords IT-driven modernization · Health care · Extended benefits · Nursing home

1 Introduction

High-quality information management represents a focal priority in healthcare. Despite significant investments in information technology (IT) in the healthcare sector, the industry continues to struggle with poor outcomes [7]. Most research on

A. Sebastiano
Università Carlo Cattaneo, LIUC, Castellanza, Italy
e-mail: asebastiano@liuc.it

A. Carugati
Aarhus University, Business and Social Sciences, Aarhus, Denmark
e-mail: andreac@asb.dk

A. Giangreco (✉)
IESEG School of Management (LEM–CNRS), Lille, France
e-mail: a.giangreco@ieseg.fr

P. Spagnoletti (ed.), *Organizational Change and Information Systems*, Lecture Notes in Information Systems and Organisation 2, DOI: 10.1007/978-3-642-37228-5_6,

IT-driven modernization focuses on sources of unsuccessful experiences [13], such as limited uses of technology or low perceived value [3] from the IT investment. In many cases though, information and data simply get mismanaged, neglected, or underused. This highly problematic scenario highlights the gap between what should happen in theory—as exemplified by studies that predict positive outcomes of Healthcare IT (HIT) [1] and what happens in practice.

Our study features the analysis of an experience at *Fondazione Santa Clelia* (FSC), an Italian nursing home that over the past decade has designed and implemented ABC, an IT tool to aid the provision and management of long-term care. The experience generated positive outcomes not only for the operators (see also Carugati et al. [5]), but also for the guests of FSC to the extent that this experience became the pilot study of a larger IT diffusion study with 100+ nursing homes using that subsequently adopted ABC. In the present study, we aim at presenting the software, its development process, and its usage in FSC. This analysis is critical to understand the elements that contribute in practice to the successful use of IT in healthcare settings.

2 Research Context and Methods

2.1 Research Context: Fondazione Santa Clelia

Fondazione Santa Clelia[1] (FSC) is a non-profit, Catholic, publicly accredited residential structure for the aged founded in 1982 and located in Vidiciatico, a small town near Bologna (Italy). A total of 85 guests benefit of FSC services, while 62 of them live at FSC (2009). The resident care philosophy that FSC adopts focuses more on animation and social activities, rather than on heavy use of pharmaceutical treatments. This choice is based on the belief that through social integration, guests can attain better standards of living [14]. The focus requires a high staff-to-guest ratio, which in FSC is 1 operator to 1.5 guests (ratio = 0.68). Labor costs account for 78 % of FSC's operating expenses and making FSC among the most personnel-intensive residences for the aged of the Region Emilia-Romagna.

2.2 ABC Software

In 1999, following the input of a new general manager (GM) the first version of ABC was developed over the course of one year by a volunteer retired software engineer. Over time, the software engineer developed new functions in ABS following the emergent requests of the nursing personnel according to a modular

[1] Acknowledgments: we thank the personnel and guests of FSC for their support.

logic. ABC's modular structure supports daily care and offers a means to record and share behavioral and health information about the guests among all users: nurses, physiotherapists, clerks, doctors, and social animators. The system computes well-being indexes for each guest on daily basis with the aim of monitoring the quality and continuity of services and goals improvement. The data and information collected by the care personnel contain the following areas for each guest: (1) the personal data including the health and the life history; (2) the history of rehabilitation, socialization and animation; (3) the level of autonomy; (4) the information and data regarding the everyday life at FSC (meals, sleeps, falls, etc.). (5) the area of current wellbeing and health conditions; and (6) a synthesis of the objectives, measures and expected results of the different types of interventions, including the current individual plan of assistance (IPA). These areas are collected independently—not to interfere with daily work—but can be analyzed cross checking data (e.g., food with falls; gymnastic with sleep etc.)

2.3 Intervention Description

Before the introduction of ABC, the information existed in paper documents but it was almost impossible to analyze and use. Only administrative staff had access to computers. This is the reason why staff involvement was considered pivotal during the entire development phase. Moreover, the programmer was asked by the GM not to be pro-active, rather he was invited to rely on the input of the most available, enthusiastic or interested operators of FSC. The first prototype was developed with a group of nurses. The development approach was to computerize existing paper documents so that users could feel comfortable with the new electronic form. The second step was that of either eliminating useless information, or adding additional information, or both. As the software evolved, it became evident that the main advantage of ABC was the ability to provide access to all the information when it occurred. This continuous development approach was used in the course of the last 13 years to develop modules to support all the remaining protocols, processes and procedures with the involvement of all the professional profiles working in FSC. The system is still (in 2012) under development, albeit at a slower pace, and the users still play the main role in the development. Personnel, managers, and guests interviewed in multiple occasions declare the implementation to be a success with 100 % rate of adoption at FSC.

2.4 Data Collection

The qualitative data were collected during two field trips, in October 2008 and September 2009 for the purpose of involving all stakeholders multiple times in our data collection [2]. During the first round of data collection, we conducted semi-structured interviews with five people: the general manager, the software developer, an administrative assistant, and two nurses. These interviews lasted 60–150 min and helped us understand how the new IT tool had been developed.

The focus of the second visit was the usage of the tool. We interviewed ten employees (approximately 60 min each) about their daily use of ABC, including a nurse coordinator, five nurses, two social animators, a physiotherapist, and the administrative clerk responsible for the interface between users and the developer. Furthermore, we interviewed two guests who had moved to FSC before the development of ABC. Moreover, we undertook a field observation of the entire working day of a nurse. Finally we carried out two interviews with the GM and the software developer.

We collected the descriptive quantitative data regarding the operators and the guests for 1999 and 2009 (Table 1). To measure changes in guests' mobility and autonomy, we used three internationally recognized parameters (Table 2). The Barthel index measures people's ability to perform normal daily activities, such as eating or walking on a flat floor from 0 (severe, no self-sufficiency) to 100 (complete self-sufficiency) [12]. The Global Evaluation Functional index similarly attempts to define self-sufficiency, partial dependency, and total dependency. Its score varies from 0 (self-sufficiency) to 1,000 (maximum dependency) [8]. Finally, the Mini Mental State Examination measures disturbances to intellectual efficiency and the potential presence of deterioration [10] with a score between 0 (max impairment) and 30 (no impairment).

2.5 Data Analysis

The data analysis involved the comparison and cross checking, over time, of qualitative and descriptive quantitative data. All interviews were tape recorded, transcribed and translated from Italian into English by a person different from the authors of this manuscript. Interview protocols are available from the authors upon request and all interviewees provided verbal consent to use their data. The content of the interviews and field notes was analyzed using Nvivo software to aid the qualitative analysis [11]. To ensure that the system development activities and the

Table 1 Organizational and guest parameters at FSC (1999–2009)

Parameters	1999	2009
Number of beds	60	62
Number of employees	38	42
Guest average age	80.5	83.1
Number of deaths per year	24	15
Employee turnover (%)	7.90	4.76
Average number of sick days	10.6	8.9
Costs/revenues (%)	82.84	94.70

Table 2 Multidimensional evaluation of guests (2003–2009)

Evaluation scale	2003	2009
Barthel index	49	63
Global evaluation functional index	281	245
Mini mental state examination	14	19

development of the organization were grounded in the data, we coded for interconnected evidence of positive and negative experiences with ABC, acceptance or resistance of the system, and evidences of organizational impacts (either positive or negative) [9] with special focus on guests related activities and performances about well being and quality of life. The qualitative data reported by interviewees were then triangulated with the quantitative data extracted from the ABC system. The data analysis involved three cycles of coding according to Charmaz's method [6]. Finally, we cross-checked our coding among authors to control for internal reliability of the analysis. Disagreements among coders were handled by double-checking with the interviewees, procedure that also helped with the external validity of subsets of the analysis, along with cross checking our results with the GM of FSC and through his agreement on the content of this paper.

3 Results: The benefits for Operators and Guests

3.1 Evidences from the Qualitative Analysis

Our qualitative investigation of the development (data collection—phase 1) and use (data collection—phase 2) of the ABC software reveals two main outcomes: (1) The software gradually responded to all the informational and operational needs of the organization, and (2) its use had tangible results for guests' perceptions of their quality of life, managerial decision-making processes, and external perceptions of the quality of care. In brief, the software is widely used, and our interviewees perceive that this use leads to positive results. According to the GM, "through the use of ABC we were able to retain our employees longer, to have more money for social interventions rather than pharmacological treatments, and above all we have prolonged and improved the lives our guests."

The employees of FSC were reticent to try a new technology, but through incremental development, they managed to gain considerable IT skills and now consider it an integral part of their work, rather than a mandated burden: "If I think how scared I was at the beginning … and now I could not live without it [ABC software]" (physiotherapist).This seemingly abnormal but positive use of HIT by the health professionals reflects the contribution of three factors that emerged from our analysis, which led to continuous, pervasive, value-adding use of ABC: (1) bottom-up design with autonomy, (2) user friendliness and job simplification, and (3) orientation toward guests.

3.2 Bottom–Up Design with Autonomy

The idea of having a software tool integrated into FSC's daily activities came from the GM. However, the interviews confirm that the software was developed by the volunteer programmer by never including anything in the program that had not been demanded by staff. Furthermore, the GM enforced a positive cycle that always provided sufficient slack resources to include enough personnel in the development process: *Take the physiotherapists for example… never before existed the concept of knowing over years how much bike a guest does, who does more often or in which days it is done. I wouldn't know what is important so all these requests and the input tables came from the operators. Then of course we had to standardize to make data entry similar for all modules. This was my suggestion to their request to make the software simple to use* (software developer).

In this respect, neither the GM, nor the software developer forced any top-down solution onto users. Users in turn took full advantage of the chance to define their own work tool with respect to their duties, processes, and organizational structure. The "showcase" module in ABC provides a good example, as summarized in the following comment: *The doctors entered the system from home and wrote the prescriptions without looking at the guests diaries. So we asked the programmer to create a rule that the doctors have to pass through the diary of a guest before accessing the prescription page* (head nurse). Over time, the bottom-up approach grew to feel so natural for the organization that initiatives to change or add new modules came only from users. Twelve years after the first test, ABC is an integral part of the activities engaged in by anyone who works at FSC; even training is done internally, such that "everybody is good at using the software perhaps because they come here and the group helps them. We do the training ourselves, on the job" (head nurse).

3.3 User Friendliness and Job Simplification

A key characteristic of ABC is that its complexity grew together with the IT skills and capabilities of the healthcare operators. Many operators (e.g., nurses, health assistants) had been IT illiterate before the introduction of ABC. However since the tool grew with them, they quickly realized its accessibility. The initiative achieved such a warm welcome that the operators even tried to enhance their capability on their own. As the GM recounted, "some of them at the beginning asked help from their sons and daughters; others went to the local computer store for help. Today training is no longer necessary but we sponsor it if they ask. I even had a cook taking an Access course." Furthermore, ABC simplifies and accelerates certain functions by fully reflecting the job of healthcare operators, which require both standard outcomes and immediate local responses. That is, it supports very complex analyses but also provides quick overviews and includes tools to help users react quickly to known problems: *If a guest has an urgent problem which requires going to the hospital, it is necessary to print an accompanying module. This is a complex document … people normally panic … especially at night. Here you see … it is sufficient to click here to print the complete document with all the information* (software developer).

3.4 Orientation Toward Patients/Guests

Finally, largely as a consequence of the previous factors, the data collected in ABC generates a positive cycle of additional value and use for analysis and planning. For example, before ABC, even the individual assistance plans were based mostly on hunches. The ABC software instead provides visual warnings related to daily issues for each guest (e.g., diet, evacuation, mobility, sleep). These warnings are organized temporally, which enables operators and managers to take proper actions according to the current situation or trends. Consider an example of how the warnings in ABC were used in a specific, actual situation to solve one of the major problems for elderly people worldwide, namely, falls [4]: *For example, who falls more than others? Mr. White has fallen 28 times this year [2009]. With ABC I can see falls per year, let's s22 2008: 82 falls in 2008… I am interested in place: 19 falls have taken place in his room. The falls happening in rooms are due to get up phase … he will never accept bedrails. Here you see it: Slipped off bed, found near the bed…. So you see, by crossing data on falls over time and personal data we are able to reflect … being more accurate with our response, grants him, and his family, a better life. Result: we put a gym mat near his bed just in case, to soften the falls: it is non-intrusive, he is happy, and it costs nothing* (general manager).

The perception of care is confirmed by the two guests whom we interviewed about their experiences with regard to the effects of ABC. For example, one guest noted: "At first I did not understand how the nurse from the day shift could know that I had a difficult night. They care a lot about me" (guest).

3.5 Evidences from the Descriptive Quantitative Data

During the first 10 years of usage, the average age of FSC guests increased from 80.5 to 83.1 years. A 3 year increase in average age entails greater complexity and costs for care and clinical services. However, even as the FSC guests grew older, mortality rates decreased significantly, from 24 deaths in 1999 to 15 in 2009, a reduction of 37.5 %. This trend emerged even though FSC moderately increased its bed capacity (+2, an increase of 3.3 %) (Table 1).

As the scores in Table 2 reveal, on all three parameters, the guests have attained improved quality of life since the ABC implementation. In this sense, FSC demonstrates its strong orientation toward rehabilitating guests' residual physical and mental autonomy. It is important to clarify that these positive differences do not refer to the same population of guests given the turnover of guests over 10 years. The ABC software played a significant role in improving FSC capability of personalizing the services through a strong orientation for recovering or maintaining the residual levels of autonomy. This resulted in a higher attractiveness for a population of guests with higher cognitive and functional autonomies. This means that FSC, also thanks to the use of the ABC software, is now more capable of attracting guests who although need to be treated for different typical illness of the aged prefer to live in a nursing home where the residual levels of cognitive and physical autonomy are stimulated.

From a HRM perspective, the adoption of ABC generated better outcomes in terms of personnel loyalty, tenure, and participation. As in many Western healthcare organizations, staff tenure has been a serious problem at FSC. In the past decade though, the extent of this problem was nearly halved, with notable positive effects for the quality and continuity of health services provided. Furthermore, average sick days taken by staff members decreased by 16 % (Table 1).

4 Discussion

FSC developed a system that fit its needs as they emerged. More advanced needs, such as cross-analyses of trends, medication lists, and hospital documentation, entered the system only later and in stepwise fashion. Each function was developed only on when users asked for them. Furthermore the development reflected the evolving needs of the guests. As the types of guests changed (i.e., older, requiring more complex treatment), the software evolved to fit these needs. The quantitative data, whose trends became visible thanks to the software, also played a pivotal role in establishing and maintaining a virtuous cycle both for guests and operators. In particular, they provided tangible, objective proof that the work was benefiting guests. These positive trends fed users' enthusiasm and thus constituted key factors for these projects: *The constant decrease of the use of drugs replaced by stronger rehabilitation and social measures, the improvement of the mobility conditions of guests, [and] the fall in the number of deaths from 24 to 15 with (in the last year) 8 people who were over 95 could not happen without the IT modernization process of the organization driven by the new software* (general manager). While not all improvements are strictly due to ABC, the organizational practices in use today are supported largely by the tool (*we could not leave without it!*) making ABC an important contributor to the organizational performances.

5 Study Limitations and Future Research

This is a promising exploratory study for a wider investigation involving part of (or all) the more than 100 other organizations that have adopted the same tool. However, we need to take into account few limitations. The first limitation refers to the absence of a control group. No solution could be provided because the presence of an internal control group subjected to a lower quality level of long-term care, due to the absence of the software use, would be unequal and discriminant and potentially cause legal problems. Second, we are aware of the fact that rather than providing the evolution of those parameters for the same population, we presented only the comparison (but also the amelioration) of two fixed situations in different times and with almost totally different populations. To overcome these limitations, future research should focus on the comparison of two or more nursing homes having similar type of population, with some using ABC while others used as external control groups.

6 Conclusions

We have presented an IT-driven modernization process for a nursing home that, through careful management and patience, managed to design an HIT system based completely on the needs of users and guests. Proper implementation and productive utilization of a new IT tool appears more likely if the system provides tangible results, obtained from (1) a design focused on the needs of patients, (2) a system that it is easy to learn and use, and (3) a bottom-up approach that considers tips and warnings provided by users. The results provide internal validity that helps maintain motivation, and external validity that supports the organization in its market. Such outcomes require more thinking and energy than money, in contrast with a complex, top-down, universal, cost-cutting IT tools traditionally implemented in health-care organization. These greater efforts realized through the three main results of our research have activated a continuous virtuous circle that brought benefits for guests and operators.

References

1. Adler-Milstein, J., & Bates, D. W. (2010). Paperless healthcare: Progress and challenges of an IT-enabled healthcare system. *Business Horizons, 53*(2), 119–130.
2. Alberg, A. C. (2008). Care recipients' Perceptions of activity-related Life space and life satisfaction during and after geriatric rehabilitation. *QLR, 17*, 509–520.
3. Bath, P. A. (2008). Health informatics: Current issues and challenges. *JIS, 34*(4), 501–518.
4. Bowen, M. E., Craighead, J., Wingrave, C. A., & Kearns, W. D. (2010). Real time locating systems (RTLS) to improve fall detection. *Gerontechnology, 9*(4), 464–471.

5. Carugati, A., Giangreco, A., & Sebastiano, A. (2011). Moving the implementation line: A nursing home's path to success with IT. *SIM, 16*(4), 73–101.
6. Charmaz, K. (2006). *Constructing grounded theory: A practical guide through qualitative analysis*. Thousand Oaks: Sage.
7. Charney, P. (2007). Computer technology and the nutrition support professional: Make it work for you! *Nutrition in Clinical Practice, 22*, 421–427.
8. Cucinotta. D., Angelin, A.& Godoli, G., et al. (1989). Proposta e Validazione di un Semplice Indice per la Valutazione Funzionale Globale dell'Anziano: il GEFI. Giornale di Gerontologia 38, 31–36.
9. Eisenhardt, K. M. (1989). Building theories from case study research. *AMR, 14*(4), 532–550.
10. Folstein, M. F., Folstein, S. E., & McHugh, P. R. (1975). Mini-mental state. A practical method for grading the cognitive state of patients for the clinician. *Journal of Psychiatric Research, 12*(3), 189–198.
11. Hutchison, A. J., Johnston, L. H., & Breckon, J. D. (2010). Using QSR-NVivo to facilitate the development of a grounded theory project: An account of a worked example. *International Journal of Social Research Methodology, 13*(4), 283–302.
12. Mahoney, F. I., & Barthel, D. (1965). Functional evaluation: The barthel index. *Maryland State Medical Journal, 14*, 56–61.
13. Mantzana, V., Themistocleous, M., Irani, Z., & Morabito, V. (2007). Identifying healthcare actors involved in the adoption of information systems. *EJIS, 16*(1), 91–102.
14. Meyer, D., Marx, T., & Ball-Seiter, V. (2011). Social isolation and telecommunication in the nursing home: A pilot study. *Gerontechnology, 10*(1), 51–58.

Legal Issues and Requirements for Cloud Computing in e-Science

Francesco Bellini, Fabrizio D'Ascenzo, Alessandra Ghi, Francesca Spagnoli and Valeria Traversi

Abstract Cloud technologies have increasingly gained momentum in recent years, primarily due to their promise of enhanced performance, such as elasticity, scalability, risk reduction and the easy deployment of end-user services. Despite the great interest and success achieved by the Cloud model, there are still some legal issues raised both in the scientific sector and the information society as a whole. The objective of this paper is to provide the needed starting points for a reflection aimed at the creation of a new governance and legislative model on data protection, privacy and security to develop an efficient strategy on Cloud Computing, notably for government and e-Science, promoting innovation and interoperability in Europe.

Keywords Cloud Computing · e-Science · Privacy · IPR · Data security · SLA · Legal requirements

F. Bellini (✉) · F. D'Ascenzo · A. Ghi · F. Spagnoli · V. Traversi
Department of Management, University of Rome La Sapienza, Rome, Italy
e-mail: francesco.bellini@uniroma1.it

F. D'Ascenzo
e-mail: fabrizio.dascenzo@uniroma1.it

A. Ghi
e-mail: alessandra.ghi@uniroma1.it

F. Spagnoli
e-mail: francesca.s@uniroma1.it

V. Traversi
e-mail: valeria.traversi@uniroma1.it

P. Spagnoletti (ed.), *Organizational Change and Information Systems*, Lecture Notes in Information Systems and Organisation 2, DOI: 10.1007/978-3-642-37228-5_7,

1 Analysis of Potential Legal Issues

On 26 August 2010 the European Parliament Commission on Industry, Energy and Research published The Digital Agenda 2020 [4], a new plan which aims to deliver sustainable economic and social benefits from a digital single market based on ultra-fast internet and interoperable applications and to eliminate the legal fragmentation of contract laws related to the ICT. Europe should build its innovative advantage through reinforced e-Infrastructures, in order to develop an EU-wide strategy on Cloud Computing for government and science, which should necessarily consider several and relevant new legal aspects related to Cloud infrastructures.

1.1 Data Protection Law in the Cloud: Personal and Sensitive Data

In the Cloud, customers and often providers do not have the power or the ability to check the real use and location of their data, which is not fixed in the infrastructure. This problem raises data protection issues related to the swift transfer of data from one data centre to another. The Directive 95/46/EC [7] protects sensitive and personal data, and imposes obligations to the actors of the transfer process. Article 6 and 8 of the Directive [7] clearly state that the collecting and processing of personal data for historical, statistic and scientific purposes is allowed, if Member States provide an adequate high level of safeguards. In the scientific Cloud setting, it is important to clearly distinguish between personal data collected in research and research data in general. The DPA applies only to personal data. Sensitive and confidential information can be shared ethically if researchers apply one or more of the following strategies to managing their data: obtain informed consent to share data, as well as for the participation to the research, obtain consent for the publication of results in which their data is included, protect the identity of the participants and decide if restrictions on data access applies to the information as a whole, researchers have also to inform participants that their data will be transmitted and processed by other researchers in the Cloud infrastructure.

The role of data controller and data processor. Within the context of personal and sensitive data protection in the Cloud, a key role is played by the data Controller. Article 17 of the Directive [7] claims that Member States have to ensure the Controller implements technical and organisational measures to protect personal data against loss and alteration, unauthorised disclosure or access. The Member States must also notify that the Controller, who has the responsibility of the processes, chooses a Processor providing guarantees to his customers. Instead, the data Processor draws personal data for the Controller, but do not exercise responsibilities or control over personal data. According to the DPA [7], data Controller is responsible for the actions of the data Processor when carrying out duties on behalf of the data Controller. As also claimed by Peter Hunstix [9], in a Cloud environment it is not simple to identify the real role of the Controller and the Processor, despite carrying out core functions for data protection. Which role is played by Cloud providers has to be determined case by case, with respect to the specific nature of the Cloud services.

1.2 Risks of Changes In Jurisdiction

Within the Cloud, customers' data may be held in multiple jurisdictions. Often the main problem is the inability to identify where data resides. This situation is more complex in the case of scientific Cloud communities that exchange data more frequently across different countries. It is important to determine whether EU law applies in every specific case. The problem is also amplified in case of international data transfers that may affect privacy. Data transfer to countries outside the EU is regulated by the 25th Article of the Directive [7] preventing the transfer to countries unable to provide an adequate level of data security. This limitation applies also to the possibility to outsource service providers outside Europe. The European Commission has the responsibility to check which specific country provides this adequate level of data and to obtain a contractual promise from the provider to keep information in that country.

Information Security Issues. Often, in a Cloud the customer may not analyse the data security. Furthermore, when the provider inspects the system of one customer, this process also involves those of other clients which are allocated in the same installation. Another relevant information security issue is related to the location of data. The decision adopted by the European Commission (EC) to develop standard clauses for the transfer of personal data outside the European Economic Area (EEA), does not consider the exchanging of combined data in the Cloud, as in the case of scientific communities. However, the Binding Corporate Rules can provide an effective solution to this issue, by developing custom-tailored solutions and eliminating the data transferring problems also between different large scientific Cloud communities. Researchers have to ensure research participants that the Cloud provider complies with these standards.

1.3 Data Security

Security in the Cloud depends on the service delivery model (SPI) and on the Service Level Agreement (SLA). All network level security challenges related to the Cloud are exacerbated by its infrastructure. Often the data stored in private and in public Clouds are not encrypted, because they are allocated only for the storage, which makes them unsafe. Service providers are subject to external audits and security certifications. Where encryption is possible, the provider should prove that their schemes have been designed and tested by experienced specialists. Encryption accidents can make data unusable. It is urgent the need to consider also server and network security, data segregation and back-up/replication policies. A Cloud provider has to ensure also business continuity, security monitoring, application and code security, incident, antivirus and patch management. A useful tool to ensure data security in the scientific Cloud environment, is the Due Diligence, the process of evaluating a prospective business decision by getting information about the financial, legal and other material state of the other party, before entering into an agreement or a transaction with another party. In the Cloud, the customer choosing between different offers should be directed against suppliers who have the effective ability to satisfy the requirements of the context. For the overall internal audit assessment, it is important to negotiate the terms of the relationship with the possibility to build a framework contract to ensure compliance with mutual obligations throughout the life cycle. Due Diligence requires the explication of controls intended to identify potential problems and risks that may arise during the relationship and evaluate the compliance of the performance.

US Safe Harbor. The US has a set of coherent privacy and data protection laws (i.e. USA Patrioct Act, Electronic Communications Privacy Act, U.S. Federal Information Security Management Act, GLBA, HIPAA, Hitech Act) in place with a number of differences compared with EU laws. This approach joins different legislation at State and Federal level. The Federal Rules of Civil Procedure [18] states that parties involved in a civil lawsuit must disclose information to support its defence, including also electronically stored information (ESI), this procedure create several issues in the Cloud context at international level. Indeed, EU legislation prevent from the disclosure of personal and sensitive data without the consent of the subject to which that data refer. This problem can be partially solved by the The Safe Harbor [19], US entities which signed up to this scheme also have to respect EU data protection principles. A US cloud provider must self-certify to the US Federal Trade Commission that it adheres to the Safe Harbor principles through a public declaration once a year. Firms must give individuals the chance to choose whether their personal data will be disclosed to third parties, ensure data integrity, access to its personal information by individuals and the possibility to change or delete personal data. For countries in which the EU Directives and the Safe Harbor may not apply, the European Commission can approve standard contracts [19], between the data exporter in the EU and the data importer outside the EU to ensure safeguards for the personal data transferred. Within the American context, the data security is protected also by the U.S. Federal Information Security Management Act [15] that obliges the U.S Federal agencies to develop, document and implement an agency information security program.

1.4 Privacy Laws

The Cloud model has significant implications for the confidentiality of business, governmental and personal information. According to Mather [12], the key privacy concerns in the Cloud are related to: access, compliance, storage, retention, destruction of data, audit and monitoring, privacy breaches. First, to protect the confidentiality of data it is needed to encrypt them. However, this is not enough to also ensure the integrity of personal information as integrity requires the use of message authentication codes (MACs). Privacy and confidentiality risks may vary depending on the terms of service and privacy policy established by the Cloud provider. Furthermore, confidentiality and privacy rights may be modified when a user discloses information to a Cloud provider. In a scientific Cloud that needs to protect the privacy and the confidentiality of data exchanged between different research communities, barriers should prevent the transferring to third parties. To protect their data, users, must ask the provider to include in the contract privacy and confidentiality clauses identifying the liability of the parties. The Directive [7] states that unauthorised listening, tapping, storage or other kinds of interception or surveillance of communications is illegal. If a third country does not ensure an adequate level of protection, the Directive requires the blocking of specific transfers. At International level, the Privacy and Confidentiality of Information is protected by the OECD [17] and the APEC [2] establishing guidelines and best practices for organizations, governments, business, industry and the civil society operating in the International Economic Area and processing personal data. These guidelines enable providers and organization to effectively move to cloud solutions complying with the legislation and ensuring an adequate level of security of personal and sensitive data.

Confidentiality in the Cloud. The National Research Council [16] assessed the disclosure of biological and social data risks online. They discovered that the degree of potential damage to shared scientific information is higher in the case of combined data. It is a problem if the data stolen cover social topics. The literature on data sharing describes two broad approaches to protect the confidentiality of individuals whose records appear in data collections: restricting access and restricting data. According to [16] the restricted access strategies are four:

1. licensing: to remove direct identifiers, researchers must sign a licensing agreement not to use the data for malicious purposes
2. remote execution systems: confidential data are stored in a computer system owned by the data disseminator. Researchers who want to use these data, submit a query to the system, which discloses only the information that is not confidential
3. data enclaves: an investigator works in a room dedicated to accessing the data. Researchers cannot take individual-level data from the enclave
4. virtual data enclaves: he data is housed in a system owned by the data disseminator. Licensed secondary researchers access the data remotely.

Instead, through the restricted data approach, many data sets containing biological or social data are shared after the identification or sensitive values of data have been altered. Scientists may protect confidentiality by obscuring relatively high-order features. The strategy has to be chosen during the process of planning for the study, to insert the consent form with the details.

1.5 Identity and Access Management Guidelines

In a Cloud environment, there is the need to plan basic user management functions [10]: account provisioning, credential and attribute management, entitlement management, compliance management, identity federation management, centralisation of authentication and authorisation, access management and log management. However, within a Cloud infrastructure it may be a loss of control and the network, systems and application can be extended into the service provider domain. IAM may help the migration of IT applications into a Cloud service model, accelerate the adoption of new Cloud services, improve operational efficiency by automating user on-boarding, control access and ensure the respect of data protection and privacy rights.

1.6 Intellectual Property Rights

According to the Green Paper [5], we have to determine who will own these rights in the Cloud and the use of this information by third-parties, especially in the case of scientific Cloud communities. With reference to collective works owned by citizens of Member States, the economic rights shall be owned by the person holding the copyright. For a database created by a group of natural persons jointly, the exclusive rights shall be owned jointly. The 2001/29/EC [8], in Chapter II, in Article 2 and 3 protects only the authors of the work. Any unauthorised communication to the public of the works is prohibited. In recent years, the EU efforts on IPR laws are increasing, particularly in the knowledge economy. The European Commission has adopted a Communication on this kind of copyright [6] aiming to provide mass-scale digitization and dissemination of books, creating new ways for researchers to access to knowledge.

According to the American legislation, Intellectual Property includes copyrights, trademarks, patents, industrial design rights and trade secrets. Intellectual Property is addressed by the U.S. Copyright Act [20] and a WTO Agreements [21] including International conventions and treaties regulating also the disclosure of data protected by IPR laws in electronic format, providing an high level of protection to American and foreign countries.

1.7 Service Level Agreements

A Service Level Agreement is a part of a Master Agreement between the service provider and its customers in reference to the availability, performance, downtime and service suspension, security, support and description of services, modification of the agreement, licenses. In a scientific Cloud if there is no individual who requires access to the Cloud, contracts must be differentiated, according to the specific services accessed by the different research communities. An SLA should contain also the indication of services delivered, the metrics to allow users to verify if the provider is complying with terms and conditions, auditing of the service, responsibilities of each party and a forecast of the changes that will occur over time. In an SLA are not included only the duties of providers, but also those of the users, such as their responsibilities, restriction on the kind of data shared.

2 Legal Requirements for e-Science

Dealing with sensitive data collection, processing and storage, scientific research on Cloud may involve serious personal and sensitive data issues. For instance, in the case of human genome research, if the data are disseminated through the Cloud outside the specific research group, unauthorised individuals may intercept these data and cross them with other information coming from other subjects, creating serious issues. Assuming the situation where a researcher is studying the "Muscular Dystrophy" and an intruder accesses to the researcher's database, the intruder, combining the sensitive data with publicly available information, may determine that John Smith is potentially affected by this hereditary rare disease. The Cloud provider is financially and legally liable for this data protection loss. As a preliminary condition, the Cloud provider must ensure to scientific Clouds that their data will be treated in accordance with the International legislation and that the third party also complies with the legislation. To avoid the legal issues related to the risks of changes in jurisdiction and personal and sensitive data, the Cloud provider should have signed a Service Level Agreement (SLA) or a Non-Disclosure Agreement (NDA). Related to data security issues, one evident problem can be represented when, for instance, an architectural research community decides to use Cloud Computing services and suddenly the infrastructure is struck by damages or interruption from earthquakes. The Cloud provider has to offer tailored disaster recovery services and ensure the compliance with the European and International regulatory framework and the security standard controls ISO/IEC series [13] and SAS70 [1]. The provider should also trigger a Due Diligence process to protect the physical server, network, encryption, back-up or replication security. A trust relationship based on transparency between members is relevant for the effective functioning of the Cloud community. If the researchers use data protected by privacy laws, he has to ensure integrity, confidentiality and availability for the data safety. For instance, assuming the case of doctors assessing somatic mutations in tumours and evaluating individual's germ line mutations using the Cloud, the related data collected and managed are protected by privacy and confidentiality laws. In this situation, researchers have to identify what kind of confidentiality risk is involved: with the identity disclosure risk the intruder is able to determine that record number 7 belongs to patient X, instead with the attribute disclosure risk an intruder learns something new about the patient in the database without knowing which specific record belongs to that patient. If patients from a specific area in the research database had a certain test result, an intruder does not need to know which record belongs to patient number X, to obtain this sensitive information about the subject. The Cloud provider and the researchers both have to ensure the privacy and confidentiality of the patients. Also the scientists using confidential data have to trigger the strategies of the National Research Council [16].

With reference to the Intellectual Property, the Cloud provider is the only subject who has the duty to ensure the protection to its customers, however in some particular cases, legal issues related to this topic may occur. For instance, let's assume the case of a pharmaceutical researcher working in the Cloud on an innovative life-saving medicine which is still under development. The researcher could receive relevant scientific awards for this discovery. But, if other subjects in the Cloud access the data and steal the information collected by the pharmaceutical researcher, the former subject could reuse the data and publish them in a scientific paper. In this case, the pharmaceutical researcher has no possibility to prove the paternity of the data and of the discovery. The confidentiality issues can occur if the Cloud provider is not compliant with Directive 2001/29/EC [8] and he has also to conform to International Copyright principles. In the scientific Cloud context, only the provider is obliged to ensure the centralisation of authentication and authorisation to large communities that can develop lacks of data protection. The Cloud provider should ensure the security of credentials, the interoperability and scalability of authentication systems and the speed of deployment and implementation of identity procedures. Each researcher should have a password and a username to access his or her community on the Cloud. The provider has also to plan and provide user management functions. However, in the Cloud, it might be possible to violate the identity credentials. Indeed, assuming the case where several aerospace engineers, residing in foreign countries, use the Cloud services in order to work together for the development of an innovative spacecraft. However if other subjects steal the identity of an aerospace engineer and access this information through the Cloud, they can use the data before the effective implementation of the spacecraft. If these subjects sell the prototype to other companies its project funding could be revoked and the high profits resulting from this discovery would be given to the other subjects. The Cloud provider must also enable auditing processes. However, also the local authorities have to consider the availability of each cloud community's node and its interoperability. All research projects should have in place also an easily accessible Data Management Policy (DMP) which contains high level statements about how data generated or compiled in the research project is to be made available for access and use. As stated in the European Union in the Opinion 05/2012 [3], there is the urgent need for an International Cloud risk management model, including the prior identification of operational risks and evaluating the potential international legal risks to to constitute an effective and secure winning strategy for the renewal of private and public companies through Clouds Computing infrastructure. This statement is in line with the US Federal Cloud Computing Strategy [11] to ensure a trustworthy environment and mitigate the legal threats in accordance with the NIST technical security guidance [15] and the US Risk Management Framework [14].

3 Conclusions

The previous legal analysis highlights a number of key considerations about Cloud Computing in scientific settings. The only predictable solution is to study a global approach to Cloud legal issues, in which international organisations design a unique regulatory framework and an open and flexible market to effectively improve the economic potential of Cloud technologies.

References

1. American Institute of Certified Public Accountants (AICPA), SAS No. 70 Audit, available at: http://sas70.com/index.html.
2. APEC Secretariat. (2005). APEC privacy framework. Available at: http://www.ema.gov.au/www/agd/rwpattach.nsf/VAP/(03995EABC73F94816C2AF4AA2645824B)~APEC+Privacy+Framework.pdf/$file/APEC+Privacy+Framework.pdf.
3. European Commission. (2012). Article 29 data protection working party, Opinion 05/2012 on Cloud Computing.
4. European Commission. (2010). Communication from the European commission to the European Parliament: A digital agenda for Europe. Available at: http://www.edps.europa.eu/EDPSWEB/webdav/site/mySiteshared/Documents/EDPS/Publications/Speeches/2010/10-0413_Speech_Cloud_Computing_EN.pdf.
5. European Commission. (2008). Green paper copyright in the knowledge economy. Available at: http://ec.europa.eu/internal_market/copyright/docs/copyrightinfso/greenpaper_en.pdf.
6. European Commission. (2009). IP/09/1544, European Commission puts challenges of books digitisation for authors, libraries and consumers on EU's agenda. Available at: http://europa.eu/rapid/pressReleasesAction.do?reference=IP/09/1544.
7. European Parliament and the Council. (1995). Directive 95/46/EC of the European Parliament and of the council of October 24 1995 on the protection of individuals with regard to the processing of personal data and on the free movement of such data, Official Journal L 281, 23/11/1995, pp. 0031–0050. Available at: http://eur-lex.europa.eu/LexUriServ/LexUriServ.do?uri=CELEX:31995L0046:en:HTML.
8. European Parliament and the Council. (2001). Directive 2001/29/EC of the European Parliament and the council on the harmonization of certain aspects of copyright and related rights in the information society. Available at: http://eur-lex.europa.eu/LexUriServ/LexUriServ.do?uri=OJ:L:2001:167:0010:0019:EN:PDF.

9. Hunstix P. (2010). Data protection and cloud computing under EU law. European Data Protection Supervisor. Third European Cyber Security Awareness Day. BSA. European Parliament. Available at http://www.edps.europa.eu/EDPSWEB/webday/site/mySite/shared/Documents/EDPS/Publications/Speeches/2010/10-0413_Speech_Cloud_Computing_EN.pdf.
10. Christian, A. Christiansen., Charles, J. Kolodgy., Sally, H., Gerry, P., (2010). White Paper: Identity and access management for approaching clouds, May 2010, IDC. Available at http://www.ca.com/us/~/media/files/industryanalystreports/cloud_security_wp_236234.aspx.
11. Kundra V. (2011). Federal cloud computing strategy. Available at: http://www.cio.gov/documents/federal-cloud-computing-strategy.pdf.
12. Mather, T., Kumaraswamy, S., & Latif, S. (2010). *Cloud security and privacy* (p. 149). Sebastopol: O'Reilly.
13. National Institute of Standards and Technology (NIST). (2010). Cloud computing standards roadmap document: NIST CCSRWG– 070 Eleventh Working Draft, 2011 National Institute of Standards and Technology (NIST), NIST Releases Guide for Applying the Risk Management Framework to Federal Information Systems (Special Publication 800-37, Revision 1). Available at: http://www.nist.gov/itl/csd/guide_030210.cfm.
14. National Institute of Standards and Technology (NIST). (2002). Statutory responsibilities for developing standards and guidelines, Federal Information Security Management Act (FISMA) of 2002, Public Law, pp. 107–347.
15. National Institute of Standards and Technology (NIST). (2002). The Federal Information Security Management Act of 2002 ("FISMA", 44 U.S.C. § 3541 enacted in 2002 as Title III of the E-Government Act of 2002 agency.
16. National Research Council. (2008). Biosocial Survey, Committee on Advances in Collecting and Utilizing Biological Indicators and Genetic Information in Social Science Surveys, Maxine Weinstein, James W. Vaupel, and Kenneth W. Wachter, Editors, available at http://www.nap.edu/openbook.php?record_id=11939.
17. Organisation for Economic Co-operation and Development (OECD). (1980). Guidelines on the protection of privacy and transborder flows of personal data. Available at http://www.oecd.org/internet/ieconomy/oecdguidelinesontheprotectionofprivacyandtransborderflowsofpersonaldata.htm.
18. The Committee on the Judiciary House of Representatives. (2010). Federal rules of civil procedures, Washington.
19. U.S. Department of Commerce. (2009). U.S.—EU safe harbor framework. Available at: http://trade.gov/publications/pdfs/safeharbor-selfcert2009.pdf.
20. U.S. Government. (1976). Copyright law of the United States and related laws contained in title 17 of the United states code. Available at: http://www.copyright.gov/title17/.
21. WTO. Agreement on trade-related aspects of intellectual property rights, available at http://www.wto.org/english/docs_e/legal_e/27-trips.pdf

Acts of Organizing and Knowledge Sharing: Key Factors Towards a Non-positivist Development of E-Service Studies

Paolo Depaoli

Abstract The purpose of this conceptual chapter is to show, within a service science approach, that the improvement of e-services (and not just of services) is based not only on further development of ICTs (e.g., band width and computing power) but on the effective exchange of knowledge (including tacit knowledge) between providers and consumers enabled by the interplay of technology and people through specific acts of organizing. To this end, e-government has been chosen as an area of investigation and exploration because of the number of heterogeneous actors involved (individuals and public and private organizations), of the extensive use of technology, and of the issues that are being debated. Furthermore, the field has been an object of study for several years so that the available literature to draw upon is rich. Results show that the basic tenets of service science developed so far are an appropriate lens to understand current concerns in e-government and, conversely, the results of research on this subject can help address some key questions in e-service studies.

Keywords Service science · e-government · Acts of organizing · Knowledge sharing

1 Introduction

In his brief note on the Harvard Business Review, when describing the reasons why the new discipline of 'services science' seemed to be a promising area of research, Chesbrough [1] stressed the role of intangibility as the specific trait of services with two main consequences: (1) the lack of a tangible artifact to test consumers needs that makes innovation a different endeavor from other sectors;

P. Depaoli (✉)
Università degli Studi di Urbino "Carlo Bo", Urbino, Italy
e-mail: paolo.depaoli@uniurb.it

P. Spagnoletti (ed.), *Organizational Change and Information Systems*, Lecture Notes in Information Systems and Organisation 2, DOI: 10.1007/978-3-642-37228-5_8,

(2) productivity is harder to measure since both inputs and outputs are intangibles. He considers these two areas of research not satisfactorily explored by other disciplines. The same occurs to the question of the transfer of tacit knowledge which Chesbrough finds particularly relevant since services promote encounters among people that have to learn from each other for an effective service to occur. The accent on tacit knowledge was kept at center stage in the article that Chesbrough co-authored with Spohrer the following year [2]. A successive article by Spohrer and other members of the Almaden IBM Research center [3] points to explicit knowledge ("information" in their wording) as the key issue. Furthermore, given the importance of information technology in services, they highlighted the need to both differentiate and find connections between computational systems and service systems since the components can be modeled and simulated in the former whereas in the latter the presence of human beings complicates matters substantially. They suggest: "*perhaps*, if we model people as components with stochastic behavior" existing theories of computational systems can be applied to service systems ([3] p. 76, italics added). The word 'perhaps' used by the authors shows that caution is necessary when proposing computational models to be applied to human behavior. The theoretical objections to the computational model of the mind have been put forth for example by Dreyfus[4]; here such objections are mentioned because they underline the role of tacit knowledge in understanding human learning, both in individuals and organizations. Furthermore, other literature on service science defines service as "the application of competences (knowledge and skills) by one entity for the benefit of another" [5, p. 145] so that knowledge is once again at center stage in the discussion concerning the development of a theoretical framework for service science. This definition of service is particularly useful since it creates the basis for a non deterministic view of technology. Information and communication technologies (ICTs) are certainly a basic part of the picture but they must be kept in a non dominant role when undertaking the design of a service, lest they take the preeminence and obscure other and as important factors. In the work of Vargo and Lusch, the ten 'Foundational Premises of Service-Dominant Logic' is another contribution that should be highlighted in the service science literature because of its relevance for a non positivist approach to e-service studies. Specifically the tenth one: "Value is always uniquely and phenomenologically determined by the beneficiary" since "Value is idiosyncratic, experiential, contextual, and meaning laden" [6, p. 9].

Drawing on service science literature, the purpose of this conceptual chapter is to show, within a service science approach, that the improvement of e-services (and not just of services) is based not only on further development of ICTs (e.g., band width and computing power) but on the effective exchange of knowledge (including tacit knowledge) between providers and consumers enabled by the interplay of technology and people through specific acts of organizing. To this end, e-government has been chosen as an area of investigation and exploration because of the number of heterogeneous actors involved (individuals and public and private organizations) and of the extensive use of technology. Furthermore, the field has been an object of study for several years so that the available literature to draw upon is rich.

The theoretical underpinnings draw on service science literature, mainly the work by Chesbrough, Spohrer, Vargo, and their co-authors [2, 3, 5, 6]. Furthermore, a non deterministic approach to technology is supported by Dreyfus [4] and Orlikowski [7] [8].

The chapter is structured in the following way. In the first section experiences and theories concerning evaluation in e-government initiatives are examined and commented on. The second paragraph explores the question of 'value propositions' in e-government. The third one considers the present characteristics of co-production in e-government and in the fourth section the paradox of policy claims concerning citizen participation are confronted with the scant participation of citizens in design activities. Concluding comments present the results obtained through the previous analyses.

2 Evaluating in a Non-positivist 'Service Science' Perspective

According to the framework proposed by Spohrer and his co-authors [3] internal and external services are considered to be key components of service systems. In the relevant literature on e-government, internal services (the vast area of 'back office', for example) are deemed to be just as important as updating front office service delivery channels [9]. A key service that can be either internal or external is managing change within public agencies since changes in ICTs have to be accompanied by organizational changes [9]. The way technology is conceived orientates priorities and the early phases of e-government projects have suffered from technologic determinism [10] so that appropriate design techniques constitute a core service to be offered in projects. In advanced countries' reform agendas, customer focus has been gained in projects whereby the needs of citizens and businesses prevail [9].

One crucial service within the e-government arena concerns how to evaluate initiatives from the ex ante phase to the monitoring of their implementation, searching for both positive outcomes and weaknesses so that experience can be gained for successive endeavors. The issue is complex but has interesting implications for the aim of this chapter. Evaluation becomes ever more critical since researchers who are investigating e-government in order to orientate initiatives in developing countries have stressed the enormous amount of resources invested in industrialized societies on government information technology: over 1 % of gross domestic product according to some estimates [11]. It is not surprising then that the evaluation approaches more commonly used are centred on return on investment, cost/benefit, payback period, and present worth which, however, have been criticized, for example, for their inability to go beyond the targeting of direct tangible costs and benefits in information systems (IS) in general and specifically in e-government [12]. When considering the issues of information systems evaluation, some authors [13] find in the dominant overarching positivist conception (basically functional or rationalistic) the origin of the inadequacy of evaluation approaches that consider IS independent of organizational components: technological and accounting aspects overweigh the social ones so that the organizational context and the process of development of IS are not properly considered. Thus the evaluation process offers incomplete indications. When, instead, technical change is considered to be interwoven with organizational change, the evaluation process cannot be considered any longer an objective and external judgment and becomes itself "a socially embedded process in which formal procedures entwine with the informal assessments by which actors make sense of their situation"[13, p. 94] Since situations evolve, sensemaking is a process by which actors give meaning to their experience and orientate their choices and actions so that the evaluation process is open-ended -whereby, from IS design onwards, outcomes are interpreted and used to guide successive action toward improved performances. As Weick and his co-authors point out [14], besides being retrospective (built on experience) and onward looking (aimed at identifying successive actions), sensemaking is also social (actors are interdependent) and it entails communication so that interactive talk and exchange of interpretations allow organizing and decision making in the different circumstances at hand. In sum, the IS evaluation cycle deals with organizational change and is a complex matter that has to do with numerous aspects besides the (however crucial) technical and accounting ones. Specifically, the mentioned research results show that important tacit knowledge is created by the interaction of people in the sensemaking process and this fact should be considered when both evaluating and designing e-services.

As in the case of several e-government initiatives, when IS dimensions are significant, the issues in organizing change (and sensemaking) to pursue a certain accomplishment become ever more crucial because of the time required for development of the specific system and of the large number of heterogeneous actors involved. An example of the complex network of interests implied and of the analyses that have to be carried out in order to evaluate such large projects is the assessment conducted by the London School of Economics [15] on the Identity Cards Project that was to be launched in 2006 by the British government to combat terrorism and reduce crime. The report concluded that the 10 year roll-out, 10.6 billion pound (minimum) cost project for "the establishment of a secure national identity system has the potential to create significant, though limited, benefits for society. However, the proposals currently being considered by Parliament are neither safe nor appropriate." (p. 5) The project was then revised, partially implemented and finally dropped at the beginning of 2011. For the aim of this chapter, the most interesting comments of that report concern the key perspective to be adopted for a successful program: "Depending on the model used, identity systems may create a range of new and unforeseen problems… The success of a national identity system depends on a *sensitive, cautious and cooperative approach involving all key stakeholder groups* including an independent and rolling risk assessment and a *regular review of management practices*." (ibid., emphasis added).

This concluding remark is particularly meaningful because it stresses that not only services are co-produced by providers and consumers (in this case the value to be co-produced was 'security'), but that also in e-services co-production is vital in order to prevent ineffectiveness and even failure. The 'new and unforeseen problems' can only be tackled by sharing information (explicit knowledge) and experience (tacit knowledge) gained among service providers in a process of 'sensemaking'.

3 'Value Propositions', Strategies and Models in e-Government Initiatives

The comments just made show that in e-government both the perspective of service-dominant logic and the concept of co-creation of value-in-use seem to be particularly useful, as the service science literature has pointed out [5, 6]. As mentioned above, the basic change undergone during the years in e-government approaches is the shift from techno-centric standpoints, where ICT was expected in itself to spur efficiency and effective services, to enabling views, where the accent is not on technology but on how public administration should change supported by technology [10]. Given the aim of this chapter, one question concerns whether or not (among policy makers and scholars) there is agreement on the core values that are leading this change since they should inform strategies and guide agents in the structures undergoing change (to generate better e-services) in the duality of organization and technology [16]. Interestingly, a recent research [10] shows that in the e-government practice the two sets of values that have been competing in the theoretical arena ('Weberian Bureaucracy' versus 'New Public Management-NPM') concerning public administration change are actually blended: elements of both approaches emerge. In fact, traditional weberian values (e.g.,: rule of law, objectivity, impartiality, high specialization, transparency) have been pursued and held together with NPM values (e.g.,: customer/citizen orientation, mission and goal orientation, cost efficiency). The following is a concluding comment expressed by the researchers in their case analysis: "[in] the project there existed value conflicts between NPM advocates of *customer centricity* and case-handling officers who relied on more traditional weberian values" (p. 55). This instance shows that different values and interests have been composed not because a superior entity in charge of e-government design decided that a new set of (blended) values had to be implemented. Rather, agents found a way to promote and safeguard their choices.

Those agents can be considered to be internal service providers that are making different (and competing) value propositions and who found a way to compose their different proposals in an integrated value proposition to internal customers (the IS designers). This process can be considered itself a service (internal of course) because a new set of values (a blend of Weberian and NPM values) was co-produced through the interaction of people with different views who shared their knowledge.

The cited study does not explain how the synthesis between the two opposing strategies came about, that is what acts of organizing and leading where enacted by relevant actors. Nor such issues seem to have been included in the other high level models present in the literature [17]. Yet, there are several unsolved problems that concern citizen-government interaction and therefore the development of an effective value propositions to citizens by public administrations. The next session considers this interaction.

4 The Quest for Increased Citizen-Government Interaction: A Way Towards Co-production?

In 2001, the Organisation for Economic Co-operation and Development (OECD) published a report that identified key issues in strengthening government-citizen relations and ongoing interactions [18].The form of citizen involvement deemed desirable is 'active participation': the direct engagement of citizens in decision-making and policymaking. However, the analysis of the impacts of ICTs (the 'new frontier' of government-citizen relations) conducted in the report confirmed that online active participation was even more limited than offline participation.

What became clear in successive studies is that the engagement of citizens and the contextualization of e-government projects require not only the bridging of the 'digital divide' but also the promotion of 'intermediate entities' to act as a go-between in connecting citizens with services [9]. The important role of 'intermediaries' becomes apparent because the attitude of people towards ICT-intensive services has not been encouraging: surveys conducted in the years 2000 in the United States showed that half of the adult population had never visited the websites of federal agencies (two thirds had never accessed state or local government websites) [19] and the users of health information technology have been few [20]. Thus, any strategy concerning the delivery of public services must leverage other resources in order to integrate digital with in-presence public services. An example of such a strategy is the 'transformational government' policy launched by the UK government in 2005 [21], whereby government is transformed through technology but is also 'transformational' because it retains the ability to innovate by using technology effectively as technology itself develops. In this approach, the appropriate channel strategy is determined for each customer group, including relevant parts of government, "use of intermediaries,…, local providers and the voluntary and community sector" [21, p. 11].

In sum, in e-government programs a service-dominant logic is being built and a number of intermediate service providers ('intermediaries') are developing their value propositions in a sort of supply chain, where different techniques are employed (both digital and in-presence). The reason for the flourishing of services within services is realizing that value is basically idiosyncratic and contextual, as was mentioned in the introduction to this chapter. Implanting a service-dominant logic in e-government, however, has to overcome a paradox.

5 The Paradox: Pursuing Citizen Participation but in e-Government Projects

At the policymaking level (at least in the OECD countries), there is: (1) a willingness to ensure higher interaction between citizens and governments; and (2) the belief that ICTs can be effective drivers and enablers of such augmented interaction. In addition, there is an awareness that the electronic channels pose problems of accessibility and usability that curtail their diffusion and use [22]. Despite such a widespread perception of the issues at stake, most existing studies on user engagement are not sensitized to the context of e-government [23]. The knowledge of how citizens are engaged in the development or selection of appropriate 'tools' (a growing phenomenon) is still inadequate since the literature on this topic is scant [24]. Clearly, the specific issue of 'citizen' engagement needs further study since 'user' participation instead has been extensively researched in information theory and practice (and its usefulness often acknowledged): as, for example, in the June 1993 issue of Communications of the ACM. Further, theoretical frameworks have been available for a long time: the socio-technical approach to IS of Enid Mumford dates back to 1983 [25].

Therefore, it is in some ways paradoxical that while e-government applications pursue interaction (and possibly active participation), the understanding of user (citizen) participation in designing e-government systems is still limited. In other words, users have little opportunity to be involved in technology design or to exercise 'ownership' over the solution provided. "There is also an inadequate appreciation of the culture of service providers and users and the context of service delivery and use" [26, p.863]. Yet, since the use of e-government services is still unsatisfactory, the engagement of citizens in the development of e-government systems and services would appear to be an essential factor, "the missing link" in generating e-government projects [27, p. 500]. Though based on the current limited evidence of citizen engagement in such projects (as the authors themselves highlight), the conclusions of the last cited study stress the importance of 'capacity building' in IS development, of leveraging the experience matured in offline citizen consultation and participation, and of circulating the emerging e-government participatory practices.

One significant problem, then, is that the actors involved in the design and implementation of e-government programs have an insufficient culture of co-production so that value-in-exchange is still dominant with respect to value-in-use: focus is more on products to be delivered (IS applications) rather than on a thorough organizing of knowledge sharing along the process that is meant to perform the e-government service.

6 Conclusions

The examination of the e-government literature, that has been considered vis-à-vis the basic principles of 'service science', has shown:

- the evaluation of programs and projects is conducted mainly on economic measures which are not capable of capturing both propulsive and limiting factors in the process of organizing and sensemaking of such initiatives (quite important especially in large and long lasting projects); this bears negative consequences on the availability and sharing of thorough experiences and in the construction of holistic theoretical approaches (i.e., not technocentric nor economicscentric);
- internal services are engaged in making value propositions which often compete with one another, particularly when overarching frameworks are at stake (e.g. NPM versus 'Weberian'); competition among different approaches is part of an effective knowledge sharing process which sustains the value-in-use principle in a service dominant logic;
- 'active involvement', which can be considered as a proxy of co-production, is still in its infancy and it encounters obstacles both in the 'digital divide' and in the territorial dispersion of end-users;
- especially at the policy level a service-dominant logic is being built which underlines the role of 'intermediaries' to respond to different needs with articulated mixes of techniques; policymakers and practitioners, supported by the findings of researchers, are realizing that also in e-services value is basically idiosyncratic and contextual.

It is therefore reasonable to conclude that e-government initiatives have much to gain from service science principles.

On the other hand, service science, especially when e-services are considered, can gain from the findings of research on e-government a higher sensitivity when considering the role of ICTs -that is when considering the interplay of technology and the acts of organizing. Following Hosking [28], the use of the word 'organizing' is better suited than the term 'organization' to illustrate the fact that service is a process rather than a condition. Furthermore, knowledge sharing and sensemaking are both processes that are helpful in improving and innovating e-services, harnessed as they appear to be by active agency.

The limits of this chapter concern mainly the fact that it stops at the surface of management theory applicable both to e-government and e-services in general. In fact theories concerning leadership and organizational learning should be examined in depth. They represent successive research activities that will complete the work done so far.

References

1. Chesbrough, H. W. (2005). Toward a new science of services. *Harvard Business Review, 83*(February), 43–44.
2. Chesbrough, H., & Spohrer, J. I. M. (2006). A reserach manifesto for services science. *Communications of the ACM, 49*(7), 35–40.
3. Spohrer, J., Maglio, P., Bailey, J., & Gruhl, D. (2007). Steps toward a science of service systems. *Computer, 40*(1), 1–46.
4. Dreyfus, H. L. (1992). *What computers still can't do* (p. 354). Cambridge: The MIT Press.
5. Vargo, S. L., Maglio, P. P., & Akaka, M. A. (2008). On value and value co-creation: A service systems and service logic perspective. *European Management Journal, 26*(3), 145–152.
6. Vargo, S. L., & Lusch, R. F. (2008). Service-dominant logic: continuing the evolution. *Journal of the Academy of Marketing Science, 36*(1), 1–10.
7. Orlikowski, W. J. (2007). Sociomaterial practices: Exploring technology at work. *Organization Studies, 28*(9), 1435–1448.
8. Orlikowski, W. J. (2010). The sociomateriality of organisational life: considering technology in management research. *Cambridge Journal of Economics, 34*(1), 125–141.
9. OECD. (2003). *The e-government imperative*. Paris: OECD Publishing.
10. Persson, A., & Goldkuhl, G. (2010). Government value paradigms—bureaucracy, new public management, and e-government government. *Communications of the Association for Information Systems, 27*, 45–62.
11. Petricek, V., Escher, T., Cox, I.J. & Margetts, H. (2006). The web structure of e-government—developing a methodology for quantitative evaluation. Public Policy, pp. 669–678.
12. Alshawi, S., & Alalwany, H. (2009). e-government evaluation: Citizen's perspective in developing countries. *Information Technology for Development, 15*, 193–208.
13. Serafeimidis, V., & Smithson, S. (2000). Information systems evaluation in practice: A case study of organizational change. *Journal of Information Technology, 15*, 93–105.
14. Weick, K. E., Sutcliffe, K. M., & Obstfeld, D. (2005). Organizing and the process of sense making. *Organization Science, 16*(4), 409–421.
15. Thomas R. (2005). The identity project an assessment of the UK identity cards bill and its implications, London.
16. Orlikowski, W. J. (1992). The duality of technology: Rethinking the concept of technology in organizations. *Organization Science, 3*, 398–428.
17. Yildiz, M. (2007). E-government research: Reviewing the literature, limitations, and ways forward. *Government Information Quarterly, 24*(3), 646–665.
18. OECD. (2001). Citizens as partners: information, consultation and public participation in policy-making. Paris, p. 253.
19. West, D. M. (2001). E-government and the transformation of service delivery and citizen attitudes. *Public Administration Review, 64*, 15–27.
20. Miller, E. A., & West, D. M. (2009). Where's the revolution? Digital technology and health care in the internet age. *Journal of Health Politics, Policy and Law, 34*(2), 261–284.
21. United Kingdom Government Cabinet Office. (2005). Transformational government—enabled by technology.
22. Dubberly, H., Mehta, R., Evenson, S., & Pangaro, P. (2010). Reframing health to embrace design of our own well-being. *Interactions, 17*(3), 56–63.
23. Chan, C. M. L., & Pan, S. L. (2008). User engagement in e-government systems implementation: a comparative case study of two Singaporean e-government initiatives. *Journal of Strategic Information System, 17*, 124–139.
24. Damodaran, L., & Olphert, C. W. (2006). *Informing digital futures: Strategies for citizen engagement*. New York: Springer.
25. Mumford, E. (1983). *Designing human systems for new technology: the ETHICS method*. Manchester: Manchester Business School.

26. McLoughlin, I., Maniatopoulos, G., Wilson, R., & Martin, M. (2009). Hope to die before you get old? Techno-centric versus user-centred approaches in developing virtual services for older people. *Public Management Review, 11*(6), 857–880.
27. Olphert, W. (2007). Citizen participation and engagement in the design of e-government services: The missing link in effective ICT design and delivery. *Journal of Association of Information Systems., 8*(9), 491–507.
28. Hosking, D. M. (1988). Organizing, leadership and skilful process. *Journal of Management Studies, 25*(2), 147–166.

Part II
New Ways to Work and Interact via Internet

Measuring the Success of E-Justice. A Validation of the DeLone and McLean Model

Rocco Agrifoglio, Luigi Lepore and Concetta Metallo

Abstract The aim of this chapter is to develop a research model to assess the success of e-justice applications in the Judicial System. Judicial System has been characterized by considerable investments in ICTs in order to improve court's efficiency and effectiveness. Despite these investments, court performances did not increase and little research has been conducted to understand the reasons. Our research model adapts the DeLone and McLean's IS success model and provides an useful contribute to understanding e-justice success.

Keywords E-justice success · IS success · Judicial System

1 Introduction

During the last two decades, there was a considerable growth of e-justice projects aimed at using information and communication technologies (ICT) to improve efficiency and effectiveness of Judicial Systems (JS).

Several computer applications are being introduced in judicial organizations to support administrative activities, evaluation of court performances and case-flows management. ICTs are considered to be important tools to implement the managerial philosophy in the JSs [1], planning and control instruments, new budgeting methods, accounting systems, performance indicators, measurement of workload,

R. Agrifoglio (✉) · L. Lepore · C. Metallo
Department of Management, Parthenope University, Naples, Italy
e-mail: agrifoglio@uniparthenope.it

L. Lepore
e-mail: lepore@uniparthenope.it

C. Metallo
e-mail: metallo@uniparthenope.it

P. Spagnoletti (ed.), *Organizational Change and Information Systems*, Lecture Notes in Information Systems and Organisation 2, DOI: 10.1007/978-3-642-37228-5_9,

etc. In many experiences, these investments in e-justice solutions have not given the expected results. In particular, Italy has been one of the European Countries that has spent the most in ICTs, but despite the modernization process and the considerable investments, to date the results achieved have been very few [2, 3]. In this context, evaluation of the success or effectiveness of the ICT investments could be useful for court administrators and presiding judges, in order to monitor the court activities, the achievement of goals and, thus, to improve court efficiency and effectiveness.

The overall goal of this study is to develop a research model to assess the success or effectiveness of Information System (IS) in JS. Among different e-justice applications used by court employers, we focus on ISs mainly used to automate the administrative tasks, such as Case Management Systems (CMS) and Case-tracking System (CtS). We analyze these applications mainly for two reasons. First, because these tools represent the field in which there has been the greatest development of e-justice. Second, because administrative activities often generate critical problems for the efficiency of JS and the use of ICTs for conducting out these activities could contribute to improve the overall performance of the JS.

This research adapts the DeLone and McLean's IS success model to assess the effectiveness of e-justice applications. Despite the increased research interest on e-justice, the field currently is poor of theoretical frameworks that can be useful for addressing important issues concerning the implementation success of e-justice solutions, such as the factors influencing the usage behavior of e-justice applications. It would seem very important to understand what factors influence the usage behavior of e-justice solutions, so that policy makers may improve the likelihood of success when introducing or refining the use of these tools in JS.

In this phase, we propose a model to assess the success of e-justice applications. In the next phase, we will test the research model and hypotheses. To date, data collection phase was finished but the data analysis is yet not complete.

The structure of this chapter is as follows. First, we deepen e-justice applications and then we introduce the theoretical background. Second, we present research model and hypotheses. Finally, we describe the research methodology and future perspectives.

2 E-Justice Applications

The introduction of ICTs in the JS is part of the wider modernization process that has involved at first the executive branch of the government all over the world. In Europe, only recently this process has also affected in a systematic way the judicial institutions. In fact, at beginning, use of ICTs in JSs has represented an isolated response to specific problems. Referring to this, the term "e-justice" was coined specifically to indicate these projects aimed at enhancing the use of computer applications in the field of justice, in order to improve the quality of judicial services, making them more accessible, faster and less expensive [4, 5].

We can categorize e-justice applications into two categories: Justice-to-Justice (J2J) and Justice-to-Citizen (J2C). The first category includes all those applications that automate the internal activities of the JS and that digitalize the communication and interaction between different actors of JS (e.g., courts, courts and ministry of justice, courts and superior council of magistracy, judge and lawyer, etc.). The second, instead, includes all the applications used to electronically deliver services to citizens (e.g., web sites/portals, on-line services, etc.). In other words, the first category includes the back office applications, while the second includes applications that support the front office activities.

E-justice applications developed to support court activities could also be classified into two main categories. The first category includes technologies for automation of administrative tasks, while the second includes the technologies to support typical activities of judges and prosecutors. However, the boundaries of the two categories are not clear, so it is possible that an application automates mainly administrative activities, but also supports some judge's activities and vice versa. The matrix of e-justice applications is showed in Fig. 1.

One of the first applications developed for the courts activities is CtS that automate court dockets and other court registers. To better support the activities of the administrative personnel, different CMSs were developed in European Countries in the last decades. These applications are principally devoted to support and automate the back-office and court staff's administrative work, the case tracking, the case planning, document management, scheduling of hearings and in this way they also support judicial activities. With the objective to improve these applications, more recently different European JSs are trying to open the CMS database to external users, such as lawyers and parties.

Some other recent applications were aimed to automate judges' activities to support document management, such as writing judgments, sentences and court orders, or overall to support decision-making process. For example, forums and

Fig. 1 E-justice applications

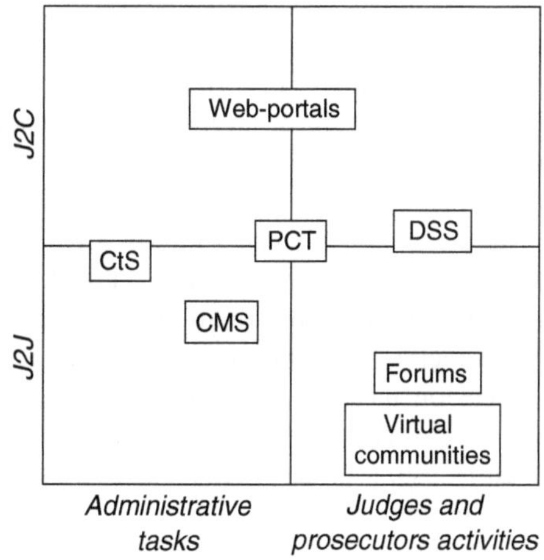

virtual communities were developed by judges in order to share knowledge and experiences [6], making the research activities faster and less expensive.

Furthermore, other applications were developed to support electronic communications and interactions in legal proceedings. For instance, the project "Processo Civile Telematico" (PCT), through use of ICTs in the courts' activities, aims to allow full on-line transaction between ministry of justice, courts, lawyers, and other actors of the JS. The implementation of these types of resources profoundly changes the ways of working and interacting of everyone involved in the JS.

As Torres and colleagues [7] highlighted in the last decade various institutions and academics have tried to evaluate the performance and characteristics of e-government initiatives. E-government initiatives have become a developing field of empirical studies. However, there are not specific studies intended to evaluate the IS success in the JSs. This consideration makes our study interesting for institutions of JSs and for academics whose studies refer to justice.

3 E-Justice Success

"IS success or effectiveness is critical to our understanding of the value and efficacy of IS management actions and IS investments" [8, p. 10]. Many scholars recognize the need to evaluate IS success (or effectiveness) and a large number of systems success measures exist [e.g., 9, 10].

DeLone and McLean [10] classified the dimensions of IS success into six categories: (1) system quality, the measurements of IS itself; (2) information quality, the measures of the IS output; (3) information use, recipient consumption of IS output; (4) user satisfaction, recipient response to the use of IS output; (5) individual impact, the effect of information on the behavior of the recipient; and (6) organizational impact, the effect of information on organizational performance. Particularly, system quality concerns the consistency of the user interface, the quality of documentation, and whether there are bugs in the system. Information quality concerns the relevance, timeliness and accuracy of information generated through the system. IS use concerns the use of the system by the user. User satisfaction, instead, is the sum of an individual's reactions to a set of factors affecting information system success [9]. Finally, individual and organizational impacts are the outcomes attributed to IS use [11] and user satisfaction [10].

DeLone and McLean's model is based on three levels: technical, the accuracy and efficiency of the communication system that produces information; semantic, the success of the information in conveying the intended meaning; effectiveness, the effect of the information on the receiver. Therefore, the systems quality dimension measures technical success; information quality dimension measures semantic success; and effectiveness success is measured from several dimensions such as use, user satisfaction, individual and organizational impacts. Since 1992, DeLone and McLean's IS success model has served as a basis for numerous studies and empirical investigations.

E-government systems diffusion has encouraged the proliferation of research on this issue. However, Wang and Liao [12] highlighted that little research has been conducted to assess the success of e-government systems.

Our study focuses on e-justice because there are not specific studies intended to evaluate the IS success in the JSs. The traditional research in this area concerned mainly descriptive analysis of the phenomenon, investigating the evolution of software applications for JS, the amounts of money invested by public sector, experience of use of ICT, and different e-justice strategies by European Union members e.g., [3, 13–15]. These studies have showed that considerable investments have been done to project, develop and implement new ICTs in the JS, with a whole body of practical experience in the courts. However, functionality and performance of technologies to support judicial administrations vary significantly across different Countries [3]. In many experiences, these investments in e-justice solutions have not given the expected results. In particular, in Italy, the results achieved have been very few, despite the considerable investments in ICT [2, 3]. This situation highlights that to understand the conditions that lead users to adopt a new application as well as the determinants of technology implementation success represents a high-priority research issue.

4 Research Model and Hypotheses

We investigate the IS success in the J2J context from the perspective of court administrative staff who uses CtS and CMS applications for their work.

Based on original DeLone and McLean's IS success model, we consider system quality, information quality, IS use, user satisfaction, and individual impact, as key variables to assess the technical, semantic, and effectiveness J2J applications. The e-justice success model is reported in Fig. 2.

As suggested by DeLone and McLean [10], system quality and information quality are two direct antecedents of user satisfaction and IS use that, in turn, determinate the individual performance.

The literature agrees that systems perceived as reliable, precise, and timely positively affect the user's usage behavior e.g. [9, 10, 16]. Within JS, J2J applications have encouraged the digitalization of documents and the streamlining of

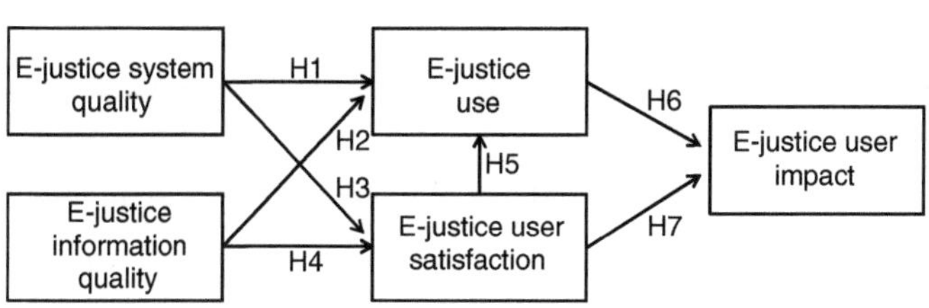

Fig. 2 E-justice success model

the organizational processes. These systems have allowed to integrate existing databases and to explore the possible uses of ICT to improve the exchange of information in JS [5]. In particular, the CtS automate court docket and other court register activities, while CMS applications have granted and integrated many courts' activities, procedures and practices, improving the work effectiveness of court administrative officers and judges [5, 15]. Thus, court personnel who perceive J2J applications as more reliable and timely will be more available to use them.

- H1. E-justice system quality will be positively related to Use in the J2J context.
- H2. E-justice information quality will be positively related to Use in the J2J context.

Furthermore, IS literature also agrees that system quality and information quality are two determinants of user satisfaction. Thus, users who perceive the system as reliable, precise, and timely will be more enjoyed and satisfied to use it. J2J applications, such as CtS and CMS, automate administrative and judges' activities. Using these applications, both administrative officers and judges could explore legal information timely and without time and spatial limits, improving the main institutional functions of judicial system such as disputes resolution and law enforcement. Moreover, the adoption of these systems has leaded to a detailed description of organization workflows, reading the codes of procedures and other relevant regulations, reinforcing the standardized application of rules by each judicial office [5]. Thus, court employers who perceive the quality of e-justice applications as well as the quality of output provided will be more satisfied with these systems.

- H3. E-justice system quality will be positively related to user satisfaction in the J2J context.
- H4. E-justice information quality will be positively related to user satisfaction in the J2J context.

DeLone and McLean [10] posited a reciprocal dependence between user satisfaction and IS use. However, to test this reciprocal dependence is very difficult because research should follow use and user satisfaction over time. Based on human behavioral approach, much research excluded the reciprocal interdependence between user satisfaction and IS use, assuming that user satisfaction is an attitude, while actual use is a behavior [8, 17]. As suggested by these studies, user satisfaction leads to system use rather than vice versa. Thus, the more satisfied users are with the system, the more they will use it. With refer to JS, we also believe that court administrative officers satisfied with e-justice applications will be more available to their usage.

- H5. E-justice user satisfaction will be positively related to use in the J2J context.

Finally, prior studies have also investigated the relationships between semantic variables, such as IS use and user satisfaction, and effectiveness variable, such as individual impact [8, 10, 16]. In particular, some empirical research shown that IS use is positively associated with individual impact. Of course, whether a system is not used at all, it will not have any impact on individual performance, while a system that is used more will have higher impact on users' performance. Moreover, other research shown that user satisfaction is positively related to user performance [8]. In particular, whether user satisfaction is individual's belief in the correspondence or fit between job requirements and IS functionality, a positive relationship between user satisfaction and individual impact is quite understandable. Within court, using J2J applications judges and court administrative officers can timely get information, decreasing the resolution time of legal cases and improving the individual and court performances. Moreover, their best estimate of the match between requirements and the J2J application's capabilities should be positively associated with individual performance.

- H6. E-justice use will be positively related to user performance in the J2J context.
- H7. E-justice user satisfaction will be positively related to its performance in the J2J context.

5 Research Methodology

Data that we will use to test research model were gathered from administrative users of two Italian Courts, such as the Court of Bari and the Court of Naples, during the period from the 20th of October 2009 to the 15th of January 2010. In particular, in data were gathered from court users of various J2J applications such as "sistema informativo della cognizione penale" (SICP), "sistema informativo della cognizione civile" (SICC), and "sistema informativo dell'area amministrativa" (SIAMM).

A structured questionnaire was developed to measure e-justice success model variables and to capture the user profile as well as the e-justice applications they used. In particular, we conducted a pre and pilot testing to verify and validate the measures used and obtained feedback by both court e-justice application users and some IS scholars in the first instance. Findings of the pre-test have highlighted the reliability and consistency of the scales used.

Then, we administered the questionnaire to users of two Italian Courts with permission of presiding judges. Of 620 court employers, of which 212 from Court of Bari and 408 from Court of Naples, we received a total of 321 complete questionnaires (59 from court of Bari and 262 from court of Naples). To minimize data entry errors, all the collected data were checked for consistency. As a result, 314 valid responses were collected. The variables used were adapted from existing IS literature. In particular, information quality was measured using Rai and colleagues' [16] seven-item scale. Two items were used to measure system quality by adapting Doll and Torkzadeh's [18] ease of use scale to e-justice system. IS use was measured with a single item based on Goodhue and Thompson [19] dependence measure. Twelve items were used to measure user satisfaction based on Doll and Torkzadeh's [18] end-user computing satisfaction scale. Finally, individual impact was measured using Etezadi-Amoli and Farhoomand's [20] user performance four-item scale. Moreover, other questions were used to capture the profile of survey respondents (e.g., age, gender, educational level, IT experience) and kinds of e-justice applications.

6 Conclusion and Future Perspectives

IS plays an important role in the "modernizing" process of the JS by encouraging the adoption of mechanisms of accountability compatible with principle of independence and by satisfying the needs of court employers and stakeholders. Through considerable investment in ICT, the European legislators sought to provide an "e-government approach" to the JS, named e-justice, forcing the courts to adopt ad-hoc applications to automate internal (J2J) and external (J2C) court activities. In particular, Italy has been one of the European Countries that has spent the most in ICTs in order to improve the efficiency and effectiveness of its JS. Despite the large amount of money invested, the court performances, in term of disposition time and case turnover ratio, are not increased overtime and little research has been conducted to understanding the reasons.

The aim of this research has been to develop a research model to measure and to evaluate the success of J2J applications. Despite data collection phase was finished, the next phase of data analysis is yet not complete to date.

This research is in response to the call for continuous challenge and validation of IS success model in different contexts [8, 12, 16]. Considering the considerable investment in ICTs and the growth of e-justice projects, the JS is a very interesting context of analysis for IS research. Our research goes along this direction and contributes to understand the relationships between e-justice applications, usage behaviors and individual performance.

References

1. Fabri, M., & Langbroek, P. M. (2000). *The challenge of change for judicial systems. Developing a public administration perspective*. Amsterdam: IOS Press.
2. Falletti, E. (2008). *E-justice*. Milano: Giuffrè.
3. Carnevali, D., Contini, F. & Fabri M. (2006). Tecnologie per la giustizia. Giuffrè, Milano.
4. Fabri, M. (2001). State of the art, critical issues and trends of ICT in European judicial system. In M. Fabri & F. Contini (Eds.), *Justice and technology in Europe: How ICT is changing judicial business*. The Netherlands: Kluwer Law International, The Hague.
5. Contini, F., & Cordella, A. (2007). Information system and information infrastructure deployment: The challenge of the Italian e-justice approach. *The Electronic Journal of e-Government, 5*, 43–52.

6. Alvino, F., Agrifoglio, R., Metallo, C., & Lepore, L. (2011). Learning and knowledge sharing in virtual communities of practice: A case study. In A. D'Atri, M. Ferrara, J. F. George, & P. Spagnoletti (Eds.), *Information technology and innovation trends in organizations*. Berlin: Springer.
7. Torres, L., Pina, V., & Acerete, B. (2005). E-government developments on delivering public services among EU cities. *Government Information Quarterly, 22*, 217–238.
8. DeLone, W. H., & McLean, E. R. (2003). The DeLone and McLean model of information systems success: A ten-year update. *Journal of Management Information Systems, 19*, 9–30.
9. Bailey, J. E., & Pearson, S. W. (1983). Development of a tool for measuring and analyzing computer user satisfaction. *Management Science, 29*, 530–545.
10. DeLone, W. H., & McLean, E. R. (1992). Information systems success: The quest for the dependent variable. *Information System Research, 3*, 60–95.
11. Seddon, P. B. (1997). A respecification and extension of the DeLone and McLean model of IS success. *Information Systems Research, 8*, 240–253.
12. Wang, Y. S., & Liao, Y. W. (2008). Assessing e-government systems success: a validation of the DeLone and McLean model of information system success. *Government Information Quarterly, 25*, 717–733.
13. Fabri, M. (2008). The Italian style of e-justice in a comparative perspective. In M. Cerrillo & P. Fabra (Eds.), *E-justice: ICT in the court system*. USA: IGI Global.
14. Cerrillo, M., & Fabra, P. (2008). *E-justice: ICT in the court system*. USA: IGI Global.
15. Velicogna, M. (2008). Use of information and communication technologies (ICT) in European judicial systems, Strasbourg, Commission for the Efficiency of Justice.
16. Rai, A., Lang, S. S., & Welker, R. B. (2002). Assessing the validity of IS success models: An empirical testand theoretical analysis. *Information Systems Research, 13*, 50–69.
17. Baroudi, J. J., Olson, M. H., & Ives, B. (1986). An empirical study of the impact of user involvement on system usage and information satisfaction. *Communications of the ACM, 29*, 232–238.
18. Doll, W. J., & Torkzadeh, G. (1988). The measurement of end-user computing satisfaction. *MIS Quarterly, 12*, 259–274.
19. Goodhue, D. L., & Thompson, R. L. (1995). Task-technology fit and individual performance. *MIS Quarterly, 19*, 213–236.
20. Etezadi-Amoli, J., & Farhoomand, A. F. (1996). A structural model of end user computing satisfaction and user performance. *Information and Management, 30*, 65–73.

The Impact of Corporate Governance on Internet Financial Reporting in Concentrated Ownership Companies

Romilda Mazzotta and Giovanni Bronzetti

Abstract In the context of agency theory this study investigates the effect of corporate governance (CG) on Internet Financial Reporting (IFR) disclosure in a concentrated ownership environment, such as Italy. We hypothesize that IFR may be explained in term of increasing transparency in order to defend minority shareholder interest, so we predict, and find, a positive association between the extent of a firm's IFR and its CG and a negative association between IFR and ownership structure. CG is measured by ownership structure, using as a proxy the share held by the first three major shareholders and by managerial ownership, and by board composition, captured through the incidence of independent director (IND) and of a Non-Executive Chair (NEC). IFR is measured taking into consideration the content and format of information present in Investor Relations sections.

Keywords Voluntary disclosure · Internet financial reporting · Independent director · Managerial ownership · Non executive chair

Though this work is the fruit of joint reflection and collaboration, for academic reasons the paragraphs 1, 2, 3, 5.2 and 6 are to be attributed to Romilda Mazzotta and the paragraphs 4 and 5.1 are to be attributed to Giovanni Bronzetti

R. Mazzotta (✉) · G. Bronzetti
University of Calabria, Calabria, Italy
e-mail: romilda.mazzotta@unical.it

G. Bronzetti
e-mail: bronzetti@exnet.it

P. Spagnoletti (ed.), *Organizational Change and Information Systems*, Lecture Notes in Information Systems and Organisation 2, DOI: 10.1007/978-3-642-37228-5_10,

1 Introduction

Usually stakeholders require companies' information to evaluate the real and potential chance to invest in them. This is, generally, financial information normally synthesized in a hard document named financial/annual report. Many companies, today, in addition to this also issue an electronic version of the report and make it available on their websites. This means that once the document is available on the internet, it is easily accessible to all stakeholders, wherever they are [1–3]. The information, at relatively low costs [4, 5] with respect to the traditional channel, can be continuously updated in real time, thus influencing the investors' decisional process [6]. The practice through which companies give available financial information on the Internet is known as Internet Financial Reporting (IFR). The main motivation which pushes companies to disclose a larger quantity of information, according to the agency theory, is connected to the necessity to reduce the information asymmetry between management and ownership [7, 8]. The latter is found in companies in which ownership is separated from control, whereby, in detail, the owner (principal) delegates management (agent) to manage the company but the manager and owner could have conflicting interests (principal-agent agency problem). Managers, in fact, thanks to more information available than the principal (information asymmetry), may act in our interests rather than in that of the ownership [9]. The presence of these information asymmetries determines the rise in costs (agency costs) in order to develop and implement control systems aimed at controlling opportunistic behavior and, as a consequence, to aligning the interests of shareholders and managers. Two related mechanisms, a transparent corporate disclosure (also IFR) and an adequate internal corporate governance system (or board of directors), can mitigate the agency problem and then reduce the agency cost. The studies that analyze the relationship between IFR and internal corporate governance show, in general, that a well-governed company tends to engage in IFR [10–13]. These researches, however, are conducted using US or UK sample firms and their results cannot be inferred in different realities that do not face the same expected agency problem. Italian listed firms, for example, are mainly family owned, with a high ownership concentration. Large controlling shareholders dominate boards or are involved directly in the management activity (managerial ownership) or, using their power, influence the nomination process of the board by appointing directors who are aligned with their own interest [14]. Under these circumstances, the agency problems may be found to be less severe between owner and manager (principal-agent problem) [15, 16] but a different agency conflict arises between majority and minority investor (principal–principal problem) [17, 18] where controlling shareholders may seek private benefits at the expense of minority shareholders [19]. As in the principal-agent problem, also in the principal–principal problem, the literature suggests that the board of directors and disclosure are the two complementary mechanisms able to reduce the agency problem, even if, in this case, between majority and minority shareholders [20–22]. To the best of our knowledge, there is no research that tests the impact of corporate governance mechanisms on IFR focusing on a context of high ownership concentration. On this basis, we choose to analyze this relationship with regard to the 182 Italian companies listed at 31/12/2011. Our main hypothesis is that the IFR disclosure may be explained in term of increasing transparency in order to defend minority shareholder interest [16–18]; consequently the expected role for the board of directors is the protection of minority shareholders' interest, increasing transparency through voluntary disclosure information. The extent of IFR disclosure is measured by a disclosure index that considers the content and format of information. Italian listed companies have, as in other countries, few regulatory references [19], we remind the reader of the general principle introduced by IOSCO's (submit all information on the web that is generally provided in hard form) and the recommendations introduced in the European Commission Directive 2003/6/EC (dissemination of inside information to the public, as soon as possible on the website). The governance variables taken as a reference are the percentage of independent directors (IND) within the board and the presence of a Chairman of the Board with non-executive functions (NEC). To take into consideration the ownership structure, we consider the percentage of managerial ownership and the share held by the leading three shareholders. Then, through a linear regression analysis were analyzed the relationship between governance mechanisms, ownership structure and IFR disclosure. We hypothesize that voluntary disclosure increases in the presence of independent directors, representing minority shareholders and free-floating capital, and of NEC, representing the impartial viewpoint all the constituent elements in the company. Therefore, we expect to find a lower level of information in those businesses with a greater concentration of ownership and high presence of shareholders on the board, with few independent directors and situation of CEO-duality. Our results highlight that IFR disclosure is positively influenced by the presence of NEC and of a high percentage of IND on the board. At the same time, we found a negative relationship between IFR and ownership concentration and managerial ownership. This finding suggests that IND and NEC representing the interest of minority and free-floating capital enhance the importance of reducing information asymmetries with alternative ways of communicating with the shareholder. Therefore, IFR disclosure can be explained in terms of increasing transparency in order to defend minority shareholder interest.

The chapter differs from existing research, because it examines the impact of corporate governance IFR mechanisms with reference to a context of high ownership concentration, such as in Italy, which has not yet been investigated. Therefore, this study helps to develop the existing literature on the relationship between voluntary disclosure, governance and ownership structure and gives evidence about the different business practices in terms of IFR. The remainder of this chapter is organized as follows: Sect. 2 reviewers the literature; Sect. 3 presents our hypotheses; Sect. 4 describes the research design and methods; Sect. 5 describes the empirical analysis and presents the results and their interpretation; finally, we summarize and conclude in Sect. 6.

2 Previous Research on IFR and Governance

Studies on IFR disclosure are mainly linked to the research on the choice of disclosure by companies [23]. Focusing attention only on studies interesting for our contribution, we find many researches that, in the agency theory framework, link the voluntary disclosure to internal governance [1, 10, 11, 24–28], as a mechanism to mitigate the agency problem [9]. The problem arises because modern companies, especially if listed, are characterized by the separation between ownership and control. This separation determines an agency problem, or a potential conflict of interest between those directly involved in corporate governance (manager or agent) and individuals who hold interests in the process of creation of the value (principal). This principal-agent problem, as the literature suggests, can be mitigated introducing appropriate governance mechanisms to monitor the managers' behavior [20, 29–31] and enhance voluntary disclosure, both as a mechanism to monitor the performance of managers and reduce information asymmetries. With the Internet, as a tool for company disclosure, the mitigation of the agency problem becomes even more possible as well as the reduction of information asymmetries owing to the larger space available, the breadth of information and the capability of real-time access [32]. The level of corporate information is, all the same, conditioned by the complex choices of internal governance mechanisms, adopted by each firm and thus firm-specific. The main internal governance mechanism is the board of directors (board) or, in detail, the board composition. The existing literature suggests that well-governed firms are more transparent and so, reducing the agency problem, potentially perform better [33–35]. Board composition, even so, may be affected by the ownership structures. In an owner concentrated firm, in fact, large owners may use their power to appoint directors or managers who are aligned with their own interests and this may lead to wealth expropriation from minority shareholder [14]. Therefore, in owner concentrated firm, board composition is a key control mechanism in order to defend minority shareholders.

There are a limited number of studies that analyze IFR and the relationships between variables of governance and IFR disclosure. Abdelsalam et al. [12], analyzing a sample of Irish listed companies, found that IFR completeness is associated with CEO duality as well as the presence of independent directors. Kelton and Yang [13] show, with reference to a sample of U.S. companies, that firms with less shareholder protection, a low percentage of block holder ownership, a high percentage of independent directors and directors with a greater presence of experience in financial audit committee are more likely to develop practical IFR. Pervan [36], with reference to 85 Croatian and Slovene listed companies, found a significant relationship with size and number of shareholders. Overall, the literature show a positive relationship between good internal mechanisms of corporate governance and level of corporate information. A good system of governance, in fact, strengthens the system of internal control of companies and makes it less likely for managers to use information for their own personal interest, leading to an improvement in the completeness of the disclosure and the quality of financial statements.

3 Hypotheses

Based on the agency theory framework, we examine the association between corporate governance and IFR disclosure, where corporate governance is analyzed with reference to ownership concentration and board composition.

Ownership structure. Ownership structure can be diffused or concentrated. In a diffused structure a separation arises between ownership and control, this increases costs associated with the agency relationship that requires greater information to improve transparency [15]. In a concentrated structure, instead, free-floating capital is in a lower proportion and owners have the access to relevant information making for a reduced need for disclosure. In other words, ownership concentration, aligning the interest of manager and control, reduces the agency cost and therefore lowers the need to enhance voluntary disclosure [28, 37]. Since Italian listed companies have a mainly concentrated structure, we mean to test the hypothesis that follows:

H1: There is a negative association between ownership concentration and IFR disclosure

The impact of ownership structure within the board is considered by managerial ownership, or the presence on the board of a large shareholder as a manager. The managerial ownership reconciles the agency conflict between managers and shareholders and reduces agency costs [9] but may lead to wealth expropriation from minority shareholders. In firms with a high ownership, managerial agency costs are low because the managers and also shareholders do not have incentives to pursue a personal interest, which implies a low level of monitoring. Therefore, managerial ownership decreases voluntary disclosure [11]. With reference to Italian listed companies we mean to test the hypothesis that follows:

H2: There is a negative association between managerial ownership and IFR disclosure

Board composition. Internal corporate governance mechanisms are principally linked to board composition. Board composition may be affected by the ownership structures. A large owner, in fact, may use his power to appoint independent directors to control managerial decisions and reduce the agency problem between the owner and managers. Therefore, board composition becomes a key control mechanism for minority shareholders. Specifically, there are two internal mechanisms that play an important role: the degree of independence of the board and the presence of NEC. The existent literature states that the percentage of independent directors on the board is positively related to the ability to influence the decision of the board of disclosure [38] and for example to the comprehensiveness of corporate disclosure [10]. A high proportion of independent directors on the board should lead to a higher level of disclosure by firms [30, 13]. In addition, the few studies focused on IFR disclosure, suggest that IFR is positively associated with the percentage of independent directors. On this basis, we test the following hypothesis:

H3: There is a positive association between the degree of board independence and IFR disclosure.

The agency theory and, in general, the existing literature, as well as generally all codes of conduct, require a separation between the roles of chairman and executive directors. When the two roles are joint the effectiveness of the board in performing its functions may be impaired, limited by the control that the Chair/ CEO [39]. Cheung et al. [40] argue that firms in which the two roles are separated tend to have higher voluntary disclosure. The Preda Code also declares a separation between Chair and CEO but also notes that the two roles can be covered by a single subject to respond to valuable organizational needs. Many Italian companies, in reality, have a joint leadership structure and when the two roles are separated, the Chair is, generally, an executive director. This reduces the need to provide more information. In our view, the level of disclosure increases when the role of CEO and Chair are separated and, more specifically, when the Chair is a non-executive director. NEC, specifically, can play a critical role in representing the different constituent elements in the company with an impartial viewpoint. On this basis, we want test the following hypothesis:

H4: There is a positive association between Non-Executive Chair and IFR disclosure

4 Research Design and Methods

4.1 Sample Selection and Regression Model

The sample was selected from Italian listed companies. From the original sample were removed, to have uniform data, the companies that: operating in financial sector (72 companies); listed in the AIM-MAC market (24 companies); foreign or suspended (6 companies); with different year date closing from December 31 (9 companies); with missing data (10 companies) and with a different model from the traditional (3). The final sample is made up of 182 valid observation companies. A list of sample companies is available from the authors. To test the hypothesis we use a research model specified in the following equation:

$$\begin{aligned} \text{IFR} = {} & \beta 0 + \beta 1\text{DCEX} + \beta 2\text{IND} + \beta 3\ \text{MGMTR} + \beta 4\text{OWNC} + \beta 5\text{NOSH} \\ & + \beta 6\text{BIG4} + \varepsilon \end{aligned}$$

where IFR is the dependent variable while DCEX (that identified the presence of an NEC); IND (which identified the proportion of independent directors on the board); MGMTR (to capture the influence of ownership structure) and OWNC (which represented the ownership concentration) are the independent variables; NOSH and BIG4 are the control variables. In the next paragraph, we identify dependent, independent and control variables.

4.2 The Dependent Variable: Internet Financial Reporting Score

Consistently to existing studies in the field, we measure the level of information on the web building an IFR non-weighted disclosure index taking into account the 37 more used items selected from the 60 most common items identified in the existing literature [41–43], [30, 44, 13, 45]. In accordance with previous studies, IFR is measured in terms of form (FORMAT) and content (CONTENT) of the information [30, 1, 7, 13], see Table 1. IFR disclosure is build assigned for each item of disclosure of the value of 1 if the item is present or 0 if not present [13]. Section FORMAT examines, through 12 items, the form of IFR disclosure and options provided on the company website that are not available in the traditional form, including the presence of different file formats, the ability to download data, hyperlinks, audio and video and e-mail alerts. Section CONTENT examines, through 25 items, the content of IFR including the presence of financial reports including previous years, the performance overview, prices and current and historical dividends, the list of financial analysts and their evaluations and information on board of director. The sum of the value assigned to an indentified item of CONTENT and FORMAT measuring the overall level of disclosure (TOTAL) of firms. Information to build IFR disclosure was collected, from each company in the sample, examining their website and more specifically the Investor Relations section. This link, generally, makes available all information of possible interest to the shareholders [46]. The company's website evolves continuously, so data collection was done in the shortest time possible, from March to April 2012.

4.3 Dependent Variables

The explanatory variables of the IFR, identified with reference to ownership concentration and internal mechanism of corporate governance, are: (1) ownership structure; (2) managerial ownership; (3) Non-Executive Chair and (4) degree of independence of the board.

Ownership structure (OWNC) is measured in term of the share of the three main shareholders, while managerial ownership, or the impact of ownership structure on a

Table 1 IFR items on format and content and descriptive statistics for each item

	FORMAT	Media	Standard deviation	Firm number	%
1	Annual report in multiple formats	0.2033	0.4036	37	20
2	Financial data in processable format	0.2473	0.4326	45	25
3	Hyperlinked table of contents	0.9890	0.1045	180	99
4	Drop-down navigational menu	0.4396	0.4977	80	44
5	Hyperlinks inside the annual report	0.1483	0.3564	27	15
6	Hyperlink to data a tirth party of web	0.1429	0.3509	26	14
7	Audio/video files	0.2198	0.4152	40	22
8	Investor e-mail alert	0.3681	0.4836	67	37
9	Automatic IR info request form	0.1593	0.3670	29	16
10	Dynamic graphic images	0.4615	0.4998	84	46
11	Internal search engines	0.5275	0.5006	96	53
12	Multiple language of website	0.8791	0.3269	160	88
	CONTENT				
13	Current year's annual report (year 201 1)	0.9341	0.2488	170	93
14	Last year's annual report (year 2010)	0.9890	0.1043	180	99
15	Recent quarterly report	0.9780	0.1470	178	98
16	Carter for the audit committee	0.5055	0.5013	92	51
17	Charters for other board committee	0.4945	0.5013	90	49
18	Code of conduct and ethics	0.8626	0.3541	157	86
19	Recent monthly financial data	0.0219	0.1470	4	2
20	Performance overview (highlights, factsheet, Faq)	0.5604	0.4977	102	56
21	Earnings estimates	0.0604	0.2389	11	6
22	Calendar of events of interest to investor	0.9231	0.2672	168	92
23	Recent financial news release	0.9508	0.2174	173	95
24	Listing of analysts following the firms	0.5220	0.5008	95	52
25	Analyst rating	0.2692	0.4447	49	27
26	Text of speeches and presentation	0.7912	0.4076	144	79
27	Same day stock price	0.4231	0.4954	77	42
28	Historical stock price	0.4396	0.4954	80	44
29	Dividend reinvestment plan	0.0824	0.2758	15	8
30	Dividend history	0.2308	0.4224	42	23
31	Corporate governance guidelines	0.9505	0.2174	173	95
32	Members of board	0.9066	0.2918	165	91
33	Quotation	0.6813	0.4672	124	68
34	Shareholder	0.6264	0.4851	1 14	63
35	Summary data	0.4560	0.4994	83	46
36	Alerts	0.9945	0.0741	181	99
37	Strategy	0.3352	0.4733	61	34
	Total item 25			182	

board, is equal to the ratio between the number of shareholders-directors and the size of the board (MGMTR). The explanatory variable related to the presence of an NEC is a dichotomous variable that takes the value 1 when the Chair is a Non-Executive director and zero otherwise (DCEX). The effect of the degree of independence at the board level (IND) is measured by the proportion of independent directors within the board [47, 28]. IND is obtained by dividing the number of independent directors by the board size. The directors are considered independent if they meet the requirements of the Preda Code (2011), or if they are not enforceable and do not have family ties with the non-executive director. The control variables are the number of commons shareholders (NOSH) and auditors (BIG4). Firms with a larger number of shareholders, in fact, are more likely to meet the needs of different stakeholders should provide more information [36, 48, 49]. The control variable audit firm is connected to the fact that the disclosure should be greater for those companies in which the auditor is one of the four large audit firms (BIG4) [30, 50, 51]. The quality of the audit is better in those entities subject to the review of a large corporation because there is less incentive to issue an opinion not appropriate to keeping the customer, because this could result in loss of reputation [52]. The BIG4 variable is measured using a dichotomous variable equal to 1 if the audit firm is one of the big 4 (KPMG, PricewaterhouseCoopers, Deloitte, Ernst & Young) and zero otherwise. This information was taken from the yearly report.

The data on ownership concentration are available on the Consob website (www.consob.it) while information on directors is taken from the annual report on the ownership structure and governance. The MGMT information and on auditors is available on the Italian Stock Exchange website in the Company Profile Corporate Governance section, while numbers of shareholders were retrieved from the DATASTREAM database.

5 Results

5.1 Descriptive Statistics and Correlation Analysis

All surveyed companies have their own website and generally is possible to find an area identified as Investor Relations or equivalent names (such as Investor or Financial Information). Table 1 presents descriptive statistical analysis for each item investigated to assess the level of IFR. With regard to the format, the most popular item is the presence of hyperlinks within the website (99 %) followed by the opportunity to view/download the documents in different languages (88 %) and keyword search in the site (53 %). In an intermediate position, we find the presence of a navigation menu drop-down (44 %), of dynamic graphs (46 %) and the opportunity to subscribe to the investor e-mail alerts (37 %).

Instead, the connection from the data to other parts of the web is less common (14 %), the presence of hyperlinks within the Annual Report (15 %) and the form request for information Investor Relator (16 %). Few companies, then, have different formats of annual reports (pdf, or others) (20 %) and with the ability to download data into usable format for analysis (xls) (25 %). These deficiencies make the information, in fact, less useful [68]. The most popular item with regard the contents are the presence of the previous years' annual reports (99 %), recent

Table 2 Descriptive statistics

Variable	Mean	Standard deviation	Minimum	Median	Maximum
TOTAL	19.77	6.11	8	19	35
FORMAT	4.79	2.44	1	4	11
CONTENT	14.99	4.22	6	15	24
IND	0.3890	0.1643	0	0.3636	0.8889
MGMTR	0.2831	0.2421	0	0.25	0.8889
DCEX	0.2253	0.4189	0	0	1
OWNC	61.11	16.57	11.276	63.569	94.668
NOSH	1335355	5402734	122	138283	520e+08
BIG4	0.8791	0.3269	0	1	1

Possible maximum value for Total is 37, for Format 12 and for Content 25

financial information (95 %), last year's report (93 %) and quarterly reports (93 %). There are very few companies that provide information on the financial data of last month (2 %) and the estimate of earnings (6 %). These data are consistent with those found by Ettredge et al. [1] and Kelton and Yang [13], and suggest the presence of a great uniformity in the information about the company provided voluntarily. Table 2 provides descriptive statistics of the whole sample. The mean score is 20 of which 16 with respect to content and 4 to format. The overall level of IFR disclosure (TOTAL) varies from 8 to 35. The presence of directors at the same time shareholders is on average equal to 28 % (median 25 %) of members of the board, while the incidence of independent directors of about 39 % (median 36 %). The ownership concentration for the firm sample is over 61 %. The 88 % of companies surveyed have one of Big4 audit firm, suggesting a limited variation in the variable Big4.

A correlation analysis was conducted to understand the magnitude of the linear relationship between the variables. The following table presents the correlation matrix between the independent variable and control variables. The level of IFR (TOTAL) has a high correlation with the percentage of independent directors on the board (IND) and with the percentage of directors at the same time shareholders (MGMTR). The level of information via the web also appears linked to the leadership structure, in particular the IFR increases when the Chair is not at the same time managing director and does not play an executive role within the company (DCEX) (Table 3).

Table 3 Correlation analysis, star (5)

	TOTAL	NOSH	BIG4	DCEX	IND	MGMTR	OWNC
TOTAL	1.0000						
NOSH	0.3538*	1.0000					
BIG4	0.2158*	0.0883	1.0000				
DCEX	0.2206*	0.1052	0.1193	1.0000			
IND	0.3071*	0.2231*	0.1410	0.2310*	1.0000		
MGMT	−0.2500*	−0.1383	−0.2034*	−0.1462*	−0.2398*	1.0000	
OWNC	−0.1654*	−0.2280*	0.0554	−0.0159	0.0045	−0.0624	1.000

5.2 Regression Analysis and Sensitivity Test

Using the items identified we created an IFR disclosure index capable of synthesizing the level of information provided on the Internet (TOTAL) ranging from 0 to 37. On the basis of this indicator we examined the association between the IFR disclosure and governance, taking into account the control variables. The results, presented in Table 4, show that IFR disclosure is negatively correlated with ownership structure, the coefficient of variable OWNC is, in fact, negative and statistically significant. Therefore the result, supporting hypothesis 1, suggests that with high ownership concentration the IFR disclosure level decreases and the attention to format and to accessibility of document decreases. Consequently, the websites of companies with highly concentrated ownership are less accurate. In non-tabulated results, we test the regression between IFR and OWNC and we find a significant and negative relationship. This test was conducted because OWNC could be interpreted also as a control variable. We find evidence also in hypothesis 2 that predicted the existence of a negative relationship between the level of IFR and the presence of director shareholders within the Board. The coefficient of the MGMTR variable is actually negative and statistically significant. This result, in line with the literature, suggests that managerial ownership aligned interest between the principal and manager and, therefore, reduced the agency problem between owner and principal giving the lowest need for IFR disclosure. This effect can be mitigated by a good internal governance structure. A first internal mechanism is identified in the presence of an NEC. We believe that the level of disclosure increases when the role of CEO and Chair are separated and, more specifically, when the Chair is a non-executive director because he can play a critical role in representing the different constituent elements in the company with an impartial viewpoint. Table 4 shows a positive coefficient for the variable DCEX, which is also statistically significant. This result suggests that firms in which the Chair does not play the role of CEO and holds executive positions tend to provide more information on the Web than those which do not possess these characteristics. Another internal mechanism able to mitigate the agency problem is an adequate degree of board independence. The literature suggested that the IFR level was related to the percentage of independent directors on the board and this hypotheses is supported by the results of the analysis. That is, by the presence of a positive coefficient for the statistically significant IND variable. In other word IFR increases when the board has a higher incidence of independent directors. Over all, the analysis highlights that a good internal governance, in terms of the presence of independent directors and of an NEC, mitigated the agency problem that arises in a context where the firm has a highly concentrated ownership structure or, in other words, between majority and minority stakeholder. Therefore, IFR disclosure can be explained in terms of increasing transparency in order to defend minority shareholder interest. The control variables have the expected sign and are statistically significant. The model was tested for heteroscedasticity and the presence of collinearity among the independent variables using the Variance Inflation Factors

Table 4 Regression results OLS—coefficient (*p* value)

	1	1bis	2	3	4	5
	TOTAL	VIF	TOTAL	TOTAL	TOTAL	TOTAL
Constant	18.81 (0,00)***		15.66 (0.00)***	16.52 (0,00)***	20.87 (0,00)***	18.88 (0,00)***
IND	5.63 (0,073)*	1.17	5.55 (0.085)*	6.77 (0,025)**		6.55 (0.029)**
MGMTR	−3.81 (0.037)**	1.13	−3.47 (0.058)*		-4.55 (0,011)**	−4.07 (0.023)**
DCEX	1.81 (0.095)*	1.08	1.88 (0.086)*	1.98 (0.069)*	2.21 (0.032)**	
OWNC	−0.051 (0.05)**	1.07		-0.04 (0.078)*	−0.05 (0,06)*	−0.05 (0,047)*
NOSH	2.76 (0.022)**	1.13	3.14 (0.010)**	2.92 (0.028)**	3.05 (0.008)**	2.81 (0.013)***
BIG4	2.62 (0.036)**	1.07	2.45 (0.047)**	3.03 (0.009)**	2.82 (0.023)**	2.79 (0.026)**
F	8.08		8.46	6.80	9.28	9.61
R-squared	0.2531		0.2357	0.2328	0.2340	0.2390
Adj R^2	0.2271		0.2136	0.2107	0.2119	0.2170

(VIF) (see Table 4 column 1 bis) suggesting the absence of inter-correlations among the explanatory variables and then co-linearity problems.

To test the robustness of the results we studied four other models in which, one at a time, we have eliminated one of the governance variables (IND, MGMTR, DCEX and OWNC); the results are summarized in the following table in columns 2, 3, 4 and 5. In all models OWNC and MGMTR have a negative sign as well as the sign being maintained, and the significance, of the other three variables of governance. Since OWNC, MGMTR, IND and DCEX variables measure different aspects of the governance structure, they should theoretically be present in the model. When the four variables (IND, MGMTR, DCEX and OWNC) are used as explanatory variables the model becomes more significant. In fact, the R-squared, and so the adjusted R2, improves when all the four variables are included in the model. The lack of correlation between the variables of governance can support the validity of our results.

6 Conclusion

The study examines whether ownership structure and internal corporate governance mechanisms affect the behavior of Italian listed companies in terms of IFR disclosure. The sample is composed, generally, of firms with a high level of ownership concentration and with the presence of a dominant shareholder, so the agency problem and information asymmetries can arise mainly between majority and minority shareholder. We hypothesize that a firm with a high ownership concentration has a weak behavior in terms of IFR but that, at the same time, internal governance mechanisms, such as the presence of independent directors and of an NEC, enhance voluntary disclosure and information transparency, reducing the agency problem between majority and minority shareholders. The presence of ownership concentration, aligning the interest of principal and manager, reduces the need for disclosures. Minority shareholders have a low level of information and it generates a high level of information asymmetries. We assume that the agency problem between majority and minority shareholder can be mitigated by an adequate presence of independent directors and of an NEC who represents the different constituent elements in the company with an impartial viewpoint. The results of analysis show that firms with a higher incidence of independent directors are more likely to choose to start practical IFR; the presence of shareholders in the board tends to reduce the level of disclosure while the presence of a Chair who holds a non-executive role tends to its increase. Overall, the results provide support for our hypothesis and show that corporate governance structure is a significant control mechanism able to affect the level of IFR disclosure, so reducing information asymmetries through greater transparency in order to defend minority shareholder interest.

The study helps to build upon the existing literature on voluntary disclosure, specifically on the web (IFR) and on corporate governance. First, because, to the best of our knowledge, there are no previous studies that with regard to Italian listed companies test the impact of corporate governance mechanisms on IFR or that specifically examine disclosure on the Internet. The study extends previous literature on ownership concentration and IFR disclosure in a single country and explains IFR disclosure in terms of increasing transparency in order to defend minority shareholders interest. At the same time, analysis can provide evidence about the different business practices in terms of IFR.

The mainly limitations of this study are the restriction of the analysis to a single year and the exclusion of financial sector companies. Moreover, we have not analyzed the full access to all information and functionality of the web pages and what information and how users might want it [53]. Future work will seek to extend the analysis to all the listed Italian companies, including the financial sector, and to develop a larger sample of the same year and refine the items used to assess the IFR by entering others. Further study, finally, could devote attention to other control mechanisms (such as executive compensation) employed by listed companies to reduce the agency problem.

References

1. Ettredge, M., Richardson, V. J., & Scholz, S. (2002). Dissemination of information for investors at corporate Web sites. *Journal of Accounting and Public Policy, 21*, 357–369.
2. Ghani, E. K., Laswad, F., & Tooley, S. (2009). Digital reporting formats: user' perceptions, preferences and performance. *International Journal of Digit Access Research, 9*, 45–98.
3. Wallam, S. M. H. (1995). The future of accounting and disclosure in an evolving world: The need for dramatic change. *Accounting Horizons, 9*, 81.
4. Wagenhofer, A. (2003). Economic consequences of internet financial reporting. *Schmalenbach Business Review, 55*, 262–279.
5. Williams, S. M., & Ho Wern Pei, C. A. (1999). Corporate social disclosures by listed companies on their website: An international comparison. *The International Journal of Accounting, 34*(3), 389–419.
6. Hodge, F. D. (2001). Hyperlinking unaudited information to audited financial statements: Effects on investor judgment. *The Accounting Review, 76*(4), 675–691.
7. Debreceny, R., Gray, G. L., & Rahman, A. L. (2002). The determinants of Internet financial reporting. *Journal of Accounting and Public Policy, 21*, 371–394.
8. Hirshleifer, D., & Teoh, S. (2003). Limited attention, Information disclosure, and financial reporting. *Journal of Accounting and Economics, 36*, 337–386.
9. Jensen, M. C., & Meckling, W. H. (1976). Theory of the firm, managerial behavior, agency cost and ownership structure. *Journal of Financial Economics, 3*, 305–361.
10. Chen, C. J. P., & Jaggi, B. (2000). Association between independent non-executive directors, family control and financial disclosures in Hong Kong. *Journal of Accounting and Public Policy, 19*, 285–310.
11. Eng, L. L., & Mak, Y. T. (2003). Corporate governance and voluntary disclosure. *Journal of Accounting and Public Policy, XXII*, 325–345.
12. Abdelsalam, O. H., & Street, D. L. (2007). Corporate governance and the timeliness of corporate internet reporting by U.K. listed companies. *Journal of International Accounting, Auditing and Taxation, 16*, 111–130.

13. Kelton, S., & Yang, Y. (2008). The impact of Corporate Governance on Internet Financial Reporting. *Journal of Accounting and Public Policy, XXVII*(1), 62–85.
14. Lim, S., Matolesy, Z., & Chow, D. (2007). The association between board composition and different type of disclosure. *European Accounting Review, 16*(3), 555–583.
15. Jensen, M. C., & Meckling, W. H. (1976). Theory of firm: Managerial behavior, agency costs, and ownership structure. *Journal of Financial Economics, 30*, 401–420.
16. Anderson, R. C., & Reeb, D. M. (2004). Board composition: Balancing family influence in S&P 500 firms. *Administrative Science Quarterly, 49*(2), 209–237.
17. Shleifer, A., & Vishny, R. (1997). A survey of corporate governance. *Journal of Finance, 52*, 737–783.
18. Park, Y. W., & Shin, H. H. (2004). Board composition and earnings management in Canada. *Journal of Corporate Finance, 10*(3), 431–457.
19. Quagli, A., & Teodori, C. (2005). *L'Informativa Volontaria per Settori di Attivita*. Milan: FrancoAngeli.
20. Healy, P. M., & Palepu, K. G. (2001). Information asymmetry, corporate disclosure, and the capital markets: A review of the empirical disclosure literature. *Journal of Accounting and Economics, 31*, 405–440.
21. Brealey, R. A., Myes, S. C., Allen, F., & Sandri, S. (2007). *Principi di Finanza Aziendale (Principles of Corporate Finance)* (Vol. V). Milan: McGraw-Hill.
22. Melis, A. (2000). Corporate Governance in Italy. *Corporate Governance: An International Review, 8*(4), 347–355.
23. Ashbaugh, H., Johnstone, K. M., & Warfied, T. D. (1999). Corporate reporting on the Internet. *Accounting Horizons, 13*(3), 241–257.
24. Marston, C. (2003). Financial reporting on the internet by leading Japanese companies. *Corporate Communications: An International Journal, 8*(1), 23–34.
25. Oyelere, P., Laswad, F., & Fisher, R. (2003). Determinants of Internet financial reporting by New Zealand companies. *Journal of International Financial Management and Accounting, 14*(1), 26–63.
26. Abdelsalam, O. H., & El-Masry, A. (2008). The impact of the board independence and ownership structure on the timeliness of corporate internet reporting on Irish-listed companies. *Managerial Finance, 34*(12), 907–918.
27. Clemente, A. G., & Labat, B. N. (2009). Corporate governance mechanisms and voluntary disclosure. The role of independent directors in the board of listed Spanish firms. *International Journal of Accounting Information Systems, 5*, 5–24.
28. Labelle, R., & Schatt, A. (2005). Structure de propriété et communication financière des entreprises françaises. *Finance Contrôle Stratégie, 8*(3), 77–104.
29. Ettridge, M., Richardson, V. J., & Scholz, S. (2001). The presentation of financial information at corporate web sites. *The International Journal of Accounting Information Systems, 2*, 148–168.
30. Xiao, J. Z., Yang, H., & Chow, C. W. (2004). The determinants and characteristics of voluntary Internet-based disclosures by listed Chinese companies. *Journal of Accounting and Public Policy, 23*, 191–225.
31. Ball, R. (2006). International Financial Reporting Standards (IFRS): Pros and cons for investors. *Accounting and Business Research, 36*(1), 5–27.
32. Al Arusi, A. S., Selamat, M. H., & Hanefah, M. M. (2009). Determinants of financial and environmental disclosures through the internet by Malaysian companies. *Asian Review of Accounting, 17*(1), 59–76.
33. Levitt, A. (1999). Quality information: The lifeblood of our market. *Quality assurance: Good Practice, Regulation and Law, 7*(2), 65–75.
34. Fama, E. F., & Jensen, M. C. (1983). Separation of ownership and control. *Journal of Law and Economics, 26*, 301–326.
35. Hermalin, B. E., & Weisbach, M. S. (2003). Boards of directors as an endogenously determined institution: A survey of the economic literature. *Economic Policy Review, 9*(1), 7–26.

36. Pervan, I. (2006). Voluntary financial reporting on the internet-analysis of the practice of Croatian and Slovene listed joint stock companies. *Financial Theory and Practice, 30*(1), 1–27.
37. Gelb, D. S. (2000). Managerial ownership and accounting disclosure: An empirical study. *Review of Quantitative Finance and Accounting, 15*, 169–185.
38. Beasley, M. (1996). An empirical analysis of the relation between the board of director composition and financial statement fraud. *The Accounting Review, 71*(4), 443–465.
39. Haniffa, R. M., & Cooke, T. E. (2002). Culture, Corporate Governance and Disclosure in Malaysian Corporations. *Abacus, 38*(3), 317–349.
40. Cheung, Y., Jiang, P., & Tan, W. (2010). A transparency disclosure index measuring disclosures: Chinese listed companies. *Journal of Accounting and Public Policy, 29*, 259–280.
41. Deller, D., Strubenrath, M., & Webber, C. (1999). A survey on the Internet for investor relations in the USA the UK, and Germany. *The European Accounting Review, 8*(2), 346–351.
42. Pirchegger, B., & Wagenhofer, A. (1999). Financial information on the Internet: A survey of the homepages of Austrian companies. *European Accounting Review, 8*(2), 383–395.
43. Marston, C., & Polei, A. (2004). Corporate reporting on the internet by German Companies. *International Journal of Accounting Information Systems, 5*, 285–311.
44. Khan, T. (2007). Internet financial reporting disclosure about companies on website. *Journal of business systems, governance and ethics, II*(2), 37–46.
45. Despina, A. C., & Demetrios, P. L. (2009). The web-based financial reporting adopted by the listed companies in the Athens stock exchange. *Journal of Modern Accounting and Auditing, 5*(7), 7–20.
46. Pendley, J. A., & Ray, A. (2009). Internet financial reporting: An examination of current practice. *International Journal of Disclosure and Governance, 6*(2), 89–105.
47. Ho, S. M., & Wong, K. S. (2001). A study of the relationship between corporate governance structures and the extent of voluntary disclosure. *Journal of International Accounting, Auditing and Taxation, 10*, 139–156.
48. Ghazali, N. M., & Weetman, P. (2006). Perpetuating traditional influences: Voluntary disclosure in Malaysia Following the economic crisis. *Journal of International Accounting, Auditing and Taxation, 15*, 226–248.
49. Cooke, S. (1989). Disclosure in the corporate annual reports of Swedish companies. *Accounting and Business Research, 19*, 113–122.
50. Bonson, E., & Escobar, T. (2006). Digital reporting in Eastern Europe: An empirical study. *International Journal of Accounting Information Systems, 7*, 299–318.
51. Wang, D. (2006). Founding family ownership and earning quality. *Journal of Accounting Research, 44*, 619–656.
52. Momany, M. T., & Al-Shorman, S. A. (2006). Web-based voluntary financial reporting of Jordanian companies. *International Review of Business Research Papers, 2*(2), 127–139.
53. Debreceny, R., & Gray, G. L. (2001). The production and use of semantically rich accounting reports on the internet: XML and XBLR. *International Journal of Accounting Information Systems, 2*(1), 47–74.

Antecedents of Willingness to Share Information on Enterprise Social Networks

Paul Leroy, Capucine Defert, Amaury Hocquet, Frank Goethals and Johan Maes

Abstract This chapter identifies four significant antecedents of an employee's willingness to share information on an online Enterprise Social Network in a knowledge intensive organization. Employees with more tenure show a higher willingness to share information. For management it is important to be aware of the importance of recognizing employees' contributions on the network and to recognize that being present on the network takes time. Finally, the fact that people who feel less involved in the company show a lower willingness to share information reveals a limitation for the success of the project.

Keywords Enterprise social networks · Willingness to share information

P. Leroy (✉) · C. Defert · A. Hocquet · F. Goethals · J. Maes
IESEG School of Management (LEM-CNRS),
3 Rue de la Digue, 59000 Lille, France
e-mail: paul.leroy@ieseg.fr

C. Defert
e-mail: capucine.defert@ieseg.fr

A. Hocquet
e-mail: amaury.hocquet@ieseg.fr

F. Goethals
e-mail: f.goethals@ieseg.fr

J. Maes
e-mail: j.maes@ieseg.fr

F. Goethals · J. Maes
LEM-CNRS, Lille, France

P. Spagnoletti (ed.), *Organizational Change and Information Systems*, Lecture Notes in Information Systems and Organisation 2, DOI: 10.1007/978-3-642-37228-5_11,

1 Introduction

More than 200,000 companies are currently using the Yammer platform, a popular online Enterprise Social Network platform (ESN), similar to Facebook but for professional use. Amongst them 85 % of the Fortune 500 companies. Recently Microsoft announced its intent to take over Yammer for 1 billion dollars. ESNs allow employees to develop a profile and connect with other users for the purpose of information dissemination, communication, collaboration and innovation, knowledge management, training and learning, and other management activities [1]. Other examples of such networks are SocialCast and Salesforce.com's Chatter. Companies' worldwide annual IT spending is $2.7 trillion with social computing being a major force driving future spending [2]. ESNs are clearly gaining momentum in companies but they have hardly been studied in academic research.

ESNs are assumed to be valuable. Yammer for example has been said to cultivate a sense of community (e.g. at Deloitte), to lead to better teamwork (e.g. at Ford), to improve informal knowledge flows (e.g. at Suncorp), etc. Global financial services provider Wells Fargo implemented a large-scale social networking platform for over 200,000 of its employees and reported significant productivity enhancements [1]. Companies especially seem to deploy enterprise social network platforms with the goal to improve collaboration among employees within departments and across departments [3]. ESNs can enhance business value as a result of providing quick access to information, enabling new forms of communication and collaboration, improving social relationships (existing and new social ties), and facilitating knowledge sharing and collaboration [4, 5].

When it comes to the adoption of ESNs, it has been observed that ESNs often attract much attention in the beginning but after some time see less and less participation. Anecdotal evidence suggests that the reality of work pushes ESN use to the side so that people pull away from ESN activities and return to their original communication pattern [3]. The conclusion is that, because the value of an ESN depends upon the correct use in the entire enterprise (because of network effects), usage is problematic. The goal of our research project is to identify antecedents of the willingness to share information on an ESN.

Given the space limitations we immediately move to the development of hypotheses in the next section. After that, we shortly explain our research method. Next the research results are presented and we discuss the findings.

2 Literature Review and Research Model

Knowledge on individual employees' abilities and motivation to contribute to knowledge networks is very limited [6]. In this paper we intend to get more insight into the antecedents of the willingness to share information. We will consider the recognition given for sharing on the ESN, the involvement in the company, having enough time to use the system and the happiness at work. The level of analysis is the individual employee.

Social exchange theory states that individuals interact with others because they assume that such interaction will give them social rewards such as status and respect [7]. Related to this, the expectancy theories of motivation suggest that people are motivated to act in some way because of the recognition through external rewards satisfying personal needs [8]. McLure Wasko and Faraj [9] investigated antecedents of the number of posts of employees on an online discussion forum. They found that the individuals would contribute more responses if they perceived their participation would enhance their reputation. Similarly, back in 1999 Donath [10] found that building reputation was a strong motivator for active participation in an organizational electronic network. Hence, we put forward the following hypothesis:

H1: If an employee is convinced that sharing information on the ESN will be recognized, his/her willingness to share will be higher.

Expressing yourself on social networks puts an employee under public scrutiny. In general, self-disclosure is perceived to be risky [11]. Enterprise social networks are supposed to create more transparency, taking away asymmetrical information, what can change power relations in the company. Also, sometimes people may not follow advices that were given by someone else. The credibility of the latter may be lowered and there are chances they will get defensive [12], as this is touching their identity. These negative effects, however, can be countered through dedication at work, or employee involvement. Past research has linked involvement positively to autonomous work motivation, a factor which recently has been shown to stimulate knowledge sharing in networks [8, 13]. Moreover, employees' involvement in the organization also increases their efforts to share knowledge as it improves their perceptions of the organizational context [14] and thus lowers the perceived risk of information sharing. Knowing this, we hypothesize:

H2: If an employees' involvement in the company is higher, his/her willingness to share information will be higher.

Sharing information on an ESN takes time. ESNs have been touted as harmful because they can create information overload [5] and selecting the information that is relevant to some employee takes time. Anecdotal evidence suggests employees often stop using an ESN after some time because they feel they should spend their time on their primary task [3]. Consequently, we put forward the following hypothesis:

H3: If an employee has the impression that time constraints do not allow him/her to take part in the ESN, his/her willingness to share will be lower.

Finally, happiness or well-being at work has been said to increase participation from employees, which concerns therefore also the rise of communication [15]. In our model, well-being at work can also be seen as a proxy for support from colleagues as this support positively affects employee attitudes at work. Such support has been found earlier to stimulate knowledge sharing [14]. Therefore, we hypothesize:

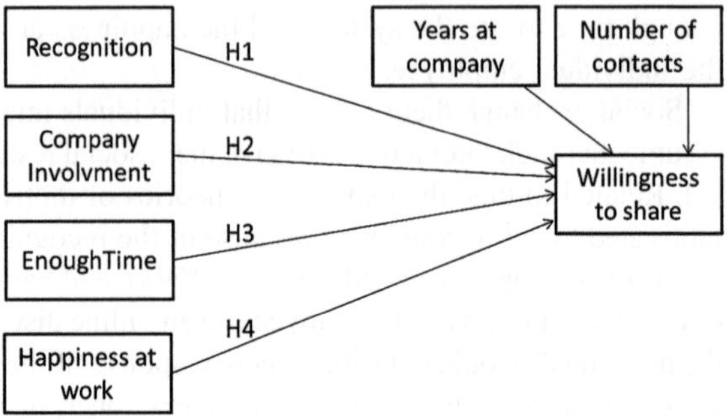

Fig. 1 Antecedents of willingness to share on an ESN

H4: If an employee is happier to be working at the company, his/her willingness to share will be higher.

The four hypotheses are shown in Fig. 1.

As shown in Fig. 1, we include two control variables in the model. A first control variable is the average number of other knowledge workers in the organization that a person has contact with per week. This variable may play a role, as it may indicate how open a person is to exchange information with others. On the one hand, a person who is exchanging information with more colleagues in the physical world is probably less closed as a person and more likely to *be open to* exchanging information with a broader set of colleagues online as well. On the other hand, a person who is sharing information with more people offline probably has a lower *necessity* to exchange information online. Secondly, the number of years one has been working at the firm may play a role. More specifically, employees with less tenure may feel like they are not the right person to post information and that it is up to employees with more seniority (and presumably more knowledge) to communicate. In fact, prior research in a related field showed that employees with longer tenure contributed more responses on an online discussion forum [9].

3 Research Setup

The research model was tested in a knowledge intensive organization with 65 knowledge workers. All knowledge workers received an e-mail to fill out an online survey concerning their willingness to participate in an ESN. Employees got one week to reply to the survey. Thirty-one employees did so. 58 % of the respondents were male; 42 % female. Given the small sample size, data was analysed using SmartPLS. SmartPLS is software for path modeling that uses Partial Least Squares.

The items that were used to measure constructs were adapted from prior research including those constructs. For each of the four independent variables and the dependent variable, several items were used. For the control variables, the number of years worked at the company and the average number of people contacted per week, a single item was used. The cross loadings shown in Table 1 do not reveal problems.

Table 2 shows the cross-correlations between the different constructs (with the square root of the AVE on the diagonal). While the correlations between involvement and happiness and between willingness to share and recognition are relatively high, the cross correlations are always lower than the square root of the AVE. Moreover, regressing involvement and happiness against another variable gives a VIF of 2.309, and regressing recognition and willingness to share against another variable gives a VIF of 2.429. This allows us to assume there is no problem of multicollinearity. All in all, there is no reason to expect issues with discriminant validity and multicollinearity.

The square roots of the AVEs shown in Table 2 are clearly above 0.7, and all Cronbach's alphas were 0.7 or above (not shown in the table), showing that there is no reason to assume problems in terms of convergent validity either.

4 Research Results

The test results are shown in Fig. 2. The R^2 of the model is high (0.749).

Hypothesis 1 is supported, showing that employees who believe they would be recognized for sharing information on the ESN would have a higher willingness to share information. Hypothesis 2 is supported as well. Employees who feel more involved in the company show thus a higher willingness to share information on the ESN. The belief that one has enough time to actually use the ESN also has a very positive relation with the willingness to share information, supporting Hypothesis 3. Happiness at work could not be shown to be statistically significantly related with the willingness to post information. The t-statistic for the relation between happiness and the willingness to share was 1.1. The insignificance of the relation may be due to the small sample and this result should be interpreted with caution.

In terms of control variables, the number of years an employee has been working at the company indeed has a positive relation with the willingness to share. The average number of co-workers that an employee contacts per week, on the other hand, could not be shown to be significantly related to the dependent variable.

5 Discussion

The fact that the model has an R^2 of 0.749 shows that the antecedents in the model are valuable to explain the variation in the willingness to share information on an ESN. While we are not aware of other research investigating the willingness to

Table 1 Cross-loadings

	Recog.	Involv.	Time	Happ.	Will.	Nr Cont.	Years
Sharing knowledge online would lead to more recognition from your superiors	**0.91**	0.20	0.51	0.26	0.58	0.15	−0.27
Sharing knowledge online would lead to increased credibility with your superiors	**0.94**	0.31	0.53	0.24	0.72	0.12	−0.08
Sharing knowledge online would lead to credit or acknowledgment in the work that follows from your help	**0.87**	0.32	0.37	0.30	0.69	0.10	−0.20
How would you characterize your professional experience at *the company*? (1 boring—7 interesting)	0.17	**0.83**	−0.07	0.59	0.19	0.13	0.10
How would you characterize the future at *the company* as you expect it? (1 dull—7 exciting)	0.32	**0.87**	−0.02	0.67	0.19	0.19	−0.38
How involved do you feel in *the company*'s environment? (1 not at all—7 really involved)	0.31	**0.92**	−0.02	0.60	0.34	0.30	−0.01
I think using an ESN would not take too much time	0.50	0.00	**0.84**	0.07	0.50	0.13	−0.22
I think I have enough time to use an ESN at *the company*	0.41	−0.06	**0.91**	0.05	0.65	0.09	0.06
Working at *the company* is (1 disgusting—7 enjoyable)	0.23	0.65	0.06	**0.95**	0.17	0.05	0.00
Working at *the company* is (1 dull—7 exciting)	0.27	0.75	0.10	**0.93**	0.14	0.11	−0.21
Working at *the company* is (1 unpleasant—7 pleasant)	0.33	0.59	0.04	**0.96**	0.20	0.10	0.04
You will want to share information on an ESN	0.75	0.25	0.61	0.14	**0.93**	0.11	−0.05
I think spending time to share information online with colleagues is useful	0.65	0.26	0.62	0.12	**0.90**	0.07	0.10
You would like to participate on an ESN between employees at *the company*	0.63	0.29	0.61	0.25	**0.92**	0.10	0.11
With how many other knowledge workers do you communicate (speak/mail) per week on average?)	0.13	0.25	0.12	0.09	0.10	**1.00**	−0.06
How many complete years have you been working at *the company*	−0.20	−0.09	−0.07	−0.04	0.06	−0.06	**1.00**

Table 2 Cross-correlations and AVEs

		1	2	3	4	5	6	7
1	HappinessWorkingHere	0.893						
2	InvolvedAtCompany	0.694	0.766					
3	NrContacts	0.093	0.254	1.000				
4	Recognition	0.295	0.308	0.132	0.827			
5	TimeEnough	0.065	−0.037	0.124	0.513	0.766		
6	Willingnesstoshare	0.182	0.294	0.105	0.740	0.667	0.842	
7	YrsAtCompany	−0.045	−0.091	−0.055	−0.196	−0.074	0.055	1.000

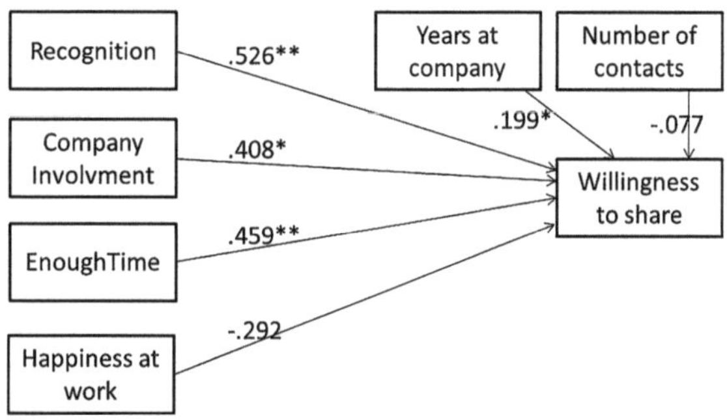

Fig. 2 Model test results (*$p < 0.05$; **$p < 0.005$)

share on an ESN, the R^2 is high compared to similar studies with other applications. For example, in their study of antecedents of the number of posts of employees on an online discussion forum, McLure Wasko and Faraj's model [9] had an R^2 of 0.37.

Two very significant antecedents are the recognition one expects to get from superiors and the feeling one has some slack time to spend on the ESN. These findings have big practical consequences, which deserve special attention in the domain of ESNs. The reason for this is the following: the initiative to start an ESN for a company often comes from the business people who feel a need for information from colleagues. It is a requirement that arises at the bottom of the organization, but in contrast to classic IT implementations, the requirement does not need to move bottom-up to get the IT platform installed: ESN platforms are usually run in the 'cloud' and offer free versions. Business people have no need (and often don't want) to get the IT department involved. This implies that the ESN initiative is often not managed at all. While business people who need more information may set up the platform, people who have knowledge to share may have little motivation or time to take part. Consequently, if management is not setting up a kind of reward system and is not admitting that being present on the ESN takes time, the ESN may only be short lived. Moreover, the consequence is that people soon would say 'we gave it a try, but an ESN did not work', jeopardizing new 'managed' attempts to set up an ESN. Hence, a lack of recognition and a lack of time are serious threats to the use of ESNs. However, management can facilitate the use of ESNs through several possible ways in terms of HR practices (rewards, retention, etcetera) and job design [6].

Although other research showed puzzling findings on the relationship between information sharing and commitment, our results point to the importance of company involvement for knowledge sharing through ESNs. Our results are therefore in line with those of Kalman [16]. People who feel like they work in an exciting firm with an interesting future, which has a project in which they can really play an important role, are more likely to share information on the ESN in order to help their organization forward. This is a property of the company-employee relationship which exists even without the ESN (in contrast to the 'recognition' and 'time' issues mentioned above, which are related directly to the ESN). Therefore, it may be harder to observe that this variable is playing a role [14] and hence companies may forget to consider this variable in their change management practices. More specifically, the people who feel very involved are likely to be the people who are taking the initiative for setting up the ESN (as mentioned in the paragraph above). They may get frustrated if other employees don't show the same passion to help the company or they may feel like their efforts are not appreciated. This could lead to less initiative taking in the future. Also, people who feel less involved in the company show a lower willingness to share information, implying that there is likely to be knowledge that remains untapped.

The most positive finding concerns the relevance of the tenure variable. The more years an employee has been working in a company, the higher his willingness to share information on the ESN. This is important, as these are typically the people who have gathered a lot of knowledge on 'stable' elements over the years and they are often in a position to have access to 'new' elements earlier than others.

In terms of limitations, we stress the fact that our research was conducted in a single institution and a single country and that the research needs to be replicated in other (and bigger) institutions and countries to guarantee the external validity. Also, given the small sample size, it would be inappropriate to conclude that happiness really is not a significant antecedent. Stepping away from ESNs, further research is needed on the way IT implementations need to be managed in the future. Change management has often been problematic in the past, even when companies still had official IT projects that were 'managed'. Now, with more software running in the cloud, including free versions, initiatives of people who care for the company may fail (because of a lack of change management), with all its consequences.

6 Conclusions

This paper identifies four significant antecedents of an employee's willingness to share information on an online Enterprise Social Network. The positive news is that employees with more tenure show a higher willingness to share information.

For management it is important to be aware of the importance of recognizing employees' contributions on the network and to recognize that being present on the network takes time. Finally, the fact that people who feel more involved in the company show a higher willingness to share information reveals a risk for the success of the project which may be harder to manage.

References

1. Turban, E., & Bolloju, N. (2011). Liang, T-P : Enterprise Social Networking : Opportunities, adoption, and risk mitigation. *Journal of Organizational Computing and Electronic Commerce, 21*(3), 202–220.
2. Gartner (2011). http://www.gartner.com/it/page.jsp?id=1824919.
3. Li, C. (2012). Making the business case for enterprise social networks. http://www.altimetergroup.com/research/reports/making-the-business-case-for-enterprise-social-networks
4. Albuquerque, A., & Soarez, A. L. (2011). Corporate social networking as an intra-organizational collaborative networks manifestation. In L. M. Camarinha-Matos et al. (Ed.), *PRO-VE* (pp. 11–18).
5. Parsons, K., McCormac, A., & Butavicius, M. (2011). Don't judge a (Face)book by its cover: A critical review of the implications of social networking sites. *Defence Science and Technology Organisation TR, 2549*, 39.
6. Reinholdt, M., Pedersen, T., & Foss, N. J. (2011). Why a central network position isn't enough: The role of motivation and ability for knowledge sharing in employee networks. *Academy of Management Journal, 54*(6), 1277–1297.
7. Blau, P. M. (1964). *Exchange and power in social Life*. New York: Wiley.
8. Porter, L. W., & Lawler, E. E, I. I. I. (1968). *Managerial attitudes and performance*. Homewood, IL: Irwin.
9. McLure Wasko, M., & Faraj, S. (2005). Why should I share? Examining social capital and knowledge contribution in electronic networks of practice. *MIS Quarterly, 29*(1), 35–57.
10. Donath, J. S. (1999). Identity and deception in the virtual community. In M. A. Smith & P. Kollock (Eds.), *Communities in cyberspace* (pp. 29–59). New York: Routledge.
11. Olivero, N., & Lunt, P. (2004). Privacy versus willingness to disclose in e-commerce exchanges: The effect of risk awareness on the relative role of trust and control. *Journal of Economic Psychology, 25*(2), 243–262.
12. Gal, D., & Rucker, D. D. (2010). When in doubt, shout! Paradoxal influences of doubt on proselytizing. *Psychological Science, 21*(11), 1701–1707.
13. Vansteenkiste, M., Neyrinck, B., Niemiec, C. P., Soenens, B., De Witte, H., & Van den Broeck, A. (2007). On the relations among work value orientation, psychological need satisfaction, and job outcomes: a self-determination theory approach. *Journal of Occupational and Organizational Psychology, 80*, 251–277.
14. Cabrera, A., Collins, W. C., & Salgado, W. F. (2006). Determinants of individual engagement in knowledge sharing. *International Journal of Human Resource Management, 17*(2), 245–264.
15. Oswald, J. A., Proto, E., & Sgroi, D. (2008). *Happiness and productivity*, IZA Discussion Paper 4645, 53.
16. Kalman, M. E. (1999). *The effects of organizational commitment and expected outcomes on the motivation to share discretionary information in a collaborative database*. Unpublished dissertation, University of Southern California, California.

Effects of Networking Activities by Internet on the Creation of a Business Network: Experimental Results of Simulimpresa Laboratory

Massimo Bianchi and Laura Tampieri

Abstract The chapter wants to discuss the results of network building activities realized by Internet in the experimental environment of "Simulimpresa" (Enterprise Simulation) laboratory managed by Bologna University—Forlì campus. The research analyses the networking of the simulated enterprise Perting Ltd operating in Forlì laboratory that reproduces the activities of a real business using Internet. The hypothesis concerns the consolidation of strong links coming from a rising selection as the business continuity over the time increases. The results outline that this process, in the analysed period, leads to the consolidation of some links that set up the more relevant framework of the enterprise business network.

Keywords Internet · Practice firm · Simulation · Networking · Customers/ suppliers

1 The Dynamic of Networking

Different models have been proposed [1–3] to reproduce the process of network building from a managerial point of view [4–6] particularly as it concerns the enterprise creation and the organizational development.

Although this paper is the result of a joint collaboration, paragraphs 1 and 2 are attributed to M. Bianchi, par. 3, 4 to L. Tampieri.

M. Bianchi (✉) · L. Tampieri
Forlì Faculty of Economics, Bologna University, Forlì, Italy
e-mail: massimo.bianchi@unibo.it

L. Tampieri
e-mail: laura.tampieri@unibo.it

P. Spagnoletti (ed.), *Organizational Change and Information Systems*, Lecture Notes in Information Systems and Organisation 2, DOI: 10.1007/978-3-642-37228-5_12,

The chapter analyses the specific field of research represented by the models based on the dynamics of relationships with customers and suppliers and its effects on the management [7].

This research stream, firstly applied to a sample of enterprises to detect its feasibility in the real environment, has been submitted to "Simulimpresa" (Enterprise Simulation) laboratory managed by Forlì Faculty of Economics in which the simulated enterprise Perting Ltd has developed, through internet, links with customers and suppliers. On this purpose the diffusion of ICTs tries to improve the reproduction of business networking activities through the web site and the e-mail that represent the main tools used by the simulated enterprises for establishing relationships with other organizations.

Many reasons could affect the prosecution or the interruption of a business link such as the competitive situation, the quality/price ratio, the reciprocal trust and the strategic choices.

Considering the process of selection as a whole we can examine the selection rate itself as (1)

$$TS_j = C(t_j)/C(t_{j-1}) \tag{1}$$

in which *TSj* is the Selection Rate concerning the *j* period considered as a year for $j = 1, 2, \ldots n$ and *C(tj)* is the number of C/S elements (Customers or Suppliers) with the result to have an active link with the enterprise at the end of the *j* year and $C(t_{j-1})$ of previous one.

We assume that among C/S elements, in the period subdivided in *n* phases or sub periods of equal dimension (year term), *n* subsets are distinguishable and each of these are characterized by the presence of that element in s phases or sub periods, with $s = 1, 2, \ldots n$.

If we suppose that each subset is submitted to a different selection rate TS, this would be described with (2) referring to the numerosity of customers or suppliers that, in the considered period, are present in *s* year

$$TS_s = C(t_{j,s})/C(t_{j-1,s)}) \tag{2}$$

$C(t_{js})$ is the number of C/S with *s* presences, selected for the passage to the following year and $C(t_{j-1,s})$ the number of C/S that in previous year *j-1* exhibits a frequency of *s* presences.

About the turnover data we can consider the progress rate of turnover TF (3) that indicates its trend on the basis of the business relationships persistence rise with $\Sigma m_{i,j}$ and $\Sigma m_{i,j-1}$ the amount of turnover with *s* presences in the considered period as regards the years *j* and $j - 1$.

$$TF_i = \left(\sum m_{i,j} - \sum m_{i,j-1}\right)/\sum m_{i,j-1)} \tag{3}$$

Previous researches allowed to point out the TS_s from the renewal data of C/S system that, distinguished on the basis of business continuity years and of the corresponding yearly medium turnover, can be represented by the curves X and Y

Table 1 Turnover of purchase or sale distinguished for C/S and years of business continuity

Code, customer/ supplier	1^ year	2^ year	.....	6^ year	Total partial for C/S	Years of business continuity of C/S	Yearly average of turnover ($m_{i,j}$)
1	$A_{1,1}$	$a_{1,2}$	…	$a_{1,6}$	$\Sigma a_{1,j}$	*count* ($a_{1,j}$)	$\Sigma a_{1,j}$ / *count* ($a_{1,j}$)
2	$a_{2,1}$	$a_{2,2}$	…	$a_{2,6}$	$\Sigma a_{2,j}$	*count* ($a_{2,j}$)	$\Sigma a_{2,j}$ / *count* ($a_{2,j}$)
…	…	…	…	…	…	…	…
Total	$\Sigma a_{i,1}$	$\Sigma a_{i,2}$	…	$\Sigma a_{i,6}$	$\Sigma a_{i,j}$	***count*** ($a_{i,j}$)	$\Sigma a_{i,j}$ / ***count*** ($a_{i,j}$)

Table 2 Medium data of turnover distinguished for years of business continuity

1^ year	2^ year	…	6^ year	
$m_{1,1}$	$m_{1,2}$	…	$m_{1,6}$	
…	…	…	…	
$m_{i,1}$	$m_{i,2}$	…	$m_{i,6}$	
$\Sigma m_{i,1}$	$\Sigma m_{i,2}$	…	$\Sigma m_{i,6}$	$\Sigma m_{i,j}$
$\Sigma m_{i,1} / \Sigma m_{i,j}$	$\Sigma m_{i,2} / \Sigma m_{i,j}$	…	$\Sigma m_{i,6} / \Sigma m_{i,j}$	**1**

(XY curves). These curves express the profile of renewal, respectively in numerosity and turnover, to which the C/S elements of an enterprise have been submitted on the basis of the mentioned selection criteria.

The first step to build the XY curves is to achieve the enterprise data of billing in the standard period of six years. These data can be deducted from the total of invoices issued and received from the enterprise and obtained, using RiXY,[1] by the management programme used for the accounting of C/S.

From the turnover data we can produce the Table 1 in which: $a_{i,j}$ is the total turnover that the customer i moves in the year j and is the result of the sum of all the total invoices to that customer and *count* ($a_{i,j}$) is the number of $a_{i,j}$ of the line i different from zero.

The formula (4) allows to obtain medium data of turnover distinguished on the basis of business continuity years (Table 2).

$$m_{i,j} = \sum a_{i,j} \Big/ count\left(a_{i,j}\right) \quad (4)$$

In a similar way we calculate the "Number of C/S per years of active link persistence" in the considered period, summarizing in Table 3 the data needed to define the XY curve.

[1] http://pyrrot.it. Francesco Pirrottina—University of Bologna, Faculty of Maths, Physics and Natural Sciences.

Table 3 Values of XY curve of C/S renewal

Years	Curve X	Curve Y
1	Σ *count* $(a_{i,1})/ \Sigma$ *count* $(a_{i,j})$	$\Sigma m_{i,1} / \Sigma m_{i,j}$
2	Σ *count* $(a_{i,2}) / \Sigma$ *count* $(a_{i,j})$	$\Sigma m_{i,2} / \Sigma m_{i,j}$
3	Σ *count* $(a_{i,3}) / \Sigma$ *count* $(a_{i,j})$	$\Sigma m_{i,3} / \Sigma m_{i,j}$
4	Σ *count* $(a_{i,4}) / \Sigma$ *count* $(a_{1,j})$	$\Sigma m_{i,4} / / \Sigma m_{i,j}$
5	Σ *count* $(a_{i,5}) / \Sigma$ *count* $(a_{i,j})$	$\Sigma m_{i,5} / \Sigma m_{i,j}$
6	Σ *count* $(a_{i,6}) / \Sigma$ *count* $(a_{i,j})$	$\Sigma m_{i,6} / \Sigma m_{i,j}$

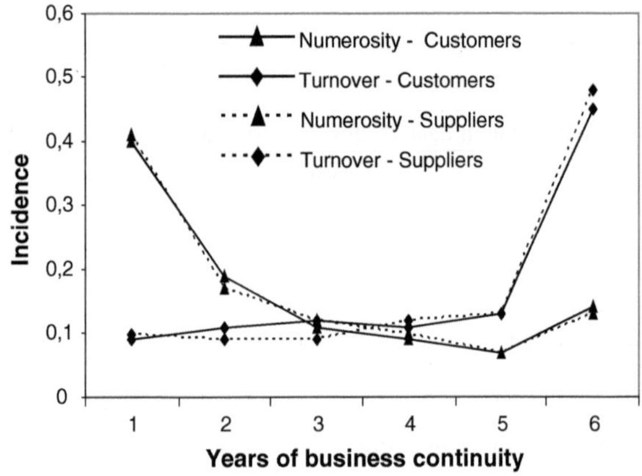

Fig. 1 XY *curve* of C/S renewal (real data) [8]

We can notice that *count* $(a_{i,j})$ gives as result the number of years in which, in the period of six years, the continuity of business emerges, justified by the invoices issued with the C/S*i*. The index *i* is assigned in arbitrary way. The medium data of turnover are indicated in the Table 2 in which the last line represents the incidence of yearly turnover of each class of C/S on the total yearly turnover and it is assumed as the vertical axe of curve Y (Fig. 1).

2 The Hypothesis

Assuming that the increase of TS and of the amount of turnover yearly managed with customers and suppliers by an enterprise it represents the strength of network links in business organizations, the hypothesis we want to test is that the continuity of business relationships enforces network links with customers and suppliers. This topic will be confirmed if the XY curves derived from the renewal model with an increasing selection ratio TS have a similar trend in the sample and, further, could be reproduced in Laboratory.

XY curves are showed in Fig. 1 and corresponding to obtained data (Table 4) with the method applied to 25 real small and medium enterprises of Emilia-Romagna region [8].

Table 4 Incidence class numerosity/turnover of C/S in small and medium enterprises [8]

	Years					
	1	2	3	4	5	6
Data numerosity						
Customers	0, 40	0, 19	0, 11	0, 09	0, 07	0, 14
Suppliers	0, 41	0, 17	0, 12	0, 10	0, 07	0, 13
Data turnover						
Customers	0, 09	0, 11	0, 12	0, 11	0, 13	0, 45
Suppliers	0, 10	0, 09	0, 09	0, 12	0, 13	0, 48

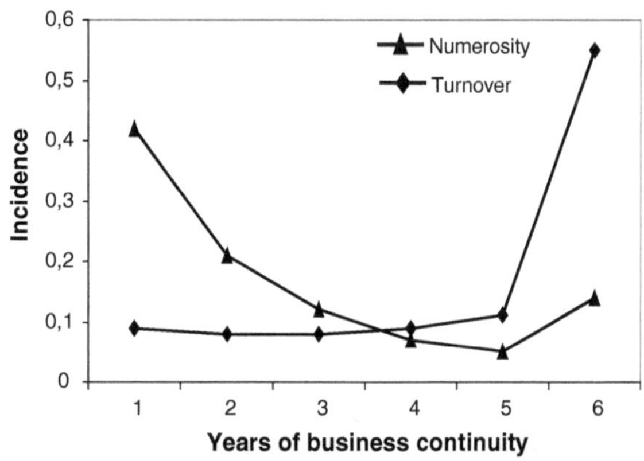

Fig. 2 XY *curve* of C/S renewal (mathematical method)

As showed in Fig. 1, the profile of customers renewal is similar to that of suppliers, confirming the symmetry in the links Customer/Supplier and Supplier/Customer, with a TS of the first year floating on average at about 43 %.

Once stated the feasibility of XY curves and the real behaviour of enterprises in managing their network links with Customers and Suppliers, we search a confirmation in reproducing them in Forlì' laboratory of enterprise simulation.

As it concerns the first topic, the profile that more fit to the renewal behaviour of SMEs in managing C/S links is the one based on an increasing TS and, symmetrically, in the decreasing of business links interruptions. This is according to the hypothesis of an enforcing of links as the continuity of business relationships increases together with the corresponding turnover (Fig. 2).

3 The Networking in Enterprise Simulation

The simulated enterprise or practice firm aims to reproduce in laboratory the activities of a real business using Internet. The simulated unit Perting Ltd operating in the laboratory of Forlì Faculty of Economics is set up and run by students as a study course under the supervision of teachers and tutors [9].

Table 5 The numerosity and turnover data incidence on the basis of years of business continuity

	Years of business continuity									
	1	2	3	4	5	6	7	8	9	10
Data numerosity										
Customers	0, 16	0, 52	0, 16	0, 06	0, 03	0, 02	0, 01	0, 05	0, 00	0, 00
Suppliers	0, 13	0, 35	0, 23	0, 15	0, 00	0, 00	0, 03	0, 03	0, 08	0, 08
Data turnover										
Customers	0, 02	0, 02	0, 88	0, 01	0, 01	0, 00	0, 01	0, 04	0, 00	0, 00
Suppliers	0, 01	0, 16	0, 26	0, 03	0, 00	0, 00	0, 28	0, 00	0, 00	0, 00

The mission of the practice firm is to trade virtual products and services with other simulated enterprises in the market economy at local, national and international basis. In this simulation the money and the financial regulatory institutions are fictitious, although the business decisions, documentation, forms and activities are of real nature [10].

So the enterprise simulation represents a form of professional and vocational training centre based on the usage of ICTs that, through Internet and mainly web site and e-mail, allow the participants to develop links with C/S.

One of the main features of Simulimpresa methodology application in Forlì Laboratory is the networking activities carried out by Perting Ltd since the academic year 2002/2003. Its mission is to trade informatics equipments (PC, printers, photo cameras, modems and software) and to deliver consultancy services in management, accountancy, labor and net field as: planning of macro and micro structures, personnel selection, keeping of pay register and pay rolls, pay-packet processing, job and skill evaluation, work cost accountancy, manpower planning and internet web sites designing.

The net of relationships with C/S developed by Perting derives by its connection to the network EUROPEN[2] that is in charge of: (1) coordinating the international practice enterprises network, (2) monitoring activities and (3) managing international telecommunications.

The operations of simulated purchase and sale carried out by Perting Ltd with the other practice firms of the network EUROPEN (Table 5) produced the X/Y Curve (Fig. 3) concerning 10 years of Simulation laboratory in Internet in the period 2001–2012. For our purposes we consider XY data of 6 years (- - - -).

The Fig. 3 shows that there is a quite similarity of the trends of the curve X and Y of C/S. A particular data is for customers the "3" period of business continuity in which Perting obtained the turnover of 14.284.506,51€ that is the highest during all the considered period (2002/2003–2011/2012), representing the 88 % of the total. In this case the high value of turnover is not justified by the high numerosity

[2] EUROPEN—Pen International is the worldwide practice firms network with over 7,500 practice firms in 42 countries. It is a non-profit association that was established on the 27th Oct 1997 http://cms.peninternational.info/.

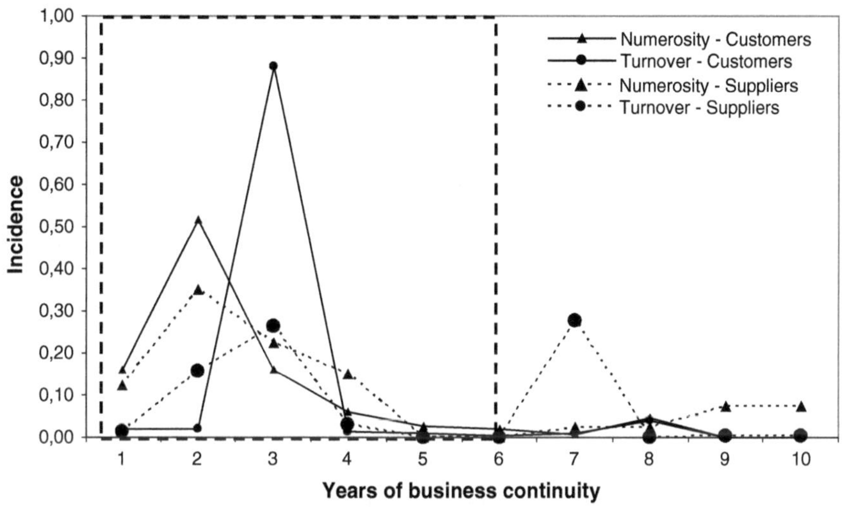

Fig. 3 XY *curve* of C/S renewal in the simulation enterprise

of customers as its value is quite low (0,16). This means that a low incidence of the numerosity could correspond to high value in the turnover.

So the process of selection applied over the time determined the continuity of some links with customers and suppliers that set up the more relevant framework of the enterprise business network and also the loss of other relationships.

4 The Research Results

In the paragraph nr. 2 we stated that the reproduction with a mathematical algorithm, according to an increasing selection rate with the continuity of business relationships, produces a profile of XY curve similar to the one detected in the reality.

The same is not possible to state as it concerns the simulation in the laboratory, almost till now. This is mainly connected to the missing of participation by Perting Ltd to national and international fairs. This barrier influenced the trend of business relationships with customers and suppliers as in the fairs Perting Ltd could develop and carry out a lot of business affairs in short term (2–3 days). Another element is the timing of the simulation enterprise methodology applied in Forlì Faculty of Economics (1 working day in the week, 25 h with a suspension of 15 days for exams) that limits the creation and the development of strong and stable relationships owing to the slowness of its fulfilment process.

[3] www.simulimpresa.com.

Although these relevant elements, the National Centre of Simulation,[3] through "suppliers shade", ensures to Perting a little continuity of some relationships rather than others.

This means that the condition of the simulation enterprise working has to be modified to better reproduce the reality and particularly through: (1) a major participation by Perting Ltd to international and national fairs, (2) an increasing number of working days and hours of simulation and (3) a better implementation of Internet applications to facilitate the communication process with customers and suppliers needed to develop and consolidate relationships. These elements would allow Perting to move towards a more C/S relationships continuity.

5 Conclusions and Research Perspectives

The chapter discussed the networking implemented by the simulated unit Perting in the experimental environment of simulation laboratory managed by Bologna University—Forlì campus.

In particular the frame of business relationships developed by Perting Ltd with customers and suppliers outlines a different trend respect to those obtained in the real context and through the mathematical method.

The main limitation derives from the consideration of only one enterprise in the simulation context that limits the generalization process of the findings. Moreover research results could be, almost till now, limited to small and medium business as this is the dimension in which the hypothesis have been tested in the sample and in the laboratory.

Further researches would address to deepen the simulation enterprise application to better reproduce the real trend of C/S relationships in order to find an adequate way, also using new technological applications as for instance virtual worlds, to stabilize them as they are considered key determinants of enterprise success.

References

1. Mielke, R. (1999). Applications for enterprise simulation. In P. A. Farrington, H. B. Nembhard, D. T. Sturrock & G. W. Evans (Eds.), *Proceedings of the 1999 Winter Simulation Conference*, (pp. 1–6).
2. Terzi, S., & Cavalieri, S. (2004). Simulation in the supply chain context: A survey. *Computers in Industry, 53*(1), 3–16.
3. Harrison, J., Lin, Z., Carroll, G., & Carley, K. (2007). Simulation modelling in organizational and management research. *The Academy of Management Review, 32*(4), 1229–1245.
4. Gallagher, K. P., Hosack, B. (2009). The role of strategy in the evolution and innovation of information systems: a simulation experiment. In S. Newell, E. Whitley, N. Pouloudi, J. Wareham & L. Mathiassen (Eds.), *A Globalising world: Challenges, ethics and practices*

information systems, The 17th European Conference on Information Systems. www.ecis2009.it.

5. Giesen, E., Ketter, W., & Zuidwijk, R. (2009). An agent—based approach to improving resource allocation in the dutch youth health care sector. In S. Newell, E. Whitley, N. Pouloudi, J. Wareham & L. Mathiassen (Eds.), *A Globalising world: challenges, ethics and practices information systems, The 17th European Conference on Information Systems*. www.ecis2009.it.
6. Schoenemann, N., Fischbach, K., & Schoder, D. (2009). P2P architecture for ubiquitous supply chain system. In S. Newell, E. Whitley, N. Pouloudi, J. Wareham & L. Mathiassen (Eds.), *A Globalising world: challenges, ethics and practices information systems, The 17th European Conference on Information Systems*. www.ecis2009.it.
7. Heller, R. (2006). Intellectual capital: Management now has to take care of not one but three varieties of intellectual capital. In E. Bono & R. Heller (Eds.), *Thinking managers*, http://www.thinckingmanagers.com.
8. Barzanti, L., Bianchi, M. (2002). *Stabilizzazione delle relazioni interaziendali e apprendimento organizzativo*. Paper presented to International Symposium on Learning Management and Technology Development in the Information and Internet Age. The convergent paths of Public and Private Organizations, University of Bologna, Forlì campus, 21th–22th Nov.
9. Gualdi, D. (2001). *L'impresa simulata*. Varese: Paravia Bruno Mondadori.
10. Moore, A. (2004). The challenge of the practice firm: Simulating a business environment in the UAE Fourth European GIS Education Seminar, Villach, Austria 02nd–05th Sep.

Revitalizing the Barter: The Case of Sardex.Net

Claudia Melis, Ernestina Giudici and Angela Dettori

Abstract "Creativity without boundaries" could be the best expression to describe the activity of an enterprise which was founded a few years ago in Sardinia (Italy). Its concept is a rediscovery of *barter*, the ancient practice to obtain goods from other people. The basic rules of barter rest unmodified nowadays: networked firms produce/sell goods or services and exchange them with goods and services provided by other firms in the network. Starting from the awareness that about barter firms has been written little, the goal of this article is to analyze this concept in order to show how information and communication technologies create new ways to make business. Our aim is in particular to understand, through the case study of Sardex.net, how this firm works, and how it improves thanks to the Internet the performance of the networked firms. We try moreover to find out whether and how the tourism is involved.

Keywords Barter · Complementary currency · Barter network · Internet · Tourism

1 Introduction

The word "barter" bears in mind the basic economic studies on the evolution of economies: From the prehistoric exchanges of goods to the developed well organized economies, from barter to monetary systems.

C. Melis (✉) · A. Dettori
University of Cagliari, Cagliari, Italy
e-mail: cmclaudiamelis@gmail.com

A. Dettori
e-mail: angela.dettori@libero.it

E. Giudici
Department of Business Economics, University of Cagliari, Cagliari, Italy
e-mail: giudici@unica.it

P. Spagnoletti (ed.), *Organizational Change and Information Systems*, Lecture Notes in Information Systems and Organisation 2, DOI: 10.1007/978-3-642-37228-5_13,

Taking this logical path, appears obvious that "barter" should be disappeared while substituted by monetary systems. We note on the contrary that it is alive and that its role is increasing in the contemporary economy. Why? How does barter work in the so called advanced economies?

There are numerous reasons for the long life of barter. They are connected with particular economic, social, and environmental situations.

An example is in the post socialist economy in Bulgaria [1], particularly in the Rhodope Mountain Villages, were people exchanged potatoes for any other kind of goods that was necessary for the daily life. Another example is *Liwac* in Ethiopia [2]: This particular kind of barter has become an attractive business opportunity for the unemployed young people.

The previous examples are only some of the multiple faces that the phenomenon may assume nowadays. The factor of the revival of barters is the economic crisis that affects occidental economies and influences SMEs negatively. The importance of the analyzed phenomenon becomes clear if we remember that SMEs are about the 98 % of all firms in the European Union [3]. In this difficult situation, SMEs create an alternative system while rediscovering barter. By the use of new technologies they net all the interested firms.

Assumed the cited phenomenon, our question is: is barter an effective way to solve the problems of economic crises and which elements are so attractive for SMEs?

The goal of this paper is to find the possible answers to the previous question by the in-depth analysis of a firm named Sardex, located in Sardinia (Italy), founded 2 years ago, which is having a real quick development.

The next point is devoted to the analysis of the most significant scholar contributions, then we analyze the case study and after that we present some comments.

2 Theoretical Background

Both economists and anthropologists have discussed about barter [2]. Nowadays, as barter occurs as well in undeveloped as in developed economies, it could be interpreted with a double, or, according to some author, [2] contrasting perspective. The first-one [2] tends to interpret this institution as an ancient practice of a primitive and moneyless [4] economy. This is interpreted as the earliest step on the path toward modern and monetized economy. According to this perspective barter is today a practice which concerns only the most undeveloped countries such as in Africa. Taking into consideration another perspective, barter is adopted as the contemporary response to the monetary systems' deficiencies, and, as such, it is a concern of the most developed economies such as USA and Europe [5]. Polanyi [6] notes that just a few economies operate without barter. It exists in several forms, and involves both large and small scale transactions. It is often adopted in the most developed countries as a complementary form of exchange. Although some scholar highlighted the difficulty in defining of barter in opposition to other forms of exchange [1, 3, 5, 7–9], there occurred several definitions. The barter practice has been defined by Appadurai [10] as the exchange of objects without reference to money and with maximum feasible reduction of social cultural political or personal transaction costs. Although having defined barter as a form of exchange with no reference to money, the author also notes that this practice can involve currency as a unit of account in the evaluation of transactions.

Anderline and Sabourian [11] defined barter as a form of non-monetary exchange in which all trades are required to balance. Taking into account what has been said so far, some authors [6] recognize common features in the barter practice. These characteristics are not intended to provide an exhaustive definition and description of barter; in fact the authors underline that this form of exchange should be situated within the social and cultural context, and on the other hand, it should be also regarded according the way in which it relates with other forms of exchange.

According to Humphrey and Hugh-Jones [5] barter implies a reciprocal interest that each side has in the good of the other. Moreover, it depends on the interest and satisfaction that both sides gain from the transaction. The same authors also note the necessity, that the exchanged goods and services have a direct consumption value for both participants. In addition: (1) It involves the demand of goods and services that are different in kind; (2) participants are free and equal and they can interrupt the deal at any time; (3) participants don't have future obligations following the fulfillment of the exchange; (4) the two parts of the transaction occur simultaneously or separated in time [1, 3, 5, 8, 9].

Among these definitions, merges the importance of two aspects in particular: The relevance of the information, social relations and reciprocity. These aspects that have characterized barter formerly are steel important for today's barter firms.

Humphrey and Hugh-Jones [5] emphasize the importance of social relations involved in barter exchanges. As we highlighted before, once the barter exchange has occurred, participants don't have future obligations and therefore there is no need for additional transaction to satisfy the wants of the actors following the fulfillment of the exchange. The purpose of each exchange in barter is to reach a double *coincidence of wants* [12]. In order to achieve such an objective, different information is needed about the item to be exchanged such as: Where is to be traded, when and by whom. Information is therefore a critical issue when barter is concerned. To this end, information and communication technologies have strongly contributed to the restoration and diffusion of this institution. According to Appadurai [10], barter in its earliest stage occurred mostly in face to face situation, but even now, although technologies have speed up the exchange of information, direct and personal contact and communication are still important.

From the analyses of old-new cases of firms that have adopted in various forms the barter practice it could be observed that the principles that have guided their proliferation are the need in the exchange system of reciprocity and inclusiveness. To this end, it seems emblematic the example of the *Red Global de Trueque*, an initiative which was establish in Argentina in 1989 and by December 2001, after the economic collapse it was widespread in the whole Country [13]. One of the peculiar aspects of this network is that the enrolled firms are called *prosumidores* (prosumers), which means that an individual or a firm is a subject that produces as well as consumes. In this way the multi-reciprocal exchange is personified in a single individual [13]. The reciprocity is underlined in the statute of the principles of the Red Global de Trueque (RGD) when it affirms: *Our aim is to mutual help* [13: 220] and also: *We believe it is possible to replace sterile competition, profit and speculation by reciprocity between people* [13: 220].

Also the principle of inclusiveness is one of the purposes of the most recent firms which operate as barter networks. The people here are encouraged to think what they could bring in the network; in this way the lack of money is not a problem for being a part of it, as people are asked to bring the products or services which they are able to produce, and to exchange it with other services or goods within the network. According to one of the founders of RGT, the contribution of these elements (reciprocity and inclusiveness), permitted the firm *To offer the world a system* [13: 219].

As far as reciprocity and inclusiveness are concerned among the most successful examples of local community currencies could be taken into consideration *Wir Bank* in Switzerland and *Ithaca HOURS* currency in New York State.

Wir Bank is an independent complementary currency which includes both small-medium firms as well as small retailers. *Wir* has a double meaning: It is the abbreviation of *Wirtschaftsring* (Wirtschaft means economic, and Ring means circle, ring) as well as the German word for "we". It was born as a response to the Great Depression of 1930s and financial instability and currency shortage with the aim to remind participants that the economic circle is also a community [14]. According to its cooperative statute Wir' purpose is: *To encourage participating members to put their buying power at each other's disposal and keep it circulating within their ranks, thereby providing members with additional sales volume* [14]. In 1934 Wir Bank started with 16 members, currently it includes more than 60,000 members becoming the fourth Swiss bank [14].

HOURS is the oldest and largest local community currency steel operating in United States; as wells as Wir Bank it has its origins in the Great Depression of the 1930s but was launched in 1991. It now accounts more than 4,000 firms enrolled in its Network [13].

From the old-new cases that has been presented, it is possible to affirm that the restoration of barter in present days could be explained as a reaction to the deficiency of the monetary system such as currency shortage and hyperinflation which has suggested the idea that money is exploitative and uncreative [5] but also as a complementary tool in order to revitalize marginal and excluded communities.

3 Methodology

In order to explore these issues, we opted for a case-study approach [15] because this methodology can be used to gain a better understanding of changing business practices in their social context [16]. With the aim to get a depth understanding of the firm, we conducted a semi-structured personal interview to Gabriele Littera, the marketing responsible of Sardex. In addition we collected some member's point of view with the purpose to acquire the motivations leading firms to join Sardex.

4 Sardex.Net

4.1 Origins and Operations

Sardex is a commercial credit circuit which makes use of a complementary currency named Sardex (SRD) as a unit of account for exchanges. One Sardex have a value of one euro. It was born in 2009, when, after the analysis of the global financial and economic crisis and its impact to the local economy (an emblemathic information is the unemployment rate of 13.5 % in 2011, against an average rate of 8.7 % in the rest of Italy [8]), four young (average age 30 years and residing in a rural area) developed a project with the aim to give a practical answer to this problem.

Before starting, the group explored other similar circuits without money, acquiring best practices from Europe and elsewhere.

The activity of the firm began on January 2010, when it achieved the first adhesions. By December 2010 the circuit Sardex.net was accounted over 200 firms and working professionals in Sardinia. In 2011 the enrolled firms reached the number of 400, and 650 by May 2012, with an increasing number of participants over 100 %, and a drop-out rate near to 5 % (among the lowest in the World) [17]. Transactions within the network, have increased exponentially achieving a record percentage on May 2012 of over 400 %: the annual average number of transaction was 357 in 2010, 425 in 2011, reaching the 800 transactions by the first quarter of 2012 [17]. The circuit involves firms from a broad variety of class of product and services ranging from grocery to advertising services. The compartment of firms directly involved on the tourism (including hotels, bed and breakfast, farm houses, residences, restaurants, catering and others) counts near 6 % of the total. To this end, Gabriele Littera says:

> Our circuit offers opportunities for firms operating in the tourism industry while giving them the possibility to purchase the needed services during the low season (for instance maintenance costs) with Sardex credits. In such a way they save cash which can be used to pay the other suppliers; in return they pay these services by providing rooms within the network.

Precisely the network operates in the following way: the firm which is interested in joining the circuit decides about the percentage of offered goods or services, that it makes available within the network; the firm is encouraged to take this decision based on an evaluation of the annual unsold stock. As an example, a hotel has a yearly turnover of one million Euros. This hotel declares to have an annual unsold stock (unsold hotel rooms) to the tune of 50,000 Euros. It means that the hotel can decide to make available within the network, product and services for an equivalent of 50,000 Euros (which means 50,000 Sardex). Next step for the enrolling firm is to make a spending review in order to evaluate which, among the cost items, it can spend on Sardex. The total credit at its disposal, is equal to the amount that it has decided to make available within the network. Hence, supposing that from the analysis emerges that the hotel previously cited, faces costs for advertising or maintenance, it can decide to purchase these services with the available Sardex credits. In return, according to a reciprocity mechanism, other firms will purchase hotel rooms until a total amount of 50,000 Euros. The output of the transaction is a loss or a gain in terms of Sardex credits. For instance, the hotel which spends 1,000 Euros purchasing brochures, will have, at the end of the deal a net situation of 49,000 SRD (50,000−1,000 SRD). On the other hand, the counter-party of the deal will have a gain equal to 1,000 credits in terms of Sardex. What is the convenience for joining such a network? An example will show why to purchase in credits within the network for a higher price than the one applied by a supplier outside the network will be more convenient. Let's suppose that the hotel has to buy a printer. It has two options: (1) Buying the printer from a supplier outside the network for Euros 800; (2) buying the printer within the network for 860 Sardex (860 Euros). Let's presume that the markup that the firm applies on its products is equal to 30 %. By choosing the first option the firm will have an expense in euro equal to 800. Instead, by choosing the second one, the firm will have an actual cost equal to 860 Euros (860 SRD) minus the markup applied to sales (30 %) for a total actual cost of 602 Euros [17].

In order to allow transactions, Sardex provides the enrolled firms with both on-line and off-line tools. Each member owns a card depicting the account number. Moreover, before starting the deal, customers can choose the suppliers among the enrolled firms by consulting the list of the subscribed firms for each class of products in the Sardex magazine or on the web site. In order to complete the deal, customers have two possibilities: (1) To contact a broker or (2) login into the Sardex portal and proceed by inserting the card number and the expiring date in order to forward the payment. The Sardex web-platform has a double function: to set the credit and debit position for each firm and to contain the profile of each member with the account of transaction and the net situation. The Sardex web site also provides a platform for the e-commerce transactions; however Gabriele Littera says that there are only few firms which have adopted it, so far. From what has been said we may observe that web technologies provide both a tool that allows transactions, as well as a powerful showcase for promotion and advertising purposes: Firms can learn about the desired products or services through descriptions and images as well as by evaluating feedbacks left by other customers.

4.2 Participant Views

> The true soul, the heart of the network are its enrolled firms, their fidelity and the way they embrace our values such as the reciprocity and inclusiveness that permitted our circuit to grow up; the true added value that the circuit can give to the island economy is to be found in its enrolled firms

says Gabriele Littera. From the analysis of these views we may deduce that the main motivations for join the network are both the increasing of sales and the number of customers as well as establish relationship with other firms in order to create a network.

> It's a dynamic and motivating system, which allows the economy to work, and reveals needs that otherwise wouldn't have emerged; an added value for the island economy, one more reason for being Sardinian! [17: 14].

This statement highlights the importance of being part of a motivating and dynamic exchange network in a context of economic recession. Being part of the network raises needs for services and products as a consequence of the increasing spending power as well as the possibility to have a variety of firms available for the exchange of goods and services. Moreover, it points out that being part of the circuit gives one more reason in order to identify the own firm with the local economy and to make it working. Another member says: "For Sardinian firms Sardex is an important opportunity for the diffusion of knowledge and for bridging relations aimed to collaboration" [17: 15]. Hence, within the network for firms, collaboration is more relevant than competition. According to another enrolled firm, Sardex: *Increasing the variety of the enrolled firms, increases also the efficacy of the network.* Thanks to the variety of the networked firms Sardex is becoming more and more a new marketplace for product and services coming from different market compartments. Therefore by joining Sardex firms have the availability of a broad range of product and services, and this constitutes the premise for building a new complementary market.

5 Conclusions

It follows from the above that we are in face of a revival of barter. Using the Net allows to fulfill better the necessities of firms in the Third Millennium.

Moreover, from the analysis of the literature emerges that barter is multifaceted. It assumes different organization depending on the field where it is used. This means that barter can be considered as a tool able to solve specific problems of well-identified areas with a specific culture that are able to accept some changes of the economic life but on line with the cultural identity. This may be one of the reasons of the Sardex' success that works in a region where the regional and culture identity is strong and where the involving of people is not easy to realize

(Sardinia). Sardex knows very well these problems and interacts effectively with the firms of its network. Taking the basic role of the environment into consideration in all its expressions (cultural, economics, naturalistic, etc.), future research may assume the aim to highlight which relationship exists (if exists) with the binding attention that is necessary devote to sustainability. Is barter able to reduce the goods transportation giving a good answer to the Km 0 perspective? And, is barter able to increase the "consume of proximity" giving a strong support to the activities of SMEs and, indirectly, to the economic development of some specific areas? This contribute constitutes the first step of a study which aims to analyze and compare similar firms in Europe and elsewhere.

References

1. Cellarius, B. A. (2000). You can buy almost anything with potatoes: An examination of barter during economic crisis in Bulgaria. *Ethnology, 39*(1), 73–92.
2. Tadele, F. (2000). Barter in practice: A case study of Liwac transaction in Addis Ababa. *Development in Practice, 10*(2), 223–228.
3. European Commission. http://ec.europa.eu/.
4. Noguera, J. (2011). Barter, centralized merchants and geographical spread. *Papers in Regional Science, 90*(1), 143–158.
5. Humphrey, C., & Hugh-Jones, S. (1992). *Barter, exchange and value*. Cambridge: Cambridge University Press.
6. Polanyi, K. (1957). *The great transformation*. Boston: Beacon Press.
7. Barnes, R. H., & Barnes, R. (1989). Barter and money in an Indonesian village economy. *Man New Series, 24*, 399–418.
8. CRENOS (Centre for North South Economic Research): Economia della Sardegna, XIX Rapporto, CUEC Cagliari (2012).
9. De Meulenaere, S.: Reinventing the market: Alternative currencies and community development in Argentina. *International Journal of Community Currencies*, http://www.geog.le.ac.uk/ijccr/.
10. Appadurai, A. (1986). Introduction: Commodities and the politics of value. In A. Appadurai (Ed.), *The social life of things: Commodities in cultural perspective* (pp. 3–63). Cambridge: Cambridge University Press.
11. Anderline, L., & Sabourian, H. (1992). Some notes on the economics of barter, money and credit. In C. Humphrey & S. Hugh-Jones (Eds.), *Barter, exchange and value*. Cambridge: Cambridge University Press.
12. Pryor, F. L. (1997). *The origins of the economy: A comparative study of distribution in primitive and peasant economies*. New York: Academic Press.
13. Pearson, R. (2003). Argentina's barter network: New currency for new times? *Bulletin of Latin American Research, 22*(2), 214–230.
14. Wir Banking Portal, Official Site http://www.wir.ch/.
15. Yin, R. K. (1999). *Case study research: Design and methods*. Los Angeles: Sage Publication.
16. Eriksson, P., & Kovalainen, A. (2008). *Qualitative methods in business research*. London: Sage Publication.
17. Sardex.Net (eds.) (2011). Un anno indimenticabile. Come trasformare tramite la colaborazione una buona idea in realtà. *Sardex.Net Magazine*, (Vol. 0, pp. 1–56).

Library Perceptions of Using Social Software Such as Blogs in the Idea Generation Phase of Service Innovations: Lessons from an Experiment

Ada Scupola and Hanne Westh Nicolajsen

Abstract This article investigates the use of social software such as blogs to communicate with and to involve users in the idea generation process of service innovations. After a theoretical discussion of user involvement and more specifically user involvement using web-tools with specific focus on blogs, the article reports findings and lessons from a field experiment at a university library. In the experiment, a blog was established to collect service innovation ideas from the library users. The experiment shows that a blog may engage a limited number of users in the idea generation process and generate a useful, but modest amount of ideas.

Keywords Idea generation · Social software · Service innovations · Blogs · Library · Experiment

1 Introduction

Concepts like Open Innovation [1] and User-driven Innovation [2] are receiving growing attention. The concepts indicate that innovation is not confined to internal organizational boundaries but involve interactive processes, where organizations interact with external partners including customers and users.

A. Scupola (✉) · H. W. Nicolajsen
Roskilde University, Copenhagen, Denmark
e-mail: ada@ruc.dk

H. W. Nicolajsen
e-mail: westh@hum.aau.dk

A. Scupola · H. W. Nicolajsen
Aalborg University, Copenhagen, Denmark

P. Spagnoletti (ed.), *Organizational Change and Information Systems*, Lecture Notes in Information Systems and Organisation 2, DOI: 10.1007/978-3-642-37228-5_14,

Libraries, and especially research libraries, are facing considerable challenges and opportunities due to the advent of the Internet and consequent digitalization of the library services [3]. According to Brindley [4] libraries must innovate their services to keep on staying competitive and service innovation must happen in close contact with the users. The aim of this article is to investigate the potentials of using social software for user involvement in service innovation in libraries. In doing so we limit ourselves to focus on the ideation phase of the innovation process in which the involvement of users has been found to have particular potentials [2]. Therefore, the following research question is addressed in this chapter: To what extent might social software such as blogs be used in academic libraries to communicate with and to involve users in the idea generation process of service innovations?

In order to investigate the research question, we conducted a study in which social software in form of a blog was used in the idea generation phase of the library services innovation process. The blog, directly allowing users to provide ideas for service innovations on an open platform, resulted in the library giving serious consideration to the ideas collected and implementing many of them. All in all, the blog was considered by the library management as a useful tool to communicate with the users and to generate a manageable amount of useful ideas.

The chapter is structured as follows. First, we theoretically discuss user involvement in service innovation and in particular user involvement through means of social software with focus on the use of blogs. Then we present our research method and the analysis and results. Finally we provide a discussion of the results and some concluding remarks.

2 Theoretical Background

Later research has focused on the role of users in relation to innovation, also in service innovation [2]. This has resulted in a clearer understanding of different types of user involvement. Alam and Perry [2] have developed a 10 stages model of the service innovation process, going from idea generation to implementation and marketing and present and discuss user involvement in each of these ten stages. They conclude that it is most profitable to involve users in the earlier and later innovation phases, because these phases are closest to the role as "service user". This role does not demand particular expertise from the customer, but only that the customer/user provides insights on his own needs and wishes or evaluates an existing or potential service. The phases in between are more work-intensive and typically demand professional qualifications. According to Alam [5], customer activities in the ideation phase include describing needs, problems and solutions. Customers may suggest wanted features and preferences or they may evaluate existing services, lacking in the market or wishes for new services.

Several researchers [5–7] argue that the direct interaction between customer and employee provides an occasion to get both ideas and an understanding of customers needs. For example Magnusson [7] argues for the benefits of physical meetings between professionals and customers because meetings may provide the professionals with insight into the customers' needs and understanding and, conversely, the users may get a better understanding of the conditions allowing them to suggest more realistic ideas. Other ways to get ideas from users include monitoring of user data such as complaints, returned products, observation of customer behavior in the so-called 'service encounter' [6, p. 336], company visits or integration of customers in development teams [5], innovation labs [8] or virtual communities e.g., [9].

2.1 Web Tools to Support User Involvement with Focus on Blogs

Prandelli et al. [10] have identified 28 different web tools that can be used in the different stages of product innovation. These web based tools range from surveys and 'complaint areas' used in the idea generation phase to 'virtual product tests' in the product test phase. In addition, Prandelli et al. [10] found that the web-based tools are mainly used by larger corporations and in the first and last stages of the innovation process and are mainly used as substitutes for the offline practices. Many of such tools have been investigated in other studies as well. For example, Franke and Piller [11] describe the use of simple toolkits to create user-adjusted design of watches, while Ogawa and Piller [12] report the use of idea competitions for t-shirts design and Franke et al. [13] describe user design of ski equipment. Virtual communities are another example where customers help organizations to innovate products or service development by using web-based interactive tools. Lego Mindstorm and online gaming are well known examples [14]. These communities may be user or company initiated. In both cases, user involvement is based on the users' own interest and prestige in the community. Some organizations develop online user communities for users to exchange knowledge, which can be seen as extension of the services delivered as in the case of NetDoctor's baby club. The interaction between an organization's customers can be an important source of knowledge regarding customers' challenges, discontent and needs relevant for new service or new product development.

As it can be seen from the above discussion, the Internet has created many opportunities for organizations to interact both directly and indirectly with their users e.g., [9]. However blogs have received limited attention as a technology to collect and discuss ideas for service innovation, even though a few studies have investigated the potential of blogs for innovation especially in the field of new product development e.g., [15].

Persons or organizations initially used blogs to write posts in chronological order about a particular theme: their life, products etc. [16]. However changes in the technology, growing experiences, combination with other tools, easy access to free platforms as well as an increasing accept and use of user-created content has opened up for new use forms including professional, medical, political, industrial and product related issues see [15]. The possibility for others to write comments has created a shift towards more interaction and discussion on the blogs (Bar-Ilan, 2007 in [17]. Transparency and documentation leads according to Kuhn [18] to accountability as well as easy and cheap access promote equality. Anonymity may also be a factor of relevance as it may affect the content in good or bad ways. It might result in more inputs especially if the content concerns taboos [19]. On the other hand anonymity or lack of knowledge about the senders might provide challenges such as difficulties in understanding the input or it might result in irrelevant or harsh input [20].

3 Research Method

The research method employed in this study consists of a pilot study investigating innovation processes and user involvement at an academic library followed by a field experiment involving users in idea generation trough a blog and finally follow-up interviews and workshops with library personnel to gain library insights about the experiment and its results. In the pilot study, conducted at Roskilde University library (Rub), we used semi-structured qualitative interviews, meetings and workshops lasting between 1 and 2 h with top managers, middle managers, and 'front-line' librarians as the main data collection methods. Other data collection methods used in this chapter includes library reports, minutes of top management meetings as well as click stream analysis.

Based on the results of the pilot study, an agreement was made with the library management to conduct an experiment inviting user ideas through an interactive web-tool such as blog (called RUbminds). This experiment was conducted as a so-called field-experiment, which is an experiment carried out in a natural context rather than in a laboratory. Field experiments are similar to other practice oriented methods such as action research, action learning, and reflexive practice [21].

A small group comprising four employees from around the library as well as the authors of this chapter designed and implemented the blog. The blog was seen as a tool accommodating for an open dialogue about the users perceptions of the library services and their wishes. Different names and layouts were discussed inspired by other blogs. It was decided to go for four topics, which were all formulated by the library personnel. The topics intended to cover the services of the library as well as the physical setting for these services. Three of the topics were formulated as questions on the blog: (1) "Do we comply with your wishes?"; (2) "If you should furnish the library….?"; (3) "Is Rub your favourite library?"; and (4) "The future of the library—give us your suggestions". The blog experiment was conducted for a period of 3 months. The success criterion for the field experiment was that the blog (the independent variable of the experiment) could function as a medium for idea generation by library users and that these ideas could result in implemented service innovation at the library (the dependent variable of the experiment). In this article we primarily look at the first part—how useful the blog is to involve users in the ideation phase from the perspective of the library.

4 Analysis

The results of the pilot study show that the library's traditional approach to innovation processes is mainly based on the use of 'internal development plans' where most ideas come from top management, collaboration with external partners and competitors but also, even though to a lesser extent, from employees. RUB had very little experience with social software at the time of the study. For RUB, meeting the users through a blog was new and different not at least due to the direct involvement of users in the idea generation of the service innovation process, signaling a different attitude towards users, which were seen as having little to contribute due to an expected low interest and conservative ideas about library services.

During the short period in which the experiment was conducted, 1,011 visits were made to the blog and 2,572 pages were looked at. On average, the visitors stayed for 1 min and 35 s. A total of 27 "useful" ideas were provided during the period of the experiment.

The ideas generated by the users on the blog were very different in nature and covered a wide range of topics. Some ideas were visions of the library fulfilling other and different functions—as a more cultural place. Some are suggestions for new services such as an EndNote course, others suggest big or small changes to services already offered such as access to computers in the library reading areas. Some comments just criticize the service offerings, without providing suggestions for improvements as for example the noise level in the silent area. This broadness of topics is in line with Alam [5] who argues that input can have many different forms.

In follow up interviews, the library management stated that the blog was a good way to get input from the users and especially to communicate online with the users. According to library management, some ideas coming from the blog addressed problems that were well known to the library but that had been forgotten or put aside. Meeting them again on the blog and knowing that many potential users could read the comments posted on the blog and become aware of the problems, motivated the library management to find solutions and fix problems neglected in the past. In a way the library personnel felt a pressure from the blog to do something about the implementation of the ideas, both those pointing to well-known problems as well as those pointing to problems/ideas that the library was not previously aware of. Some ideas were investigated further; a few were completely dropped like the establishment of open-air library services. Overall, the ideas provided by the users were not major breakthroughs, but rather could be classified as ideas suggesting incremental service innovations. RUB has seen the relative low activity on the blog as an advantage because they could manage it by engaging few resources. According to the blog manager, they would probably had closed the blog if they got overwhelmed by a huge number of posting/ideas that would have required a huge amount of resources both in terms of employees time to handle the blog and money/other resources to investigate and eventually implement the ideas suggested by the bloggers.

In addition the blog manager said that the blog had had several internal positive spin-offs such as increased collaboration among colleagues of different departments both in order to find appropriate answers to the blogs' questions/postings and to investigate/implement solutions. The blog had overall increased collaboration and communication among the library employees. Finally, the blog gave the library also the image of an institution that was open to ideas and critique from the users.

In a top management meeting to evaluate the outcome from the blog experiment, the library management decided to keep the blog on RUB's website because "The blog invites for open discussion of suggestions and opinions in opposition to just e-mails" (Minutes from a RUB meeting). The blog is still used to communicate with the users.

5 Discussion and Conclusions

Our experiment shows that RUBminds blog is perceived by RUB to be a useful web-based interactive tool in order to communicate with the users and to engage the users in the idea generation phase of the service innovation process. So our study supports, even though with big caution, the results of the study conducted by Droge et al. [15]. However, our experiment shows that it is difficult to engage a huge amount of users to contribute ideas and therefore to generate a huge amount of ideas on the blog. There could be several reasons for this: the library users are not really burning to provide ideas about how to improve the library services; library users are in general satisfied; or it could also be due to the design of the RUbminds blog, lacking knowledge of RUbminds, lacking interest or qualifications to communicate using blog. Nevertheless, the ideas and insight generated during the 3 months experiment were considered important by library management that considered them as an eye opener for what services the library users might wish from them. For RUB the relative low activity on the blog was seen as an advantage because they could manage it with relatively few resources. The balance between the value gained through the blog and the resources spent on it was also the reason for the decision to continue the blog after the experiment period. The library received some valuable insights into what users like, dislike, what they need and some suggestions about what to do. Some ideas point to implementable solutions. Others point to problems or needs that need further investigation. Some critiques and needs even led to further inquiry to understand what the problem is. The blog thus becomes a platform to understand the users, their way of thinking and their values. These results are in line with what argued by Magnusson [7]: that understanding user needs and wants is a first step to develop good solutions. On the other hand the blog becomes also a platform to provide feedback to the users on the conditions and limitations' regarding what is doable [7]. The library felt obliged to take into serious consideration the ideas posted on the blog, due to the transparency, documentation and archiving function of the blog as also stated by Kuhn [18] meaning the blog gives the users a voice that are difficult to be overheard. We can conclude that the answer to the research question—To what extent might social software such as blogs be used in academic libraries to communicate with and to involve users in the idea generation process of service innovations? is: it depends on the expectations to the blog.

If the blog has to be used to generate a modest, but useful number of ideas, then the blog has potential to engage users in the service innovation process. If the purpose is to generate a huge number of ideas or engage a huge number of users, then the answer is that probably blogs are not a good tool. Blogs can eventually be used in combination with other more traditional tools for involving users in idea generation in libraries as for example workshops.

However, our results have found a number of spin offs advantages that blogs can generate in addition to user involvement for idea generation, namely increasing internal collaboration among the employees and giving the organization an image of a more "open to critique and new ideas" kind of organization.

However, our study is not free of limitations. One limitation is represented by the fact that it is difficult to generalize these results to the whole library sector since we only have conducted one experiment in one library for a limited amount of time. Similarly it is impossible to generalize these results to other settings. More experiments in several libraries would need to be conducted in order to better understand and to some extent be able to generalize regarding the use of blogs for user involvement in library service innovations. Alternatively, a survey could be conducted to identify libraries that have engaged in similar kinds of experiments and interview them to get insights into their experiences. These could be subject for further research. Finally, more research also in other service sectors could be carried out in order to fully exploit the potential of social software such as blogs for user involvement in the service sector.

Acknowledgments We wish to thank employees and the management group at Roskilde University Library for their openness and collaboration. In addition we would like to thank all the colleagues participating to the ICE project (ice-project.dk) for interesting discussions and suggestions. Finally, and especially, we would like to thank the Danish Strategic Research Council for financial support for the ICE project, without which this study would not have been possible.

References

1. Chesbrough, H. W. (2003). *Open innovation: The new imperative for creating and profiting from technology*. Boston: Harvard Business School Press.
2. Alam, I., & Perry, C. (2002). A customer-oriented new service development process. *Journal of Services Marketing, 16*(6), 515–534.
3. Carr, P. L. (2009). From innovation to transformation: A review of the 2006–7 serials literature. *Library Resources and Technical Services, 53*(1), 3–15.
4. Brindley, L. (2006). Re-defining the library. *Library Hi Tech, 24*(4), 484–495. Bradford.
5. Alam, I. (2006). Removing the fuzziness form the fuzzy front-end of service innovations through customer interactions. *Industrial Marketing Management, 35*, 468–480.
6. Narver, J. C., & Slater, S. F. (2004). Responsive and proactive market orientation and new-product success. *Journal of Product Innovation Management, 21*, 334–347.
7. Magnusson, P. (2003). Benefits of involving users in service. *European Journal of Innovation Management, 6*(4), 228–238.
8. ICE project, http://www.ice-project.dk.
9. Prandelli, E., Sawhney, M., & Verona, G. (2008). *Collaborating with customers to innovate: Conceiving and marketing products in the networking age*. Cheltenham: Edward Elgar.
10. Prandelli, E., Verona, G., & Raccagni, D. (2006). Diffusion of web-based product innovation. *California Management, 48*(4), 109–135.
11. Franke, N., & Piller, F. (2004). Value creation by toolkits for user innovation and design: The case of the watch market. *Journal of Product Innovation Management, 21*, 401–415.
12. Ogawa, S., & Piller, F. T. (2006). Reducing the risks of new product development. *MIT Sloan Management Review, 47*(2), 65–71.
13. Franke, N., Keinz, P., & Schreier, M. (2008). Complementing mass customization toolkits with user communities: How per input improves customer self-design. *Journal of Product Innovation Management, 25*, 546–559.
14. Jeppesen, L. B., & Molin, M. (2003). Consumers as co-developers: Learning and innovation outside the firm. *Technology Analysis and Strategic Management, 15*(3), 363–383.
15. Droge, C., Michael, A., Stanko, M. A., & Pollitte, W. A. (2010). Lead users and early adopters on the web: The role of new technology product blogs. *Journal of Product Innovation Management, 27*(1), 66–82.
16. Newson, A., Houghton, D., & Patten, J. (2009). *Blogging and other social media: Exploiting the technology and protecting the enterprise*. Farnham: Gower Publishing.
17. Aharony, N. (2009). Librarians and information scientist in the blogosphere: An exploratory analysis. *Library and Information Science Research, 31*, 174–181.
18. Kuhn, M. (2007). Interactivity and prioritizing the human: A code of blogging ethics. *Journal of Mass Media Ethics, 22*(1), 18–36.
19. Tyler, T. R. (2002). Is the Internet changing social life? It seems the more things change, the more they stay the same. *Journal of Social Issues, 58*(1), 195–205.
20. Alonzo, M., & Aiken, M. (2004). Flaming in electronic communication. *Decision Support Systems, 36*(3), 205–213.
21. Baskerville, R., & Wood-Harper, A. T. (1996). *A taxonomy of action research method working paper*. Copenhagen: Institute of Informatics and Management Accounting, Copenhagen Business School.

A Best Practice of Enterprise 2.0: The Photoviva Case Study

Domenico Consoli and Walter Del Prete

Abstract Nowadays, a new model of Enterprise 2.0, an open enterprise that dialogues with customers, using Web 2.0 tools (blog, chat, forum, social network), is affirming. The customer could be fully involved in the innovative process and express opinions and suggestions to improve the product/service. In the paper we analyse a case study that operates in this context. Photoviva is a brand of a small company where users themselves can design the cover of their own iPhone and they can also gain royalties when other customers choose their personal designed image. In this way the boundaries of the company is open. Between company and customers a strong relationship and collaboration, in reaching business goals, is established. The customer becomes an active prosumer, producer and consumer at the same time.

Keywords Web 2.0 · Enterprise 2.0 · Virtual channel · Customer involvement · Prosumer

1 Introduction

The Enterprise 2.0 is an open enterprise that collaborates and exchanges information with customers by interactive channels.

By web 2.0 tools, customers can express suggestions and recommendations that may be useful to the company for the improvement of the product/service and also

---

D. Consoli (✉)
Department of Economics, Society and Politcs, University of Urbino, Urbino, Italy
e-mail: domenico.consoli@uniurb.it

W. D. Prete
E-leva s.r.l, Pesaro, Italy
e-mail: walter@e-leva.com

P. Spagnoletti (ed.), *Organizational Change and Information Systems*, Lecture Notes in Information Systems and Organisation 2, DOI: 10.1007/978-3-642-37228-5_15,

for strategic goals. There are many websites such as epinions.com, cnet.com, complaints.com, ecomplaints.com where consumers share their opinions on their shopping experience [1].

In this way, between customer and manufacturer a bidirectional channel, that stimulates a process of co-creation and co-production, is established.

Nowadays, in the global world, to innovate, companies must exchange information with other subjects like individuals, employees, partners, customers and suppliers. In an innovation process, open and oriented towards the external environment, it is possible to acquire knowledge and other skills that are not present inside the company. In the Enterprise 2.0, the customer can be involved in all processes [2]: design, development, production, testing and marketing.

This is the new formula for reducing the time to market and meet users requirements.

The Ducati company (ducati.com) gives to loyal customers the first opportunity to test ride new products. Lego (lego.com) is a good example of a company that involves customers in projects of open innovation. In 2004 the company decided to develop a new line of robots "Mind Storms" with the cooperation of customers from the planning stage of the new product. Approximately 10,000 customers responded to the invitation to participate in the design of Lego and 100 users were selected and worked inside the internal R&D department.

In a Canadian company John Fluevog (fluevog.com), customers participate actively and creatively in designing new models of shoes. The Mulino Bianco (mulinobianco.it) is available to consider any proposal on the conception of new biscuits. Ideas can be proposed and voted; the best one will be realized. In the website "Fiat 500" (500 Wants You—fiat500.com) consumers contributed creatively to the design of the new car.

In this chapter we describe a case study, the Photoviva brand of a small company, where users are involved in the productive process. This is a best practice of an Enterprise 2.0 that involves customers in an open innovation process.

The analysis of this innovative case is useful to show how in a small company with few employees it is also possible to involve the customer in the business process. In the literature usually successful case histories are referred to medium and large enterprises.

The chapter presents the following structure: Sect. 2 focuses on the literature review. In Sect. 3 we analyse the Photoviva case study. In Sect. 4 we describe the web 2.0 strategy of Photoviva. Finally some conclusions are drawn.

2 Literature Review

The first author who defined the Enterprise 2.0 was McAfee [3]. He affirmed that "Enterprise 2.0 is the use of emergent social software platforms within companies, or between companies and their partners or customers".

In this new model of enterprise, the customer has an active role in the company and becomes prosumer [4], producer and consumer at the same time, user generated content (UGC) [5] or consumer generated media (CGM) [6].

In the web, the contents' production is no longer the prerogative of media centres but everyone, by web 2.0 tools, can participate in the discussion and produce contents by simple platforms like Flickr, YouTube, Second Life, Facebook, Wikipedia.

In the Cluetrain Manifesto [7], authors affirm that "markets are conversations" and with the digital revolution there was a change of role of the customer from passive consumer to active prosumer.

The Enterprise 2.0 model can be interpreted as a new way of doing business, a participative business where the company and the customer work together (cooperate, co-create, co-produce) [8] to improve the final product/service.

Exchanging information with all subjects of the supply chain allows the enterprise to acquire new ideas and competitive advantages. The new concept of Open Innovation [9], an innovation opens towards the external environment, is spreading.

Chesbrough [10] argued that the innovation is increasingly a result of collaborative efforts with other parties (individuals, customers, partners). Innovating means also that an enterprise coordinates, in a flexible way, a large portfolio of innovation projects and patents [11].

Recent empirical evidence argues that the exploitation of the internal and external knowledge stimulates the innovation not only in large and high-tech companies [12] but also in small and medium ones and in sectors of medium–low technological intensity [13] like the Danish *Quilt of Denmark*, Belgium *Curana* or Italian *Lago*.

In the context of Open Innovation it is important that the company recognizes the value of the external knowledge. For assimilating this knowledge the enterprise must have specific organizational dynamic capabilities [14] and an absorptive capacity (ACAP) that represents the ability to acquire the value of the new knowledge and to assimilate and apply it for commercial goals [15, 16].

Von Hippel in Democratizing Innovation [17] has studied the phenomenon of users who innovate by themselves and are later followed, with delays from 1 to 5 years, by manufacturing companies. In this book the author describes many cases in which users were true initiators and implementers of innovation and other cases in which large communities expressed a "collective wisdom" to develop better products.

Nowadays, the enterprise should develop internal skills to engage talents and build relationships with innovation service providers. In a global market the best way to innovate is to refer to every individual contribution of the external environment.

The crowdsourcing [18] addresses the development of specific projects or solutions to a distributed team of people (crowd), not centrally organized, usually by posting ads on specific websites. Crowdsourcing is a process of problem-solving and idea generation that the company launches to outsiders. Solvers who bring winning solutions are rewarded.

The web and in particular the web 2.0 has facilitated a progressive customer empowerment [19]. Companies can communicate directly with their customers and involve them in the productive process [20]. A direct relationship with customers is an important advantage but at the same time it involves a reorganization: the organization must be able to satisfy, in real time, customer requests [21].

3 The Case Study: The Photoviva Brand

Photoviva is a brand owned by an Italian company DB Prospettive s.r.l. It is a small enterprise with 3 employees. Its traditional core business was a Business to Business (B2B) activity concentrated on objects and gadgets (like mugs, t-shirts, pillows, ect…) for photography shops and retailers. Later the company launched the brand Photoviva to allow customers to customize iPhone covers therefore implementing a mass customization process. The target of the brand is the end customer and hence a Business to Consumer (B2C) market.

DB Prospettive s.r.l. has trained and supplied a subcontractor with its original system and technology to produce the covers. Now, the covers are physically produced in North Italy and sent to Europe.

The brand is promoted and published with an e-commerce website (photoviva.it) that permits customize covers for iPhone and in the future also for other mobile devices. An English version of the website will be launched in the next months for the whole European market.

On Photoviva.it, users can choose to design their covers from scratch or to modify one created by other designers.

Users can load images from PC and immediately, by a 3D simulator, he/she can visualize the preview (Fig. 1).

In the websites, users have got a tool to design their own products; in a 3D model they can rotate the preview and check, in every detail, the customized cover.

The Photoviva case study can be considered a good example of the mass customization. Recently the mass customization process has received great attention from the business community [22].

Several companies like Procter and Gamble, Lego, Nike, Adidas, have started large-scale mass customization programs implementing a model of customer-centered enterprise [23]. In this context it is possible to follow an interdisciplinary approach, where scientists, practitioners and customers share their findings, concepts, ideas and technical solutions in the innovation management.

To obtain the customized cover a sublimation printing process is used. This technology allows to have a high resolution image on the cover made of a rigid plastic material.

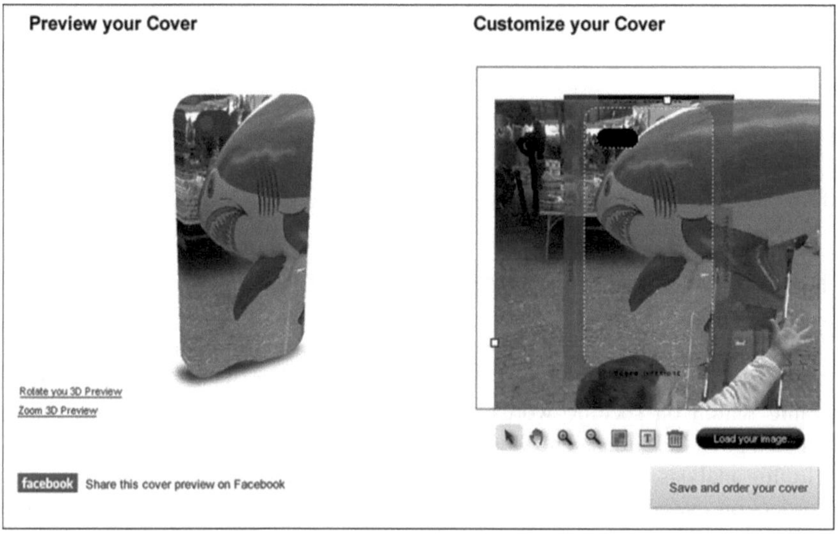

Fig. 1 Photoviva's tool to design and customize iPhone covers

When a new order is submitted it is immediately sent to the company and to the subcontractor that execute it producing the new cover. The subcontractor has got a system to download the high resolution image to print with the customized layout. Once the cover is ready, it is packaged and delivered in 3–4 working days. All the delivery process is managed very carefully and inserted in a tracking system, so the customer can check, at any time, the delivery flow. The consumer can pay for the personalized product by credit card, PayPal or cash on delivery.

4 The Web 2.0 Strategy of Photoviva

This business activity, that is having a great success, implements different emerging trends: mobile technologies, product customization and open innovation. In this context the social, participative and interactive web 2.0 plays the main role.

The marketing strategy of Photoviva is managed by the web agency e-leva s.r.l.. Most of the structure of the website, the contents, the communication, the web marketing with advertising campaigns and the management of social networks are designed by the agency.

E-leva s.r.l. has implemented for the website the Search Engine Optimization (SEO) that actually ranks very well mainly for the most important Italian keywords in this business field like "cover iPhone", "cover iPhone 4", "cover iphone personalizzate", "cover iphone 4 personalizzate".

Photoviva was launched in March 2011 and the traffic grew from 2,815 visits in March 2011 to 15,882 visits in December 2011 (Fig. 2).

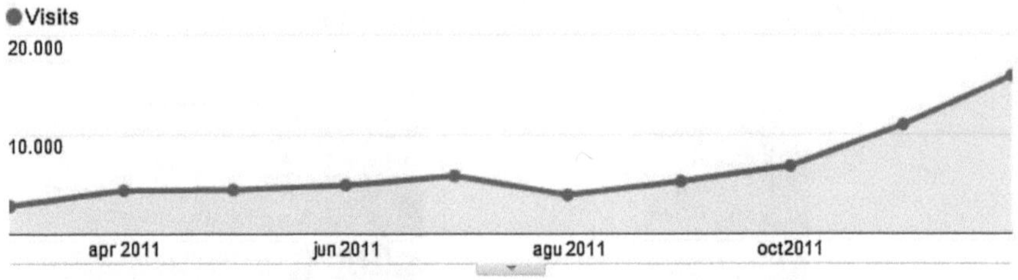

Fig. 2 Traffic growth by Google Analytics (Mar 2011–Dec 2011)

Users who visit the website Photoviva.it comes from different sources (Fig. 3).

As we can see from the Fig. 3, the highest percentage (44 %) of visits is by an organic search on specific words. This means that the web agency has implemented a good SEO plan. The 9 % of visits comes from blogs and social networks.

In this analysis, an important factor to consider is the conversion rate (the ratio of orders on overall visits) of this e-commerce website: 3.73 %. About 4 persons of 100 who visit the website become customers. Some users, when entering the website, are ready to design and buy the cover, probably because they found positive opinions on blogs and social networks.

Other users, trying the internal image configurator, are satisfied with their own creation and so they order it.

Once users have customized their cover, to continue, they can click on two different buttons. The most important button lets them buy the cover, the other one to share the new creation on Facebook and so it is possible to show the cover to friends. Users ask their friends if they like the cover and so the brand has an advertising viral effect.

Fig. 3 Visits from different sources. (Mar 2011–Dec 2011)

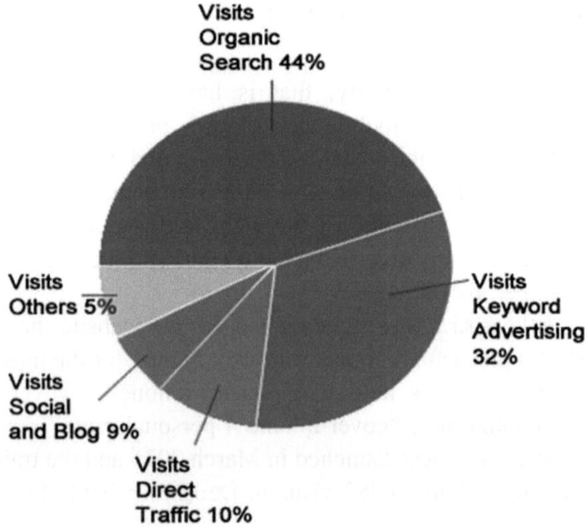

The marketing strategy is fully focused on web 2.0 activities with a great possibility to share information and contents. For promoting the brand online, improving the customer care and to collect feedback, the company uses social networks like Facebook (the most used), Google+ and Twitter.

The web agency also manages the Fan Page (facebook.com/photoviva), writes news and posts concerning some creative ideas and it stimulates the discussion on a specific topic of the virtual community. The community manager [24] (CEO of the web agency) knows very well the company's brand and so he can answer specific questions relative to all phases of the product development.

The Facebook page is full of posts written by satisfied customers. Of course this aspect encourages new customers to try the 3D simulator on the website. The community creates a strong trust between the company and customers. The lack of trust is one of the main obstacles for the e-commerce success.

In the Fan page there are also negative opinions and constructive critics. For example, some customers found it difficult to remove the covers; they did not push the right corners. The web agency, understanding that the process was not so intuitive, has produced a video to post on Facebook just to explain the right way to remove the cover.

The company, over time, has established various collaborative partnerships with other enterprises and subjects to improve the relationship with end customers.

It has contacted many bloggers writing about Mac, Apple or iPhone devices but also on fashion and trends. Most of them consider the Photoviva's idea very interesting and develop together some initiatives. For examples apple.hdblog.it organized a contest for their readers and another blog sells brand covers with the note "Powered by photoviva.it".

A very particular partnership was developed with an another brand (Eroticpink) that, with a great creative energy, communicates, through a female perspective, a new symbol of the modern sensuality. The website Photoviva presents, in a specific section, covers designed by this commercial brand, completely customized.

For Valentine's Day the company has presented 19 new covers inspired by love. Users could select their favourite cover, clicking on "customize the cover" and use the 3D configurator to add, for example, the name of their boyfriend or girlfriend.

Nowadays, there are a lot of magazines, blogs focused on mobile phones, fashion, trends like iPhoneItalia.com, applemobile.it, style.it, tobrepel.com, modalizer.com, ciao.it that publish news relative to the Photoviva brand.

Photoviva fully involves the customer in the productive process and gives to end users also the possibility to entry in the business. Some users "want to be" or already are professional designers. So they will be involved in the "ready covers" section to present different graphic solutions. The company will pay royalties to these persons for any cover that is sold. The designer user must sign a declaration that the images are personal and not copied from others and he/she can obtain also the copyright on the images.

Another project to implement in the next months is the *Cover Art* section, where the cover will be designed by professionals: designers, graphics, painters and artists. In the section of the website the profile of the artist will also be included.

5 Conclusions

In this chapter we have analyzed a best practice: the brand Photoviva of a small company. The photo lives not only on the paper but also on mobile devices. These photos are part of everyday life; they are personal icons that tell a personal story. The company involves customers in the productive process designing unique and personal covers by the website. In this way the community grows, in a social, authorial and creative perspective. The company also lets customers participate in the business through royalties, when their designed cover are bought by other persons. The enterprise communicates with end users by social network. The web agency actively manages the Facebook community and responds quickly to customer requests. The DB Prospettive s.r.l. company, owner of the Photoviva brand is an example of Enterprise 2.0 where the customer participates in the productive process. If Youtube, Facebook or blogs allow people to express their creativity in videos and communications, in our case study, customers express their originality in designing creative covers. This small company can implement inside advanced business concepts: prosumer, co-production, mass customization and open innovation. Generally in the literature many success cases are related to companies of medium and large sizes. This best practice instead refers to a small enterprise that continually applies new and innovative ideas in the business exploiting the contribution of customers.

References

1. Cho, Y., Im, I., Hiltz, R., Fjermestad, J. (2002). An analysis of online customer complaints: Implications for web complaint management. *35th Hawaii international conference on system sciences in New York* (pp. 2308–2317). New York: IEEE.
2. Consoli, D. (2009). The totally customer centred enterprise supported by web technology. *Journal of International Scientific Publication: Materials, Method and Technologies, 3*(1), 80–93.
3. McAfee, A. (2006). Enterprise 2.0: The dawn of emergent collaboration. *Sloan Management Review, 47*(3), 21–28. MIT, USA.
4. Toffler, A. (1980). *The third wave*. USA: Bantam Books.
5. Strobbe, M., Van Laere, O., Dauwe, S., Dhoedt, B., De Turck, F., van Demeester, P., et al. (2010). Interest based selection of user generated content for rich communication services. *Journal of Network and Computer Applications, 33*(2), 84–97.
6. Sumi, K. (2008). Anime de Blog: Animation CGM for content distribution', *Proceeding of the 2nd international conference on advances in computer entertainment technology in Japan* (vol. 352, pp. 187–190). Yokohama, Japan: ACM.
7. Levine, R., Locke, C., Searls, D., & Weinberger, D. (2001). *The cluetrain manifesto: The end of business as usual*. New York: Perseus Books.
8. Tapscott, D., & Williams, A. D. (2006). *Wikinomics: How mass collaboration changes everything*. USA: Portfolio (Penguin Group) Publisher.
9. Chesbrough, H. (2003). *Open innovation: The new imperative for creating and profiting from technology*. Harvard: Harvard Business School Press.

10. Chesbrough, H. (2006). *Open business models: How to thrive in the new innovation landscape*. Harvard: Harvard Business School Press.
11. Faems, D., Van Looy, B., & Debackere, K. (2005). Interorganizational collaboration and innovation: Toward a portfolio approach. *The Journal of Product Innovation Management, 22*(3), 238–250.
12. Chesbrough, H., Vanhaverbeke, W., & West, J. (2006). *Open innovation: Researching a new paradigm*. Oxford: Oxford University Press.
13. Enkel, E., Gassmann, O., & Chesbrough, H. (2009). Open R&D and open innovation: Exploring the phenomenon. *R&D Management, 39*(4), 311–316.
14. Eisenhardt, K. M., & Martin, J. A. (2000). Dynamic capabilities: What are they?'. *Strategic Management Journal, 21*(10–11), 1105–1121.
15. Cohen, W. M., & Levinthal, D. A. (1990). Absorptive capacity: A new perspective on learning and innovation. *Administrative Science Quarterly, 35*, 128–152.
16. Vega-Jurado, J., Gutiérrez-Gracia, A., Fernández-de-Lucio, I., & Manjarrés-Henríquez, L. (2008). Analyzing the determinants of firm's absorptive capacity: Beyond R&D. *R&D Management, 38*(4), 392–405.
17. Von Hippel, E. (2005). *Democratizing innovation*. USA: MIT Press.
18. Stewart O., Huerta, J. M., Sader, M. (2009). Designing crowdsourcing community for the enterprise. *Proceedings of the ACM SIGKDD workshop on human computation* (HCOMP '09).
19. Kucuk, S. U., & Krishnamurthy, S. (2007). An analysis of consumer power on the internet. *Technovation, 27*(1/2), 47–56.
20. Sharma, A., & Sheth, J. N. (2004). Web-based marketing: The coming revolution in marketing thought and strategy. *Journal of Business Research, 57*(7), 696–702.
21. Vescovi, T., Checchinato, F., & Gazzola, P. (2010). Invading customers: New markets relationships. *Journal of Marketing Trends, 1*, 41–57.
22. Tseng, M. M., Jiao, J., & Merchant, M. E. (1996). Design for mass customization. *CIRP Annals—Manufacturing Technology, 45*(1), 153–156.
23. Tseng, M. M., & Piller, F. (2003). *The customer centric enterprise: Advances in mass customization and personalization*. Heidelberg: Springer.
24. Consoli, D. (2011). The web community manager in SMEs: A key figure to implement a model of enterprise 2.0. *Proceedings of ITAIS 2011*, Oct 7–8, Rome.

Part III
e-Business, Communities and Social Networks

Municipalities 'Like' Facebook: The Use of Social Media in Local Municipalities

Camilla Guttormsen and Øystein Sæbø

Abstract The use of Facebook in local municipalities has grown dramatically over the last few years. Local municipalities enter social media to meet people where they already are, in order to inform, discuss and receive feedback. The use of such services is rarely an integrated part of the municipalities' communication strategies, and more knowledge is needed to explore how local municipalities could use such services to their benefit. This chapter contributes to this area of research by, based on current literature, classifying municipalities' use of social media into six thematic areas. The explanatory potential is illustrated by conducting a qualitative case study in which a local municipality's use of Facebook is analysed based on the suggested thematic areas. We argue that instead of viewing social media as a silver bullet, its implementation should be adapted to obtain specific achievements in one or several of the categories suggested here. Local municipalities could be more specific about the potential achievements in order to avoid a mismatch between external and internal stakeholders' use and expectations of social media.

Keywords Social media · Facebook · Local municipalities

1 Introduction

This chapter focuses on the use of social media in local municipalities. There are several reasons for why this area of interest should to be investigated. The public sphere is an essential part of a well-functioning democracy [1]. Media and

C. Guttormsen · Ø. Sæbø (✉)
University of Agder, Agder, Norway
e-mail: Oystein.Sabo@uia.no

C. Guttormsen
e-mail: milla_g_88@hotmail.com

P. Spagnoletti (ed.), *Organizational Change and Information Systems*, Lecture Notes in Information Systems and Organisation 2, DOI: 10.1007/978-3-642-37228-5_16,

societies' communication networks are core components of the public sphere in a modern society [2], rendering possible the formation of new opinions that can influence public decisions. If the interaction between the government and civil society is not working properly, or the communication channels are inhibited, citizens' affiliation to public institutions may disintegrate [3]. Therefore, it is of critical importance to utilise, develop and maintain well-functioning communication channels to serve the public discourse.

Municipalities have long since initiated projects where Internet-based technologies are used to increase citizens participation, but very few have been successful [4]. There is still the challenge of turning the audience into active users, and the emergence of social media is seen as promising, since such media attract large numbers of users sustaining a great deal of interaction [5]. Thus, social media is a promising tool for municipalities to inform, discuss and receive feedback from their surroundings, and maintain and augment local democracies. Moreover, the use of social media is a key component of governments' strategies on digitalising the governmental sector.

Even though social media has emerged in recent research literature [6], more work is clearly needed to explore how local municipalities may design, organise and benefit from social media for deliberative purposes [7]. In this chapter we propose a framework identifying six thematic areas through which social media may influence local municipalities. We illustrate the explanatory potential of these thematic areas by analysing a qualitative case study focusing on a local municipality's use of Facebook.

2 Theoretical Approach

The framework is based on literature with various theoretical approaches. A detailed review of these theories is beyond the scope of this chapter, and they are only very briefly introduced here. Castells work [2] on the public sphere as the network society shed light on the influence of information technology on social networks, elaborating on the seminal work by Habermas [1], which discussed social processes in the digital age, and Giddens' [8] theories on time and space. Work on e-democracy models [9] illustrate how information technology could be used to support various democratic contexts. Finally, the system theory focuses on the changes occurring in communication processes, moving from a one-way communication pattern to a two-way dialogue.

The six thematic areas introduced below explore how social media can influence local municipalities. As demonstrated later on when discussing the case study, online activities may relate to more than one category. Consequently, criticisms could be made regarding the mutual exclusiveness of the distinct areas. We would argue that even though some activities may relate to several of these thematic areas, the idea here is to identify and categorise distinct areas of *influence* that social media may have, not to categorise distinct area of online *activities*.

2.1 From One- to Two-Way Dialogue

Social media provide municipalities with the opportunity to develop ICT-based services for people to inform themselves, locate each other and interact [5], independently of borders concerning time, space and location [8]. Based on technological drivers (broadband access and development of ICT-based services), social drivers (changed media consumption habits) and institutional drivers (new legal means to create and distribute content) [5], the municipalities utilise social media primarily to support dialogue between the government and their stakeholders.

2.2 Digitalised Administrative Governance

Social media do not only provide opportunities for two-way dialogue, but also influence how municipalities design their services. In a digitalised world, government services are most effectively designed and developed to utilise the opportunities provided by online services, not to reflect internal workflow in the government sector [10]. New services should therefore be designed based on a self-service model, in which online support and the possibility to discuss and enter into a dialogue with the municipality and other stakeholders are an integrated part of the online services, rather than isolated stand-alone services with only scattered integration to the decision-making processes.

2.3 Digital Participation

A major objective for municipalities' use of social media is to invite citizens and other external stakeholders to participate in the use of online services. In a society where traditional public arenas are decreasing in strength (such as political parties, face-to-face public meetings and participation in various associations), and citizens' political interests are changing from a holistic perspective towards a focus on certain political aspects [11], it is important to invite external stakeholders to participate in the public debate on an individual basis. In turn, this allows them to use social media to debate, inform the municipality and add issues to the political agenda, as well as control and evaluate the decisions being made.

2.4 Attentive Municipality

Ideally, the municipalities are not only communicating with the citizens, but also invite them to participate in and influence the decisions being made [1]. A well functioning public sphere is decisive in a system where politicians and citizens ideally share an interest in dialogue and discourse, leading to the formation of political opinion in which the input and cooperation between citizens and politicians constitute the legalisation of power [9]. Thus, an attentive municipality goes beyond the idea of only listening to external stakeholders; their input and ideas should also be reflected in the decisions being made, preferably by explicit integration of decision-making processes and the online political discourse [12].

2.5 Developing Democracy

Based on the activities classified above, local democracy may develop into a more deliberative way of thinking [12]. Moreover, the new networks rendered possible through globalisation and technological development, in which borders concerning time, space and location are eliminated, can heavily influence local democracies. The municipalities' stakeholders could be located all over the world with the same interest in participating and influencing local democracies. The globalised world also changes the municipalities' opportunities to collaborate and learn from each other, independently of traditional restrictions concerning time- and location-related issues.

2.6 Organisational Culture and Change Management

To be able to utilise the new borderless opportunities provided by the introduction of social media, local municipalities need to consider change management and their organisational culture, in order to explore their willingness and responsiveness to change based on signals from the external world [13]. A question related to the use of social media is the municipality's ability to invite external stakeholders to comment on their work processes and act according to the signals received [7, 14].

3 Introducing the Case, Data Collection and Analysis Strategy

To illustrate the explanatory potential of this framework, we conducted an analysis of a local municipality's use of Facebook. Porsgrunn municipality, with approximately 35,000 inhabitants, was awarded a prize for the best local municipality's web pages in 2011, based on their citizen-oriented services and easy access to core services [15]. From a Norwegian perspective, Porsgrunn has been innovative in their use of digital media, and were early adopter of using Facebook as part of their communication with external stakeholders.

Since the conducted study (spring 2012) is exploratory by nature it was appropriate to design a qualitative study. We aimed to explore the use of Facebook, placing emphasis on understanding the phenomenon within its real-life context [16]. The major data source was semi-structured interviews with major stakeholders, both internal (employees and politicians) and external (citizens). Other sources included the online postings on the municipality's Facebook pages, and written material provided by the municipality. Ten interviews were conducted, selected by using a snowball technique [16] to identify interviewees who were knowledgeable on the topic being investigated. Interviews were transcribed, coded and analysed based on the categories presented above, whereas analyses of the online-postings increase our understanding of contextual issues.

4 Findings

4.1 From One- to Two-Way Dialogue

The main motivation for the municipality's use of Facebook is to increase the dialogue between the municipality and their stakeholders: *There are new ways to communicate which we would like to employ actively in the municipality to support the public discourse* (employee). The municipality would like to arrange for digital meeting places where everyone could meet and discuss political issues. One reason for this is to become aware of criticism from the citizens: *It is important to work actively to notice the critical talk taking place in the discussion between neighbours, and to be able to respond coherently with one voice* (employee).

The internal interviewees tend to disagree on the extent to which the municipality will have an active role in the discussions, by initiating discussions, posting questions and participating in on-going discussions. A quite common apprehension is that the municipality needs to be on Facebook in order to provide information and listen to a dialogue of which it is not an active part, whereas the external interviewees more clearly expect the municipality to participate actively, and not only listen to whatever citizens do discuss. Despite acknowledging the importance of the municipality's presence, employees do realise the lack of dialogue: *We do not encourage citizens to ask question through Facebook since we currently don't have an instrument to follow up questions being posted. As a matter offact it is still information from us to them.*

4.2 Digitalised Administrative Governance

Porsgrunn is about to introduce new administrative support systems where e-mail is fully integrated. The municipality is no longer printing numerous brochures to inform their citizens; as such information is now primarily accessible for the citizens online. Facebook is not yet an integrated part of the governmental processes, since services cannot be exclusively provided through social media. The main focus is to provide mobile services for citizens to read, communicate and discuss through a mobile application from their smartphones. They have started to use Quick Response (QR)-coding to provide links to information and services to simplify access for external stakeholders: *Now you may have the information needed stored on your mobile phone, which is much easier than bringing brochures and paper-based plan-schedules. We may also link our Facebook pages through the QR-codes.*

4.3 Digital Participation

A few online services are provided by the municipality, such as Fix my street and the QR-coded services, focusing on administrative processes and service provision. An ePetition system is currently being developed, allowing the citizens to promote causes for the municipality to consider. The ePetition services are designed for Facebook integration to attract more citizens and lower the threshold for citizens to sign. Facebook is considered instrumental in engaging citizens to participate and discuss: *Traditionally the municipality has only disseminated information to the citizens with few, if any, arenas for citizens to discuss and add their suggestions. We need to diminish some barriers to get the citizens running.*

4.4 Attentive Municipality

Even though the municipality's web pages allow for two-way dialogue, discussions and public discourse between the municipality and its citizens are not the primary focus here. Thus, Facebook could provide opportunities not offered through their traditional web pages. A major challenge from the employees' point of view is to decide who is going to represent the municipality's opinion in online discussions: *Porsgrunn municipality has 3,000 employees. All of these can't represent the municipality's views externally through social media* (employee). As a result, the external stakeholders are frustrated by the lack of participation from the municipality's side on the issues being discussed, which is considered problematic: *It doesn't make sense to introduce social media if you don't have a plan or your product is bad. It is actually more harmful than anything. You have to eliminate reasons for negative publicity before you enter the scene* (citizen).

The employees argue that Facebook is added on top of everything without being integrated as a part of daily life in the municipality. Consequently, attendance in social media is not an integrated part of the daily routine, and relies on employees being highly dedicated: *It requires great dedication to maintain and work with Facebook the way we would like to. You have to read and keep yourself updated in a way that we unfortunately are not presently able to* (employee). A lack of time and resources is not seen as a sound argument among external interviewees: *You don't need much time or money; it is about spending half an hour updating their Facebook pages. Everyone is able to dedicate the minimum amount of time needed.*

4.5 Developing Democracy

The interviewees tend to disagree on Facebook's potential role in the local democratic debate. Whereas one group (dominated by external stakeholders) argue that social media is the next big thing for political discourse, where the presence of local politicians is self-evident, another group of interviewees (dominated by the municipality's employees) voice their concerns about the amount and quality of online political discussions: *I'm not quite sure about the number of people who are using Facebook to discuss political issues. And we have to keep in mind that there are many inhabitants who are still not using such services* (employee). For the latter group, Facebook is considered tiresome, with very few topical contributions among a huge number of tedious postings.

Another main concern relates to how to censor online postings (and who to censor), and what to expect from the municipality's employees when discussing politics. Guidelines on how to behave are seen as important in order to reduce the amount of insults towards named employees or politicians. While everyone acknowledges the importance of including more people in the public debate by using Facebook, there is disagreement on how to manage negative comments and harassments posted online: *If we were going to respond to the negative enquiries, such postings would increase, bringing about successive un-reflected statements.*

4.6 Organisational Culture and Change Management

The process of developing an open and alternative-oriented municipality, as well as being citizen-oriented and responsive to suggestions made by external stakeholders, is an on-going process in Porsgrunn municipality. More effort is needed to encourage employees to share: *The main challenge is to get everyone interested in informing and dissemination online, not only among external stakeholders, but also to encourage employees to do so* (employee).

When it comes to change management, internal use of social media is of comparable importance to external use. Even though internal use of Facebook to distribute information and discuss internal concerns has so far not been prioritised, the employees are aware of the importance of doing so. The municipality needs to listen to internal as well as external stakeholders in order to stay dynamic over time: *We do have well-educated and qualified employees who are perfectly capable of conducting the services provided by the municipality. But we are very much aware that it is instrumental for us to utilise citizens' competence and to engage them in our daily routine for us to stay adaptive and competent in the future as well* (employee).

5 Discussion and Conclusion

Table 1 summarises findings from the case study.

The thematic areas introduced here contribute to the theoretical understanding of how social media may influence a local municipality, thus contributing to the need for more detailed criteria to evaluate municipalities' use of such media [6, 7]. Hence, we subscribe to an established line of IS research warning against viewing any application of IT as a generic black box, orientating instead towards analysing

Table 1 Case findings summarised

Thematic area	Main findings	Main challenges
From one- to two-way dialogue	The main motivation for introducing Facebook is to enter into a dialogue with external stakeholders.	Lack of allocated resources and strategic foundation inhibits the transformation from dissemination into dialogue.
Digitalised administrative governance	The integration of social media is not prioritised, mainly since public services cannot *only* be provided through social media.	Administrative systems are traditionally organized to support municipalities' needs, not as citizen-centric systems.
Digital participation	Very few services are provided for the citizens to participate, but present services are well received by the citizens.	Services are needed where citizens are invited to participate in the democratic dialogue, not only to perform tasks needed or to provide feedback to the municipality
Attentive municipality	There are few possibilities for citizens to provide feedback or to discuss with municipality's officers.	To decide whom to represent the municipality and to allocate resources needed.
Developing democracy	Some argue that the use of social media is important for the democratic debate, whereas others voice scepticism due to scattered quality on the postings, censoring issues, and a lack of representativeness.	The use of social media should be designed as an integrative part of the decision-making processes, in a way that addresses issues related to harassment and representation.
Organisational culture and change management	Despite good intentions, the use of Facebook is so far not organised to support a dynamic municipality.	Facebook is introduced to strengthen the municipality's reputation, but the lack of feedback may lead to the opposite result.

the use of social media in the municipality as a structural process in which technologies and organisational contexts develop in an interwoven manner [17]. Our work points to the need for a particular technology in a particular context to understand how a particular communication medium can be effective in various contexts [9].

We would encourage researchers to take up some of the many issues that our study raises. An improved theoretical foundation might incorporate influences from political science, social theory, public governance theory, and communication studies. Whereas seminal work by Habermas [1], Castells [2] and Giddens [8] prove the importance of understanding the public sphere and the importance and characteristics of the networked society, more work is needed to further explore how social media could be utilised by local municipalities. One issue to look at is to explore the resistance to change among government officials when introducing social media like Facebook. Whereas it might be tempting to criticize municipalities' limited use of such services, more research is needed to fully understand why such resistance exists, and the (maybe well-argued) reasons for such resistance.

Some practical recommendations can be drawn. Firstly, municipalities must consider what they wish to achieve by using social media. The thematic areas introduced here may guide the process of identifying potential benefits. Secondly, there is a need to allocate resources when entering social media; efforts are needed to gain benefits. Being present without being responsive may be worse than non-presence, and may do more harm than good for the municipalities. Thirdly, municipalities need to consider the use of social media as an integrated part of their information exchange and their services. The real benefits may be achieved when the strengths of social media (to support dialogue) are integrated into administrative services, providing feedback mechanisms and services for citizens to discuss issues related to on-going decision-making processes. Finally, most emphasis so far has been on the *external* use of social media in the government sector, whereas *internal* uses have been investigated less. Both practitioners and researchers may bring the internal use of social media into focus to understand how highly educated and competent public sector employees may be encouraged to develop dynamic work environments in local municipalities.

References

1. Habermas, J. (1989). *The structural transformation of the public sphere: An inquiry into a category of bourgeois society* (p. XIX, 301 s). Cambridge: Polity Press.
2. Castells, M. (2008). The new public sphere: Global civil society, communication networks, and global governance. *The ANNALS of the American Academy of Political and Social Science, 616*(1), 78–93.
3. Sassen, S. (2006). *Territory, authority, rights: from medieval to global assemblages* (p. XIV, 493 s). Princeton, N.J.: Princeton University Press.
4. Sæbø, Ø., Rose, J., & Flak, L. S. (2008). The shape of eParticipation: Characterizing an emerging research area. *Government Information Quarterly, 25*(3), 400–428.

5. Sæbø, Ø., Rose, J., & Nyvang, T. (2009). The role of social networking services in eParticipation. *Electronic Participation*, 46–55.
6. Medaglia, R. (2012). eParticipation research: Moving characterization forward (2006–2011). *Government Information Quarterly, 29*(3), 346–360.
7. Rose, J., & Sæbø, Ø. (2010). Designing deliberation systems. *The Information Society, 26*(3), 228–240.
8. Giddens, A. (1997). *Sociology* (p. XIV, 625 s). Cambridge: Polity Press.
9. Päivärinta, T., & Sæbø, Ø. (2006). Models of E-democracy.
10. Norwegian Ministry of Government Administration (2012). R.a.C.A., Public administration to be fully digitalised.
11. Castells, M. (2010). *The rise of the network society, volume I of the information age: economy, society and culture* (p. LVII, 597 s). Chichester: Wilwey-Blackwell.
12. Held, D. (2006). *Models of democracy* (p. XII, 338 s). Cambridge: Polity Press.
13. Ihlen, Ø., & Robstad, P. (2004). *Informasjon & samfunnskontakt: perspektiver og praksis* (p. 242 s). Bergen: Fagbokforl.
14. Charalabidis, Y., & Koussouris, S. (2012). *Empowering open and collaborative governance: Technologies and methods for online citizen engagement in public policy making*. Berlin, Heidelberg: Springer.
15. (Difi), A.f.P.M.a.e. Kvalitet på nett. (2001). [cited 2012 15.05]; Available from: http://kvalitet.difi.no/resultat/prisutdeling2011/-kommunal.
16. Yin, R. K. (2009). Case study research: Design and methods. Rev. ed. Applied social research methods series (4th ed., Vol. 5). Newbury Park, California: Sage Publications.
17. Orlikowski, W. J., & Iacono, C. S. (2001). Research commentary: Desperately seeking the "IT" in IT research—a call to theorizing the IT artifact. *Information Systems Research, 12*(2), 121–134.

Trust as Individual Asset in a Network: A Cognitive Analysis

Francesca Marzo and Cristiano Castelfranchi

Abstract One of the most addressed kinds of relationships able to generate value in a network is trust (studied in different ways, for different purposes, by different disciplines). While it is very important to keep on investigating this issue using an interdisciplinary and integrated approach, it is also crucial to study the value-generation involved from a perspective able to disentangle what happen both at macro and micro level. In other terms we need a clear distinction between what is commonly called social capital and what is better known as relational capital. In this chapter we focus on the latter by analysing the point of view of the trustee on the bases of the goal oriented theory of trust. We developed a cognitive model of trust to explain why it represents a form of power and, then, a strong asset for individuals acting in a network. Finally, we propose some experimental future works based on this analysis and involving both laboratory experiments and multi-agents systems simulations.

Keywords Trust · Relational capital · Cognitive analysis · Multi-agent systems

1 Introduction

The next generation of pervasive and adaptive ICT applications will need to be *designed for trust*, to fulfill their expected impact on future Information Society [1]. Trust-oriented technologies imply a two-pronged challenge. First, pervasive and adaptive applications need to elicit adequate levels of trust in users, that must be willing to rely on largely autonomous devices and self-organized systems

F. Marzo (✉)
CeRSI, LUISS Guido Carli, Rome, Italy

C. Castelfranchi
ISTC-CNR, Rome, Italy

P. Spagnoletti (ed.), *Organizational Change and Information Systems*, Lecture Notes in Information Systems and Organisation 2, DOI: 10.1007/978-3-642-37228-5_17,

(users' trust) [2, 3]. Second, system components need reliable trust heuristics for autonomously coordinating with each other, in order to strike an optimal balance between flexibility and dependability (trust technologies). Hence this second basic condition asks for a detailed formal and computational model of trust that will be integral part of the digital pervasive environments of the future [4] but that will be also tractable for the computational units embedded in the environment. These distributed devices in fact must be designed for trusting each other despite the volatility of their interaction situations, the uncertainty intrinsic to real environments, the novelty of the contexts and of the possible peers but given their limited computational power. In this perspective, trust is a crucial decision criterion for agents with finite resources: it enables agents to decide whether to perform actions or delegate activities, evaluating risks and utilities. According to different perceived trust levels agents may adopt the proper policies, using different strategies. But to serve this purpose, the metrics and methods used for trust assessment must prove reliable also in highly dynamic and largely unknown environments [5]. On the contrary, current computational trust models are usually built either on the agent's direct experience of an interacting partner (interaction trust) [6, 7], or on reports provided by third parties about their experiences with a partner (witness reputation) [8–10]. Both these models present critical drawbacks when they need to cope with open, highly dynamic environments. Whenever starting a new session, for instance, agents are often engaged with totally unknown peers, and they must decide whether to trust them or not in a situation of partial ignorance, high uncertainty, and lack of prior knowledge: in such conditions neither witness reputation nor interaction trust provide significant guidelines for the agent's decisions [11]. It is important to overcome these critical shortcomings of existing models and applications of trust in computational systems, by investigating the critical cognitive capabilities needed for a quick and effective process of trust formation in open environments [5]. Our study is a step on this direction. One of the main objectives of our cognitive approach, in fact, is to build artificial agents which are able to reason about trust, that is, to improve actual computational and formal models of trust in online interaction between autonomous artificial agents and in human–machine interactions in such a way that they can account for sophisticated social processes of trust formation, revision, attribution, and circulation in open environments. In order for artificial agents to be able to take into account the complexity and multi-factoriality of trust they need to be built as agent able to find adaptive strategies and integrate different features for trust attribution and inducement. This will lead to a step change in computational, mathematical and logical models of trust for multi agents systems, ubiquitous computing, and human–machine interaction.

In this preliminary study we will focus on a specific side of trust relationship, the trustee, to reach two different aims: on one side, we will underline the intrinsic importance of trust links in a network, on the other, we will propose a theory that can explain how these links, that represent a real asset for nodes in the network, can be manipulated in order to accumulate power.

2 Social Capital and Relational Capital: Different Assets for Different Beneficiaries

Trust is sometimes a property of an environment, rather than of a single agent or even a group: under certain conditions, the tendency to trust each other become diffused in a given context, more like a sort of acquired habit or social convention than like a real decision [2, 12]. These processes of 'trust spreading' are very powerful in achieving high level of cooperation among large population, and should be studied in their own right. In particular, it is crucial to understand the subtle interaction between social pressures and individual factors in creating these 'trusting environments', and to analyze both advantages and dangers of such diffused forms of trust. In fact, considering collectivity and individuals as two different stakeholders, it is possible to say that in building trust their goals can, under certain circumstances, not only be different, but also contradictory: while the population of agents as a whole might gain more benefits from a spread diffusion of trust in the society as a whole, individual agents might seek for concentrating trust relationships on itself. In the first case we are dealing with what we commonly call "social capital", in the second one we are talking of what we call "relational capital".

The notion of social capital suggests an abstract hidden resource, which can be accumulated, tapped, attained when people value relationships among each other, interact, collaborate, learn and share ideas. This is a valuable stock of capital. Productive resources can reside not just in things but also in social relations among people [13, 14]. Resnick [15] argues that social capital is a residual side effect of social interaction and the enabler of future interactions. Brehm and Rahn [16] have developed a structural model that shows how social capital manifests itself in individuals as a relationship between levels of civic engagement and interpersonal trust. Starting from the assumption that if interpersonal trust increases then also civic engagement increases, there is a common agreement that we need to address the issue of trust to study the origin of social capital. It is possible to consider separately what are the connections between people (communities' fundamental characteristic) and what is the added value of these connections (economic aspect of social capital). These practices foster powerful norms of generalized reciprocity: the implication is that past collaboration is the basis for future collaboration, and refusal to take or give increases one's chances of being sanctioned or even removed from the society [17]. Hence social capital is essential for both personal and community development in the society. Nevertheless, individuals can also use their capital of trust for anti-social purposes. In order to study the individual form of this capital and then to start understanding how the two can be in contrast, we believe we need to analyze what it means that trust represents a strategic resource for agents that are trusted, proposing a model of 'trust as a capital' for individuals and suggesting the implication for strategic action that can be performed. Our thesis is that to be trusted: (1) increases the chance to be requested or accepted as a partner for exchange or cooperation; (2) improves the 'price', the contract that the agent can obtain. Since the term "capital" refers to a commodity itself used in the production of other goods and services and the adjective "social" is used to claim that a particular capital not only exists in social relationships but also consists in some kind of relationships between subjects, it is clear that for the capital goods metaphor to be useful, the transformative ability of social relationships to become a capital must be taken seriously. This means that we need to start by finding out what is the competitive advantage not simply of being part of a network, but more precisely of being trusted in that network.

3 Cognitive Model of Trust Network

Trust is a multi-factorial and highly dynamic notion: it depends on many concurrent factors, it changes over time due to a variety of reasons, and it involves both specific mental states, cognitive capacities, and characteristic social attitudes and relations [18]. As a corollary, the influence of a single factor on trust dynamics is rarely linear: a given relevant feature (e.g., high competence) often fails to affect trust attribution, or do so in indirect and complex ways, due to interference of other significant elements (e.g., lack of motivation). In order to account for the intrinsic complexity and dynamicity of this crucial notion, we need to adopt a multi-factorial theory of the formation, revision, attribution, and circulation of social trust [5]. Such a theory is important not only to face a major conceptual challenge, but also to develop ground-breaking technologies addressing important priorities in the present societal and economical context, that will become even more pressing in the future. The new generation of distributed, agent-oriented systems requires the evolution of capabilities for cognitive and social interaction in "open" environment and systems where agents can freely join and leave at any time, and where the agents are owned by various stakeholders with different aims and objectives [19]. The aim of achieving robust social interaction is thus especially challenging in open environments, like the web (with its serious problem of unknown possible partners), virtual social spaces, and physical environments inhabited by many distributed 'intelligences' and agents. To face this challenge, we need to cope with the dynamicity of trust, by defining its lifecycle within the agent mind as part of the entire social system. We need to individuate the rational foundations of trust attribution, along with internal dynamic of trust formation and its relations with: (1) experiences of prior actions and outcomes of previous interactions; (2) communication and perception of specific "markers of trust"; (3) shared and/or certified reputation; (4) reasoning, i.e., analogy, deduction; (5) transferability of trust attribution within and between different domains.

A "trust network" is the network of the trust relationships among several agents [5]. Each node is the source of possible trust attitudes and acts towards other agents, but it is also the trustee, which means that it receives several trust attitudes/ evaluations (and potential trust acts and relationship). This create a specific topology of the net that can assume a very centralized shape (converging net) or a quite decentralized one. If a node is very central with many afferent links, the effect on the network will be greater, by affecting many nodes, than if it is a local and marginal node. More specifically, the trust links towards a node can have alternatives (being in an "or" relation with other links) and, then, generates competitors in the network [20].

We say that a node can trust other nodes for different domains and performances (independent trust links), or for the same task, as possible alternatives (alternative trust links), or a mixed form: one node can trust other nodes for given tasks (their co-power and coordination) and need all of them for the same outcome (interdependent trust links). Although it is important to consider such structural differences, what needs to be represented and managed are also the specific semantics of trust links, together with their intentionality and arguments. The trust relationship between nodes is then relative to a specific task (action, performance, service etc.) for a given goal in given context of the action. Trust dynamics and structural relations are affected by those multiple dimensions and arguments. For example, if y and z are possible referents (trustees) of x for the same need and task they are in competition with each other, and the crisis of y's trustworthiness might affect very much the relationship of x towards z. On the contrary, if x trusts y for a given thing and z for a different thing, the disappointment towards y will not necessarily affect x–z relationship [21]. Moreover, trust (which is based on beliefs of different kinds: evaluations, expectations, attribution beliefs, dependence beliefs) has certain "sources"; those beliefs are credible because of the sources they derive from. From what has been said so far, it is clear that the trust network, build on tasks, goals etc., is basically connected with another network: the dependence one.

The theory of dependence includes two type of dependences: (1) The objective dependence, which says who needs who for what in a given society. This dependence has already the power of establishing certain asymmetric relationships in a potential market. (2) The believed dependence, which says who is believed to be needed by who. This dependence is what determines relationships in a real market and settles on the negotiation power. The importance of dependence network for negotiation power has already been proved: the bigger is the number of people who depend on me for a given goal and the smaller is the number of those I depend on, the bigger will be my negotiation power. But this model is incomplete, since, although it is important to consider dependence relationship between agents in a society, there will be not exchange in the market if there is not trust to enforce some connection. That is to say that if a node is strongly needed by other nodes, but not trusted, her negotiation power does not improve [20].

4 Trust as Relational Capital

Thanks to a structural theory of what kind of beliefs are involved it is possible not only to answer some very important questions about agents' power in network but also to understand the dynamical aspects of relational capital. In addition, it is possible to study what a difference between trustee's beliefs and others' expectations on her implies in terms of both reactive and strategical actions performed by the trustee. First, let us consider what kind of strategies can be performed to enforce the other's dependence beliefs and his beliefs about agent's competence. Since dependence beliefs is strictly related with the possibility of the others to see the agent in the network and to know her ability in performing useful tasks, the goal of the agent who wants to improve her own relational capital will be to signaling her presence and her skills. While to show her presence she might have to shift her position (either physically or figuratively like, for instance, changing her field), to communicate her skills she might have to hold and show something that can be used as a signal (such as certificate, social status etc.). This implies, in her plan of action, several and necessary sub-goals to make a signal. This sub-goals are costly to be reached and the cost the agent has to pay to reach them can be taken has the evidence for the signals to be credible (of course without considering cheating in building signals). It is important to underline that using these signals often implies the participation of a third subject in the process of building trust as a capital: a third part which must be trusted. We would say the more the third part is trusted in the society, the more expensive will be for the agent to acquire signals to show, and the more this signals will work in increasing the agent's relational capital. We will see later how this is related with the process of transferring trust from an agent to another (building reputation).

Let us now consider how willingness beliefs can be manipulated. In order to do so, consider the particular strategy performed to gain the other's good attitude through gifts. It is true that the expected reaction will be of reciprocation, but this is not enough. While giving a gift the agent knows that the other will be more inclined to reciprocate, but she also knows that her action can be interpreted as a sign of the good willingness she has: since she has given something without being asked, the other is driven to believe that the agent will not cheat on him. Then, the real strategy can be played on trust, sometimes totally and sometimes only partially—this will basically depend on specific roles of agents involved. On the other hand, relational capital can also decrease. Losing relational capital means to be discredited and it can be imputed to the fact that some of the strategies performed to make the others trust fail. In fact it is possible that if the goals of signaling competences fail to be reached (because the signs chosen is bad, for instance) it is not necessarily true that the agent will just not increase her relational capital, but she can also lose some (since the agent who should trust her can valuate the sign particularly badly, for some reason). Also, if the tentative to enter the dependence network of some agents does not get true, it could be the case of losing relational capital in another market, both for the effort put in the action, which is time consuming, and for the fact that agents in the existing network can feel "betrayed". Finally, if the agent's attempt to show her willingness is interpreted as opportunistic exchange, the agent who was supposed to trust her can react badly and harmed her reputation. Another important feature of the dynamic of relational capital is the possibility of transferring from agent to agent. In fact, relational capital can also circulated inside a given society. If somebody has a good reputation and is trusted by somebody else, she can be sure this reputation will pass and transfer to other actors—and this is always considered in marketing strategies. What is not clear yet is how these phenomena work. But when trust on an agent propagates, it is strategically important for the agent to know very well how this happens and which ways trust takes to expand. That said, it should be clear the importance of understanding if and how much an agent is able to manage this potentiality of her capital, also taking into account the fact that there might exist several type of discrepancies in subjective valuation (i.e., differences between how the others trust an agent and the level of trustworthiness that agent perceive in herself) and that these discrepancies can deeply influence in terms of strategical actions that can be performed.

5 Conclusion

Online interactions can be described as embodied in three foundational pillars (other than the technological one): regulative, normative, and cognitive [22]. Regulative aspects are thought to be based upon legal sanction. Normative aspects are morally grounded and people will comply with these elements based on social obligation. Cognitive aspects are individual mental states that can be assumed or modeled and that contribute to the collective constructions of social reality via meaning systems and other rules. It is this cognitive aspect that emphasizes the taken for granted beliefs to which individuals will conform. The different interaction conceptions should be viewed as frames for understanding the underlying tensions in online society rather than independent categories or alternatives. Our focus in this chapter has been on cognitive aspects of interactions and on a particular concept that has been recognized as crucial for any kind of interaction between individuals: trust. This concept has been extensively studied in several disciplines and, in particular, in the context of e-services the focus has been mostly on how trust affects users' intention to buy or re-use online services and on designing computational trust models to predict degrees of trust. The aim of our study is, instead, to study these processes in an environment constituted by heterogeneous agent (being it a condition already diffused but that will be the very standard in future) the models developed following the cognitive analysis presented in this chapter are intended to be tested on empirical bases (e.g. through experiments aimed to verify the actual strategies applied by humans to manipulate their relational capital under different circumstances, or collecting evidences in the interaction between human agents and artificial agents). At the same time, future work will produce advanced agent-based test-beds and social simulations, to test and verify not only interaction between artificial agents but also whether systems endowed with different simple strategies/heuristics for trust assessment and inducement in a trust network are better in performance than systems that manipulate trust only on the basis of previous experiences and/or reputational information. Both this test can be run by using a very interesting framework already used in multi-agent systems: Colored Trails [23–25]. It is in fact an open source very adaptable framework designed to be used both for laboratory experiments (with the possibility of using tasks more complex than those usually used in laboratory investigation about interaction) and for agent-based simulation [26].

References

1. Ramchurn, S.D., Huynh, D., Jennings, N.R. (2004). Trust in multi-agent systems. *The Knowledge Engineering Review 19*(1), 1–25.
2. Ricci, A., & Omicini, A. (2004). Engineering trust in complex system through mediating infrastructures. WOA.
3. Castelfranchi, C., & Tan, Y. H. (Eds.). (2001). *Trust and deception in virtual societies*. Dordrecht: Kluwer Academic Publisher.
4. Kagal, L., Finin, T., & Joshi, A. (2001). Trust based security for pervasive computing environments. *IEEE Communications, 34*(2), 154–157.
5. Castelfranchi, C., & Falcone, R. (2010). *Trust theory: A socio-cognitive and Computational model*. UK: Wiley.
6. Witkowski, M., Artikis, A., & Pitt, J. (2001). Experiments in building experiental trust in a society of objective-trust based agents. In R. Falcone, M. Sing, & Y.-H. Tan (Eds.), *Trust in cyber-societies*. Berlin: Springer.
7. Jonker, C. M., & Treur, J. (1999). Formal analysis of models for the dynamics of trust based on experiences. In F. J. Garijo & M. Boman (Eds.), *Multi-agent system engineering: Proceedings of the 9th European workshop on modeling autonomous agents in a multi-agent world, lecture notes in artificial intelligence* (Vol. 1647). Berlin: Springer.
8. Carbó, J., Molina, J. M., & Dávila, J. (2005). Fuzzy referral based cooperation in social networks of agents. *AI Communications, 18*, 1.
9. Yu, B., Singh, M.P., Sycara, K. (2004). Developing trust in large-scale peer-to-peer systems. In *Proceedings of the First IEEE Symposium on Multi-Agent Security and Survive-ability*.
10. Sabater, J., & Sierra, C. (2005). Review on computational trust and reputation models. *Artificial Intelligence Review, 24* (1).
11. Billhardt, H., Hermoso, R., Ossowski, S., Centeno, R. (2007). Trust-based service provider selection in open environments. In *proceeding of the he 22nd Annual ACM "Symposium on Applied Computing"*.
12. Arcos, J. L., Esteva, M., Noriega, P., Rodríguez, J. A., & Sierra, C. (2005). Engineering open environments with electronic institutions. *Journal on Engineering Applications of Artificial Intelligence, 18*(2), 191–204.
13. Coleman, J.S (1988). Social capital in the creation of human capital. *American Journal of Sociology*, 94.
14. Putnam, R. (1993). The prosperous community: social capital and public life. In American Prospect, Vol. 13.
15. Resnick, P. (2002). Beyond bowling together: Sociotechnical capital. In J. M. Carroll (Ed.), *HCI in the new millennium*. New York: Addison-Wesley.
16. Brehm J., & Rahn W. (1997). Individual-level evidence for the causes and consequences of social capital. *American Journal of Political Science, 41*(3).
17. Bowles S., & Gintis H. (2002). Social capital and community governance. *Economic Journal, 112*.
18. Falcone, R., Singh, M., & Tan, Y. H. (2001). *Trust in cyber-societies: Integrating the human and artificial perspectives, LNAI 2246*. Berlin: Springer.
19. Wooldridge, M. (2002). *An introduction to multi-agent systems*. Chirchester: Wiley.

20. Castelfranchi, C., Falcone, R., & Marzo, F. (2007). *Being trusted in a social network: Trust as relational capital, Lecture notes in computer science*. Germany: Springer.
21. Castelfranchi C. (2012). Earthquakes in trust networks: Basic dynamic principles (3 Apr 2012) SSRN Working Papers Series.
22. Scott, W. R. (1995). *Institutions and organizations*. CA: Sage.
23. Gal, Y., Grosz, B., Kraus, S., Pfeffer, A., & Shieber, S. (2010). Agent decision-making in open mixed networks. *Artificial Intelligence, 174*(18), 1460–1480.
24. Gal Y., Pfeffer A., Marzo F., Grosz B. (2004). Learning social preferences in games. In *proceeding of the National conference on artificial intelligence* (AAAI). San Jose: California.
25. Grosz B.J., Kraus S., Talman S., Stossel B., Havlin M. (2004). The influence of social dependencies on decision-making: Initial investigations with a new game. In *Third International Joint Conference on Autonomous Agents and Multi-Agent Systems* (pp. 782–789). New York.
26. Gal Y., Grosz B., Kraus S., Pfeffer A., Shieber S. (2005). Colored Trails: a Formalism for Investigating Decision-making in Strategic Environments. In *proceeding of the IJCAI Workshop on Reasoning, Representation, and Learning in Computer Games* (pp. 25–30). Edinburgh, Scotland, August 2005.

Design Science and eTrust: Designing Organizational Artifacts as Nexus of Social and Technical Interactions

Francesco Bolici and Luca Giustiniano

Abstract Our research aims to investigate an open problem: the difficulty to build a virtual system in which trust-relationships can be created and managed. To address this problem in a manner consistent with the Design Science (DS) approach, we design a model for trust-based interactions in online distributed networks (e.g., online collaborative environments) that takes into consideration both technical and social factors. Simultaneously considering artifact's characteristics and individual behavior, we build our model on the consideration that technology and social aspects are not dichotomous, but rather inseparable [1]. The proposed model would offer a conceptual contribution in addressing the problem of generating and managing trust in distributed settings.

Keywords Design science • Digital trust • eTrust • Virtual collaboration • Virtual teams

1 Introduction: Design Science and eTrust

Design Science (DS) is a problem-solving paradigm that has been originated in engineering and the sciences of the artificial [3]. Design means "to create, fashion, execute, or construct according to plan"[1], and indeed, *learning through building* is

This chapter is based on a previous study [2].

[1] Merriam-Webster Dictionary, 2012.

F. Bolici (✉)
DIAM-Orgalb, Visiting at IESEG Business School, Università degli Studi di Cassino e del Lazio Meridionale, Paris-Lille, Italy
e-mail: francesco.bolici@eco.unicas.it

L. Giustiniano
DIM, Luiss Guido Carli University, Rome, Italy

P. Spagnoletti (ed.), *Organizational Change and Information Systems*, Lecture Notes in Information Systems and Organisation 2, DOI: 10.1007/978-3-642-37228-5_18,

the characteristic that clearly differentiates DS from others paradigms. In line with [4] contribution on design process modeling, our research starts rising the awareness of a research problem: the difficulty to build a virtual system in which trust-relationships can be created and managed. To address this problem in a manner consistent with the DS approach, we design a model for trust-based interactions in online distributed networks (e.g., online collaborative environments) that takes into consideration both technical and social factors. Simultaneously considering artifact's characteristics and individual behavior, we build our model on the consideration that technology and social aspects are not dichotomous, but rather inseparable [1]. The proposed model would offer a conceptual contribution in addressing the problem of generating and managing trust in distributed settings.

In information systems field, DS mainly addresses *wicked problems* "characterized by unstable requirements and constraints based upon ill-defined environmental contexts: (1) complex interactions among subcomponents of the problem and its solution; (2) inherent flexibility to change design processes as well as design artifacts; (3) a critical dependence upon human cognitive abilities to produce effective solutions; (4) a critical dependence upon human social abilities to produce effective solutions" ([5], p. 81). The previous description clearly fits our research problem characterized by: (1) the mutual interdependency between several factors in a distributed environment (actors' preferences and behavior, propensity to trust, artifacts' characteristics, reciprocal interactions, etc.); (2) the difficulty in standardizing or rooting into a system a peculiar and fluid human function as trust; (3) the dependence upon human cognitive capability to collect and process all the information needed to start and manage a trust-based relationship; (4) the importance of individual propensities and preferences towards social relationships based on trust. Recognizing our research domain as an *ill-structured problem* [6], we also explain the reason for adopting DS as our analytical paradigm: it is precisely in the investigation of wicked problems, for which diverging or scarce theoretical roots exist, that DS excels [7, 8].

This chapter's main contribution consists in the design of a conceptual model of trust-based interactions among actors and artifacts in distributed networks. Indeed, our research outcome is in line with [8] widely cited research, where the authors identify four general outputs for DS research: constructs, models, methods, and instantiations. In details, our contribution belongs to the *model* category, defined as "a set of propositions or statements expressing relationships among constructs. In [DS] models represent situations as problem and solution statements" ([8], p. 256). They are proposals for how things are or should be. Thus our aim is to use "constructs to represent a real world situation, the design problem and its solution space" ([5], p. 79) applied to distributed settings where trust-based relationships have been generated.

Following DS paradigm, in the next section we will present a focused literature review on trust in online environments, from which *the awareness of the problem* will emerge [4]. Indeed, while there are multi-perspectives studies on *etrust* (we will use this word as synonymous of online trust and technology-mediated trust), there is still a lack of a shared understanding of the dynamics of etrust and of the characteristics of the systems that could trigger and support it. Thus, following [9] suggestions about how to conduct a DS research, we will mainly focus our activities on the "problem identification and motivation" and "define the objectives for a solution" phases. These activities will be described in the following sections, while conclusions about this research and their limitations and future works are going to be presented in the last section.

2 Trust: Genesis and Evolution of a Socially Built Construct

Trust is a socially built construct [10] at the foundations of human action and organization [11, 12]. In its simplest configuration, trust requires the interplay between an actor (trustor) and another entity to be trusted (institution, person or environment). However, the structure of such trust-based relationships could be very complex and articulated (multiple actors involved in mutual and enduring interactions), and therefore difficult to explore. This phenomenon has been investigated from several different perspectives, e.g., social psychology, behavioral economics, sociology, and organizational theory [13–16], but little consensus has been reached about its definition and characteristics [17]. The scope of this chapter is to address trust in distributed settings, thus we will first provide a brief (and not exhaustive) recognition of offline trust in literature. This activity is accomplished in order to collect concepts, ideas and references needed for the analysis of etrust dynamics. Online trust is the object of a more focused literature review, where the main research streams and contributions are collected and analyzed. Furthermore, we study in details the reasons for which trust in distributed network can be considered a puzzling problem (*awareness of the problem*) before proposing the constructs of our model.

2.1 (Offline) Trust: An Overview

The researches on trust, as well as its definition and characteristics, have significantly evolved along time. Trust has been considered mainly an individual characteristic that can influence the possibility to establish a (social or business) relationship (e.g. 11, 26, 40, 44). Given the variety of contributions on trust, there are several dimensions through which a literature review can be conducted.

A first conventional distinction can be done between "confidence in institutions" and "social trust". Confidence in institutions comes from people's sense of how these institutions work. Social trust, sometimes known as interpersonal trust, means trust in people. Furthermore, some researchers define two categories of social trust: particularized trust and generalized trust [18] Particularized trust, which is social trust in small scale, means people trust their friends, relatives and others who they interact closely together. It is based on personal, first-hand knowledge of the trustee. Generalized trust means "trust in strangers", which is social trust in large scale. Another distinction proposed by researchers is the difference between trust and trustworthiness [19]: while the first one refers to an "encapsulated interest" of someone toward someone else (and thus is a relational characteristic), trustworthiness is an attribute of an actor. The application domain of trust dynamics can be seen as another possible analytical dimension. Trust has been studied inside organizations as a principle for managing activities and social interactions [20, 21], as well as outside the organization in the relationships between customer and sellers [22, 23]. As last dimension, we identify a consistent bulk of researches that investigates the link between trust and socio-demographic characteristics of the actors involved in the relationship, as the studies on trust and national culture [24], or trust and different categories of modern societies [25–28]. A novel research stream [29], has also investigated trust through an empirical methodology (neuroimaging) that allows the direct measurement of brain activity and relies on the cognitive neuroscience literature.

2.2 Technological and Organizational Networks: A Parallel Between ICT Diffusion and Trust

Luhmann [10, p. 8] defined trust as "an effective form of complexity reduction". The same characteristic, the capability to simplify and support human activities, is often applied to the use of information and communication technology (ICT). This analogical parallel between ICT and trust as complexity-reduction mechanisms is even more interesting since the diffusion of ICT tools have deeply influenced the evolution of some forms of trust in our society. The ICT impact on social settings has been one of the dominant themes since the early 1980s [30]. Progressively, both the deterministic explanations of a technological or organizational "imperative" drawn by [31] have decreased their explanatory effectiveness, while wider and more open perspectives of the interaction between humans and technology have become predominant. The original idea of the "emergent approach" [31] has been declined and further deepened by several studies. As result, soft factors as reputation, culture, and trust increase their importance in the definition and design of ICT and organizations.

Together with the ICT diffusion, the organizational forms have been deeply redesigned. The idea of an organization as an isolated and independent social setting is coherent and respondent to the 1980–1990s scenario. Instead, networks are recognized as the dominant organizational form in the post-Fordist era [32]. This transition has already produced several effects both at the organizational level: large number of M and A, outsourcing, business networks, online marketplaces; and at the social level: new communication forms, the emergence of social network, the virtualization of relationships and work, the emerging communities of practices [33]. Thus, the increasing of the potential number of relationships among organizations (and people) makes even more urgent to focus to trust factor, able to reduce the complexity of the trades and to decrease the transactions costs. The parallel between networks as organizational forms and networks as technological infrastructures [34] permits us to refer to all those studies and perspectives based on the network analysis in order to take into account the evolution in the relationship among organization, people, and technology. This is also coherent with [35, p. 139] call for contributions that will focus on "science of subjective experience", rather than objective/mechanistic. Networks are traditionally defined as specific types of relations linking sets of persons, objects, or events [36]. The ties between such entities are usually referred to as the network structure. Social networks are conceptualized as the relations between actors and are, therefore, specifically social in nature. The adoption of new technologies enables both the reinforcement of the ties connecting different actors (nodes) and the creation of new emerging networks whereas it overtakes some physical barriers (distance, language, etc.) constraining the network formation. Following this line of reasoning we will introduce in Sect. 3 the design of an etrust model in network settings where both social and technical factors are simultaneously taken into consideration.

2.3 Trust and Online Settings: The Problem Awareness

In this section we focus on etrust showing that the general concept of trust presented in the previous sections cannot be mechanically adapted to the online settings, and to reach a conceptualization of trust models in technology mediated network further research efforts are needed. Some scholars argue that there is a natural link between offline and online social trust because they share many characteristics [37]. People who possess high degree of offline trust seems also to have high degree of online trust, thus they are more likely to feel comfortable with online activities [18]. However there is still little empirical evidence to support the transfer of trust from an offline to an online setting, and there are analytical issues that suggest just a partial and not complete fit between the two concepts. The argument that offline trust does not entirely overlap the etrust concept is sustained by at least three considerations: (1) online social dynamics differ from those in physical/offline settings; (2) the trust-based relationship is always technology mediated (and thus, not based on face to face interaction); (3) virtual settings are characterized by a large number of artifacts, and often they play an active role in online human interactions.

The first consideration relies on the fact that trust dynamics are influenced by the evolution of social factors. As social conditions change, so do the appropriate mechanisms for giving, receiving and managing trust. For example, trust can be shaped by new abilities and tools that enable individuals to collect and to access larger bulks of information, by the modern propensity to get in touch with people and environments outside our usual circles [38], and by the development of new forms of communication and collaboration mediated by technologies. Thus, there is the possibility that radical change in social and organizational relationships could appreciably modify what we know about trust [39]. The second argument takes into consideration the nature of online relationships: they are always technology-mediated, and often asynchronous. This is a key point, since several articles pointed out that face-to-face meetings are the most suitable means to establish trust, at least in physical settings [40, 41]. As a consequence of technology mediation, in online settings face-to-face interactions are relatively scarce (when possible), thus, etrust literature cannot rely only on the established background developed for general trust to elaborate an etrust-structured model [42, 43]. As summarized by [44], other trust mechanisms have to be taken into considerations for online settings, focusing on the presence of shared norms and values among the actors, and by the implicit identification of the parts involved in the interactions, artifacts included. The third consideration focuses on the importance of artifacts as trust-broker in online relationships. Being interactions often asynchronous and always ICT mediated, the role of artifacts as nexus of meaning is relatively higher that in the physical context. The lack of face-to-face interactions requires that the actors will *reificate* [45] some of their meaning (social norms, coordination mechanisms, information) in online artifacts that can be accessed and understood by the counterpart. Thus, also trust can be embedded into artifacts, in order to reduce the dependence from a synchronous interaction and the costs of communication (an artifact can be accessed at any time by multiple actors). The previous arguments, showing that there is a potential gap between trust in physical settings and online trust, evidence the need for a research effort toward a deeper understanding of etrust. There is also another consideration that even better clarifies the contribution of this article: most of the researches focused on digital trust have been very specific, and with a very narrow research focus (e.g. 5). However, while researchers have started to provide some insights about the characteristics of etrust, a clear and general frame is still missing [41, 46]. The consequence of such a lack of common and stable understanding is a conceptual puzzle where the different research-pieces sometimes overlap and at other times do not fit together, making it difficult to gain a wide and shared view on the whole phenomenon. We classified the articles on digital trust along three different classes: (1) eCommerce/Purchasing: etrust is considered as the enabling factor for using a system or closing an online transaction [47, 48]; (2) Socio-Demographic Factors: analysis of the influence of several socio-demographic factors on etrust [49–53]; (3) Privacy and Security: analysis of the relationship between trust and privacy [54–57].

As emerge by our literature review there are not comprehensive and exhaustive contribution trying to frame the understanding of the main characteristics of online trust and how those can be embedded in an analysis for the design of effective systems. However, a growing number of scholars is engaged in "reconsider[ing] the construct of trust in the context of online environments" [58, p. 276] rather than just translating old concepts and mechanisms into ICT-mediated interactions. For instance, [44] claims that the idea that "trust needs touch", typical of the face-to-face settings, has to be abandoned and digital trust should be founded on other aspects as information sharing or actors' attitude toward interactions. At the same time, the importance of both human and nonhuman actors for digital trust is receiving an increasing attention by researchers that are recognizing the active role of artificial agents also in social interactions [59, 60]. In developing the conceptual model of digital trust, we will follow this line of reasoning, taking into considerations the peculiarities and the specific characteristics of online environment and social interactions.

3 Designing eTrust Model

This chapter contributes to the systematization of this research stream designing (through the DS paradigm) a conceptual model focused on digital trust. Following a well-established tradition, this chapter grounds on the social dimensions of information systems related to the interplay between social and technological drivers [61, 62]. The present reality shows that the interaction between human beings and technology does not always allow a clear distinction of the roles of human and nonhuman entities[2] [59, 60]. In fact, ICT-sustained networks seem to generate new actors rather than mere ties [63, 64]. Coherently, drawing upon the work of actor-network theorists, such as Callon, Latour, and Law, we argue that the investigation on digital trust dynamics requires a new conceptual framework [65] for understanding online social network relationships; in doing this we adopt [66] Murdoch's approach [66, p. 731] "to seek to follow network builders as they weave together heterogeneous materials". Designing the model's constructs: social and technical factors

Designing the model of digital trust, we follow a DS approach, and we also notice the potential contributions that Actor Network Theory (ANT) can provide to our research stream as conceptual perspective of investigation. ANT is defined as the "sociology of translation" [67–69] and it focuses on explaining how social processes are developed and are reciprocally influenced, rather than investigating the reasons behind actors' behaviors. This approach is coherent with our research issue and with our DS paradigm, since the ties connecting different entities (networks of relations) can be both humans and of nonhumans (ICT). Thus, when ICT mediated, trust might emerge in two different classes: a) social trust, and b) technological trust.

---

[2] The distinction between human and nonhuman actors (or entity) is typical of the study adopting the Actor-Network perspective. We prefer keeping such a taxonomy acknowledging the fact that thanks to the ICT nonhuman entities could embed any form of ICT-supported communication, knowledge sharing, virtual tie, social networking, etc.

Social trust ties humans interacting trough the ICT platforms (e.g. Intranet, Groupware, Virtual Community spaces). Any kind of order, association, or network can only emerge from a range of different, human and nonhuman, tangible and intangible, resources. Considering [69] framework, trust can be considered as a form of social order, that to be effective and stable must spread across space and time, maintaining and developing the networks at the same time. In Law's words, without forms of order "human actions and words do not spread very far at all" (1994, p. 24). The idea of "translation" refers to the definition and redefinition of the actor's roles within the network [70]. Social trust enhances the quality of translation of actors' identities and behaviors and consequently tends to stabilize the network itself.

Technological trust is the trust of human actors in technology. Recalling [69, p. 24] "materials, such as texts and technologies, surely form a crucial part of any ordering". The role of technology itself switches then from a pure enabler to an active actor. Callon [70, p. 133] notion of techno-economic network refers, in fact, to "a coordinated set of heterogeneous actors which interact more or less successfully to develop, produce, distribute and diffuse methods for generating goods and services". The idea of technological trust emphasizes the role of the interaction, whereas actors define one another in interaction and in the intermediaries that they put into circulation. The more tightly the various entities (human and nonhuman) are tied in, the stronger the network. Among the possible intermediaries, ICT has a crucial role since its pervasive nature and its innate potential of binding actors together, "cementing" the links. Furthermore, ICT has the potential to define the roles played by other human and nonhuman entities in the network. According to this perspective, the actors and the flow of intermediaries define the network itself. Therefore, trust that human beings attribute to ICT is a significant enabler of the relation within the network. In conclusion, ANT supported us in explaining how two level of trust (social and technical) have to be taken into consideration in designing an etrust model. In the next section we will introduce the model.

If in the physical world it is quite normal to refer to local and global points or local and global networks, when it comes to the virtual world the physical distance tends not to matter. The idea of close and remote actors is then replaced with the distinction between strategic and operative centers (nodes). Such a perspective is consistent with the idea of network governance defined by Latour [68, p. 223] that proposes to solve the problem of linking global and local actors by: (a) render[ing] them mobile, so they can be brought back; (b) keep[ing] them stable so that they can be moved back and forth without additional distortion, corruption or decay; and (c) [making them] combinable so that whatever stuff they are made of, they can be accumulated, aggregated, or shuffled like a pack of cards".

ICT infrastructure might work in this way by reducing the variety of activities in one place to a set of predetermined features that can then be transmitted to another place to be further elaborated. Similarly to what is represented in [71], also trust-based relationships can be represented as a whole. The etrust model presents two levels: the social and the technological layers. The social level embeds the interactions occurring between two or more individuals who mostly use ICT as a communication channel On the other hand, the technical level requires no direct interaction among actors since it is characterized by the creation of a shared artifact that will act as broker in the etrust relationship. In this case the relationship among actors is mediated by rules, roles, norms and instruments (or in general by shared institutions).

In order to provide a better understanding of our etrust model, we will propose a brief example of an application domain. Free/Open Source Software (FLOSS) is characterized by a network of distributed actors collaborating in software development activities. In most of the cases the developers do not know each other and had not ever met face to face. However, the decision to invest a consistent amount of time and efforts in developing software require a certain level of reciprocal trust since the individual work is tightly interdependent to other developers' work. Each developer has to be reasonably sure that the others will develop their own lines of code in keeping with the project and that time constraints will be respected. As shown by our model, the developer has two possible ways to establish etrust interactions: the social and the technological level. The developer will use the social level through the direct interaction with the others developers (chat, emails, video call or past common experiences), but s/he will also use the technical level through the access and the control of the code itself. Being the code visible to everybody, each developer can check what are the changes introduced by other developers and in this way to create her/his individual representation of their actions, that will constitute the enabler to the genesis or the maintenance of a trust-relationship. Thus, the design of an effective environment, where to facilitate the creation and management of etrust, should take into consideration the interactions between the social and technological level and the role of the artifacts as e-trust brokers. Along these lines technology could be considered as a moderator in the etrust relationship between actors and communities. The same reasoning could be applied to different levels of hierarchical control, intervention and supervision. In this sense, ICT contributes to the visibility and the comparability of actions among actors, so that the networks can be "governed" from the place where decisions are made. Given the centrality of the translation in the governance of such processes, the above recalled concepts of "institutional thickness" [72] and "institutional trust" [73] become crucial. In fact, through translation processes it is possible to concentrate activities and decisions in one place (e.g., strategic center—headquarter) that gains dominance over another place (the operative nodes—peripheries—subsidiaries). The recall of trust as a form of social order helps avoid any technological determinism or imperative [31]. The point has been effectively enlightened by Webster [74] who shows that as ICT solutions come to be applied they need to fit the existing structure of the work organization and may be modified by the requirements of local users. Further, consistently with the socio-technical approach, [63] show that ICT solutions can deliver the expected results only when they are accepted by the final users and are compatible with the legacy systems and the existing organizational procedures. If such solutions are not trusted (technological trust) by the final users and/or are unable to sustain the existing social network (social trust) this situation might lead to dysfunctions, misusage, and unexpected problems. Alternatively, when ICT infrastructures result successfully integrated with the existing social networks they can generate positive synergies through their interrelationships and mutual dependency [75, 76] .

4 Conclusions

This chapter focuses on trust-based relationships in online context. While the initial attempts to simply translate offline trust models to online settings seems to be gradually abandoned by researchers, the analyses on etrust are very specialized and balkanized into three main subsets (security and privacy, socio-demographic antecedents, and influence on the online purchasing). This chapter represents a first step in calling for the awareness of the problem: online trust can be analyzed as a complex and comprehensive concept. Thus, our first contribution relies on the literature review on online trust and the subsequent identification of a gap in the research consisting in the lack of a comprehensive framework for understanding of etrust as a whole phenomenon. In order to facilitate this line of research we propose a first model through which etrust relationships can be understood and systems designed. We propose this model along with the DS paradigm, thus as a conceptual model that can be taken into consideration in building effective online environments where collaboration and trust relationships have to be managed. As possible application domains, for example we can consider some online social networks as LinkedIn, CouchSurfing, Twitter. They have different aims, functionalities and structures, but they all share the same need for building and maintaining etrust systems: in LinkedIn we need to trust the info about the professional skills and the references other left to one profile; in CouchSurfing we need to believe that a person that we never met before will host us; in Twitter we need to know if some of the info we are receiving can be trusted or not. Those are just some examples of systems that could benefit in designing their structure according to the proposed model, where both social interactions among actors and the relationship between an actor and the online artifacts are determinant of etrust. The main limit of this chapter consists in the lack of an evaluation empirical-phase of the proposed model. However, the chapter's aim is to reach the awareness that a comprehensive model on etrust is needed and in designing the first constructs (social and technological interactions) for its development. Further research can start from this model in order to define and test the characteristics of the systems to design. Despite the limit described above, the design of an etrust model through DS represents a further step in the research field, filling existing gaps. First of all, the proposed conceptual model takes explicitly into consideration the human side of the organization, an aspect that is often neglected in those studies still deeply rooted in the technological imperative [31]. For the same reason, this approach decreases the risk of focusing on a pure "illusion of control" [63, 77], by turning the attention on the governance mechanisms of trust as a very complex social phenomenon. Moreover, our conceptual framework recognizes the active role of artifacts (ICT systems) in shaping and influencing human interactions. Thus, we contribute to the discussion about the role of ICT in social contexts, claiming that technological artifacts could have a "social shaping" function [64, 78], and that ICT itself can be molded by the contents shared by the participants [79]. Finally, similarly to other organizational factors (such as perceived equity, reputation, empowerment) [80], trust might have a moderating, buffering or even and enabling effect in shaping the social dimension of IT investments [81]. In more general terms, by following actors and networks as they coevolve, we may establish a deeper understanding of the human action (trust as a purely human feeling) in the construction of reality, even when it comes to technological artifacts.

References

1. Lee, A. (2000). Systems thinking, design science and paradigms. keynote address at the 11th ICIM. http://www.people.vcu.edu/~aslee/ICIM-keynote-2000.
2. Giustiniano, L., & Bolici, F. (2012). Organizational trust in a networked world: Analysis of the interplay between social factors and information and communication technology. *Journal of Information, Communication and Ethics in Society, 10*(3), 187–202.
3. Simon, H. A. (1996). *The sciences of the artificial*. Cambridge: MIT Press.
4. Takeda, H., Veerkamp, P., & Yoshikawa, H. (1990). Modeling design process. *AI magazine, 11*(4), 37.
5. Hevner, A. R., March, S. T., Park, J., & Ram, S. (2004). Design science in information systems research. *Mis Quarterly, 28*(1), 75–105.
6. Pries-Heje, J., & Baskerville, R. (2008). *The design theory nexus. MISQ, 32*(4), 731.
7. Carroll, J. M., & Kellogg, W. A. (1989). *Artifact as theory-nexus: Hermeneutics meets theory-based design* (Vol. 20). ACM.
8. March, S. T., & Smith, G. F. (1995). Design and natural science research on information technology. *Decision support systems, 15*(4), 251–266.
9. Peffers, K., Tuunanen, T., Rothenberger, M. A., & Chatterjee, S. (2007). A design science research methodology for information systems research. *JMIS, 24*(3), 45–77.
10. Luhmann, N. (1979). *Trust and power*. New York: Wiley.
11. Thomas, R. (1994). *What machines can't do: Politics and technology in the industrial enterprise*. CA: University of California Press.
12. Walsham, G. (2001). Knowledge management: The benefits and limitations of computer systems. *European Management Journal, 19*(6), 599–608.
13. Kramer, R. M., & Tyler, T. R. (Eds.). (1996). *Trust in organizations: Frontiers of theory and research*. CA: Sage Publications.
14. McDermott, R. (2000). Why information technology inspired but cannot deliver knowledge management. In E. L. Lesser, M. A. Fontaine, & J. A. Slusher (Eds.), *Knowledge and communities*. Woburn: Butterworth-Heinemann.
15. Rousseau, D., Sitkin, S. B., Burt, R. S., & Camerer, C. (1998). Not so different after all: A cross-discipline view of trust. *Academy of Management Review, 23*, 393–404.
16. Walsham, G., & Hayes, N. (2001). Participation in groupware-mediated communities of practice: A sociopolitical analysis of knowledge sharing. *Information and Organization, 11*, 263–288.
17. Fehr, E. (2009). On the economics and biology of trust. *Journal of the European Economic Association, 7*(2–3), 235–266.

18. Uslaner, E. (2004). Trust online, trust offline. *Communications of the ACM, 47*(4), 28–29.
19. Brower, H. H., Scott, W., Lester, M., Korsgaard, A., & Dineen, B. R. (2009). A closer look at trust between managers and subordinates: Understanding the effects of both trusting and being trusted on subordinate outcomes. *Journal of Management, 35*(2), 327–347.
20. Mayer, R. C., Davis, J. H., & Schoorman, F. D. (1995). An integrative model of organizational trust. *Academy of Management Review, 20*(3), 709–734.
21. Mcevily, B., Perrone, V., & Zaheer, A. (2003). Trust as an organizing principle. *Organization Science, 14*(1), 91–103.
22. Chaudhuri, A., & Holbrook, M. B. (2001). The chain of effects from brand trust and brand affect to brand performance: The role of brand loyalty. *The Journal of Marketing*, 81–93.
23. Van der Heijden, H., Verhagen, T., & Creemers, M. (2003). Understanding online purchase intentions: Contributions from technology and trust perspectives. *European Journal of Information Systems, 12*(1), 41–48.
24. Srite, M., & Karahanna, E. (2006). The role of espoused national cultural values in technology acceptance. *MIS Quarterly, 30*(3), 679–704.
25. Barber, B. (1983). *The logic and limits of trust*. New Brunswick: Rutgerts University Press.
26. Giddens, A. (1984). *The constitution of society: Outline of the theory of structuration*. Cambridge: Polity Press.
27. Giddens, A. (1990). *The consequences of modernity*. Cambridge: Polity Press.
28. Huff, L., & Kelley, L. (2003). Levels of organizational trust in individualist versus collectivist societies: A seven-nation study. *Organization Science, 14*(1), 81–91.
29. Benbasat, I., Gefen, D., & Pavloua, A. (2008). Trust in online environments [special issue]. *Journal of Management Information Systems*, *24*(4), 5–11, (spring).
30. Carnall, C. A. (1986). Toward a theory for the evaluation of organizational change. *Human Relations, 39*(8), 745–766.
31. Markus, M. L., & Robey, D. (1988). Information technology and organizational change: Causal structure in theory and research. *Management Science, 34*(5), 583–598.
32. Schoenberger, E. (1988). From Fordism to flexible accumulation: Technology, competitive strategies, and international location. *Environment and Planning D: Society and Space, 6*, 245–262.
33. Bolici, F. (2011). The role of information sharing and social community in the evolution of collaborative food networks. *Agribusiness and Information Management, 3*(1), 1–10.
34. Weill, P., & Broadbent, M. (1998). *Leveraging the new infrastructure*. Cambridge: Harvard Business School Press.
35. Weiss, H. M., & Rupp, D. E. (2011). Envisioning a person-centric work psychology. *Industrial and Organizational Psychology, 4*(1), 138–143.
36. Knoke, D., & Kuklinski, J. (1982). *Network Analysis*. CA: Sage.
37. Wang, Y. D., & Emurian, H. H. (2005). An overview of online trust: Concepts, elements, and implications. *Computers in human behavior, 21*(1), 105–125.
38. Priem, R. L., & Nystrom, P. (2011). *Exploring the dynamics of workgroup fracture: Common ground, trust-with-trepidation, and warranted distrust*. June: Journal of Management.
39. Festré, A., & Giustiniano, L. (2011). Relational capital and appropriate incentives: A recipe for human resources sustainability. In *Proceedings of the 2011 International Conference on Human Resources Development* (pp. 101–112). 28–30 Sept 2011, Taiwan.
40. Rocco, E. (1998). Trust breaks down in electronic contexts but can be repaired by some initial face-to-face contact. In C. M. Karat, et al. (Eds.), *Proceedings of the SIGCHI conference on Human factors in computing systems (CHI '98)* (pp. 496–502). New York: ACM Press/Addison-Wesley Publishing Co.
41. Wilson, J. M., Straus, S. G., & Mcevily, B. (2006). All in due time: The development of trust in computer-mediated and face-to-face teams. *Organizational Behavior and Human Decision Processes, 99*(1), 16–33.
42. Bos N. et al. (2002). Effects of four computer-mediated communications channels on trust development. In *Proceedings of the SIGCHI conference on Human factors in computing*

systems: Changing our world, changing ourselves (CHI '02) (pp. 135–140). ACM: New York.
43. Kimble, C. (2011). Building effective virtual teams: How to overcome the problems of trust and identity in virtual teams. *Global Business and Organizational Excellence, 30*(2), 6–15.
44. Taddeo, M. (2009). Defining trust and E-trust: Old theories and new problems. *International Journal of Technology and Human Interaction, 5*(2), 23–35.
45. Brown, J. S., & Duguid, P. (2001). Knowledge and organization: A social-practice perspective. *Organization science*, 198–213.
46. Jøsang, A., & Bewsell, G. (2010). Trust and trust management [special issue]. *Journal of Theoretical and Applied Electronic Commerce Research*, 5(2), I–II.
47. Deng, L., & Poole, M. S. (2010). Affect in web interfaces: A study of the impacts of web page visual complexity and order. *MIS Quartely, 34*, 711–730.
48. Vance, A., Alie-Dit-Cosaque, C., & Straub, D. (2008). Examining trust in information technology artifacts: The effects of system quality and culture. *Journal of Management Information Systems, 24*(4), 73–100.
49. Kim, D. J. (2008). Self-perception-based versus transference-based trust determinants in computer-mediated transactions: A cross-cultural comparison study. *Journal of Management Information Systems, 24*(4), 13–45.
50. Neveen, F., & Ragowsky, A. (2008). Establishing trust in electronic commerce through online word of mouth: An examination across genders. *Journal of Management Information Systems, 24*(4), 101–121.
51. Sia, L., Lim, K., Leung, K., Lee, M., & Benbasat, I. (2009). Web strategies to promote internet shopping: Is cultural-customization needed? *MISQ, 33*(3), 491–512.
52. Sun, T. (2011). The roles of trust and experience in consumer confidence in conducting e-commerce: A cross-cultural comparison between France and Germany. *International Journal of Consumer Studies, 35*, 330–337.
53. Yoon, C. (2009). The effects of national cultural values on consumer acceptance of e-commerce. Online shoppers in China. *Information and Management, 46*, 294–301.
54. Joinson, A. N., & Paine, C. B. (2007). Self- disclosure, privacy and the internet. In A. N. Joinson, K. McKenna, T. Postmes, & U. Reips (Eds.), *Oxford handbook of internet psychology* (pp. 237–252). Oxford: Oxford University Press.
55. Nosko, A., Wood, E., & Molema, S. (2010). All about me: Disclosure in online social networking profiles: The case of FACEBOOK. *Computers in Human Behavior, 26*(3), 406–418.
56. Tang, Z., Hu, Y., & Smith, M. D. (2008). Gaining trust through online privacy protection: Self-Regulation, mandatory standards, or caveat emptor. *Journal of Management Information Systems, 24*(4), 153–173.
57. Verhagen, T., Meents, S., & Tan, Y. H. (2006). Perceived risk and trust associated with purchasing at electronic marketplaces. *EJIS, 15*, 542–555.
58. Gefen, D., Benbasat, I., & Pavlou, P. A. (2008). A research agenda for trust in online environments. *Journal of Management Information Systems, 24*(4), 275–286.
59. Durante, M. (2010). What is the model of trust for multi-agent systems? Whether or not e-trust applies to autonomous agents. *Knowledge, Technology, and Policy, 23*(3–4), 347–366.
60. Grodzinsky, F., Miller, K., & Wolf, M. (2011). Developing artificial agents worthy of trust: Would you buy a used car from this artificial agent? *Ethics and information technology, 13*(1), 17–27.
61. Orlikowski, W. (1992). The duality of technology: Rethinking the concept of technology in organizations. *Organization Science, 3*(3), 398–427.
62. Zuboff, S. (1988). *In the age of the smart machine*. New York: Basic Book.
63. Ciborra, C., & Hanseth, O. (2000). Introduction: From control to drift. In C. Ciborra, K. Braa, & A. Cordella (Eds.), *From control to drift* (pp. 1–11). Oxford: Oxford University Press.
64. Hanseth, O., & Monteiro, E. (1995). Social shaping of information infrastructure. In W. Orlikowski, et al. (Eds.), *Information technology and changes in organizational work* (pp. 325–343). London: Chapman and Hall.

65. Cropanzano, R. (2009). Writing nonempirical articles for Journal of Management: General thoughts and suggestions. *Journal of Management, 35*(6), 1304–1311.
66. Murdoch, J. (1995). Actor-networks and the evolution of economic forms: Combining description and explanation in theories of regulation, flexible specialization, and networks. *Environment and Planning A, 27*(5), 731–757.
67. Callon, M. (1986). Some elements of a sociology of translation. In J. Law (Ed.), *Power, action, belief: A new sociology of knowledge?* (pp. 196–233). London: Routledge and Kegan Paul.
68. Latour, B. (1987). *Science in action*. Milton Keynes: Open University Press.
69. Law, J. (1994). *Organizing modernity*. Oxford: Basil Blackwell.
70. Callon, M. (1991). Techno-economic networks and irreversibility. In J. Law (Ed.), *A sociology of monsters: Essays on power technology and domination* (pp. 132–161). London: Routledge.
71. Bolici, F. (2005), "Analyzing the link between technology and organizational knowledge from a social-practice perspective, *Proceedings of EGOS'05 (European Group on Organizational Studies)* (pp. 1–20). June 30th–July 2nd, Berlin.
72. Amin, A., & Thrift, N. (1992). Neo-Marshallian nodes in global networks. *International Journal of Urban and Regional Research, 16*, 571–587.
73. Spagnoletti, P., Za, S., & D'Atri, A. (2007). *Institutional trust and security, new boundaries for Virtual Enterprises*. Paper presented at the 2nd International Workshop on Interoperability Solutions to Trust, Security, Policies and QoS for Enhanced Enterprise Systems. 26 Mar 2007. Madeira, Portugal.
74. Webster, J. (1991). Advanced manufacturing technologies: Work organisation and social relations crystallized. In J. Law (Ed.), *A sociology of monsters: Essays on power technology and domination* (pp. 192–222). London: Routledge.
75. Dosi, G., & Salvatore, R. (1992). The structure of industrial production and the boundaries between firms and markets. In M. Storper & A. Scott (Eds.), *Pathways to industrialization and regional development* (pp. 171–195). London: Routledge.
76. Nelson, R., & Winter, S. (1982). *An evolutionary theory of economic change*. London: Harvard University Press.
77. Ciborra, C. U. (1996). Platform organization: Recombining strategies, structures, and surprises. *Organization Science, 7*(2), 103–118.
78. Barret, M., Grant, D., & Wales, N. (2006). ICT and organizational change. *The Journal of Applied Behavioral Science, 42*(1), 6–22.
79. Orlikowski, W. J., & Barley, S. R. (2001). Technology and institutions: What can research on information technology and research on organizations learn from each other? *MIS Quarterly, 25*(2), 145–165.
80. Bauer, T. N., & Erdogan, B. (2010). Differentiated leader-member exchanges: The buffering role of justice climate. *Journal of Applied Psychology, 95*(6), 1104–1120.
81. Clarioni, G., & Giustiniano, L. (2011). Outsourcing, business performance and vertical integration boundaries: An empirical analysis. *Proceedings of the World Business and Social Science Research Conference.* 27–28 Oct 2011, Las Vegas, USA,

Knowledge Creation Processes in Information Systems and Management: Lessons from Simulation Studies

Stefano ZA and Paolo Spagnoletti

Abstract This chapter aims to contribute to the debate on the relationship between Information Systems (IS) and other Management (MGT) fields of studies. We present the preliminary results of the publication statistics, co-citation, and cross-citation analyses performed on a dataset of 54 and 169 "simulation related studies" published in top IS and MGT journals in the last thirty years. The analysis shows that this stream of research allows to comparatively analyze the evolutionary trends of research outcomes and impact, and to better understand the cumulative tradition of the knowledge creation process in the IS and MGT communities. Although research in IS is unlikely to build on and cite prior research, its influence on other fields is proportionally similar in magnitude to the external influence of MGT studies.

Keywords Simulation · Cross-citation · Network analysis · Hierarchic complex systems

1 Introduction

The relationship between Information Systems (IS) studies and other sub-fields of management has been widely debated with some controversial positions. This debate started at the infancy of the IS field, when the concepts of "work points" and "reference points" have been introduced to refer to the structure and the nature of the field [1]. Some authors have advocated a two-way relationship in which IS plays the role of both a referee discipline and a reference discipline [2]. Other studies have found evidences that IS has left a modest imprint on other sub-fields of Management [3]. However there is a common agreement on the potential of IS in terms of its external influence on other fields [4].

S. ZA (✉) · P. Spagnoletti
CeRSI, LUISS Guido Carli University, Rome, Italy

P. Spagnoletti (ed.), *Organizational Change and Information Systems*, Lecture Notes in Information Systems and Organisation 2, DOI: 10.1007/978-3-642-37228-5_19,

Previous studies on this topic are based either on conceptual analysis [2], or on the quantitative analysis of citations trends [3], and in some cases on post hoc content analysis aimed to understand how IS works are being utilized by other disciplines [4]. These studies share an holistic approach to the study of this phenomenon, in which the whole body of knowledge developed in the IS field has been considered as unit of analysis instead of focusing on a specific topic. These contributions aim to provide a general assessment of the IS field in order to define general guidelines for enhancing the discipline. We claim that a further contribution to this debate can be provided by gaining insights into the dynamics of knowledge creation processes in scholar communities.

In this chapter we start a discussion on this matter by showing how a citation analysis focused on a specific topic can help in the exploration of such dynamics. We thence begin an investigation on the relationship between the knowledge creation process of a research community and the impact of its research results. To achieve this goal we first restrict the scope of our analysis to a specific stream of research, which represents the source of data for this study. This stream of research must be (1) old enough to show its evolutionary trends, (2) present in two different fields of research to enable a comparative analysis, (3) narrow enough for allowing the adoption of both quantitative and qualitative bibliometric analysis methods and techniques. According with these criteria, our case study addresses the knowledge creation process of the IS and the Management (MGT) research communities within the particular domain of "simulation related studies". This stream of research includes both articles adopting simulation as a research method and articles providing contributions at the meta-level. Simulation is intended as using computer software to model the operation of "real-world" processes, systems, or events [5]. Simulation methods have been adopted as theory development methods in both Management and Information Systems studies. Davis et al. [6] have discussed the strengths and weaknesses of simulation methods for theory development and have defined a roadmap for executing and evaluating research using simulation methods in the broad Management field. Simulation is also considered as being one of the available evaluation methods for design research studies [7, 8].

Our assumption is that a comparative exploration of trends and connections between articles referred to "simulation related studies" in the IS and MGT fields can set up the basis for a subsequent discussion on the emergent aspects of their generation processes. The chapter starts with a description of the research method and the dataset. Then the results of the analysis are illustrated by the means of descriptive data and network diagrams. Finally a discussion summarizes the findings by providing insights and suggestions for further investigation.

2 Method and Data

Institute for Scientific Information (ISI) Web of Science [9] was used to conduct the searches and retrieve publication data taking into account the first three citation databases: Science Citation Index Expanded, Social Sciences Citation Index and Arts and Humanities Citation Index. They fully cover nearly 12,000 major journals adding up to over 40 million searchable records [9]. In addition, ISI Web of Science search seems to merge duplicate results when searching from multiple indexes, so there was no great fear of redundant data in the search results. These citation indexes also contain a record of the references cited by the authors of the covered publications. This enables the use of cited reference searches and various citation analyses.

For this work, we performed two queries on ISI Web of Science search, both based on "what" (topic) and "where" (publication name) searching attributes. For both queries the topic is the same whereas they differ for the set of selected journals. With respect to the topic, we adopted the classification provided by Davis et al. [6], about the different simulation approaches. Therefore the following keywords have been identified: "system dynamics", "NK fitness landscape", "genetic algorithm", "cellular automata", and "stochastic processes", plus the more generic term "simulation". With respect to the journals' selection, we adopted the Senior Scholars' Basket of Journals published by AIS[1] for the IS query. Whereas, for the MGT query we based the selection on the list of top journals published by the Italian National Agency for the Evaluation of Universities and Research Institutes (ANVUR[2]). The two final search strings are formulated as:

IS query: `Publication Name = (''European Journal of Information Systems'' OR ''Information Systems Journal'' OR ''Information Systems Research'' OR ''Journal of AIS'' OR ''Journal of Information Technology'' OR ''Journal of MIS'' OR ''Journal of Strategic Information Systems'' OR ''MIS Quarterly'') AND Topic = (''system dynamic*'' OR ''NK fitness landscape'' OR ''genetic algorithm*'' OR ''cellular automat*'' OR ''stochastic process*'' OR ''simulation*'')`

MGT query: `Publication Name = (''academy of management review'' OR ''academy of management journal'' OR ''organization science'' OR ''organizational behavior and human decision processes'' OR ''journal of organizational behavior management'' OR ''strategic management journal'' OR ''behaviour & information technology'') AND Topic = (''system dynamic*'' OR ''NK fitness landscape'' OR ''genetic algorithm*'' OR ''cellular automat*'' OR ''stochastic process*'' OR ''simulation*'')`

Asterisk-characters are used to include singulars search and plurals of each search term. The search is not limited to any specific year, thus everything from 1985 to 2012 has been retrieved and no other restrictions are applied. All searches were performed on 14th June 2012.

This resulted in 54 hits for the IS query (with 1,080 citations) and 169 for the MGT query (with 5,076 citations). Furthermore the "Create Citation Report"-link was

---

[1] http://home.aisnet.org/displaycommon.cfm?an=1&subarticlenbr=346

[2] http://www.anvur.org/

used to get detailed data on citations to the retrieved publications. The relative paucity of simulation studies, which are not a mainstream topic in both IS and MGT, provides us the opportunity to perform a longitudinal analysis over a thirty year period without losing the possibility for further studies to analyze details of articles' connections. This also does not avoid us to analytically generalize our findings.

Before to start the analysis of the results, we performed the same queries without any filter on the topic. In this way we obtained the following output in terms of the two overarching sets:

- IS query: 3,462 articles, cited 95,580 times
- MGT query: 9,556 articles, cited 527,821 times

Therefore the ratio of publications in IS to MGT is about 1–3, whereas it is about 1–5 with respect to the number of citations. These proportions reflect the ones founded in the subset of simulation related articles.

For further analyses the search results of the queries were exported from the ISI Web of Science in text format as full records, including cited reference data. These data have been then imported into a bibliometric analysis tool called Sitkis [10]. Sitkis is a free Java-based program that utilizes Microsoft Access database to store and analyze data exported from the ISI Web of Science. Various analyses can be made with Sitkis using the exported data. After analyzing the articles, Sitkis can generate some text file containing a matrix representation of some citation analysis results. These text files can be imported to UCINET 6, a social network analysis software, to make them visualized in NetDraw (included with UCINET 6). NetDraw was then used to draw the various network diagrams provided in this work.

3 Analysis and Results

3.1 Publication Statistics

There are two categories of bibliometric indicators: descriptive indicators, and relational indicators having an analytical function [11]. We start our analysis by presenting some general figures representing descriptive indicators.

Even though the first article in IS was published in 1988, the trend in this area actually starts in 1994, almost 10 years later with respect to the MGT area (1986). This delay also reflects the different ages of these two fields. The number of publications per year and their citations trends for both IS and MGT areas are depicted in Fig. 1.

The number of publications and citations per year in the two sets shows a similartrend. Indeed the publishing rate increases as a sine wave trend with peaks in 1996, 2003, and 2010 in both cases (left side of Fig. 1). Whereas the number of citations increases yearly in a continuous manner. Two are the main considerations about the topic:

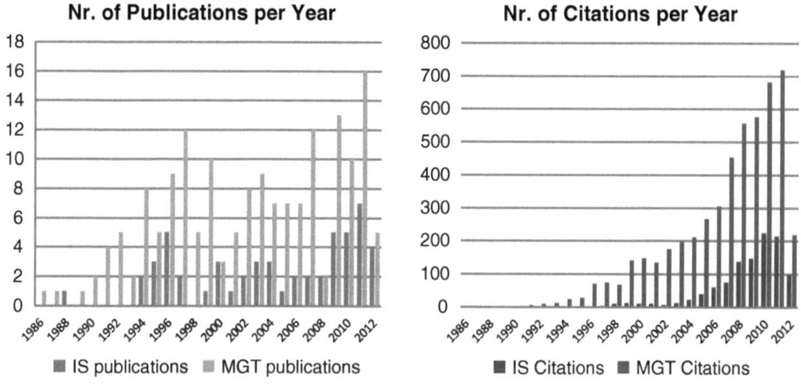

Fig. 1 Number of publications and citation per year

- on the basis of the number of publications per year, simulation studies still represent a research topic in which both communities show a growing interest;
- the trend of the number of citations of papers in the two sets, is a proxy of the importance of these contributions for the whole research community.

3.2 Co-Citation Analysis

The ISI Web of Science citation indexes also record the citations to references made by retrieved publications. By analyzing these citations, the most influential works in the IS and in the MGT areas can be identified. Table 1 lists the most cited references, among those retrieved with the IS query, that are cited at least 3 times by other articles belonging to the same set. On the other side, Table 2 refers to the MGT query, and shows the references cited at least 13 times. These thresholds have been fixed for obtaining a similar number of papers (14 and 13 for IS and MGT respectively). By observing these two tables, a high degree of convergence emerges in the MGT area in which some influential works are cited about 30 times. On the other side, in the IS area the maximum number of repeated citations is 5. The co-citation analysis can depict better this behavior considering the co-citation network.

Co-citation analysis is a relational bibliometric indicator, which provides a picture of scientific activity and helps in monitoring and identifying emerging research topics and the relevant contributors [11]. Co-citation analysis involves tracking pairs of papers that are cited together in the source publications, forming relations and clusters of research [12]. Figures 2 and 3 show the co-citation network of the most cited references for IS and MGT subsets respectively. The nodes represent the common references and the ties, with their thickness, show how many times two articles are cited together. Despite the number of nodes is quite similar the co-citation networks are fairly different. Within the IS set, the number

Table 1 The most cited references (cited by the search result publications for IS area)

Citations	Author(s)	Title	Year	Type
5	Diamantopoulos A, Winklhofer H.M.	Index construction with formative indicators: an alternative to scale development	2001	Journal article
4	Jarvis C.B., MacKenzie S.B., Podsakoff P.M.	A critical review of construct indicators and measurement model misspecification in marketing and consumer research	2003	Journal article
4	Majchrzak A., Rice R.E., Malhotra A., King N., Ba S.L.	Technology adaptation: the case of a computer-supported inter-organizational virtual team	2000	Journal article
3	Ba SL, Stallaert J., Whinston A.B.	Research commentary: introducing a third dimension in information systems design the case for incentive alignment	2001	Journal article
3	Boehm B.W.	An experiment in small-scale application software engineering	1981	Journal article
3	Cohen J.	Statistical power analysis for the behavioral sciences	1988	Book
3	DeMarco T.	Controlling software projects: management, measurement & estimation	1982	Book
3	Dewan S., Mendelson H.	User delay costs and internal pricing for a service facility	1990	Journal article
3	Fornell C., Larcker D.F.	Evaluating structural equation models with unobservable variables and measurement error	1981	Journal article
3	Forrester J.W.	Industrial dynamics	1961	Book
3	Hardin A.M., Chang J.C.J., Fuller M.A.	Formative versus reflective measurement: comment on Marakas, Johnson, and Clay (2007)	2008	Journal article
3	Jöreskog K.G., Yang F.	Structural equation modeling	1996	Book Chapter
3	Malone T.W.	Modeling coordination in organizations and markets	1987	Journal article
3	Mayer R.C., Davis J.H., Schoorman F.D.	An integrative model of organizational trust	1995	Journal article
3	Milgrom P.	Auctions and bidding—a primer	1989	Journal article

Table 2 The most cited references (cited by the search result publications for the MGT area)

Citations	Authors	Title	Year	Type
28	Nelson R.R., Winter S.G.	An evolutionary theory of economic change	1982	Book
27	Cyert R.M., March J.G.	A behavioral theory of the firm	1963	Book
22	March J.G., Simon H.A.	Organizations	1958	Book
21	March J.G.	Exploration and exploitation in organizational learning	1991	Journal article
16	Levitt B, March J.G.	Organizational learning	1988	Journal article
15	Baron R.M., Kenny D.A.	The moderator mediator variable distinction in social psychological-research - conceptual, strategic, and statistical considerations	1986	Journal article
15	Cohen M.D., March J.G. and Olsen J.P.	A garbage can model of organizational choice	1972	Journal article
15	Thompson J. D.	Organizations in action	1967	Book
14	Levinthal D.A.	Adaptation on rugged landscapes	1997	Journal article
14	Rivkin J.W.	Imitation of complex strategies	2000	Journal article
13	Gavetti G. and Levinthal D.	Looking forward and looking backward: cognitive and experiential search	2000	Journal article
13	Locke E.A., Latham G.P.	A theory of goal setting & task performance	1990	Book
13	Teece D.J., Pisano G, Shuen A.	Dynamic capabilities and strategic management	1997	Journal article

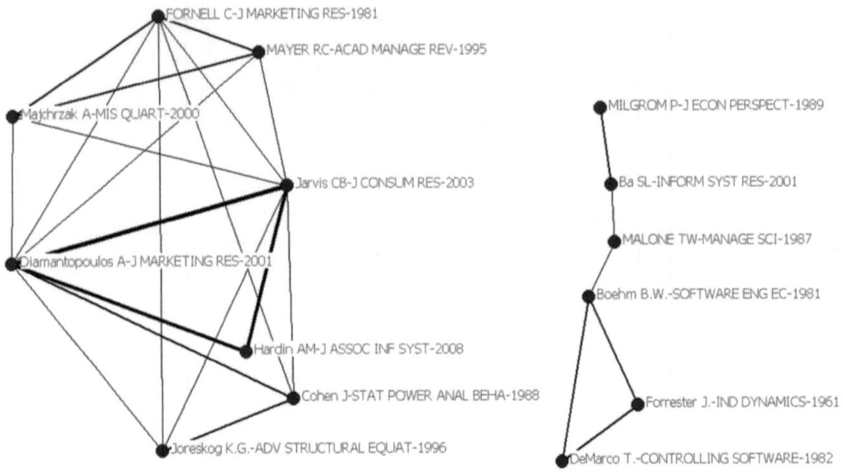

Fig. 2 Co-citation network of the most cited reference for IS query

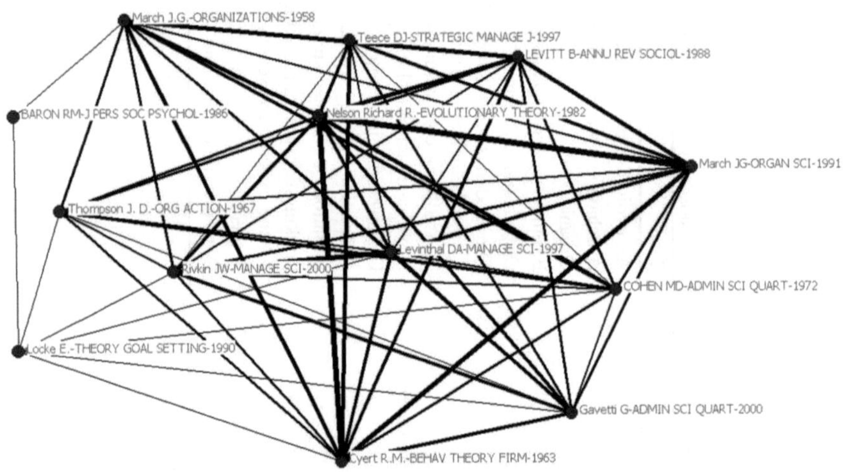

Fig. 3 Co-citation network of the most cited reference for MGT/OS/OB query

of ties is 25 and their maximum thickness is 4 (4 times two references are cited together). Moreover the network is composed by two separated graphs (also identified by different colors in Table 1). On the other side, in the MGT area there are 62 ties and two references are cited together 14 times.

This result suggests to further analyze the extent to which the most popular IS references are sparse and scattered in comparison with the MGT area. In order to investigate this issue we evaluate the connectedness or density index of both graphs. The level of connectedness (also named density) can be considered as the simplest index of the amount of relationships among the nodes in a network. It is defined as the ratio of observed links to the total number of links possible [13, 14].

Connectedness is a variable that takes on a value of 0 when there are no links in the network and it reaches a value of 1 when every node is linked with everyone. To calculate the level of connectedness C, the first step is to identify the number of possible ties T in the network. T can be calculated considering the total number of nodes (named N) and the directionality of the graph:

- $T = N \times ((N - 1)/2)$ for a non-directional graph
- $T = N \times (N - 1)$ for a directional graph.

The co-citation network is a non-directional graph, then the connectedness or density for both networks is:

- for IS $C = 25/[14 \times ((14 - 1)/2)] = 0.27$;
- for MGT $C = 62/[13 \times ((13 - 1)/2)] = 0.79$.

As suggested before, the connectedness index confirms that the level of common references usage is higher in MGT than in IS. This parameter does not take into account the "quality" (size: how many times two nodes are cited together) of each tie.

From the IS co-citation network there is only one co-cited "triangle" within the selection of the most cited references: Diamantopoulos et al. 2001, Jarvis et al. 2003 and Hardin et al. 2008. They are cited together 3 times in the retrieved publications. There are also two additional co-cited "triangles" which are less frequent and belong to two separated sub-graphs; one is formed by Majchrzak et al. (2000), Mayer et al. 1995 and Fornell et al. 2001 and the second one by DeMarco 1982, Forrester 1961, and Boehm 1981.

In the MGT co-citation network, the more co-cited "triangle" is composed by: March 1991, Nelson and Winter 1982, and Cyert and March 1963. These references are cited together in 12 publications. If we set the minimum number of cited times to 7, all the nodes are connected through one or more ties, except Baron and Kenny 1986, and Locke and Latham 1990 (cited only two times together also with the remaining publications).

As mentioned before, the nodes in the MGT co-citations network are more strongly connected (high density degree and great ties thickness) than in the IS co-citation network. This means that in MGT, the research community has identified a common set of references on the topic.

3.3 Cross-Citation Analysis

The co-citation analysis shows the main network of references cited by the articles retrieved in the two areas: Information Systems (Fig. 2) and Management (Fig. 3). It can be considered as the basis (mainly outside the set of retrieved publications) upon which the authors have built their contributions. However it is also interesting to observe whether the selected publications do relate to each other. By tracing these links it is possible to identify the evolution paths of the knowledge creation process and to compare the two fields of study.

This can be achieved by adopting the cross-citation analysis. This analytical technique depicts whether and to what extent a publication within a set is cited (does have an impact) by the others in the same set. The cross-citation network is created as a result of the cross-citation analysis. It is a way for having an idea on the "relative impact" of each publication inside the same set. The nodes represent a publication and the ties, formed by arrows, indicate "who cites whom". For example, if the paper A cites paper B there is an arrow from A to B. The cross-citation network can be considered as a snapshot of the citations links among the members of the same community. For describing this kind of graph we adopt some concepts borrowed from the social network analysis studies [14, 15].

Figure 4 shows the cross-citation network for the IS field. There are 20 nodes and 13 ties, which are distributed in 4 Isolated Dyads (a pair of nodes linked together but isolated from the rest of the network) and 3 Trees (a subset of node with minimal connections; if any single node is removed the result will separate the tree structure in two parts). Figure 5 shows the cross-citation network for the MGT field. There are 79 nodes with 111 ties, distributed in 10 Isolated Dyads, 1 Tree, and two groups of nodes: the smaller is formed by 11 nodes and 13 ties and it is quite similar to a tree structure; the bigger includes 44 nodes and 85 ties and it is a typical "scale-free" or "Power law" structure, in which very few nodes have a huge number of connections, some nodes with moderate connections and many with very few ties.

From Fig. 5 it is possible to observe a hierarchical structure between articles grounded on previous articles that are recursively grounded on additional levels. The graph suggests that the members of the MGT community build their body of knowledge incrementally, by taking into account the previous works done within the community itself. A totally different behavior can be observed in the IS field. In fact, the cross-citation graph in Fig. 4 shows a sparse network with very few ties linking a small number of papers.

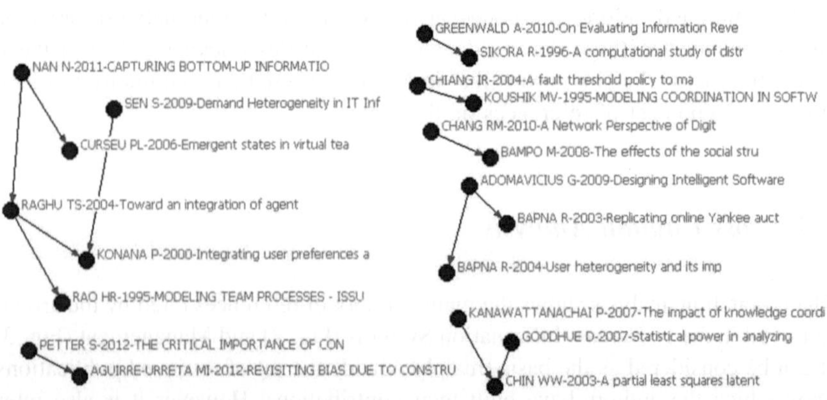

Fig. 4 Cross-citation network of the most cited reference for IS query

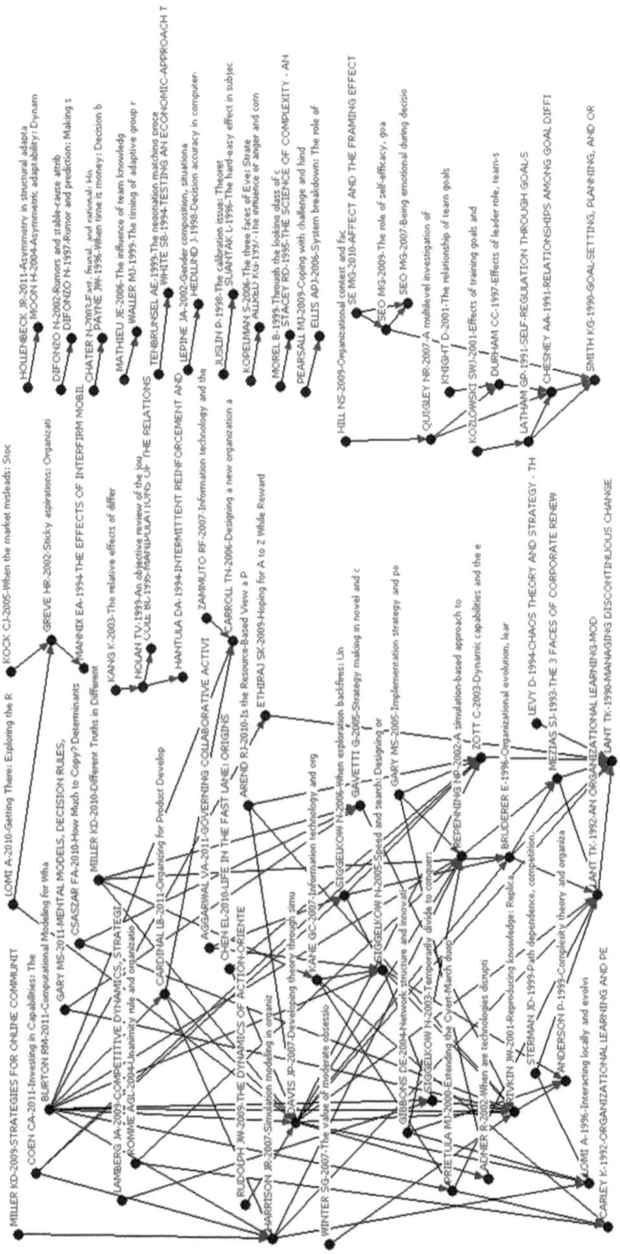

Fig. 5 Cross-citation network of the most cited reference for MGT/OS/OB query

The transitivity degree is used in social network analysis for describing the extent to which nodes are taken into account by other nodes in the same set. We start from the following definition [14]:

- Triad: a triple of actors with their ties
- Transitivity: the triad involving actors A, B, and C is transitive if whenever A– > B and B– > C then A– > C (in our case, if A cites B and B cites C then A cites C).

Starting from these definitions we can introduce the transitivity degree as the number of transitivity triads or paths present in the graph divided by the potential

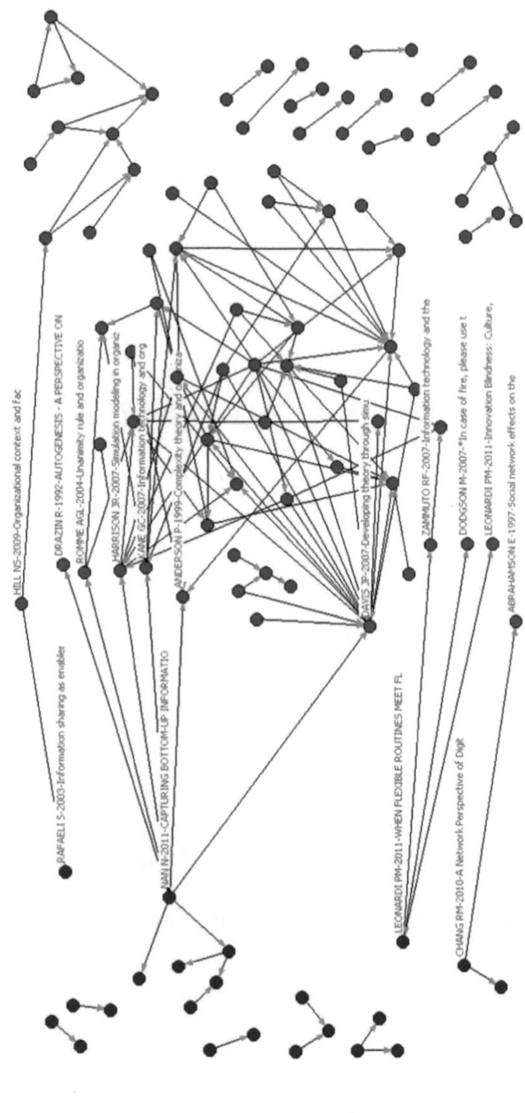

Fig. 6 Cross-citation network of the most cited reference in the IS (*left*) and MGT (*right*) fields

number of them. This index is equal to 1 when each triad in a directional graph is transitive.

We used UCINET for calculating this index with a resulting value of 0 for the IS field cross-citation network and 0.2 for the MGT field. These values confirm the hypothesis on the behavior of the MGT research community described before.

Finally, we adopt cross-citation analysis for investigating the reciprocal influence between the two communities. With this purpose we merged the two datasets and we built a holistic graph, using different colors for characterizing the original set of each node. Figure 6 shows on the left side the IS publications (blue) whereas on the right side the MGT (red) ones. From this graph is interesting to observe that 10 out of 11 "bridges", meaning the group members with a link to a member of a different group, come from the IS field and are linked towards the MGT field. Furthermore the most cited publications in the MGT area are often linked to (cited from) articles in the IS area. This highlights the different behaviors of these research communities with respect to the knowledge creation process in this specific domain. Indeed the IS community has the propensity to cite external publication, even though in this case we are considering only the MGT ones.

4 Conclusion

In this chapter we present the preliminary results of a bibliometric analysis of "simulation related studies" published in top IS and MGT journals in the last thirty years. Although a discussion of these findings against previous works on the knowledge creation processes of scholar communities is out of the scope of this chapter, it can be considered as a first step towards a better understanding of such complex phenomenon. In fact a deeper exploration of the mechanisms leading to similar evolutionary trends starting from different cumulative research traditions emerges as the main finding of our analysis.

The concept of hierarchy in complex systems [16] can provide the lens for interpreting the results of our cross-citation analysis that shows how the majority of scholarly contributions in the MGT field are firmly grounded on previous studies published within the same field. As opposed to this hierarchic incremental behavior characterizing the knowledge creation process in the MGT field, IS studies seldom refer to a hierarchical body of knowledge. When this is the case, MGT studies act as a reference discipline upon which new knowledge is created in the IS domain.

In spite of this different behavior, citation data show that the two body of knowledge have a similar impact on subsequent research. In fact, the number of citations from other fields can be considered as a proxy of the research importance [17] and the analysis of this research stream shows a similar ratio number of publications versus number of citations. This means that although research in IS is unlikely to build on and cite prior research, its influence on other fields is proportionally similar in magnitude to the external influence that MGT studies. This conclusion asks for further investigations on the relationship between the knowledge creation process of a research community and its external influence and evolutionary dynamics. A qualitative analysis on the same dataset or the analysis of further streams of research can provide additional insights on this research problem and contribute to the debate on the development of the IS field.

References

1. Culnan, M. J., & Swanson, E. B. (1986). Research in management information systems, 1980–1984: Points of work and reference. *MIS Quarterly, 10*, 288–302.
2. Baskerville, R., & Myers, D. (2002). Information systems as a reference discipline. *MIS Quarterly, 26*, 1–14.
3. Wade, M., Biehl, M., & Kim, H. (2006). Information systems is not a reference discipline (and what we can do about it). *Journal of AIS, 7*, 247–269.
4. Grover, V., Ayyagari, R., Gokhale, R., & Lim, J. (2006). A citation analysis of the evolution and state of information systems within a constellation of reference disciplines. *Journal of AIS, 7*, 270–325.
5. Law, A. M., & Kelton, D. W. (1991). *Simulation modeling and analysis* (2nd ed.). New York: McGraw-Hill.
6. Davis, J. P., Eisenhardt, K. M., & Bingham, C. B. (2007). Developing theory through simulation methods. *Academy of Management Review, 32*, 480–499.
7. Hevner, A. R. A. R., March, S. T. S. T., Park, J., & Ram, S. (2004). Design science in information systems research. *MIS Quarterly, 28*, 75–105.
8. Spagnoletti, P., Baskerville, R., Marco, M.D. (2012). The contributions of Alessandro D'Atri to Organization and Information Systems Studies. In: R. Baskerville, M. De Marco, & P. Spagnoletti (Eds.) Designing organizational systems, LNISO Vol. 1 (pp. 1–18). Heidelberg: Springer.
9. ISI: ISI Web of Knowledge [v.5.6]—Web of Science Home.
10. Schildt, H.A. (2006). SITKIS software for bibliometric data management and analysis v2.0. Institute of Strategy and International Business, Helsinki.
11. Gauthier, É. (1998). Bibliometric analysis of scientific and technological research: A user's guide to the methodology. Statistics Canada.
12. Garfield, E. (1993). Co-citation analysis of the scientific literature: Henry small on mapping the collective mind of science. *Current Comments, 9*, 3–13.
13. Tutzauer, F. (1985). Toward a theory of disintegration in communication networks. *Social Networks, 7*, 263–285.
14. Wasserman, S., Faust, K. (1994). Social network analysis: Methods and applications. Cambridge: Cambridge University Press.
15. Richards, W. (1981). The NEGOPY network analysis program. *Social Networks, 3*, 215–223.
16. Simon, H.A. (1996). The sciences of the artificial. Cambridge: MIT Press.
17. Loebbecke, C., & Leidner, D. (2012). The Contribution of top IS publications to subsequent research: A citation analysis. *Communications of the Association for Information Systems, 30*, 423–438.

Solar System: A New Way to Model Online Communities for Open Innovation

Alberto Francesconi, Riccardo Bonazzi and Claudia Dossena

Abstract Online communities are becoming an important way to support innovation through an open approach. Knowledge shared in online communities can be explored and exploited through adequate absorptive capacities. The chapter explores which factors allow an assessment of a firm's absorptive capacity to exploit an online community as a source of innovation.

Keywords Absorptive capacity · Knowledge exploration and knowledge exploitation · Open innovation

1 Introduction

In this chapter we focus on innovation nourished 'from the outside', highlighting the role of online communities (OCs). Recent studies [1] outline that opening the innovation process to external knowledge can improve in-house activities [2]. This is linked to the concept of 'absorptive capacity' (ACAP) [3]. **Our research question is: which factors allow the assessment of a firm's ACAP to exploit an OC as a source of innovation?** Trying to answer this question, we take a pragmatic approach and we do not take a social or political stance with respect to firm exploitation of knowledge, which users decide to share with the firm and that is

A. Francesconi (✉) · C. Dossena
Faculty of Economics, University of Pavia, Pavia, Italy
e-mail: afrancesconi@eco.unipv.it

C. Dossena
e-mail: claudia.dossena@eco.unipv.it

R. Bonazzi
HEC, Information Systems Institute, University of Lausanne, Lausanne, Switzerland
e-mail: riccardo.bonazzi@unil.ch

P. Spagnoletti (ed.), *Organizational Change and Information Systems*, Lecture Notes in Information Systems and Organisation 2, DOI: 10.1007/978-3-642-37228-5_20,

stored in its repositories. The chapter is structured in six sections. We briefly recall the literature around three concepts (innovation, OC, ACAP) to underline a set of gaps. In the third section we present the method used to obtain a model, which is described in the fourth section. Preliminary results from a case study are presented in the fifth section. The last section reports a brief summary and a set of future research directions.

2 Theoretical Framework

Innovation. Innovation is recognized as a primary means for organizational renewal [4] and a key lever for sustainable competitive advantage [5]. Innovation studies have developed mainly within the conventional context of organizational hierarchies. Various types of innovation can be highlighted: market [6], technological [7], organizational [8], product [4], process [9], service [10], and strategic innovations [11]. Other studies focused on the distinction between incremental or radical innovations [12] and the different sets of mechanisms which drive them. Researchers have often substituted innovation generation for innovation adoption, used the terms interchangeably [13] and considered firms as either innovation-generating [7] or innovation-adopting [14]. Although innovativeness includes at its core the degree of being 'new' [15], most new ideas emerge as novel recombination of old ideas. Restricting the definition of innovation only to those ideas that are utterly new to the world would make this concept almost empty [15]. Therefore, the degree of innovativeness needs to be specific to a particular domain. In our work, we focus on firm's innovativeness which manifests itself in the ability to transform knowledge and ideas from OCs in novel products, services, processes conceived also as upgrades, modifications, extensions, and new applications of existing ones. We adopt Van de Ven and Poole's [16] definition of innovation process as the invention and implementation of new ideas, which are developed by people, who engage in transactions with others over time within an institutional context, and who judge outcomes of their efforts and act accordingly. We examine the temporal sequences of activities which involve an OC, trying to light-up part of the 'black box' that exists between innovation inputs and outcomes [16]. March [17] launched the argument that the firm's innovation capabilities include both explorative and exploitative abilities. Exploration includes things captured by terms such as search, variation, risk taking, experimentation, play, flexibility, discovery [17]. Exploitation includes things such as refinement, choice, production, efficiency, selection, implementation, execution [17]. Based on this literature, the integration of external knowledge appears crucial but such process should be further studied. In brief, literature argues the innovation locus can lie across traditional firm's boundaries, between the closed hierarchical model of innovation and the open market-based model [18], in locus where technical knowledge, marketing experience and customer activities intersect. This, in turn, requires also that knowledge spread within OCs might be not only explored but also exploited.

Online communities. An OC is a virtual community, a group of people brought together by common interests or goals through taking part in membership ritual. The community is virtual in that its members mainly interact using IT (i.e., software tools), and are brought together through a network which alleviate the constraints of the physical distance [19]. A fundamental distinction exists in the production versus consumption orientation of OCs. On their intersection can be located the concept of a community of creation, which "is governed by a central firm that acts as the sponsor and defines the ground rules for participation" [19: 25]. The OC of creation blends the benefits of hierarchies and markets by offering a governance compromise between too much structure and complete chaos. The OC of creation model relies on extended participation and distributed production [18]. The creation of new idea significantly benefits from the high number of OC members and the voluntary flows of ideas among them. However, a firm needs to develop adequate organizational capacities to concretely benefit from this knowledge. These capacities are linked to an 'ideal process' that starts with the idea generation, which is focused on the identification and generation of opportunities, fresh ideas and novel concepts. The contributions of OC members can be added to suggestions created by the firm itself. The collection of ideas, suggestions and concepts can be evaluated, selected and refined in the following stages. Within the design stage, the OC's members can be involved as co-creator or co-designer [20]. In the test and launch stage (of product, services, processes), OC's members may take on the roles of end users or buyers. Thus, the innovative potential of OCs can be utilized throughout all stages of the innovation process. Moreover, by integrating selected OC members more than once or iteratively in different stages, these users may even get the status of development advisors which strengthens the idea of collective invention and trust building [21]. The idea generation mainly refers to the concept of knowledge exploration. However this knowledge have to be assimilated, transformed and exploited by a firm to be useful. To our knowledge, most chapters so far considered the exploitation task as mostly internal, without exploring the role played by the OC. Hence, there is a need for a model that explores the role of OCs not only for knowledge exploration but also for knowledge exploitation.

Absorptive capacity. The exploration and exploitation of external knowledge is linked to the concept of ACAP, defined as the collective abilities of a firm "to recognize the value of new information, assimilate it, and apply it to commercial ends" [3: 128]. Despite other several theoretical [22, 23] and empirical studies [24] of ACAP, this field is still under-investigated. Furthermore, while some studies try to explain and to refine the concept of ACAP, its determinants and consequences [25], there is still a lack of support in terms of ACAP assessment, especially related to the online environment. To a large extent this is probably due to the fact that the qualitative nature of ACAP makes it a very difficult concept to be measured quantitatively. Aimed at contributing to fill this gap, we start from the point that ACAP can positively influences innovation [26]. Therefore, trying to answer our RQ, we use an expanded definition of ACAP, re-conceptualized as a set of organizational routines and processes by which firms acquire, assimilate, transform, and exploit knowledge to produce a dynamic organizational capability [23]: (1) acquisition refers to a firm's capability to identify and acquire externally generated knowledge that is critical to its operations; (2) assimilation refers to the organizational routines and processes that allow it to analyze, process, interpret and understand the information obtained from external sources; (3) transformation denotes a firm's capability to develop and refine the routines that facilitate the combination of existing knowledge with newly acquired and assimilated knowledge; and (4) exploitation denotes the firm's ability to use consistently the new knowledge gained for commercial use over an extended period of time. Acquisition and assimilation provide the potential ACAP (PACAP) of the firm, close to the concept of explorative ability already proposed by March [17]. Transformation and exploitation provide the realized ACAP of the firm (RACAP), closer to the March's concept of exploitative ability [23]. Thus, PACAP and RACAP have complementary roles and this is consistent with the concept of 'ambidexterity' [17]. In fact, a firm, whose resource and possible investments are limited, can become agile and resilient managing well the trade-off and balancing these two innovation capabilities. An OC can be used by a firm as a knowledge source to expand its PACAP. Nevertheless, a high PACAP does not necessarily imply enhanced performance. RACAP involves transforming and exploiting the assimilated knowledge by incorporating it into the firm product, services and processes, thereby improving its performance (i.e., the cost or the time for innovation). In the end, reviewing the existing literature, we have identified the following gaps: (1) OCs are often identified as a source of 'idea exploration' but only recently they have been considered as candidate for 'idea exploitation'; (2) no metrics currently exist to assess the knowledge process for OC. Therefore, in the following section we are going to propose a model that relates to the OC's role in knowledge exploration and exploitation using a process view.

3 Method

According to Morgan view [27], we use the explicative power of metaphors to explain the process through which an OC's innovative idea is 'attracted' by a firm to be exploited for innovation purposes. We adopt the solar system metaphor illustrated in Fig. 1: the innovative idea can be seen as a meteor that crosses the solar system, which symbolizes the OC. In the centre, the sun represents the firm, which 'influences' all solar system activities. The planets of our systems symbolize the firm's 'experienced employees' (as individuals or groups), who verify the quality of ideas. All around the planets, there are some OC members, external to the firm's staff, who gravitate around them as satellites (because 'attracted' by topics they are interested in), forming clusters specialized in one or some topics of discussion. Clusters may be more or less stable (depending on the strength of the network ties and the permanent or temporary purposes they follow). The satellites, even if not so powerful as the planet in assessing the idea, can support the idea

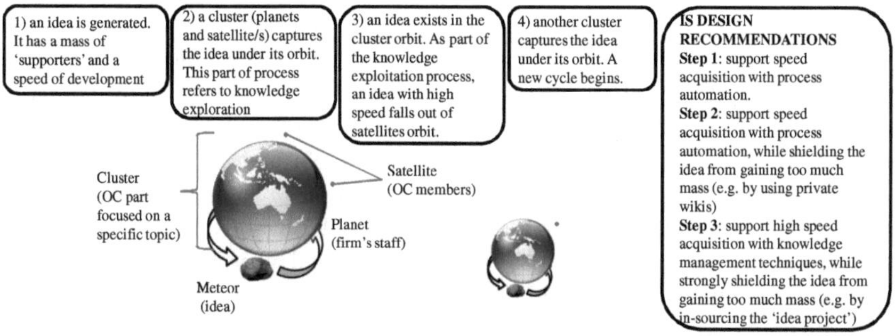

Fig. 1 Trip of a meteor (i.e., an idea) across the orbits of different planets (i.e., groups)

with their consensus (i.e., through feedbacks, comments, ratings and so forth), thus increasing the mass of the meteor.

In our metaphor the innovative idea/meteor can originate from outside the solar system and be attracted by the sun or through a more heuristic process, it can be generated from a satellite or, more probably, it can be the result of an encounter/collision among satellites. Each innovative idea/meteor has a mass, which we define as the number of supporters associated to it within an OC, and a speed in moving through the solar system, i.e., the time an idea takes to pass from exploration/conceptualization to exploitation. When the innovative idea/meteor passes close enough to the planet, it can be attracted by its gravity force, i.e., the 'constant effect' associated to an OC. This force is directly proportional to the fit between the cluster specialization and the topic of the innovative idea. It can be seen as a sort of 'absorptive capacity' of the cluster in recognizing the value of the idea. In other words, an idea is understood and caught by the cluster if there is a sufficient level of ACAP between the idea and that part of the OC. The cluster ability in effectively catching and maintaining the innovative idea depends upon the right balance between the meteor mass and speed. If the speed is too high and the mass too small (the consent among community members is not enough), the meteor goes out of the planet's orbit. If the speed is too low, the gravity force can drop the meteor to the planet, i.e., the idea is not perceived as sufficiently mature to be concretely exploited and stays as a simple proposal shared within the OC. Therefore, the correct match between planet and meteor characteristics leads to an effective exploitation of the idea for innovation purposes. This effectiveness is also influenced by the meteor 'distance' from the sun: if the innovative idea is too close the sun—that is, the idea is too little innovative and poor knowledge is gained,—it burns (it is dissipated); if the idea is too far—that is, the idea is too innovative and radical because of its knowledge content or too much disruptive with regard to the status quo, which represents the core business of the firm—the system is too 'cold' and the meteor cannot be 'attracted'. In brief, an idea can be no innovative at all, incremental or radical and ACAP acts at two different levels in our solar system. From one hand, the idea should be close enough to the topic of the cluster to be understood and caught. From the other hand, the idea should be close enough to the sun, the core of the firm (i.e., quite innovative but not too much disruptive). Through this interpretation, a firm could increase its explorative abilities improving its PACAP in two different ways. The first way is to act on the ability of the clusters in understanding and attracting innovative ideas. For example, this can be done working on planets' attractive power (i.e., through trainings of moderators, who play a key role within the idea evaluation process) or increasing the number of satellites, that support each planet through off-line and online activities (thus increasing the visibility of the OC). The second way is at firm level, i.e., trying to build clusters increasingly far from the sun, which might be able to catch more disruptive ideas for radical innovations.

4 Model

Our model has three constructs. The first one is **mass**, which we define as the number of supporters within an OC associated to an idea. This concept is linked to knowledge exploration and it is meant to measure the PACAP supported by the OC. The second constructs is **speed**, i.e., the time an idea takes to pass from conceptualization to development. This concept is linked to knowledge exploitation and it is meant as a proxy for RACAP supported by the OC. The third construct is the **software tool**, aimed to increase its ACAP. We start by testing the causal effect of speed over mass. Hence, our first hypothesis is: **the mass of an idea is proportional to its speed, with a fixed effect given by the fit between the idea and each planet (H1).** If the H1 is confirmed, a system that increases the speed, such as a process automation solution, will increase the performance of the process. Therefore, our second hypothesis is: **a software tool that increases the speed of an idea will increase its mass (H2).** One could assume an effect of reverse causality between speed and mass (ideas with large mass gets higher speed, whereas ideas with higher speed gets greater mass). We represent this claim using the constructs of software tool to obtain a mediation effect. Therefore, we claim that: **a software tool that increases the mass will increase the speed (H3).** To test our model we have developed a program written in Java, which analyses the posts in a forum. Forums are often associated to software that manages the users' feedbacks, which are usually used by companies to allow users to propose improvements for their products (or services). Our software currently focused on forums managed using the User Voice feedback management solution, and it is able to parse the (HTML) code of a page, to identify the different posts, to assign a unique identifier to each post and to extract the age of the post and the number of supporter to the post (i.e., people that vote it, or people that contributed with a comment). To support our three hypotheses we have used the Stata 10 statistical package to perform correlation analyses, linear regressions and quadratic regressions with fixed effect (using the xtreg function). In order to test our model we adopt a single case-study methodology [28], which is proper for the explorative aims of this study. As Lee and Baskerville [29] provided numerous examples, the belief that the study of a single case is undesirable or deficient is widespread among information systems researchers, even among case researchers themselves. However, requiring case study research to involve multiple sites or multiple cases for the sake of substantiating a theory is mistaken [30]. Since our study is currently ongoing, we test our model using second-hand data from Mendeley, a firm founded in November 2007 and based in London, which produces a free desktop and web program for managing and sharing research chapters, discovering research data and collaborating online. The software is combined with an online social network. The user base includes mainly affirmed academics, professional researchers, and students. Users are required to store all basic citation data on Mendely servers—storing copies of documents is at the user's discretion. Upon registration, 1 GB of free web storage space is provided, upgradeable at a cost. More than 163,000,000 chapters are shared and the network links more than 1,600,000 people and holds about 35,000 institutions as universities, business schools and research institutes. We chose Mendeley as case-study suitable for our aims because of the high number and quality of information available in its website, where user's feedbacks and suggestions are left to improve the firm processes/services. Suggestions can be classified in: (1) 'under review' by Mendeley staff; (2) 'accepted and planned' for future implementation; (3) 'accepted and transformed' in projects; (4) 'transformed' in completed projects; (5) 'refused'; (6) 'not taken into account' yet. Each suggestion can be voted and commented by other OC members. Our spider has extracted from the Mendley feedback page 1,297 posts (as of June 2012), which refer to ideas/projects that we classed into five groups: 170 under review; 214 accepted; 103 started; 678 completed; 132 declined. For each post we were able to extract the number of votes, which we associated to the idea's mass, and the idea's date of creation, which we associated to the speed. According to this choice, we took only the first three groups of ideas to avoid possible mistakes due to the lack of end date.

5 Results

For the three chosen groups of feedback posts, the distribution of the mass and the speed was skewed, with the mean and medians set respectively at 76 and 5 votes (for the mass) and 856 and 901 days (for the speed). Therefore, all the following analyses have been done using robust regressions. As shown in Table 1, there is an effect between mass and speed, which is statistically significant for the first three groups of posts on Mendeley ($p < 0.01$). We have also defined the fixed effect associated to each group, identified in our model as the different gravity forces of planets. Accordingly, the second group has a fixed effect on speed, which is negative, while the third group has a negative fixed effect which is even greater than the one of the second group. This occurrence can be easily explained by the fact that ideas takes more time to be reviewed than to be included in the overall development planning and developed.

Table 1 Overall and detailed analysis for hypothesis 1 and 2 (***$p < 0.01$; **$p < 0.05$; *$p < 0.1$)

Speed =	Overall (N = 486)	Overall (N = 486)	Step 1 (N = 170)	Step 2 (N = 214)	Step 3 (N = 103)
Mass	0.21***	0.45***	0.19	1.07***	0.55***
Mass^2		−0.0001***	−0.00002	−0.0004***	−0.0009***
Step 2	−76.35***	−78.74***			
Step 3	−136.44***	−136.44***			
Cons	902.10***	894.85***	905.28***	797.86***	748.59***
R2	0.10	0.12	0.03	0.13	0.18

Table 2 Overall and detailed analysis for hypothesis 3 (***$p < 0.01$; **$p < 0.05$; *$p < 0.1$)

Mass =	Overall (N = 486)	Overall (N = 486)	Step 1 (N = 170)	Step 2 (N = 214)	Step 3 (N = 103)
Speed	0.33***	−1.20***	−1.47	−0.68**	−2.44**
Speed^2		0.001***	0.001	0.0005**	0.002**
Step 2	28.51	8.05			
Step 3	122.12**	80.14			
Cons	−246.46***	316.12***	533.26	202.36*	601.11**
R2	0.08	0.13	0.06	0.10	0.27

Hence, one could say that **the first hypothesis is supported**. The third column of Table 1 shows that a polynomial regression has a greater explanatory power (as shown by the greater R2 associated to the second model). This quadratic effect corresponds to an inverted parabola. That implies the need to find a software tool to increase the mass until a certain level (the critical mass to achieve speed) and to avoid gaining too much mass (the beginning of internal disagreements within the community). Thus, one could say that **the second hypothesis is supported**. The following columns shows that the polynomial regression works best for the second and third step, which have an R2 greater than 0.10. As shown in Table 2, there is a reversed effect between speed and mass. By looking at the polynomial model, we see an increase in the R2 and the description of a normal parabola. That implies the need of a software tool to fine tune the speed of the idea (e.g., slow for brainstorming sessions, whereas fast during prototyping). Thus, one could say that **the third hypothesis is supported**. The following columns shows that the even this polynomial regression works best for the second and third step, which have an R2 greater than 0.10.

6 Conclusions

After having assessed the existing literature, we developed a model with three components (mass, speed and software tool) and empirically tested it. We refer to the principle of parsimony to justify our choice to initially limit our model to a few concepts. The results lead us to suggest that the system we envisage should have two main functions: (1) a 'booster' function that should automate the ideas scanning process and increase speed, whereas (2) a 'shield' function that should protect ideas from gaining too much mass in the second and third steps. Although preliminary and explorative single case-study, we believe our work represents a twofold contribution on open innovation. Firstly, **scholars can built on this new perception of knowledge as a trajectory across pole of attraction, rather than a linear process**. Secondly, **practitioners can profit from the specifications of a system, which has been already tested once, and whose specifications are grounded into existing theories**. We are aware of the limitations of our work. 'Mass' and 'speed' are naively described and are a poor simplification of the social dynamics surrounding the emergence of innovation in specific social groups. A deeper specification of the 'software tool' is needed. The measure of the 'fit with the planet' has to be deepened. And, what types of feedback do 'satellites' generate? A study in this direction would help to understand a possible insight into the relationship between exploitation and incremental innovations or exploration and radical innovations in the output of the OC. We also would explore in depth the types of ideas shared in the OC and their degree of innovativeness as well as the impacts on internal efficiency, data which are currently not available.

References

1. Chesbrough, H. W., & Crowther, A. (2006). Beyond high tech: Early adopters of open innovation in other industries. *R&D Management, 36*(3), 229–236.
2. Cassiman, B., & Veugelers, R. (2006). In search of complementarity in innovation strategy: internal R&D and external knowledge acquisition. *Management Science, 52*, 68–82.
3. Cohen, M. W., & Levinthal, D. A. (1990). Absorptive capacity: A new perspective on learning and innovation. *Administrative Science Quarterly, 35*, 128–152.
4. Dougherty, D. (1992). A practice-centered model of organizational renewal through product innovation. *Strategic Management Journal, 13*, 77–92.
5. Brown, S. L., & Eisenhardt, K. M. (1995). Product development: Past research, present findings, and future directions. *Academy of Management Review, 20*(2), 343–378.
6. Levitt, T. (1962). *Innovation in marketing: New perspectives for profit and growth*. New York: McGraw-Hill.
7. Utterback, J. (1971). Process of technological innovation within firm. *Academy of Management Journal, 14*(1), 75–88.
8. Daft, R. L. (1978). Dual-core model of organizational innovation. *Academy of Management Journal, 21*(2), 193–210.
9. Davenport, T. H. (1994). *Process innovation*. Boston: Harvard Business School Press.
10. Frambach, R. T., Barkema, H. G., Nooteboom, B., & Wedel, M. (1998). Adoption of a service innovation in the business market: An empirical test of supply-side variables. *Journal of Business Research, 41*(2), 161–174.
11. Tushman, M. L., & Anderson, P. (2004). *Managing strategic innovation and change: A collection of readings*. New York: Oxford University Press.
12. Swan, J., Scarbrough, H., & Robertson, M. (2002). The construction of "communities of practice" in the management of innovation. *Management Learning, 33*(4), 477–496.

13. Rogers, E. M. (1995). *Diffusion of innovations* (4th ed.). New York: Free Press.
14. Damanpour, F., & Schneider, M. (2006). Initiation adoption, and implementation of innovation: Effects of context, organization, and leaders. *British Journal of Management, 17*, 215–236.
15. Gupta, A. K., Tesluk, P. E., & Taylor, M. S. (2007). Innovation at and across multiple levels of analysis. *Organization Science, 18*, 885–897.
16. Van De Ven, A. H., & Poole, M. S. (1990). Methods for studying innovation development in the minnesota innovation research program. *Organization Science, 1*, 313–335.
17. March, J. G. (1991). Exploration and exploitation in organizational learning. *Organization Science, 2*(1), 71–87.
18. Sawhney, M., & Prandelli, E. (2000). Communities of creation: Managing distributed innovation in turbulent markets. *California Management Review, 42*(4), 24–54.
19. Piccoli G. (2012). *Information Systems for Managers: Texts and Cases*, (2nd ed). Wiley Publishing.
20. von Hippel, E. (2002). Horizontal innovation networks-by and for users. Working paper 4366-02, MIT Sloan School of Management (2002).
21. Prahalad, C. K., & Ramaswamy, V. (2000). Co-opting customer competence. *Harvard Business Review, 78*(1), 79–87.
22. Todorova, G., & Durisin, B. (2007). Absorptive capacity: Valuing a reconceptualization. *Academy of Management Review, 32*, 774–786.
23. Zahra, S. A., & George, G. (2002). Absorptive capacity: A review, reconceptualization, and extension. *Academy of Management Review, 27*, 185–203.
24. Jansen, J. J. P., Van den Bosch, F. A. J., & Volberda, H. W. (2005). Managing potential and realized absorptive capacity: How do organizational antecedents matter? *Academy of Management Journal, 48*, 999–1015.
25. Cadiz, D., Sawyer, J. E., & Griffith, T. L. (2009). Developing and validating field measurement scales for absorptive capacity and experienced community of practice. *Educational and Psychological Measurement, 69*, 1035–1058.
26. Newey, L. R., & Shulman, A. D. (2004). Systemic absorptive capacity: Creating early-to-market returns through R&D alliances. *R&D Management, 34*, 495–504.
27. Morgan, G. (1986). *Images of organization*. Beverly Hills: Sage.
28. Yin, R. K. (1994). *Case study reserach: Design and methods* (2nd ed.). CA: Sage Publications.
29. Lee, A. S., & Baskerville, R. (2003). Generalizing generalizability in information systems research. *Information Systems Research, 14*(3), 221–243.
30. Lee, A. S., & Hubona, G. S. (2009). Scientific basis for rigor in IS research. *Management Information Systems Quarterly, 33*(2), 237–262.

Developing Web-Based Dynamic Negotiation towards Collective Innovation: the Open Contract Mechanism

Alessandro Avenali, Giorgio Matteucci and Fabio Nonino

Abstract The scope of this chapter is to propose the design and the implementation of an innovative web-based tool, the Open Contract Mechanism (OCM). OCM allows client companies and suppliers to dynamically and simultaneously bargain the clauses and the characteristics of distinct innovation contracts in general open innovation and collaborative crowdsourcing environments. The OCM can be implemented inside open innovation web-based platforms for evaluating offers and determining the winning one, and therefore guaranteeing valuable binding contract clauses.

1 Introduction

Internet and the web-based technologies have facilitated the collaborative approaches for innovation enabling the emergence of large networks of potential contributors (i.e. the so-called "crowd"). A high number of new innovative enterprises promoted innovation and allowed the collaboration of individuals and companies and the so-called crowdsourcing through open innovation web-based platforms [2]. The most recent innovation model is then the collaborative crowdsourcing (also referred to as the collective innovation), which integrates the crowdsourcing approach with the open innovation paradigm [3]. The collective innovation process involves three typologies of actors: (1) the individuals or companies forming the crowd (workers, solvers and know-how providers), (2) the

A. Avenali (✉) · G. Matteucci · F. Nonino
Department of Computer, Control and Management Engineering "Antonio Ruberti", Sapienza University of Rome, Rome, Italy
e-mail: alessandro.avenali@uniroma1.it

G. Matteucci
e-mail: giorgio.matteucci@uniroma1.it

F. Nonino
e-mail: fabio.nonino@uniroma1.it

P. Spagnoletti (ed.), *Organizational Change and Information Systems*, Lecture Notes in Information Systems and Organisation 2, DOI: 10.1007/978-3-642-37228-5_21,

individuals or client companies (seekers) and (3) the open innovation intermediary platforms (OIPs) which act as brokers between the crowd and the seeker (e.g. Innocentive, NineSigma, CrowdSpring, etc.). The problem to reach an agreement on the quality and quantity of work to be performed among outsourcers and suppliers and on the value of the knowledge provided by solvers is typical to all markets and is often resolved through negotiation. But negotiation is not easily practicable in all situations. In open distributed markets, the work performed by any single worker is often vanishingly small. For this reason buyers' take-it-or-leave-it prices tend to predominate, and negotiations are rare [4]. Moreover open innovation and crowdsourcing requires web-based platform able to protect the intellectual property, but also to support the negotiation phase and the definition of terms of agreements in the contracts in order to motivate companies and individuals in participation both as seekers and solver and prevent disputes. A solution can came from patents, but patenting is costly and, in the collective innovation, the mechanisms for collecting and enforcing patent rights and licensing royalty income, are complex and impose high transaction costs. The user agreements and contracts should be used as a deterrent to opportunistic behaviour, while patents can be employed too late, i.e. in the final stages of the innovation process [1].

The objective of our research has been to design and to implement an innovative tool able to guarantee the solvers/providers that their ideas are protected in order to create a "win–win" scenario. The chapter presents the design (Sect. 2) and the implementation (Sect. 3) of the Open Contract Mechanism (OCM), an innovative web-based tool which allows innovation seekers and solvers to dynamically and simultaneously bargain the clauses and the characteristics of distinct innovation contracts in general open innovation and crowdsourcing collaborative environments. Finally, we draws conclusions (Sect. 4).

2 The Design of the Open Contract Mechanism

The design of OCM starts from a general open innovation and crowdsourcing scenario where an organization (from now on referred to as seeker) does not possess specific skills and technical knowledge (hereinafter referred to as know-how items) which are crucial for an innovation or for a part of NPD project (e.g. work, solutions to problems, patents, licenses, prototypes). Using the OCM tool the seeker can acquire these missing know-how items by posting a *challenge* inside an open innovation platform, where selected organizations and individuals (hereinafter referred to as solvers) are requested to submit bids to provide their work or know-how according to some conditions specified by the seeker. In particular, the seeker can specify the quantity demanded, the required quality, the terms of delivery, of warranty and of payment and clauses to safeguard possible intellectual property rights. Moreover, in order to select reliable solvers both in terms of owned know-how and economic performances, the seeker can impose agreements which strictly require solvers with suitable characteristics (special certifications, constraints in term of key financial ratios, etc.). To avoid solvers' post-contractual opportunistic behaviour, the agreements can be enforced by an appropriate set of penalties for not fulfilling the related undertakings. There exist different ways of exchanging skills and technical knowledge between the seeker and the solvers: sell of existing patents, licensing, development and patenting of the design of a crucial input described in terms of abstract and general ideas and/or a fixed amount of money to solve a specific technical problem. Furthermore the OCM allows the seeker and the solvers to bargain the features of an innovation contract (contract amendments) by applying an *open contract model.*

2.1 Design of the Seeker and Solvers Client Side

The seeker clicks on OCM tool which displays two sections, respectively labelled "My contracts" and "My bids". In the first section, the tool permits the seeker to create a new challenge to acquire know-how items. The challenge will allow the seeker to acquire all the specified know-how items from exactly one solver after a competition among all solvers invited by the seeker (possibly suggested by a suitable procedure based on the semantic engine of the OIP which selects potential solvers on the basis of the keywords representing the know-how items desired).

In the second section the seeker can:

- Monitor the current round of a challenge which the seeker himself has created. Since it is still running, the challenge is referred to as an *open challenge*.
- Look through a challenge created by him and that is ended. Since there are no more rounds, the challenge is referred to as a *closed challenge*.
- On the solver side the OCM displays a section where the solver:
- Attends the current round of an open challenge which a seeker has created and which the solver is taking part in.
- Attends the amending phase of an open challenge which the seeker has created and which the solver is taking part in.
- Attends the *boarding phase* (namely, the period when the invited solvers are accepting or rejecting the invitation to take part in the challenge) of a challenge and which the solver has been invited to take part in.
- Can investigate whether there are or not new challenges (still in the boarding phase) which the solver could be interested in. The tool allows the solver to contact the seeker in order to be invited before the boarding phase ends.

2.2 Process Description

The OCM functioning can be divided in three phases: (a) the creation, (b) the boarding and (c) the negotiation. During the *creation phase* the tool allows the seeker to define:

- The name of the challenge and a description of the required know-how items.
- A bunch of keywords related to every know-how item.
- The maximum number of rounds of the challenge. In every round the seeker and the solvers will bargain contract features. The challenge ends after a given maximum number of rounds. However, depending on the competition level among solvers, the challenge can end in a fewer number of rounds.
- The maximum running time of any round of the challenge. Each round automatically ends after a given maximum time.
- The timetable of the challenge, that is, the beginning and the end of the boarding phase, of the amending phase, and the beginning of the 1st round.

At the end of the creation phase the OCM asks the seeker to design the contract scheme (see Sect. 2.3). Once the contract scheme is definitively carried out, OCM allows the seeker to invite the solvers to take part in the challenge. When the list of all solvers to be invited is ready, the seeker can write a letter of invitation. Then, the tool automatically contacts all the solvers and communicates them the seeker's letter of invitation. Then the *boarding phase* starts and the OCM tool waits for the solvers answering to the seeker's invitation. The tool displays to any invited solver the list of the names of the open challenges which he has been invited to take part in and which are in the boarding phase. Once solver has clicked on the challenge he is interested in, the tool allows him to accept or to reject the invitation. At the end of the boarding phase, the OCM contacts the seeker providing the list of the solvers who have accepted the invitation. The tools don't provide this list to any solver so as to reduce collusion among solvers. Subsequently the *amending sub-phase* begins the tools waits for the solvers submitting their amendments. When the amending phase is over the seeker decides which amendments can be accepted and which ones have to be rejected. Afterwards the tool communicates the definitive formulation of the contract scheme to any solver and no information about which solvers have proposed the submitted amendments (so as to reduce collusion among solvers). Then, when it is the time for the beginning of the *negotiation phase*, the tool contacts the solvers and informs them for the beginning of the first round. For any current round the tool waits for the solvers submitting their contract bids. If any solver has definitely carried out his contract bids (or quit the challenge), or the maximum running time of the round is over, the tool stops the current round. Then the tool compute a *score* for every submitted contract bid (see Sect. 2.4). At the end of the negotiation phase the tool communicates:

- To the seeker, the details of the winning contract bid and of the solver.
- To the solver who has submitted the winning contract bid, the details of the winning contract bid.
- To all other solvers, the details of the winning contract bid and no information regarding which solver has submitted the winning contract bid (so as to reduce collusion among solvers).

2.3 Contract Design

The tool allows the seeker to design the *contract schemes* to acquire all the desired know-how items and provide their details. In particular:

The seeker uploads files which can be applied (inserting links in the contract scheme) to design the clauses (i.e. ".pdf", ".avi") and enclosed in the contract. Any contract clause, which makes up the contract scheme, is a string.

Every contract clause can also be parametric. The seeker can insert parameters, that is, unspecified quantitative data of the clauses which every invited solver will specify through values selected among those the seeker has defined as feasible. In order to highlight which parameters are more crucial than others, the seeker assigns a weight to each introduced parameter. Therefore, if r is the overall number of parameters which characterize the contract scheme and $w_i \geq 0$ are the weight associated by the seeker to parameter i for $i = 1, \ldots, r$; the weights decided by the seeker are subject to the constraint $\sum_{i=1}^{r} w_i = 1$. For any parameter, the seeker has to specify if the parameter is ascendant (descendent), in the sense that the higher (the lower) the parameter, the better the resulting contract scheme for the seeker. The seeker has also to specify which values can be taken into account for it (the feasible values for the parameter); to do this, the seeker associates to any parameter i a lower bound lb_i, an upper bound ub_i and a minimum step ms_i. Consequently, if parameter i is ascendant the tool will show in the drop-down menu of the parameter all and only these values (ordered from the lowest value to the highest):

$$\begin{gathered} lb_i + 0 \cdot ms_i \\ lb_i + 1 \cdot ms_i \\ \vdots \\ lb_i + f_i \cdot ms_i \end{gathered}$$

where $f_i = \frac{ub_i - lb_i}{ms_i}$.

If the parameter is descendant the tool will show in a drop-down menu of the parameter all these numbers (ordered from the highest value to the lowest):

$$\begin{gathered} ub_i - 0 \cdot ms_i \\ ub_i - 1 \cdot ms_i \\ \vdots \\ ub_i - f_i \cdot ms_i \end{gathered}$$

where $f_i = \frac{ub_i - lb_i}{ms_i}$.

For example, let us assume that the know-how item is the production of a specific component which has been designed by capital company Solinnovation. The component is critical, but the expected demand is highly uncertain. The seeker Solinnovation proposes a challenge to negotiate the risk sharing between the seeker and the solver who will produce the component. Solinnovation defines a contract scheme (Fig. 1), where Clause 7 contains links to some enclosed files, while clauses 12 and 13 are parametric (in the example all and only the parameters of the contract scheme are those proposed by the seeker in these two clauses).

2.4 Bid Score Calculation

The score of a bid is computed as follows:

- Let l be the number of solvers who have submitted bids in the current round. Let d_k be the number of contract bids submitted by solver k in current round for

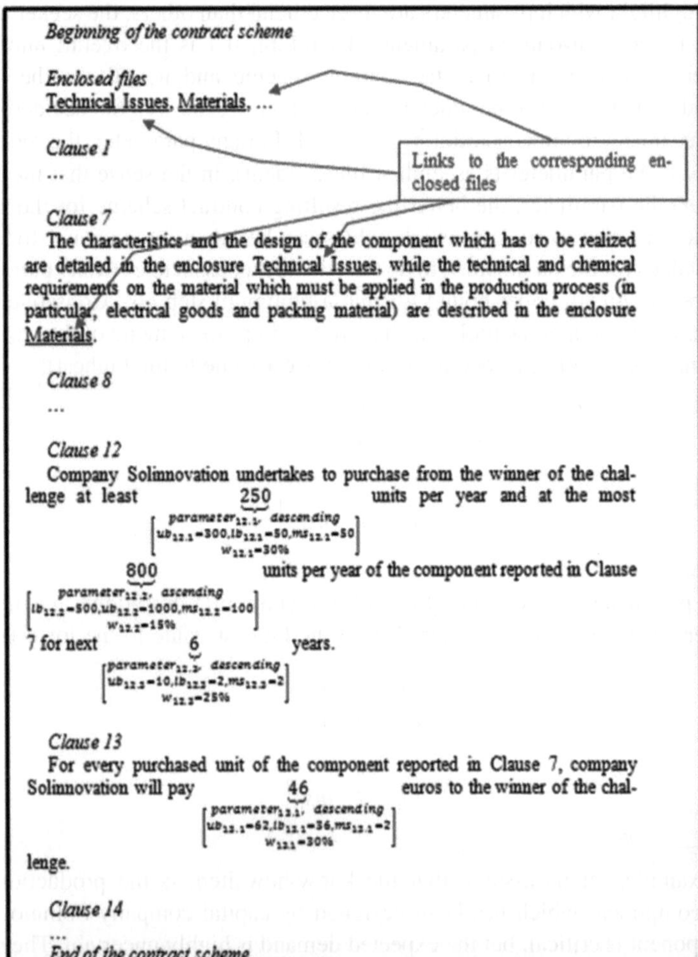

Fig. 1 Example of a contract scheme

$k = 1, \ldots, l$, and let $d = d_1 + \cdots + d_l$ be the overall number of contract bids submitted by all solvers in current round. Let $k(j)$ denote the solver who has submitted bid j. Every contract bid j for $j = 1, \ldots, d$ consists of an ordered list of values $(v_{1,j}, \ldots, v_{r,j})$, where any $v_{i,j}$ for $i = 1, \ldots, r$ is the value offered, by solver $k(j)$, in contract bid j for parameter i. First, the OCM computes for $i = 1, \ldots, r$ both average m_i and standard deviations σ_i of the values offered for parameter i by all solvers. For $i = 1, \ldots, r$, the OCM computes:

$$m_i = \frac{\sum_{j=1,\ldots d} v_{i,j}}{d} \qquad \sigma_i = \sqrt{\frac{\sum_{j=1,\ldots d} \left(v_{i,j} - m_i\right)^2}{d}}$$

- The OCM defines the new weights of the parameters ($\overline{w}_i = w_i$ if parameter i is ascendant and $\overline{w}_i = -w_i$ if parameter i is descendant).
- Then, the tool sets the score of contract bid j equal to:

$$sc_j = \sum_{i=1}^{r} \overline{w}_i \frac{v_{i,j} - m_i}{\sigma_i}$$

Among all bids which have been stored so far (i.e. from the beginning of the challenge until this round), the tools select as winning the contract bid with the highest score (ties are broken randomly).

3 The Open Contract Mechanism (OCM) Tool

The OCM has been implemented as a standalone web-based tool which can be integrated inside an OIP. The overall architecture is depicted in Fig. 2.

OCM has been implemented using a web service approach where a number of HTTP verbs have been developed implementing the basic operations that are needed in order to create, manipulate and negotiate contracts. The communication between the client and the server through HTTP is performed with the exchange of appropriate JSON documents. Everything in the OCM data model is built around the concept of the contract. Inside the contract, a number of metadata are defined, e.g. information regarding the seeker, a list of solvers that the seeker decides to call to participate and a number of parameters that constitute the negotiable values of the contract. These entities are related to the contract creation and boarding phases. Finally, for the modelling of the negotiation phase, the concept of round is introduced. The final element is the scheduler. The various phases and the rounds of the negotiation are defined by a starting and ending time provided by the seeker. At the beginning of each round specific actions have to be performed, e.g. the change of the contract status from creation to boarding and from boarding to negotiation. These kinds of actions are performed by the scheduler in pre-defined time intervals based on the values provided by the seeker during the contract

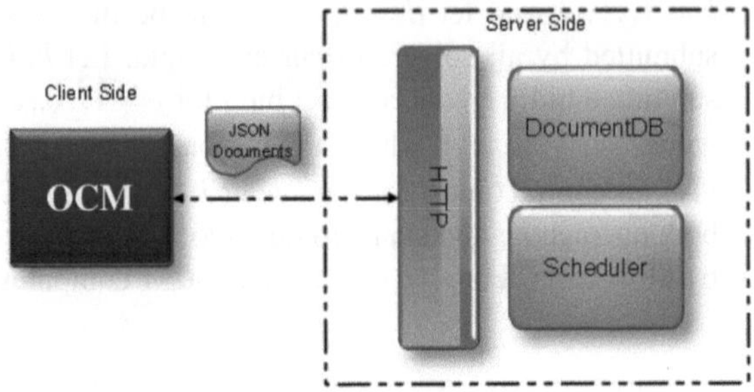

Fig. 2 The open contract mechanism overall architecture

creation. A relational database is used to store the jobs. The current version of the OCM consists of the three distinct phases described below.

3.1 Creation Phase

During this phase the seeker defines all the defined parameters of a contract and invites the potential solvers who would participate in the negotiation of the specific contract. The contract creation phase consists of four distinct sub-phases:

1. Creation of a new contract with a title and a brief description (Fig. 3–left).
2. Definition of an arbitrary number of parameters that will be negotiated for the contract together with their attributes (Fig. 3–center).
3. Selection of the potential solvers who will participate in the negotiation.
4. Definition of the number of rounds the negotiation phase will have, when the boarding phase will start and end and the duration of each negotiation round.

3.2 Boarding Phase

During the boarding phase, when the user submits the newly created contract, two scheduled jobs are created: one for the initialization of the phase and one for its conclusion. Both the date and time for these two states are provided by the seeker

Fig. 3 Contract creation, definition of parameters and of the number of rounds (screenshots)

during the creation phase. When the scheduled job is fired, a number of e-mails are sent to the candidate solvers. The status of the solver has three potential states, (a) pending, (b) accepted and (c) rejected. Initially the system assigns the state pending. By either accepting or rejecting the participation, the user alters the status either as accepted or rejected. At the end of boarding phase, another scheduled job is fired and the invited solvers are scanned. If their status is still in pending state, it is changed into rejected, while if no one accepted the invitation, then the current state of the contract is changed into closed and the whole procedure ends. If one or more potential solvers have accepted the invitation, the status of contract changes into negotiation.

3.3 Negotiation Phase

During the negotiation phase the actual process of negotiating a contract is performed. Initially the seeker is able to create a new negotiation round (Fig. 4–center). When this happens a new scheduled job is created and scheduled using the round duration provided by the seeker at the creation phase. During the creation of a new negotiation round, notifications are sent to the solvers so they can submit new offers for the current negotiation round. The solvers can create new offers using the OCM interface. After deciding about the values of each parameter, they are able to submit their offers (Fig. 4–right). At the end of the round the scheduled job is fired and a number of actions occur; initially the system parses all the offers together with any past winning offers and calculates the various scores based on the scoring algorithm (see 2.4).

On the basis of these scores the winner is retrieved and then the system sends e-mails and notification to both the seeker and the solvers. The mail to the seeker contains all the details regarding the last negotiation round together with the information about the current winner. The solvers receive an e-mail which contains only the information of the winning contract but without the credentials of the winning solver. At this point the seeker can initiates again a new negotiation round unless all the solvers have left the negotiation phase: in this case the winner is found and the contract status changes to closed.

Fig. 4 Notification for participating in the negotiation of a contract, initiation of a new negotiation round and creation and submitting an offer (screenshots)

4 Conclusions

The open contract mechanism can be implemented inside open innovation web-based platforms, or directly used by the companies. OCM can become a powerful tool for evaluating offers and determining the winning one, and therefore guaranteeing valuable binding contract clauses. Moreover it can enhance confidence in decision making and flexibility in dealing with negotiation issues developing the company's ability to confront with the complexity of the collective innovation in open innovation web-based platforms. On the basis of several simulations run up to now using the software prototype developed, we found improvements achieved in negotiation performance in terms of reduction of purchasing costs and increase of quality and quantity of know-how items acquired.

Acknowledgments The research leading to these results has received funding from the European Community's Seventh Framework Programme managed by REA-Research Executive Agency http://ec.europa.eu/research/rea [(FP 7—SME 2008—2)] under grant agreement n [243593], project COLLECTIVE—Emerging communities for collective innovation: ICT Operational tool and supporting methodologies for SME Associations. For details, see www.collectiveproject.eu.

References

1. Avenali, A., Matteucci, G., & Nonino, F. (2010). *Contract clause dynamic bargaining and procurement design*. In: Proceedings of the International Public Procurement Conference 26–28 Aug 2010, Seoul, Korea.
2. Battistella, C., & Nonino, F. (2012). "What drives collective innovation?—Exploring the system of drivers for motivations in open innovation, web-based platforms". Information Research, Vol. 17, No. 1, paper 513, Univ. Sheffield, Dept. Information Studies, Western Bank, Sheffield, UK.
3. Chesbrough, H. (2003). *Open innovation: The new imperative for creating and profiting from technology*. Boston: Harvard Business School Press.
4. Horton, J.J. & Zeckhauser, R.J. (2010). *Algorithmic wage negotiations: Applications to paid crowdsourcing*. In: Proceedings of CrowdConf, 4 Oct 2010, San Francisco, CA.

Using Social Network as Organizational Storytelling: A Narrative Analysis of Dooced Employees' Blogs

Giuseppe Scaratti and Michela Cortini

Abstract The present chapter aims at analysing the narratives of dooced bloggers. Doocing is the name we use to mean "to be fired from job for something written on or posted within a personal blog"; a name in honour of the www.dooce.com blog owned by a worker who has been fired in 2002 for having written something about her workplace her organization did not like at all. We have collected 10 blogs of dooced employees, 5 female and 5 male and we have analysed, in comparative terms their narratives after having been dooced. In particular, we present both a discourse analysis and a content analysis of the textual material we have collected. We have done the analysis of metaphors and the analysis of word occurrences and co-occurrences. For what concerns the results, it is interesting to note the different guilty perceptions and the narrative analysis of the events causing doocing.

Keywords Blogs · Doocing · Narrative analysis

1 Employee Blogs and Doocing: Definitions and a Critical View

By employee blogs we refer to personal blogs where individuals talk as corporate employees or by personal blogs where the blogger makes continuous reference to her/his working experiences, talking also about her/his organization. These blogs, even if they are not official corporate tools, communicate company images, which may be in some cases very different from the desiderata of the company itself.

G. Scaratti (✉)
Università Cattolica del Sacro Cuore, Milan, Italy

M. Cortini
Università di Chieti, Pescara, Italy

P. Spagnoletti (ed.), *Organizational Change and Information Systems*, Lecture Notes in Information Systems and Organisation 2, DOI: 10.1007/978-3-642-37228-5_22,

Since employees' blogs do not transmit official communications of the company but rather the personal view of employees, they are, and for some researchers, they should be [1], deeply controlled by organizations themselves [2]. From the employers' point of view, this pretty unfair behaviour is justified making reference to the possibility that an unsatisfied or even tired worker may express a very bad picture of themselves, very often not conformed to the truth [3]. Concerning the possibility of saying something true or untrue in a blog post, we have to cite the case of counter-employer-blogs or defamatory blogs, about a corporation, individuals, or a competitor that may lead to libel suits [4]. In this sense corporations have been improving an additional alternative to internal employees blogs and to blog monitoring, or blog policies, that is to say doocing, namely "to be fired from job for something written on or posted within a personal blog"; a name in honour of the www.dooce.com blog owned by a worker who was fired in 2002 for writing about her workplace [4].

Doocing, of course, has a pretty pragmatic value in order to prevent other employees from doing the same but, with such behaviour, the employer may, in turn, lose its attractiveness for potential employees and lose its ability to retain skilled employers, showing lack of the possibility to express oneself. Also for the above cited reason, even if there have been a lot of dooced employees [4], it is still a matter of discussion if it is opportune or not, from a corporation point of view, to terminate an employee because of something said in a personal blog.

2 The Research Design and the Rationale for Adopting a Mix-Method Approach

When we talk about a mixed-method approach or triangulation [5], we refer to the idea of melting different points of view and perspectives, by using different researchers, different research paradigms or different data analysis tools.

By proposing the triangulation of methods, we intend to propose a third way which is rarely approached and estimated, beyond the qualitative and quantitative analysis.

The first proposal of triangulation has been, at least at our knowledge, that of Wilson, who states: "qualitative and quantitative approaches are complementary rather than competitive methods (…and the) use of a particular method (…) rather must be based on the nature of the actual problem at hand" [6, p. 58].

In 1990 Patton [7] deepened this idea with the so called *methodological appropriateness*, according to which the choice for a specific analysis tool or technique has to respond not to the researcher's limits but rather to the reality; in other words, it is the object of analysis to suggest the right method. For what concerns in particular the analysis of doocing, it seems to us particularly interesting to adopt a mix method approach on the same textual dataset, made up by the posts of different dooced bloggers. In other words, on a corpus which is qualitative in nature, we have used 2 different analysis paths; the first one refers to a classical discourse analysis approach, with a particular reference to the critical tradition; the latter, on the other hand, refers to the content analysis, which can be meant as a particular quantitative analysis (based on different word-association indexes) done on the basis of a qualitative data set like texts do represent. In different words, with the discourse analysis we will focus mainly on the ways specific concepts are transferred and narrated, while with the content analysis we will focus on the most represented word associations.

The corpus of data is made up by the transcriptions of all the blog posts written by 10 dooced bloggers concerning the phenomenon of doocing; we chosen the blogs with the idea of collecting data from employees of different kind of organizations (universities, ICT companies, etc.)

3 Results of the Discoursive Analysis

For what concerns the critical discourse analysis, it seems to us important to remark, at least, 2 different interpretations emerging from the data analysis. In addition, it appears important for dooced people to celebrate the dooced day, as it is evident in the following examples.

Example 1 "This week marks one year since I was "dooced."

This need of remarking the day during which the dooced employee has fund out of having being fired frames the dooced people as victims, or better popular saints (example 2) and it seems a way to let this event become eternal, something to celebrate, or better something that has to be remembered in order to become something useful.

Example 2 "That's blogworld parlance for being outed and fired from one's job for something written on a blog. A blogger named **Heather B. Armstrong** coined the term and she serves as a sort of patron saint of anonymous bloggers."

Concerning the name "doocing", which is in honour of the above mentioned dooced blogger, it is interesting to note that someone in the blogsphere has tried to change the name for being fired due to own blog by adopting his name Karl, and litterally proposing to use "karling" (example 3), something that stresses the narcissistic vein of every blogging phenomenon.

Example 3 "But the fact of the matter remains that Dooce inadvertently coined the term "dooced" when she got fired from her job... she got it on the ground floor, so to speak. Now anytime someone gets fired because of their blog, they call it getting dooced. I'm here to change that. From now on, we are going to call it getting karled".

Finally, it is important to show how dooced bloggers search for the audience support and, in some sense, live by the post and comments the readers send (example 4).

Example 4 "Did I suffer from the doocing? Can't say I have. The university tried to shame me, but failed. They couldn't keep me from getting another teaching job (part-time but wonderful). And they only exposed their own hypocrisy in trying to punish me.

My community of readers has grown beyond my craziest expectations. And your encouragement is the honey on the biscuit. When I get mail from Lebanon, Israel, Ireland, New Zealand, Canada—golly, y'all. I don't know how you found me, but I'm glad you did".

3.1 Results of the Content Analysis

Before going into deep details of analysis, it is important to remark that the analysis unit is the singular lemma with its co-occurrences and that we have prepared our text for analysis doing what is known under the name of *lemmatization*, which gives a reorganization of the T-LAB database, creating different tables used to analyze data; in particular the idea is that of cluster together words that have the same meaning root, like for example "family" and "familial". Such an operation, of course, has been done only for the words (lemmas or categories) considered interesting for the subsequent analyses, like work, training, and so on.

3.2 Results of the Analysis of Word Occurrence and Co-occurrence

The most cited word is "blog", with 60 occurrences; besides the mere datum of occurrences, it is interesting to analyse in detail the relationships of the word "blog", the so-called co-occurrences (Fig. 1, where words with high cosine coefficients are displayed closed one another in the multidimensional space); it is important here to remark that in the multidimensional space the more 2 words are closed one another the highest is their co-occurence in the text under analysis.

For what concerns the associations of the most cited word, "blog", it is important to stress the high association with "tell", "think", "comment" and "story" (respectively Cosine's coefficient of 0.25, 0.24, 0.32 and 0.32), associations which, in turn, stress the idea that blogging is a need for the employees, especially after a docking phenomenon.

It is interesting to note that actually few words make explicit references to the employer (just the word "employer" with a Cosine's coefficient of 0.29), like the

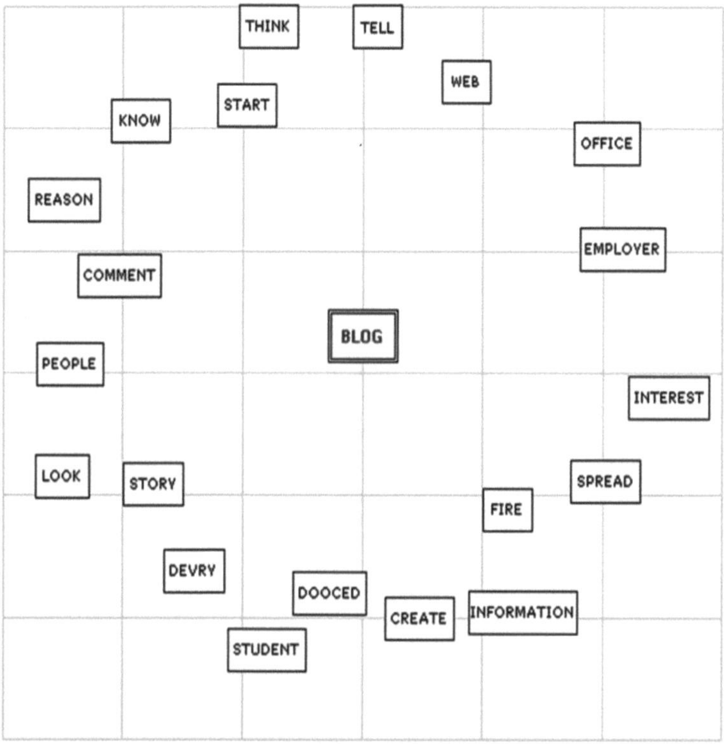

Fig. 1 The association of the word "Blog"

dooced blogger would like to exert her/his power of giving importance and live to the words she/he states, and silencing the employer, saying nothing about it seems to us more an attacking strategy rather than a defensive one (remember the dooced employees have been actually fired out and in such a sense after the doocing they have not to worry about what they say) (Fig. 2).

For what concerns the association of the stimulus word "dooced", it is interesting to note the high Cosine's coefficient of 0.32 with the word "blog", which is actually pretty auto-evident since blogging is the cause of doocing. In addition, "dooced" presents an high association with "job" (Cosine's coefficient of 0.29), "fired"(Cosine's coefficient of 0.24). Finally, it is interesting to note the high association with the word "today" (Cosine's coefficient of 0.21), and with a series of words that refer to the dimension of storytelling (like, for example, "story", with a Cosine's's coefficient of 0.19 and "comment" with a Cosine's coefficient of 0.19). This last result seem to show the need for storytelling and outing concerning the fact related to doocing, like writing on becomes a first way to cope with the fact of having been fired.

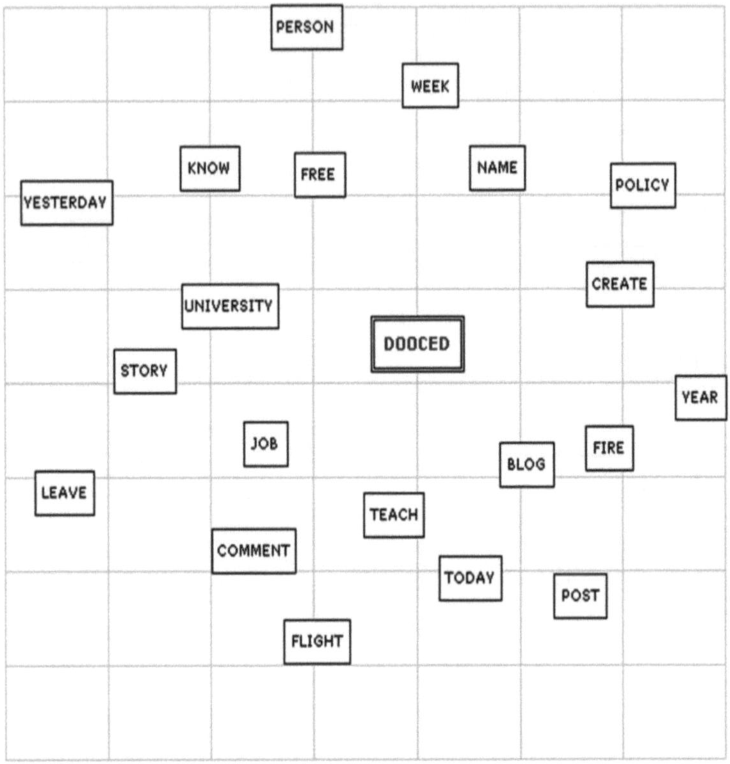

Fig. 2 The association of the word "Dooced"

4 Conclusion and Future Research Agenda

We have analysed the personal blogs of 10 dooced employees, adopting a mix-method approach of narrative analysis, based on the one hand on critical discourse analysis and on the other one on content analysis.

It emerges the need for expressing own personal experiences and for having some form of support by the audience, clearly marked by the co-occurrence of the word "doocing", which is represented, very often, in the form of storytelling. By using the framework of stories, the blogger "forces" the event of doocing within the storytelling categories, such as the hero (herself/himself) and the villain (the employer), in order to depict in a clear way the causal attributions.

In terms of future research agenda, it would be useful, beside the effort of enlarging our sample of participants, to collect additional data on blog policies and to collect data about employer perspectives on doocing. In particular, an important question arises concerning blog policies: is it really possible to prevent doocing by adopting them? And if so, how can this employer control over employee speech be managed within the framework of ethical and philanthropic concerns able to not impede free self-expression? Elsewhere we have proposed blog policies as a valid alternative to doocing, a sort of psychological contract by which employees know what they can and cannot say on their personal blogs, in order to avoid getting fired from work for something related to blog activities [3], now it would be useful to better understand how employees and employers consider and actually use blog policies.

References

1. Scott, A. (2005). *Blogging and your corporate reputation: Part one- listen to the conversation*. Factiva: Dow Jones and Reuters.
2. Cortini, M. (2008). From corporate websites to corporate weblogs: New frontiers of organizational communication. *International Journal of Knowledge, Culture and Change Management, 2*, 1–8.
3. Cortini, M. (2009). New horizons in CSP and employee/employer relationship: Challenges and risks of corporate weblogs. *Employee Responsibilities and Rights Journal, 21*, 291–303.
4. Mercado-Kierkegaard, S. (2006). Blogs, lies and doocing: the next hotbed of litigation? *Computer Law and Security Report, 22*(2), 127–136.
5. Fielding, N. G., & Fielding, J. (1986). *Linking data*. London: Sage.
6. Wilson, T. (1981). Qualitative "versus" quantitative methods in social research. In: Küchler, M. et al. Integration von qualitativen und quantitativen Forschungsansätzen (pp. 21–35), Zuma, Mannheim.
7. Patton, M. Q. (1990). *Qualitative evaluation and research methods*. Newbury Park: Sage.

Part IV
Information Systems, Innovation Transfer, and New Business Models

How Small and Medium Healthcare Assistance Structures Should Leverage Cloud Computing Technology for Optimizing Their Processes and Reducing Costs

Gustavo Barresi and Massimo Villari

Abstract Cloud Computing is becoming the most famous *buzz term* in the IT world. It is causing a high level of expectation for Quality Of Life improvements that may derive from its wide usage on more human activities. In the near future, also IT in the healthcare scenarios should deal with Cloud Computing. However for hospitals, medical centers, healthcare assistance structures it is not easy at all to deploy all services on cloud due to the Security and Private constrains. Looking at efforts recently pursued from World Wide IT standardization boards, a markable convergence on cloud standards is noticed, thus for encouraging the cloud adoptions in many fields. We strongly believe even the healthcare contexts might benefit of clouds. This chapter represents the description of a first approach of Cloud Resources utilization in the context of e-Health management. In particular a real use case is described where to provide basic solutions easily applicable in more similar scenarios.

Keywords e-Health · Cloud computing · Datacenter optimization · Medical cares

1 e-Health Evolution

The use of IT is, by now, widespread in all human activities. In the healthcare field, in particular, it is helped not only by the ever faster evolution of information and communication technology (ICT), but also by a set of variable, dynamic intrinsic values within the system (see [1]). With regard to services offered, the

G. Barresi (✉) · M. Villari
University of Messina, Piazza Pugliatti I, Messina, Italy
e-mail: barresig@unime.it

M. Villari
e-mail: mvillari@unime.it

P. Spagnoletti (ed.), *Organizational Change and Information Systems*, Lecture Notes in Information Systems and Organisation 2, DOI: 10.1007/978-3-642-37228-5_23,

dynamics of change are complex and mixed, fundamentally involving organizational models of the healthcare system. In this setting, we have seen, for some years now, the destructuralization of welfare processes. The system is further fragmented into a system of micro-phases, which while being part of a single diagnostic-therapeutic course, tends to acquire an "identity" of its own, by virtue of specificity of competence, structure and technology used. Along with recourse to increasingly specialist technologies and healthcare skills, this dynamic evolution renders the capacity of healthcare structures to manage collection, selection and distribution systems of information, all the more crucial. It is through communication that exchanges take place between operators, who, in different contexts and times, are involved in different areas of the welfare process. The evolution of IT systems, hence, allowing participation of an unknown number of specialists in increasingly intangible diagnostics and care, has widened the traditional boundaries of the welfare process, to the point of making it potentially indefinite (see [2]). An even sharper and more radical driver of change has been the way in which patients have participated in these processes. Today, and even more so in the future, they have taken on an active role, of organic producer of information for the system. This can be traced back to the progressive de-hospitalization of some welfare processes, with the aim of an increasing amount of services being directly managed in the patients home. All western healthcare systems have seen hospital assistance costs raising, hence the current priority given to services, which allow home care. Thus, new types of services are emerging, stemming from the concept of diagnostic and therapeutic self-administration (see [3]). Information sharing, thanks to the Internet, has thus led to many new approaches to management of disease, deriving from User Generated Care (UGC) and User Generated Health (UGH), already consolidated in many contexts. In this scenario of rapid, deep transformation we define e-health as an emerging field in the intersection of medical informatics, public health and business, referring to health services and information delivered or enhanced through the Internet and related technologies.

1.1 Why Healthcare ICT Should Benefit of Cloud Infrastructure

Cloud Computing can be seen as a new way for providing services hiding the actual implementation. We are assisting at cloud offerings for computation, storage and networking at three levels (IaaS, PaaS and SaaS). Nowadays on-site installations constitute a considerable cost-factor both in terms of capital expenditure (CAPEX) as well operational costs (OPEX). Cloud computing allows to scale storage infrastructures on-demand as well as the integration of several stakeholders. Example many mobile devices are producing a lot of sensing data [4]. The healthcare domain, however, has particular requirements which may prevent the utilization of current cloud systems. Privacy, confidentiality, data mobility, availability are quality attributes which play a minor role in most current cloud applications, yet are mandatory for the healthcare domain. Moreover, complex data models and specific access patterns on large volumes of data rely on certain capabilities of the cloud infrastructure. This chapter is aimed at describing a first approach for the deployment of medical ICT services on Cloud, focusing on IaaS level. It represents the starting layer where it is possible to leverage cloud resources. Furthermore this layer strongly exploits the virtualization of these physical resources (Virtual Machine—VMs—deployed at IaaS level). In this shape, IaaS ensures high elasticity in the usage of available resources, thus determining higher efficiency to all e-Health activities.

2 Aims and Methodology

This work represents an investigation activity aimed at the partial deployment of medical cares IT system on cloud computing. The focus is on considering Small and Medium Healthcare Assistance Structures (SMHASs) who often provide support to public healthcare infrastructures (i.e. Hospitals and Medical Centers) for a subset of health processes. The work we are dealing with is rather different of the cloud model in which a common platform is shared with more heath cares operators (see Google Health [5], Microsoft HealthVaulth [6], etc.).

Our analysis has been carried out through the observation of a small-sized hospital, characterized for its noted use of ICT in the healthcare services offering. It is therefore a qualitative analysis, carried out through a case study, aimed at verifying potentialities and opportunities arising from use of cloud computing in a hospital setting. The use of case studies to construct theories has been well studied in literature (see [7–9]). In particular, Eisenhardt proposes organizing constructed theories starting from case studies in the wider field of the methodology of social science research, highlighting strengths and weaknesses (see [2]). In this framework, the case study approach can be defined in different ways. In Eisenhardts definition, it can be intended as a research strategy which focuses on understanding the dynamics present within a single setting. With regard to the case in hand, a case study approach was adopted according to Yins suggestions. This method appeared to be coherent with the specific research question assumed in this chapter. Moreover, the approach is frequently used, as it can be particularly apt in studying the implementation of IT-based organizational contexts.

In the next section, the early part describes the healthcare structures highlighting its activities and aims, whereas in the latter part, its IT infrastructure is presented. We remark, the IT under assessment represents the typical IT backbone of common SMHAS. Hence, this description may be adapted on whichever SMHAS.

2.1 *Use Case Description:* Cure Ortopediche and Traumatologiche *(COT)*

Our work gives a look at the current IT infrastructures of common SMHAS, for understanding how and which services may leverage Cloud Computing Technology minimizing the risk of disclosing neither patients personal data nor healthcare employee activities.

The hospital chosen for study is a private, poly-specialist structure in Messina, called COT (Orthopedics and Traumatology Cures). It has been operating since 1973 and, since 1977, works in agreement with the National Healthcare Service. It also works in collaboration with the University of Messina and other leading Italian healthcare structures. The 82 bed-places are divided as follows:

- Operative Unit (OU) Orthopedics and Traumatology 26
- OU General Medicine 9
- OU Cardiology 4
- OU Rehabilitation 29
- OU Vascular Surgery 4
- Post-operative Intensive care 2

In addition, there are 8 places in Day Hospital shared among various departments. The company mission clearly expresses that high quality service is its aim, through continual improvement of the structure and technology, and updating of all operators. In May 1998 a quality process was initiated which, in November 1999, led to obtaining the UNI EN ISO 9001:1994 international certificate of conformity (and successive updates). During the continual improvement of quality, particular attention was paid to clinical risk management. In the past few years, the hospital has undertaken to improve clinical practices for patient safety, with particular attention to the six goals as defined by the Joint Commission International:

1. Identify patients correctly
2. Improve effective communication
3. Improve high-risk drug safety
4. Ensure right-site, right-patient, right-procedure surgery
5. Reduce risk of healthcare-associated infections
6. Reduce the risk of patient harm from falls

2.2 *IT Infrastructure in COT*

In pursuing the objectives described in the previous section, along with the introduction and periodical revision of specific procedures, ample space is given to use of technology and computer tools. In particular, with reference to the previous *goal* 1, a system based on the use of the electronic bracelet with an inserted microchip was implemented. The microchip is read by an electronic tablet used by nurses, able to open the patients' electronic chart.

The use of radio frequency identification (RFID) allows:

- Univocal and continual patient identification
- Chronological traceability of activity
- Therapy prescription with direct access to pharmaceutical codex
- Identification of administration
- Identification of prescription
- Monitoring of consumption

Moreover, the information system in use oversees the efficiency of the operating block, all Operating Units, and specialist services. Access to the system is only permitted by an operators individual password. This is to ensure patient privacy and improved traceability of operations carried out within the system.

Figure 1 depicts the composition of the IT infrastructure in COT. Two main sites guarantee all mechanisms for IT fault-tolerance and disaster recovery capabilities. Nowadays all IT system administrators need to configure at least another twin place respect to the main one, where to deploy service and transmit replicated data. Thus for avoiding issues that may occur in the primary site. The right part of the picture shows this twin site. Looking at the left side of the figure, we recognize the two main parts compounding the system, that is *Mobile Side* and *Servers Side*. In the Mobile part belong tablets, laptops, RFID readers and bracelets, up to all wireless accessing devices (APs Wi-Fi). The Server part is wired interconnected and its aims are to process, store and communicate all data produced in the

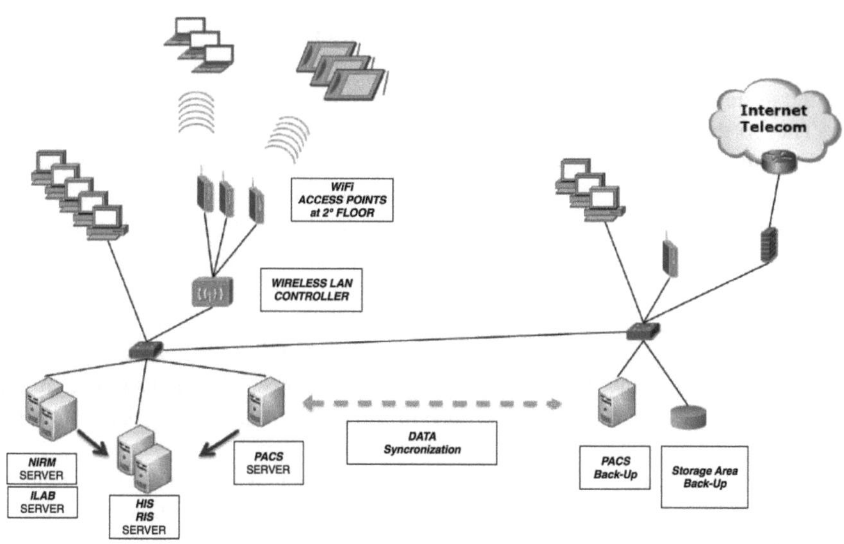

Fig. 1 IT infrastructure of a small medical assistance operator operating in Messina

medical center achieved from the Mobile Side. All data management involves the following sub-sets IT:

- PACS: Picture Archive and Communications Systems.
- HIS/RIS: Health/Radiography Information System.
- ILAB: Analysis Lab.
- NIRM: Nurse Information System with Pain Monitoring and Clinic Risk Analysis.
- IPSOA: Management control and performance assessment.
- TELECLIC: Tele-Consultation (for Doctors) and Tele-Reservation (for Patients).

There is a pool of servers for the PACS management. This pool is characterized by a considerable amount of storage. In COT, the storage of images has started in 2001 and right now it sizes 1 TB. The overall Information System relies on a Relational Database where 500 GB of data are stored since 1991. The HIS data are managed in HL7 format, XML based. The TELECLIC platform offers a Web interface Internet based useful for patients needing healthcare services (i.e. they can make reservation for consultations) and at the same time the system allows external Doctors (i.e., primary care physicians) to monitor the medical treatments of a patient under their supervision.

3 All Possible Cloud-Based Solutions for e-Health

For any kind of profit organization and enterprise, try to leverage the full cloud computing capabilities means outsource all IT needs on external cloud operator using the well-known *pay-per-use* model. Cloud operators are responsible for the maintenance and upgrade of their systems. Cloud customers are not aware neither of the system complexity, nor of costs for maintain IT infrastructures.

The correct cloud model relies on services deployed on not-well-internally-defined infrastructure (cloud), with a powerful network using mobile device for accessing these resources. Let's try to apply this model for SMHAS under our assessment. The first main constrain in using cloud for a medical center is about the management of *sensible data*. These clinic structures have to satisfy many laws for guarantee Security and Privacy to Patients. Many insurance companies, banks and so on are really interested to this data. Giving an example it is possible to imagine the value of knowing a disease of a patient that has to sign a contract with an insurance company for a Mortgage Life Assurance. Cloud operators might easily get this data and in the worst case of a fraudulent access, the date might be stolen.

In Cloud Computing the network covers a fundamental role for accessing cloud services. Whether we consider the full services deployment on cloud it is necessary to have continuous connectivity among the parties. Let's assume the hospital using clouds we have to guarantee to all departments, offices and room cares a reliable network backbone to the cloud. Any issue in the network communication determines the total block of any activities in the hospital. This is a compelling scenario but in our view it is still futuristic, as an example, the network in Italy so far does not provide these capabilities. Italy still suffers of the *Digital Divide* issue, not all places in the country are covered by the broadband access.

Keeping in mind these issues and risks, hereby we briefly analyze the possible exploitation of Cloud resources ranging from a weak involvement (we define it as at a first stage) towards an ideal futuristic cloud scenario (scenario with a full network connectivity).

The following items show the different levels of cloud utilizations:

- *Weak Coupled*: we define this level as a cloud at a first stage. This determines a weak involvement for minimizing the risks on its adoption. However the amount of saving costs is particularly limited.
- *Medium Coupled*: in this case applications deployed on cloud rely on encrypted data stored in another cloud. A cloud operator *X* executes the services whereas the data are encrypted on cloud *Y* and the medical care center *Z* has all keys for decrypting all data (see [10]). The scenario is quite complex, but information and security keys are spread among more parties.
- *Strongly Coupled*: this represents the typical use of Clouds in Software as a Service configuration. The same web application is shared among more Tenants (i.e., hospitals, medical centers, healthcare structures, etc.). In this model there is not a markable separation among Cloud Customers. The network is fundamental for accomplishing all activities. This services are like Google Health [5], Microsoft HealthVaulth [6], etc.

3.1 Cloud for COT: A Possible Solution for Impacting as Less as Possible the SMHAS Constrains

We introduce the concept of Cloud solution at first stage in which the deployment of SMHAS IT services involves the twin site depicted in Fig. 1, right side. In the COT example a twin site has been adopted for addressing problems of fault-tolerance and disaster recovery. All elements and devices falling into the *Server Side* area may be deployed in cloud. The network has to be operative but without having restricted requirements. Looking at Fig. 2, it is possible to notice that the right part of Fig. 1 is replaced by a cloud shape. We are considering the Cloud as a back-up area, where to enforce strong security policies. In the figure, the lockers icons on the cloud shape highlight the needs to guarantee a high level of security. The cloud provider is not aware of what data are stored in, he/she sees a wrapper of encrypted data. However one of the main issues about the encryption technology represents the following problems:

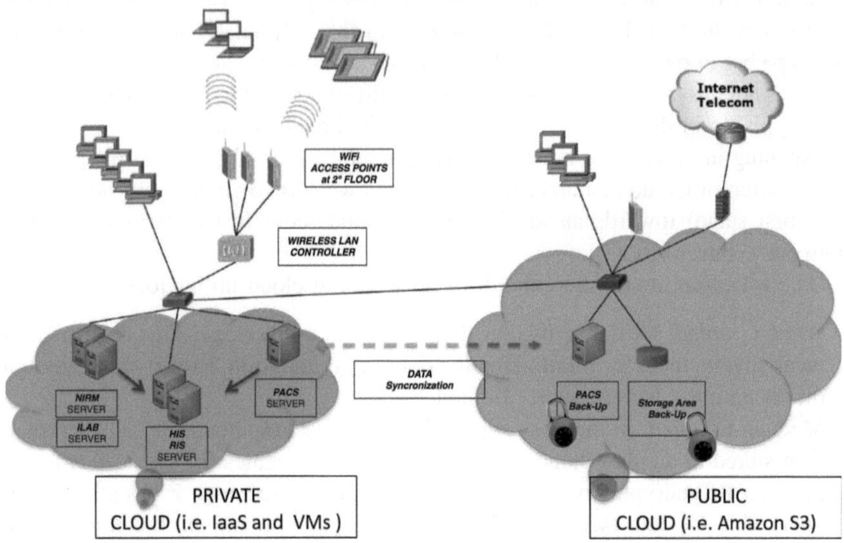

Fig. 2 IT infrastructure of a small clinic assistance operator operating in Messina.

- the difficulty to manage keys and
- the incremental management of changed of data.

To avoid these issues, in the early case we suggest the use of crypto tokens with Asymmetric Keys. Private keys remain stored in the primary site (the main site, see left side of Fig. 1), whereas public keys can be distributed to cloud operators. (i.e., for evaluating the integrity of data stored on clouds).

For the latter case, because cloud computing strongly exploits the concept of Virtualization technology for increasing its flexibility, we need to find a solution linked to the Virtualization technology. Virtual Machines are logic elements where it is possible to confine Operating Systems (useful for managing computation resources and file systems), Software Applications and Services exposed to the Internet. In our case we can imagine to install the PACS (as well HIS/RIS, etc.) inside a VM (one, or more VMs). These VMs may be transferred on Cloud Storage, e.g. *Amazon S3* (i.e. during the night for saving the network bandwidth), after the encryption occurred in the primary site, the VMs can land on Cloud. However this approach causes the issue related to the update of changed data. In order to describe what the problem raises the use of VMs, let's assume this example: if the size of a VM is 1 GB, to back-up it on cloud we have to transfer the total amount of 1 GB of data. Whatever internal operation inside this machine, even the simple modifies of a single Byte, yields to the changing of the whole VM. Thus means a new update of the whole VM loosing the same time utilized at the first time. The concept of VM snapshot and the incremental file system feature prevents this issue. In this form it is not necessary to re-upload the entire VM, but the differential elements respect to the early version are taken into account. 1 Byte of modifies implies the transfer of an incremental file portion with a limited size. Confine services into VMs helps the System Administrator to restore services as soon as possible. The SyS-Admin of COT in using Amazon S3 needs to transform the real Servers into VMs, hence, with an OpenSSL Script encrypting them and finally with a *Cron Process* transmit them every night on Amazon S3. This solution guarantees a high degree of security and a good opportunity to save costs.

4 Related Works

Generally there are many potential benefits on ICT adoption, even the field of e-Health takes advantages in using cloud technologies. If we consider the situation in which many data are acquired from Cameras, Sensors and Mobile Devices, the overall information that might be treated for making clear pictures of ongoing events in medical care scenarios is really huge. Cloud computing seems to be the new compelling technology able to manage this amount of data, where the massive processing is effectively addressable.

Looking at the initiatives on cloud and health, in Pandey et al. [11], the authors propose the use of cloud for collecting personal health data, in particular for monitoring the ECG (ElectroCardioGram) values. Authors have designed a real-time health monitoring and analysis system that should be scalable and economic for people who require frequent monitoring of their health. They focused on the design aspects of an autonomic Cloud environment that collects health data and disseminates them to a Cloud based information repository, facilitating analysis on the data using software services hosted in the Cloud. Persons under their assessment have to wear PDAs with sensors able to catch some physiological data. Thanks to Wi-Fi/UMTS network connections PDAs are able to send to clouds data they aggregated on board. One of the main concerns in using public cloud services (see Amazon storage), is about the level of security and privacy that cloud companies can offer to customers. In particular the security aspect is crucial all the times personal health data are collected.

Internet of Things (IoT, see [12]) and e-Health is becoming a new IT scientific field where many works are appearing. In particular the Near Field Communication (NFC) is one of the technologies, in conjunction with Bluetooth and 6LoWPAN, which makes feasible the wireless transmission of information from small objects and sensors to Internet-enabled devices. The work in Antonio et al. [13] is focused on the evaluation of the capabilities from the mentioned technologies for the integration of a continuous data transmission. The works deals with the possibility that sensors with high requirements in data transmission, i.e. an electrocardiogram (ECG), continuously transmit data over the Internet. It is interesting to notice how this data are compressed for reducing the amount of information to be transmitted and stored within the cloud. An interesting work is presented in Fabio and Corradi [10] in which an accomplishment of a Software as a Service (SaaS) application with the fully-exploiting of elastic Cloud computing infrastructures is described. As the authors claimed, SaaS applications typically require to transfer data and resources to the Cloud infrastructure site; that raises several challenging issues spanning from access control to resources to privacy protection, ownership, and security of the data of the final SaaS users. Although encryption of personal and enterprise data is strongly recommended by existing Cloud infrastructures, such as Amazon Web Services (AWS), typically they do not provide yet adequate encryption and key management support. The chapter that authors have presented reports a real use case of Vitaever, a home healthcare SaaS application deployed on Amazon AWS, and discusses the challenges and changes needed to add cryptography and key management capabilities to the standard AWS Web/database offer so to enable SaaS data protection.

5 Conclusions

In this chapter we have presented a Cloud-based solution aimed at Small and Medium Healthcare Assistance Structures (SMHASs). These medical centers need to update quite often their IT systems. Cloud computing thanks to its *pay-per-use* model allows to reduce IT costs on Capital Expenditure and Operational Costs. However it is not possible yet to deploy all e-Health services on cloud due to the Security and Private constrains, especially in scenarios where sensible data are treated. Here, a real use case has been described, useful for providing basic solutions applicable in more similar scenarios. We described the first level of Cloud Computing adoption. However, in the near future, we believe the cloud technology will widely adopted.

References

1. Buccoliero, L., Nasi, G., & Caccia, C. (2005). E-health.
2. Eisenhardt, K. (1989). Making fast strategic decision in high velocity, environments.
3. Kerkhove, D. (2009). In M. Moruzzi (ed.), *E-health e fascicolo sanitario elettronico*.
4. Fazio, M., Paone, M., Puliafito, A., & Villari, M. (2012, March). Huge amount of heterogeneous sensed data needs the cloud. In: 9th International Multi-Conference on Systems, Signals and Devices.
5. Solution, G. H. (2012, January). Public Google Health site www.google.com/health/.
6. Solution, M. H. (2012, June). Public HealthVault site http://www.healthvault.com/personal/index.aspx
7. Yin, R. (1981). The case study crisis: Some answers.
8. Yin, R. (1984). The case study research.
9. Glaser, B., & Strauss, A. (1967). The discovery of grounded theory: Strategies of qualitative research.
10. Fabio, B., Corradi, A., & Foschini, L. (2012). Database security management for healthcare saas in the amazon aws cloud.

11. Pandey, S., Voorsluys, W., Niu, S., Khandoker, A., & Buyya, R. (2011, June). An autonomic cloud environment for hosting ecg data analysis services. *Future Generation Computer Systems, 55*(6).
12. Fazio, M., Paone, M., Puliafito, A., & Villari, M. (2012, July). Heterogeneous sensors become homogeneous things in smart cities. In 2012 Sixth International Conference on Innovative Mobile and Internet Services in Ubiquitous Computing (IMIS).
13. Antonio, J. J., Pablo, L., David, F., Benito, ò., Miguel, A. Z., & Antonio, F. S. (2012, July). Interaction of patients with breathing problems through nfc in ambient assisted living, environments.

Learning from Patents: An Application of Technology Intelligence in Nanotechnology

Fabrizio Cesaroni, Daniela Baglieri and Luigi Orsi

Abstract Technology is a strategic asset for an increasing number of firms that nurture their competitiveness through innovation. Accordingly, fostering innovation, exploiting technological opportunities and avoiding threats are increasingly important issues within their strategies. Firms need to support their decision-making processes by investing in technology intelligence system in order to protect their products from competitors' aggressive actions or to exploit new emerging technological trajectories. This chapter presents some actions that a Technology Intelligence System (TIS) can accommodate, drawing upon patent analysis. The main purpose of patent analysis is to enable firms to monitor and assess technological developments and other areas of concern. Such technology management activities assist firms in evaluating their environment while taking advantage of new emerging technological trends. The methodology is described in detail using an application conducted in nanotech patents.

1 Introduction

Over the last decades, the advent of general purpose technologies, such as biotechnology and nanotechnology, has blossomed a wide range of entrepreneurial opportunities and nurtured their application in several domains. Accordingly,

F. Cesaroni (✉)
Department of Business Administration, Carlos III University, Madrid, Spain
e-mail: fabrizio.cesaroni@uc3m.es

D. Baglieri
University of Messina, Messina, Italy
e-mail: dbaglieri@unime.it

L. Orsi
Department of Economics, Management and Quantitative Methods
and TTO "UNIMITT", University of Milan, Milan, Italy
e-mail: luigi.orsi@unimi.it

P. Spagnoletti (ed.), *Organizational Change and Information Systems*, Lecture Notes in Information Systems and Organisation 2, DOI: 10.1007/978-3-642-37228-5_24,

exploiting these technological opportunities and facing patent race are increasingly crucial issues for gaining competitive advantage in several industries. To achieve these goals, an increasing number of firms is investing in technology intelligence systems in order to improve capabilities to scrutinize technological and competitive environments. Technology intelligence has been defined as "the capture and delivery of technological information as part of the process whereby an organization develops an awareness of technological threats and opportunities" [1]. Technological information relies on data that comes both from internal and external sources. Among the external sources, firms may take advantage of a lot of useful, unstructured data coming from patents. Although patent information exhibits intrinsic limits [2], systematic patent analysis allows firms to identify and assess entrepreneurial opportunities. This strategic task requires robust technology intelligence systems supporting firms' R&D decision-making, which include proper actions taken by the intelligence actors.

In this chapter, among those various actions, we provide a practical application of the "assessment of the state-of-art" action, by analyzing 5,002 family patents on nanotubes, which is one of the most important classes of nanotechnology in terms of potential market. Nanotechnology has been recognized as a key technology of next decades and more than 60 countries have adopted national projects or programs partially stimulated by the establishment of the US-based National Nanotechnology Initiative (NNI, http://www.nano.gov) [3]. The US National Science Foundation predicts that the market for products involving nanotechnology will reach $1 trillion in 10–15 years. Accordingly, more than 100 companies around the world today are manufacturing carbon nanotubes and this number is expected to increase to more than 200 within the next five years, while there are more than 1,000 companies and institutions that are actively engaged in CNTs R&D. As a result, nanotubes patent information is mostly unstructured, and analysis and interpretation requires robust technology intelligence systems to understand market opportunities.

In this vein, we suggest that patent information can be perceived as a learning tool supporting firms' R&D strategies. Within the Technology Intelligence Framework, the assessment of the state-of-art represents a pre-condition to identify promising technological opportunities, to show their potential as well as their limits and, more in general, to take advantage of technological change.

2 Actions of Technology Intelligence System

A technology intelligence system can effectively be described by a three-level model consisting in: (a) a framework level; (b) a system level; and, (c) a process level [1]. While the framework level defines which information is required and knowledge gaps of the decision-makers, the system level clarifies the specific operations that have to be implemented to make the technology intelligence system effective, and the process level refers to all the tools and metrics needed to conduct the various activities pertaining to the previous level. Accordingly, the system level refers to the proper actions R&D managers have to perform to assess and monitor technology trends, namely: (1) assessment of state-of-art; (2) profile of trends; (3) identification of opportunities; (4) awareness of threats.

At the end, technology intelligence system will generate a reporting focus for each of these actions, by analyzing primary and secondary data gathered mostly from publicly available white sources. Patents fall into this category. Accordingly, the Technology Intelligence System includes some actions related to the technological landscape assessment whose main purpose is to make relevant technological information available to decision makers in order to anticipate future developments. This action requires two major processes: (1) the scanning process and (2) the monitoring process.

The scanning phase refers to the gathering of all relevant patent data in order to get R&D employees aware of new technological trajectories. This information will be in turn communicated to top management involved in R&D strategies formulation.

The monitoring phase deals with the detection of the observed and potentially new technological trends. To achieve this goal, this process includes assessing the emerging and competing technologies that could potentially disrupt a business.

The opportunities and threats arising from this environment are the analyzed. Opportunities may be considered for further R&D strategies, by assessing market potentialities and consequent technology investments. Threats should receive mitigation plans and be treated appropriately.

Although a Technology Intelligence System could work as an independent tool supporting R&D strategies, it does require predefined inputs. Key prerequisites are: market needs, legislative and social issues regarding the new technology adoption, core technologies, and the assessment of the state-of the-art (Fig. 1).

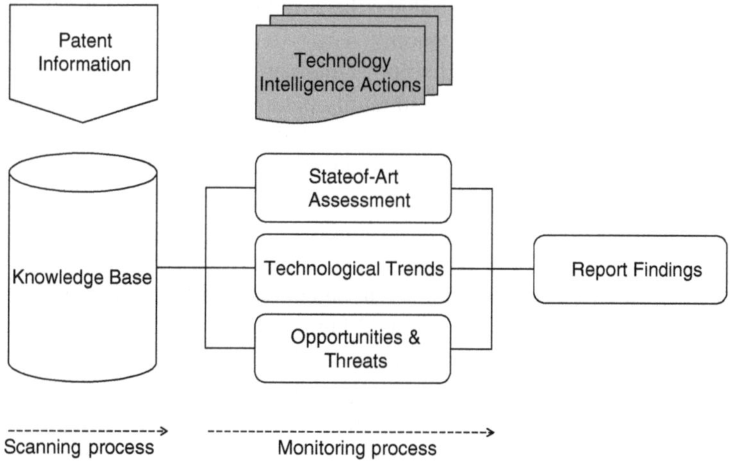

Fig. 1 Actions of technology intelligence system

3 Methods

We provide in this section a practical application of the assessment of the state-of-art in the nanotech field, and offer an overview of the analytical methods we employed.

Our statistical approach is based on patent data. A critical starting point of any patent-based analysis is clearly related to the availability of reliable data, according to two important dimensions: the coverage of the database and the quality of the data available for patents. QPAT database is one of the currently available patent databases that satisfy all these characteristics across the world. QPAT is a Questel/Orbit's Internet database providing the searchable full text of patents from 1974 to the present in about 80 countries. For the industrial researcher, QPAT offers invaluable competitive intelligence and market knowledge. Often, a competitor's patents will provide in-depth and comprehensive information about strategies, production costs and product limitations. In a more general sense, examining patent information for a given industry will highlight important trends and directions within the industry [4].

We focus our analysis on nanotechnology due to its market potentialities. Because nanotechnology concerns the scale of materials rather than a particular application, the scope of nanotechnology is extremely broad. A measure of the breadth of nanotechnology relates to the classes assigned to each patent. The World Intellectual Property Organization (WIPO) divides the entire set of patents into searchable collections based on the technology claimed. The primary groupings are referred to as classes. Classes are divided into relatively small collections of patents called subclasses. One of the most important classes, in terms of potential market, is carbon nanotubes (CNTs). Used across a wide range of industries including plastics and composites, electrical and electronics, and energy as well as a range of industrial sectors, CNTs have become an essential ingredient or reinforcement material for these industries, with its usage growing broadly in line with the global economy.

Starting from the B82 (nanotechnology) International Patent Classification code (IPC), we obtained a sample of 16,930 family patents. Standard IPCs exhibit some problems. Class hierarchies are revised in batch about once every 5 years, old patents are not reclassified, and one must check old editions of the IPCs if he/she plans to search them over an extended time period. To avoid such problems and to restrict the search area to the nanotube technology, full Boolean capabilities can be used by combining multiple fields. In our search we looked for this kind of technologies searching for "nanotubes" in patent title, abstract, keywords and IPC code, so the final sample consists of 5,002 family patents related to nanotubes (for a total of 16,343 individual patents), from 1974 to present. This type of research allowed us to capture the use of these technologies in different technology fields.

First, analyzed nanotubes patents at three analytical levels: country (country group), assignee institution, and technology field (represented by IPC subclasses).

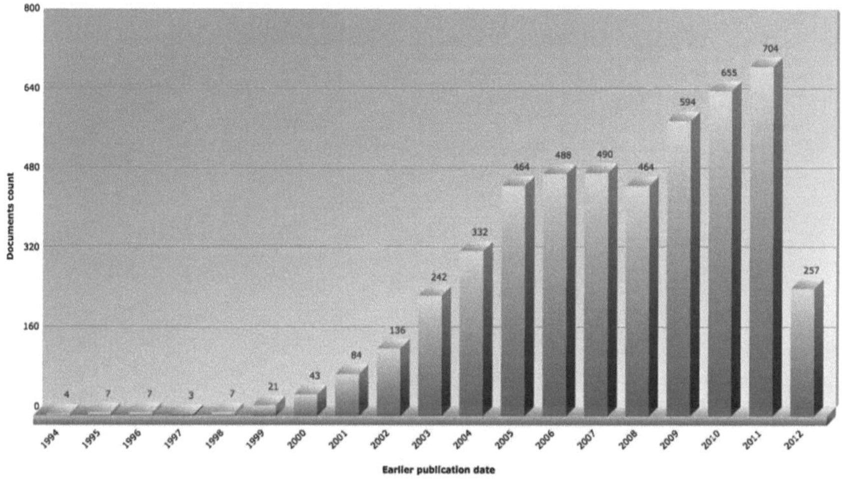

Fig. 2 Nanotubes patents trend (1994–2012)

Figure 2 shows the total number of patent publications in the last 18 years. It is worth noting that nanotube patents took their peak in 2011, and highlight a growth stage of technology life cycle. During the introduction stage (1994–2004) there was a modest and slow increase in nanotube patent applications. The growth stage, on the other hand, is typically characterized by exponential growth. In our case, after a four-year stability, patent applications started to rapidly grow from 2008. As a result, nanotubes have not entered the saturation stage.

Figure 3 shows the geographical distribution of nanotube patents, based upon publication date in the latest twenty years (1992–2012), and reveals that US and Japan are the two relevant countries investing in nanotubes.

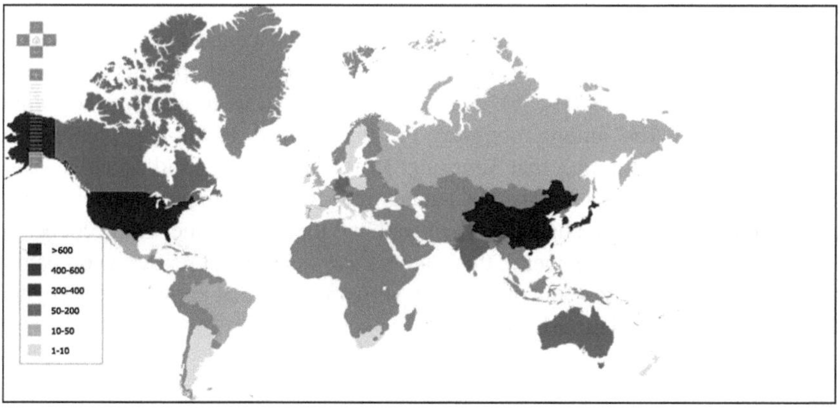

Fig. 3 Nanotube patents around the world

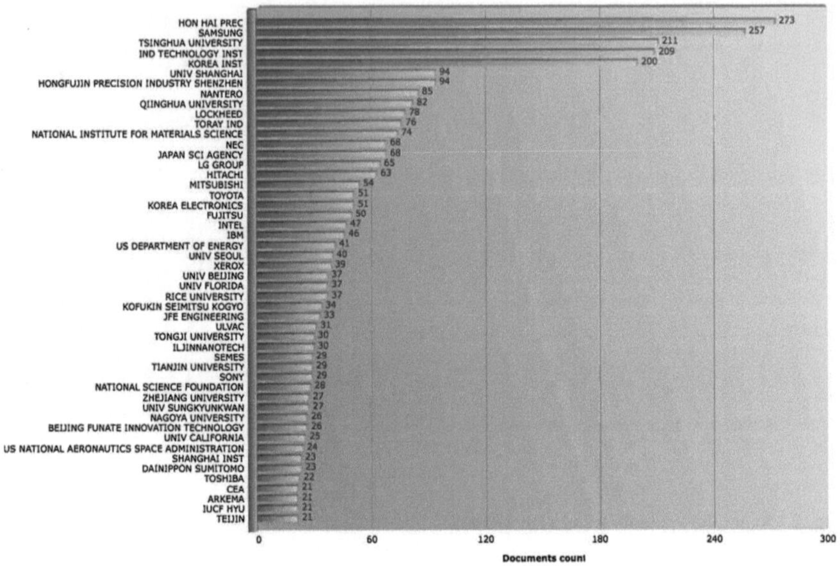

Fig. 4 Assignees ranking

For these two countries, the trend for nanotube patents has increased sharply since 2002, followed by Korea (2006) and China (2009). Even though they are followers, their patents are more than the world-wide average. China is also catching-up. Among the European Union, France is expected to take the lead in CNTs production. Despite more than 100 CNTs manufacturing companies, the majority of nanotubes patents is held by Hon Hai Precision Industry, which is a Taiwan-based holding working for big companies (i.e. Apple, Motorola, Sony, Microsoft, Dell), followed by Samsung (South Korea), Tsinghua University (China), and the Indian Technology Institutes (India). Figure 4 shows assignees' ranking.

We also conducted a network analysis to describe connections among technology fields. We detected such fields by deploying both patents' keywords (Fig. 5) and IPC classes (Fig. 6). This analysis allowed us to identify the salient competitive patterns among assignee institutions and technology fields. For example, it is worth noting that Samsung, Hon Hai Precision and Tsinghua University share the highest number of patents referring to carbon nanotubes. Thus they compete in this technology field and, at the same time, may cooperate forming a patent pool. In general, this analysis shows both that research companies and universities are key actors in nanotech networks, and that knowledge is created through their close relationships.

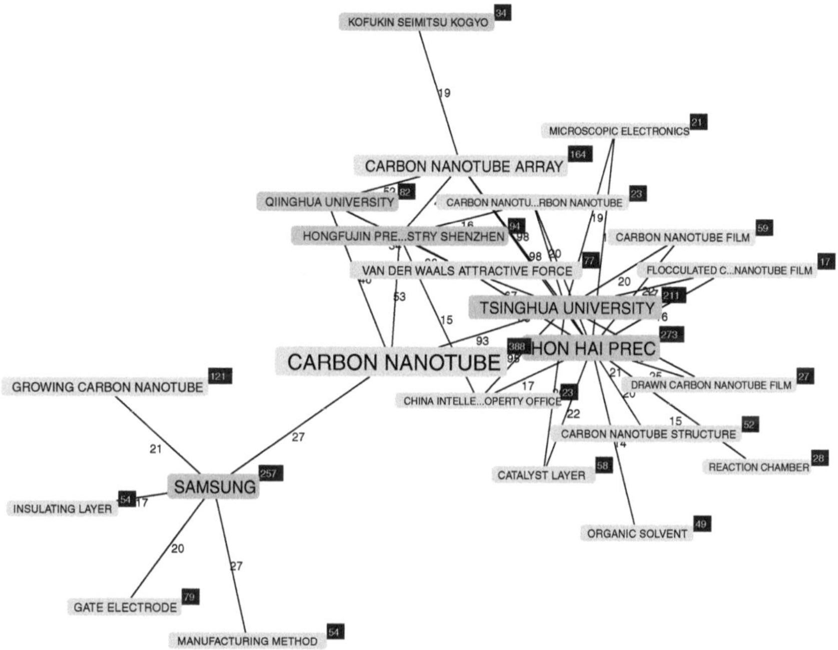

Fig. 5 Keyword-based and IPC-based network analysis

4 Discussion and Conclusion

Promoting technological innovation requires both exploiting technological opportunities and avoiding threats. Firms need to assess current and potential future technological advances, which might affect their products, services and processes. Nevertheless, the accelerating pace of technological change increases the risks faced by technology-driven companies. To alleviate these risks, it is crucial to provide early warnings of potential change. This chapter provides an exemplification of practical tools that can be used to monitor the external technological environment.

Using a series of patent clustering methods implemented on the QPAT database, the nanotubes patent documents from 80 countries were clustered into general technology families. A close analysis of these clusters reveals the patent development strategies of competing nanotubes technology developers. Currently, carbon nanotubes account for a 28 % market share of overall nanomaterials' demand. In terms of production capacity, Asia–Pacific leads, followed by North America and the European Union. In a fierce competitive business environment, the main advantage of a company and, consequently, of a country is to create intellectual property continuously; therefore, companies need to work on developing innovative technology, increase holdings of key intellectual assets, organize patent alliances and elaborate patent benefits to enhance their competence. As

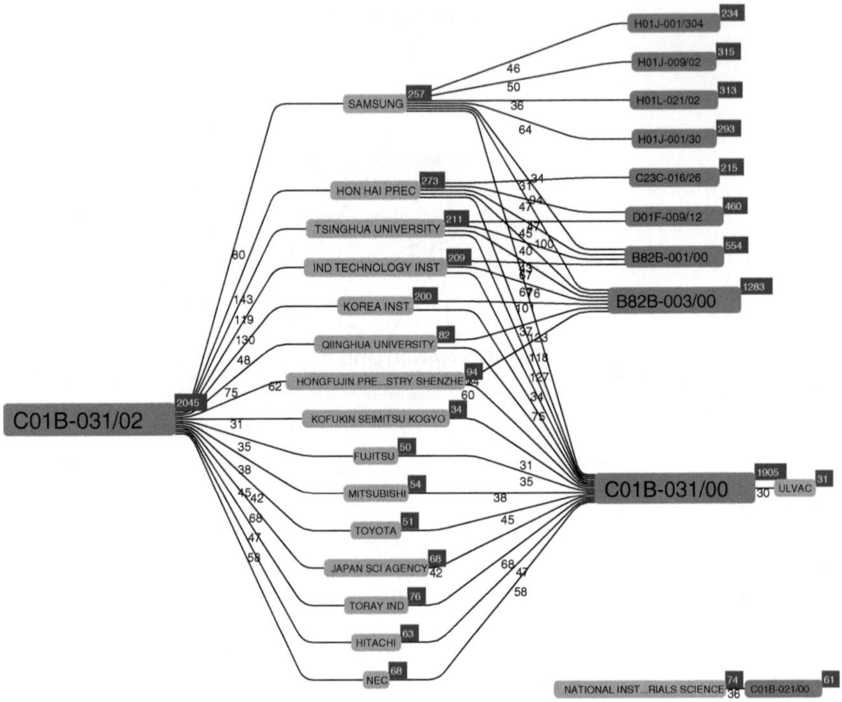

Fig. 6 Keyword-based and IPC-based network analysis

known, intellectual property is designed to protect an inventor's right of ownership [5]. If a company owns a patent, no other companies can use the patented technology without an authorization from the patent holder.

Research shows that through proper intellectual property management, companies can be at the leading position and gain competitive advantage. Hagelin [6] proposes a method called competitive advantage valuation as one way of assigning value to the intellectual property assets. The Author also considers that the intellectual property can increase a company's competitive advantage and that the effective intellectual property management is the key to profitability. By analyzing patent data, extracting patent information and gathering patent intelligence, companies can realize related patent development in the past and advance future R&D directions [7]. Patent content analysis could be a useful tool to compare and contrast the technical competence between companies and to establish technical strategy planning of a company [8, 9]. Thus, it is not how many patents a group holds but the contents of the patents that create a profitable intellectual asset and competitive advantage.

The evidence presented here suggests a possible link between quality of patents obtained and competitive dominance. In line with this reasoning, patent analysis could be used to direct R&D efforts and to shape partnering strategies. While this study covers only one action—the state-of-art assessment—, it emphasizes the crucial value of intellectual property and, in particular, the value of patents and methodologies of patent analysis as learning tools.

References

1. Kerr, C. I. V., Mortara, L., Phaal, R., & Probert, D. R. (2006). A conceptual model for technology intelligence. *International Journal of Technology Intelligence and Planning, 2*(1), 73–93.
2. Cesaroni, F., & Baglieri, D. (2012). Technology intelligence: New challenges from patent information. In M. De Marco, D. Te'eni, V. Albano, & S. Za (Eds.), *Information systems: Crossroads for organization, management, accounting and engineering*. Heidelberg: Springer.
3. Roco, M. C., Williams, R. S., & Alivisatos, P. (2000). *Nanotechnology research directions*. Dordrecht: Kluwer Academic Publishers.
4. Lambert, N. (2004). Internet patent information in the 21st century: A comparison of Delphion, Micropatent, and Qpat, presented at the 2004 International Chemical Information Conference & Exhibition, Annecy, France.
5. Hall, B. H. (2004). Exploring the patent explosion, NBER Working Paper, National Bureau of Economic Research.
6. Hagelin, T. (2003). Competitive advantage valuation of intellectual property assets: A new tool for IP managers. *IDEA: The Journal of Law and Technology, 44*, 79–103.
7. Ernst, H. (1998). Patent portfolios for strategic R&D planning. *Journal of Engineering and Technology Management, 15*(4), 279–308.
8. Ernst, H. (2003). Patent information for strategic technology management. *World Patent Information, 25*, 233–242.
9. Lin, C. Y., & Chen, M. Y. (2007). Does innovation lead to performance? An empirical study of SMEs in Taiwan. *Management Research News, 30*(2), 115–132.

The Determinants of Knowledge Transfer: The Study of a Refined Model

Maurizio Cavallari

Abstract Starting form previously research findings this chapter investigates the determinants of knowledge transfer. The intention of the present research is to refine a previous proposed model, in order to utilize it for further empirical research. Personal traits and the concept of trust, along with absorptive capacity, dependency and availability to share, are stressed out in order to enhance the proposed model. The outcome of the chapter is a theoretical model, which will serve as a torch bearer for future empirical research.

Keywords Knowledge · Transfer · Sharing · Trust · Dependency · Absorptive capacity · Ability · Availability

1 Introduction

In recent years, knowledge sharing and knowledge transfer received increasing attentions by researchers and scholars. The aim of this research work, given the constraints in term of length, is to refine a previous published theoretical model pertaining the knowledge transfer construct and subsequent latent variable definition, with respect to its role as a predictor for creativity [1]. The foreseen outcome is a model of investigation on one of creativity's subtle predictors: knowledge transfer. Based on the previous work, knowledge transfer is regarded as a complex organizational dynamic that cannot be easily identified, nor imitated. As Ciborra taught us, knowledge assets in organizations represent an intangible part of organizational culture that can lead—but not all the time—to a sustainable competitive advantage [2, 3]. Scholars like Gabbay et al., and Espinosa et al.,

M. Cavallari (✉)
Università Cattolica, Milano, Italy
e-mail: maurizio.cavallari@unicatt.it

P. Spagnoletti (ed.), *Organizational Change and Information Systems*, Lecture Notes in Information Systems and Organisation 2, DOI: 10.1007/978-3-642-37228-5_25,

proved that individuals couldn't rely, efficiently, only on their personal knowledge resources [4–7].

In many organizational contexts knowledge transfer is not explicitly defined [8] and often takes place informally and spontaneously [9], while knowledge sharing and knowledge transfer are constantly present in a large variety of organizational dynamics and inter-relations. For this reason the current chapter only focuses on individual knowledge transfer. Within this chapter the concept of "knowledge sharing" precede the concept of "knowledge transfer" as the "sharing" is a condition, needed but not sufficient, that leads to eventual and actual "transfer" of knowledge; sharing is a half-way process, transfer is a full-way process involving both actors [1]. Hindes and Pfeffer identify one of the hindrances to knowledge sharing as the *lack of motivation* to share knowledge, which in turn will lead to *lack of intention* at individual levels [10]. Different research have focused so far on the intention to share knowledge among individuals [11–15], while other studies have researched into inter-organizational knowledge sharing [16–19].

The arising *Research Questions* that guide the research are, therefore:

R.Q.1 What are the major factors facilitating the *intention* to share knowledge between employees?
R.Q.2 What are the major factors facilitating the *ability* to share knowledge between employees?
R.Q.3 What are the major factors facilitating the *availability* to share knowledge between employees?

All of the three above mentioned concepts, are finally regarded as predictors of knowledge transfer.

The reminder of the chapter is: in Sect. 2, we examine the relevant literature and highlight the basic concepts; in Sect. 3, we conclude and discuss the conceptual model for further empirical investigation, explaining variables and inter-correlations among them; in Sect. 4, we outline the limitations and the scope for future research.

2 The Basic Concepts

2.1 Knowledge Transfer

Knowledge transfer among individuals on a work place is very rarely formalized and usually takes place spontaneously [20, 21]. Scholars like Nahapiet and Ghoshal [22], elaborating the concepts proposed by Burt [23], identify three dimensions of social capital that influence knowledge transfer, that are, respectively, the structural dimension (organization structure and network configuration), the cognitive dimension (language, case studies), and the relational dimension (trust, norms, identification). For the aim of the present research chapter we adopted the relevant definitions proposed by Portes [24] and Tsai [25], which point to the "instrumental" and the "consummatory" (Tsai uses this terminology) views [24, 25]. The instrumental view, utilized by Adler and Kwon [26], sees the establishment of knowledge transfer as based on reciprocal relationships, while the "consummatory" view, as further elaborated by Leana and Van Buren [27], interprets knowledge transfer as the outcome of the strengthen of social ties and the identification within a group. According to this previous results then, the instrumental view includes the "social network" aspect of knowledge transfer. The "consummatory" view sees knowledge transfer more as an emerging phenomenon that is created through a socialization process of members in a group. A remarkable feature of Portes's work [24] is the statement that these different views represent important and frequently coexisting aspects of knowledge transfer. In the present research chapter we have adopted, and adapted, Portes's [24] ideas.

Two major requirements must be met before knowledge transfer can take place, according to Husted and Michailova [28]. These are: intention to share, and ability to share knowledge. These requirements are met only if motivational and cognitive limitations toward knowledge sharing are overcome, according to Grandori and Kogut [29]. We learn from the works of Hindes [10, 30] that cognitive limitations are associated with the "ability to share" knowledge, while motivational limitations are related to the "intention to share" knowledge [30]. According to the theory of motivation [14], only if individuals will gain incentives, they will intensify the sharing of knowledge and their expertise. Motivational limitations that inhibit sharing of knowledge are related, by contrary, to disincentives such as risk and uncertainty. It is evident that only the intention to share knowledge is not enough, as organizations and individuals should also "be able to share" the knowledge they possess and that are willing to share [14, 30]. The mentioned "ability to share knowledge" is directly influenced by the individual and collective traits of being capable to make their knowledge available and to learn the knowledge that is put at their disposal. As mentioned before, "cognitive limitations" can cause hindrances in knowledge sharing and as a result they have a definite impact on the ability to share knowledge. Cognitive limitations are directly related with the way in which individuals with a certain grade of expertise are conscious of their knowledge, store it and knowingly process it. These kind of cognitive limitations curb and subdue sharing of knowledge, and are frequently due to unconscious patterns. Hau and Evangelista argument about explicit and tacit knowledge, and point out that "cognitive problems", are crucial to understand the difficulties in sharing [14]. Howells [31, 32] describes tacit knowledge as an important factor of innovation, and highlights the difficulties that arise, specifically, in order to share tacit knowledge. Following Howells' path, Martin and Salomon [33] identify a streamline of factors (concepts and requirements) affecting knowledge transfer. For the aim of the present research chapter we have considered, an adapted streamline, derived from the mentioned research findings (Table 1).

Table 1 Factors and literature references

Factor/concept/requirement	Elements/characteristics/key	Author(s)
Structural dimension	Organization structure	Nahapiet and Ghoshal [22]
	Network configuration	Burt [23]
Cognitive dimension	Language, case studies	*ibidem*
Relational dimension	Trust, norms, identification	*ibidem*
"instrumental" view	Reciprocal relationships	Portes [24], Tsai [25]
	Social network	Adler and Kwon [26]
"consummatory" view	Social ties	Portes [24], Tsai [25]
	Identification within a group	Leana and Van Buren [27]
Intention to share	Cognitive limitations	Husted and Michailova [28]
		Grandori and Kogut [29]
Ability to share	Motivational limitations	Grandori and Kogut [29]
		Hindes [10, 30]
Motivation to share	Incentives	Hau and Evangelista [14]
Explicit and tacit knowledge	Expertise gap bridging	Hau and Evangelista [14]
	Tacit knowledge articulation	Howells [31, 32]
Individual traits	Availability of sharing	Hindes [10, 30]

2.2 Trust

We argue that knowledge sharing among individuals in an organization can only be fostered if mutual trust is a persistent character among those individuals or their group(s). The concept of trust [34–39] has received a lot of attention in organizational studies for the wide variety of relapses on organizational aspects like, e.g., network forms of organization [40], social capital [22], the social aspects of knowledge transfer [41, 42]. Knowledge sharing depends on the forging of trusting relationships that are qualitatively different than those prescribed by formal and bureaucratic systems. True knowledge transfer requires the existence of highly trusted personal relationships [43, 44].

Literature on trust formation in organizations, like in Rousseau et al. [45], has converged on structural conditions such as interdependence and risk that tend to coincide with high levels of trust. Others, like Doney et al. [46], have focused on cultural conditions such as informal expectations or obligations prescribing a system that rely on trust. Apart from *conditions* for trust, literature has also examined the *processes* by which trust is formed and maintained in organizational contexts. Scholars like Dooley and Fryxell [47] as well as Elsbach and Elofson [48] suggest that trust is a delicate phenomenon that is highly sensitive to interaction and organizational context. Some research point out that trust represents also a drawback in knowledge transfer between particular organizational context such as information systems security, which is characterized by a highly competitive work environment among professionals, often not willing to share their knowledge, acquired in years of hard work, expertise and for which they might be paid higher wages then other professionals [1, 49].

2.3 Dependency

This concept relates to the different skills that different individuals retain within their expertise. This concept points toward the differentiation of knowledge and the specialization of jobs [11, 12, 50].

Dependency occurs when individual(s) need to cooperate with each other, in order to be able to complete the job or to remain competitive on the job market. The levels of dependency will also affect the future of collaboration, as being aware that a mutual advantage is springing from past interaction, would encourage individuals to search for new ways of collaboration [50].

2.4 Absorptive Capacity

The concept of absorptive capacity was first defined as a firm's "ability to recognize the value of new information, assimilate it, and apply it to commercial ends" by Cohen and Levinthal in 1990 [51] and re-conceptualized by Zhara and George in 2004 [52].

Most recently, scholarly work from Volbreda et al. [53], points out the conceptual gaps and propose to differentiate "micro-antecedents" and "macro-antecedents" in order to fully exploit the concept of absorptive capacity. In the present context the concept is intended as a measure of the ability to understand and utilize new knowledge held at other individuals' party. We assume that the higher the absorptive capacity, the more successful would be the knowledge transfer.

2.5 Availability to Share

One individual trait that is argued to be of influence is the availability to share knowledge within a group or individuals. Das and Teng argue that, within this relationship, availability means that the individual is intimately open because he/she is able, correspondingly, to reliably act and meet the expectations of other individuals and, most notably, vice versa [54].

3 The Proposed Model

Following the line of our discourse, we argue that: (hypothesis 1a) Trust relates positively to knowledge transfer; (hypothesis 1b) Trust can act as a mediator of absorptive capacity; (hypothesis 1c) Trust can mediate the intention to share towards knowledge share; (hypothesis 2a) Higher levels of dependency tend to

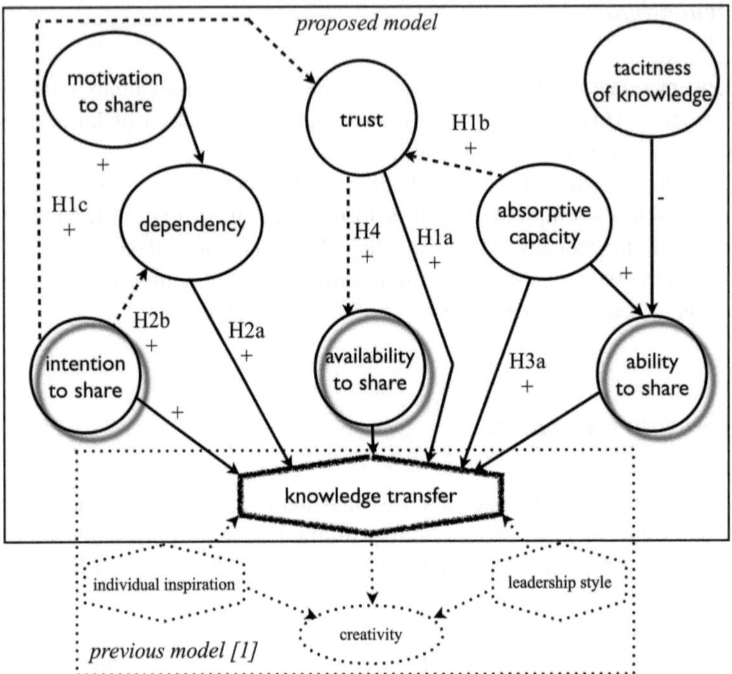

Fig. 1 Proposed model of investigation, with connection to previous published model, adapted from Cavallari [1] and Daneshgar and Seyyedeh [55]

correspond to higher levels of knowledge transfer, so dependency among individuals will positively relate to knowledge transfer; (hypothesis 2b) Intention to share is mediated by dependency; (hypothesis 3a) Absorptive capacity acts as a predictor for knowledge transfer; (hypothesis 4) Repeated positive interactions enable the members of the group(s) to better assess the reliability of each individual member and thus, enhance their individual trait of availability to share knowledge, hence availability to share is a mediator between trust and knowledge share. The proposed model is shown in Fig. 1.

4 Limitation and Future Research Work

The present chapter arguments reside on a solid baseline of previous research findings, both theoretical and empirical, and constitute a refinement of a the knowledge transfer part of a previously published model. As the aim of this work is the building of the theoretical part of a more complex investigation, evidence is needed to validate the assumptions. It is foreseen therefore an empirical test of the assumptions argued within the present research.

References

1. Cavallari, M. (2012). Creativity and the mediating role of social capital in the domain of information systems security. In C. Rossignoli (Ed.), *Proceedings of XIII Workshop dei Ricercatori e dei Docenti di Organizzazione Aziendale, WOA 2012, Desperatly Seeking Performance in Organizations*, Verona (VR) Italy.
2. Ciborra, C. (2002). The labyrinths of information. Oxford: Oxford University Press.
3. Lu, L., Leung, K., & Koch, P. T. (2006). Managerial knowledge transfer: The role of individual, interpersonal, and organizational factors. *Management and Organization Review, 2*, 15–41.
4. Nieminen, H. T. (2005). Successful inter-organizational knowledge transfer: Developing preconditions through the management of the relationship context.
5. Gabbay, S. M., & Leenders, R. Th. A. J. (1999). The structure of advantage and disadvantage. In R. Th. A. J. Leenders, & S. M. Gabbay (Eds.), *Corporate social capital and liability* (pp. 1–14). London: Kluwer Academic Publishers.
6. Espinosa, J., Slaughter, S., Kraut, R., & Herbsleb, J. (2007). Team knowledge and coordination in geographically distributed software development. *Journal of Management Information Systems, 24*(1), 135–169.
7. Kwaśniewska, J., & Nęcka, E. (2004). Perception of the climate for creativity in the workplace: The role of the level in the organization and gender. *Creativity and Innovation Management, 13*, 187–196.
8. Hendriks, P. (1999). Why share knowledge? The influence of ICT on the motivation for knowledge transfer. *Knowledge and Process Management 6*(2).
9. Bain, P., Mann, L., & Pirola-Merlo, A. (2001). The innovation imperative: The relationship between team climate and performance in research and development teams. *Small Group Research, 32*(1), 55–73.
10. Hinds, P., & Pfeffer, J. (2003). Why organizations don't "know what they know": Cognitive and motivational factors affecting the transfer of expertise. In M. Ackerman, V. Pipek, & V. Wulf (Eds.), *Beyond knowledge management: sharing expertise* (pp. 3–26). Cambridge, MA: MIT Press.
11. Bock, G. W., & Kim, Y. G. (2002). Breaking the myths of rewards: An exploratory study of attitudes about knowledge transfer. *Information Resources Management Journal, 15*(2), 14–21.
12. Zhou, J., Shinm, S. J., Brass, D. J., Choi, J., & Zhang, Z. (2009). Social networks, personal values, and creativity: Evidence for curvilinear and interaction effects. *Journal of Applied Psychology, 94*(6), 1544–1552.
13. Lu, L., Leung, K., & Koch, P. T. (2006). Managerial knowledge transfer: The role of individual, interpersonal, and organizational factors. *Management and Organization Review, 2*, 15–41.
14. Hau, L. N., & Evangelista, F. (2007). Acquiring tacit and explicit marketing knowledge from foreign partners in IJVs. *Journal of Business Research, 60*(11), 1152–1165.
15. Tagliaventi, M. R., & Mattarelli, E. (2006). The role of networks of practice, value sharing, and operational proximity in knowledge flows between professional groups. *Human Relations, 59*, 3.
16. Scott, E. B. (2005). The impact of peer mentoring on organizational knowledge creation and sharing: An empirical study in a software firm. *Group & Organization Management, 30*(3), 319–338.
17. Cramton, C. D. (2001). The mutual knowledge problem and its consequences for dispersed collaboration. *Organization Science, 12*(3), 346–371.
18. Cooke, N. J., Salas, E., Cannon-Bowers, J. A., & Stout, R. J. (2000). Measuring team knowledge. *Human Factors, 42*(1), 151–173.
19. Cramton, C. D. (2001). The mutual knowledge problem and its consequences for dispersed collaboration. *Organization Science, 12*(3), 346–371.

20. Cummings, J. (2004). Work groups, structural diversity, and knowledge transfer in a global organization. *Management Science, 50*(3), 352–364.
21. Tiwana, A., & McLean, E. R. (2005). Expertise integration and creativity in information systems development. *Journal of Management Information Systems, 22*(1), 13–44.
22. Nahapiet, J., & Ghoshal, S. (1998). Social capital, intellectual capital, and the organizational advantage. *Academy of Management Review, 23*, 242–266.
23. Burt, R. S. (1997). The contingent value of social capital. *Administrative Science Quarterly, 42*, 339–365.
24. Portes, A. (1998). Social capital: Its origins and applications in modern sociology. *Annual Review Sociology, 24*, 1–24.
25. Tsai, W. (2000). Social capital, strategic relatedness and the formation of intraorganizational linkages. *Strategic Management Journal, 21*, 925–939.
26. Adler, P. S., & Kwon, S. W. (2002). Social capital: Prospects for a new concept. *Academy of Management Review, 27*, 17–40.
27. Leana, C., & Van Buren, H. (1999). Organizational social capital and employment practices. *Academy of Management Review, 24*, 538–555.
28. Husted, K., & Michailova, S. (2002). Diagnosing and fighting knowledge-sharing hostility. *Organizational Dynamics, 31*, 60–73.
29. Grandori, A., & Kogut, B. (2002). Dialogue on organization and knowledge. *Organization Science, 13*, 224–231.
30. Hinds, P., Patterson, M., & Pfeffer, J. (2001). Bothered by abstraction: The effect of expertise on knowledge transfer and subsequent novice performance. *Journal of Applied Psychology, 86*, 1232–1243.
31. Howells, J. (2002). Tacit knowledge, innovation and economic geography. *Urban Studies, 39*(5–6), 871–884.
32. Howells, J. (2006). Intermediation and the role of intermediaries in innovation. *Research Policy, 35*(5), 715–728.
33. Martin, X., & Salomon, R. (2003). Tacitness, learning and international expansion: A study of foreign direct investment in a knowledge-intensive industry. *Organization Science, 14–3*, 207–311.
34. Barnes, L. B. (1981). Managing the paradox of organizational trust. *Harvard Business Review.*
35. Elsbach, K. D., & Elofson, G. (2000). How the packaging of decision explanations affects the perceptions of trustworthiness. *Academy of Management Journal, 43*, 80–89.
36. Rousseau, D. M., Sitkin, S. B., Burt, R. S., & Camerer, C. (1998). Not so different after all: A cross-discipline view of trust. *Academy of Management Review, 23*, 393–404.
37. Sitkin, S. B., & Roth, N. L. (1993). Explaining the limited effectiveness of legalistic remedies for trust/distrust. *Organizational Science, 4*, 367–392.
38. Mayer, R. C., Davis, J. H., & Schoorman, F. D. (1995). An integrative model of organizational trust. *Academy of Management Review, 20*, 709–734.
39. McKnight, D. H., Cummings, L. L., & Chervany, N. L. (1998). Initial trust formation in new organizational relationships. *Academy of Management Review, 23*, 473–490.
40. Powell, W. W. (1990). Neither market nor hierarchy: Network forms of organization. In B. M. Staw, & L. L. Cummings (Eds.), *Research in organizational behavior* (vol. 12, pp. 295–336).
41. Bromiley, P., & Cummings, L. L. (1995). Organizations with trust. In R. Bies, R. Lewicki, & Sheppard, B (Eds.), *Research in negotiations* (pp. 219–247), 5th Edn.
42. McKnight, D. H., & Chervany, N. L. (1995). Trust building processes in organizational relationships. In C. T. Ragsdale & E. C. Houck, R. T. Sumichrast (Eds.), *Proceedings Decision Sciences Institute* (vol. 2, pp. 751–753).
43. Mishra, A. K. (1996) Organizational responses to crisis: The centrality of trust. In R. M. Kramer, & T. R. Tyler, (Eds.), *Trust in organizations: Frontiers of theory and research* (pp. 261–287).

44. Mishra, A. K., & Mishra, K. E. (1994). The role of trust in effective downsizing strategies. *Human Resource Management, 33*(2), 261–278.
45. Rousseau, D. M., Sitkin, S. B., Burt, R. S., & Camerer, C. (1998). Not so different after all: A cross-discipline view of trust. *Academy of Management Review, 23*, 393–404.
46. Doney, P. M., Cannon, J. P., & Mullen, M. R. (1998). Understanding the influence of National culture on the development of trust. *Academy of Management Review, 23*, 601–620.
47. Dooley, R. S., & Fryxell, G. E. (1999). Attaining decision quality and commitment from dissent: The moderating effects of loyalty and competence in strategic decision-making teams. *Academy of Management Journal, 42*, 372–388.
48. Elsbach, K. D., & Elofson, G. (2000). How the packaging of decision explanations affects the perceptions of trustworthiness. *Academy of Management Journal, 43*, 80–89.
49. Mcallister, D. J. (1995). Affect and cognition-based trust as foundations for interpersonal cooperation in organizations. *Academy of Management Journal, 38*, 24–59.
50. Van Wijk, R., Jansen, J. J. P., et al. (2008). Inter-and intra-organizational knowledge transfer: A meta-analytic review and assessment of its antecedents and consequences. *Journal of Management Studies, 45*(4), 830–853.
51. Cohen, W. M., & Levinthal, D. A. (1990). Absorptive capacity: A new perspective on learning and innovation. *Administrative Science Quarterly, 35*(1), 128–152.
52. Zahra, S. A., & George, G. (2002). Absorptive capacity: A review reconceptualization, and extension. *Academy of Management Review, 27*(2), 185–203.
53. Volberda, H. W., Foss, N. J., & Lyles, M. A. (2010). PERSPECTIVE—absorbing the concept of absorptive capacity: How to realize its potential in the organization field. *Organization Science, 21*(4), 931–951.
54. Das, T. K., Teng, B. S. (2004). The risk-based view of trust: a Conceptual framework. *Journal of Business and Psychology, 19*(1).
55. Daneshgar, F., & Seyyedeh, N. (2010). What drives organizations to share knowledge with their supply chain partners?. In *Proceedings of the 18th European Conference on Information Systems ECIS*, Pretoria.

Organizations and New IT Paradigms: Processes and Organizational Implications Related to Cloud Computing Projects

Roberto Candiotto and Silvia Gandini

Abstract Recently, the remarkable success of the Cloud Computing inspires reflections related to the introduction and the development of new technologies. The relevant turmoil around this phenomenon is not always supported by a complete understanding of its peculiarities, potentialities, opportunities offered to companies and of its consequent organizational implications. Actual market propositions of Cloud solutions include not only the supply of infrastructures and applications as a service, but also the availability of business platforms, to design business processes and to realize integrated inter-organizational processes. Managers can, in fact, improve their companies productivity and competitiveness through the implementation of Cloud and Business Process Management technologies. This work, through the methodology of multiple case study and the coherent analysis of some providers, is aimed to point out Cloud Computing peculiarities, and different organizational approaches that actually characterize projects' planning and implementation, to identify, apart from various offer typologies, standardized procedures for process management and to deduce and suggest a common, hoped organizational behaviour.

Although this work is the result of a common will, every paragraph has been written by a single author; particularly:
1st and 2nd sections by Roberto Candiotto.
3rd and 4th sections by Silvia Gandini.

R. Candiotto
University of Eastern Piedmont, Novara, Italy
e-mail: roberto.candiotto@eco.unipmn.it

S. Gandini (✉)
Researcher at the Department "Studi per l'Economia e l'Impresa",
University of Eastern Piedmont, Novara, Italy
e-mail: silvia.gandini@eco.unipmn.it

P. Spagnoletti (ed.), *Organizational Change and Information Systems*, Lecture Notes in Information Systems and Organisation 2, DOI: 10.1007/978-3-642-37228-5_26,

1 Introduction

Cloud Computing can be defined as a set of technologies, typically in the shape of a service offered to a client by a provider, which enable to store, to file away and to process data items, thanks to the use of hardware and software resources, distributed and shared in a virtual platform on line.[1]

This phenomenon represents the logical consequence of the nineties' technological progresses and of the succeeding technologies pervasiveness, thanks to which each final consumers can process data and pass information, even without having high technological competencies and understanding of computing contents of operations carried out. Related authors have, in fact, identified, the most relevant features of Cloud Computing, the prevalence of economic variables [1] and of organizational implications and goals [2, 3] over purely technological aspects.[2]

The study of Cloud can be particularly interesting not only for its multidisciplinary character, determined by the involvement of different disciplines in data collection, data processing, and data storage operations, and for the use of Information and Communication Technologies (ICT) [4], but also for its transversality toward different organizational research themes, typical features of studies about Information Systems' Organization. It is noteworthy to remark that Cloud technologies are strictly related to specific aspects, like: (a) ≪management and organization of information systems≫, for what concerns the planning of infrastructures and applications, and the relationships between information system and organization, (b) ≪development of information systems≫, with regard to the definition of technical and organizational requirements, and the management of project risks [5, 6].

In the light of previous considerations, this chapter's objective is to answer, through a multiple case study, the following research questions:

1. What are the main characteristics of Cloud market;
2. What are the organizational implications of project management, and particularly:
   - is there a relative uniformity among providers concerning the projects management?

---

[1] In short, from now on the term ≪Cloud≫ will be used as ≪Cloud Computing≫.

[2] Literature analysis has been realized on the abstracts of 837 paper, in the years from 2010 to 2011, of these publications: *European Journal of Information Systems*, *Information Systems Journal*, *Information Systems Research*, *Journal of AIS*, *Journal of MIS*, *MIS Quarterly* [first 6 excellence journal and review according to the ranking of Association for Information Systems (AIS)] and *Information and Management*, *Management Science* [class A review for ≪Organization≫ area according to the ranking 2011 of Accademia Italiana di Economia Aziendale (AIDEA)]. The analysis has shown that only 9 paper are related to Cloud topics, and not focused on organizational aspects of ICT as a Service.

The same results has been produced by the analysis of the first 15 available *Google Books*, related to the keyword ≪Cloud Computing≫, and on the first 20 pages of *Google Scholar*, related to the same keyword.

- are there standardize procedures for processes related to projects management?
- if it is possible to identify and take up common organizational behaviours, what are the effects on the clients' organizations?

2 Characteristics of the Cloud Market

Cloud Computing has had a strong impact on ICT market, with particular regard to the reconsideration of procedures, through which services are created, supplied, and, then, employed. In this connection the Cloud market can be analyzed under different perspectives. The main ones, according to the literature analysis, emphasize, both the goals of Cloud services, and technological components, through which services are provided.

According to the first perspective, the attention is drawn to the best conditions of use, in order to assure the greatest flexibility and effectiveness. For this matter, providers make use of a large pool of virtualized and easily accessible resources (such as hardware, development platforms and/or services), that can be dynamically reconfigured. This pool of resources is typically supplied by a *pay per use* model, fully respecting predetermined Service Level Agreements (SLA) [7, 8].

According to the second perspective, instead, providers' infrastructures consist of Internet-connected servers, located either in a single area or distributed across several locations, which host applications and data in order to obtain efficiency and innovation. Those infrastructures are virtualized and they include different types of software, they use interfaces and communication tools with final users, and lastly they are based on monitoring mechanisms for SLA [9, 10].

A third perspective, developed by *American National Institute of Standards and Technology* (NIST), reconciles the two previous mentioned ones, by defining Cloud Computing as ≪a model for enabling ubiquitous, convenient, on-demand network access to a shared pool of configurable computing resources (networks, servers, storage, applications, and services) that can be rapidly provisioned and released with minimal management effort or service provider interaction≫.[3]

NIST has also offered important contributions to the determination of the cloud computing concept:

- *essential characteristics of Cloud*; according to standards, it's possible to talk about Cloud when: (a) the service is offered through *self-service* and *on-demand* modality; (b) services are available on line and the distribution occurs through mechanisms of standards supply (c) the provider's physical and virtual resources are gathered to serve multiple consumers using a *multi-tenant* model; (d) the supply of resources and services can be elastically provisioned and released, in order to assure timeliness of supplying; (e) resources usage can be monitored,

[3] Source: http://www.nist.gov/.

controlled, and reported, guaranteeing transparency for both provider and consumer.

- *service model*; the consumer can buy: (a) provider's applications running on a Cloud infrastructure (*Software as a Service—SaaS*); (b) processing, storage, networks, and other fundamental computing resources (*Infrastructure as a Service—IaaS*); (c) applications created using programming languages, libraries, services, and tools supported by the provider (*Platform as a Service—Paas*);
- *deployment models*; it's possible to distinguish between: (a) a *public Cloud*, when the infrastructure is provisioned for an open use by the general public, resources are shared, and dynamically allocated, according to customers' real needs; (b) *private Cloud*, when the infrastructure is offered to the exclusive use of a single organization; (c) *community Cloud*, when the infrastructure is shared by several organizations associated with some common interests (for instance, mission values, security requirements, policy, and compliance considerations); (d) *hybrid Cloud*, when infrastructure is a composition of two or more distinct Cloud deployment models (private, community, or public).

3 Organizational Peculiarities in Cloud Project Management

The analysis of some Cloud providers has enabled us to identify some guidelines, that characterized the service offers which reflect the strong diversity within the organizational approaches used by supplier companies.

Analyzed companies[4]: Altea, Asystel, Cosmic Blue Team, Eid, Gruppo Zenit, IBM, Kelyan.

Research methodology: multiple case study.

Goals:

- the provider positioning in the Cloud market;
- phases and activities of Cloud projects;
- constraints/opportunities related to projects;
- the impact of projects on business opportunities of clients companies.

The analysis showed how the market is currently characterized by a great number of providers, aware that some changes are taking place in the ICT market,

[4] We thank all companies' managers that have allowed the realization of this work with their willingness, professionalism, attention, and sensitivity. Particularly: for Altea Gian Carlo Pera and Giovanni Rota, for Asystel Danilo Formaggini and Paolo Sito, for Cosmic Blue Team Manuela Branz and Paolo Zanolini, for EID Giuseppe Volta, for Gruppo Zenit Alessandro Barbero and Roberto Pagano, for IBM Mariano Ammirabile and Mario Moccia, for Kelyan Andrea Bouchard and Luca Ferraris.

The interviews has been planned by defining a specific scheme, predisposed through preliminary conversations (May–July 2011), and then realized (October 2011–January 2012).

and prepared to transform themselves from licence producer to supplier of applicative services (SaaS), present in their own infrastructure. Other vendors have began as an IaaS provider, by placing infrastructures composed of servers and storage tools, and supplying traditional programming services.

A first consideration, in the light of interviewed providers' contributions and of their main organizational variables, carries on the identification of:

- *utility provider*: generally equipped with relevant infrastructures and economic capabilities, they can be provider of applications, conceived as Cloud services, or provider of functions for the elaboration of data and for basic business processes. They are able to better standardize offered processes and services, thus assuring a greater flexibility, an easier pay per use services' quantification, and becoming more coherent with the above mentioned Cloud's peculiarities;
- *niche provider*: generally skilled in services for the support of specific functional activities, they use their specialization to offer personalized services and organizational behaviours closer to IT outsourcing logics.

This classification shows how, still today, Cloud is interpreted in different ways, as regards goals and project activities, and how providers can variously manage modular architectures, thus being able to integrate themselves with solutions from other providers.

The strong points of the package on offer by the utility providers are mainly represented by the efficiency, achievable through the complete services' availability,[5] the recovery capability in case of damage, the celerity of the service's resetting of service capability, the data security, and lastly the chance to offer it at economic and favourable conditions.

The main strength of niche provider is, instead, the ability to project personalized services and applications, configurable in a rapid and secure way, in relation with final consumer's contexts, needs, and business goals. They are able to offer the most recent software releases, adapting them to clients' specific requirements, but often they are unable to include these applications as modular components in a wider solution.

However, the above analysis permits one to define a prevailing behaviour, particularly for the management of SaaS projects, articulated in the following phases:

1. *Definition of the solution* (*contracting phase*). In reference to the service chart, indicating service typologies and general service conditions, the commercial definition can involve three different professional resources: commercial figures for relations, the specialists (technical figures with commercial competencies for project propositions) and the planners (for the proper definition of the project); they are all coordinated by a Cloud manager. In this phase, the provider can use information systems to manage offer activities, which give a

[5] The activation of Cloud solutions requires the availability of the broadband Internet connections, to assure high service levels, and particularly a reliability threshold closed to 99,999 %.

support to specialists in collecting consumer's bills, and plan for the involvement of adequate business resources, to assure the formulation of an optimal proposition. Concerning this, a direct interaction between resources of provider and client is pretty common, in order to better analyze management directives of existing information systems, expected levels for security and compliance, the required autonomy in the applications' development, and lastly the sought service level related to the business.

2. *Activation of the service*. The order is received and processed into the informative system of the delivery unit (i.e. a team for the implementation of solutions, coordinated by a Data Center responsible), for the effective service supply, respecting pre-defined guidelines. Resources involved in the delivery structure are not only responsible for the implementation, but also for the integration of clients' different solutions, in order to coordinate internal applications and software/hardware managed as a Service. In this phase, people responsible for the monitoring have to assure a continuous assistance; in case of damage and malfunctioning they have to be ready to manage those problems, by involving their own specific competencies, both on damage related to the hardware and to applications.

The diffusion of the above mentioned project management procedures, is justified by the fact that a great number of niche providers, extremely professional in the sector of specific functional solutions, has capitalized their deep experience in the field of IT outsourcing, by finding an alternative way to be competitive in the Cloud market; in fact, even with limited investments, they are able to better analyze final markets, to satisfy peculiar requirements of the final consumer, and to offer personalization of components. On the other side, the same approach presents some incoherence with the main features of Cloud market, as defined by NIST. Particularly, personalization activities, both in the formulation of the offer and in the implementation of contracts, contrast with the idea that service has to be offered through *self-service* and *on-demand* modalities.

4 Considerations About Provider Organizational Reassessment

Currently, given the service models previously identified (SaaS, IaaS and PaaS), and the conditions of modularity and pay per use, Cloud Computing can be seen as a way of interaction between the *Business Process Management* (BPM) and the so called *Service Oriented Architectures* (SOA).[6] This reflection implies that each provider must avail itself of infrastructures able to support both single applications

[6] A *Service Oriented Architecture* (SOA) is a set of principles and methodologies for designing and developing software in the form of interoperable services; these services are well-defined business functionalities that are built as software components that can be reused for different

and BPM platform, to facilitate clients in reaching their specific goals, but leaving them autonomous in the configuration/integration of their business processes.

The real challenge for the provider consists in the capability to project their own services in the most coherent way with regards to the more relevant market *business drivers*,[7] and then to provide those services with standardized procedures. From an organizational point of view, the above mentioned approach requires the involvement of the following resources:

- *service creation team*; it's the most innovative organizational unit, characterized both by technical and managerial competencies; particularly, if there is a high degree of interaction between: (a) a developer of the single service components, that uses specific tools for software design and development; (b) a compositor, responsible for the configuration of different solutions, by assembling various components; (c) an offer manager, for the offer planning;
- *service delivery team*; it's the operative organizational unit, integrated, through different portals, both to the service creation team and to the final consumers; it's composed of: (a) business supporters, responsible for the implementation of the offer, as planned by the offer manager, by defining, in a catalogue, the typologies and characteristics of supplied services, and the related contractual conditions; (b) operative supporters, responsible for the offer publication over the Internet, for the management of all operations required by the effective service activation and delivery, and for all consequent monitoring (mainly on service continuity and security levels) and help desk activities; (c) a service manager, responsible for the coordination of all resources involved in the team;
- *service promoters*[8]; they directly interact with final consumers (consolidated or potential) to present new solutions' opportunities, configuring themselves as consultants for a revising of existing strategies and of related processes, and activating Cloud solutions.

The defined organization can be effectively operative only if the provider possesses servers, storage tools, and networks, all implemented over a specific infrastructure, in order to enforce required services. Providers that cannot respect this condition, can find a secure infrastructures environment available in the offer of the so called *global provider*,[9] which gives on-line the availability of Cloud applications and services. In this case the provider uses the global provider's infrastructures, delivering either its own services directly or becoming a pure indirect offer innovator.

(Footnote 6 continued)
purposes. SOA also generally provides a way for consumers of services, such as web-based applications, to be aware of available SOA-based services.

[7] For instance, reduction of development and activation costs, solutions' flexibility, quality of supplied services, new competencies development, etc.

[8] These professional figures can be used in a first moment, mainly if final consumers aren't so ready to have an autonomous access to the provider's resources.

[9] For instance: Cordys, Pega, Appian, HumanWave, Longjump.

In both cases, the on-line presence of BPM tools, comprehended in the global provider's offer and implemented in its infrastructure, lets final consumers autonomous in the design of their own business processes, or in the modification of pre-configured business processes, published on digital libraries. In the light of these considerations, it is possible to extend the previous classification, about the service models, by introducing the *Business Process as a Service* (BPaaS) modality; the latter, by positioning itself on various software components, infrastructures, and platforms, leads to an interpretation of those items as instruments to investigate and to test new business opportunities, and lastly as tools to be used under a service perspective.

The limits of our research are shown in both a reference sample scarcely large and in the lack of a criticality analysis related to projects managed with an organizational behaviour well defined. For these reasons, future steps will consist in finding a confirmation of results achieved so far through the realization of further interviews and in carrying out, still with the support of the interviewed providers, an analysis process based on the model *Failure and Mode Effects* (FMEA) [11] which, due to the criticalities showed, might be able to identifiy consequences and appropriate corrective actions.

References

1. Chellappa, R. K., & Gupta, A. (2002). Managing computing resources in active intranets. *International Journal of Network Management, 12*(2), 117–128.
2. Aymerich, F., Fenu, G., & Surcis, S. (2008). An approach to a cloud computing network. *Proceedings of the* 1*st International Conference on the Applications of Digital Information and Web Technologies*.
3. Ahronovitz, M. et al. (2010). A white paper produced by the cloud computing use case discussion group. *Cloud Computing Use Cases*, 10.
4. Avison, D. A., & Pies-Heje, J. (1995). *Research in information systems: A handbook for research students and their supervisors*. Oxford: Elsevier Butterworth-Heinemann.
5. Baskerville, R. L., & Myers, M. D. (2002). Information systems as a reference discipline. *MIS Quarterly, 26*(1), 1–14.
6. Davis, G. (2000). Information systems conceptual foundations: Looking backward and forward. In R. L. Baskerville, et al. (Eds.), *Organizational and social perspectives on information technology*. Boston: Kluwer.
7. Catteddu, D., & Hogben, G. (2009). *Cloud computing benefits, risks and recommendations for information security*. http://www.enisa.europa.eu/act/rm/files/deliverables/cloud-computing-risk-assessment.
8. Vaquero, L. M., Rodero-Merino, L., Caceres, J., & Lindner, M. (2009). A break in the clouds: Towards a cloud definition. *ACM SIGCOMM Computer Communication Review, 39*(1), 50–55.
9. Armbrust, M., et al. (2010). A view of cloud computing: Clearing the clouds away from the true potential and obstacles posed by this computing capabilities. *Communication of the ACM, 53*(4), 50–58.
10. Leavitt, N. (2009). Is cloud computing really ready for prime time? *Computer, 42*(1), 15–20.
11. Stamatis, D. H. (2003). *Failure mode and effect analysis: FMEA from theory to execution*. United States: ASQ Quality Press.

An Innovation Transfer's Network: University Spin-Offs, Venture Capital and Public Funds

Michela Piccarozzi

Abstract The third mission of universities, the one that allows the commercialization of research results, has assumed a strategic role and primary importance in government policies, in Europe as well as in the rest of the world. Although this attention has raised interest around topics such as technology transfers and university spin-offs, the scarcity of available resources and the conventional university culture still did not allow us an optimal use of the opportunities related to this type of activity. It is necessary to develop a network among university, public sector, business and finance to create value and transform into business projects the result of years of academic research. The aim of this work is to investigate the phenomenon of USOs and the possible link with the private equity and public funding emphasizing that this network creates value for universities, investors and the community itself.

Keywords USOs · Innovation transfer · Private equity · Public funding · Network · Case study

1 Introduction and Methodology

In recent years the world has witnessed a growing interest in the search results and especially in their possible uses in the industrial field. Thus were born the USOs, firms with the objective to commercialize and implement the results of years of studies and discoveries in the universities. Most of these companies operating in the Information Technology (IT); we can think at the famous Helwett Packard, Siemens, Intel and so on [1]. The complexity of the phenomenon is widely

M. Piccarozzi (✉)
Dipartimento Economia e Impresa (D.E.Im), University of Tuscia, Viterbo, Italy
e-mail: piccarozzi@unitus.it

P. Spagnoletti (ed.), *Organizational Change and Information Systems*, Lecture Notes in Information Systems and Organisation 2, DOI: 10.1007/978-3-642-37228-5_27,

investigated in the literature [2–6]. The USOs should not be considered a separate reality in relation to universities or to the market but they are instead an integral part of it and, for their growth and achievement, they need an environment rich in links, contacts and opportunities. This requires in our view that universities consider, among their strategies, the possibility of creating a network that links universities, businesses, local authorities and funders. A close collaboration between funders and universities is especially important in this context because, as we shall see in the work, the greatest obstacle to the development of business projects in the university sector derives from the lack of financial resources and managerial skills. Private equity firms and USOs, because of their characteristics and peculiarities seem to be able to become the center of this network, and as we will see in the following pages, investment funds can be considered the best way to realize it. The purpose of this study is to analyze the link between university, public funding and private equity as the principal mean for development and growth of USOs as well as for the creation of value within the network. The analysis will be conducted from two points of view. First of all from the side of the USOs, to understand what issues arise and what strategies can be implemented to involve institutional lenders in the activity. Secondly, we will investigate the views of private equity trying to capture their perceptions about USOs and then analyze the reasons and procedures to be adopted to create a communication channel between the two. The first part of the chapter will allow us to describe the phenomenon of USOs, also through the study of literature, to individuate their distinctive features and most common problems. The second part will focus on the role of private equity to highlight how, in our point of view, the involvement of an institutional lender, not only in the financial area, but especially in managerial aspects, can contribute to the growth and development of USOs. So, we will investigate the role of closed-end investment funds, and the role of public funding and support as a means for the realization of a network between companies and lenders, especially by focusing on the case of PharmEste, a biopharmaceutical spin-off of the University of Ferrara. The case will be analyzed using a qualitative methodology, describing the stages of financing and development company, focusing on the intervention of venture capital firms [7].

2 University Spin-Offs: A National and International Literature Review

Universities have always been considered important players in the process of transferring knowledge and technology to the industrial sector especially for their contribution to regional development. This role has historically been dominated by the granting of patents by universities to outside parties, but this is not the only way to gather benefits from commercial exploitation of academic discoveries; the USOs may indeed be considered an alternative, surely efficient, way of exploitation of scientific research. When we speak about USOs, we refer to those realities in which we find the following features [8]: a new company, an entity independent from the university a separate legal identity, created by the university, thus excluding all other research organizations or institutions; for the exploitation of results arising from the academic activity (not just patentable results, but also all technical and scientific knowledge acquired during the academic activity); whose aim is to obtain profits (this then allows us to exclude all non-profit activities). The fact that we consider only those businesses spun from universities allows us to develop the right framework of reference of the USOs, excluding all other contexts (technical schools, departments of R&D laboratories and private research institutes) for whose is preferable to speak of research-based USOs [3, 9]. The first example of academic spin-off companies can be find in the development of Silicon Valley; it can be attributed to the action of scientists who left their industrial or academic lab, for example Helwett and Packard or the Basf company. The majority of those firms operates in Information Technology (IT). The spin-off activated in Italy in 2011 are 990, and about one third of these enterprises (31.2 % to be precise) is active in the field of ICT where we can find the older companies (mean age of 13.4 years) [1]. One of the main aspects about USOs investigated in literature is the problems that exist in these realities, from the moment you start to develop your business idea, up to the stages of growth and development of the company [6, 10]. The most complex phenomena are of course those related to sources of funding. This problem is consistent throughout the European context [11, 12]. The funding represents the most frequently cited obstacle to innovation by companies of all sizes in all sectors. In Italy the problem of funding seems to be the result of a mix of issues ranging from lack of financial literacy that characterizes firms and entrepreneurs, the inefficiency of these markets through the excessive burden of indebtedness in finance especially for small and medium enterprises [13].

The lack of financial resources and shortage of funds for research and innovation results in difficulties for the growth and development and often the start-up of USOs.

Often it is difficult for research USOs to finance their own activity because of the limited resources available to the companies. Also it is almost impossible to refer to self-financial support because those companies are rarely able, especially in their early stages, to produce adequate cash flows. Thus they resort directly to external sources. USOs have two main funding streams: first public resources especially dedicated, second, institutional investors or banks. Public funds for research and technology transfer are often scarce and not always able to fill the actual needs, also the procedure for the award is long and complex and also in recent years, universities have seen a significant reduction in the funds available for their activities and in particular those related to research initiatives and inevitably USOs [14]. If instead we look at the resources coming from private investors, we can say that in recent years we have had an increase in private equity funding and business angels to the side of funding from entrepreneurs or banks. But there is an information gap between the USOs and the lender that often prevents the conclusion of the funding operation [10].

This information asymmetry occurs because of the lack of entrepreneurial culture of the researchers who have difficulties in appropriately transforming their knowledge into an attractive business plan. Also, in the case of banks, the lack of adequate grants is seen as a major problem to the concession of the funding. Furthermore, the financing of an innovative company has substantially higher risk profile than any other company. The uncertainty about the actual application of research results and the difficulties linked to a commercial use of the results present a risk-return ratio too unbalanced (especially in the early stages of development) which often discourages donors. That is why the hierarchy of sources of financing of USOs, and more generally firms that base their activities on research and technology, differs from that of other realities. Also in relation to each life stage of a company we can identify the most appropriate source of funding.

While under normal business you start with internal sources for the early stages of birth and then move on to credit institutions and only secondarily to institutional investors, in the case of innovative firms and thus the USOs, the use of internal sources is almost absent as well as those coming from the banks. Private equities play therefore a major role as those are preferred to bank, both because of the lower amount of guarantee needed to access credit, both because of the managerial support that private equities are able to provide to spin-offs. The managerial support and strategic guidance provided by private equity funds assume an even greater importance in those firms who originate from the university environment especially because of the genetic lack of solid entrepreneurial basis. Often indeed the support provided by specialized center for the exploitation of research or specific bureaus created by universities (Technology Transfer Office, TTO) to support start-ups are not enough.

3 The Private Equity's Point of View and the Role of Closed-End and Public Funds for the Research

The approach of universities to the financial world must meet with a reluctance of investors to finance this particular enterprise reality. Institutional investors are always been looking for business projects, start-up, highly innovative companies with high prospects of development to be funded with the aim of achieving high capital gain.

In this regard we can notice that the ideal profile of the company, which an institutional investor intends to support and to participate to, are represented by [15]: a management whit abilities and unquestioned entrepreneurial experience; a company with an analytical business plan and innovative market strategies; a holding opened to new financing partners; high corporate performances; corporate management transparency.

It is easy to see that these are just ideal characteristics, difficult to find in companies or to predict with certainty, but at the same time it is evident that USOs, compared to traditional companies, present much less these profiles. The process that institutional investors must follow in selecting projects to be supported, includes a series of evaluative steps.[1] To create this process of evaluation of the characteristics of USOs can allow an approach between the two realities, and give to this kind of companies the possibility to have chance of growth and development. Also the instrument for financing must be suitable for company and competitive in order to use the new ideas that spring from the academic world, to create value for investors, researchers and for the territory. Then you need not only to have an assessment process which considers the characteristics of USOs, but also an ad hoc tool to properly manage the funding. The main tool that institutional investors make available to the development of USOs are closed-end funds. The strategy of a fund is made through two basic premises: first of all a new enterprises are necessary to create and develop new technologies and new markets and the high-tech company, and then also, and especially, the USOs are the means by which we can increase competitiveness and achieve significant capital gain. There are numerous cases of funds devoted entirely to the start-up of the research; these funds allow universities an easier access to the network of venture capitalists just because they are set on loans less onerous and more slender.

This kind of funds are created and regulated by the company's asset management, using the logic of network contacts and the links between university and business, and also to build tools that are designed to fund the research for industrial and commercial use of the exploitation of academic work. The understanding of a model of excellence based on public and private sectors is the main reason for the creation of these funds: to the one side, in fact, we find a network of groups and organizations directly involved in research and universities, to the other, a society and a team of experts to the management and the support of enterprises, institutional investors, stakeholders, etc. The network allows to have entities that provide different skills at different stages of the birth and development of enterprises. In particular, research centers assist the proponents in the implementation phase of the idea supporting them in relation to contracts, patents and marketing; the TTO assists the incubation step with advices aimed to support the ideas and to analyze the potentiality of projects [16].

In this network are very important not only closed-end funds but also public funds.

Public funds are essential in the initial phase of the research activity; they are often insufficient to follow also the development phase, so, it is important that they are also added to other funds, in particular private funds. Public funds finance activities for a maximum of 500,000€, resources available increase when it comes

[1] The first phase is the analysis of deal flow, during which most of the initiatives are being discarded, criteria are dictated by the strategic guidelines of the investor, then the geographical location, industry, type of product or service must be assess. Proposals that pass to the second step are subjected to further analysis about the economic and financial aspects, market outlets and the amount of funding. Finally, for all the initiatives that pass the first two steps, the due diligence phase opens, ad it will end with the careful selection of projects to be funded.

to particular areas, for example underdeveloped areas; this amount covers 50 % of the costs of industrial research and 25 % of the costs of development. So at last, the network of venture capital, through investment funds, acts as the operating arm for funding and therefore the possibility of commercialization and industrialization of research results. The use of the funds allows to adjust the relationships between the company management and investors that will combine the resources, represented not only by banks and banking foundations, but in recent years, mostly from funds of funds. The development of such network permits to use simultaneously the different responsibilities of various parties that compose it, helping to fill the gaps in the USOs that we have previously analyzed, while stimulating the development of the entire economic system of the territory. Development strategies of universities and institutional investors find a meeting point in the network which, although it is virtuous requires a difficult constitution. It relies heavily on the belief first of all by the proponents of entrepreneurship initiative, of all the other involved partners. We have already seen the difficulties in relying together USOs and institutional investors, and equally complex is make the institutions, consortia and especially the market to perceive the potential of initiatives.

It's then necessary for the operation of the network we are considering, the projects' firm to be able to capture the trust of all stakeholders by diversifying itself every time in order to focus more on the expectations inherent in the individual subject to whom addresses it. While talking to institutional investors economic and financial prospects of the project must been shown, while addressing to a public or local authorities, it is important to highlight the possible beneficial effects on the territory (for example for employment, development or image, etc.).

4 Case Study: PharmEste Ltd

An example of the synergy between universities (in particular public resources and founds) industry and finance is the PharmEste Ltd, a spin-off of the University of Ferrara. PharmEste, founded as a USOs of the University of Ferrara is a private drug development biopharmaceutical company based on a unique Transient Receptor Potential (TRPs) ion channel technology platform that brings together strong expertise on TRPs area and industrial competences in research and development process applied to small molecule therapeutics. The company mission is to play a leading role in the discovery and development of fully proprietary high affinity and selective TRP channel therapeutics for the treatment of neuropathic pain, overactive bladder and other TRP-mediated diseases. The TRPV1 receptor is the best known member of the TRP ion channel family TRPV1 is present on primary sensory neurons and is activated by low pH, by noxious heat and by endogenous chemical mediators such as lipids, whose action is also mimicked by exogenous substances including capsaicin. TRPV1 is up-regulated following inflammation and nerve damage and is a key factor in the pain response. Neuropathic pain has no satisfactory treatment because standard therapy either work poorly or produce unacceptable side effects. TRPV1 antagonists may represent a new safe and effective treatment for neuropathic pain and other TRPV1–related diseases. The TRPV1 antagonist, PHE377, is the candidate drug under Phase I clinical trial, characterized by high activity and selectivity on target, high efficacy and long lasting effect in experimental models of pain, no relevant toxicity in vitro and in vivo and favorably compares with other TRPV1 antagonists under development.

Second generation of TRPV1 antagonists are at lead optimization stage and a discovery program on TRPs antagonists is on going in order to identify new drug candidates for the treatment of other TRP-mediated diseases. The innovative idea generated by university research was supported by a team of donors who have supported the activities from the earliest stages of life; the same firm has also had the opportunity to use five patents owned university itself. PhamEste is managed by an industrial and multidisciplinary team with many years of experience and account of 12 people. The company is supported by an outstanding international advisory board with scientific, clinical and industrial competences.

PharmEste started with 200.000€, because of the accent put by researches on the IP system, PharmEste was able to raise considerable venture funds in a very short period of time. Later, PharmEste has raised two round financing from International Venture Capitals for the different development phases:

1. Phase 1 (toxicity verification) €6 million (January 2007);
2. Phase 2 (efficacy verification) €12 million (September 2008);
3. Phase 3 (clinical experimentation) €20 million.

The first one, on January 2007 PharmEste closed a €3.2 million Round A financing with Z-Cube s.r.l as lead investor and Quantica Sgr, Zernike Meta Ventures, Fondamenta Sgr as co-investors. In the second phase, on September 2008, PharmEste closed the second financing stage (Round B) for a total of €6 Million, to be mainly used for the pre-clinical and clinical development of the PHE377 compound.[2] The investment is supported by two of the financial partners of the first round financing, namely Z-Cube s.r.l., the corporate venture of the Zambon Company S.p.A, and Quantica Sgr (Italian leading vc Company), the Asset Management Company dedicated to innovative Venture capital activities and by two new financial partners: Emilia Venture, managed by MPS Venture Sgr (Montepaschi Group) and MP Healthcare Venture Management Inc., the Boston Venture fund jointly owned by Mitsubishi Tanabe Pharma Corporation and Mitsubishi Chemical Holdings Corporation in Japan. In early 2009 PharmEste has continued discussions with pharmaceutical companies and venture capitalists who had shown interest in the activity. These contacts are also strategic in view of future funding of the company. By the end of 2011 PharmEste expects to have: completed Phase II (trials for PHE377 in DNP and PHN); completed FTIM with a

[2] PHE377 is a small molecule TRP1 receptor antagonist highly effective in several pain models, including pain of neurophatic origin.

second generation TRPV1 antagonist; pre-clinical development for a new TRPs antagonist and provide an exit for the investors. To reach this goal PharmEste is planning a round C financing. The focus for USOs is evident from the many funders and contact of PharmEste; in particular in this case is a clear relationship between public and private funds both contributed to the development of the project that otherwise could not have done the testing phases. The importance of this network is evident both in the availability of different funds and also in the various skills made by entities.

5 Conclusion

The benefits of innovation processes have an impact, with positive effects both on subjects directly involved in the ideal network analyzed, and on society and economic system. As for the USOs and institutional investors we would have benefit in terms of economic returns, i.e. the ability to reinvest the profits of a business in further research; brokering of scientific knowledge innovation; internationalization.

The fallout on the entire economic system and the territory in which this network develops and operates, can be expressed in terms of cultural growth and prestige, just for the key role that universities have in the social context. On the enterprise system, the strong innovative capacity of USOs can contribute to the development of skilled and emerging sectors such as the one related to IT or to biotechnologies, and thus creating new jobs and new professional opportunities for specialists and researchers.

The innovation and the link between research and business world are then the best answer to the problem of competitiveness on markets and the need for internationalization. The essence of the knowledge based economy is exactly expressed through technological transfer and exploitation of university research; the network between universities, markets and investors, nor are the primary vehicle for contributing to the economic development and to the overcoming of moments of crisis and difficulty of the market. The analysis of PharmEste case allows to highlight the strength of the network and of the multidisciplinary of skills and relations for development and success of the USOs. Just in relation to this, USOs can be considered the best tool available, if inserted into a network of success as that proposed, which allows these companies to gain even more strength and ability to achieve success in the international context. So, the network described can be an excellent opportunity for all USOs and in particular for those working in IT that seem to be the firms most successful and with more development capabilities. The analysis of the role of information systems in this network can be a future development of the research.

References

1. Piccaluga, A., et. al. (2012). Pronti per evolvere. IX Rapporto Netval sulla valorizzazione della ricerca pubblica italiana. Online http://www.netval.it.
2. Carayannis, E., Rogers, E., Kurihara, K., & Allbritton, M. (1998). High technology spin-offs from government R&D laboratories and research universities. *Technovation, 18*(1), 1–11.
3. Clarysse, B., & Moray, N. (2004). A process study of entrepreneurial team formation: the case of a researched-based spin-off. *Journal of Business Venturing, 19*, 55–79.
4. Rasmussen, E., & Borch, O. J. (2010). University capabilities in facilitating entrepreneurship: A longitudinal study of spin-off ventures at mid-range universities. *Research Policy, 39*(5), 602–612.
5. Roberts, E., & Malone, D. (1996). Policies and structures for spinning off new companies from research and development organizations. *RtScD Management, 26*(1), 17–48.
6. Steffensen, M., Rogers, E. M., & Speakman, K. (2000). Spin-offs from research centers at a research university. *Journal of Business Venturing, 15*, 93–111.
7. Yin, K.R. (2002). Case study research: Design and methods. Applied social research methods series. (3rd ed.,Vol 5).
8. Klofsten, M., & Johnes-Evans, D. (2000). Comparing academic entrepreneurship in Europe—the case of Sweden and Ireland. *Small Business Economy, 14*(4), 299–309.
9. Degroof, J. J., & Roberts, E. B. (2004). Overcoming weak entrepreneurial infrastructures for academic spin-off ventures. *The Journal of Technology Transfer, 29*(3-4), 327–352.
10. Shane, S. (2004). *Academic entrepreneurship: University spinoffs and wealth creation*. Cheltenham: Edward Elgar.
11. Ndonzuau, F. N., Pirnay, F., & Surlemont, B. (2002). A stage model of academic spin-off creation. *Technovation, 22*, 281–289.
12. Wright, M., Clarysse, B., Mustar, P. E., & Lockett, A. (2007). *Academic entrepreneurship in Europe*. Cheltenham: Edgar Elsevier.
13. Nicolaou, N., Birley, S. (2000). Academic networks in a trichotomous categorization of university spinouts. *10th Annual Global Entrepreneurship Research Conference*. Imperial College, London.
14. Grossi, G., Ruggiero, P. (2008). Lo spin-off accademico. Attori ed ambiente nella fase di gestazione aziendale. Cedam, Padova.
15. Giovannini, R. (2004). *La gestione del venture capital e dell'early stage financing*. Roma: Bancaria editrice.
16. O'Shea, R., Allen, T. J., Cheavalier, A., & Roche, F. (2005). Entrepreneurial orientation, technology transfer and spin-off performance of U.S. universities. *Research Policy, 34*, 994–1009, Elsevier, Amsterdam, ISSN: 0048-7333

Open Innovation for Technological Transfer

Pasquale Ardimento, Vito Nicola Convertini and Giuseppe Visaggio

Abstract This chapter presents a framework aiming to support a cooperative "innovation chain" in an Open Innovation (OI) perspective. To this end we propose a Knowledge Management System (KMS) which consists of a set of processes that constitute the Experience Factory (EF) and a platform that is the Knowledge Experience Base (KEB), which collects Knowledge Experience Packages (KEP). The KMS thus formed supports the formalization and packaging of knowledge and experience of producers and innovation transferors encouraging gradual explanation of tacit information of bearers of knowledge to facilitate the transfer while minimizing costs and risks.

Keywords Knowledge base · Open innovation · Business model

1 Introduction

The necessity to exchange knowledge between different public and private organizations causes the generation of new approaches to innovation transferring. The proposed approach to knowledge generation and exchanging is based on OI [1, 2]. The logic of OI characterizes the end of the 20th century and forecasts that

P. Ardimento (✉) · V. N. Convertini · G. Visaggio
Department of Informatics, University of Bari Aldo Moro, Bari, Italy
e-mail: ardimento@di.uniba.it

V. N. Convertini
e-mail: convertini@di.uniba.it

G. Visaggio
e-mail: visaggio@di.uniba.it

P. Ardimento · G. Visaggio
Ser and Practices, Spin-off of the University of Bari Aldo Moro, Bari, Italy

P. Spagnoletti (ed.), *Organizational Change and Information Systems*, Lecture Notes in Information Systems and Organisation 2, DOI: 10.1007/978-3-642-37228-5_28,

enterprises develop their projects in collaboration with other enterprises. As contrast to the principles that had characterized the Closed Innovation, the divulging idea is that of: internal R&Ds holding part of a knowledge that comes from external R&D; creation of a business model that assumes a primary role in the knowledge development lifecycle; sharing knowledge with other enterprises in order to achieve higher quality levels. The diffusion of any innovation goes through all or at least part of the phases of what is known as Knowledge Lifecycle because it must first be acquired by single individuals and then gradually transferred to the rest of the technical staff, up to the entire organization. The original definition of this lifecycle [3] has been considered and interpreted in relation to introduction and transfer of a new technology; let it be a process or product, within an industrial environment. We have defined it Knowledge Lifecycle during Innovation (KLI). At first the innovator internalizes the knowledge related to the new technology he is willing to introduce (tacit knowledge and individual learning occurs); tacit knowledge is then socialized between the innovator and other project team members, and among them, during training sessions or team work (informal communication and group learning occur); during externalization acquired knowledge is formalized and made independent from the innovator. Tacit knowledge is made explicit to all stakeholders of the organization (explicit knowledge and formal learning occur); once new knowledge is acquired and formalized, each individual can combine it to previous one.

So, abstract knowledge models are extracted from explicit ones. An innovation is completely acquired when it is integrated and combined with previous knowledge. Summarizing, innovation diffusion transforms tacit knowledge, e.g. operational skills that few stakeholders possess, including practical judgment capabilities, into explicit knowledge, e.g. formalized knowledge through documentation, manuals, workflow and so on. This transfer occurs through learning at both an individual and group level, e.g. modification in stakeholders' behaviour according to experience and acquisition of new knowledge following to adoption of the new technology. In KLI knowledge transfer is critical during the stage of Internalization, and the stage of externalization and socialization. Indeed, in the first phase tacit knowledge has to be extracted and formalized in all its essential parts. During internalization transcribed knowledge has to be rapidly acquired, so it must be cut depending on the skills of the recipients, in addition, its acquisition must be attractive to the recipient in order to reward the person who required it, to overcome his cultural inertia, and acquire new knowledge. Socialization is encouraged if the tools which support the OI enable to lead recipients to acquire new knowledge. Obviously the attractiveness of the vehicle used for technology transfer is important at this stage too.

The PROMETHEUS Project [4] (Practices Process and Methods Evolution Through Experience Unfolded Systematically), is a model of Experience Factory (EF) to collect experimental knowledge in a repository Knowledge Experience Base (KEB) in the form of Knowledge Experience Package (KEP). The KEP is the vehicle suggested for the transfer of knowledge while the EF is the set of processes that make the OI. This chapter describes:

- the structure of the KEP and the features that make the contents to be tailored and attractive for the target of the innovation;
- the characteristics of the EF processes that ensure the extraction of tacit knowledge and its formalization in KEP.

The rest of the chapter is structured as follows: Sect. 2 discusses related works and research activities; Sect. 3 presents the proposed approach, focusing on the KEP structure. Section 4 describes the attractiveness of Prometheus contents. Finally, in the conclusions some observations are made about Prometheus and possible future research pathways are identified.

2 Related Works

The problem of knowledge packaging for better usage is being studied by both research centers [5–8] and companies [5, 8] demostrating in this way a common interest to the same problem. Knowledge bases sometimes have a semantically limited scope. This is the case of the Daimler-Benz base [7, 8], that collects lessons learned or mathematical prediction models or results of controlled experiments in the automobile domain only. In other cases the scope is wider but the knowledge is too general and therefore not very usable. This applies to the MIT knowledge base that describes business processes but only at one or two levels of abstraction. There are probably other knowledge bases that cover wider fields with greater operative detail [8] but we do not know much about them because they are private knowledge bases. Our approach focuses on a knowledge base whose contents make it easier to achieve knowledge transfer among research centres; between research centres and production processes; among production processes. The knowledge base must be hybrid, public, as we wish, or private, depending on KEP authors preferences. The public KEB allows to one or more interested communities to develop around it and exchange knowledge.

3 Proposed Approach

The KEP term refers to an organized set of: knowledge content, teaching units on the use of the demonstration prototypes or tools and all other information that may strengthen the package's ability to achieve the proposed goal. The KEP contains knowledge content integrated with an e-learning function. In the proposed approach, the KEP must include all the elements shown in Fig. 1. A user can access one of the package components and then navigate along all the components of the same package according to her/his training or education needs. Search inside the package starting from any of its components is facilitated by the component's Attributes.

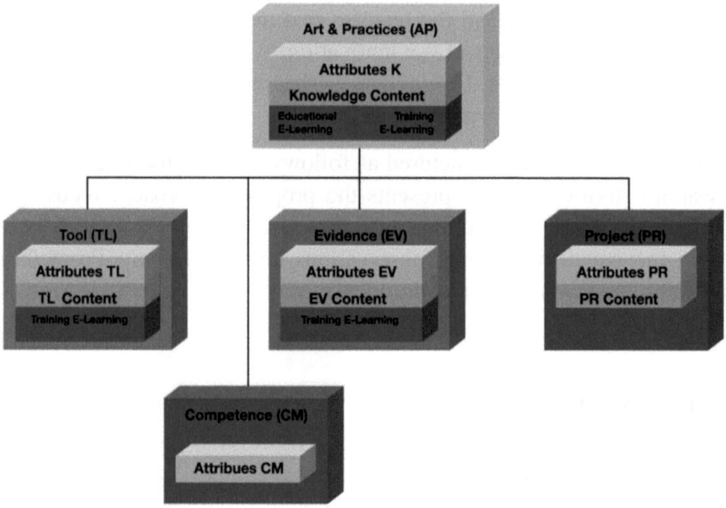

Fig. 1 A knowledge/experience package

It can be seen in the figure that the Art and Practices Knowledge Content (KC) is the central one. It contains the knowledge package expressed in a hypermedia form in order to include figures, graphs, formulas and whatever else may help to understand the content. The KC is organized as a tree. Starting from the root (level 0) descent to the lower levels (level 1, level 2, …) is through pointers (Fig. 1). The higher the level of a node the lower the abstraction of the content, which focuses more and more on operative elements. The root node is made up of the following sections:

- Thoughtful Index: tells the reader how the package suggested will practically change, with a list of processes and activities, case the whole process is not innovating or has to be modified.
- Problem (one or more): describes the problem of KEP. A problem may belong to one of the two following types: decision and optimization. If the problem is the decision there should be the possibility to make a choice, and the aim for this choice. If the problem is optimization, the resources of which you want to improve the performance and the objective function of optimization have to be indicated. For each problem, the context has to be defined, that is to say all facts and circumstances which cause and condition a certain problem.

The leaf nodes have the answers to the problems: the solution or solutions suggested for each problem set. Figure 2 shows an example of contents of a KEP. The KEP does not contain the conceptual basis of the subject, because it is considered as the background of the user's knowledge, and can be found in conventional sources of knowledge such as technical reports, papers and books. Anyway, when users needs some of the basic concepts for understanding the contents of the KEP they can use educational e-learning course. And if users should need more information, they can use the “attachments” regarding reports, papers and books about basic topics of KEP. Instead, if the use of a demonstrational prototype is required to become operational, the same package will point to a training in e-learning course (Fig. 1.) As stated above, the use of these courses is flexible, to meet individual user’s needs. When a package also has support tools, rather than merely demonstration prototypes, KC links the user to the available tool. For the sake of clarity, we point out that this is the case when the knowledge package has become an industrial practice, so that the demonstration prototypes included in the archetype they derived from have become industrial tools. The tools are collected in the Tools Component (TL). Each tool available is associated to an educational course, again of a flexible nature, in the use of the correlated training e-learning course. Should the user need support from whom has knowledge of the contents of the KEP, a list of resources is a reference. The list is collected in the Skills component (CM). To ensure control of completeness and lack of ambiguity in the contents of KEP, the vocabulary of the KEP, i.e. concepts and relations between there meanings, has been formalized by the W3C XML Schema [9].

In line with OI, the research results integrated by a package may be contained within the same knowledge base or derive from other knowledge bases or other laboratories. If the knowledge package being read uses knowledge packages located in the same experience base, the relations will be explicitly highlighted. As shown in Fig. 1, each component in the knowledge package has its own attributes structure. For all the components, these allow rapid selection of the relative elements in the knowledge base. The focus in this work is on the attributes in the KC. In fact, these have been defined during research conducted by the authors and by

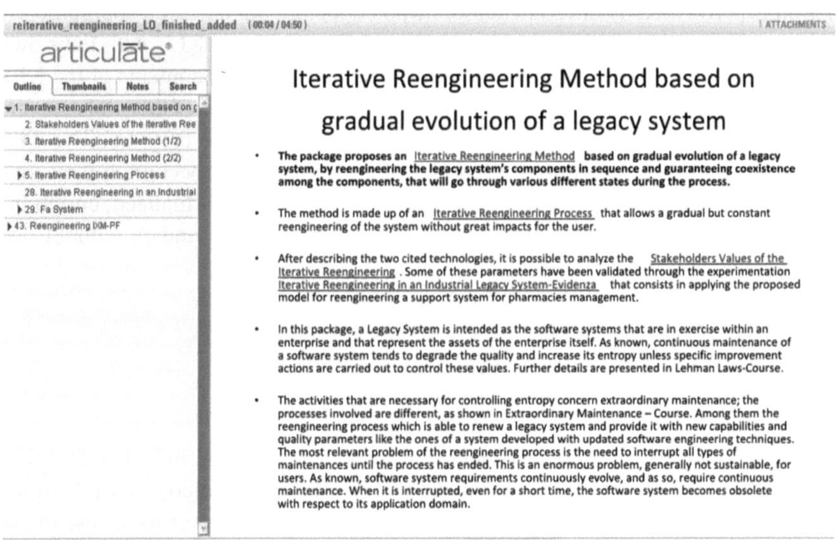

Fig. 2 Sample of content of a knowledge/experience package

other authors. To facilitate the research, we used a set of selection classifiers and a set of descriptors summarizing the contents. The classifiers include: the key words and the problems the package is intended to solve. The summary descriptors include: a brief summary of the content and a history of the essential events occurring during the life cycle of the package, giving the reader an idea of how it has been applied, improved, and how mature it is. The history may also include information telling the reader that the content of all or some parts of the package are currently undergoing improvements. The interested reader can find further details on the contents of the KEP and the management and use of the KEB on the technical report [10, 11–13].

4 PROMETHEUS as Support to Open Innovation

A KEP is generally based on conjectures, hypotheses and principles. As they mature, their contents must all become principle-based. The transformation of a statement from conjecture through hypothesis to principle must be based on experimentation showing evidence of its validity. The experimentation, details of its execution and relative results, are collected in the Evidence component (EV), and duly pointed to by the knowledge package. Finally, a mature knowledge package is used in one or more projects, by one or more firms. At this stage the details describing the project and all the measurements made during its execution that express the efficacy of use of the package are collected in the Projects component (PR) associated with the package. A KEP is undergoing a process of incremental improvement that aims to reach all parts described above. The incremental completion is performed by different authors who cooperate but that are geographically and temporally spread. Authors (A_1, A_2, …, A_n) produce the KEP with their own knowledge. Researchers and practitioners, beneficiaries of the contents of the KEP and reported as (D_1, D_2, …, D_m), with or without the knowledge of the $\{A_i\}$, acquire the innovation contents contained in the KEP, whatever stage they are. The KEP evolve since then, through their research or their experiments becoming their own authors. The results of the research or experiments, properly formalized, enrich the KEP. Such a process, therefore, provides an OI between D and A without any geographical and time constraints.

5 Conclusions and Future Works

The public and private organizations need to be linked to the information cycle. For this reason, the proposed approach PROMETHEUS includes an e-learning System teaching knowledge of the packages and training the user in the use of the demonstration prototypes or tools supporting an innovation. We propose PROMETHEUS, a demonstration platform that integrates a Knowledge Management

System and a Learning System, allowing navigation among all its components. Obviously, to generalize the validity of the KEP proposed in this work many experimentations and studies to different contexts are needed. For this reason, the authors intend making instruments and material available to other interested researchers.

References

1. Chesbrough, H. W. (2003). *Open innovation: The new imperative for creating and profiting from technology*. Boston: Harvard Business School Press.
2. Amidon, D. M. (1998). Blueprint for 21st century innovation management. *Journal of Knowledge Management, 2*(1), 23–31.
3. Ikujiro, N., Hirotaka, T. (1995). The knowledge creating company: How Japanese companies create the dynamics of innovation (p. 284, ISBN 978-0-19-509269-1). Oxford University Press, Oxford.
4. Ardimento, P., Caivano, D., Cimitile, M., & Visaggio, G. (2008). Empirical investigation of the efficacy and efficiency of tools for transferring software engineering knowledge. *Journal of Information and Knowledge Management, 7*(3), 197–208.
5. Jedlitschka, A., Pfahl, D. (2003). Experience-based model-driven improvement management with combined data sources from industry and Academia. *Proceedings of the 2003 International Symposium on Empirical Software Engineering*.
6. Klein, M. (2001). Combining and relating ontologies: An analysis of problems and solutions. In: A. Gomez-Perez et al. (Eds.) WS on Ont. and Inf. Sharing, Seattle, USA.
7. Malone, T. W., Crowston, K., & Herman, G. A. (2003). *Organizing business knowledge-the MIT process handbook*. Cambridge: MIT Press.
8. Schneider, K., & Schwinn, T. (2001). Maturing experience base concepts at DaimlerChrysler. *Software Process Improvement and Practice, 6*(2), 85–96.
9. W3C XML Schema available at http://www.w3.org/XML/Schema.
10. Ardimento, P., Baldassarre, M. T., Cimitile, M., & Visaggio, G. (2009). Empirical validation of knowledge packages as facilitators for knowledge transfer. *Journal of Information and Knowledge Management, 8*(3), 229–240.
11. Ardimento, P., Cimitile, M. (2008). An empirical study on software engineering knowledge/experience packages. In: Lecture notes in Computer Science (including subseries lecture notes in artificial intelligence and lecture notes in bioinformatics), 5089 LNCS, pp. 289–303.
12. Ardimento, P., Baldassarre, M., Bianchi, A., Visaggio, G. (2003). Empirical studies as a means for technology transfer. *Proceedings of the second workshop series on empirical engineering*, p. 8.
13. Ardimento, P., Boffoli, N., Cimitile, M., Masone, A., Tammaro, A. (2007). Empirical investigation on knowledge packaging supporting risk management in software processes. *Proceedings of the IASTED international conference on software engineering*, SE 2007, pp. 30–36.

The Dynamics of Innovation: Linking Corporate Entrepreneurship and IT-Enabled Value Co-creation

Enrico Angioni and Francesca Cabiddu

Abstract We offer a theory of innovation that links corporate entrepreneurship and value-co-creation, theories usually separated in the management and organizational literature. We show how firms' innovations are shaped by the relationship between organizations and customers and how information technology (IT) can enhance this process. We then introduce a new construct, corporate customership, to convey the joint process of innovation realized by the firm and the customer and enabled by IT.

1 Introduction

Innovation is recognized as a primary source of competitive differentiation for organizations [1], and the management and organization literature has used various ways of investigating the process of innovations [2, 3]. The literature has shown that the type of innovations (radical or incremental) has an impact on creating the conditions for firms to have superior performance, and on imposing the conditions to sustain it in the long run [4, 5]. Yet, innovators must be attuned to customer needs and agile in their ability to assemble new value propositions that meet those needs [6].

Moreover, innovation is increasingly IT-enabled and spans beyond dyadic relationships to include suppliers, complementers and even competitors [7]. While the literature has begun to investigate novel customer service arrangements [8, 9] and electronic interfaces for service provision [10] there has been very limited work aimed at systematically understanding how the cooperation between firms and customer enables innovation and the role of IT in this process.

To help fill this theoretical gap we offer a theory of innovation that links corporate entrepreneurship (CE) and IT value-co-creation, theories usually

E. Angioni (✉) · F. Cabiddu
University of Cagliari, Cagliari, Italy

P. Spagnoletti (ed.), *Organizational Change and Information Systems*, Lecture Notes in Information Systems and Organisation 2, DOI: 10.1007/978-3-642-37228-5_29,

separated in the management and organizational literature. CE has been defined as the "formal and informal activities aimed at creating new business in established companies through product and process innovations and market developments…with the unifying objective of improving a company's competitive position and financial performance" [11]. IT value, "co-creation represents the idea that (a) IT value is increasingly being created and realized through actions of multiple parties, (b) value emanates from robust collaborative relationships among firms, and (c) structures and incentives for parties to partake in and equitably share emergent value are necessary to sustain co-creation" [12].

We show how firms' innovations are shaped by the relationship between organizations and customers and how information technology can enhance this process. We then introduce a new construct, corporate customership. Corporate customership puts the attention directly on costumer-company interaction as the locus of innovation. We contribute to the service innovation literature in that we provide insights into the process of innovation. Future research should both extend and complement our approach.

2 Corporate Entrepreneurship

The Corporate Entrepreneurship (CE) must be understood as a process of innovation aimed at a renewal of the existing organization, whose main purpose is to maintain or improve their competitive potential in the market [13, 14]. This process of renewal, it should be understood as an operation that potentially encompasses every type of organization of any size, whose main connotation part by the need to innovate and innovate themselves, so that the same can cope the high dynamism and competitiveness arising from the market [15, 16]. Research has found that CE initiatives can materially improve an existing organization's agility and are positively associated with financial performance [11].

The basis of the CE can be found in Schumpeter [17], who stated that the main perpetrators of economic growth are the entrepreneurs, who are the principal architects of the introduction of new products, methods, methodologies and other important innovations, which are stimulating for economic activity. According to this perspective, the CE is a process of creative destruction, denoted by the fact that innovations are typically an improvement in terms of usefulness of process and product [16]. The CE today, is one of the phenomena that characterize most of the internal dynamics of entrepreneurship, which has found its way, or rather a more substantial growth, only in the last twenty years.

Is essential starting from the concept of entrepreneur, a figure which is characterized by high risk appetite, typical of its function, which in the words of Schumpeter [17] cited above, is one who is constantly looking for opportunities earnings enhancing situations which permitting the introduction of factors of innovation.

The concept of entrepreneurship begins with two assumptions underlying or two orders of questions:

- The presence of lucrative opportunities;
- The presence of individuals who perform the entrepreneurial function.

Consequently, especially nowadays, entrepreneurship is accompanied by the important connotations as the innovative potential, which is unexplored, the ability to realize at a glance the needs expressed by the market and risk-taking. The centrality, however, is the fact that the entrepreneurial function is innovation. Entrepreneurship is not limited in small businesses, but also permeates the act of medium and large sizes. In this case we talk about entrepreneurship and internal corporate entrepreneurship [18].

The CE according to the preceding definitions can be defined as an innovative process creative, which, by means of the entrepreneur, tries to obtain the results of growth of its value using new operational processes. These new processes must be characterized by that innovation which allow them to exploit the same as a strategic lever for future growth potential.

Therefore you can understand what are the main features of the CE, which assume that the main architect of this process is the entrepreneur. So it might be defined as a unilateral process that starts from the ability of the entrepreneur to assume the risk of innovative renewal of its organization. Logically, this process, called unilateral above, has as principal aim is to implement these processes in order to enhance and create value for the firm, but are always a processes that can not be separated from the market, or best from actors within the same, consumers.

Finally, the CE, is always a process that is free from one of the most important developments of the last century, technology. The exploitation of technology, regardless of whether the renewal in question relate to different situations or size, must necessarily pass on the exploitation of technologies. The technology is one of the most important means by which it is possible to develop entrepreneurship internal. Through the same entrepreneur can develop processes and methodologies present in the company in order to obtain an output denoting an increase in firm value and logically achieve results that can meet those expectations and needs are of the market.

The CE, therefore, is seen as an innovative process of renewal of the existing organization, which is being implemented through his leading actor, the entrepreneur, who, through the use of technology, seeking to increase the value and potential of his business, can get positive results in its target market, among which there is customer satisfaction.

3 IT-Enabled Co-creation of Value

The basis of value co-creation theory are mainly given by the interaction between two main actors, the firm and the client [19]. This is a new perspective for marketing, named service dominant logic (S-D), that attributes particular importance to the value-creating processes which involve the customer as a co-creator [19].

This theory also suggests that all actors in the process of value creation are considered as dynamic, operant and active resources, enabling reticular/networked interactions [20] in which value co-creation is not limited to the supplier and the customer, but also involves a network of interested stakeholders. In order to shape these personalized interactive experiences the firm must implement an infrastructure that allows the communication between firm and customers [21].

The building blocks of this kind of communication are represented by the dialogue, access, transparency and acceptance of risk and are the starting points that must be met to impress this type of approach [21]. Logically they are not the only items on which is based this kind of strategic and cooperative communication with the customer, but must be accompanied by the scaffolding to ensure this policy. While many past studies have demonstrated a relationship between IT and some aspects of firm value, only recently some researchers have focused their attention on the co-creation of value through IT rather than on IT value alone. The notion of IT-enabled co-creation of value emerges from the realization that organizational boundaries are increasingly permeable and that novel arrangements are emerging that enable previously unattainable value propositions [22]. Based on service-dominant logic [6, 19], value is always co-created by customers and firms, and IT enables such arrangement of the actions and offers the potential to reshape how much value can be created in collaborative relationships. Information technology (IT) enables those arrangements and offers the potential to combine competences, capabilities and knowledge [22]. One example of this support can be represented by the multi-channel Nike approach. The web-sites provide the possibility to deliver the whole Nike's supply information, sale and distribution integrating their online channel with existing physical operations in order to leverage the benefits arising from potential synergies between the two [23].

4 Main Differences and Similarities

The previous evaluations about the theories of CE and Value co-creation, have highlighted several factors which point to a fundamentally different nature of themselves, but also have shown some aspects in common. Among the firsts, the dichotomy between the two main theories is the fact that they have a different nature, a statement dictated by the fact that while the first one, the CE, is a theory that emphasizes a strong one-sided connotation, because the actor leading innovator is the entrepreneur; while in the second one, Value Co-creation, we can safely speak of a bilateral nature, because we have two main players, firms and its customers, among which there is interaction. This is the main difference between the two theories but it is possible to find also points in common and complementary. Firstly, it is essential to establish that both theories can exploit the technologies for their operations. The technology, in both cases, is the key element. In the CE is useful in the development of internal entrepreneurship in order to cope and exploit innovative and competitive context. Through technology we can develop an internal process so that there is a streamlining of the product life cycle and internal relationships that enable the enrichment of the value of the firm. The technology we can safely state that takes part in the second theory, Value co-creation. In fact, the creation of shared value can be possible only through a continued exploitation of technologies, which allow to engage approaches through different channels, or points of contact, between company and client. Also through the exploitation of technologies is possible to develop services aimed at continuous communication with the client, such as software that allows the customer to customize the product. Another common element is the fact that both theories have as their ultimate goal to achieve a maintenance or improvement of its position in the market. It can be defined as the research of value accretion, which on both theories it can be assessed by quantitative data relating to the performance of the market. Logically, this research is affected by the different nature of the two theories, which can be defined as an unilateral value improvement in the first one and is being sought by the sharing of skills in the second one. Finally the last element is the fact that both theories have as their principal aim, customer satisfaction. In both cases we speak of two circumstances that starts from a distinct nature, but which have as their main objective the customer satisfaction and its relative ethical responsibility due to this opening to the outside. The approach of both theories exploit the technology in order to renew itself into satisfy those who are the market requirements, which are represented by the needs of customers. So they are two theories that depart from a purely different point, but that share these elements: technology exploitation; value creation and competitiveness; customer satisfaction. These points in common may be useful in order to obtain a new construct: corporate customership.

5 Corporate Customership

The already outlined theories (CE and IT value co-creation) suggest that the process of innovation lie at the intersection of entrepreneurial and customer innovation. Based on these aspects we wanted to try a new perspective, which comes from the crossover study between the two theories and points of contact between them. We have defined this new perspective as corporate customership to convey the joint process of innovation realized by the firm and the customer and enabled by IT. The birth of this new perspective is based on the assumption that the changes of view on theories are common in this area, the most common example is represented in the value co-creation and the change from G-D logic to S-D logic [24] that involves a metamorphosis of the base, which comes to define how services represent the key elements of co-creation of value.

The corporate customership starts from two fundamental assumptions. In the CE, we have a renewal of the organization, more specifically the internal entrepreneurship, through targeted strategies implemented by the entrepreneur through the use of technologies. The entrepreneur could exploit technologies, or IT in general, in order to use it as a leverage to become more entrepreneurial [25, 26].

In the value co-creation, however, always through the exploitation of technology, there is the pursuit of value based on a collaborative contribution by both parties, which has among the main goals to develop the position of the client, which becomes a active part of the report, whose contribution is essential. However, this kind of collaborative contribution is made possible by an IT approach [12], which is supported sometime by a multichannel strategy [23].

Through the corporate customership we propose a new construct resulting from the conditions mentioned above. The development of this new construct starts from the basis that the CE, using the support of a more particular theory as the value co-creation, can be extended.

The CE is based on a theory that is unilaterally implemented by a single actor, the entrepreneur [27], but thanks to the support of value co-creation, in particular the common points analyzed above, mainly the exploitation of technology, may present new points of view.

Firstly, this new construct is based on the fact that the CE can use the value co-creation in order to develop its traditional position, trying to see entrepreneurship no longer by the exclusive point of view of the entrepreneur but from the point of view of the client and considering the last one as an entrepreneur.

Secondly, the view of the client as an entrepreneur is possible only if there is a good support of the technology. The client can do its part as a new entrepreneur only with the presence of a good infrastructure, that using the technology as a mean to guarantee a communication with the firm. This structure can allow the client to give its contribution to the firm growth, because lay their ideas on the same field of firm. An example of this kind of relationship is offered by Nike ID service, that allows the communication between the company and their customers through a specific software of product customization [23]. The technology, or rather the IT in general, can be a perfect mean in order to put in contact firm and client and to exploit the ideas of latter, so that can be possible to create a bilateral contribution to the firm value development [27] (Fig. 1).

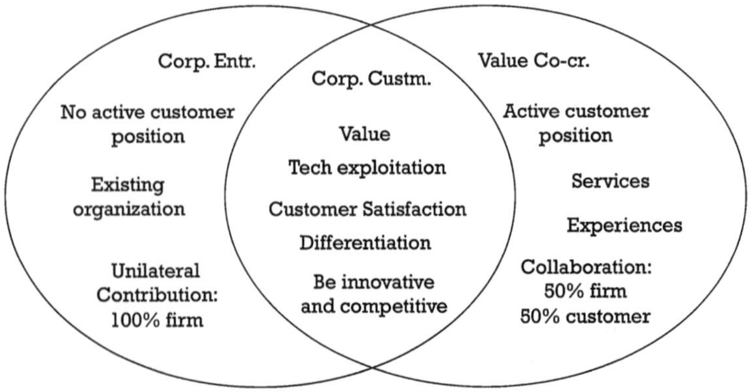

Fig. 1 Corporate customership

6 Conclusions

Given that consumers' needs and requirements are evolving rapidly, the traditional, closed innovation paradigm, generating new ideas only internally and marketing them slowly through a single path, is inefficient and inflexible in a fast-changing environment. In light of this recognition, in this study we seek to contribute to our understanding of innovation introducing a new construct: corporate customership. Corporate customership conveys the joint process of innovation realized by the firm and the customer and enabled by IT. It is a powerful concept in the analysis of where innovation reside because links corporate entrepreneurship and value-co-creation theories. In particular, it enables simultaneous understanding of technology and innovation ability of entrepreneur and customer.

References

1. Brown, S. L., & Eisenhardt, K. M. (1995). Product development: past research, present findings, and future directions. *Academy of Management Review, 20*(2), 343–378.
2. Romanelli, E., & Tushman, M. L. (1994). Organizational transformation as punctuated equilibrium: An empirical test. *Academy of Management Journal, 37*(5), 1141–1167.
3. Anderson, P., & Tushman, M. L. (1990). Technological discontinuities and dominant designs: A cyclical model of technological change. *Administrative Science Quarterly, 35*, 604–633.
4. Dewar, R. D., & Dutton, J. E. (1986). The adoption of radical and incremental innovations: An empirical analysis. *Management Science, 32*(11), 1422–1433.
5. Ettlie, J. E., et al. (1984). Organizational strategy and structural differences for radical versus incremental innovation. *Management Science, 30*(6), 682–695.
6. Vargo, S., Maglio, P. P., & Archpru, A. (2008). On value and value co-creation: A service systems and service logic perspective. *European Management Journal, 26*(3), 145–152.
7. Straub, D., Boudreau, M. C., & Gefen, D. (2004). Validation guidelines for IS positivist research. *Communications of the Association for Information Systems, 14*, 380–426.
8. Cenfentelli, R. T., Benbasat, I., & Al-Natour, S. (2008). Addressing the what and how of online services: Positioning supporting-services functionality and service quality for business to consumer success. *Information Systems Research, 19*(2), 161–181.
9. Brohman, M. K., Piccoli, G., Martin, P., Zulkernine, F., Parasuraman, A., & Watson, R. T. (2009). A design theory approach to building strategic net-based customer service systems. *Decision Sciences, 40*(3), 403–430.
10. Rayport, J. F., & Jaworski, B. J. (2004). Best face forward. *Harvard Business Review, 82*(12), 47–58.
11. Zahra, S. (1991). Predictors and financial outcomes of corporate entrepreneurship: An exploratory study. *Journal of Business Venturing, 6*(4), 259–285.
12. Kohli, R., & Grover, V. (2008). Business value of IT: An essay on expanding research directions to keep up with the times. *Journal of the Association of Information Systems, 9*(1), 23–39.
13. Covin, J., & Miles, M. (1999). Corporate entrepreneurship and the pursuit of competitive advantage. *Entrepreneurship Theory and Practice, 23*, 47–63.
14. Dess, G. G., Ireland, R. D., Zahra, S. A., Floyd, S. W., Janney, J. J., & Lane, P. J. (2003). Emerging issues in corporate entrepreneurship. *Journal of Management, 29*(3), 351–378.

15. Michelini L., Fiorentino D. (2011). Nuovi modelli di business per la creazione di un valore condiviso: il social e l'inclusive business. *Electronic Journal of Management* (January), *1*. http://www.impresaprogetto.it/issues/2011-1
16. Covin, J. G., & Slevin, D. (1989). Strategic management of small firms in hostile and begin environments. *Strategic Management Journal, 10*, 75–87.
17. Schumpeter, J. (1934). *Capitalism, socialism and democracy*. New York: Harper and Row.
18. Garzoni A. (2010). Corporate entrepreneurship. Stimolare l'imprenditorialità nelle aziende complesse". Milano, Egea. pp. 1–185.
19. Lusch, R. F., & Vargo, S. L. (2006). The service-dominant logic of marketing: Reactions, reflections, and refinements. *Marketing Theory, 6*(3), 281–288.
20. Payne, A. F., Storbacka, K., & Frow, F. (2008). Managing the co-creation of value. *Journal of the Academy of Marketing Science, 36*(1), 83–96.
21. Prahalad, C. K., Ramaswamy, V. (2004). *The future of competition. Co-creating unique value with customers* (pp. 1–272). Boston: Harvard Business School Press.
22. Srivastava, M. K., & Gnyawali, D. R. (2011). When do relational resources matter? Leveraging portfolio technological resources for breakthrough innovation. *Academy of Management Journal, 54*(4), 97–810.
23. Angioni, E., Cabiddu, F., Di Guardo, M.C. (2012). Value-co-creation through multichannels distributions: The Nike ID case. In: M. De Marco, D. Te'eni, V. Albano, S. Za (Eds.), Information systems: crossroads for organization, management, accounting and engineering, Heidelberg, German: Springer.
24. Vargo, S. L., & Lusch, R. F. (2004). Evolving to a new dominant logic for marketing. *Journal of Marketing, 68*(1), 1–17.
25. See, S. L. (2004). Corporate entrepreneurship: Exploiting technologies for innovation discovery and brake through. *International Engineering Management Conference 2004*.
26. Van de Velde, E., Clarysse, B., Wright, M. (2008). Entrepreneurial origin, technology endowments and the growth of spin-off companies. CMBOR working paper.
27. Guth, W., Ginsberg, A. (1990). Guest editors' Introduction: Corporate entrepreneurship. *Strategic Management Journal, 11*(S), 5–15.

Instant Messaging and Social Network Sites: Combining Coopetition Strategies and Network Externalities

Maria Chiara Di Guasrdo and Gianfranco Ennas

Abstract In recent years, Instant Messaging (IM) and Social Network Sites (SNS) have became the most important social platform for computer-mediated communication. This study proposes an integrated theoretical framework by combining network externalities and coopetition theory to investigate the strategic behavior of IM and SNS service providers. We show how firms generally coopete instead of competing in order to overcome local network externalities and avoid market segmentation, rival firms divide or partition the overall market into separate segments, with each firm selling to different segments. This indirectly produces network effects between competing products.

Keywords Local network externalities · Coopetition · Social networks · Instant messaging

1 Introduction

Since their introduction, Instant Messaging (IM) and Social Network Sites (SNS) – i.e. online settings that allow users to register and connect to each other in order to communicate or share resources with primary focus on social interpersonal communication—have attracted millions of users, currently representing the world's fastest developing personal networking tool. Not surprisingly, this phenomenon has been receiving growing attention from industry and academia for the innovative mode in which IM and SNS operate [1].

Researchers have highlighted how network externalities have significant effect on expanding social network potential [2, 3]. Conventional wisdom, in fact, suggests that network effects should drive faster market growth due to the bandwagon

M. C. Di Guasrdo · G. Ennas (✉)
University of Cagliari, Cagliari, Italy
e-mail: gianfrancoennas@unica.it

P. Spagnoletti (ed.), *Organizational Change and Information Systems*, Lecture Notes in Information Systems and Organisation 2, DOI: 10.1007/978-3-642-37228-5_30,

effect. Recently, economic literature has explained that, in particular markets, such mobile, software or financial products as credit cards, consumers have a preference for staying in the same network as people they are communicating with [4, 5]. However, in the IM and SNS markets, network externalities may also create an initial slow-down effect on growth because, generally, potential users wait for early adopters to provide them with more utilities, before joining in [1, 5].

In this line, previous research has seldom studied how IM and SNS service providers rely on increasing network externalities to propagate their business model. This question is critical, however, because the strategic behavior of IM and SNS providers affects the competitive landscape and the network externalities effects.

Our aim is to explore the behavior of the IM and SNS providers and in doing so we combine network externalities and coopetition theory [6]. We show how firms generally coopete instead of competing in order to overcome local network externalities and avoid market segmentations negative effects, otherwise rival firms divide or partition the overall market into separate segments, with each firm selling to different segments [4]. This indirectly, as we will see later, produces network effects between competing products.

This chapter is structured in three parts, in the first part we define IM and SNS and recall the basic aspects related to network externalities and coopetition, in the second part we present some data supporting our hypothesis and discuss related economics implications. In the third part we give our concluding remarks.

2 IM and SNS: Definitions and Properties

Social network sites (SNS) can be defined as web-based services that allow individuals to construct a public or semi-public profile within a bounded system, articulate a list of other users with whom they share a connection, and view and traverse their list of connections and those made by others within the system. The nature and nomenclature of these connections may vary from site to site [7]. There are many different categories of social network: generalist as Facebook or Google Plus, for professional use as LinkedIn, for dating and so on. Sociologists have studied many properties of social networks, such as the shortest path, the small-world effect, transitivity or clustering, degree distribution, assortative mixing, and community structure. Recently it was observed that characteristics of a physical social network also appear in online social networks [8].

Instant messaging (IM) is near-synchronous computer-based one-on-one communication. With a fast network, transmission times are fractions of a second and the experience is of near-synchronous interaction. Like chat, IM allows users to type messages into a window, but like the phone, it is based on a dyadic "call" model. Users do not go into "rooms" to converse with whoever is there; instead there is a single individual with whom they communicate (although they may have several concurrent dyadic conversations with different individuals in progress at a given time). Some IM systems support multiparty chat but our data concern the more typical dyadic communications. As with the phone, the intended recipient of an instant message may or may not "answer" [9]. For instant messaging programs (IM), segmentation is the same there are generalist such Windows Live Messenger, or Yahoo Messenger, for professional use such Skype but, in comparison with SNS, boundaries in this market are less defined.

2.1 Theoretical Background

In this chapter to explore the behavior of the IM and SNS providers, we combine network externalities and coopetition theory. A recent web research shows there are over 350 SNS and IM,[1] showing an highly fragmented market. People choose a SNS or IM service based on how many other friends (or new friends) can meet. By definition a network externalities is *the value or effect that users obtain from a product or service will bring about more values to consumers with the increase of users, complementary product, or service* [1]. IM and SNS markets are characterized by strong positive network externalities, they arise from the specific patterns of interaction between groups of users, because advantage grow with increasing of other users. The value of the good or service to the purchaser also depends on the purchaser's expectations about the future size of the network [10]. We argue they are subjected to local effects, in this way as mentioned in introduction, literature is not well structured and there are no contributions in business study. Banerji and Dutta [4] show that in the presence of local network externalities, the market can end up being segmented between competing firms. In literature, market segmentation, is intended as the partition of the market with the purpose of selecting one or more market segments which the organization can target through the development of specific marketing mixes that adapt to particular market needs [11] When goods or services are subjected to local network externalities segmentation can limit or completely deny the possibility of interoperate, so consumers are affected by the consumption choices of their neighbors. Use of such packages e.g. words processor or data analysis package depends at least partly on the number of her research collaborators who use the same package, rather than on the total number of users of the package, the same is true for SNS or IM, hence we can say they are local by nature. We argue, in this market, network externalities effects are simultaneously direct and indirect, explain the first assumption it is relatively easy because direct network externalities exists when an increase in the size of a network increases the number of others with whom one can interact directly. The subscriber effect occurs when the benefits to society from the addition of an individual subscriber are larger than those recognized by the subscriber in her decision to join a network [12].

[1] http://wiki.answers.com/Q/How_many_social_networks_are_there

In literature indirect network are only considered as the utility of consumers in the variety of complementary products available for it [2], classic examples are between hardware/software, adoption of the hardware by one purchaser confers external benefits on other users of the same hardware, because it expands the installed base of the hardware, stimulating demand for compatible software [1]. A possible increase in utility may occur through market mediation (e.g., the number of DVD rental outlets), which in turn is a function of the number of adopters, consumers will wait for a hardware adoption until there is enough software [13].

Coopetition describes the nature of the inter-firm interdependences where both competitive and collaborative issues co-exist. It is a synthesis between two opposite paradigms: the competitive paradigm, postulating that firms interact on the basis of a fully divergent interest structure, and the cooperative paradigm, assuming that firms interact on the basis of a completely convergent interest structure [14]. The competitive perspective is represented by Porter and particularly his seminal book "Competitive Strategy" (1980) and by Williamson and his major contributions on the field of "transaction cost economics" (1975, 1985). On the other side, the cooperative perspective is shown by Contractor and Lorange [24], who strongly emphasize on the benefits of cooperation and regard them as sufficient incentive to be not seduced by possible benefits of opportunism [15]. Coopetition is a matter of incomplete congruence of interests and goals concerning firms interdependence; in other words, defines the modern corporate strategy that combines competition and cooperation [16]. Competing firms can then work together, not only to make their products mutually compatible, but to overcome lock-in problems as they arise [17]. The distinction between the concepts of strategic alliance and coopetition is also interesting. Bengtsson and Kock [25] associate strategic alliances with cooperation. Furthermore, Jorde and Teece [26] have defined such alliances as bilateral or multilateral relationships characterized by the commitment of two or more partner firms to a common goal. It is evident that in their thinking the strategic alliance is nearer to cooperation than competition. A strategic alliance is coopetitive if it includes competitive moves, with regard to at least one strategic variable and collusion or a cartel is coopetitive if the firms involved compete [18]. Coopetitive relationships are complex as they consist of two diametrically different logics of interactions. These two logics of interactions are in conflict with each other and must be separated in a proper way to make a coopetitive relationship possible. Coopetitive relationships are enacted by two types of interactions. On one hand, hostility characterizes actors relationships due to conflicting interests, on the other hand "friendship" is part of their relationships since they have to pursue common interests and, accordingly, a collective action [19].

We claim that understanding interfirm interdependences for the IM and SMS providers as a coopetitive game provides new challenges in the strategic behavior of the firms because reduce market segmentation [18]. In this turbulent markets strongly innovative and subjected to rapid changes the only way to survive is to gain and keep a critical mass of users, market fragmentation may lead the effects that only few competitors survive. The cooperative aspect of such knowledge sharing refers to the collective use of shared knowledge to pursue common interests. The competitive aspect refers to the use of shared knowledge to make private gains in an attempt to outperform the partners [20]. In this way coopetition arise from the need to keep and share users, friendship is the capacity to attract the largest number of users as possible, with the function "import friend" lists and in second by possibilities to log in with a common account, in order to easily permit to known their services with a short registration and then keep user by hostility that is characterized by maintain they own identities limiting "connect account feature". After coopetition between global players is established, the cooperative and competitive element mix does not necessarily remain constant over time.

3 Data Analysis

To support our assumptions, we decided to analyze 10 majors SNS and 4 majors IM, 3 of which are also email providers. For SNS, as expected, get data about ranking was not easy, there are no specific survey about that, just online research and in most cases only regional data, so we decided to intersect the numbers of members and the Alexa[2] global sites ranking (Table 1). An important exclusion refers to Chinese SNS (Qzone has over 480,000,000 subscriber); this choice was made because censorship in that country does not allow the use of many global platforms, so this is not a limitation but a need in order to have a vision as little as possible distorted by exogenous factors as such political choices. Table 2.

We have focused on three characteristics: the first is the possibility to import friend lists, the second is the possibility to log-in with other accounts provided by a competitor or to do a short registration using other accounts, and the third is the possibility to connect the accounts, this feature allows to see friends' activities from a SNS into another. As we can see, looking at the above tables, the first characteristics is allowed and encouraged during registration process by 7 out of 10 SNS analyzed and by the two bigger IM. On the second feature there are 4 SNS out of 10 permitting log-in with competitor accounts and all of these 4 admits Facebook, for the second group there are 3 out of 4. For the third characteristic, the situation is reversed since Facebook allows all SNS by third party applications and Google+ allows Facebook by third party applications, for the second group 2 out of 4 permit this feature.

It is important to notice that Twitter and Google+ do not allow the possibilities to connect with all others accounts. This feature give the possibility to the users to see all activities on their account, hence it is a strategy to keep users as long as possible in their sites. Probably, causes are that Twitter offers a particular service "share short messages", so connect with other accounts may go out of the services aim, therefore it is not a weaknesses. For Google+ reason could be that it is

[2] Alexa provides traffic data, global rankings and other information on thousands of websites, and claims that 6 million people visit its website monthly.

Table 1 List of SN sites

	Name	Approximated registered users	Global alexa page ranking	Import friends list	Log in with or short registration	Connect account
1	Facebook **(G)**	901.000.000	2	A,B,C,D	/	All by apps
2	Twitter **(G)**	480.000.000	9	B,C,D	/	/
3	Google+ **(G)**	170.000.000	N/A	B,C,D	C[a]	1,2 (3rd party apps)
4	LinkedIn **(P)**	160.000.000	13	/	/	/
5	Habbo **(D)**	200.000.000	6545	/	1,2,3,8,B,C	/
6	Badoo **(D)**	150.000.000	117	B,C,D	1,7,B,C,D	/
7	Vkontakte **(G)**	112.000.000	44	/	/	/
8	Myspace **(G)**	100.000.000	131	C,D	1	/
9	Tagged **(D)**	100.000.000	281	B,C,D	1	/
10	Netlog **(D)**	94.000.000	296	B,D	/	/

Data at April 2012

[a] Not relevant because Gmail account is required to join in Google+

G General, *P* Professional, *D* Dating/Discovery (Social discovery is the process by which a user finds and connects with another)

Table 2 List of IM programs

	Name	Approximated registered users	Import friends list	Log in with or short registration	Connect account
A	Skype	665.000.000	1	1	1
B	Windows live[a]	369.000.000	1,4,9	All emails	1,2,4
C	Gmail/gtalk[a]	350.000.000	/	/	/
D	Yahoo[a]	310.000.000	/	1,C	/

Data at April 2012

[a] Global users, not just instant messaging users

relatively recent and there are not yet much apps developed. It is clear that this situation increases Facebook leadership because, offering this feature, it continue to keep its competitive advantage.

As we can see in the above tables, firms coopete at different intensity; according to Luo [21], intensity of coopetition is a measure of the vigor of a specific coopetitive relationship with a leading competitor. He proposes four basic types of coopetition's intensity, giving heterogeneity to SNS and IM that we think they are applicable. Coopetition intensity's degree can be a choice or a need, but this element is not static, rather dynamic in response to changing parameters in both their external and internal environments [21].

A contending situation exists when the firm races with another major global player for market power, competitive position, and market share in critical international markets, maintaining high competition and low cooperation with its counterpart. This case arises between direct competing firms e.g. general–general SNS or IM–IM, reason is why they are competing in the same market segment.

A partnering situation exists where a global player voluntarily maintains high cooperation and low competition with another major global player. Both are searching joint synergies created by each one, complementary resources and capabilities. This seems to be the case between SNS and IM e.g. Skype's members can make video and voice calls, as well as send instant messages, to all Facebook friends direct from Skype.

An isolating situation arises when the firm does not interact significantly with other global rivals, maintaining low competition and low cooperation with another leading global player. As we can see in the above tables, this strategy is adopted only by few firms; reasons could be a previous competitive advantage in their segment or the firm is in a specific market niche without competitors.

An adapting situation refers to the case in which two global players mutually depend on each other to achieve their respective goals, maintaining high cooperation as well as high competition with each other. This case is typical between firms that coopete in different market segments e.g. SNS-IM or general-dating SNS.

Given the results of analyzed characteristics, we can see that benefits to join in a SN or IM x turn also in a potential benefits for SN or IM y because members could extend their network or join directly or indirectly into another local network. This seems to be an important and singular way to look at indirect network externalities, because in this case, we can observe indirect network effects between competing products.

The economic logic behind sharing applications and friend lists is given by Metcalfe's law, which states that the value of a network is the square of the number of nodes in the network [22]. In the same way, it states that when a network loses users the value decrease exponentially. A corollary to Metcalfe's law is that when two networks connect or interoperate the smaller network benefits more than the larger network does. If network A has 50 members according to Metcalfe's law its value is 2,500 (50^2). If network B has 100 members its value is 10,000 (100^2). If they interoperate, theoretically, network A could gains 10,000 in value, but network B only gains 2,500 in value. This is the reason why 4 out of the 10 SNS analyzed permit log-in with Facebook that is the SN with the major number of members. However, it's demonstrated that Metcalfe's law is too optimistic: some scholars [23] show that the incentives to interconnect cannot be too strong, and so Metcalfe's Law cannot be valid. But, as they argue, it is still true that interconnection between two or more networks generate benefits for all networks, but in a less way than t previously thought (incentives are in logarithmic scale instead of square scale). This deserves a separate and much depth analysis that is beyond this chapter's purposes.

4 Conclusions

This study proposes an integrated theoretical framework by combining network externalities and coopetition theory to investigate the strategic behavior of IM and SNS service providers, and proposes possible factors to better understand the firms competitive behaviors. We claim that understanding interfirm interdependences in the IM and SMS markets as a coopetitive game provides new challenges in the strategic landscape. This behavior in fact indirectly produces network effects between competing products and reduces the market segmentation. Profitable online service performance depends on understanding factors influencing strategy behaviors. So far, few studies have investigated these factors.

References

1. Katz, M. L., & Shapiro, C. (1985). Network externalities, competition and compatibility. *American Economic Review, 75*, 424–440.
2. Lin, C. P., Tsai, Y. H., Wang, Y-J., Chiu, C. K., (2010). Modeling IT relationship quality and its determinants: A potential perspective of network externalities in e-service. Elsevier p. 2.
3. Doganoglu, T., & Grzybowski, L. (2007). Estimating network effects in mobile telephony in Germany. *Information Economics and Policy, 19*(1), 65–79.
4. Banerji, A., & Dutta, B. (2009). Local network externalities and market segmentation. *Elsevier International Journal of Industrial Organization, 27*, 605–614.
5. Fjeldstad, Ø., Moen, E. R., Riis, C., (2009) Competition with local network externalities norwegian school of management.
6. Brandenburger, A. M., & Nalebuff, B. J. (1996). *Co-opetition*. New York: Doubleday.
7. Boyd, D. M., Ellison, N. B., (2008). *Journal of Computer-Mediated Communication* 13 210–230 International Communication Association.
8. Chen, C-C., Chiu, T. H-Y., Joung, Y-J., and Chen, S., (2011). An examination of online social networksproperties with tie-strength. *PACIS* 2011 *Proceedings Paper* 41.
9. Nardi, B., Whittaker, S., Bradner, E. Interaction and Outeraction: Instant Messaging in Action. Proceedings of *CSCW*'00, (pp. 79–88).
10. Page, W. H., & Lopatka, J. E. (2000). Network externalities. In B. Bouckaert & G. D. Geest (Eds.), *Encyclopedia of law and economics* (pp. 952–980). Aldershot: Edward Elgar.
11. Goyat, S. (2011). The basis of market segmentation: A critical review of literature. *European Journal of Business and Management, 3*(9).
12. Mayo, J. W., & Wallsten, S. (2011). *From network externalities to broadband growth externalities: A bridge not yet built.* LLC: Springer Science + Business Media.
13. Goldenberg, J., Libai, M., & Muller, E. (2010). The chilling effects of network externalities Elsevier Intern. *Journal of Research in Marketing, 27*, 4–15.
14. Dagnino G. B., Padula, G. (2002). Coopetition strategy—A new kind of interfirm dynamics for value creation, in EURAM "Innovative Research in Management". Stockholm, 9–11 May.
15. Stein, H. D. (2010). Literature overview on the field of co-opetition. *Business Theory and Practice, 11*(3), 256–265.
16. Bigliardi, B., Dormio, A. I., & Galati, F. (2011). Successful co-opetition strategy: evidence from an Italian consortium. *International Journal of Business, Management and Social Sciences, 2*(4), 1–8.

17. Caplan, B., Stringham, E., (2003). Networks, law, and the paradox of cooperation *The Review of Austrian Economics*, 16:4, 309–326.
18. Rusko, R. (2011). Exploring the concept of coopetition: A typology for the strategic moves of the Finnish forest industry. *Industrial Marketing Management* 40 311–320.
19. Bengtsson, M., & Kock, S. (2000). "Coopetition" in business networks–to cooperate and compete simultaneously. *Industrial Marketing Management, 29*, 411–426.
20. Khanna, T. R., & Gulati, N. N. (1998). The dynamics of learning alliances: Competition, cooperation, and relative scope. *Strategic Management Journal, 19*(3), 193–210.
21. Luo, Y. (2007). A coopetition perspective of global competition. *Journal of World Business, 42*, 129–144.
22. Metcalfe, B. (1995). Metcalfe's law: A network becomes more valuable as it reaches more users. *Infoworld*, Oct. 2.
23. Odlyzko, A., & Tilly, B. (2005). *A refutation of Metcalfe's law and a better estimate for the value of networks and network interconnections*. Digital Technology Center: University of Minnesota.
24. Contractor, F. J., & Lorange, P. (1988). Why should firms cooperate? The strategy and economics basis for cooperative ventures. *Cooperative strategies in international business*, 3–30.
25. Bengtsson, M., & Kock, S. (2003). Tension in Co-opetition. *Developments in marketing science*, *26*, 38–42.
26. Jorde, T. M., & Teece, D. J. (1990). Innovation and cooperation: implications for competition and antitrust. *The Journal of Economic Perspectives*, *4*(3), 75–96.

Part V
Information Systems Management: A Critical Perspective

Coping with Power of Control: The Role of IS in an Italian Integrated Tariff System

Mario Pezzillo Iacono, Marcello Martinez, Gianluigi Mangia, Paolo Canonico and Ernesto De Nito

Abstract The study explores the role of the Electronic Ticketing Systems in the Integrated Tariff Systems (ITS), focusing on the relationship between technology and control from the perspective of the Critical IS Research. More specifically our work reflects upon the impact of the "smart card technology" on the process of control and power centralization from the perspective of the ITS meta-organizer. It is for this purpose that a case study of UnicoCampania, an Italian ITS, is analyzed and discussed. We show that UnicoCampania's power to control the transport operators is not only extended through technology, but also becomes more pervasive and more effective. So the electronic ticketing could be considered an artifact which enabled the power relations within the tariff network, establishing itself as the strength of the process that the drive the network. Our chapter provides an empirical example of the application of critical approach to an Italian local transport system, confirming that the two categories analyzed—political and technological—do not denote a specific and separated belonging.

Keywords Transport · Electronic ticketing · Power of control · Critical · Centralization

M. P. Iacono (✉) · M. Martinez
Department of Economics, Second University of Naples, Capua, Italy
e-mail: mario.pezzilloiacono@unina2.it

M. Martinez
e-mail: marcello.martinez@unina2.it

G. Mangia · P. Canonico
Department of Management, University of Naples Federico II, Naples, Italy
e-mail: mangia@unina.it

P. Canonico
e-mail: pcanonic@unina.it

E. De Nito
Department of Scienze Giuridiche, Storiche, Economiche e Sociali,
University Magna Græcia of Catanzaro, Catanzaro, Italy
e-mail: denito@unicz.it

P. Spagnoletti (ed.), *Organizational Change and Information Systems*, Lecture Notes in Information Systems and Organisation 2, DOI: 10.1007/978-3-642-37228-5_31,

1 Introduction

In Italy in the past 10 years the demand for mid and short distance transport has increased exponentially, especially in metropolitan areas. The public administration has been forced to rationalize the supply of public transport to improve its accessibility, lessen the pressure on traffic in city centers and optimize the provision of this type of service in terms of economy. One of the tools typically used to achieve these objectives in various Italian regions is the institution of Integrated Tariff Systems (ITSs). In coordination with the local authorities, these systems connect the various companies that operate in Local Public Transport (LPT) through a shared ticketing system.

Furthermore by the late 1990s there was a gradual realization in the Italian transport systems that there may well be some real benefits for public transport in exploring the adoption of electronic ticketing, following the success of large-scale electronic ticketing schemes in Europe, leading examples being London, Paris and Brussels. So, the use of an electronic smart card as an alternative means for users to access and pay for transport services is emerging as a viable option for many Italian operators. In particular Electronic Ticketing Systems (ETSs) represent a highly important area of technological innovation in terms of the development of ITSs and LPT in general, increasing the flexibility of use of mobility services, safety, ease of payment, modal integration and checks on fare avoidance.

In recent years a very intense debate on ITSs has been taking place, both in politics and in the managerial literature. Many issues were at stake: the quality and the evaluation of services provided [1], the pressure for efficiency [2], the effects of integrated ticket policies on transportation demand [3, 4], the governance of structure [5, 6] and, obviously, the technology adopted [7].

Nevertheless, managerial and organisational literature has rarely been concerned with the relationship between technological evolution and power relations within the domain of public transport and, more specifically, in reference to inter-organisational relations in ITSs.

Transport technological innovations have led to the availability of data, so that abundant information for control purposes seems to be available. The question is to whom is the information available and for which purposes the information can be used. We rarely ask who uses the control data and for which purpose.

Stemming from the problem of power of control, we face the need of understanding the theoretical perspectives through which analysing the role of IS within an integrated tariff network. We selected the Foucauldian/post-structuralist perspective of Critical IS Research (CISR) [8, 9].

Our study explores the role of the ETSs in the ITSs, focusing on the relationship between technology and control from a critical perspective. More specifically our work reflects upon the impact of the "smart card technology" on the process of control and power centralization from the perspective of the ITS meta-organizer. It is for these purposes that a case study [10] of an Italian ITS is here analyzed and discussed. The analysis is based on a qualitative investigation conducted in terms of grounded theory.

The article follows an inductive logic and is organized in six sections. First of all, the theoretical background is analysed, presenting the main assumptions related to the relationship between IS and organizational control according to CISR (Sect. 2); after describing the methodology used for the empirical analysis (Sect. 3), the research context is explained (Sect. 4) and the case study is illustrated and analysed (Sect. 5); finally the main conclusions of this study are presented (Sect. 6), making a number of suggestions regarding future research on the topic and a description of the limitations.

2 Theoretical Background: Critical IS Research and Control

Information Systems (IS) are often described as a disciplinary technology intended to regulate the actions of workers and produce information to improve the ability of managers and/or organizations for surveillance of the outcomes of those activities [11]. In particular, CISR aims at revealing, criticizing and explaining how the development and use of IS in organizations and society in the pursuit of efficiency and rationalization increase social and organizational control, with potential detrimental consequences for some stakeholders and society as a whole [12]. Adopting an inclusive view, Howcroft [13] encompasses critical research on IS as the branch of IS studies in opposition to technological determinism, which assumes that technological development is autonomous and that societal development is determined by the technology. On the contrary, critical approach seeks to challenge (rather than justify) technological imperatives as natural and inescapable, interpreting the adoption of IS by recourse to a wider social, political, historical, economic and ideological context [14].

CISR typically emphasizes the effects of ICT on people (e.g., on their thinking, working conditions and identities), organizations and societies (e.g., highlighting the fetish of statistics and preoccupation with targets which ICT facilitate and feed).

The basic assumption of this view is that technology—interpreted as both a body of artifacts and practices and as a specific artifact/object—is not neutral, but it is "socially shaped". In other words, it has embedded beliefs, values, culture and perceptions of both the designers and the consumers. In this context, technological artifacts can be viewed as culturally constructed and interpreted, not only in how technology is thought of but in its design and implementation [15]. In the opinion of Cecez-Kecmanovic [16] the main aim of CISR is to transform the social/organizational systems in terms of actors, IS, organizations (including their dynamic and relationships), by revealing and explaining how an IS, supposedly implemented with the purpose to increase efficiency and effectiveness, increased power of control and decreased autonomy and human agency.

In CISR literature, interpretations of power and control are significantly influenced by Foucauldian/post-structuralist approach [17] and our analysis is developed according this view.

The post-structuralist perspective bases its essential theories on social constructivism [18], subjectivist studies [19], and the theoretical elaborations of structuration theory [20]. Applying this approach, social reality is not objective (it is not a thing or a reification), but consists of the interaction between individuals and emerges as a conflict of power and construction of meanings, in a logic in which the creation of meaning and organization are characterized as interchangeable concepts. The basic concept behind a post-structuralist approach is to be found in power of control as interpretative key to processes, analyses and organizational design. These studies typically explore shift from simple control to technical control to bureaucratic control and, most recently, to normative control [21–23].

The Faucauldian literature on IS and control [24, 25] suggests that the design and the implementation of ICT might affect organizational control at least in two interdependent ways: (i) controlling workforce and (ii) controlling organizational processes/structures. Consistently with the purpose of our chapter, here we are interested above all on the latter issue. According to CISR, in fact, an important way in which IS affect organizational control is linked to the influence on organizational processes and/or structures, facilitating control and coordination of activities at different levels, simultaneously enabling and constraining those activities. This concept is based on the idea that the integration of information determined by ICT facilitates the process of standardization and centralizing of organizational power, increasing the polarization between a broad range of "controlled" actors and a tight range of "controlling" subjects. Moreover, this concept appears to be consistent with the Weberian approach that identifies the availability of data, information and skills, the primary source of organizational power.

Furthermore, in terms of control relating to organizational processes, it is worth noting Ciborra's [26] work. In contrast to the prevailing view in IS literature, he suggests that IS artifacts may drift, i.e., "they deviate from their planned purposes for variety of reasons often outside anyone's influence" (p. 4) and puts forward a notion "of technology with a certain degree of autonomy and inner dynamics; of technology both as a drifting system and as an organism to be cultivated" (p. 32).

In short, ICT infrastructures tend to have a life of their own: they drift as a result of their usages, design choices, organizational routine, human resource management, user resistance, and/or other unforeseeable behaviors of both systems and humans [27]. Building on this perspective, Rajao and Hayes [28] claim that this drift can be understood as a result of power relations and negotiations between diverse conceptions of controls [29]. Under this idea, the design and use of ICT artifacts tend to reflect the dominant conceptions of control [30]. In other words, ICT both create new conditions of possibility, e.g., new ways of organizing, and are implicated in different control mechanisms, e.g., they enable and constrain what we do and how we do it. Introna [31], for instance, interprets the relationship between IS and organizations not only as an electronic panopticon, but also as embedded in the "micro physics" of everyday life, power relations, discourse and knowledge.

Finally we have to point out that some critical studies have shown that IS are designed to support existing structures and that their use tends to strengthen the structures and ways of organizing which are already in place [32]. To understand where the power of control is embedded (or where it should be embedded) in a group, organization or network requires first analyzing the distribution of decisional power, or rather the level of centralization/decentralization. Evaluating a network's (or company's) level of centralization or decentralization requires discovering where the decisions that influence its characteristic activities are made.

3 Methodology

Our study adopts an interpretive approach. The empirical basis of this article comes from a case study: we have studied UnicoCampania, a Consortium composed by 14 local public transport companies, operating both rail and bus services in Campania Region (Italy).

We selected this case study within a set of 10 Italian ITSs analyzed during a research project funded by *Cesit—Centre for the Study of Transport Systems "Carlo Mario Guerci"*. We present the main evidences related to the ITS in Campania because it represents, at same time, one of the most complex and widest ITSs in Italy and one of few where the electronic ticketing technology based on smart cards was implemented.

The analysis is based on a qualitative investigation conducted in terms of grounded theory. In the opinion of Jabar et al. [33], the qualitative research methodology approach is viewed as significant in IS research due to the value of capturing and explaining what is going on in real organization and "it enabled us to understand the interaction of social organization and information systems" (p. 50). In particular, the characteristics of grounded theory, inductive, contextual and processual, fit with the interpretive rather than positivist orientation of this research [34].

The collection of empirical data was carried out using a heterogeneous plurality of instruments. The methods include: document analysis, semi-structured interviews and participant observations. Fieldwork was carried out between September 2011 and early February 2012.

In particular, the analysis is based on a total of 9 semi-structured interviews with 1 manager and 2 managerial staff members of UnicoCampania and 6 managers of transport operators. The interviews were guided by a questionnaire of wide-ranging, including questions about: the governance model, the fare structure and the fare evasion, the transportation demand trend, the key element of the technological side, the problem of revenue distribution (clearing), the response of some managers to the application of electronic ticketing, and the socio-technical interplays within the network (e.g., how can a "certain" characteristic of the IS influence the inter-organizational relationship?).

4 Research Context

In public transport domain the word "integration" may refer to informative integration, where users have easy access to information about the different networks, timetables and tariffs, physical integration among different networks (infrastructures), and tariff integration, that allows passengers to utilize several transport modalities by buying one ticket only, which can be used in either a short time period or can have a seasonal validity [35].

Historically, the rise of ITS in local public transportation systems tooks place at the end of the 1960s. The principal reasons for this may be found in the economic development of Western Europe, which was accompanied by a growth in urbanized areas, and therefore a rise in mass transit needs.

Activating ITS increases the need to establish relations with new organisational actors. Inclusion in a ITS, in fact, has immediate effects on the actions of each operator, who loses margins of manoeuvrability and has to redesign its organisational boundaries. So within an ITS there is a phenomenon of growing dynamism in inter-organisational relations, which presents elements of competition and cooperation at the same time.

Stemming from these regards, the issue of the structure and regulation of the tariff network (governance) gains in importance. On the basis of the transport literature [36, 37], it is possible to distinguish two different ITS governance models:

1. transport operator centered;
2. authority centered.

The two different organisational models share the presence of a focal organization. In the first case, this role is played by a transport operator (e.g., Pegaso Tuscany, SITAM Milan, STIB Brussels, Formula Turin). Typically, by the most important one for dimension, resources etc. In the second category the coordination and control role is played by an *ad hoc* structure (e.g., an authority and/or a consortium) introduced with this specific purpose (e.g., AMT Barcelona, CRTM Madrid, Stif Paris Ile-de-France, Stimer Emilia Romagna, UnicoCampania Consortium). The introduction of an authority entity implies the setting up of a network of relationships with local bodies and institutions.

From another point of view, the public transportation ticketing system represents a key element of an ITS: it must be able to handle large volumes of passenger transactions while providing the minimum possible impedance to travel. Ticketing is a tool for the implementation of a pricing policy with the consideration of operational, commercial and social objectives. In particular, contactless ticketing appeared in Italy in the 1990s.

The technology has many advantages. In the perspective of the ITF governance body (e.g., an authority), smart cards might alleviate the problem of revenue distribution between participating companies because they make it possible to count each passenger. They are a strong marketing tool since they enable detailed data collection on the mobility behavior of customers, which helps to develop targeted products. Moreover electronic control devices allows for better information and electronic screens with actual times. This could reduce problem of search for interconnection which is often encountered in long short distance combinations [38].

From the transport operators' perspective, e-ticketing might be able: (i) to increase the medium term operating profit and reduce fraud; (ii) to increase speed at boarding; (iii) to supply opportunities to add "new services"; (iv) to improve cash flow, etc.

To sum up, in public transport electronic ticketing systems are not only means of payment but process huge amount of information which offer a large range of possibilities to make ITS easier to use, to manage and to control. They offer as well opportunities to introduce integrated pricing structure that are not easy to implement with traditional payment tools. In particular, the information provided with smartcard systems can be used for patronage monitoring and network planning. Under this respect, electronic ticketing transformed sense-making around the governance of mobility, reinforcing and stabilizing new perspective about it.

5 Data Analysis

The governance and technological analysis Campania ITS carried out in this paragraph is limited to a description of the object *per se* and its intrinsic characteristics without considering the political dimension (aim of the analysis in the following paragraph).

The LPT tariff policy in the Region of Campania is essentially unique and is governed by the UnicoCampania Consortium, which coordinates 78 % of the regional road-based supply and 100 % of the rail supply. The Consortium manages and coordinates the ITS and the ticketing technological standards of 14 operators (9 of which offer road-based services and 5 rail-based). Specifically, the Consortium's areas of activity are as follows:

- management of the printing and distribution of travel tickets;
- distribution of the revenues between the consortium companies (clearing);
- management of travel ticket checks on consortium vehicles;
- management of promotion and communication activities;
- management of administrative aspects relating to the above activities;
- definition of the technological standards for on-board systems, automatic ticket machines and communication systems, and management thereof;
- introduction and dissemination of new electronic ticketing technologies in the area.

Under this respect, UnicoCampania could be conceptualize as a ''meta-organization'' [39] whose members are other organizations. The Consortium, acting as a meta-organizer, has the crucial role of organizing, governing and tuning the ITS network in synergy with operators.

The tariff structure is based on the definition of concentric zones in relation to a pole of attraction (Naples), which represents the center of the 11 zones into which Campania is subdivided for all movements.

The clearing system, which typically forms the basis of one of the most critical questions (and point of contention between the operators) in the ITS, is founded on a parameter that keeps count of the travellers transported and the km travelled by each operator.

The integrated tariff was formally established on 19 December 1994 as a system that only related to the urban area of Naples (Napolipass). The travellers transported every day by the companies in the Consortium increased from 250,000 in 1994 to 750,000 in 2000. In 2003 the UnicoCampania ITS was extended to the whole region (Naples and 550 municipalities, with a catchment area of approximately 55 million residents) and the number of companies in the consortium increased from 6 to the current 14. Parallel to this, there was a significant increase in the travellers transported until 2010.

It should be noted that the foundation and development of the regional ITS were linked to choices and guidelines shared between the LPT institutions and operators: on one hand, the political will of the various local bodies (first the Municipality of Naples, then the Region) and on the other the "voluntary" choice of the LPT operators. In fact, the 14 LPT operators chose (at different times) the contractual form of the Consortium as a mechanism for inter-organizational coordination for managing tariff policies. In other words, unlike many European and Italian forms of ITS whereby the coordination is delegated to the biggest operator (see below), a form of governance was adopted in which the resulting organization is an autonomous subject in relation to all the operators. This model of governance therefore represents a *strong* option in that it removes several keys functions from operator control so that they are carried out in a joint and unified manner by Unicocampania.

Furthermore the path of technological evolution followed by the Consortium can be described starting from 5 basic technological steps:

- the exclusive use of paper (1994);
- the introduction of magnetic media—*step 1* (January 2001);
- the introduction of contactless technology—*step 2* (December 2001);
- openness and security of the system—*step 3* (January 2003);
- introduction of the Consortium's Data Processing Centre (DPC)—*step 4* (January 2008).

In particular, in December 2001 UnicoCampania introduced an actual ETS and since that time annual travel cards have been managed through Smart Card Contactless. Contactless type travel tickets are swiped on the validator's reading device, which recognizes the type and validity and makes validation and access significantly faster than the magnetic ticket adopted 12 months earlier. Monthly travel cards are also currently managed with the same technology.

In January 2003 the Consortium installed an SAM—*Secure Access Module*[1]—management module to recognize and validate electronic tickets, creating an "open and secure" system in which each company can implement its own ticketing system compatible with the UnicoCampania tickets. The operating system and the security keys were therefore transferred to the SAM hardware, which the Consortium customizes with the management module and then distributes to the consortium companies. The SAM belonging to the Consortium is used in all the components of the ticketing system for the Consortium and the companies—ticket punchers, portable verification readers, issue and top-up terminals—and also in the production phase for the smart cards themselves.

In 2008 the electronic ticketing system was completed with the introduction of a Consortium DPC. The central DPC processes the information on ticket sales and on obliterated tickets in order to compute the revenues and to divide them among different carriers on the basis of the carried passengers. In particular the DPC dialogues with the 14 company DPCs: the operators' sales networks directly provide the Consortium with information relating to user profiles, the validation of the travel tickets used, the total demand, online purchases, theft/loss and extensions. The UnicoCampania system periodically receives the data for the validations carried out on the operators' means of transport, automatically generating a set of reports, including the total number of validations per individual operator, per means of transport (rail/road), per line, as well as indicators on the use of each individual type of tariff. Furthermore, the data on ticket validation are completed with other indicators (attendance, fare avoidance, etc.) required for clearing. The Clearing server uses a database Oracle to gather and store the data on validation and attendance.

6 Discussion and Conclusion

The technological path described is not seemed to be the outcome of a logical plan of a chain of rational decision, but rather result of the interactions between actors inside and outside the Consortium (e.g., operators, Regional Institution) and of an integration (and negotiation) process of the interest expressed by these different organizational actors.

Moreover such IS were not anchored either to the classical parameters or the financial-economic ones, nor to the more evolved system of performance indicators. It were rather more a visioning system. An engineer who had been responsible for the technologic implementation asserted that: "If we had faced smart cards in a rigid way, with business plan and ROE objectives, we would never have

[1] A *Secure Access Module* is based on SmartCard ICs and is used to enhance the security and cryptography performance in devices, commonly in devices needing to perform secure transactions, such as paying terminals. It is widely used as a secure data carrier in the financial, telecommunications, transportation and other areas.

realized it. The project's complexities and the amount of time that it required were such that we were involved in the project for nearly 8 years without seeing any economic advantages".

In essence, the technical evolution implemented by UnicoCampania to manage ticketing marks a progressive increase in the Consortium's power to monitor and control in relation to the operators. The Consortium first defined a standard—the SAM management module (step 3)—to which the operators had to conform (with the possibility of choosing the hardware supplier to be used, however), and then introduced a central DPC—step 4–that allowed data (e.g., validation data) to be automatically transmitted from the operators to the Consortium. In particular, the progressive development of the ETS marks a significant change in the ability to control the distribution of revenues from traffic. In fact, there was a shift from a phase in which the data relating to the transported travellers were defined on "historical" data provided by the operators, adjusted based on periodic sample studies, to the adoption of a system that, by directly communicating with the operators' various computer systems, is able to define data and reports of a various nature (see below) relating to each operator and each line etc., in real time. It should also be noted that in a phase such as the present one, the revenues from traffic are increasingly more importance for the public transport companies in the Region than the total revenues because of the significant reduction in public funding for the management.

It can therefore be said that the Consortium's power to control the transport companies is not only *extended* through technology (potentially expanding to include new types of data and information), but also becomes more *pervasive*, increasing the visibility of data and information that was previously only acquired indirectly, and more *effective*, for example, reducing the risks of manipulating the processed data through sample studies carried by individual operators. In other words, ICT is used by UnicoCampania managers to extend and deepen the ability to exert control on the actors of the tariff network [40].

Electronic ticketing, due to its "pervasiveness" drastically affects the properties of the tariff network, generating paths which lead to power relations. It could be considered an artifact which enabled to renew and transformed the power relations within the ITS, stabilizing and reinforcing them. In other words, electronic ticketing intervenes on the dominant structure redesigning the power relationships inside the ITS governance and it has gradually established itself as the strength of the process that the drive the network. In other words, the development of technological innovation recreates the ways for the emersion of the political dimension. We have showed that the two dimension—technical and political—are co-present, appearing in association, even when one of them seem hidden [41]. They are mutually enabling and interact in a symbolic relationship where it was not possible to identify border lines which stated where one finished and the other started.

These conclusions are consistent with CISR perspective [42]. In the light of this framework and in keeping with the poststructuralist paradigm, IS are viewed as a lever used by management and, more generally, by dominant actors to consolidate or increase their control over other organizational actors. In the opinion of Myers and Klein [43] critical researchers should identify power relations and social practices, and challenge them.

Our study contributes to the CISR literature because we analyze the relationship, rarely theoretically and empirically examined in literature, between IS and power of control from the network perspective. Moreover CISR has, at times, been criticized for its lack of engagement with empirical issues. Our case study provides an empirical example of the application of this approach to an Italian LPT, focusing on the implementation of an electronic ticking system in ITS and confirming that the two categories—political and technological—do not denote a specific and separated belonging. From this point of view, the case illustrates the presence of a degree of alignment between dominant conceptions of control and IS artifacts.

References

1. Mercurio, R., Martinez, M., & Iacono, M. P. (2011). *Cambiamento e crisi delle ferrovie regionali in Italia: La difficile ricerca di un modello organizzativo per conciliare interessi pubblici e risorse private nel trasporto pubblico locale*. Naples: Editoriale Scientifica.
2. Mangia, G., Iacono, MP., Martinez, M., Canonico, P., Mercurio, R. (2012). The human side of organizational change: Compliance and management control systems in Italian public utilities. *Human Factors and Ergonomics in Manufacturing and Service Industries*.
3. Matas, A. (2004). Demand and revenue implications of an integrated public transport policy: The case of Madrid. *Transport Reviews, 24*, 195–217.
4. Dargay, J. M., & Pekkarinen, S. (1997). Public transport pricing policy: Empirical evidence of regional bus card systems in Finland. *Transportation Research Record, 1604*, 146–152.
5. Canonico, P., De Nito, E., Mangia, G., Mercurio, L., & Iacono, M. P. (2011). Regulation issues in the Italian local transport industry: Aligning transactions and governance structures. *Journal of Management and Governance, 15*, 1–23.
6. Canonico, P., De Nito, E., Mangia, G., Mercurio, L., & Iacono, M. P. (2012). Modelli di governance nei servizi pubblici: il trasporto pubblico locale in Italia, Impresa Progetto—Electronic. *Journal of Management, 1*, 1–27.
7. Mallat, N., Rossi, M., Tuunainen, V. K., & Örni, A. (2008). An empirical investigation of mobile ticketing service adoption in public transportation. *Personal Ubiquitous Computing, 12*, 57–65.
8. Kvasny, L., & Richardson, H. (2006). Critical research in information systems: Looking forward, looking back. *Information Technology and People, 19*(3), 196–202.
9. Doolin, B. (2002). Enterprise discourse professional identity and the organizational control of hospital clinicians. *Organization Studies, 23*(3), 369–390.
10. Yin, R. K. (2003). *Case study research: Design and methods* (3rd ed.). Newbury Park, CA: Sage.
11. Doolin, B., & McLeod, L. (2005). Towards critical interpretivism in IS research. In D. Howcroft & E. M. Trauth (Eds.), *Handbook of critical information systems research: Theory and application* (pp. 244–271). Cheltenham, UK: Edward Elgar.
12. Cecez-Kecmanovic, D., Klein, H. K., & Brooke, C. (2008). Exploring the critical research agenda in information systems research. *Information Systems Journal, 18*(2), 123–135.
13. Howcroft, D. (2009). Information system. In M. Alvesson, T. Bridgman, & H. Willmott (Eds.), *Oxford handbook of critical management studies*. Oxford: Oxford University Press.

14. Bednar, P. M. (2000). A contextual integration of individual and organizational learning perspectives as part of IS analysis. *Informing Science Journal, 3*(3), 145–146.
15. McLoughlin, I., & Harris, M. (1997). *Innovation, organizational change and technology*. London: International Thompson Business Paper.
16. Cecez-Kecmanovic, D. (2005). Basic assumptions of the critical research perspectives in information systems. In D. Howcroft & E. Trauth (Eds.), *Handbook of critical information systems research: Theory and application* (pp. 19–46). UK, Aldershot: Edward Elgar.
17. Avgerou, C., Mansell, R., Quah, D., & Silverstone, R. (2007). *The oxford handbook of information and communication technologies*. Oxford: Oxford University Press.
18. Berger, P. L., & Luckmann, T. (1966). *The social construction of reality: A treatise in the sociology of knowledge*. Garden City: New York Doubleday.
19. Weick, K. E. (1977). Enactment processes in organizations. In B. M. Staw & G. R. Salancick (Eds.), *New directions in organizational behaviour* (p. 300). Chicago: St. Clair Press.
20. Giddens, A. (1991). *Modernity and self identity: Self and society in the late modern age*. Cambridge: Polity Press.
21. Sveningsson, S., & Alvesson, M. (2003). Managing managerial identities: Organizational fragmentation, discourse and identity struggle. *Human Relations, 56*(10), 1141–1193.
22. Alvesson, M., & Willmott, H. (1992). On the idea of emancipation in management and organization studies. *Academy of Management Review, 17*(3), 432–464.
23. Alvesson, M., & Willmott, H. (2002). Identity regulation as organizational control: Producing the appropriate individual. *Journal of Management Studies, 39*, 619–644.
24. Brooke, C. (2002). Critical research in information systems. *Journal of Information Technology, 17*(2), 45–47.
25. Martinez, M., & Iacono, M. P. (2012). Dealing with critical IS research: Artifacts, drifts, electronic panopticon and illusions of empowerment. In R. Baskerville, M. De Marco, & P. Spagnoletti (Eds.), *Designing organisational systems: An interdisciplinary discourse* (pp. 83–102). Berlin: Springer.
26. Ciborra, C. U. (2000). A critical review of the literature on the management of corporate information infrastructure. In C. U. Ciborra (Ed.), *From control to drift: The dynamics of corporate information infrastructures* (pp. 15–40). Oxford: Oxford University Press.
27. Ciborra, C. U. (2002). *The labyrinths of information: Challenging the wisdom of systems*. Oxford: Oxford University Press.
28. Rajao, R., & Hayes, N. (2009). Conceptions of control and IT artefacts: An institutional account of the Amazon rainforest monitoring system. *Journal of Information Technology, 24*(4), 320–331.
29. Fligstein, N. (1990). *The transformation of corporate control*. Cambridge, Mass: Harvard University Press.
30. Martinez, M. (2011). ICT, productivity and organizational complementarity. In C. Rossignoli & A. Carugati (Eds.), *Emerging themes in information systems and organization studies* (pp. 271–281). Berlin: Springer.
31. Introna, L. D. (1997). *Management, information and power*. London: Macmillan.
32. Orlikowski, W. J. (2000). Using technology and constituting structures: A practice lens for studying technology in organizations. *Organization Science, 11*(4), 404–428.
33. Jabar, M. A., Sidi, F., Selamat, M. H., Ghani, A. A. A., & Ibrahim, H. (2009). An investigation into methods and concepts of qualitative research in information system research. *Computer and information Science, 2*(4), 47–54.
34. Orlikowski, W. J. (1993). CASE tools as organizational change: investigating incremental and radical changes in systems development. *MIS Quarterly, 17*(3), 309–340.
35. Abrate, G., Piacenza, M., & Vannoni, D. (2009). The impact of integrated tariff systems on public transport demand: Evidence from Italy. *Regional Science and Urban Economics, 39*, 120–127.
36. Piacenza, M., & Carpani, C. (2003). *Esperienze di integrazione tariffaria nel trasporto pubblico locale in Italia*. Moncalieri, Turin: HERMES Research Report.

37. Mangia, G., De Nito, E., Pezzillo Iacono, M., Canonico, P. (2009). Governance models in the local transport industry: An empirical research on tariff integration systems. *Proceedings EIASM, the Naples forum on services: Service-dominant logic, service science and network theory*, Capri, Italy.
38. D'Atri, A. (2010). *Management of the interconnected world.* Berlin Heidelberg: Springer.
39. Revellino, S. (2010). *Enabling innovation: Essay on intellectual capital, control, and the ontology of IT artefacts*. Milan: Franco Angeli.
40. Canonico, P., De Nito, E., Mangia, G., Mercurio, R., & Esposito, V. (2009). Interpreting projects: Bureaucratical mechanisms to enforce control or lever for change. *Organizacja I Zarzadanie, 3*(7), 5–16.
41. Ahrne, G., & Brunsson, N. (2005). Organizations and meta-organizations. *Scandinavian Journal of Management, 21*(4), 429–449.
42. Brooke, C. (2009). *Critical perspective on information systems*. Oxford: Elsevier.
43. Myers, M. D., & Klein, H. (2011). A set of principles for conducting critical research in information systems. *MIS Quarterly, 35*(1), 17–36.

Challenging the Power Balance Between Governments and Citizens: The Role of Information Diffused Through the Internet

Tommaso Federici and Alessio Maria Braccini

Abstract A new phenomenon is rapidly spreading in the world: original, or even official, data regarding the governments' policies and the behaviour of their leaders are diffused onto the Internet to everybody by unofficial agents. Such novelty has already provoked some change, and may profoundly alter the relationship between citizens and governments or their leaders. Because of the newness of its nature, traditional theories may not be able to fully explain this innovation.

Keywords Governments · Citizens · Information multicasting · Power balance · Critical management studies

1 Introduction

Since years, the Internet is increasingly allowing individuals and groups to collect and disseminate original data and information. Such data and information diffused through the Internet by private citizens or organizations, and possibly stemming from direct sources, are available at a very low cost, and can even be used to confute or compare data or information disclosed by public administrations. This new possibility can modify the way the communication with the stakeholders of governments, public administrations, and their representatives is traditionally settled.

For example, citizens can put more pressure on politicians or public administrations, thanks to the availability of more official data and information on their

T. Federici (✉) · A. M. Braccini
Dipartimento di Economia e Impresa, Università degli Studi della Tuscia, Viterbo, Italy
e-mail: tfederici@unitus.it

A. M. Braccini
e-mail: abraccini@unitus.it

P. Spagnoletti (ed.), *Organizational Change and Information Systems*, Lecture Notes in Information Systems and Organisation 2, DOI: 10.1007/978-3-642-37228-5_32,

work. The idea is that data intended to be confidential can be revealed, and incomplete data can be completed, integrated, or confuted by similar or complementary data shared by Internet users. This contributes to a potential, even when unintentional, empowerment of individual or associated citizens, who have new ways to control politicians' decision-making and behaviour, and administrations' actions. An increased transparency and some policy changes may then be fostered. Some scholars already studied the relationship between transparency and public government actions as a solution to reduce corruption, and improve accountability [1, 2]. Rich and clear information improve the quality of the society, because more informed citizens demand to be better governed and such pressure positively influences governments [3].

We argue that a scenario like the one described here—new ways to diffuse information regarding the activity of politicians or public administrations—can, with time, change the way communication between a government or a public administration and its stakeholders is performed. Instead of having few central points managed by government or administrations from which official data and information are broadcast, several independent and unofficial agents cooperate and compete in a multicast fashion to share data and information. We argue that this novelty has also the potential to challenge the power balance between citizens and political leaders, and it might require major revisions in current management styles.

This emergent phenomenon has already provoked some changes, like for example in the cases, later described, of the Mayor of Bari, and of the Fukushima crisis. Not all the actors interested by this phenomenon are anyhow aware of this, and even fewer are prepared to manage it, like the "Cablegate" case of WikiLeaks, see below, demonstrates. At the same time, many constraints and hurdles could potentially impede the change in progress. For example (the list is not exhaustive) possible barriers against the change in progress are:

- Difficulties in using, interpreting, or processing the information, due to language, required skills, and quantity of information available;
- Inaccessibility of information, due to the behaviour of media operators which may choose what, if, and when to publish;
- The blocking or hindering of information diffusion by service operators that may close servers, connections, and/or bank accounts of the subject who exposes the information [4].

For all the aforementioned reasons we believe this to be a new interesting research topic, which can be investigated moving from different scientific realms, like politics, communication science, and organization science. In this chapter, our aim is to start to identify the changes that this new phenomenon may provoke in the organizational structures of public administrations, in the behaviour of politicians, and even in the politics processes. This chapter follows a draft research agenda [5] drawn to describe this phenomenon under diverse aspects, and to delineate a research program to investigate it under several different perspectives.

This chapter is however only a first step of a research effort still in progress. Its structure is the following: in Sect. 2 we will describe the research design clarifying the purpose of the chapter, the methodology, and the theory addressed; in Sect. 3 we will briefly describe the empirical cases analysed, which will be discussed in Sect. 4. In Sect. 5 we will draw preliminary conclusions and provide information on future research steps.

2 Research Design

While firstly considering evidence of the most relevant events involving diffusion of original data or information on the Internet by subjects other than governments or public administrations, our impression was that we were in front of a completely new situation, where the potentially incoming changes may be really strong and radical.

In such scenario, organisational structures built upon consolidated and normally accepted mechanisms, like the pyramidal power structure, a sole source of official information, and an usually undisclosed decision making process, may no longer fit into the organization's environment with its new pressures. Consequently, we believed the traditional "mainstream" theories not worth adopting, even when applicable, like for example the Agency Theory [6], as they are not intrinsically capable to fully interpret the possible modifications.

We then turn to refer to the Critical Management Studies (CMS) as a potentially more proper theoretical framework. CMS are a rich body of research [7, 8], whose limits and characteristics are not precisely defined [9]. CMS offer a theoretical background alternative to mainstream management theories to discuss, even from the grass roots, the transformation of management practices [10]. In fact, differently from mainstream research, the CMS do not take any organizational structure nor perspective for granted, not even the most accepted ones, which in the common world end to be considered as "natural" or "eternal". The underlying assumption in CMS, even in their great variety, is that framing an organizational context (i.e.: the structures of control in a firm) always under the same specific perspective (i.e.: the control level of the CEO), like the mainstream theories do, often implicitly, drives to severe issues and losses. The observer is forced to consider such representation, with its vertical organizational design, as the only option, in this way reinforcing its "necessity". At the same time he/she misses other perspectives, possibly rich of insights and brand new suggestions.

Regarding the methodology, CMS do not involve a well defined way to operationalize research. However, also recalling the claims by Visser [9] about the validity of adopting mainstream methodologies, we decided to use the multiple case-study methodology [11]. The chapter then discusses four cases, each one focusing on the role of the Internet in the diffusion of official or original data or information. The data for the cases were of different nature every time, and gathered from different sources as illustrated in Table 1. In the table, the sources

Table 1 Information sources used in the four cases

Case	Data	Sources
Mayor of Bari	Pictures Comments	Facebook profile of the Mayor of Bari (direct) Newspapers (indirect)
Cablegate on WikiLeaks	Cables (official documents)	WikiLeaks website (direct) WikiLeaks cables (direct) Newspapers (indirect)
Fukushima nuclear crisis	Radiation levels Video/audio files Comments Posts	Website of the Italian Embassy in Tokyo (direct) Fukushima nuclear accident update log of the international atomic energy agency (IAEA) (indirect) Reports of the Japan Ministries of education and of economy, trade and industry (indirect) Various blogs (eBuroggu, GiappoPazzie, RischioCalcolato) (direct) Newspapers (Repubblica, and Sole 24 Ore) (indirect)
Riots in Kenya on Ushahidi	Video/audio files Comments	Ushahidi website (indirect) Newspapers (indirect)

that reported original data (audio/video files, or official/original documents) are indicated as "direct", while sources that reported second hand data (like comments) are indicated as "indirect". In each case we focus on the sequence of actions that shows the behaviour of political leaders and citizens in the circumstances of a specific event or in its aftermath.

3 The Cases

As already mentioned in the introduction, the common ground of the phenomenon we are investigating in this chapter consists in the diffusion, through the Internet, of original data and information, by a group of independent actors who sometimes remain anonymous. Traces of this phenomenon can be found in some recent events as testified by the following cases of study. The cases we are referring to are: the Mayor of Bari and his use of Facebook, "Cablegate" case on WikiLeaks, the Fukushima nuclear crisis, and the history of the riots in Kenya on the Ushahidi website.

3.1 The Mayor of Bari and Facebook

The Mayor of Bari (Italy) opened his own Facebook profile and started to use it as an open forum to communicate with his citizens. On January 2011 he received from a citizen a picture of a group of dustmen chatting in the street during their working shift. The picture does not clearly show whether the dustmen are just messing around or organizing their work. In spite of that, citizens and trade unions immediately reacted to the sharing of the picture the Mayor made on his Facebook profile. Lots of citizens posted comments on the Facebook page to complain about a poor efficiency of the public sweeping service. In reply to this mobilization, the trade unions blamed the Mayor for his possible will to run down the work of honest workers. The Mayor on his side invited both groups to come to a necessary clarification, either on Facebook or anywhere else. Other examples of this kind of usage of the Mayor's of Bari Facebook page, are for instance the reports of protests related to town hall employees' cars being parked on pedestrian crossings, or double-parked in the streets of the city.

After about one year of experience, being strongly convinced of the usefulness of this channel to open the communication with citizens, the Mayor of Bari forced his councillors to create a personal page on Facebook, to make it public, and even to spend at least an hour per day on it [12].

3.2 The Cablegate on WikiLeaks

WikiLeaks is an international non profit organization which, through its website, receives and subsequently shares confidential documents containing information on the actions of large organizations and/or governments. WikiLeaks verifies the information received and protects the identity of the person who discloses the documents, thanks to the usage of Internet technologies.

On November 2010 WikiLeaks began publishing part of 251.287 documents with confidential information on the work of the US government and diplomacy in the world. WikiLeaks also sent all the documents to the dailies El Pais, Le Monde, The Guardian, The New York Time, and to the weekly Der Spiegel. The documents contained information and comments on the habits and on the work of leaders of the most influent international countries expressed by diplomatic representatives of the US government. Such event was given the name of "Cablegate" case.

The reactions of administrations and leaders interested by the disclosures showed unpreparedness (a European government even claimed to "deny WikiLeaks" [13]), and were of embarrassment, minimization, and contradiction. Following this event, and in reaction of the potential threat of further leaks being disclosed, attacks were moved against WikiLeaks and its founder. The website was obscured, the founder was accused of sex crimes and eventually arrested, and since December 2010 a financial blockade made WikiLeaks activities harder. Since then the WikiLeaks website is still running, but the organization has lost about 95 % of its financial revenues.

3.3 The Fukushima Nuclear Power Plant Crisis

On March 2011, a massive tsunami wave triggered by the Sendai earthquake in Japan started a sequence of events and incidents that led to a nuclear crisis at the Fukushima Dai-ichi power plant. As a consequence of the damage the tsunami wave caused to the power plant, nuclear radiations were released in the environment surrounding the power plant for a prolonged period of time. The difficulties in restoring a safe condition in the reactors, and the suspicion that the government was not telling the whole truth on the incident, have created a big concern on the safety of the nuclear technology and also on possible local and global consequences of this incident. In the aftermath of the event, several unconfirmed communications regarding radiation levels around the power plant and in Tokyo created a big safety concern in public opinion, both concerning living conditions in Japan, and the nuclear power plant technology.

In response to this uncertainty several individuals and organizations started to publish on websites and blogs data on radiation levels they manually detected around the nuclear power plant, and in Tokyo. These initiatives forced public authorities to regularly detect and publish official data on radiations. At first the Italian civil protection measured radiation levels near the Italian embassy in Tokyo. Later, both the Japanese Ministry of Economy Trade and Industry, and the Ministry of Education, started to publish official data on radioactivity levels. Finally the International Atomic Energy Agency published regular and detailed reports on the evolution of the incident.

3.4 Riots in Kenya on Ushahidi

The word Ushahidi means witness in Swahili. Ushahidi is also the name of a non profit organization that develops open source software for information collection, visualization, and interactive mapping. Ushahidi created a website to collect reports and eyewitnesses of violence sent by persons, by e-mail and text massage, and eventually placed on a Google map.

The website was firstly created and used in the aftermath of Kenya's disputed 2007 presidential election. In that circumstance president Mwai Kibaki was declared the winner, but supporters of his opponents alleged electoral manipulations. An increasing number of violent protests from the opposition supporters leaded to fights in several parts of the country. During these protests the police shots a number of demonstrators, including a few in front of TV cameras. Citizens who were witnesses of such troubles documented them through posts and photos, that were geo-referenced on the website.

The Ushahidi software later became an open platform available for every group of citizens or associations who wants to report politicians misbehaviours.

4 Challenging Stakeholders Relations with Organizations

The four analysed cases come from as many countries, involve diverse levels of government, face different problems and present various issues. In Table 2 we classified the characteristics of such cases so far identified as relevant for our scope. Even in such diverse contexts, we can observe some commonalities in the occurred changes:

- An increased availability of original data (not comments or opinions) provided by unofficial subjects about events of interest for central or local governments;
- A modification in the communication, from a broadcast (highly controlled) mode, to a multicast (substantially uncontrolled) one;
- An increased possibility for citizens of addressing pressures on institutions.

It must be noted that we are considering public organizations, formally submitted to the social control of the respective population. The above-mentioned changes suggest that constructs taken for granted in public organization, like those below discussed, are neither natural nor eternal [10] and may be altered in presence of new conditions. In a nutshell, in the presented cases the great novelty is twofold represented by: the possibility for citizens to have more information on events and actions regarding their government, and the circumstance that such data and information were delivered by other citizens and no longer by the same government as in the past. We argue that both of them may substantially alter the relationships between citizens and their government and leaders, increase the number of knowledge sources related to governments' actions or decisions available for citizens, and influence the behaviour of the administrations' leaders or managers.

Table 2 Analyzed dimensions in the cases

Variables	Mayor of Bari	Cablegate on WikiLeaks	Fukushima nuclear crisis	Riots in Kenya on Ushahidi
Year	2011	2010	2011	2007
Original source	Citizens	Whistleblower	Citizens and institutions	Citizens
Disseminator	The Mayor	WikiLeaks, TVs, and press	Private blogs	Ushahidi
Stakeholders interested	Citizens of Bari	International citizens, governments, community	Japan citizens, international community	Kenyan people, international community
Type of interested administration	Local government	Diplomatic institutions	Central government and private companies	Central government
Problem nature	Inefficient services	Diplomatic relations	Public health	Violation of rights

As regards changes in the relationships, we can mention (the list is not exhaustive): the alteration in the power balance between the two sides, particularly when referring to the power of knowledge, and to the compilation of the government (or administration) agenda, based on more detailed, freshly collected requirements.

The knowledge about the events and the related political decisions is traditionally possessed and managed by central and local governments' leaders: they decide how to use it, and when and in what measure to diffuse it to their citizens. Up to now this has represented a fundamental source of power [14], sometimes even giving space to a sort of domination [10] by the leaders with corrupted moral responsibility over their people. Apparently, thanks to the cited new opportunities, citizens seem to become more powerful because of the availability of more information about the actual behaviour of institutions (like in the WikiLeaks and Ushahidi cases), or the possibility to force the disclosure of more data (like in the Fukushima crisis case).

The opening of new channels to exchange requirements, like with a Facebook page in the Bari case, allows to constantly put pressure on an administrator to update his/her agenda, and also giving to him/her an immediate and public visible feedback about the performed actions. Again, the opportunity for the citizens to directly interact with their leaders about requirements seems to create a new, more equilibrated, power balance. This could also give a different answer to the well-known question by Dahl "who actually governs?" when knowledge and access are highly unbalanced [15].

When dealing with the effects of the discussed changes on the behaviour of political leaders or governors, we can refer to the greater evidence of ethical and political (in a broader, more democratic sense) questions in their decision making process and in their management style. On the one hand, when little information is disclosed about a decision made, the decision maker might be more oriented towards a performance target to show (like in the Fukushima case, the energy national independence), following a typical mainstream means-ends rational process [10], than to the underlying ethical aspects (i.e.: in terms of related hidden social costs). On the other hand, scandals and misbehaviours might decrease when the actor clearly knows that his/her actions could possibly be officially documented and publicly disclosed (like in the WikiLeaks case). Mainstream theories usually consider scandals and misbehaviours as a consequence of poor individual or organizational ethics [10]. The cited case instead critically suggests that a different approach to organizational design (more transparency, more down-up control) can reduce their frequency.

We can observe a, still initial, change of the management style promoted by the Mayor in the Bari case. Having remarked the huge participation of citizens in dialoguing with him using his Facebook page—expressing critiques, requests and proposals to solve issues about city services and status, the same Mayor decided that also its councillors had to use it, stating that: "Facebook is just another channel to keep in touch with citizens… and even elderly people now use it".

In the Fukushima nuclear crisis we can also notice another instance of the mainstream theories weakness, already predicted by Perrow about 30 years ago in a famous study [16], which adopted in a critical fashion contingency theory. The nuclear power has demonstrated to be too risky to be controlled with usual organizational structures, and "normal accidents" may then be devastating.

5 First Conclusions and Limitations

This chapter deals with the new arising phenomenon of the diffusion on the Internet by private subjects of original data and information about policies, decision making processes, and behaviours of governments or public administrations and their leaders. The novelty in this case consists in the overcoming of the traditional broadcasting model, where official data and information are diffused only by a single official source, like a government or a public administration. Such a model does not fully keep its previous power, as it has now to fight against what we call the "multicasting" model. This shift in the relationship between a government (or a public administration) and its citizens could produce changes in the organizational structures of the involved institutions, and in the management style of their leaders. In our opinion, such changes may be so innovative and significant that mainstream theories, with their usual frameworks, seem inadequate to investigate them. For these reasons we suggest to turn to Critical Management Studies body of theories, which for its openness seems to fit better when studying big changes and the rethinking of consolidated systems.

On the basis of the results of the analyzed four cases, we address as main fields of change the alteration in the power balance between governments and citizens (with particular regard to the power of knowledge), and the compilation of the government (or administration) agenda, based on more detailed, freshly collected requirements.

This work is part of a much larger research effort devoted to investigate the phenomenon of the diffusion of data and information from direct sources through the Internet under several, complementary, perspectives. In particular this work addresses the perspective of changes of power balance between citizens and governments. This work has to be considered as a first step: further research will be addressed to deepen the analysis and the discussion of the cases investigated in this chapter, to identify new cases, and to thoroughly investigate in critical terms the change in action.

References

1. Kaufmann, D., & Bellver, A. (2005). Transparenting transparency: Initial empirics and policy applications. *Working Paper Series*, The World Bank. Retrieved December 22, 2011, from: http://ssrn.com/abstract=808664 or http://dx.doi.org/10.2139/ssrn.808664.
2. Gant, D. B., Gant, J. P., & Johnson, C. L. (2002). *Enhancing E-service delivery*. Pricewaterhouse: Pricewaterhouse Coopers Endowment.

3. Islam, R. (2003). *Do more transparent governments govern better? Policy Research Working Paper, 3077*. Washington: World Bank.
4. Federici, T. & Braccini, A.M. (2012) Internet, Citizens, and Public Organizations: The Power of Service Providers in Fostering or Hampering Transparency. In M.B. Nunes, P. Isaias and P. Powell (eds.) *Proceedings Information Systems–IADIS International Conference 2012*, Berlin, Germany, 10–12 March.
5. Federici, T. & Braccini, A.M. (2012). How internet is upsetting the communication between organizations and their stakeholders: A research agenda. In M. De Marco, D. Te'eni, V. Albano, S. Za (Eds.), *Information systems: crossroads for organization, management, accounting and engineering*, Berlin, Germany: Springer.
6. Eisenhardt, K. M. (1989). Agency theory: An assessment and review. *Academy of Management Review, 14*(1), 57–74.
7. http://en.wikipedia.org/wiki/Critical_management_studies [last accessed: 10.2.2012].
8. http://www.criticalmanagement.org/ [last accessed: 10.2.2012].
9. Visser, M. (2010). Critical management studies and "mainstream" organization science: A proposal for a rapprochement. *Journal of Organizational Studies, 18*(6), 466–478.
10. Adler, P. S., Forbes, L. C., & Willmott, H. (2007). Critical management studies. *Academy of Management Annals, 1*, 119–179.
11. Yin, R. K. (1994). *Case study research: Design and methods*. CA: Sage Publishing.
12. http://corrieredelmezzogiorno.corriere.it/bari/notizie/cronaca/2011/15-novembre-2011/su-facebook-a-tutti-costiemiliano-obbliga-assessori-1902185542070.shtml [Accessed: 10.2.2012].
13. Governo Italiano (2011). "Governo Italiano–Il Governo Informa," [Online]. Available: http://www.governo.it/Presidenza/Comunicati/dettaglio.asp?d=61569 [Accessed: 19.1.2012].
14. Foucault, M. (1975). *Surveiller et punir*. Paris: Gallimard.
15. Dahl, R. A. (1961). *Who governs? Power and democracy in an American cty*. New Haven, CT: Yale University Press.
16. Perrow, C. (1984). *Normal accidents: Living with high-risk technologies*. New York: Basic Books.

A Case for Holistic, Multicriteria Benefit Analysis

Peter M. Bednar and Christine Welch

Abstract This chapter discusses the ways in which a critical systemic approach to systems analysis can provide support for a holistic, multicriteria benefits analysis. It highlights the importance of inquiry into the nature and boundaries of a perceived organizational problem space, taking into account unique perspectives of the living, engaged actors who desire beneficial change in their working systems. The role of the IS professional within a collaborative inquiry is explored, taking into account creation of relevant methodological frameworks (in contrast to uncritical, rigorous application of standardized methods). The chapter discusses the ways in which collaborative teams can approach identification of desirable benefits.

Keywords Benefits analysis · Critical systemic thinking · Systems analysis · Methodologies

1 Introduction

An important question to ask in relation to information system design is what is the role of an IS professional? Is it to 'deliver' what the 'client' 'wants'? If this is the proposition, then we need to question carefully what we mean by these terms. It is also important to examine the activities of professionals. In relation to project management, for instance, the Standish Group report 'Cobb's Paradox,' attributed

P. M. Bednar (✉)
University of Portsmouth, School of Computing, Portsmouth, UK
e-mail: peter.bednar@port.ac.uk

C. Welch
Portsmouth Business School, University of Portsmouth, Portsmouth, UK
e-mail: christine.welch@port.ac.uk

P. Spagnoletti (ed.), *Organizational Change and Information Systems*, Lecture Notes in Information Systems and Organisation 2, DOI: 10.1007/978-3-642-37228-5_33,

to Martin Cobb of the Treasury Board of Canada Secretariat, who reportedly said *We know why projects fail, we know how to prevent their failure—so why do they still fail*? [1] It is often considered that well-trained professionals who apply recognised methods with sufficient rigour will 'deliver' effective results. However, we suggest that it is important to ask the questions 'effective for whom?' and 'effective in what circumstances?' This chapter examines the role of IS professionals in supporting developments that are found to be useful in context. In doing so, the importance of inquiry into relevance, and a need for critical perspectives on professional 'practice' are highlighted.

2 The Role of the IS Professional

It is, of course, important for an IS professional to consider for what purpose(s) a proposed system is required. Should they attempt to deliver what the client wants? Or perhaps what the client needs? Without understanding these factors, it is unlikely that 'useful' systems will evolve. Who, though, is the client? Are we talking about a problem owner in the sense indicated by Checkland [2] in his Soft Systems Methodology? This would be a person with power to sponsor or prevent change. In an organizational setting, it is of course important to know who has ultimate understanding of the constraints within which a development is situated, e.g. budgets and timescales. However, a focus on problem owners potentially excludes 'users' of a proposed system from involvement in its creation. Nissen [3] warns against labeling engaged actors as 'users' for two reasons. First, because it disqualifies their own identities—few people define themselves professionally as users of information systems; and secondly because, in doing so, genuine dialogue about their ideas, ambitions and desires becomes inhibited.

If systems are to be created which are experienced as useful in the context of daily working life, the desires of those who will use them must be explored. As pointed out by Ciborra [4], people do not enter their workspace as ciphers, playing out mimes as described in a formal job description, but are present as *themselves*. All human beings experience multiple *Weltanshauungen* (worldviews), built from their contextual understandings of the world they inhabit, which are shifting, emergent properties of their interpretations of relationships [5]. Not only are our views and wishes opaque to other people, but we ourselves are not perpetually aware of the interacting perspectives, both rational and emotional, which shape our judgments. In our decision-making, we often seek to apply some kind of bounded rationality [6] which must be an emergent property of our own ongoing sense-making processes. Argyris [7] makes the observation that human beings may hold espoused theories about their behavior in social context(s), which can differ radically from their theories-in-use—what would make that exhibited behavior explicable to others. Desire is linked to motivation and also (prejudiced) value judgments about expectations from what is 'delivered'. Individuals will need support to explore and surface their own contextual understandings in order to shape their needs and desires from any proposed system.

An Information System can be considered as a particular example of a Human Activity System [8] (HAS). This term has given way in Checkland's work to that of Purposeful Activity System (PAS) [9]. It is worthwhile to reflect here on the difference in use of these terms. *Purposeful* behavior, which Checkland [10] describes as action that is willed or voluntary, can be contrasted with *purposive* behavior, i.e. that to which an observer can attribute 'purpose'. This distinction is important to our current purpose since it may be tempting for an IS professional to attribute meaning to a situation and in consequence assume that certain 'requirements' are the relevant properties of the system to be created. We prefer the term Human Activity System, since this emphasizes the presence of unique human individuals whose perspectives on the purpose of any system are formed through their expert understandings of context. It may become easier to engage with a multitude of differing understandings of an organizational problem space if we do not pre-determine (assume, or pre-judge) some objective, bounded rationality of what we perceive.

As practitioners, we are not limited in our own practices by other people's descriptions. We must make efforts to take responsibility for our interpretations and applications of methods and methodologies. We should not be promoting method over methodology as a logical consequence of experience in practice, but focus on co-creating an inquiry into unique, contextual understandings. It is crucial to remember the relative expertise of those involved in developing new systems. The 'client' has experience and understanding of constraints. However, as Jayaratna has pointed out [11], it is the 'users' who have contextual understanding of the problem space within which the new system will be experienced as relevant. As neither of these participants are likely to be experts in the processes of inquiry, which are an infrequent aspect of organizational life, it is here that the expertise and experience of an IS professional become crucial. It is the professional's job to facilitate a collaborative inquiry into the problem space, in order to co-create a resolution which is experienced as meaningful in context. The holders of all three types of expertise must be participating actors in this process, since none of them is an expert in the experience of any 'future desired solution space'. We can draw an analogy from the field of medicine. A patient has competence in the experience of her 'problems'. However, she may need guidance through consultation to express what 'feels wrong'. The patient may think that her symptoms indicate a particular disease and that she knows what will make her feel better, e.g. a particular drug or procedure, and this may or may not be the case. It would be a really bad idea for every doctor to assume that the patient is always right! Equally, it would be a bad doctor who assumed she knew better than the patient about the contextual experience of 'the problem'. However, the doctor is (hopefully) more competent than the patient in facilitating both a problem inquiry and an exploration into potentially valid future problem resolutions (e.g. what might be suitable medication and possible desirable outcomes). Such exploration will depend upon available resources, e.g. a hospital in which treatment can take place or drugs dispensed from a pharmacy.

3 Methodology and Method

When we apply methods, especially for IS development or project management, we are mainly concerned to produce a particular 'outcome' or 'product'. This can easily seduce managers into believing that meaningful progress is being made so that they suspend their judgment activities. However, efforts to apply methods, without first inquiring what are relevant problem spaces to address, are unlikely to meet with 'success'. We could use an analogy of a fighter who chooses and wields a weapon, without first inquiring who is the enemy, how is he armed and what is the terrain? Engaged actors cannot abrogate their responsibility to make inquiries into relevance before they make choices relating to rigor; yet such an obvious conclusion has frequently evaded project teams, resulting in all kinds of real world problems for IS practitioners and their clients for more than forty years. It is important, therefore, to recognize that choices relating to the format of 'method' are subordinate to concerns for 'methodology'.

In the field of information systems, as in other areas of expertise, we might expect to find practitioners who exhibit both personal integrity and ambition for excellence. Over the past 25 years, many practitioners have been quite successful in integrating relevant aspects of different methods and methodologies into their activities. For example, many authorities recommend use of a soft method for inquiry into a problem area before committing to application of hard methods [12]. It is difficult, therefore, to comprehend the actions of those practitioners who ignore such suggestions for good practice. However, the authors have observed that a focus on methods deemed to be fashionable can lead to a situation in which IS professionals behave like Lemmings, ignoring historic commentary that highlights phenomena such as Cobb's paradox (see [1] above). Referring again to our discussion about HAS and PAS, it is clear that a person who wishes to bring about change cannot exclude from the field of inquiry her own engagement with that change. You cannot engage with any human activity system without including your own engagement in such a system. Just as a map is not the same thing as the territory it is intended to represent, so we cannot describe a system change and at the same time exclude from consideration what could potentially bring it about. Thus, to draw up an action plan may be satisfying, but it is not a substitute for creation of a meaningful dialogue among people who want to engage with a desired change. This exploration and dialogue (about HAS and PAS) can be supported through discussions and co-creation of 'models', rich pictures or other visualization techniques that can help individuals and groups in their sense-making and informed judgment about possible action related to a desired potential future system.

Unfortunately, it is not unusual to find confusion between choice of methodologies and application of methods. On one hand, it is extremely important to understand methods well. When discussing methods, the problem of competence is often given attention. People need to be skillful in their ability to apply tools and techniques or their efforts will be disqualified by definition. This is why rigor in problem solving and inquiry are actively promoted–we want our artifacts to work. On the other hand, however, it is extremely important to understand that methods should not be used without contextual adaptation and change. In other words, while it is necessary to know the 'rules' it is also important to know when to bend or even to ignore them [13]. Contextual judgment and informed decision-making are indispensible to professional practice. A further issue for professionals is which tool from the toolbox (which method) to draw upon in any given context. How can we set the boundary of what is 'relevant' in context? It is at this point that we consider what the concept of 'methodology' is (or should be) all about. A methodological framework enables us to address the questions of 'when', 'why' and 'in what way(s)' relating to method. We can express this by saying that the job of methodology is to engage the issue of relevance.

4 A Focus on Benefits?

It has been suggested [14] that there has been too much focus on interpretation of context in IS research and that a more pragmatic focus on benefit realization (problem-solving) is needed. This has led to the body of work known under the label of design science. However, when we contemplate the benefits that may accrue from creation and introduction of new IT artifacts, we always return to the questions 'In what ways and from who's point of view can this be regarded as useful or beneficial?' Just as it is necessary to question the nature of the problem space to be addressed (see, e.g. Checkland [2]) so we cannot take for granted that we, as analysts or developers, can decide on someone else's behalf what benefits they are seeking from a proposed system. Much work has been done, for instance, within a socio-technical framework by, e.g. Mumford [15]. The ETHICS methodology involves steps and techniques intended to help individual participants to express their wishes and desires for the work systems within which they interact, in order to promote job satisfaction. Living individuals have unique perspectives, which are comprised of multiple worldviews which shift and re-form over time. Our individual values and desires are emergent properties of the total life situations we experience, our interactions with the world around us and the sense-making processes we engage in [5]. Thus, our desire for 'benefits' from a proposed system emerge from many influences. Some of these belong to the world of rationality but they also derive from the affective zone [16]. The authors have expressed this elsewhere in the following terms [17]:

> Knowing that systems with potential for meaningful use are available is a necessary, but not sufficient, condition to bring about desire for use in any particular individual. Work of developers is often perceived within a narrow, largely (socio-) technical definition of information systems. However, it must be recognized that such systems are inherently dependent not only upon their social but also individual and cultural sense-making context.

Ciborra discussed the search for benefits from developments in organizational systems, emphasizing a role for *bricolage* (tinkering) in efforts to bring about beneficial change. He related this to a concept of 'mood' that is essential in relation to creativity. Ciborra was concerned to distance creative processes from mythical 'appearances' of cognitive strategies. For him, a playful creative dance among actors is what generates progress, rather than a deliberate plan of action [4]. The concept of 'mood' represents a deliberate attempt to emphasize the affective dimension in human interactions, distancing improvisation from 'appearances' of cognitive problem solving to incorporate feelings as a state of being.

> Looking at improvisation as a special disposition or attunement with the situation, a special way of being amidst the world and being thrown into it, opens up a different point of access to the phenomenon: improvisation as mood [18].

A critical systemic approach to benefit analysis must encompass a number of factors. A focus on interpretation by engaged actors and critique of the boundaries of a perceived problem space [19] are essential, as is consideration of what would constitute beneficial change from particular points of view. In order for individuals to reflect upon a problem situation, they will need to create scale for evaluation by which critique becomes meaningful and relevant benefits can be envisioned. These factors cannot be separated—processes of human reflection leading to a creative learning spiral must involve interpretation, creation of scales of measurement and judgments based upon these measures [20].

Multicriteria benefit analysis from a critical perspective must allow for paraconsistent logic in a process of defining and managing benefits. In other words, living individuals, when asked what it is that they want, are likely to answer 'It depends' [21]. As living human beings, we are tolerant of degrees of ambiguity, reflecting our multiple and shifting worldviews. Efforts to establish desired benefits must be equally tolerant of such ambiguity, rejecting either a rush to premature consensus [22] or the kind of coercive organizational environment in which actors receive the message 'Don't rock the boat' or 'Anyone who isn't with us is against us.' An organizational culture of 'mindfulness' [23], in which expression of ideas and a range of opinion is welcomed, will clearly be helpful.

In carrying out holistic, multicriteria benefit analysis it is necessary to consider different dimensions on which benefits may be judged: e.g. economic, ergonomic, measurable, experienced, intangible, etc. Stakeholder analysis is important, but this should go beyond the question of stakeholder identification. Who are the stakeholders and what worldviews to they hold *in this context*? This analysis must be both participatory and client-led (i.e. collaborative) in order to yield meaningful information for the process of inquiry, taking into account individual, subjective value systems. For each such value system, efforts are needed to explore and to discuss boundary setting (e.g. in relation to Ulrich's suggested approach in critical systems heuristics [20]). An analysis may also embrace negative perspectives, i.e. what the stakeholders do not want, since this can also trigger fruitful dialogue that illuminates the problem space.

5 Conclusion: A Critical Systemic Approach

As we have seen, a critical perspective on IS analysis involves interpretation of an organizational problem space, and goes beyond this to challenge and question underlying assumptions about the experienced 'problem' to be addressed. However, it goes further to seek for understandings that support efforts to achieve beneficial change [24]. Of course, all IS development work, from whatever perspective, has a stated aim to deliver benefits. However, a critical systemic perspective is further distinguished by concern with emergent properties of interactions among unique individuals, whose perspectives are shaped by multiple levels of contextual dependencies, e.g. organizational power, culture and values. It does not seek to generalize from the particular, but to gain a richness and depth of understanding which may add to transparency in reflection on desirable change [25]. Critics of such an approach have tended to suggest that they are too time-consuming to be practical or that they privilege reflection over action to an undue extent [26]. However, it is now possible to point to much experience from the field which shows that giving a voice to living, engaged individuals generates productive and useful results [27, 28]. A discussion of human knowing (as a facet of both being and informing) is important when considering systemic analysis. Too often, inquiries focus upon ontologies: what is the problem? what are the requirements? However, a critical systemic analysis will involve questioning and exploring sense-making processes, i.e. highlighting epistemology [21]. Contextual inquiry is conducted in collaboration with engaged actors, investigating the boundary of a perceived problem space. It considers multiple perspectives and world views within and between participating actors. The role of a professional in such an inquiry is to support creation of a methodological framework which is relevant to the perceived problem space, not to pursue rigorous application of 'standard' methods. The purpose of the inquiry is to work together with engaged actors to identify and seek for desired beneficial change–not to 'give the clients what they want'.

References

1. The Standish Group. (1996). *Unfinished Voyages: Follow-up to the CHAOS report*. http://www.umflint.edu/~weli/courses/bus381/assignment/vo.pdf, acc. May 20 2012.
2. Checkland, P. B. (1993). *Systems thinking, systems practice*. UK: Wiley.
3. Nissen, H.-E. (2002). Challenging traditions of inquiry in software practice. In Y. Dittrich, C. Floyd, & R. Klischewski (Eds.), *Social thinking, software practice*. MIT: MIT Press.
4. Ciborra, C. U. (2004). Encountering information systems as a phenomenon. In C. Avgerou, C. Ciborra, & F. Land (Eds.), *The social study of information and communication technology: Innovation, actors, and contexts*. Oxford: Oxford University Press.
5. Bednar, P. M. (2007). Individual emergence in contextual analysis, problems of individual emergence: Special issue of systemica. *Journal of the Dutch Systems Group, 14*(1–6), 23–28.

6. Simon, H. (1991). Bounded rationality and organizational learning. *Organization Science, 2*(1), 125–134.
7. Argyris, M., & Schön, D. (1974). *Theory in practice: Increasing professional effectiveness*. USA: Jossey-Bass.
8. Bednar, P.M. & Welch, C. (2006). 'Incentive and desire: covering a missing category.' MCIS 2006. *Proceedings of the Mediterranean Conference on Information Systems*, Università degli Studi di Trento, San Servolo, Venice, Italy. 5–9 Oct, 2006.
9. Checkland, P. B., & Poulter, J. (2006). *Learning for Action: A short definitive account of soft systems methodology and its use*. Chichester: Wiley.
10. Checkland, P.B. (1993) ibid.
11. Jayaratna, N. (1994). *Understanding and evaluating methodologies: NIMSAD–a systematic framework*. UK: McGraw-Hill.
12. Sommerville, I. (2010). *Software engineering* (9th ed.). Boston, MA: Adison-Wesley.
13. Bednar, P. M., & Welch, C. (2008). Hypermodernist travellers in a postmodern world. *Electronic Journal of Business Research Methods, 6*(1), 1–9.
14. Hevner, A., March, S., Park, J., & Ram, S. (2004). Design science in information systems research. *MIS Quarterly, 28*(1), 75–105.
15. Mumford, E. (2003). *Redesigning human systems*. Hershey, PA: IRM Press.
16. Ciborra, C. U., & Willcocks, L. (2006). The mind or the heart? It depends on the (definition of) situation. *Journal of Information Technology, 21*(3), 129–139.
17. Bednar, P.M. & Welch, C. (2006) ibid p. 53.
18. Ciborra, C. U. (2002). *The labyrinths of information* (p. 162). Oxford: Oxford University Press.
19. Ulrich, W. (1983). *Critical heuristics of social planning*. New York: Wiley.
20. Bateson, G. (1972). *Steps to an ecology of mind*. New York: Ballantine.
21. Bednar, P.M., Anderson, D., Welch, C. (2005). 'Knowledge creation and sharing—complex methods of inquiry and inconsistent theory'. *Proceedings of 6th European Conference on Knowledge Management*, University of Limerick, 8–9 Sept 2005.
22. Bednar, P. M. (2000). A contextual integration of individual and organizational learning perspectives as part of IS analysis. *Informing Science, 3*(3), 145–156.
23. Weick, K., & Sutcliffe, K. (2002). *Managing the unexpected*. USA: Jossey-Bass.
24. Klein, H. K. (2007). *4th Leverhulme lecture*. UK: Salford Business School. Jan 12 2007.
25. Nissen, H.-E. (2007). 'Using Double Helix Relationships to Understand and Change Informing Systems'. In H.-E. Nissen, P. Bednar, & C. Welch (Eds.), *Informing science journal, 10, monograph, use and redesign in IS: Double helix relationships?* (pp. 21–62).
26. Fuller, R. B. (1992). *Cosmography: A blueprint for the science and culture of the future*. New York: Macmillan.
27. Resca, A., D'Atri, A., De Marco, M., & Casolino, N. (2008). Re-configuring the fashion business: The "Yooox" virtual boutique case study. In A. D'. Atri, P. Bednar, & C. Welch (Eds.), *Interdisciplinary aspects of information systems studies* (pp. 155–161).
28. Whitaker, R. (2007). Informing science journal, 10, monograph, use and redesign in IS: Double helix relationships? In H.-E. Nissen, P. Bednar, & C. Welch (Eds.), *'Applying phenomenology and hermeneutics in IS Design: A report on field experiences'* (pp. 63–96).

Part VI
Professional Skills, Certification of Curricula, On-line Education

The Catchers in the Rye: Students Model Enterprise Architectures

Gianmario Motta and Daniele Sacco

Abstract We illustrate how graduate students ("the catchers") are able to model the enterprise architecture of a real organization ("the rye") by a grid of analysis techniques. These techniques design a model driven architecture, and are easy to learn by students and to understand by enterprise users. The grid includes three levels. The Aggregate Strategic Level (ASL) uses list and matrix models in the domains of information and business processes. ASL schemas are then mapped on a much more detailed Rich Semantic Level (RSL), that is still independent from the underlying technology. Finally, RSL schemas are mapped on executable models, that reflect technology. The illustration is backed by a case study on small-medium enterprise.

Keywords Enterprise architecture · Business architecture · Information systems architecture · Information requirements analysis · Requirements analysis techniques

1 Living the Rye

"The Catcher in the Rye" is a famous novel (over 65 million copies sold) on the adventures of the teen-ager Holden Caulfield, who, after being expulsed from his college, lives an intensive experience in New York. As Holden well knows "Life is a game, boy. Life is a game that one plays according to the rules" [1].

G. Motta (✉) · D. Sacco
Dipartimento di Ingegneria Industriale e dell'Informazione University of Pavia, Via Ferrata 1, Pavia, Italy
e-mail: motta05@unipv.it

D. Sacco
e-mail: daniele.sacco01@ateneopv.it

P. Spagnoletti (ed.), *Organizational Change and Information Systems*, Lecture Notes in Information Systems and Organisation 2, DOI: 10.1007/978-3-642-37228-5_34,

So, at the end of a MS degree in Computer Engineering or alike majors, students typically enter the unknown world of organizations, where often they have to play an analyst's role—i.e. a catcher's role. Now, our idea is to prepare students to the wild world through a project managed by the University. The project is on enterprise architecture[1] and uses a set of techniques that have been developed and integrated by our lab.

This approach has two objectives: to test university's analysis techniques and provide value to students. Organizations are a critical test field, where you test not only the theoretical robustness of the model, but also how practical are the approaches and how real are the theoretical benefits. Of course, a project in an organization should be a win–win game. The organization should get a workable outcome, and the project impact should fit the always very limited time that managers have.

In the following sections we illustrate our analysis grid; specifically, we survey some home developed techniques. In the final section we illustrate a case study.

2 The Analysis Grid

2.1 The Structure of the Analysis Grid

Our analysis grid concerns the systems architecture of an enterprise. This architecture of an enterprise, as defined by TOGAF, [2] includes three domains: business, information systems, and technology. Business Architecture defines the structure and flow of business processes an enterprise performs to manage and deliver its products and services and the structure of its organization. Information Systems Architecture defines the information that systems process and, also, the structure of the processes. Finally, Technology Architecture defines the building blocks and the layers on which information systems are deployed.

To define an enterprise architecture, the analyst generally to start at a very high level, that embraces the whole enterprise and, also, can be expressed by a notation that the managers easily understand. So, an ideal analysis grid should include several abstraction levels. At the highest level, e.g. when you talk with a Vice President, the notation cannot be detailed. At the lowest level, the notation shall be an executable language—as BPEL. In short, we assume three description layers:

1. Aggregate Strategic Layer (ASL), where the architecture is aggregate and expressed by the simplest possible notations, as grids or lists;
2. Rich Semantic Layer (RSL), where the architecture is expressed by detailed diagrams; notwithstanding the detail, RSL is conceptual, and neglects the

[1] The enterprise architecture reflects the orientation of our curriculum "Services Engineering" that allocates 24 of 48 credits on Enterprise Systems architecture and Business Process/Business Service Analysis (for a discussion on Services Science Curricula see [16]).

implementation; however, because of detail and the rich notation, it is much less user friendly;
3. Software Engineering Interface (SEI), that transforms RSL into a notation that is understood by software engineers and defines software functions; in most cases the notation is executable.

On the other side, the analysis has to cover functional aspects, essentially because user managers are interested in the content of information systems and not in underlying technology deployment. The functional aspects includes (a) the information the system shall use, (b) the workflow of the business processes and related execution rules, and, finally, (c) the user interface, through which information is distributed to (or collected from) users. We call these functional aspects as "domains".

By combining domains and levels, you have a grid with nine quadrants, each identifying one specific analysis segment, that implies a specific analysis technique. In Table 1 we list these techniques, that include both usual techniques as UML and, also, home-developed techniques as SIRE [3] and GEF [4]. As you can easily assume, the analysis grid covers enterprise architecture in the two upper levels, while the lowest level is for implementation.

The analysis roadmap typically proceeds top-down and right to left. This implies (a) vertical integration and (b) horizontal integration. Let us consider each point. Vertical integration means that an ASL model can be transformed into a RSL model, and, also, a RSL model into a SEI model. Of course, each top down step implies a certain amount of enrichment and a set of rules. Horizontal

Table 1 The analysis grid

Level		Domain		
		Information	Processes/rules	User interface
Architectural steps	ASL—Aggregate Strategic Level	Strategic Information Requirements Elicitation (SIRE) [3]	General Enterprises Framework (GEF) [4]	——
	RSL—Rich Semantic Level	Entity Relationship (ER) [5] Dimensional Fact Modeling (DFM) [6]	Business Process Management Notation (BPMN) [7–9] UML—Erikson Penker extension (UML—EP) [10]	Goal Oriented Analysis (GOA) [11]
Implementation steps	SEI—Software Engineering Interface	Relational database [12], UML [13]	Business Process Execution Language (BPEL) [14] UML [13]	Web Manipulation Language (WEBML) [15]

integration means that models of different are linked by cross references. E.g. use cases and information entities of a given system are cross referenced by a table that shows which entities are created, read, updated or deleted by which use cases. The table pinpoints the life cycle of information within the system and unveils potential integrity issues—e.g. an entity that is read but not created in the system.

Let us now focus on the two techniques of ASL, namely Strategic Information Requirements Elicitation (SIRE) and General Enterprise Framework (GEF).

2.2 The Information Architecture by SIRE

Strategic Information Requirements Elicitation (SIRE) is an universal technique to analyze information needs at the enterprise level [3, 17]. Its purpose is to identify a grid of information needs $N_{t,d,k}$ where t is the information type, d is information domain, and finally, k is an ordinal number assigned to each need. Table 2 shows the graphical shape of the SIRE grid. The grid crosses the information domains d_i with the information types t_i. Information domains include all universes on which an enterprise processes information—e.g. Customer. Of course the 16 generic information domains (Law, Competitor, Customer, Supplier, Broker, Shareholder, Personnel, Equipment, Raw Materials, Cash, Structure, Project, Region, Process, Product, Service) should be customized to the specific company through specialization and decomposition. Domains are layered into information types t_i, namely (1) Master information, that represents structural properties of an object (e.g. the customer name) (2) Event information, that describes transactions concerning the object (e.g. orders by made the customer) (3) Analytic information, that describes statistical properties of the object (e.g. the amount of sales). In short, relevant enterprise information is identified by domain and type. Similar grids have been proposed for specific industries. However, SIRE is simpler than SID/eTOM for telecommunications [18], and not limited to one sector, as it happens with ARTS [19] that focuses on retail (Table 3).

Table 2 The SIRE grid

Information domain	Information type		
	Master	Event	Analytic
[Domain]	[Need 1, 2, ...]	[Need 1, 2, ...]	[Need 1, 2, ...]

Table 3 SIRE and eTOM/SID grids

	SIRE	eTOM/SID
Information types	Master, event, analytic	Not defined
Information domains	Generic list (universal)	Telecommunications oriented list
Topdown analysis	Procedure from ASL to RSL (and SEI)	Not defined

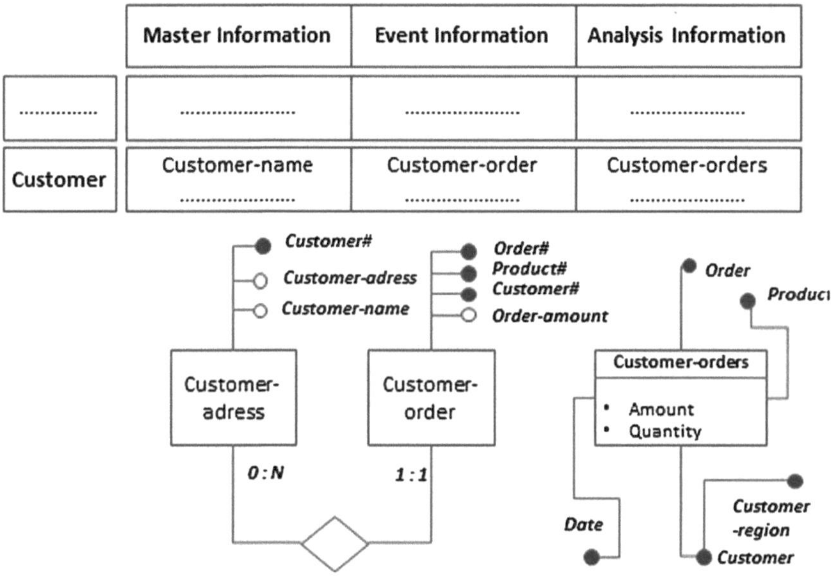

Fig. 1 Information modeling steps (oversimplified)

SIRE follows a top down approach. At ASL, the analyst identifies a list of information a given domain e.g. the customer (e.g. customer-name, customer-order, customer-sales). At the RSL, the analyst will generate, through a set of rules, ER and DFM schemas, where the first one represents the relation between customer and order, while the second one represents the keys by which customer-sales are analyzed.

While going top down from the ASL to RSL diagrams, the analyst adds details. For instance, in Fig. 1 the analyst has transformed the row "Customer-address" into a corresponding entity, to which has linked the event information on the orders issued by the customer. This relation is typically implemented in a database. The analytic information about "Customer-orders" has been enriched by the search keys on Order, Date, Product, Customer. This fact table is typically implemented in a data warehouse. In short, ASL identifies the information elements while the RSL deploys their semantics.

2.3 The Business Process Architecture by GEF

General Enterprise Framework (GEF) is a technique to analyze activities of a business process, that was developed in Pavia University during 2011 [4]. Its purpose is to identify the activities of business processes $A_{l,p,i}$ where l is the activity level, p is the business process domain, and finally, i is a sequential

Table 4 The GEF grid

Business process	Activity level				
	Plan (set plan/ goals)	Execute (perform tasks)	Monitor (check and track execution workflow)	Control (appraise results)	Manage information (collect, store and distribute)
[Business process]	[activity]	[activity]	[activity]	[activity]	[activity]

Table 5 SCOR and GEF frameworks

Model	Main activity levels	Domain	Activity level analysis
SCOR [20]	1. Plan 2. Source 3. Make 4. Deliver 5. Return 6. Source return 7. Deliver return	Supply chain (manufacturing and alike industrial sectors)	Activities are predefined at three levels: 1. Top (main activity levels) 2. Configuration (detail of level 1) 3. Process element (detail of level 2) Customization on the individual enterprise is performed at (4) Implementation level
GEF [4]	1. Plan 2. Execute 3. Monitor 4. Control 5. Manage information	Whatever industrial sector	No predefined individual activities Individual activities within each level are identified by the analyst and detailed through decomposition and specialization operations

number assigned to the activity within a given quadrant of the grid. Table 4 shows the graphical shape of the GEF grid, that is similar to the SIRE grid. Here also, as in SIRE, levels of activity are predefined.

GEF is universal. By contrast SCOR [20], a very popular framework, targets the sector of supply chain organizations. It proposes a reference framework based on the two operational levels of Planning and Execution, that is further subdivided in Source, Make, Deliver, Source Return, Deliver Return. The analyst customizes SCOR on the individual organization and identifies the gap between the ideal situation (i.e. SCOR) and the current situation, thus accomplishing the so called fit-gap analysis. SCOR is very effective on its domain but it does not fit service organizations (Table 5). With GEF the analyst follows a similar path. He customizes the grid on the individual organization and then measures the gap between the ideal and current situation.

3 A Case Study: Crossing the Rye

Jones & Jones (JJ) is the disguised name of a large vendor of Human Resource software with a wide range of customers, which include (a) advisors servicing minor companies, (b) organizations running JJ software on their premises (c) organizations that outsource the service. JJ has a wide geographical network of agents and service centers, with a central sales organization and customer care. Most customer information is decentralized, and headquarters have a limited control (Fig. 2).

The assistant of the CEO, at the first meeting, asked to improve efficiency and effectiveness of customer management, by leveraging IT. She asked also to use easy and documented analysis techniques to define an overall enterprise architecture. This request fitted perfectly ASL and RSL levels of our analysis grid.

The analysis group included 4 graduate students, which, even if they had been already familiarized with the techniques in their courses, were at their first field experience. So they started to to meet all departments (Marketing, Central Sales, Sales Agency, Customer care, Service Center, IT, Accounting) and gathered their needs. The meetings were carefully prepared to have an efficient confirmatory interview, no longer than 2 h. The interview steps were (a) Confirm Mission, Tasks, Responsibility, Authority of the department; (b) Fill and discuss the SIRE grid on the white board (we selected the applicable information domains and we put own the information needs) (c) Discuss information access requirements (GOA method [11] at RSL level of the analysis grid) to understand the use of the information included in the SIRE grid.

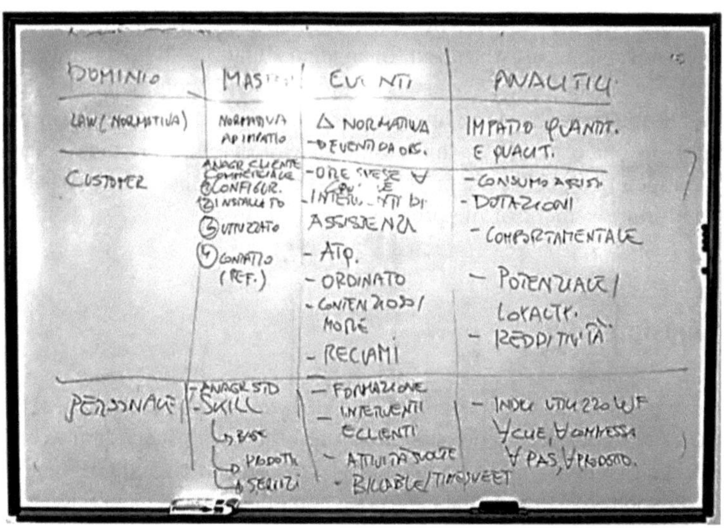

Fig. 2 A customized SIRE grid put down on the whiteboard

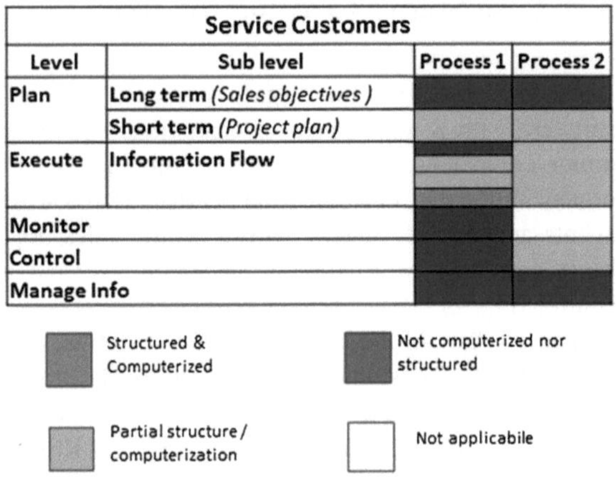

Fig. 3 An example of GEF table

This simple and agile approach—to be agile we discarded the software tools we had developed for SIRE—was highly welcome. User enjoyed to discuss and see something they really understood; also they realized immediately the gap between the reference information and the information that was really available. Students then integrated the users' views and developed a catalogue of the information and related ER and DFM schemas.

This filled the information requirements, but the architecture of business processes had to be analyzed and assessed. The related evidence was taken from the ISO 9000 manuals and from checking the completeness of this manuals trough flash interviews to the user departments. In parallel we collected a similar evidence on the existing software applications. At this pointy we knew which business process was covered by which software. By using the GEF grid we mapped each process on the activity levels. The resulting map is shown in Fig. 3, where, for privacy reasons, names are disguised. In an ideal situation, all boxes are green. The coverage in Fig. 3 reflects a paperwork automation, without support to planning and with a limited database (no analytic information and only partial information on events). In our experience, this profile is typical of early stages of business process computerization, where priority is given to clerical automation and not to a control and improvement of the process.

4 Conclusions

We have presented an enterprise analysis grid and a case study where students successfully defined an enterprise architecture– they were successful "catchers in the rye". The two home-made components of the grid SIRE and GEF can roughly measure the maturity stage of the enterprise computerization. Generally, one could assume that the higher the coverage, the more advanced the stage. This recalls similarities with CMMI [21], that was born to assess the maturity of the software development process. Of course, a complete maturity oriented enterprise architecture assessment requires further development.

References

1. Salinger, J.D. (1951). The catcher in the Rye, Little, Brown and Company.
2. The Open Group. 2009. TOGAF Version 9, The Open Group Architecture Framework, ISBN 978-90-8753-230-7. Document Number G091. Published by The Open Group.
3. Motta, G., & Pignatelli, G. (2010). *From strategic to conceptual information modelling: a method and a case study*. Naples: ITaiS.
4. Motta, G., Barroero, T., Sacco, D. (2012). General Enterprise Framework (GEF): an agile framework to define the business architecture of enterprises, SOLI, Suzhou, China.
5. Chen, P. (1976). The entity-relationship model-toward a unified view of data. *ACM Transactions on Database Systems, 1*(1), 9–36.
6. Golfarelli, M., Maio, D., & Rizzi, S. (1998). The dimensional fact model: a conceptual model for data warehouses. *International Journal of Cooperative Information Systems, 7*(2–3), 215–247.
7. Briol, P. (2008). BPMN, the Business Process Modeling Notation Pocket Handbook, LuLu, ISBN 978-1-4092-0299-8.
8. Debevoise, N.T., Geneva R. (2008). *The micro guide to process modeling in BPMN*, BookSurge Publishing, ISBN 978-1-4196-9310-6.
9. Ryan, K.L., Lee, S.S.G., Lee, E.W. (1995). Business Process Management (BPM) standards: a survey. *Business Process Management Journal*. Emerald Group Publishing Limited, *15*(5).
10. Penker, M., Eriksson, H.E. (2000). *Business modeling with UML: business patterns at work*. New York: Wiley, ISBN 0471295515 .
11. Bolchini, D., Paolini, P. (2004). Goal-driven requirements analysis for hypermedia-intensive web applications. *Requirements Engineering*. (9:2), 85–103.
12. Codd, E. F. (1970). A relational model of data for large shared data banks. *Communications of the ACM, 13*(6), 377–387.
13. Fowler, M. (2003). *UML distilled: a brief guide to the standard object modeling language* (3rd ed.). Addison-Wesley, ISBN 0-321-19368-7.
14. Juric, M.B., Krizevnik, M. (2010). *WS-BPEL 2.0 for SOA composite applications with Oracle SOA Suite 11 g*. Birmigham: Pack Publishing Ltd.
15. Ceri, S., Fraternali, P., & Paraboschi, S. (1998). Design principles for data-intensive web sites. *ACM Sigmod Record, 27*(4), 74–80.
16. Choudaha, R. (2008). Competency-based curriculum for a master's program in Service Science, Management and Engineering (SSME): an online Delphi study, Doctoral Dissertation, University of Denver.
17. Motta, G., Pignatelli, G. (2010). Information strategy: an analysis framework. *Journal of US-China Public Administration, 7*(2), 39–46.
18. TM Forum, Enhanced Telecom Operations Map (eTOM). (2005). The business process framework: for the information and communication industry, Release 6.0.
19. Arts, NRF's IT Standards Division, www.nrf-arts.org.
20. Bolstorff, P., Rosenbaum, R. (2007). *Supply chain excellence: a handbook for dramatic improvement using the SCOR model*, (2nd edn). Amacom.
21. CMMI Guidebook for Acquirers Team. 2007. Understanding and leveraging a supplier's CMMI efforts: a guidebook for acquirers, software engineering institute, Carnegie Mellon University.

References

Coaching and Mentoring for IT Project Managers

Pier Luigi Guida

Abstract In spite of the very questioned success rates of Information Technology projects, one may argue that relatively low investment and focus are still devoted to the human resources in the software business. The Chapter aims to address the subject of Coaching and Mentoring (C&M) as a means to improve the individual project managers, teams and hence project performance. In this perspective some historical references and current evolutions are considered (agile development) stressing that more involvement in this direction should be sought by IT organizations. An educational approach blending psychology, coaching and mentoring is proposed while the chapter can represent a mini-tutorial on the subject for project managers and other stakeholders in IT industry.

Keywords Coaching · Mentoring · Software psychology · Project management

1 Introduction

The chapter introduces the concepts of coaching and mentoring in the context of Information Technology (IT) project management. It is well known that the IT sector is characterized by relevant records of unsuccessful projects and looks like a risky business. According to the well known CHAOS report [1], two-thirds of IT projects are not successful in terms of the critical 'triangle' objectives (time–cost-quality), and literature is plenty of epic failures. There are several reasons for this phenomenon, but one can infer that the most cases are due to "human factors": being too much risk appetizers and not giving proper considerations to so called soft skills, may be the major cause of so many project failures. Being an IT project

P. L. Guida (✉)
Rete Ferroviaria Italiana, Rome, Italy
e-mail: pl.guida@rfi.it

P. Spagnoletti (ed.), *Organizational Change and Information Systems*, Lecture Notes in Information Systems and Organisation 2, DOI: 10.1007/978-3-642-37228-5_35,

a very human value added business, the same "content" should give account of its historical rate of unsuccessful ventures. Psychological attitudes and other human factors of the leading stakeholders—i.e. sponsors, project managers and organizations—may be accountable of so many failures; a strong hypothesis to deal with for deeper understanding and maybe more scientific verification. But if that is the case, we should be working much more on the human side of the projects to help these be successful.

During the last decades the "soft skills" have been increasingly addressed as important elements of the project management discipline, in addition to so called "hard skills". The latter are traditionally related to quantitative aspects of project management—such as scheduling, cost budgeting, quality measures etc…—while the formers are more human and behavior centered, such as leadership, motivation, negotiation, and alike. If we would provide a project analysis in terms of its human versus other costs, we certainly would understand how much care should be given to human resources and their characteristics (attitudes, personal traits, training and experience).

The present essay will focus on two concepts of human resource management, which are having increasing interest in IT project management: coaching and mentoring (C&M), with some insight of psychology. Our scope is to introduce these concepts, which are sometimes misused or misunderstood, and provide a mini-tutorial for those who would be willing to dedicate more study and (in)formal attention to these themes, assuming they can improve their own and projects life. The subject is not specific to IT, but this sector can record relevant developments and experiences, which can provide a new methodological chapter of the discipline, in terms of the software engineering and project management "bodies of knowledge". As it is often the case, these can formalize into more conscious knowledge, methods and practices which may have been naturally applied by practitioners in their working experience.

The chapter is organized as follows. Following the present introduction, Sect. 2—Definitions and descriptions—surveys basic principles on coaching and mentoring. Section 3 introduces the "Psy-Co-Men" approach, attempting to synthesize the subject and motivate its adoption; moreover we provide some references of C&M opportunities, project management standards and specific applications traced in the IT business (agile coaching). Finally Sect. 4 points out some of author's experience in the field and Sect. 5 provides some conclusions.

2 Definitions and Descriptions

Mentoring and coaching are words sometimes used interchangeably; moreover they are adopted in practical applications with some differences or "dialects" in respect of original settings and definitions of the disciplines.

As recalled in [2], the concept of mentoring dates back to the earliest stages of human civilization. The origin of the term can be traced back to the legendary history of Ancient Greece. According to "The Odyssey" by Homer, Ulysses, king of Ithaca, before leaving for the Troy war, delegates his house and the education of his son Telemachus to Mentor, one of his friends.

Mentoring implies relationships between two individuals, the mentor and the mentee or protégé, where the former provides his own experience and knowledge in favor of the latter. The mentee can achieve improvement in his professional learning, while the mentor can also benefit in other ways (income, more satisfaction and social acceptance in the working environment). The "third" and sponsoring actor, organizations, can finally gain more productivity, motivation, stability in the workforce, know-how transfer and shorter time for developing skills. In particular Landaeta et al. [3] refer to formal mentoring as management practice to support knowledge transfer across projects. Some types of informal or natural approach of mentoring may also develop in working environments, more or less acknowledged and encouraged by the management, particularly for apprentices. In broader acceptance, mentoring is an improvement process concerning both aspects related to a professional career and more global development of the individual.

Coaching in management jargon is a much more recent concept, introduced in the 80s, when it was imported from other sources, namely academic training and sport.

Wikipedia helps us about the etymological origin of the English term "coach", derived from a transport vehicle that traces its origins to the Hungarian word "kocsi", a particular carriage, named after the village where it was first made [4]. The first use of the term in relation to sports came in early '800 and is nowadays very well known. The facilitative approach to coaching in sport was pioneered by Gallwey [5] and divulgated in more management oriented style by Whitmore [6]. This author reports one of the most known methods of coaching, which favors a style in which the coach asks questions and offers opportunities that will challenge the coachee to find answers from within himself. This also has some historic origin from the so-called "Socratic method", after the Greek philosopher Socrates (5th cent. B.C.) who facilitated the learner to discover answers and new ways of being, based on their own perspective and values. According to this literature, the coach is a motivation builder and should not intervene or even be expert of the coachee's world.

Other contexts, forms and schools for coaching have since developed, including: executive or business coaching, life coaching, team coaching, wealth coaching, emotional intelligence coaching, even self-coaching and so on. Since the mid-90s, coaching has developed into more independent discipline and professional associations. Needless to say the evolution of coaching has been influenced by many other fields of study including those of personal development, adult education, psychology (sports, clinical, developmental, organizational, social and industrial) and other organizational or leadership theories and practices; another sister discipline to coaching for human motivation and behavior improvement is the Neuro Linguistic Programming (NLP), first pioneered by Richard Bandler and others.

Moreover the "pure" concept of coaching, where the coach should be not be cognizant of the coachee's professional knowledge and experience, has evolved indeed into more "contextual" forms, where the motivation builder is required to have knowledge of his/her coachee business environment. This is also the case of the sport coach, who is not required to be great performer in the athletic field, but should be expert of the methods and techniques in the discipline, in addition to having other qualities, such as leadership, team building and alike. The contextualization of coaching—as we would describe it—has therefore introduced new coaching practices and professionals aimed at specific roles and applications. Through the marketing pages of internet, today one can thus find coaches who promote themselves for projects and project management. Furthermore the IT world and literature have been fairly open to the new discipline, particularly related to more recent evolutions, like the Agile movement, which have originated agile software engineering and agile project management. Finally the first books on Agile coaching have been delivered [7, 8].

The embedding of contextual or technical know-how into some schools of coaching is not a mistake by itself, given that one can reconcile this to the true origins of the discipline, and the human more than engineering side of the coin is duly taken into account. Eventually following the coaching contextual path, some combination of coaching and mentoring competences can be produced, the level and depth of each practice being appropriately considered for any specific project intervention.

2.1 Coaching and Mentoring in Project Management Standards

Coaching and mentoring already appear in the project management reference standards, or so-called "Bodies of Knowledge", respectively by Project Management Institute (PMI), International Project Management Association (IPMA) and Association of Project Management (APM). For instance in PMBoK [9] these terms are cited among the techniques of the "Develop Project Team" process, as a means of improving the team's performance. In the ICB (Competence Baseline) [10], one reads that the project director coaches project managers, and coaching actions are relevant in several competences (teamwork, leadership and personnel management) and the APM BoK [11] includes this topic too. Some of these generic standards acknowledge C&M among the activities of project management offices (PMOs).

Another point of interest is assessing the project management or organizational "maturity" as a means to measure the level of growth and mastering of the industry core processes. In this regard one of the more complete models focused on human resources is the People-CMM [12] which aims to broaden the CMMI model to organizational maturity. It is noteworthy that in the P-CMM framework,

Mentoring is one of the 22 key processes against which enterprise "capability maturity" should be evaluated.

Once appraised the importance of introducing (better) formal C&M programs, we would like to focus on some project situations where planning and putting at work some coaching activities can be beneficial.

2.2 Projects Difficult or "In Crisis"

There are projects which can be difficult and complex at their initiation or any intermediate phase of the life cycle. In these cases the management should consider the intervention of coaching in support of project managers and other team members, particularly if they are novice to these venture or may require to strengthen specific abilities. This may be more convenient and in the end beneficial than hiring full or part-time consultants. Another case is when the project is in crisis, and some actions are needed in the area of human resources; a snapshot from the author's experience is given in following Sect. 4.

2.3 Organizational Project Changes

This can be an extension of the foregoing, for instance regarding the situation where the project or the project manager are faced with particular transition or transformation program (e.g. acquisitions and mergers, organizational change management) or even project closure or anticipated termination, which may have particular impact on human resources. In the case it is important that the team members do not feel "left alone" and best competences and mental energies are preserved for next project ventures.

2.4 Specific Project Environments

There are specific project environments which may require some coaching as well. In a conference the author recently attended on so called "mega projects" we were exposed to some case studies, like building of a new oil-and-gas plant in the desert, where manpower had to peak 20.000 units, being multi-ethnic and coming from all parts of the world. In the round table which followed, the subject of having a project manager coached for this mission was particularly addressed. Ideally large companies may resort to already experienced professionals in the task, but the opportunity may not always occur.

In the IT sector, as already said, some forms of specialist coaching have emerged, as one queries the literature databases on the subject, like IEEEXplore.

One of the best chapter is by Paasivaara [13], who presents a multiple-case study on how various globally distributed software projects introduced agile practices with the help of company internal coaching team. The case of some projects in crisis is also discussed. The chapter describes an organizational approach how to organize and learn lessons from agile coaching in international, multi-site project context, where a large IT company set up a coaching team for the benefit of their distributed projects.

Current low-cost technologies, like real-time world-wide chatting and Skype videoconferencing can also favor coaching programs in efficient and economical way, say with one professional or internal coach taking care of several project managers worldwide.

2.5 Project Management Career Development

One of the more classical uses of mentoring/coaching is in the area of support to career development of the mentee/coachee. This may be generic for any kind of application and management roles, but again the IT sector can provide specific opportunities for personal and professional development. It is well known the case where technical professionals and senior team leaders may find difficulties in dressing the new project management roles, and "old habits" remain on so called technical project managers. We are not venturing in the long debate about the generic competencies of an IT project manager, which may be a false problem due to very different project context and conditions; but we should point out the question how to transport, say coach, a promising individual from the technical to management career.

It is known the condition that, particularly for small projects, one cannot have only project "managers". Even in small projects, however, where some re-organization occurs—say in agile perspective—and several projects follow the agile paradigm, the project manager would increasingly detach from the technical issues, left to the Scrum-master, and be freed to manage more projects. In the agile model the project manager would thus be playing more coaching roles, with appropriate leadership styles.

In more general terms, increasing the dimension, complexity and global dispersion of projects, the project manager is required to improve his/her management competencies, shifting to more soft and general management skills. For some persons this may be more difficult to achieve, as Pressman [14] and others have already discussed. "And yet,—remarks Pressman—few senior managers would argue that poor project management is the number one cause of project failure. (…*omissis*…) I've come to believe that successful projects have much more to do with the person leading the team than with project management techniques and tools". The author stresses the learning necessity of rookie project managers, receiving formal training in negotiation and communication.

The art of communication, as touched passing by in previous notes, is at the heart of coaching and mentoring, in its more diverse aspects. Therefore one could assume that a project manager or any team member coached by this art, would in turn be able to better communicate and coach others as well. The sub-art of listening, in addition, is a building block of coaching, and this can also become part of the training programs.

3 The Psy-Co-Men Approach

Another question that may arise spontaneously is how C&M relate to psychology, its Greek etymology meaning the discourse (*logos*) on soul (*psukà*). In fact psychology is the study of the mind, occurring via the study of behavior, aiming at understanding individuals and groups and establishing general principles. The discipline has many subfields, in social, behavior and cognitive applications, while interpretation of mental functions can help understand and cure mind diseases and pathologies (counseling and clinical therapy). Excluding this side of the discipline about treatment of mental health, study of individuals and groups in work environments in principle can aid coaching and mentoring programs.

Among the many different spheres of human activity, psychology has also developed a specific stream of research and studies in computer and software engineering, thanks to the seminal book by Weinberg [15].

Some exposure to psychology studies by anyone playing some organizational role is desirable, and may complement any management curriculum, though it is not the scope of the chapter to explore this immense field with reference to coaching and mentoring. However we do not abstain from noticing how modern and interesting remains the reading of some sections by Weinberg after four decades he published his *The Psychology of computer programming*, with particular reference to characteristics of the Group, Team and Project within the software industry, linked to personality factors, motivation, leadership and training of the "programming" resources., The same author points out some traits of the software psychology that should be taken into account when considering any coaching or mentoring approach. In particular, among the factors which go into satisfaction of working groups, the competence of supervisors and leaders looks like to play a fundamental role. To summarize the Weinberg's conclusions for our theme, three concepts are worth summarizing:

- project managers and team leaders, where not specifically involved as "gurus" in the technical project work, should best direct their energies towards democratic leadership style, where more appreciation and value should come from their soft management capabilities;
- democratic groups, where knowledge sharing and informal collaboration are practiced as normal rule, are more stable and to be preferred over more authoritatively leaded groups;

- "it is useful to consider the work of the team in two categories, work directed at accomplishing the team goals and work directed at maintaining the effective functioning of the team (…) To social psychologists, these activities are designated as "task-oriented" and "maintenance-oriented". In certain types of groups, and often in programming teams, the group tends to choose two complementary leaders—a task specialist who sets, allocates and coordinates the work; and a maintenance specialist, who irons out conflict among group members or between individual goals and group goals" [15, p. 85].

According to this model, the task-specialist position should be internal or "elected" by the group and replaced by this if not displaying the necessary competence; and the maintenance-specialist can come from anywhere.

It is amazing how this text is so close (forerunner ?) to more current and renovated literature on agile principles, like the "Self-Organizing Roles on Agile Software Development Teams", described in the more recent chapter by Hoda et al. [9]. Specifically, one should outline that the maintenance-oriented leading role could be assigned to the coach-project manager of IT agile projects, and this figure should demonstrate coaching skills for being accepted by democratic groups.

The analysis of the role played by individual and group socio-psychology helps understanding why the persons manifest some kinds of behavior and their expected reactions once exposed to certain environment or human relations. Moreover psychology can introduce better ways to have the mentee learn and the coachee be motivated. As Weinberg puts it, psychologists know that human performance on a given task is a function of the task itself and *as understood* by the subject. They also know that performance will be influenced by individual differences in such areas as personality and intelligence. Once these are given, along with all the training and experience, the "residue" left of unexplained performance is called "motivation" [15].

To integrate the three aspects introduced so far, i.e. psychology, coaching and mentoring, we would like to introduce the "Psy-Co-Men" term to memorize into one figure the various concepts, and look at the continuum of techniques used for the purpose of improving the human performance. The following picture (Fig. 1) is adapted from a note by Pitcher [16], with addition of the psychological frame; this reference may be adapted by the learner according to his/her own view with other specific techniques as appropriate.

The *Psycomen* term is introduced for the first time in this chapter, and the proposed framework could represent the basis for designing specific educational programs for sponsors, IT project managers and other team members.

In particular some points are worth further elaborating on this scheme:

- how psychology will relate to the other elements;
- how to implement a methodology based on this approach;
- how to view the IT project manager as coach and coachee.

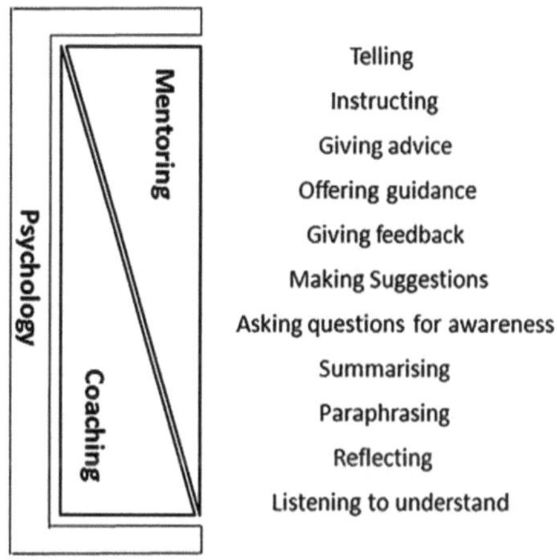

Fig. 1 *Psycomen* approach

3.1 Psychology Contribution

The theme may be very broad for the purpose of this introductory chapter. In our view the main contribution is from Weinberg's remind of two group leaders, i.e. task and maintenance oriented, since a coaching and/or mentoring function supporting the project manager might work, in very simple terms, as the latter (the maintainer).

In addition the psychology contribution to the benefit of project teams could come from three mainstream topics of the discipline:

- knowledge of social or group psychology for team management. This is also discussed in team building and team dynamics flavor found in project management textbooks, based on seminal models by Tuckman [17], Satir [18] and others. However more recommendation should be provided in operational terms to the project manager readership, e.g. as to behave proactively for relieving group conflict and enhancing performances;
- improve the awareness of cognitive psychology. This could help decision making fallacies be recognized and more easily tackled, and improve risk taking attitudes and risk management processes; furthermore recognition of so called cognitive traps could support decision making in more appropriate way;
- facilitate motivation in distressed team. This may often occur in very demanding projects and should be managed in more contextual and higher level perspective than projects alone (i.e. aiming at broader organizational level).

3.2 Methodological Approach

The issue how to implement in more methodological terms the PsyCoMen approach can follow three paths.

First is the buy-in of the IT management and governance, that is looking at IT projects as complex socio-technical undertaking than difficult software engineering ventures. This chapter would like to contribute and extend discussion on this perspective.

Another path is more structured research on the PsyCoMen opportunity in IT industry. Besides past and already quoted works, a research project should be carried out to finalize this synthesis into more complete methodology. Within this framework, one should set the objective of laying out a method for assessing the project status in regard to its human related traits and requirements. As we are already used to adopt "health check" questionnaires and templates to assess the project or organizational maturity with reference to some methodological scale; a similar approach could be sought to assess the deeper human aspects of project teams. The methodology would have more general audience, however the IT sector would appear an appropriate field of application, due to aforementioned trends and other features of interest. The sector has been forerunner of related project management methodologies (agile methods) putting in crisis "old models" and can facilitate some field development where many teams are at work in large corporations. Nevertheless, some approach in this direction could also be experienced in less structured way by IT project managers, Project Management Offices and consultants providing specific training.

3.3 The IT Project Manager, Coachee and Coach

From the foregoing, it should be clear how the Project Manager would benefit from the proposed approach. Being the joint figure between the organization and the team members, the PM would become the "object" of some Psycomen program by the Organization, that would aim to improve the performance of this figure, and hence have better managed projects. On the other hand it is natural thinking of PM as the subject or actor of the program, becoming and being the coach of his team. This does not preclude having other or complementary persons playing this role, but it would be normal that a PM, after being grown by some professional coach, would in turn become and provide some coaching to the benefit of the project team, mainly as the maintenance leader. Incidentally we recall that GROW is a specific acronym used in coaching circles as: Goals, Reality, Options, Will [6].

4 The Naïve Coach

This author thinks to have become a naïve coach after his 25 years of work experience in IT, essentially devoted to system analysis, project and program management. At this time the author understood that having a more formal training in coaching when he was younger should have provided him with better knowledge, methods and consciousness to his working life.

Our last (at the moment) experience was a project-in-crisis which could not reach its final delivery after a troubled life, for several reasons that would be too long to discuss here.

We have been working in the Client organization, where the IT projects are outsourced to an external supplier. The latter also supplies (and is paid for) the project manager (PM), while the Client plays the role of sponsor and product owner (PO, say the writer of this chapter). Among others, this project suffered from a lot of change requests, even in its final phase, and a very "administrative" management humiliated creativity and motivation of team members. The PM, and his higher management, used to restrain resources for the fixed-price contract, had delegated the most work to subcontractors and used to set milestones seldom respected. Members of the project teams were severely understaffed and the life cycle management was relatively undisciplined; moreover some key persons from the subcontractors had become the technical owners of the project know-how, inducing leadership problems. Application of contractual penalties on the Outsourcer could not resolve the question but interrupting the work and likely putting it into a never-ending legal spiral. In this context, the project could hardly be able to be over. The Client was frustrated for the visible illness of the project, until a breakpoint was reached by introducing a quasi-agile approach.

First a "conference" of all project stakeholders was organized by the product owner (PO), as a moment to recollect ideas, freeze objectives/requirements, and set up new issue log/change request procedures. A new users focus group was set up and a new external subcontractor was hired by the Client in order to provide testing, independent verification and validation (IVV) and supporting the acceptance tests by the users; this IVV team was co-located with the development (Outsourcer's) project team. A new procedure for structured daily issue log, time-boxed software release and weekly progress review meetings was agreed between the PM and the PO, in order to provide better project governance.

In particular, for the interest of this chapter, a schedule of informal coaching sessions was carried out with the subcontractors' team leaders by the product owner, being the PM apparently intolerant and suspicious about the interference of the Client PO (who however had some governance role, being responsible of certifying work progress and releasing payment notes).

The project organization was slowly transforming from a traditional and bureaucratic client-supplier model, to more agile and coupled project team between client and supplier's team members. Other internal politics were fairly hard to manage, i.e. roles respectively played by the Supplier's PM and Client's PO, which may be fairly usual situation. Though at the time we were not very aware of the "two leaders" model anticipated by Weinberg, in fact we had been drifting to it.

In fact the PO, being neither technical manager nor software guru, but counting on some referential leadership from his Client role, tried to manage the key technical experts on other grounds. During the "coffee machine" and more formal meetings, the PO behaved as a naïve coach trying to improve the motivation and self-esteem of the team leaders, shaping and putting them questions like these:

- *Do* **you** *think it is difficult to work on this change request ? If so, why ?*
- *Do you think the user is right in raising this issue ? If not, why ?*
- *What would you like to do to improve your task progress status ?*
- *What would you recommend to raise the users' trust in the project ?*
- *Would you have any issue you'd like to discuss with the project manager ?*
- *Etc …*

Some these points were not only addressed to improve personal motivation, but also relieve project pressures and tensions, which may be blocking factors of human actions. Moreover, did also help introducing more project discipline through process than personal management. Another area of team and self improvement through C&M should regard the risk attitude and ability to manage it (though it would take another chapter to discuss this).

5 Conclusions

The emergent project model of the reported experience followed the Weinberg's hints and some Psy-Co efforts. A more structured case would require to envision this organizational option since the beginning or as prerequisite to better manage difficult or in-crisis projects, where some individual or group coaching would be working alongside the project manager.

When played by two individuals—task and team maintenance managers, though the latter being part-time—appropriate agreement and mutual acceptance should be granted, with frictionless and no overlapping influence. In particular the maintainer, i.e. person dressing the coach habit, should be regarded as external advisor and supporter of the same project manager, given appropriate investiture by the company management or project sponsor. As already pointed out, evolution towards more agile project management would be better prone to accept this socio-behavioral model, which might recast the "two-parents diarchy".

Also when playing alone, the project manager should be constantly serving the two roles, task and maintenance manager, as necessary or deserved by the team. Progress status meetings are good and natural occasions where the project team would be exposed to motivation stimulus, same as basket teams are manifestly seen "recharging" and shaking their hands after the break called up by their coach.

The calibration between mentoring and coaching actions should be considered, but some general rules could not be given and remain dependent upon the context and organizational policy, in addition to situations and persons being addressed. In the case, a psychological profile or assessment could help in tailoring the support program, at least from a methodology point of view. As a general principle, the coaching content (see Fig. 1) would increase as project managers and team member would grow their seniority and competence level; while mentoring would have increasing effect as more juniors would be accompanied and more actions toward organization values and culture creation should be required. Mentoring and coaching should overall be regarded as best practices and professional values of the company and their intervention be so gentle and well accepted by the human resources with no reaction or sense of frustration; which might be the main issue for psychological attention. For instance actions for C&M could be outlined in organizational policies and procedures, and divulgated in regular training programs, besides audits and quality assurance reviews. Efficiency and coherence should be as present as usual. A very healthy project or capable project manager, maybe well trained or skilled as coach as well, would likely deserve no additional support. Medium to large corporations, where IT development workforce outnumber hundreds or a thousand, should consider this approach as organizational rule, and smaller realities be supported by some consultancy or professional services. When important projects are at the stake, so are the human resources, being the project quality dependent on the latters'.

It looks like that the actions summoned in the above short experience had some beneficial effect on the project health, though not being the only ones, to recover this venture; that, according to the CHAOS metric, should be classified as partially failed project. For the Client and Supplier, it can have been a success in the end. Recovering a trembling project can be a greater success, which is likely not taken into proper weight by CHAOS. Further we would like to remark that definition of "naïve coach" was introduced only to the benefit of this chapter, being not yet recognized by the formal accreditation of professional associations.

References

1. Eveleens, J., Verhoef, C. (2010). The rise and fall of the Chaos report figures, *IEEE Software*.
2. Soto-Acosta, P., et al. (2010). Shaping human capital in software development teams: the case of mentoring enabled by semantics, *IET Software*, *4*(6).
3. Landaeta, R.E., et al. (2008). Formal mentoring: a human resource management practice that supports knowledge transfer across projects. International Journal of Learning and Intellectual Capital, *5*(3/4).
4. "Coaching" in Wikipedia (English), accessed in Internet, en.wikipedia.org.
5. Gallwey, T. (1974). *The inner game of tennis*. New york: Random House.
6. Whitmore, J. (2009). *Coaching for Performance* (4th Ed.). London: Nicholas Brealey, 1992.
7. Davies, R. (2009). Agile Coaching, O'Relly.
8. Adkins L. 2010. Coaching Agile Teams.
9. PMBOK. (2008). *A guide to the project management body of knowledge*: PMBOK® Guide (3rd ed., p. 390). Bruxelles
10. (2006). IPMA, ICB (International Competence Baseline), 3rd Version.
11. (2006). APM, BoK (Body of Knowledge), (5th Ed.).
12. Curtis, B., Hefley, B., & Miller, S. (2009). People Capability Maturity Model (P-CMM) Version 2.0. No. CMU/SEI-2009-TR-003. Carnegle-Mellon Univ Pittsburgh Pa Software Engineering Inst
13. Paasivaara, M. (2011). *Coaching Global Software Development Project*: Sixth IEEE International Conference on Global Software Engineering.

14. Pressman, R. (1998). Fear of trying: the plight of rookie project managers. *IEEE Software*.
15. Weinberg, G. (1971). *The psychology of computer programming*. New York: Dorset House.
16. Pitcher, H. "Mentoring vs. Coaching", accessed at website www.iddas.com.
17. Tuckman B.W., Jensen M.A.C. (1977). Stages in Small Group Development revisited. *Group and Organizational Studies, 2*.
18. Hoda, R., Noble, J., Marshall, S. (2013). Self-Organizing Roles on Agile Software Development Teams. *IEEE Transactions on Software Engineering*, 422–444.

Mentoring and Technology in the Learning Process: E-mentoring

Luisa Varriale

Abstract The aim of this chapter is to investigate the technology inside the learning process by evidencing how these new tools can improve this significant and critical process examining one innovative technique: mentoring. I want to examine mentoring, recognized as a learning and competence development goal-driven process, supported by new technology in order to understand context and factors of technology that affect mentoring relationships within learning process in any organizations considering their own specific characteristics. This is a theoretical study conducted through a review of the literature, in order to systematize and clarify the main contributions on this topic and to identify new research perspectives.

Keywords Technology · Learning · E-mentoring

1 Learning Process, New Technologies and Mentoring

Individuals learn a great deal through interactions with others, especially those with different background, expertise, and seniority in their organizations [1]. One important relationship that serves as a forum for personal learning is mentoring [2]. Somewhat surprisingly, personal learning has not been empirically studied in the mentoring literature [3]. In the management literature, learning has generally been studied in the context of information seeking during socialization [4]. Some scholars recognize the importance of "learning to learn" [2, 5]. Kram [2] defined "personal learning" as knowledge acquisition, skills or competences contributing to individual development, including the interpersonal competences of self-

L. Varriale (✉)
Department of Management, Parthenope University, Naples, Italy
e-mail: Luisa.varriale@uniparthenope.it

P. Spagnoletti (ed.), *Organizational Change and Information Systems*, Lecture Notes in Information Systems and Organisation 2, DOI: 10.1007/978-3-642-37228-5_36,

reflection, self-disclosure, active listening, empathy, and feedback. Mentoring is also described as a learning and competence development goal-driven process [6]. Furthermore, the quality of individual and collective learning is a key for the organizational success. Lank and Lank [7] advocate the "continuously learning organization" and de Geus [8] argues that the ability to learn faster than competitors maybe is the only sustainable competitive advantage [1]. According to research, mentoring is an innovative learning technique that is affected from new technologies too.

In the traditional learning and training process, many educators consider that physical contact with learners (students, employees, etc.) is necessary. This medium by which educators touch and partner with students is changing dramatically with the Internet as a vehicle to deliver course content [9]. Hence, with new technologies, academics and practitioners in educational system and in each organizational setting talk about e-learning process, with different rules, instruments and procedures, and also with several effects. People use e-learning programs because they can save time and money [10]. In the last decade the use of the Internet especially for management education has increased, but the research on technology-mediated learning has not connected with this practice [11–13].

Mentoring within organizational context is a relationship where there are two individuals, a senior person (mentor) who, thanks to his/her advanced experience and knowledge and maturity, has the duty to guide, to advise, to suggest junior individual (protégé/mentee) in his/her professional and personal development; it's an exclusive relationship "person to person" between protégé and mentor, there is a dyadic personal and constant relationship (one-to-one) [14–18]. Last studies evidence that a protégé can establish relationships with more than a mentor within organizational context with a different vision of mentoring relationship [19, 20] as a multiple developmental relationship phenomenon [20], where a protégé has not only one mentor, but he/she has multiple relationships with a variety of mentors who give more contributions in terms of perspectives, knowledge and skills.

Regarding mentoring functions, mentors provide career development support, which involve coaching, sponsoring advancement, providing challenging assignments, protecting protégés from adverse forces, and foresting positive visibility. Moreover, mentors provide psychosocial roles, which include such functions as personal support, friendship, acceptance, counseling, and role modeling [21].

Within organizational settings mentoring has positive outcomes in terms of higher levels of job satisfaction and promotions [18, 21, 22] and support, counseling, friendship in terms of psychological dimensions [15].

Mentoring as instrument of human resources management is an innovative learning instrument or instrument for organizational socialization. In this direction, because of the need to formalize mentoring relationships, some studies distinguish formal or informal mentoring programs in terms of formality and length of the relationship, and purpose of the relationship meant like specific objective [3, 21]. In terms of choice of techniques or systems of communication, face-to-face or with other typologies, protégé can build their relationships with mentor thanks new technologies, for example, thanks to channel internet/e-mail [23] developing innovative typologies of mentoring programs, e-mentoring, also named electronic mentoring or mentoring online or telementoring, we know still little about this new approach because prior studies consider above all traditional mentoring (t-mentoring) schemes.

2 E-mentoring: Characteristics and Functions

Single and Mueller [24] defined e-mentoring as "a relationship that is established between a more senior individual (mentor) and a lesser skilled or experienced individual (protégé), primarily using electronic communications, and that is intended to develop and grow the skills, knowledge, confidence, and cultural understanding of the protégé to help him or her succeed, while also assisting in the development of the mentor" [24, p. 108]. According to Bierema and Merriam [25] e-mentoring is ''a computer mediated, mutually beneficial relationship between a mentor and a protégé which provides learning, advising, encouraging, promoting, and modeling, that is often boundaryless, egalitarian, and qualitatively different than face-to-face mentoring'' [25, p. 212]. In e-mentoring programs, traditional mentoring scheme is over, because the relationship between mentor and protégé uses no traditional face-to-face scheme but considers distance communication ways, internet, email, chat rooms, and so on. E-mentoring is not limited by organizational or geographical boundaries and can thus pair individuals or groups from organizations that may be totally dissimilar. Any problems inherent in doing this can be more easily addressed if a cross-boundary code of practice is in place.

There is a lack of empirical evidence from schemes that exploit the full potential of computer-mediated-communication (CMC) [26, 27]. Developing online communities involves a blend of technical planning and social development [28].

E-mentoring can support more effectively career process for individuals, especially for women [29, 30]. Thompson and colleagues' study [31] explored the viability and effectiveness of e-mentoring for an e-learning module development within arts and humanities.

McLoughlin and colleagues [32], in their study, created a peer-to-peer e-mentoring framework, facilitated by a Web 2.0-based technology model that is integrated with the university's learning management system. This framework had to support students completing their practicum placements as part of a one-year Graduate Diploma of Secondary Education. They adopted a community of practice (CoP) approach to facilitate and support interactions among students with virtual mentors hence it could establish "an effective peer support system offering mentoring capacities such as emotional support, feedback and encouragement that can help mitigate issues related to professional isolation and anxiety" [32, p. 1]. Other scholars analyze online discussions in a course portal that supplemented class discussion in three continuing education courses; they emphasized the role of e-mentors in promoting and mediating the discussions among students [33].

Mueller [30] describes MentorNet (www.MentorNet.net), a large-scale e-mentoring network for women in engineering and related sciences. Also Kasprisin and colleagues [34] focused on MentorNet to investigate the benefits in terms of time and distance. Otherwise, the literature evidences that the first large-scale e-mentoring program was the Electronic Emissary Project, founded in 1993 with the main focus to match K-12 public school students working on discipline-specific projects with subject-matter experts in those disciplines [35]. In the next years, other e-mentoring programs emerged such as the Telementoring Young Women in Engineering and Computing Project (Telementoring Young Women Project), founded in 1994, that was the first federally funded research project; this project examining the efficacy of using e-mentoring, encouraged female high school students' interests in computers and computer-related fields, fields in which women were (and are) underrepresented [36, 37]. Another e-mentoring program was the International Telementoring Project that was being piloted in 1994 as the Hewlett Packard Email Mentoring Project [38], which paired K-12 public school students with professionals in partnering corporations to assist students with their class projects. Many other e-mentoring programs were founded in public and private organizations in the last three decades with many important positive effects that support the interesting and numerous studies on this topic.

It is possible to identify five clear advantages of online mentoring: greater access, reduced costs, and equalization of status, decreased emphasis on demographics and a record of interactions. E-mentoring also allows flexibility with time and space since protégés and mentors do not have to be in the same place at the same time, thanks to the overcoming of geographic, space and time limitations, e-mentoring also facilitates the development of a professional network [39] by supporting the career process [40]. In particular, de Janasz, Ensher and Heun [40] studied e-mentoring in a population of business students that were mentored by practicing managers showing the positive effects of this program evaluated in terms of similarity and frequency of interactions. In addition, interactions needed to address complex problems can be facilitated more thoughtful by the asynchronous nature of e-mentoring [41]. Otherwise, considering the issues of personal contact, "protégés in any context learn from their mentors by directly or indirectly observing their behaviors, discussing professional challenges and receiving performance-related feedback" [40, p. 395]. In a virtual context the observational component is difficult to replicate given the current constraints of technology and accessibility, for this reason protégés in e-mentoring programs are less likely to receive the role modeling available in fate-to-face mentoring programs (traditional mentoring or t-mentoring) [40]; paradoxically, this limited personal contact in e-mentoring can be advantageous, in fact, "because electronic communication lacks the visual cues that can lead to or reinforce bias or stereotypes based on demographic or status differences" [40, p. 395], e-mentoring, as opposed to t-mentoring, helps and supports considerably disadvantaged groups such as women and people of color and any minorities especially at the upper levels of organizations [26, 42]; "the use of electronic means to establish mentoring relationships reduce the salience of observable differences in favor of value similarity" [40, p. 405].

Single and Single [43] evidenced that e-mentoring, in the literature, "is not a panacea, neither is it an inexpensive alternative to face-to-face mentoring".

The main advantage, as with other e-learning programs, is the cost effectiveness with high start-up costs but low operational costs. Costs related to travel or time away from the job and costs of updating learning resources can be reduced [26]. Even if there are many experiences of e-mentoring in several organizational contexts, "we not only wonder whether face-to-face mentoring can be replaced by an electronic doppelganger (i.e. a phantom twin), but also encounter questions that deal with the fundamental nature of mentoring" [44, p. 119].

By operating in a virtual environment without hierarchies, e-mentoring offers an organizational and personal means of minimizing status barriers and of challenging the power relations evident in the physical world [29]. These benefits in terms of overcoming barriers of different typology, are more important for women; who receive an indirect benefit of e-mentoring as the development of skills and confidence in using information and communications technologies (ICT) [26].

Furthermore, some authors recognize two critical forces that affect this relationship: the human dynamic of two people interacting, and the environment of the individuals and their relationships. While the mentor-protégé dyad is central to e-mentoring, CMC also offers opportunities to establish a community of practice [45, 46]. While e-mentoring is clearly a godsend to such groups, others perceive its value in complementing face-to-face meetings and contact by telephone. Other scholars compare the relative impact of peer-mentoring that took place either face-to-face or through electronic chat, more specifically they tried to evidence also the impact of e-mentoring on gender effects in the effectiveness of mentoring relationships in terms of its functions [47].

Moreover, e-mentoring benefits should be greater in number and available to a larger audience utilizing a range of mentors throughout the organization for different objectives. Hence, e-mentoring provides flexibility and easy access which is highly beneficial to those who would normally face barriers to being mentored because of their gender, ethnicity, disability or geographical location. The flexibility offered by its asynchronous communication methods also means that it does not have to interfere with other daily commitments. A further advantage of e-mentoring is that the protégés are able to take responsibility for initiating contact and to play an active role in online discussions. E-mentoring offers the opportunity to set up dynamic two-way learning networks, and, in online group mentoring, the opportunity for the learning networks to be multidimensional [26].

Some studies evidence that e-mentoring has a number of key challenges, such as the likelihood of miscommunication, a slower development of relationships online, negative effects of computer malfunctions, issues of privacy and confidentiality [39]. However, the main negative outcomes of e-mentoring programs concern the lack of feedback and the lack of training and support for mentor.

3 Conclusions

Previous studies evidence that technology may have high value and important results, but the quality of mentoring is the main factor for a success of the relationship scheme. Sometimes, many protégés prefer to use only emails and not chat rooms or message boards, because they consider them too impersonal. It is possible to help e-mentoring programs with a relevant preparatory training to ensure that participants acquire sufficient information technology (IT) skills. In this case, e-mentoring has built a community in which the participants can communicate in confidence and share information, but mentoring is, and should remain, a very personal experience. Technology should help to achieve this goal [48].

E-communication can be useful for both participants and can overcome some difficulties of t-mentoring, such as power differences, especially the level of formality that is present in some hierarchical organizations such as Military school, educational organizations or manufacturing industry. People can reflect before responding thanks to the asynchronous nature of e-mail. There are not barriers in terms of geographical distance; location is not an issue, for the participants at e-mentoring programs, it is very important because mentors and protégés are usually all over the world, i.e. in academic settings scholars tend to receive support and share knowledge and skills with colleagues abroad. Furthermore, race, power, and other barriers are removed. Time is easier to manage, no costly meetings; and a record of the discussion exists for later reflection and learning.

This chapter shows the viability of an innovation in education process, especially in a process of personal and professional development with the implementation of two different innovations: new technology and mentoring programs, together they form an e-mentoring program. Final considerations of the study are: using IT we can create valued-added relationships between mentors and protégé; the protégé have an innovative learning experience with multiple sets of resources and technology and the possibility to consider new skills and knowledge; this experience is very important also for their future, professional and personnel development.

As evidenced, this is a theoretical study that can be considered as a research starting point in order to examine in the future perspective, through a quantitative method, the effectiveness of technology for mentoring programs with the application of an evaluating model after defining a clear research design. In particular, it will be useful and more effective to examine some empirical case studies in order to better identify the main factors that affect the effectiveness of an e-mentoring program, in terms of both real e-mentoring experiences and a specific software that supports the program. In the future development of this study, the intention is to identify and measure the main variables in a wide research design on e-mentoring also investigating if and how communities of practice and more specifically "legitimate peripheral participation" [49] could play a central role in e-mentoring programs in the learning processes by contributing to a more interesting debate in the human resources management policies.

References

1. Hayes, J., & Allinson, C.W. (1998). Cognitive style and the theory and practice of individual and collective learning in organizations. *Human Relations*, *51*(7), 847–871.
2. Kram, K.E. (1996). A relational approach to career development. In D.Hall & Associates (Eds.), *The career is dead-long live the career* (132–157). San Francisco: Jossey-Bass.
3. Lankau, M.J., & Scandura, T.A. (2002). An investigation of personal learning in mentoring relationships: content, antecedents and consequences. *Academy of Management Journal*, *45*(4), 779–790.
4. Morrison, E.W. (1993). Newcomer information seeking: exploring types, modes, sources, and outcomes. *Academy of Management Journal*, *36*, 557–589.
5. Rawson, M. (2000). Learning to learn: more than a skill set. *Studies in Higher Education*, *25*(2), 225–238.
6. Godshalk, V.M., Sosik, J.J. (2003). Aiming for career success: the role of learning goal orientation in mentoring relationships. *Journal of Vocational Behavior*, *63*(3), 417–437.
7. Lank, A.G., & Lank, E.A. (1995). Legitimising the gut feel: the rose of intuition in business. *Journal of Managerial Psychology*, *10*(5), 18–23.
8. De Geus, A. (1988). Planning as learning. Harvard Business Review. March-April, 71.
9. Brower, H.K. (2003). On emulating classroom discussion in a distance-delivered OBHR course: creating and on-line learning community. *Academy of Management Learning and Education*, *2*(1), 22–36.
10. Dobbs, K. (2000). Too much Learning.com. Training. February.
11. Alavi, M., & Leidner, D.E. (2001). Research commentary: technology-mediated learning-a call for greater depth and breadth of research. *Information Systems Research*, *12*(1), 1–10.
12. Eastman, J.K., & Swift, C.O. (2001). New horizons in distance education: The online learner-centered marketing class. *Journal of Marketing Education*, *23*(1), 25–34.
13. Arbaugh, J.B. (2005). Is there an optimal design for on-line MBA courses? Academy of Management Learning and Education, *4*(2), 135–149.
14. Levinson, D. J., Darrow, C. N., Klein, E. B., Levinson, M. A., & McKee, B. (1978). *Seasons of a man's life*. New York: Knopf.
15. Kram, K.E. (1983). Phases of the mentor relationship. *Academy of Management Journal*, *26*(4), 608–625.
16. Burke, R.J. (1984). Mentors in organizations. *Group and Organization Studies*, *9*(3), 353–372.
17. Thomas, D.A., & Kram, K.E. (1988). Promoting career-enhancing relationships in organizations: the role of the human resource professional. *The human resource professional and employee career development*, *49*, 66.
18. Fagenson, E.A. (1989). The mentor advantage: perceived career/job experiences of protégés v. Nonprotégés. *Journal of Organizational Behavior*, *10*(4), 309–320.
19. Higgins, M.C. (2000). The more, the mentor? Multiple developmental relationships and work satisfaction. *Journal of Management Development*, *19*(4), 277–296.
20. Higgins, M.C., & Kram, K.E. (2001). Reconceptualizing mentoring at work: a developmental network perspective. *Academy of Management Review* *26*(2), 264–288.
21. Kram, K. E. (1985). *Mentoring at work: developmental relationships in organizational life*. Glenview: Foresman and company.
22. Riley, S., Wrench D. (1985). Mentoring among female lawyers. *Journal of Applied Social Psychology*, *15*, 374–386.
23. Whiting, V. R., & de Janasz, S.C. (2004). Mentoring in the 21st century: using the internet to build skills and networks. *Journal of Management Education*, *28*(3), 275–293.
24. Single, P.B., & Muller C.B. (2001). When email and mentoring unite: the implementation of a nationwide electronic mentoring program. Implementing successful coaching and mentoring programs. pp. 107–122

25. Bierema, L. L., & Merriam, S. B. (2002). E-mentoring: using computer mediated communication to enhance the mentoring process. *Innovative Higher Education., 26*(3), 211–227.
26. Ensher, E.A., Heun, C., Blanchard, A. (2003). Online mentoring and computer-mediated communication: new directions in research. *Journal of Vocational Behavior, 63*(2), 264–288.
27. Headlam-Wells, J., Gosland, J., Graig, J. (2005). There's magic in the web: e-mentoring for women's career development. *Career Development International, 10*(6–7), 444–459.
28. Rossignoli, C. (2009). The contribution of transaction cost theory and other network-oriented techniques to digital markets. *Information Systems and E-Business Management, 7*(1), 57–79.
29. Wadia-Fascetti, S., & Leventman, P.G. (2000). E-mentoring: a longitudinal approach to mentoring relationships for women pursuing technical careers. *Journal of Engineering Education, 89*(3), 295–300.
30. Mueller, S. (2004). Electronic mentoring as an example for the use of information and communications technology in engineering education. *European Journal of Engineering Education, 29*(1), 53–63.
31. Thompson, L., Jeffries, M., & Topping, K. (2010). E-mentoring for e-learning development. *Innovations in Education and Teaching International., 47*(3), 305–315.
32. McLoughlin, C., Brady, J., Lee, M.J.W., Russell, R. 2007. Peer-to-peer: an e-mentoring approach to developing community, mutual engagement and professional identity for pre-service teachers. Paper presented at the Australian Association for Research in Education (AARE) Conference Fremantle, Western Australia. 25–29 November.
33. Wong, L.-H., & Looi, C. K. (2010). Online discussion and e-mentoring strategies in continuing education courses. In E. M. W. Ng (Ed.), *Comparative blended learning practices and environments* (pp. 146–169). Hershey: IGI Global.
34. Kasprisin, C. A., Single, P. B., Single, R. M., & Muller, C. B. (2003). Building a better bridge: testing e-training to improve e-mentoring programmes in higher education. *Mentoring & Tutoring, 11*(1), 67–78.
35. Harris, J., Rotenberg, L., & O'Bryan, E. (1997). *Results from the electronic emissary project: telementoring lessons and examples*. Denton: Texas Center for Educational Technology.
36. Bennett, D., Hupert, N., Tsikalas, K., Meade, T., & Honey, M. (1998). *Critical issues in the design and implementation of telementoring environments*. New York: Center for Children and Technology.
37. Bennett, D., Tsikalas, K., Hupert, N., Meade, T., & Honey, M. (1998). *The benefits of online mentoring for high school girls: telementoring young women in science, engineering, and computing project, Year 3 evaluation*. New York: Center for Children and Technology.
38. Bennett, D., Harris, J., Klemmer, D., Neils, D. (1997). Telementoring ways of learning. Panel presented at the BBN National School Network Conference, Cambridge, MA.
39. Milne, J. (2005). Personal computing: how can mentoring or coaching by e-mail help leaners get more out of e-learning. IT Training, January.
40. De Janasz, S. C., Ensher, E. A., & Heun, C. (2008). Virtual relationships and real benefits: using e-mentoring to connect business students with practicing managers. *Mentoring and Tutoring: Partnership in Learning., 16*(4), 394–411.
41. Wade, S., Niederhauser, D. S., Cannon, M., & Long, T. (2001). Electronic discussions in an issue course: expanding the boundaries of the classroom. *Journal of Computing in Teacher Education., 17*(3), 4–9.
42. Hamilton, B. A., & Scandura, T. A. (2003). E-mentoring: Implications for organizational learning and development in a wired world. *Organizational Dynamics, 31*(4), 388–402.
43. Single, P. B., & Single, R. (2005). E-mentoring for social equity: review of research to inform program development. *Mentoring and Tutoring: Partnership in Learning, 13*(2), 301–320.
44. Kealy, W. A., & Mullen, C. A. (2003). Epilogue: unresolved questions about mentoring and technology. *Mentoring and Tutoring, 11*(1), 119–120.
45. Wenger, E. (1997). *Communities of practice: learning, meaning and identity*. Cambridge: Cambridge University Press.

46. Wenger, E., McDErmott, R., & Snyder, W. M. (2002). *Cultivating communities of practice*. Boston: Harvard Business School Press.
47. Smith-Jentsch, K. A., Scielzo, S. A., Yarbrough, C. S., & Rosopa, P. J. (2008). A comparison of face-to-face and electronic peer-mentoring: Interactions with mentor gender. *Journal of Vocational Behavior, 72*, 193–206.
48. Hunt, K. (2005). E-mentoring: solving the issue of mentoring across distances. *Development and Learning in Organizations*, 19(5).
49. Lave, J., & Wenger, E. (1991). *Situated learning: legitimate peripheral participation*. Cambridge: Cambridge University Press.

Public Policy Innovation in Distance and On-Line Learning: Reflections on the Italian Case

Enrico Maria Mosconi, Cecilia Silvestri, Stefano Poponi and Alessio Maria Braccini

Abstract The dynamic evolution of competences required by professions has to match ever-evolving contexts, in which the growth of the demand of new professionals, poses the threat of a skill shortage. The role of learning and training is strategic to this regard, also thanks to the use of on-line and distance learning that use Internet based technologies to allow learning to be administered in context different than the traditional face-to-face. Literature highlights that e-learning has to be implemented following specific strategies. Within this perspective, this chapter presents and discusses the recent experiences of the public policies for e-learning in Italy.

1 Introduction

Innovation on the one side, and economic turmoil on the other, make competences required by professional in current working activities ever-evolving. There is a continuous demand for new professionals that, in some fields, poses a skill shortage problem. The role of continuous learning and training are crucial to this regard. Especially in learning, Information and Communications Technologies (ICT), and especially Internet technologies, were since a long-time implemented

E. M. Mosconi (✉) · C. Silvestri · S. Poponi · A. M. Braccini
Dipartimento di Economia e Impresa, Università degli Studi della Tuscia, Viterbo, Italy
e-mail: enrico.mosconi@unitus.it

C. Silvestri
e-mail: c.silvestri@unitus.it

S. Poponi
e-mail: poponi@unitus.it

A. M. Braccini
e-mail: abraccini@unitus.it

P. Spagnoletti (ed.), *Organizational Change and Information Systems*, Lecture Notes in Information Systems and Organisation 2, DOI: 10.1007/978-3-642-37228-5_37,

both in academic and professional settings [1, 2], such applications go under several names like e-learning technologies, web based technologies, Internet based training technologies [3]. In the reminder of the chapter only the “e-learning” term will be used to indicate all these kinds of technologies.

E-learning technologies make use of e-learning platforms to provide a virtual space capable of distributing course-related contents, using either the Internet [4], or other digital media like satellite transmission, interactive TV, or audio/video media (tape, CD-ROM, DVD) for communication [5].

Within the framework of e-learning technologies and e-learning theories this chapter presents and discusses the public policies for innovation in e-learning in Italy. The structure of the chapter is as follows: Sect. 2 will discuss theoretical contribution regarding the application of ICTs to e-learning, Sect. 3 will provide some brief considerations regarding the research methodology, the public policies adopted by the Italian government will be introduced and described in Sect. 4, these policies will be briefly discussed in Sect. 5, and some final thoughts will conclude the chapter in Sect. 6.

2 Technology Applied to Learning Processes: E-learning

As already mentioned, the application of a set of different technologies to learning processes goes under the name of e-learning [1–3]. The set of technologies used include almost every kind of multi-media technologies that allow learning processes to be performed over the distance (where distance indicates both geographical and temporal distance) [5]. The most traditional technologies applied to e-learning are audio–video media (like CD-ROM or DVD) for asynchronous transmission, or other media that also involve synchronous and interactive transmission like satellite communication, interactive TV, and the Internet [5, 6]. More recently also more innovative media like 3D virtual platforms were used for e-learning purposes [7].

Usually these technologies are assembled in the form of platforms called learning management systems (LMS) that are used both by administrative personnel, instructors/professors, and students. These LMS offer features and functionalities that allow administrative personnel and instructors to manage the training process and to distribute learning contents and lectures on-line, and, on the other side, allow students to receive learning contents and administrative information [8]. Even though LMS were created with the intention to manage all aspects of learning processes, it has been reported that they are mainly used to manage administrative aspects of traditional learning processes [8]. Moreover due to their nature of document repositories they limit instructors in the design of more innovative courses falling back on traditional course centered approaches [9].

E-learning is not only about technology. To be effective e-learning must be applied following specific e-learning strategies. Usually there are three different strategies with which e-learning can be applied [10]. These are: the open and flexible learning, the distributed learning, and the collaborative learning. In each of these strategies the role of the different actors involved, and of the underpinning learning processes, changes [11]. An e-learning application following an open and flexible strategy focuses on the creation of a learning environment that better suits students' need. This is a student centered perspective in which the student is free to navigate into learning contents whenever and wherever it is more convenient form him/her. The distributed learning is similar to the open and flexible learning strategy since it still focuses on the role of the student. The idea is again to provide an environment where students can access training contents wherever and whenever they want, thanks to the use of an appropriate mix of technologies [12]. Learning contents are in this case grouped in learning paths students can follow. Finally the collaborative learning strategy sees an active role of the students who, together with professors and tutors, are all part of learning communities where learning takes place in a cumulative knowledge generating process [13, 14].

3 Research Methodology

This chapter aims at describing and discussing recent public policies for the application of technologies to learning and education, at all levels from primary school to university, in Italy. The chapter adopts a qualitative research methodological approach based on the descriptive case study protocol defined by Yin [15]. The sources of information adopted for this case study are mainly formed by policies and official documents released by the Italian central government. Previous study and personal experience complement these information sources. While analyzing these information sources we have focused mainly on the policies, and on the subsequent projects started, that could affect, in different ways, Italian education institutions (primary schools, secondary schools, and universities) how and when e-learning technologies shall be used by them in their traditional education offering and activity. Such discussion is of course made in the light of the characteristics of the Italian education system which were also described.

4 Public Policies for E-learning in Italy

Within the landscape of the evolution of learning needs, products, and offerings, in Italy education in general is positioned below the level of the European average. According to recent data:

- A quota equal to 20.6 % of the total population of age 18–24 with at maximum an Italian primary school degree is not involved in further learning activities in spite of the 14.9 % UE-25 average, and of the objective (to be achieved in 2010) of 10 %;

- A quota equal to 74.8 % of the total population of age 20–24 has a high school degree compared to the 77.5 % UE-25 average;
- The percentage of people with an academic degree in scientific and technological topics per 1,000 inhabitants of age 20–29 was, in 2005, 10.7 %, lower than the UE-25 average of 12.6 %.

The government recognized the need of necessary systematic interventions (both in terms of access, inclusion, and fairness) on the overall Italian training and education system. One of the principles identified as suitable to achieve such objectives was identified in the use of ICT. Learning and training are indeed one of the main fields of ICT applications since:

- The body of knowledge used in learning initiatives is more and more digitalized, and ICTs are the best tools to manage it;
- The competences required by the job market need a continuous update, and they necessarily include ICTs;
- ICT is a tool to sustain inclusion and accessibility policies that are crucial in the field of learning.

4.1 The Primary and Secondary Education System

The Italian education system is composed by different actors with different tasks, roles, and responsibilities: the central government, the regions, the provinces, the municipalities, ad the single—independent—education institutions. This fragmented organizational landscape in practical terms discharges responsibilities and decisions concerning didactic activities, education paths, and also the development and use of ICTs in the Italian education system to the base. Single institutions, their managers, and their teaching staffs are frequently addressing these problems. This produced in the recent years a fragmented development of single initiatives all targeted to stimulate the use of ICTs in single institutions, with a low level of reuse, with necessary restrained objectives, and without and integrated development plan.

In the recent years the numerous projects started contributed to improve the informatics endowment of Italian education institutions that were insufficient in many cases, and in some others even absent as indicated by the Permanent Observatory on Learning Technologies: in the 10.293 schools investigated (about 94 % of the total) in the period 2005–2006, the number of desktop PCs and notebooks reached the level of 580.900 units, and the number of students per PC decreased from 28 (2000–2001) to 11. An improvement of the accessibility to the Internet network was also achieved, since almost all schools have now access to the Internet connection, and 54 % of them use broadband connections.

The progresses made are anyhow not homogenous on the whole Italian territory. The distribution of the equipment is for example uneven since the majority of PCs are polarized in highs schools. Also the use of Internet and network shows

Table 1 Major ICTs projects on e-learning in Italy (*Source* Net Consulting)

ITC provision	ITC for school community	ITC For teaching and learning
	Innova Scuola	Scuole in rete
PON—UE	Digiscuola	Didattica digitale
Società dell'informazione—UE	Piano Min. ForTic2	Servizi Scuola famiglia via Web
		Compagno di classe
		Anagrafe Scolastica Nazionale

significant differences from primary schools (where in 96 % of the cases these technologies are used in didactic activities) to secondary schools (where the technologies are used in 80 % of the cases). In general there are teachers that do not make use of Internet technologies and resort to traditional didactic methods. Moreover, the use of ICTs and Internet technologies in Italian schools is activity, and location, dependent. For example the role of laboratories is still relevant: 77 % of the laboratories in Italian schools are connected to the Internet, and the laboratories connected to the network are mainly informatics laboratories (that are the 82 % of all the laboratories presents in primary schools), and linguistic laboratories (Table 1).

4.2 Market Trends and Policies of Italian E-learning Services

At the international level the e-learning market is continuously evolving with positive trends due to a growing use of e-learning as a support to continuous learning, and to the increase of the training needs of markets. In Italy, in 2011, the total amount of the market for Education and Training services was of € 416 millions, and showed a decrement of about 7 % compared to the amount of the previous year.

A proper implementation of e-learning technologies in education and learning systems necessarily requires an initial phase of study and evaluation of the project, with the objective of calculating its strategic convenience. Effectiveness is then more important than efficiency, and aspects like learning contents, and learning services quality are relevant (Table 2).

The objectives identified by the e-Gov 2012 Plan, presented by the Italian government in 2009, were first to provide a complete diffusion of Internet technologies in Italian schools, and then to provide technologically advanced tools and services for learning and didactic to families.

In particular the projects included in the plan were:

- Networked schools: to allow each Italian school to have secure broadband, even mobile if necessary, Internet connection;
- Digital didactic: to introduce digital contents and online textbooks in didactic; to allow schools to access to platform on which learning contents distributed by

Table 2 Composition of IT service market in Italy

	2009	Var (%)	2010	Var (%)	2011
Sistemi embledded	986	−0.4	982	1.1	993
Education and training	489	−8.6	447	−6.9	416
Counselling	950	−3.2	920	−2.5	897
Sviluppo manutenzione	1.957	−5.3	1.854	−3.7	1.786
System integration	993	−3.0	963	−2.4	940
Servizi di elaborazione	827	−8.2	759	−6.7	708
Outsourcing/FM	2.548	−1.6	2.507	−1.4	2.472
Total	8.750	−3.6	8.432	−2.6	8.212

Source Assinform 2012

editors, and also freely usable by teachers, are made available; to improve the technology facilities of Italian school, and diffuse distant learning;
- School-Family Services via Web: to simplify the communications between schools and families (i.e. electronic record, electronic colloquia, electronic forms for enrolment), digitalization of administrative services, and use of multiple channels for communications (i.e. web, e-mail, sms);
- National Schools Registry Office: to create of a registry office for Italian schools to improve the national monitoring of education policies, and to allow the publication of performance evaluations of schools;
- Project "Compagno di Classe": to give each primary school student a sturdy, secure, and low cost, personal PC as a didactic tool.

Table 3 provides a quantitative overview of the projects started in Italian schools following the e-Gov 2012 Plan.

4.3 E-learning Services in Italian Universities

Generally speaking, e-learning services in Italian Universities is still under development. The main characteristics of the current e-learning offering are the flexibility and quality. E-learning services are used with the intent of improving the quality of didactic, and to respond to worker students' needs.

Specific digital governance projects, following the e-Gov 2012 plan, were addressed to Italian universities, stimulating and investment program that, before the year 2012, should have seen all Italian universities employ advanced services for students, professors, and administrative personnel, including a complete WiFi coverage, and the availability of VoIP services on all their locations.

In particular, the projects included in the plan were:

- Online services and WiFi networks: to boost the adoption of online didactic and administrative services by Italian universities, using also WiFi technologies, and reducing the fragmentation of services provision;

Table 3 Current state of projects in the e-Gov 2012 plan

	2009	2010	2011	2012	Total program
Networked schools					
Connection of plexes	11	14	14	14	53
Connection of classrooms		5	15	20	40
Internet in classrooms	5	10	10	10	35
Digital didactic project					
Computer Labs	25	20	10		55
Platform Innova Schola	4	6	9	10	29
Project school-family services via web					
Development and diffusion	4	4	6	6	20
Project "Compagno di Classe"					
Tutoring ad communication	1				
Project national schools registry office					
Development and diffusion	2	2	2	2	8
Total	52	61	66	62	240

Source elaboration CSI&T on Osservatorio Attrezzature Tecnologice, Italian Education Ministry

Table 4 Projects for universities in the e-Gov 2012 plan, values in millions of euros

	2009	2010	2011	2012	Total program
On-line services					
Iniziative wi-fi Sud	6				6
Iniziative digital campus	3.15				3.15
Iniziative digital campus (extension)	1				1
Iniziative AFAM WiFi	1.5		1		2.5
Project digital university					
Tor Vergata—La Sapienza university protocol	0.9				0.9
Iniziative digital university	2.5				2.5
Iniziative digital university 2009	2.5				2.5
Iniziative digital university—subsequent phases		10	10	10	30
Total	17.55	10	11	10	48.55

Source elaboration CSI&T on Osservatorio Attrezzature Tecnologiche, Ministero dell'Istruzione

- Digital University: to make simplification and digitalization systematic in Italian universities through a complete WiFi and VoIP coverage, online services for students, the standardization of internal processes, and the avoidance of chapter based information and communication flows involving universities and the Italian Ministry of Education, University, and Research.

Table 4 shows an overview of all the projects started in Italian Universities following the e-Gov 2012 Plan.

5 Discussion

The data described provided in Sect. 4 depict an improving situation. On the one side it can be noticed that in the recent years there was a remarkable effort in reducing the gap in this area with the rest of the EU. Moreover the actions taken at the level of national policies are addressed to homogenize the landscape of informatics endowments of Italian schools. Given the characteristics of the Italian education system, and the current situation of education in general in Italy, the use of e-learning technologies is potentially relevant since it could contribute to absorb into continuous learning processes the quota of people who are no longer receiving learning after their degrees, and could help in overpassing burdens imposed by work or family problem.

The focus of the identified policy is anyhow still too shifted to the technological perspective. It emerges quite clear the necessity to catch up with the gap in terms of technological equipment of Italian schools. A large part of the objectives and of the action areas of the policies are in fact targeted to improve network coverage, and computers diffusion in schools (both in laboratories and at the individual level).

Regarding a more systemic perspective of the actions proposed and stimulated by the Italian public policies, it emerges quite clear, at all levels of the Italian education system, that the main advantages sought are those of simplification and rationalization of administrative processes. In particular many actions are target to the reduction of chapter-based interaction between schools and students or their relatives. This is also strengthened by the recent simplification actions taken by the current government, specifically regarding information that Universities must distribute to students enrolled or enrolling at their courses.

These are the most generic advantages that the application of e-learning technologies might produce for the education system. This application is of course in line with what is stated by the literature, but this has to be intended, according to us, as a necessary starting point for a more fruitful application of e-learning technologies in the Italian education system.

6 Conclusion

In this chapter we described and discussed the recent public policies adopted by the Italian government for the improvement and the diffusion of e-learning technologies in the Italian education system. In the discussion of the characteristics and of the contents of the policies, and of the subsequent actions, we highlighted a strong focus on the technological perspective with the intent of providing benefits in terms of simplification of administrative burdens for schools and university. While the need to fill the gap in term of technology facilities for schools and universities is a necessary step for a profitable application of e-learning technologies, we argue that this is not the only aspect necessary, and that, even in the light of the current policies, innovative e-learning applications are still left to the initiative of single professors and/or institutions, without a potential comprehensive approach that might help in circulating best practices or in creating a critical mass for e-learning investments.

References

1. Khan, B. H. (1997). Web-based Instruction: What is it and why is it? In B. Khan (Ed.), *Web-based Instruction*. Englewood Cliffs: Educational Technology Publications.
2. Wang, Y. (2003). Assessment of learner satisfaction with asynchronous electronic learning systems. *Information and Management, 41*, 75–86.
3. Khan, Badrul H. (2001) A framework for web-based learning. *Web-based training*, 75–98.
4. Nichols, M. (2003). A theory of e-learning. *Educational Technology and Society, 6*, 1–10.
5. Urdan, T., & Weggen, C. (2000) .Corporate e-learning: exploring a new frontier. WRHAMBRECHT +CO.
6. Cohen, E. B., & Nycz, M. (2006). Learning objects and e-learning: an informing science perspective. *Interdisciplinary Journal of Knowledge and Learning Objects, 2*, 23–34.
7. Za, S., & Braccini, A.M. (2012). Designing 3D virtual world platforms for e-learning services. *New Frontiers of Organizational Training*. In Snene, M. (Ed.) IESS 2012, LNBIP 103, pp. 284–296. London: Springer.
8. Dalsgaard, C. (2006). Social software: e-learning beyond learning management systems. *European Journal of Open, Distance and E-Learning*, 2.
9. Kemp, J., & Livingstone, D. (2006). *Putting a Second Life "Metaverse" Skinon Learning Management Systems. Proceedings of the Second Life Education Workshop at the Second Life Community Convention*, pp. 13–18, San Francisco.
10. Dabbagh, N. (2005). Pedagogical models for e-learning: a theory-based design framework. *International Journal of Technology in Teaching and Learning., 1*, 25–44.
11. Hannafin, M. (1992). Emerging technologies, ISD, and learning environments: critical perspectives. *Educational Technology Research and Development, 40*, 49–63.
12. Knoweldge, J. (2000). Distributed learning evolves to meet needs of lifelong learners. *Education Edition, 1*, 1–15.
13. Rogoff, B. (1994). Developing understanding of the idea of communities of learners. *Mind, Culture, and Activity, 4*, 209–229.
14. Ke, F., & Hoadley, C. (2009). Evaluating online learning communities. *Educational Technology Research and Development, 57*, 487–510.
15. Yin, R. K. (1994). *Case study research: design and methods*. CA: Sage Publishing.

Does Technology-Mediated Learning Matter for Effective Teams?

Leonardo Caporarello and Giacomo Sarchioni

Abstract Many research and studies have discussed the importance of understanding and measuring the effectiveness of technology-mediated learning initiatives. Most of the research analyses the effectiveness of such initiatives at the individual level [1, 2]. This research aims to provide insights on the effectiveness of technology-mediated learning (TML) when working in teams. In particular, we intend to investigate whether the usage of "new technologies" might have a beneficial impact on the activities of university students when organized as a team. The "new technologies" considered in the study belong to the following list: blog, e-learning platform, online encyclopaedia, e-mail, online word processing/spreadsheet/presentation software (e.g. Google Docs), smartphone, tablet, gaming console, Internet-connected TV, chat and/or VoIP, Wiki, social network and web hosting/syncing services (e.g. Dropbox). The first results of this research confirm our expectations. Technology allows teams of students to significantly improve their performances on all the dimensions considered.

Keywords Technology-mediated learning · Team learning · Enhancing learning processes

This chapter intends to formalize and share first findings of a research-in-progress.TML is referred "to a learning experience that is significantly moderated through the use of information and communication technology" [2].

L. Caporarello (✉) · G. Sarchioni
SDA Bocconi, School of Management, Learning Lab, Milan, Italy
e-mail: leonardo.caporarello@unibocconi.it

G. Sarchioni
e-mail: giacomo.sarchioni@gmail.com

P. Spagnoletti (ed.), *Organizational Change and Information Systems*, Lecture Notes in Information Systems and Organisation 2, DOI: 10.1007/978-3-642-37228-5_38,

1 Introduction

The role of technology in education has been a "hot" topic in the last 20 years. In 1999 an article by Dr. Constance A. Mellon was published in the *Journal of Research on Computing in Education*. The author presented the interesting theory of "The Great Pendulum of Education" according to which educational paradigms continuously shift from one extreme to another. "When the idea loses favor, the pendulum swings again, all the way to the other side" [3]. The author claimed that the pendulum of education was focusing on technology. In her work, Mellon presents the two—only apparently—contrasting views of Richard Clark and Robert Kozma. While the former, in fact, believes that educational media (e.g. textbooks, computers, the Internet) are mere vehicles that do not alter the way we learn [4], the latter simply shifts the level of analysis from the media to the ways media themselves can be used to influence learning [5]. Mellon [3] agrees with the fact that technology is "one of the tools for learning" and "… may not even be the best tool for learning".

Those studies, however, probably suffered from being pioneering researches in a relatively new field. Recent findings, in fact, demonstrated how technology-based education could actually improve learning performances. Joy and Garcia [6] explained how educational media comparison and research presented flaws in the experimental research. They selected five studies cited in a previous study [7], and related to the effectiveness of technology in schools, and recorded numerous errors regarding sampling techniques and non-usage or erroneous usage of control variables.

Bryant et al. [8] found significant differences in the creation of a better learning environment when web technologies are used. In a dissertation given at Fielding Graduate University in f, it was proved the existence of "significant differences in final exam and overall course scores between the traditional and online learners taking nearly identical introductory environmental science courses with the same instructor" [9].

An interesting research [10] showed that culture—and not cost factors—does represent the biggest impediment to effective TML implementation in schools. The fact that some TML initiatives do not work as expected can be the result of a refractory culture rather than the inefficacy of the technology itself. This implies that when it comes to evaluating the effectiveness of TML there might be hidden factors—e.g. culture—that could explain not significantly different or even lower performances.

In this research, following Kozma's philosophy, it is necessary to "reframe" the debate over the influence of media on learning [5]. Technology would be considered as a supportive—and not alternative—tool to be used in educational environments. In particular, we will look for the existence of a possible ancillary role that technology might have in the context of team working in the academic environment.

2 Background

Referring to the *team behaviorial integration* model [11], we intend to test differences in the way students communicate, collaborate, decide and perform in both the situations of usage and non-usage of technology-mediated learning when working in team. This research will address the effectiveness of TML in the very specific situation of student team working in University contexts. Aziz et al. [12] have demonstrated that use of computers help "students in being more actively engaged in learning" and increases "student interactions with fellow students and/ or instructors", but their analysis did not measure the ultimate students' performances and, additionally, had the individual—and not the team—as the point of reference. While Easley et al. [13] demonstrated that a well performing team (in terms of communication, coordination, balance, support, effort and cohesion) is more likely to use technological collaborative systems, the authors of this research aim at finding the existence of the opposite relationship, i.e. the impact of the usage of technology itself on variables such as communication (Comm.), collaboration (Coll.), joint decision making (JDM) and overall performance (Ov. Perf.) in a team of learners.

The figure below shows the research framework, and hypotheses (Fig. 1).

More precisely the hypotheses that will be tested are:

- H1: the higher the usage of technology, the higher the perceived communication level when students are organized in teams.
- H2: the higher the usage of technology, the higher the perceived collaboration level when students are organized in teams.
- H3: the higher the usage of technology, the higher the perceived decision making effectiveness when students are organized in teams.

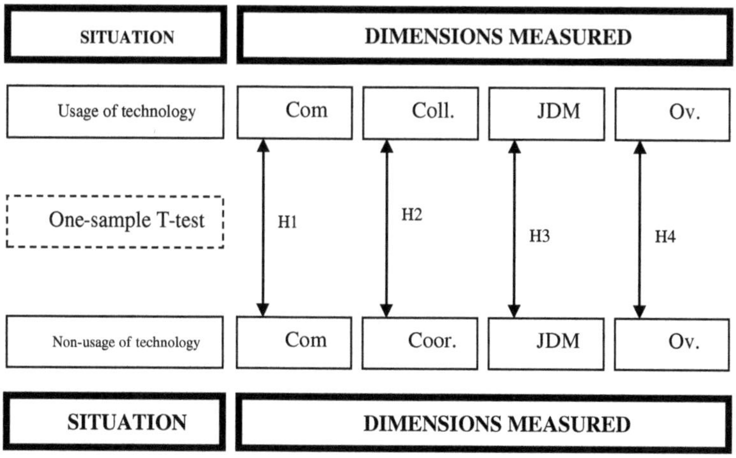

Fig. 1 Research framework and hypotheses

- H4: the higher the usage of technology, the higher the perceived overall performance level when students are organized in teams.

3 Methodology and Data Analysis

The study is conducted through an online questionnaire. We have already analysed the literature to find appropriate measures for our model.

Fourteen items aim at measuring the dimensions highlighted in the framework of *behavioral integration* [10]—communication among team members, collaboration and joint decision making—and a synthetic variable of overall performance always with regards to the context of team working at university.

Items are measured through a five-point Likert scale.

The link to the online questionnaire was sent to university students attending Italian academic institutions.

Respondents were asked to measure items in both the two situations of non-technology mediation, and of technology mediation.

One-sample *T* test analysis will be run to look for any significant difference ($p < 0.05$) on the four dimensions above mentioned for the cases of usage and non-usage of technology.

We expect to obtain significant differences for all the dimensions. This implies that student teams should prove that they communicate, collaborate, decide and, overall, perform better when using the technology in their learning activities.

4 Results and Implications

The sample obtained is composed of 141 students attending Italian universities.

As expected all the T-tests are significant. The following table compares the mean scores (on a 1–5 Likert scale) for the four dimensions measured, both in the case of usage and non-usage of technology. *P* values for H1, H2, H3 and H4 are reported in the last column.

Hypothesis	Mean scores		*P*-value
	Technology usage	Technology non-usage	
H1, perceived communication	3.9096	2.8706	0.0000
H2, perceived collaboration	3.6619	2.7423	0.0000
H3, perceived decision making effectiveness	3.5035	3.0307	0.0000
H4, perceived overall performance	3.8422	3.3209	0.0000

The results confirm that using technology in teams improves communication, collaboration, decision making effectiveness and overall performance.

Accordingly, the usage of technology in students' team activities does guarantee superior performances.

The most immediate implication is that of favouring the adoption of such technological tools among students who are required to work in teams. In particular, communication and collaboration are the dimensions that benefit the most from the usage of technology. Accordingly, Facebook, Twitter, Dropbox, Google Docs, Blogs, Wikis and all the other tools addressed in this study should be seen as "good partners" in the students' activities rather than potential "enemies".

5 Possible Limitations and Future Research

The findings of this research demonstrate that technology does have a positive impact on student-teams' performances. However, the reader should be aware that simply forcing students to use technology might not be sufficient to increase their team performances. Statistics confirm the positive impact of technology, but problems in the implementation of TML solutions should be seriously taken into account. In other words, the mere presence of technology may not be sufficient to increase team performances. Future research should investigate the eventual effect of other factors that ultimately operate as *catalysts* for the beneficial effect of technology.

In addition to that, it would be interesting to replicate the same research in other contexts. While maintaining the focus on the impact of technology on team performances, future researches might broaden the scope of the study beyond that of the academic world.

References

1. Slatin, J. M. (1990) Reading hypertext: Order and coherence in a new medium. *College English, 52*(8), 870–883.
2. Leidner, D., & Jarvenpaa, S. (1993). The information age confronts educations: Case studies on electronic classroom. *Information Systems Research, 4*(1), 24–54.
3. Mellon, C. A. (1999). Technology and the great pendolum of education. *Journal of Research on Computing in Education, 32*(1), 28–35.
4. Clark, R. E. (1993). Reconsidering research on learning from media. *Review of Educational Research, 53*(4), 445–449.
5. Kozma, R. B. (1994). Will media influence learning? reframing the debate. *Educational Technology Research and Development, 42*(2), 7–19.
6. Joy, E. H., & Garcia, E. F. (2000). Mesauring Learning Effectiveness: A New Look at No-significant-difference Findings. *Journal of Asynchronous Learning Networks*, *4*(1), 33–39
7. Sivin-Kichala, J., & Bialo, E. R. (1994). *Report on the effectiveness of technology in schools, 1990–1994*. New York: Interactive Educational System Design, Inc.

8. Bryant, K., Campbell, J., & Kerr, D. (2003). Impact of web-based flexible learning on academic performance in information systems. *Journal of Information Systems Education, 14*(1), 41–50.
9. Vroeginday, B. J. (2005). *Traditional vs. Online Education: A Comparative Analysis of Learner Outcomes*. ProQuest Digital Dissertations.
10. Alavi, M., & Gallupe, R. B. (2003). Using information technology in learning: Case studies in business and management education programs. *Academy of Management Learning Education, 2*(2), 139–153.
11. Hambrick, D. C. (1994). Top management groups: A conceptual integration and reconsideration of the team label. In B. M. Staw & L. L. Cumming (Eds.), *Research in organizational behavior* (pp. 171–214). Greenwich, CT: JAI Press.
12. Aziz, T., Khan, M. B., & Singh, R. (2010). Effects of information technology usage on student learning: An empirical study in the United States. *International Journal of Management, 27*(2), 205–217.
13. Easley, R. F., Devaraj, S., & Crant, M. J. (2003). Relating collaborative technology use to teamwork quality and performance: an empirical analysis. *Journal of Management Information Systems, 19*(4), 247–268.

Part VII
Human-Computer Interaction

Building Social Life Networks Through Mobile Interfaces: The Case Study of Sri Lanka Farmers

Pasquale Di Giovanni, Marco Romano, Monica Sebillo, Genoveffa Tortora, Giuliana Vitiello, Tamara Ginige, Lasanthi De Silva, Jeevani Goonethilaka, Gihan Wikramanayake and Athula Ginige

Abstract The development of mobile applications is paramount to support users living in developing countries to improve their lives. One of the major research challenges is to develop a user interface suitable for such users. In this chapter we present the design process we applied in order to develop a mobile application oriented to farmers living in Sri Lanka. The application prototype developed so far has been evaluated against usability requirements and a usability evaluation

P. D. Giovanni (✉) · M. Romano · M. Sebillo · G. Tortora · G. Vitiello
University of Salerno, Salerno, Italy
e-mail: pdigiovanni@unisa.it

M. Romano
e-mail: marromano@unisa.it

M. Sebillo
e-mail: msebillo@unisa.it

G. Tortora
e-mail: tortora@unisa.it

G. Vitiello
e-mail: gvitiello@unisa.it

T. Ginige
Australian Catholic University, North Sydney, Australia
e-mail: Tamara.Ginige@acu.edu.au

L. De Silva · J. Goonethilaka · G. Wikramanayake
University of Colombo, Colombo, Sri Lanka
e-mail: lnc@ucsc.lk

J. Goonethilaka
e-mail: jsg@ucsc.lk

G. Wikramanayake
e-mail: gnw@ucsc.lk

A. Ginige
University of Western Sydney, Sydney, Australia
e-mail: a.ginige@uws.edu.au

P. Spagnoletti (ed.), *Organizational Change and Information Systems*, Lecture Notes in Information Systems and Organisation 2, DOI: 10.1007/978-3-642-37228-5_39,

framework has been devised, which can be used to replicate the tests as the application iteratively reaches its final release. This work represents a pilot study within a wider international research project aiming to provide real-time information to support activities related to livelihood delivered using mobile phone applications targeted to meet the needs of people in developing countries.

1 Introduction

The Social Life Networks for the Middle of the Pyramid (SLN4MoP) is an International Collaborative research program that aims to provide real-time information to support activities related to livelihood delivered by mobile phone applications targeted to meet the needs of people in developing countries [1]. These applications are expected to harness the rich information available in social networks, public data sources including spatio-temporal sensor data as well as the emerging cloud infrastructure.

The goal of SLN4MOP project is to leverage the enormous reach of mobile phones equipped with myriads of sensors such as GPS and camera, to develop the next generation of social networks that not only connect people to people, but also have the capability of providing real-time, context-sensitive local information by aggregating data from a variety of sources. In order to move towards that goal, we chose the agricultural area as the context were a pilot research study could start.

Agriculture in most developing countries represents a major economic sector, employing the largest share of the workforce, while suffering from low productivity. The reasons for this low productivity may include land fragmentation, lack of postharvest infrastructure, weak market linkages, information and knowledge asymmetries (or lack thereof), and, most important, low technology utilization. A

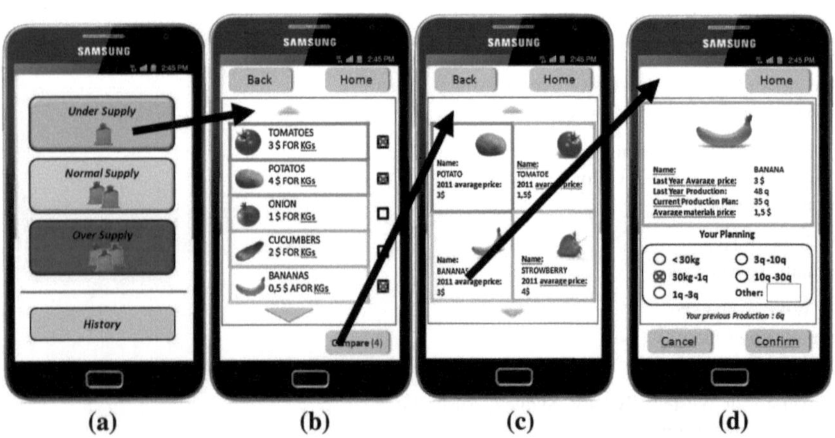

Fig. 1 The crop selection activity

recent survey conducted in Bangladesh, India, Sri Lanka and Thailand investigated the information and knowledge needs as well as the communication patterns among farming stakeholders [2]. It revealed that while sources of information and advice for farmers at present mainly consist in self-knowledge, family and friends, and other traders, the potential benefits which may come from delivering the unmet information needs through the ubiquitous mobile technology are well understood.

The goal of our pilot study was to develop a usable and useful mobile user interface to help Sri Lankan farmers improve their rural activities and gain higher incomes. We followed a user-centered design approach: we studied potential users and included them in the initial conceptual design activities. Relying on a scenario-based methodology, as suggested in [3], the research work evolved from a contextual inquiry we conducted with real stakeholders in Sri Lanka to investigate the possible causes for an oversupply of products, which is giving rise to a drastic lowering of selling prices when products are sold at the markets.

In this chapter we present the user-centered design activities, which have followed and have given rise to the present prototype of mobile application. In order to devise appropriate usability field tests with Sri Lankan farmers, we have designed a scenario-based usability evaluation framework, which we have experimented with a group of Sri Lankan immigrants living in Italy. The results of the experiment will allow us to identify the relevant usability evaluation goals and decide what data to collect before starting the usability testing phase of the project in Sri Lanka. The same evaluation framework will be used later on to replicate tests.

2 The Usability Focused Requirements Engineering Phase of the SLN4MOP Project

The initial activities of this pilot research project concerned the usability requirements elicitation, analysis and specification. In particular, the project goal led us to a completely user-centered approach, were potential users were studied in detail and their needs considered throughout the development process.

Initially a survey was conducted with real stakeholders to investigate the possible causes for an oversupply of agricultural products. The survey involved 20 farmers and 1 agri-officer from the main government seed distribution center. The farmers were selected to represent different cultivation regions in Sri Lanka. All the participants had over 3 years of farming experience and owned a farmland between half and four acres. All were less than 50 years old and 90 % of the farmers were Sinhalese. All participants were able to read and write while none had failed Ordinary level examination. Moreover, some had successfully completed Advance levels, whereas one had obtained a degree. In addition to that, 70 % of the farmers were mobile phone users.

Sri Lanka has a tropical climate and rich soil. This has made agriculture the most dominant sector in Sri Lankan economy [4]. Thus, the necessity to focus on this community, identify existing problems associated with farming and develop solutions using the existing and emerging technology is crucial for the sustainability of this sector. Further details on the survey can be found in [5].

2.1 Application Requirements

We capitalized the knowledge gained from the fieldwork and envisaged some scenarios of working practices, from which we could start our brainstorming activity for the design of a possible solution. In Ref. [5], we envisaged a scenario of truck farming practices which gave us the opportunity to reason about what were the major requirements that emerged from the rural Sri Lankan context. We were therefore able to elicit an initial set of requirements divided into five categories according to the classification described by Preece et al. [6]. Due to space limitation we cannot describe in detail each requirement in the list. We will only mention the relevant requirements for the crop selection module (Table 1).

Since users are distrustful of technology with the exception of mobile devices, developing a mobile application seemed to be the right direction. The application should receive the geographic coordinates of user's land location and should provide him/her with valuable information about the crops from neighboring farms. Users may use that information to decide what crops to cultivate.

Table 1 Application requirements

Application requirements	Rationale
The application allows the exchange of heterogeneous data between neighboring users guaranteeing anonymity	By sharing valuable information on crop cultivations, users would be able to make better decisions during the crop selection activities. Furthermore, because of social phobia and the competition among farmers, users are more conformable by preserving anonymity
Users may need training provided by experts	Users are not in habit to work with advanced technological instrumentation. Therefore, they may need training
The application has the access to data related to the distribution of crops located around user's farm	Farmers are interested to get information just about neighboring crops that are supposed to be sold to the same market
The application should be easy to use and should require a little training effort	The application is used mainly in specific and not frequent tasks
The user interface should be effective: it should provide a simple management of users mistakes	The application provides support to a critical task on the basis of data updated directly by users. Therefore, it is paramount to reduce the number of possible unintentional user mistakes

The brainstorming activities led us to identify a set of interface design scenarios from which the relevant design claims were derived. Among others, two most significant claims were:

Design claim 1. Data presentation should exploit the communicative power of images and color language to provide users with complex information through the small screen of mobile devices.

Design claim 2. The interface should provide users with a small number of menu levels and operations. Farmers need to be able to use the application without a long training effort.

2.2 Designing the Mobile User Interface

The two categories we mention in this chapter, namely *data presentation* and *data entry* cover the two aspects of a traditional user interface. The former is related to the information output that has to be clear and fully comprehensible for users of different cultural levels; the latter is related to the input modalities. The complete list of requirements can be found in [5].

Following the list of requirements, a first prototype has been developed as a mobile application running on the Android 2.2 platform. In the remaining part of this section we describe an interaction scenario we developed to specify the mechanisms for accessing and manipulating task information and show the effectiveness of the developed interface.

Personal

Sirisena is a 45 years old farmer with long experience in truck farming. Sirisena is part of Sinhalese ethnic group. He does not have advanced technical skills; the only technological instrument is his mobile phone that he uses everyday. Sirisena lives in Sigiriya, a village in the central Matale District of Sri Lanka, where he owns four acres of farmland. Since Sirisena has a long experience in truck farming he manages the crop production of his family farm. His role is to make decisions on critical aspects of the production. He takes decisions on the kind of production, the time to start it and he establishes an indicative selling price

Scenario

Sirisena is interested in producing convenient crops, i.e. crops which produce high yield within a short time. He launches the application that displays the three colored buttons, green for undersupplied products, amber for average supplied products and red for oversupplied products (Fig. 1a). Siresena selects the green buttons and the list of products in that category is displayed. Products are framed in a variety of decreasing intensity of green, with the darkest corresponding to the highest demand and the lightest to the lowest demand (Fig. 1b). Observing the proposed list, Sirisena is primarily interested in the production of tomatoes and potatoes and secondly in the production of bananas and strawberries. So he selects these four products of interest and taps on the *compare* button. On the basis of the information provided by the application, as illustrated in Fig. 1c, Sirisena decides to grow bananas. Selecting the desired product, the application displays the form where he can enter the amount of product he wishes to cultivate (Fig. 1d). The green frame around the desired product still confirms that the selected quantity does not move crop production level from under supply level to a higher level. Therefore Sirisena decides to confirm his choice

---

In order to satisfy the interface requirements, we have taken into account a set of specific design guidelines for mobile applications as well as a precious collection of design patterns [7]. As an example, for the initial interface, the traffic lights colors are used, as a universally understood metaphor. To display all products in the given scenario, the virtual page pattern has been chosen, with the aim to avoid using nested menus to search for a product. The application uses icons to describe crops and a colored frame to indicate the approximate quantity of each crop already in production. The selection of a product triggers a textual description of the product. Furthermore, a vibration is used as a further confirmation of the selection. Finally, after the selection, the color of the frame may change to amber or red, if the specified amount moves the product to a different category of demand.

3 The Usability Evaluation

In order to devise appropriate usability field tests with Sri Lankan farmers, we have designed a scenario-based usability evaluation framework, which can be later used to replicate the tests at different stages of the development process. The idea was to use the prototype developed in the HCI lab of the University of Salerno to conduct a pilot study which could help us tune the usability evaluation goals. The results of the study will be used to set up the usability testing activities.

The pilot study involved people belonging to a Sri Lankan ethnic group living in Salerno, in Italy. This group is composed of approximately one hundred people. After the presentation of the SLN project during a plenary meeting of that community, we were able to select 20 people who were motivated and knowledgeable enough to play the role of farmers in our experiment.

In order to gauge the potential effectiveness and usefulness of the application, we applied a "think-aloud" technique, inviting participants to perform some representative tasks with the current prototype with the twofold aim to gain precious suggestions on how to improve it and to verify whether the appropriate data are being collected.

During the pilot study, we focused on three aspects of the interface, namely

1. the *capability to understand the interface*: we checked whether the information clues and their layout are effective to guide users in accomplishing their tasks. The interface must not confuse user or make him/her feel awkward.
2. the *capability to navigate the menu*: we needed to determine the best way to structure the menu in order to avoid user getting lost during the interaction.
3. the *capability to analyze results*: we wanted to evaluate whether the information provided by the application is appropriate to lead users towards the selection of the most convenient crops.

Users and instrumentation

The pilot test has been performed simulating the real environment in the rural area around the city of Salerno. We used a Huawei Ideos smartphone, an entry level model with a 600 MHz processor, 256 megabytes of central memory and a 2.8 inches screen with a resolution of 320 × 240 pixels. This choice is consistent with the kind of smartphones really available in countries where people cannot afford big expenses.

The 20 participants belong to the Sinhalese ethnic group and are members of an acceptance center for Sri Lankan immigrants. All of them are well-integrated in the local Italian society. Nevertheless, they are all knowledgeable about the rural issue in Sri Lanka, in most cases being the reason for their emigration, and they appeared to be highly motivated in performing the tests.

As part of the study, the scenario described in Sect. 2 was decomposed into three critical subtasks. Each subtask represents a key feature that influences user's capability. To this aim, we asked subjects to adopt the perspective of Sirisena and to simulate the scenario activity by carrying out the tasks while commenting any critical step. We decided to start the experiment with no preliminary training on the application module, overall aiming to verify the learn ability degree of the interface.

Subtask description	Usability evaluation goal
1. The user explores the application. He/she presses one of the three buttons in the initial page and visualizes the list of products in the corresponding category. Considering the first ten items in the catalog he/she annotates what is the current "production level" he/she perceives for each item	Understand whether the color intensity scale used in the list is perceived by user as a measure of the current product demand
2. The user finds and selects four specific kinds of crop displayed in the catalog. He compares them	The aim is to verify whether the user is able to navigate the one level catalog menu
3. He ultimately makes a selection	We want to verify whether the user can correctly interpret the feedback received from the application and make the right choice

The results were compared against a set of usability specifications, which we elaborated for the envisaged scenario (see Table 2). As usual, the performance measures are based on time to perform a subtask and number of errors. Satisfaction is measured on a 5-point attitude scale. For example, "predictability" after the first subtask was rated on a scale from 1 = "not at all predictable" to 5 = "fully predictable".

Some relevant results are reported in Table 3. For the first subtask, it shows that the use of the traffic light metaphor to group the products combined with the

Table 2 Excerpt from the usability specifications related to the given scenario

Subtask	Worst case	Planned	Best case
1. Deduce the expected production level for the envisioned crops	3 errors 2 min 2 on predictability	1 error 1 min 3 on predictability	0 errors 30 s 4 on predictability
2. Select and compare 4 specific products	3 errors 4 min 3 on complexity	1 error 2 min 2 on complexity	0 errors 1 min 1 on complexity
3.Select the best crop out of 4 specific products	Bad choice 5 min 3 on confusion	Optimal choice 2 min 2 on confusion	Optimal choice 1 min 1 on confusion

Table 3 Some relevant results from the pilot study

Subtask no	Participants results
1	Mean errors: 2 Mean time to completion: 74 s
2	Mean errors: 1 Mean time to completion: 170 s
3	Percentage of participants who made the right choice: 70 % Mean time to completion: 105 s

intensity color scale, proved to be a good choice, also supporting predictability of the interface. Users were able to easily guess the production level of a crop by simply observing the color of the frame around it.

Regarding the second subtask, while the average number of errors is comparable to that of the first subtask, the execution time suggests that the use of the virtual page pattern might be too complex for our target users. This was confirmed by the rating assigned by users to complexity and by their comments during the think-aloud session. Some users also suggested a subdivision of the product catalog by type of crop: tubers, vegetables and fruits, asserting that such a division could facilitate the search.

Finally, the last subtask shows how the majority of participants was able to select the product for which the highest income can be expected. The interviews revealed that participants were satisfied with the choice of graphics and color usage. High appreciation received the possibility to compare two or more products. When information such as average price or quantity sold in the previous year were similar for more than one product, the frame indicating the production level was used as a discriminating factor in selecting the best product. Finally, perhaps the most interesting outcome of the experiment was the identification of changes needed in the current usability evaluation framework. Thus, for example, we realized that before starting the testing activities in Sri Lanka, the usability evaluation goal "verify whether the user is able to navigate the one level catalog menu", should be tuned towards a comparative evaluation of the virtual page solution against alternative design solutions, such as a grid layout interface, with or without the suggested subdivision of products into categories. The test also revealed that the ease of use should be considered as a primary usability specification feature and its qualitative measure added to the satisfaction parameters in the evaluation framework.

4 Concluding Remarks

The development of mobile applications is paramount to support users living in developing countries to improve their lives. One of the major research challenges is to develop a user interface suitable for such users.

In the first part of this chapter we presented the design process we applied in order to develop a mobile application oriented to people living in Sri Lanka. During the design process we took in account several factors such as users level of literacy, familiarity in using the device, users cultural background, language beliefs.

In the second part of the chapter we described a pilot study for an experimental usability evaluation we have performed involving a group of Sri Lankan users living in Italy. The analysis of the experimental results and the comments given during the think-aloud session by participants, allowed us to draw major claims on which we should focus when planning the usability evaluation activities in Sri Lanka.

Even if the participants differ from our target users, having higher confidence in technology and living in a different social context, their cultural background and their motivation reduced the biases to validity of the test and were useful to understand how to improve the developed usability evaluation framework before going onto the actual testing phase of the project.

References

1. R. Jain., Sing, V., & Gao, M. (2011). *Social life networks for middle of the pyramid.* Available from: http://ngs.ics.uci.edu/whitepapers/SLN_whitepaper%20110212.pdf.
2. Lokanathan, S., & Kapugama, N. (2012). *Smallholders and micro-enterprises in agriculture: Information needs and communication patterns.* LIRNE asia, Colombo, Sri Lanka pp. 1–48.
3. Rosson, M. B., & Carrol, J. M. (2002). *Scenario-based design, the human-computer interaction handbook : Fundamentals, evolving technologies and emerging applications.* Mahwah, NJ: Lawrence Erlbaum Associates, Inc.
4. Central Bank of Sri Lanka Annual Report. (2010). Central Bank: Sri Lanka.
5. Di Giovanni, P., Romano, M., Sebillo, M., Tortora, G., Vitiello, V., De Silva, L., Goonethilaka, J., Wikramanayake,G., Ginige, T., & Ginige, A. (2012) *User centered scenario based approach for developing mobile interfaces for social life networks. Proceedings of the*

1st International Workshop on Usability and Accessibility focused Requirement Engineering. Zurich 2012.
6. Preece, J., Rogers, Y., & Sharp, H. (2004). Interaction Design. Apogeo.
7. Hoober, S., & Berkman, E. (2011). *"Designing mobile interfaces" O'Reilly*.

Can Design Science Research Bridge Computer Human Interaction and Information Systems?

Laura Tarantino and Paolo Spagnoletti

Abstract The initial view of the Information System (IS) community was to consider IS as an "applied" discipline borrowing theories and methods from more mature "reference disciplines". As ISs shifted from a techno-centric focus to a more balanced view of technology, organizational, management, and social focus, traditional reference disciplines proved to be poor models for emergent goals of IS studies, and the IS field began to pose itself as independent of them. A further shift was advocated in 2002 by Baskerville and Myers who suggested that IS was mature enough to start to create a bidirectional flow of knowledge with other fields. Though this view has been recently challenged by some empirical studies, in this Chapter we contribute to this intellectual discourse through a conceptual analysis of links between the IS and the HCI body of knowledge. In particular we discuss about a possible role of Design Science Research as a cultural and methodological bridge between the two disciplines.

Keywords Information systems · Computer human interaction · Design theory

1 Introduction

Many studies have investigated the relationships of the Information System (IS) field with other interrelated disciplines. The initial view of the IS community is well represented by Keen, who in 1980 argued that ISs, as an "applied" discipline,

L. Tarantino (✉)
University of L'Aquila, L'Aquila, Italy
e-mail: laura.tarantino@univaq.it

P. Spagnoletti
CeRSI-LUISS Guido Carli University, Rome, Italy
e-mail: pspagnoletti@luiss.it

P. Spagnoletti (ed.), *Organizational Change and Information Systems*, Lecture Notes in Information Systems and Organisation 2, DOI: 10.1007/978-3-642-37228-5_40,

had to borrow theories, methods and research best practices from more mature "reference disciplines" upon which the field was drawn [1]. If the initial list of references disciplines was quite restricted (including engineering, computer science, mathematics, management science, cybernetic systems theory and behavioral decision theory), while the field grew the list expanded considerably, with, e.g., political science, psychology, sociology, accounting, and finance included in the classification proposed by Culnan [2]. Gregor observes that IS shows commonalities also with architecture, which concern people and artifacts, or with applied disciplines as medicine, where the products of scientific knowledge (e.g., drugs, treatments) are used by people [3].

Notwithstanding this great bunch of relationships, the conventional view in the 1980s and 1990s was to pose IS near the end of an intellectual food chain, consuming theories and results from other disciplines, with a flow of knowledge and information entirely one way [4]. Scholars then changed their position and started to recognize that the IS field had fully emerged as a discipline in its own right. In 2000 Davis, in an analysis of bodies of concepts, theories, processes, and application systems (somewhat) unique to ISs, identified five bodies of knowledge that had developed in the IS tradition [5]. In 2001 Lee observes that the reference disciplines "are actually poor models for our own field. They focus on the behavioral or the technological, but not on the emergent socio-technological phenomena that set our field apart" and for this reason suggests to refer to these disciplines as "contributing disciplines" [6].

The shift in perspective is then further underlined by Baskerville and Myers that suggested a new scenario in which not only did the IS field pose itself as independent from traditional reference disciplines (with IS research serving as a foundation for further IS research), but it could also issue a challenge to become itself a reference disciplines for others, even for fields previously serving as IS reference disciplines [4]. This opportunity arises because, given the growing impact of information technology in business and society as a whole, almost every other human discipline is now a potential consumer of IS research discoveries. In this new model the flow of knowledge among inter-related fields become multi-directional, and IS scholars, instead of just importing knowledge, should consider the possibility to cooperate with scholars in other fields. IS ceases to be the end of the chain and becomes "one of the many reference disciplines exchanging ideas in an intellectual discourse" [4].

Subsequent empirical studies based on citation analyses have either challenged [7, 8] or supported [9] such optimistic view of cross-contamination. These studies have addressed the problem from a general perspective by analyzing a broad spectrum of scientific publications and defining strategies for increasing the external influence of IS contributions. We adopt a narrower perspective by arguing that a more focused exploration of some of these links can provide useful contributions to this debate by guiding authors in both fields to exploit the benefits of intellectual bridges. In this chapter we focus on the relationship between Human Computer Interaction (HCI) and IS studies for achieving a better understanding on the nature of this link and on the possible benefits of a cross-contamination between these two fields. To this aim, we first discuss in Sect. 2 interrelationships between IS and HCI (in particular trying to underline reasons for existing distances among scholars of the two fields), and then, in Sect. 3, we argue for a possible role of IS Design Science Research (ISDSR) and IS Design Theory (ISDT) results as a conceptual framework bridging the two communities. As conclusions underline in Sect. 4, rather than proposing a "closed reference framework" we aim at opening a discussion to which scholars of the two communities can contribute bringing their field's specificity, in a mutual enrichment.

2 IS and HCI do Relate

In the view of Avison and Fitzgerald ISs concern "the effective design, delivery, use, and impact of information technology in organizations and society" [10, p. xi]. Gregor contrasts Webster and Watson's view of IS being just another management field like organizational behavior [11] by observing that a characteristic that distinguishes IS from these fields is that it concerns the use of artifacts in human–machine systems, so that "we have a discipline that is at the intersection of knowledge of the properties of physical objects (machines) and knowledge of human behaviour" [3]. With the words of Lee, "research in the information systems field examines more than just the technological system, or just the social system, or even the two side by side; in addition, it investigates the phenomena that emerge when the two interact" [6, p. iii]. On the other hand HCI is defined by ACM-SIGCHI (Special Interest Group on Computer Human Interaction) as "the discipline concerned with the design, evaluation, and implementation of interactive computing systems for human use and with the study of the major phenomena surrounding them" [12], with a clear overlapping between IS and HCI intents and goals. This overlapping is witnessed also by the achievements of leading scholars that have contributed across the two fields of research (e.g., [13]).

The overlapping between the two fields suggests to investigate, both at the theoretical/methodological level and at the empirical level, possible contaminations enriching the body of knowledge on which HCI and IS rely and, in particular, to investigate whether and to which extent can the research on IS contribute to the design of interactive systems. Whilst we have already addressed this problem in a previous work on the design of user centered systems [14], we maintain here that fueling a more general debate on this matter can be relevant for achieving a more effective cross-contamination between these two fields.

IS-oriented HCI issues have been debated in the literature since IS's early studies, whether focused on user attitudes, perceptions, acceptance of Information Technology (IT) (e.g., [15]) or on the interrelation between human-factors, usability, and HCI on the one side, and the systems development life cycle on the other side (e.g., [16, 17]). Zhang and Li present HCI as a sub-discipline of the Management Information Systems (MISs) field [18], specifying that HCI studies in MIS are "concerned with the ways humans interact with information, technologies, and tasks, especially in business, managerial, organizational, and cultural contexts" [19]. They also propose an overview of the broad HCI research area composed by five main players: *human*, *technology*, *interaction* (relating the first two), and *task/job* and *context*, which together assign dynamic meaning to the interaction experience. Located within *interaction* authors single out the two subareas denoted *design* and *use impact*, referring to studies traditionally carried on by the CHI and the IS communities, respectively.

It is quite unlikely, anyhow, that CHI scholars may identify their research work as a sub-discipline of IS, given also the growing diffusion of personal-use oriented IT products, and the consequent great differences in designing and evaluating IT for non discretionary job use and discretionary personal use. An overview of HCI studies under this perspective is offered by Grudin [20] who recognizes the existence of three major (non converging) research threads in HCI that, though sharing some issues and methods, emerged at different times within distinct "parent disciplines" and relying on different approaches, attitudes and terminology: the first thread origins from the *Human Factors and Ergonomics* field and focuses predominantly on nondiscretionary use; the second one is *HCI in MIS* (or IS) and, developed when mainframes spawned business computing in the 1960s, focuses on relatively nondiscretionary use; finally, the third one is *CHI* (and its antecedents) that, arisen with minicomputer and home computer and burgeoned with personal computing in the 1980s, focuses predominantly on individual discretionary use. Grudin observes that, despite a significant common focus, there has been limited interaction among the three threads, because different perspectives, priorities, and generational attitudes reduced enthusiasm for building bridges and exploring each other literatures. Furthermore, both Grudin [20] and Baskerville and Myers [4] underline the linguistic divide as a crucial problem that sets apart different disciplines: Grudin brings the examples of the terms *task analysis* and *implementation*, used with different meanings by IS and CHI, and of the lack of agreement even on basic terms likes *operator*, *user*, and *end user*.

Notwithstanding distances, a cultural bridge between IS and CHI is desirable, also considering that the pace of evolution in IT rapidly makes mandatory today what was discretionary yesterday. Cross-contaminating discourses between the two fields would add efficacy to the transition, thus laying down foundations for usability. In the next section, we reason on a possible role of ISDSR as a bridge between the two fields.

3 HCI Paradigms and ISDT Schools do Mirror

A growing stream of research in IS is characterized by the design science paradigm, which has been also recently advocated by Lee as being the theoretical orientation that needs more developments in the next years [21]. With the words of Hevner, March, Park, and Ram, design science research "seeks to extend the boundaries of human and organizational capabilities by creating new and innovative artifacts" instead of analyzing existing phenomena [22]. According to this paradigm, knowledge and understanding of a problem domain and its solution are achieved in the building and the application of the desired artifact. Theories play a dual role in this design process: they constitute the ground of the artifact construction, but they can also be the outcome of the design process ("IS design theory", ISDT). Given the centrality of the design of artifacts in HCI research, in this section we discuss possible parallels among ISDT schools of thought and HCI paradigms. Actually, design, prototyping and evaluation of interactive systems are based on the knowledge of users, technology and tasks, that, at least for meta-requirements, comes in the form of analytical, explanatory or predictive rules resulting in design prescriptive rules (e.g., knowledge on the human eye and the visual perception may result in rules about where to put a visual item on the screen, or knowledge about the human memory may result in rules about the optimal length of chunks of visualized information). With respect to Gregor's framework for classifying theories in Information Systems [3], the knowledge base to which HCI methods and methodologies belong can be rooted in the design science research tradition and it is therefore reasonable to try to look at them from a design theory perspective.

3.1 The Three Paradigms of HCI

Following Kuhn's view of scientific revolutions as a succession of overlapping waves in which ideas are re-framed [23] and with the aim of bringing clarity in the broad research in HCI and its evolution, Harrison, Sengers and Tatar order the field into three "paradigms" [24]. The paradigm shift from a wave to another is traced by tracing shifts in the underlying metaphors of interaction, according to Agre's theory of generative metaphors in technical work [25] developed for analyzing the typical questions of interest for a research stream and the corresponding methods and criteria for knowledge creation: each metaphor of interaction bring certain phenomena into the center of investigation, while marginalizing others. Phenomena of interest, questions, methods and validation procedures are the main constructs used by Harrison et al. to single out and characterize three paradigms in HCI literature.

The first paradigm is based on the metaphor of "interaction as man–machine coupling": the central goal of the design is to optimize the fit between man and machine and a typical question of interest would be "how can we fix specific problems that arise in interaction?". This human factors perspective is an a-theoretic and pragmatic approach to which engineering, programming and ergonomics disciplines provide the grounding for empirically validated objective hypotheses.

The second paradigm dominates the HCI discourse and is based on the metaphor of "interaction as information communication": the primary goal is optimizing the accuracy and the efficiency of information transfer among computers and their users, and typical questions of interest are "how can we accurately model what people do?" or "how can we improve the efficiency of computer use?". This objective is achieved through the definition of abstract models of interactions that enable to systematically compare alternative design solutions.

The third paradigm, rooted in the concept of embodied interaction as introduced by Dourish [26], is based on the metaphor of "interaction as phenomenologically situated": its main focus is on the construction of meaning and on the complexity around the system and typical questions of interest are "what existing situated activities in the world should we support?" or "how do users appropriate technology, and how can we support these appropriations?". The paradigm refocuses attention from single user/single computer paradigm that dominated the 1st and 2nd paradigms towards collaboration and communication through physically shared objects. A specific characteristic of the 3rd paradigm is a preference for multiple interpretations and, for this reason, rather than adopting a single, correct set of methods and actions, it relies on a variety of approach that Harrison et al. denote *phenomenological matrix.*

The three paradigms highlight different questions and methods for answering them, and may clash. For example, while the 1st and the 2nd paradigms emphasize the importance of objective knowledge, the 3rd paradigm sees knowledge as arising from situated viewpoints in the world. While laboratory and theoretical behavioral science can be an appropriate discipline for the 2nd paradigm, the 3rd paradigm would rather rely on ethnography, action research, and practice-based research. It is emphasized in [24] that to allow the 3rd paradigm to bear full fruit, it is necessary to recognize and accommodate its notion of validity, and that it is desirable that research works in the 3rd paradigm explain their phenomenological matrix and their measures of success.

3.2 The Design Theory framework

In a seminal chapter of 1992, Walls et al. [27] asserted that design research (DR) provides a theoretical contribution in the form of an ISDT (defined as "a prescriptive theory based on theoretical underpinnings which says how a design process can be carried out in a way which is both effective and feasible") having five components (meta requirements, meta design, design method, kernel theories, testable hypothesis). Gregor and Jones revise this work and define a set of six core components (purpose and scope, constructs, principles of form and functions, artifact mutability, testable propositions, justificatory knowledge) and two additional components (principle of implementation, expository instantiations) for specifying a design theory so that it can be communicated, justified, and developed cumulatively [28]. These two chapters share the view of considering an ISDT as grounded on kernel theories and being itself the main outcome of a DR effort.

A different perspective has been proposed by Hevner et al. [22] who put the IT artifact at the center of a DR effort, maintaining that constructs, models, methods and instantiations are "the concrete prescriptions that enable IT researchers and practitioners to understand and address the problems inherent in developing and successfully implementing information systems within organizations". They provide seven guidelines (Design an artifact, Problem relevance, Design evaluation, Research contributions, Research rigor, Design as a search process, Communication of research) and propose an IS reference framework based on environment, IS research and knowledge base (which is the base of the Hevner "three cycle view" of ISDSR [29]). According to this view, ISDSR is not necessarily grounded on kernel theories and, although not clearly expressed, an artifact should satisfy a certain degree of generality.

A third position is by Goldkuhl who emphasizes the importance of artifact impact and utility with respect to artifact grounding, although considering the contribution of external explanatory theories in enhancing the design theory validity [30]. As to ISDTs, he argues that practical knowledge per se is not necessarily a design theory and that "only theorized practical knowledge should be conceived a design theory".

By referring to these three views on the input and output role of theories with respect to a DR process, a recent contribution of Fischer, Winter, and Wortmann has identified three schools of thought: for "kernel theory fundamentalists" ISDTs are necessary output of an ISDSR and kernel theories are mandatory components, for "design theory opponents" ISDTs are not necessary output of an ISDSR and kernel theories are not emphasized, and, finally, for "kernel theory pragmatists" ISDTs are necessary output of an ISDSR, and kernel theory are only one way of grounding [31].

3.3 ISDT Schools as Lens on HCI Paradigms

The role of theories in the HCI field is somehow evolving with consequences on the epistemological positions of the different paradigms. Referring to the current debate on ISDSR, we argue that analyzing the relationships among design components within the HCI paradigms can lead to achieve a better understanding on these positions. In fact, since almost any HCI development can be seen as an instantiation of the general ISDT concept, a deep investigation on the nature of its components can set up the floor for generating new theories bridging the HCI and the IS fields.

The analysis proposed in [24] represents a first step in this direction since, as authors says, "recognizing a set of ideas as a paradigm is important because it allows us to perceive and discuss the organization of thought at the level of a system rather than just as component pieces". Our goal is to move one step further, with the final goal of providing a framework for systematically analyzing the ontological and epistemological nature of HCI contributions. As a first move in this direction we draw here a parallel with the three schools of thought characterizing the ISDT literature (Fig. 1).

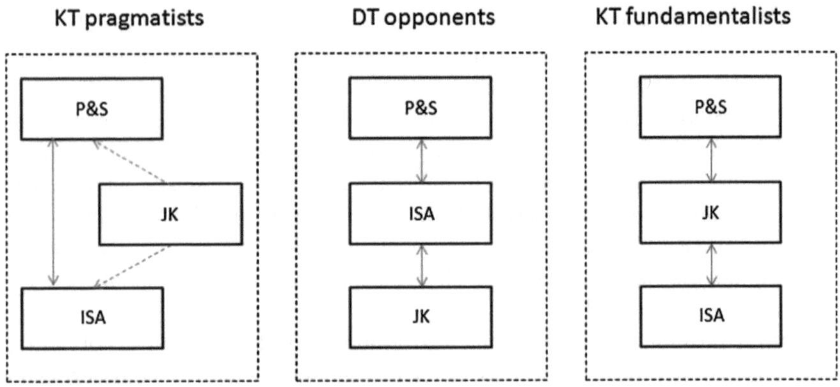

Fig. 1 Design Theory schools (*P&S* Purpose and Scope, *JK* Justificatory Knowledge, *ISA* IS Artifact)

In HCI contributions belonging to the 1st paradigm theories may (not necessarily) inform both the purpose and scope definition and the principles of form and function. This condition can be assimilated to the KT pragmatists school where the focus is on solving the problem of maximizing some utility function by the means of a technological tool with a pragmatic approach.

A different epistemological position can be assigned to most of the 2nd paradigm HCI contributions. These indeed share the characters of the DT opponents school, in which the knowledge base has the twofold role of providing input and receiving feedbacks in the form of scientific theories and methods, experience and expertise and previously developed design product and processes. In this case the design and the evaluation of the IT artifact plays the central role and the process for creating knowledge is well represented in Hevner's three cycle view [29]. In this view an iterative process bridges the design science activities with the contextual environment of the research project on the one side, and with the knowledge base of scientific foundations, experience, and expertise that informs the research project on the other.

The third paradigm is more difficult to conceptualize since purpose and scope of the theory and its principles of form and function are dependent on the context and on the construction of meaning that surrounds the situated activities in which technology is appropriated: the justificatory knowledge becomes a fundamental tool for providing the researcher with a palette of situated design and evaluation strategies and at the same time it is enriched by the better understanding of situated complex phenomena.

4 Conclusions

This chapter intends to be a first step of an intellectual discourse among IS and CHI scholars. Rather than at providing a closed reference framework, it aims at opening a debate on possible mutual enrichments. To this aim, we surveyed the epistemological positions of the two disciplines trying to underline distances and points of contact, and drew a parallel among HCI paradigms as delineated in [24] and the ISDT schools as proposed by [31], which we suggest as a possible "field for contaminations". Additional works surveying evaluation methods and results' generalization can further contribute to this debate informing the activities of researchers in these two fields.

References

1. Keen, P. G. W. (1980). *MIS Research: reference disciplines and a cumulative tradition* (pp. 9–18), in *Proceedings of the 1st International Conference on Information Systems*, E. McLean (Ed.), Philadelphia.
2. Culnan, M. J. (1987). Mapping the intellectual structure of MIS, 1980–1985: A co-citation analysis. *MIS Quarterly, 11*, 341–353.
3. Gregor, S. (2006). The nature of theory in information systems. *MIS Quarterly, 30*(3), 611–642.
4. Baskerville, R. L., & Myers, M. D. (2002). Information systems as a reference discipline. *MIS Quarterly, 26*(1), 1–14.
5. Davis, G. (2000). Information systems conceptual foundations: Looking backward and forward. In R. Baskerville, J. Stage, & J. DeGross (Eds.), *Organizational and social perspectives on information technology* (pp. 61–82). Boston: Kluwer.
6. Lee, A. S. (2001). Editorial. *MIS Quarterly, 25*(1), iii–vii.
7. Loebbecke, C., & Leidner, D. (2012). The contribution of top IS publications to subsequent research: A citation analysis. *Communications of the Association for Information Systems, 30*, 423–438.
8. Wade, M., Biehl, M., & Kim, H. (2006). Information systems is not a reference discipline (and what we can do about it). *Journal of AIS, 7*, 247–269.
9. Grover, V., Ayyagari, R., Gokhale, R., & Lim, J. (2006). A citation analysis of the evolution and state of information systems within a constellation of reference disciplines. *Journal of AIS, 7*, 270–325.
10. Avison, D., & Fitzgerald, G. (1995). *Information systems development: Methodologies, techniques and tools* (2nd ed.). London: McGraw-Hill.
11. Webster, J., & Watson, R. T. (2002). Analysing the past to prepare for the future: Writing a literature review. *MIS Quarterly, 26*(2), xiii–xxiii.
12. ACM SIGCHI (1996). *Special interest group on human-computer interaction curriculum development group*, Technical Report, http://old.sigchi.org/cdg/.
13. Spagnoletti, P., Baskerville, R., De Marco, M. (2012). The contributions of Alessandro D'Atri to organization and information systems studies. In: Baskerville et al. (Eds.), *Designing organizational systems: an interdisciplinary discourse*. LNISO, vol. 1, Heidelberg: Springer.
14. Spagnoletti, P., Tarantino, L. (2012). User centered systems design: The bridging role of justificatory knowledge. In: Baskerville et al. (Eds.), *Designing Organizational Systems: An Interdisciplinary Discourse*. LNISO vol.1, Heidelberg: Springer.

15. Lucas, H. C. (1975). Performance and the use of an information system. *Management Science, 21*(8), 908–919.
16. Mantei, M., & Teorey, T. (1989). Incorporating behavioral techniques into the system development life cycle. *MIS Quarterly, 13*(3), 257–274.
17. Zhang, P., Carey, J., Te'eni, D., & Tremaine, M. (2005). Integrating human-computer interaction development into the systems development life cycle: A methodology. *Communications of the AIS, 15*, 512–543.
18. Zhang, P., Li, N. (2005). The intellectual development of human-computer interaction research: A critical assessment of the MIS. *Information Systems Journal, 6*(11), 227–292. Citeseer. Retrieved from http://aisel.aisnet.org/jais/vol6/iss11/9/.
19. Zhang, P., Benbasat, I., Carey, J., Davis, F., Galletta, D., & Strong, D. (2002). Human-computer interaction research in the MIS discipline. *Communications of the Association for Information Systems, 9*(20), 334–355.
20. Grudin, J. (2005). Three faces of human-computer interaction. *Ieee Annals of the History of Computing, 27*, 46–62. IEEE educational activities department. doi:10.1109/MAHC.2005.67.
21. Lee, A. S. (2010). Retrospect and prospect: Information systems research in the last and next 25 years. *Journal of Information Technology, 25*, 336–348.
22. Hevner, A. R., March, S. T., Park, J., & Ram, S. (2004). Design science in information systems research. *MIS Quarterly, 28*(1), 75–105.
23. Kuhn, T. S. (1970). *The structure of scientific revolution* (2nd ed.). Chicago: University of Chicago Press.
24. Harrison, S., Sengers, P. Tatar, D. (2007). The three paradigms of HCI, *Proceedings of CHI 2007*, April 28–May 3, 2007, San Jose, USA.
25. Agre, P. E. (1997). *Computation and human experience*. Cambridge: Cambridge University Press.
26. Dourish, P. (2001). *Where the action is*. Cambridge: MIT Press.
27. Walls, J., Widmeyer, G. El., & Sawy, O. A. (1992). Building an information system design theory for vigilant EIS. *Information Systems Research, 3*(1), 36–59.
28. Gregor, S., & Jones, D. (2007). The anatomy of a design theory. *Journal of the Association for Information Systems, 8*(5), 312–335.
29. Hevner, A. (2007). A three cycle view of design science research. *Scandinavian Journal of Information Systems, 19*(2), 87–92.
30. Goldkuhl, G. (2004). Design theories in information systems—a need for multi-grounding. *Journal of Information Technology Theory and Application (JITTA), 6*(2), 7.
31. Fischer, C., Winter, R., & Wortmann, F. (2010). Design theory. *Business Information Systems Engineering, 2*(6), 387–390.

Enabling Domain Experts to Develop Usable Software Artifacts

Daniela Fogli and Antonio Piccinno

Abstract End-user development techniques are recently becoming a fundamental added value of information systems, since they allow system adaptation to the evolving needs of a company's users. To adequately manage the life cycle and code quality of software created through end-user development activities, end-user software engineering literature proposes a variety of methods. However, the underlying assumption is that end users carry out end-user development activities to adapt or develop software artifacts for their personal use. For this reason, the usability of the software artifacts resulting from the end user's work becomes a secondary issue. But, this is not true for multi-tiered proxy design problems, where the usability of software artifacts created by domain experts for other people is instead a fundamental issue. In this chapter, we analyze the approaches presented in literature that address this kind of problem, and propose a preliminary solution based on meta-design and meta-modeling.

Keywords End-user development · Meta-design · Meta-modeling · Usability

1 Introduction

The human–computer interaction (HCI) community has promoted user-centered design (UCD) approaches for more than twenty-five years, in order to favor the development of systems that end users find easy to use and to learn [1]. While in

D. Fogli (✉)
Dipartimento di Ingegneria dell'Informazione, Università degli Studi di Brescia, Brescia, Italy
e-mail: fogli@ing.unibs.it

A. Piccinno
Dipartimento di Informatica, Università degli Studi di Bari, Bari, Italy
e-mail: piccinno@di.uniba.it

P. Spagnoletti (ed.), *Organizational Change and Information Systems*, Lecture Notes in Information Systems and Organisation 2, DOI: 10.1007/978-3-642-37228-5_41,

UCD potential end users are only interviewed or observed, thus playing a passive role in design, participatory design (PD) approaches make a step further, by promoting a more active involvement of end users throughout the system design process [2].

On the other hand, private and public companies are more and more frequently requiring information systems that are flexible enough to be adapted to the variety of their users and to the dynamic markets in which they need to operate [3]. End-user development (EUD) methods are recently proposed to build such flexible systems and support their adaptation directly on behalf of end users [4]. More specifically, EUD leads to transfer to end users part of the activities that are traditionally performed by software developers, namely, not only software adaptation and extension by means of end-user programming (EUP) techniques, but also interaction design, system prototyping, and software design, customization, and maintenance. Particularly, EUD research focuses the attention on those people who use software systems as part of their daily life or daily work, but who are not interested in computers per se [5]. These people have no or few competencies in information technologies and often are not willing to acquire them. This aspect raises many doubts in the software engineering community, which insists on the importance of skilled, professional software developers to guarantee software correctness, efficiency, maintainability, and security [6].

The issue of software quality in EUD is being addressed in the so-called end-user software engineering (EUSE) area [7]. A variety of methods are proposed for requirement analysis and specification, system design and reuse, verification and testing, code debugging, which could be easily applied by non-professional software developers. However, a further and important issue related to EUD that has not been adequately addressed yet is the usability of the software artifacts developed by end users. In fact, in this research area, the term 'usability' is usually referred to the easiness of use of the end-user programming language/paradigm [8] or to the engaging metaphor of the EUD environment [9]; whilst, few words are spent for the usability of the results of the EUD activity.

On the other hand, EUSE mainly considers EUP and EUD as activities that create programs for personal rather than public use, thus distinguishing them from professional programming, which has the goal of developing code for others to use [7]. In this perspective, the usability issue may not be a priority. However, this distinction becomes blurred when the so-called multi-tiered proxy design problems are considered [10]. These kinds of problems can be described as follows: (1) in a given domain there are end users who need software artifacts to carry out some personal activity, but who are neither able nor interested in participating in their development; (2) in the same domain, there are also domain experts, who are able to describe the software artifacts that should be designed for the end users, but who are not able to create the needed technologies; (3) finally, there are software professionals who know how to develop technical systems, but who are unable to offer this service directly to end users without the help of domain experts. This situation occurred for example in the MAPS project, which aimed to provide a simple, PDA-based device that prompts instructions to support a person with cognitive disabilities in the accomplishment of her/his daily tasks [10]. Software professionals created a simple editing tool to allow caregivers (domain experts) developing prompting systems customized to the characteristics of the disabled people (end users). The use of the editing tool does not require caregivers to have programming skills.

As the MAPS project, most proposals addressing multi-tiered proxy design problems are based on a meta-design paradigm [11] and on the development of a hierarchy of interactive environments (e.g., [12–14]). Particularly, in this hierarchy, EUD environments are crucial to support domain experts to play the role of end-user developers by creating software artifacts for the actual end users. As a consequence, the usability of such software artifacts goes back to being a fundamental feature. Here, we have a situation similar to that one leading to UCD and PD approaches: "designers are not users" [15] and this favors the development of systems that users find difficult to use. In addition, when such designers are end-user developers, the creation of usable systems becomes a greater challenge, because end-user developers are often unwitting programmers and have a vague understanding of the usability concept. In fact, the knowledge needed to design an effective and usable interactive system is usually distributed among domain experts, software engineers and HCI experts. Hence, the design of an interactive system should be a multi-facet activity requiring the collaboration of experts from these communities [16].

To cope with the multi-tiered and multi-facet design problem, we need a design approach where the usability of software artifacts is guaranteed in advance by the approach itself. In the following, we propose an approach that capitalizes on the ideas at the basis of the software shaping workshop (SSW) methodology [14], but that generalizes them to take care of the usability issue. For the sake of chapter clearness, let us briefly recall here the main characteristics of the SSW methodology. SSWs are software environments where professional or non-professional software developers find all and only the objects and tools necessary to shape their software artifacts. SSWs are organized according to a three-level hierarchy: (1) at the meta-design level, there are SSWs used by software engineers to create system workshops for domain experts; (2) at the design level, domain experts use system workshops to cooperate in the design, implementation, and validation of application workshops for end users; (3) at the use level, end users carry out their tasks through application workshops created at the design level and customized to their needs, culture, and skills.

In this chapter, we describe an approach to enabling domain experts to cope with the usability of the software artifacts they develop (application workshops, in the SSW terminology). Then, we show how the proposed solution has been implemented in two different domains.

2 Addressing Usability Through Meta-Design and Meta-Modeling

With respect to the SSW methodology, the approach proposed here deepens the activities to be carried out in the meta-design phase. Particularly, a (meta-)design team, including not only software engineers, but also HCI specialists and domain experts, defines at first the conceptual model of the software environments devoted to end users. This activity should be carried out through participatory design techniques [2], such as meetings among all stakeholders to perform task and scenario-based analysis, or mock-up development. Metaphor and interaction style of the environments for end users are thus defined; they will strongly depend on domain characteristics and users' habits. For example, in Ref. [12] the logbook metaphor was proposed to support the work of epathologists: a virtual logbook is the digital counterpart of a paper-based archive used by physicians to record their data and activities. In the mechanical engineering domain, we adopted the metaphor of the artisan workshop [9]; whilst, in the neuroradiology field, a workbench enriched with a virtual diaphanoscope became the metaphor to support medical image annotation and consultation exchange [14].

After the conceptual model definition, the design team must define a meta-model that describes and generalizes the structure and properties of the software environments devoted to end users. This meta-model could be represented as a UML class diagram, an ontology, or an XML schema. Then, members of the design team will collaborate to the development of the EUD environment that supports the creation of instances of the meta-model, namely of specifications of the software environments for end users. To conclude the meta-design phase, software engineers must create an interpreter of the meta-model instances, capable of generating the software environments described by such instances. This interpreter must generate environments that satisfy the conceptual model previously defined by the design team. In this way, the usability of EUD products does not depend anymore on the capability of end-user developers, but is a responsibility of the design team that designs the conceptual model, defines the meta-model and creates the EUD environment, and of the software developers who develop the software generator according to the defined conceptual model. Even though one can object that this approach may limit end user developers' creativity, this is a way to have more control on their activity and avoid the creation of unusable products.

3 First Case Study: EUD in the e-Government Domain

In Ref. [17] we presented a meta-design approach to the development of e-government services. Here, software engineers, HCI specialists and civil servants (domain experts), i.e., the design team, have collaborated to define the characteristics of online services for booking appointments at the different

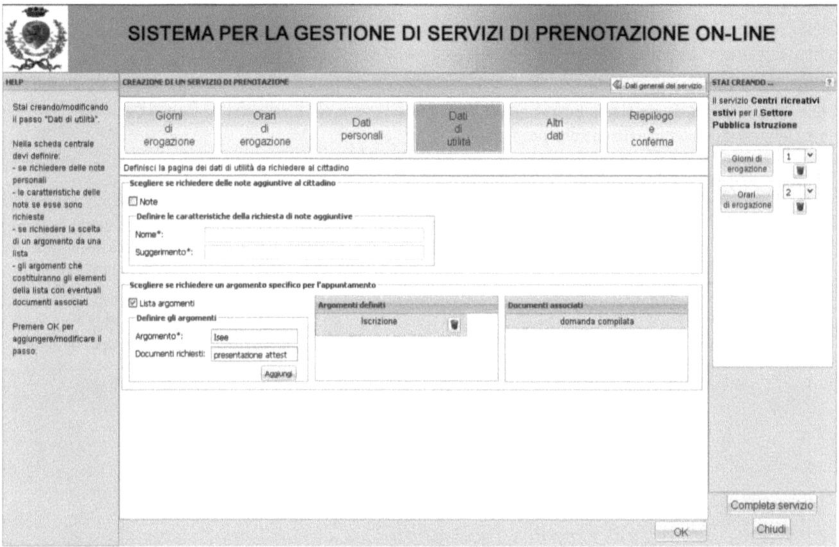

Fig. 1 EUD environment for the e-government case study

counters of a government agency. The conceptual model of these services is based on a form-based, step-by-step interaction style; indeed, it recalls the traditional way of communication between citizens and government agencies. The design activity led then to define a meta-model representing the considered class of services, which was then represented by software engineers through an XML schema. Then, the team designed an EUD environment able to support civil servants in creating instances of the XML schema, namely XML documents describing the steps of the appointment reservation services. The EUD environment does not force domain experts to write any XML code, neither to know the underlying meta-model, but just requires them filling in forms that allow defining the requests for citizens in each interaction step of the service under creation. Steps may be mandatory or optional, and the civil servant can decide their sequence order.

A screenshot of the EUD environment is shown in Fig. 1. Here, the user has just created two steps of the e-government services: (1) the step for choosing the date of the appointment among a set of dates specified by the civil servant through a set of constraints, (2) the step for choosing the time of the appointment from a list of times. These two steps have been created by selecting the respective buttons in the toolbar on the top of the page, and have become available for future access and modification as selectable widgets in the summary section on the right side of the page. In the current state (Fig. 1), the domain expert is defining the step "Topics and Notes", by creating the list of appointment topics among which the citizen can make a selection and by associating text that indicates the papers the citizen must bring to the appointment. The domain expert can also add a request for notes, but,

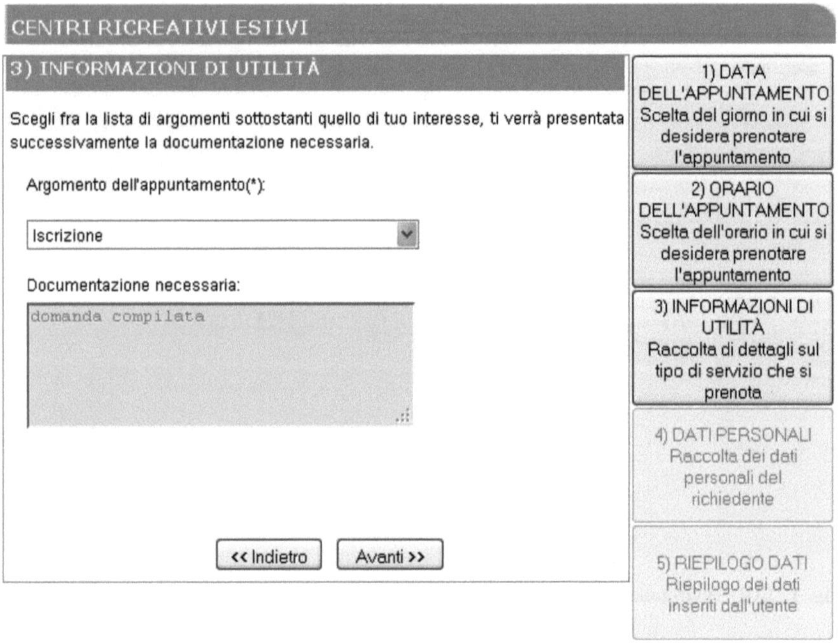

Fig. 2 A step of a web application for citizens

in this case, she decided not to include it. The XML document obtained after the interaction with the EUD environment is interpreted by a software application developed by software engineers to generate the actual web pages of the service. For example, Fig. 2 shows the page implementing the "Topics and Notes" step defined in the EUD environment.

Both the EUD environment and the web applications created through EUD have been judged usable by civil servants and citizens respectively [17]. In particular, we have conducted a test with four citizens to assess the usability of two appointment reservation services created with our EUD environment. Only the two oldest participants (age ranging from 60 to 70) encountered some minor problems, due to their low familiarity with computer technologies. However, their performance improved significantly during the use of the second service, thus demonstrating that a little experience is sufficient to interact easily with e-government services generated with this approach.

4 Second Case Study: EUD for Mass Customization

The second case study is in the classic style furniture domain [18]. In this case, a company (Maiellaro s.r.l.) producing classic style furniture only produces those pieces that are ordered by a customer. Customers provide a description of the piece of

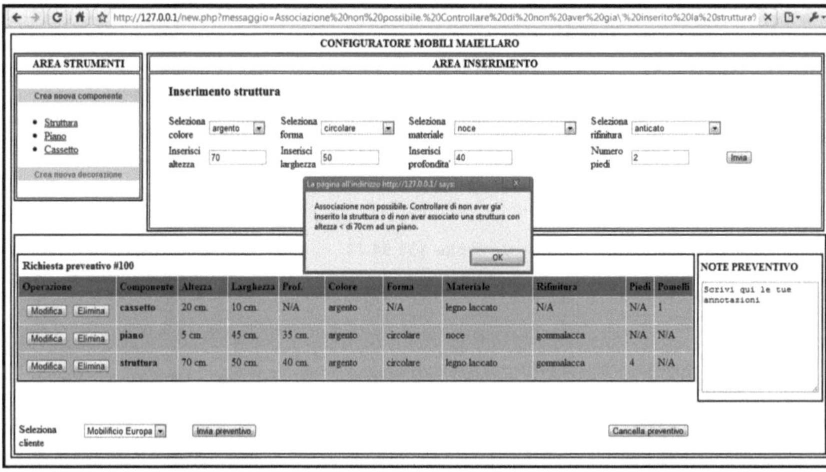

Fig. 3 EUD environment for the classic style furniture case study

furniture they want, which may be composed of parts chosen from different items in the available catalogues, by possibly specifying dimensions, type of wood and other characteristics. One of the main problems in this case study is that the information needed to customize a piece of furniture are scattered in different archives, i.e., the catalogue of Maiellaro company and the catalogues of Maiellaro's suppliers. These suppliers' catalogues are very diverse and heterogeneous because they refer to various crafts and arts (e.g., glass suppliers, wood artisans). Thus, it is really difficult to have an overall view on all existing information. Another problem is driving customers in selecting components of items in the catalogues and allowing them to assemble such components in reasonable ways to create a new piece.

To cope with this problem, the design team including software engineers, HCI experts, and domain experts (managing director, technical department employees, sales office employees) defined the conceptual model of a software environment for customers (end users). This conceptual model resembles the current end-user practice: the sales office employee helps customers choose and customize their pieces of furniture by showing pieces in different catalogues taken from a bookcase and put on a bench; customers are thus allowed to customize the desired furniture by replacing and personalizing components chosen from different pieces of furniture belonging to possibly different catalogues.

As a consequence, the adopted meta-model consists of an ontology describing the components of each piece of furniture and their properties. The ontology allows also setting all rules and constraints to assemble various components in order to generate all and only those pieces of furniture that are considered by the ontology.

The design activity then led the design team to develop a prototype of an environment able to support technical department employees in accessing and updating ontology properties and rules (Fig. 3), without being aware that they are manipulating an ontology.

Fig. 4 The customization of classic style furniture by end users

The design team finally developed the software environment for customers, whose specific instantiation depends on the underlying ontology. A possible environment for customers is reported in Fig. 4, which shows a bench providing a unified view of all available catalogues of Maiellaro and Maiellaro's suppliers and allowing the shaping of the desired piece of furniture by means of piece selection and composition. A preliminary usability evaluation of this environment, involving three customers, has been conducted with very positive results.

5 Discussion and Conclusion

The approach presented in this chapter does not conceive EUD as direct creation of code on behalf of end-user developers, but as the instantiation of a meta-model that represents a domain-dependent class of software environments for end users. Usability of the resulting environments is achieved through a meta-design activity, carried out through user-centered and participatory methods. To guarantee usability, however, flexibility of the EUD activities must be restricted. In our approach this is obtained by creating domain-dependent conceptual models and by driving and controlling end-user developers' interaction with the EUD environment. The trade-off between the flexibility of EUD tools and the usability of EUD products is an important aspect that deserves, in our opinion, an additional reflection within the EUD community in the next years. This aspect is even of particular importance in the case of information systems, where end-user developers are often business managers who must design or customize software artifacts for other users, such as company employees or customers. Maybe the trade-off could be balanced by realizing the vision of "EUD as a learning process" discussed in [19]. Anyway, the approach proposed in this chapter tries to respond to the doubts of the software engineering community with respect to EUP and EUD [6]: the responsibility of developing the meta-model and its interpreter should remain on the shoulder of software engineers, who may thus guarantee that what is created by end-user developers is not only usable, but also effective and efficient.

References

1. Norman, D. A., & Draper, S. W. (1986). *User-centered system design: New perspectives on human–computer interaction*. Hillsdale: Lawrence Erlbaum Ass.
2. Schuler, D., & Namioka, A. (1993). *Participatory design. Principles and practice*. Hillsdale: Lawrence Erlbaum Ass.
3. Dörner, C., Heß, J., & Pipek, V. (2007). Improving information systems by end-user development: A case study. In: *Proceedings ECIS 2007* (pp. 783–794). St. Gallen, Switzerland.
4. Lieberman, H., Paternò, F., & Wulf, V. (2006). *End-user development*. Dordrecht: Springer.
5. Cypher, A. (1993). *Watch what i do: Programming by demonstration*. Cambridge: The MIT Press.
6. Harrison, W. (2004). The dangers of end-user programming. *IEEE Software*, *21*, 5–7.
7. Ko, A. J., Abraham, R., Beckwith, L., Blackwell, A. F., Burnett, M., Erwig, M., Scaffidi, C., Lawrance, J., Lieberman, H., Myers, B., Rosson, M. B., Rothermel, G., Shaw, M., & Wiedenbeck, S. (2011). The state of the art in end-user software engineering. *ACM Computing Surveys*, *43*(3), 21:1–21:44.
8. Blackwell, A. F. (2006). Psychological issues in end-user programming. In H. Lieberman, F. Paternò, & V. Wulf (Eds.), *End-user development* (pp. 9–30). Dordrecht: Springer.
9. Fogli, D., & Piccinno, A. (2005). Environments to support context and emotion aware visual interaction. *International Journal of Visual Languages and Computing, 16*, 386–405.
10. Carmien, S., Dawe, M., Fischer, G., Gorman, A., Kintsch, A., Sullivan, & J. F. J. (2005) Socio-technical environments supporting people with cognitive disabilities using public transportation. *ACM Transactions on Computer-Human Interaction*, *12*, 233–262.
11. Fischer, G., Giaccardi, E., Ye, Y., Sutcliffe, A. G., & Mehandjiev, N. (2004). Meta-design: A manifesto for end-user development. *Communication of the ACM, 47*(9), 33–37.
12. Mussio, P., Finadri, M., Gentini, P., & Colombo, F. (1992). A bootstrap approach to visual user-interface design and development. *The Visual Computer, 8*(2), 75–93.
13. Ginige, A., & De Silva, B.: CBEADS©: A framework to support meta-design paradigm. In: *Proceedings HCII 2007. LNCS* (Vol. 4554, pp. 107–116). Heidelberg: Springer.
14. Costabile, M. F., Fogli, D., Lanzilotti, R., Mussio, P., & Piccinno, A. (2006). Supporting work practice through end-user development environments. *Journal of Organizational and End User Computing, 18*(4), 43–65.
15. Nielsen, J. (1993). *Usability engineering*. San Diego: Academic Press.
16. Fogli, D., Marcante, A., Mussio, P., Parasiliti Provenza, L., & Piccinno, A. (2007). Multi-facet design of interactive systems through visual languages. In: F. Ferri (Ed.), *Visual languages for interactive computing: Definitions and formalizations* (pp. 174–204). Hershey: IGI Global.

17. Fogli, D., & Parasiliti Provenza, L. (2012). A meta-design approach to the development of e-government services. *International Journal of Visual Languages and Computing, 23*(2), 47–62.
18. Ardito, C., Barricelli, B. R., Buono, P., Costabile, M. F., Lanzilotti, R., Piccinno, A., & Valtolina, S. (2011). An ontology-based approach to product customization. In: *Proceedings IS-EUD 2011. LNCS* (vol. 6654, pp. 92–106). Heidelberg: Springer.
19. Repenning, A., & Ioannidou, A. (2006). What makes end-user development tick? 13 design guidelines. In H. Lieberman, F. Paternò, & V. Wulf (Eds.), *End-user development* (pp. 51–85). Dordrecht: Springer.

Interactive Visualization Modeling with CoDe: An Application to Entomological Data

Stefania Laudonia, Marina Margiotta and Maurizio Tucci

Abstract A taxonomy of typical interaction techniques is proposed in [1], where seven categories of information visualizations provided by commercial systems are considered. This framework gives an initial foundation toward a deeper understanding of interaction in Information Visualization, helping discussion and evaluation of interaction techniques. In this chapter we propose a methodology for the specification and design of complex interactive visualizations as an extension of the graphic language CoDe [2]. Based on the seven categories introduced in [1], we add new interaction operators to CoDe, to enable a visualization designer to specify multiple perspectives of a data set, without losing the underlying mental map of the considered information. The new version of CoDe allows to manage some interaction techniques which are difficult to classify and do not quite fit into any of the categories above. Some applications of the proposed methodology to design interactive visualizations of entomological data are provided as a case study.

Keywords Information visualization · Visual analytics · Interaction model · CoDe language · Entomology

---

S. Laudonia (✉) · M. Margiotta
Dipartimento di Entomologia e Zoologia Agraria "Filippo Silvestri", University of Naples "Federico II", Portici, Naples, Italy
e-mail: laudonia@unina.it

M. Margiotta
e-mail: ma.margiotta@studenti.unina.it

M. Tucci
University of Salerno, Fisciano, Salerno, Italy
e-mail: mtucci@unisa.it

P. Spagnoletti (ed.), *Organizational Change and Information Systems*, Lecture Notes in Information Systems and Organisation 2, DOI: 10.1007/978-3-642-37228-5_42,

1 Introduction

Information Visualization systems provide users with a broad set of interaction techniques to achieve a variety of views that help understanding of the represented information amplifying human cognitive capabilities [3, 4].

Observing that many different styles of interaction serve a relative small set of user purposes, in [1] the authors propose seven categories of interaction techniques denoted as: *Select, Explore, Reconfigure, Encode, Abstract/Elaborate, Filter, Connect*. This taxonomy classifies several types of interactions with respect to the user objectives and the visualization techniques used to accomplish them. However, some techniques are difficult to classify and do not quite fit into any one of the categories, as the "water level" feature, a technique that adds a layer to mark a threshold, which play the role of a cognitive aid to augment user's ability to compare values.

On the other hand, faced with the considerable attention to the development of new techniques for interaction, less emphasis is placed on the definition of methodologies that allow the user to effectively manage the *mental map* associated with each complex view, both to control the effects of modifications of dynamic interactions and to orient the choice in the large number of available techniques.

With the aim of providing a contribution to these issues, this work proposes an approach to model interaction by exploiting the design methodology of complex visualizations based on the graphic language *Co*mplexity *De*sign (CoDe) introduced in [2]. This methodology allows designers to specify the structure of a complex visualization, named *CoDe Model*, by means of the relationship connections between the considered information items that the user aims to highlight in the view. Then, the design of the visualization is completed by a choice of aesthetic features concerning the representation of information items by means of standard graphs properly interconnected.

The CoDe graphic language is based on the First Order Logic paradigm. Several *functions* allow the designer to build complex graphic terms using the available information items which are represented by standard graphs that may overlap, even by sharing part of the display area. A different kind of functions, named *visualization operators*, do not concern the structure of terms since only modifies viewing parameters to improve the efficiency and the aesthetic impact of visual representation. The design process based on the CoDe Model has an interactive part. Indeed, the user can iteratively edit the CoDe Model by adding or deleting items and relations that, through a user interface, are connected to the available data and are consistently displayed. A first system that allows the construction of the CoDe Model and the implementation of its views has been developed in order to visualize static reports extracted from a data warehouse by using OLAP operations [5].

In this work the CoDe Model is exploited to model interactive visualizations. This can be achieved by extending the set of *visualization operators* on the basis of the taxonomy proposed in [1]. Interactive operators, explicitly represented in the

CoDe Model, support data exploration and enable users to have multiple perspectives and gain insight on the data set, without losing the underling *mental map* of the considered information items. In other words, a CoDe Model represents in the same framework both the relationship network of the information items, and the temporal characteristics of the interaction which involves changes over time of the visualization [1].

In Sect. 2 we describe the main features of the CoDe Model and its ability to model interaction. Defining two levels of interaction, we also clarify the notion of equivalence between views obtained through interaction techniques. Section 3 provides some examples of application of the proposed methodology on various kinds of entomological data. Section 4 gives some concluding remarks and future works.

2 Modeling Interaction with the Graphic Language CoDe

The graphic language CoDe [2] aims to provide an easy translation medium between the ground data and the conceptual organization of their visualization. The definition of CoDe is based on the idea that a visual representation of complex information should be considered as a "statement" of a formal language in the *First Order Logic paradigm* [6]. Thus, by an ontological point of view, a graphic visualization can be considered as made of *terms*, i.e. *information items* represented by means of suitable graph structures, and *relations* between these terms. According to this paradigm, the architectural organization of a display can be described at an abstract level by a graphic representation named *CoDe Model.*

Following [7], we define a *graph* the visualization of information carried out by a double-entry table. Graphs are the starting set of terms in *CoDe*. These information items are represented by blue rectangles with a label denoting the related double-entry table, as shown in Fig. 1.

To increase the information carried out by a graph, additional visual elements can be obtained by using composition or transformation *functions* applied to information items. These functions are constructors of graphs representing more complex information, and are represented as blue arrows connecting the involved terms. Another kind of functions, named *visualization operators*, do not concern the structure of the considered data, and are introduced to modify the aesthetic impact or to add labels and cognitive aids. They are represented as green ellipses and are connected to the involved terms by green arrows. Some examples of CoDe Model representing the structure of complex visualizations are given in [2, 5].

In [2] the syntactic and semantic formal definitions of the CoDe language can be found. Here we provide an intuitive idea of the basic features by describing the

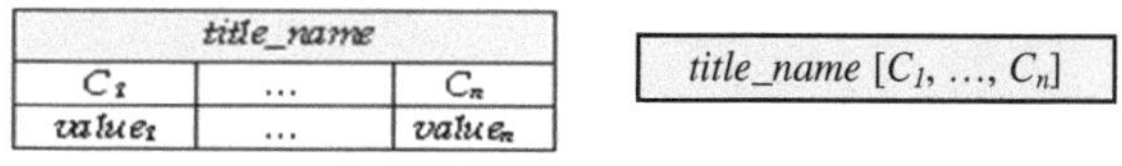

Fig. 1 A double entry table and the related term in the graphic language CoDe

SUM_i function. This function applies to a couple of double entry tables such that the value of the *i*th component in the first table is the sum of the data series in the second one. As an example, let a first table contain the total numbers of enrolled, no longer enrolled and graduate students at the end of a fixed period of three years, and let a second table contain the number of graduate students in each year of the fixed period.

Since the third component of the first table is the sum of the values in the second one, we can use the *SUM_3* function to construct a more complex information item to summarize the two tables in a single structure. A new CoDe term represents the relation between the two tables as shown in the left side of Fig. 2. The right side shows two possible visualizations by standard graphs Bar-Chart, Pie and Histogram.

Changing the choice of graph types, we obtain visualizations that can appear very different, but that are semantically equivalent, as they represent the same information. Thus, the CoDe model can be considered as a sort of *conceptual map* providing a tool to manage the complexity of visualized information, in order to organize them in efficient graphical view, according to the definition of *efficiency* of a visualization given by Bertin [7]: "The most efficient (graphic) construction are those in which any question, whatever its type and level, can be answered in a single instant of perception, that is, in a single image".

By adding suitable visualization operators to the CoDe Model, we can represent the application of several types of interaction techniques. To this aim, we have extended the set of visualization operators to include the taxonomy proposed in [1] based on a classification of the interaction techniques into seven categories called: *Select, Explore, Reconfigure, Encode, Abstract/Elaborate, Filter, Connect.* Then, the label of a visualization operator provides both the name of the interaction technique and the category to which it belongs. As an example, the category *Encode* includes the interaction technique which allows to represent values by using a spectrum of color, and this technique is represented by the visualization operator of the CoDe language named *COLOR*. Thus the label is *Encode COLOR*.

It is also possible to represent interaction techniques that do not fit easily into any category proposed in [1]. In that chapter, the authors mention the "water

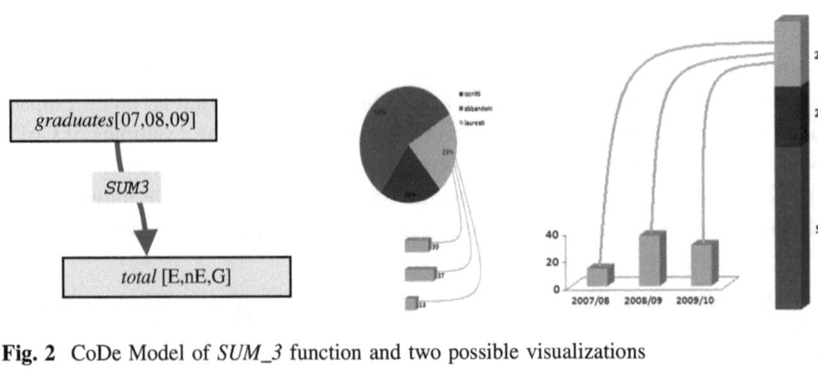

Fig. 2 CoDe Model of *SUM_3* function and two possible visualizations

level" technique which adds a layer to only visualize the values over a given threshold in order to make easier to compare the displayed values. This technique can be represented by the *ADD* visualization operator, which allows to enter user-defined graphic elements in the view.

To represent the various kinds of interaction techniques in a CoDe Model, let us define two *interaction levels*:

- *Bottom-level interactions*, that modify aesthetic features or introduce cognitive aids, without changing the information items and their relationships in the CoDe Model;
- *Top-level interactions*, that introduce new items or relations which change the CoDe Model structure.

The bottom-level interactions provide *equivalent* visualizations, while the top-level interactions provide *non equivalent* visualizations. In the next section some examples of these interaction levels are given.

3 Statistics and Relational Network Visualization in Entomology

The CoDe based approach to the design of visualizations can be applied to display statistical data in a very intuitive way, enhancing the communication impact of visualization. As a case study, we have applied the methodology based on CoDe model extended with interactive operators to design views of statistical analysis in Entomology. In a first example of application, the average number of eggs of *Glycaspis brimblecombei* Moore (Hemiptera: Psyllidae) is considered, where the data are collected in a series of samples on eucalyptus plants in a given site [8].

The aim of data visualization is to display data in a form that emphasizes the connections between the four types of standard graphs given in Fig. 3. Each graph separately represents one of the following statistical concepts: (1) sample values, (2) frequency distribution, (3) cumulative frequency function, (4) statistical indexes given by minimum, maximum and quartiles (box-whiskers plot).

We notice that it is usual to see separate representations of these concepts with a wide variety of techniques, but there is a lack of visualization techniques to represent functional ties that exist between these notions. While expert users develop their own conceptual maps to read the proper connections between separate graphs, this information is not apparent to people not familiar with statistical concepts. In addition, even an expert user can benefit from the unitary view of the four graphs with related functional links, since it provides an organic framework and an overall representation of all considered information.

In Fig. 4 the four graphs are suitably connected and this view allows to stress the functional relationships existing between data. In particular, the position of quartiles is included consistently in all charts, explicitly highlighting its meaning.

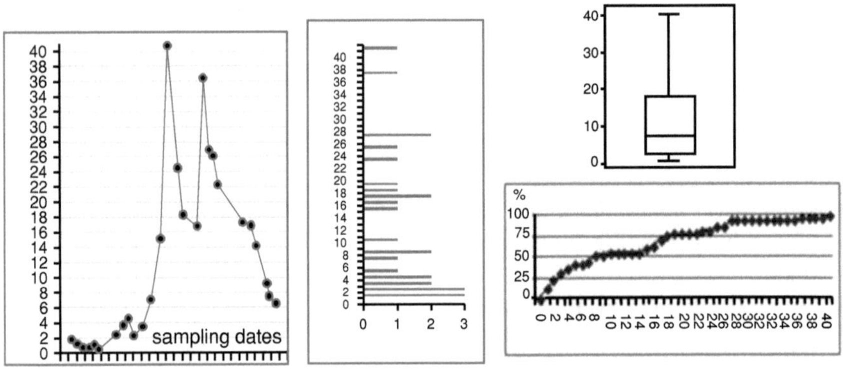

Fig. 3 Sample values, frequency distribution, cumulative frequency distribution, quantiles

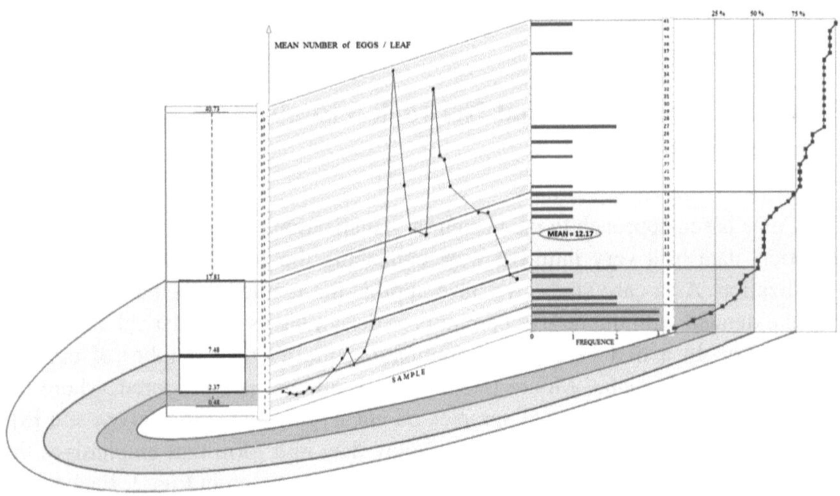

Fig. 4 A first visualization of the CoDe model of Fig. 5

The CoDe Model of complex visualization in Fig. 4 is given on the right side of Fig. 5.

The interaction operator Reconfigure in the CoDe Model allows the application of interaction techniques belonging to this category. As an example, we can overlap the two graphs providing the frequency distribution and the cumulative function. This is a bottom-level interaction that does not change the relationships layout represented in the CoDe Model of Fig. 5. Then, a possible equivalent visualization obtained by applying this interaction operator is given in the left side of Fig. 5.

The position of the mean value can be marked exploiting the "water level" interactive technique, in order to aid an easy comparison with quartiles in each graph. This kind of interaction does not fall into the categories considered in [1],

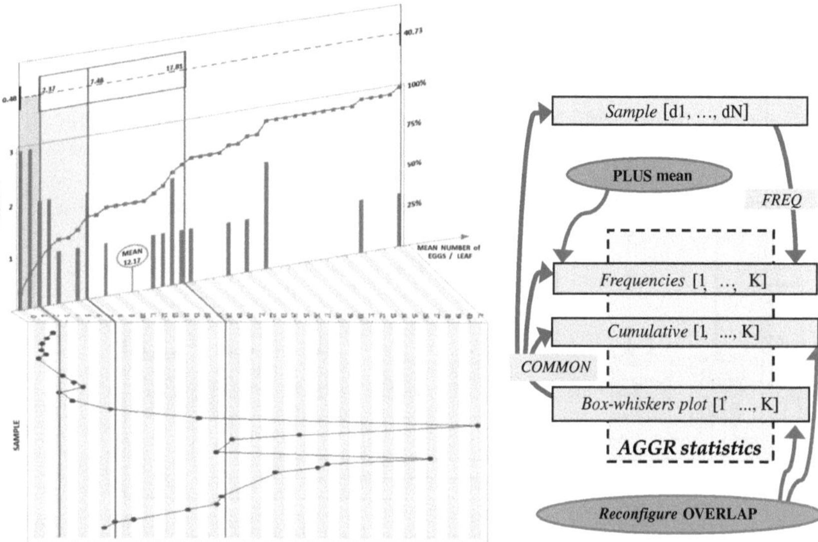

Fig. 5 Visualization of the CoDe model by applying a *Reconfigure* operator

but it can be represented in CoDe using the visualization operator *PLUS*, which allows the insertion in the view of user-defined graphic elements.

As another example, let us consider the entomophagus enemies of the *Phyllonorycter* (=*Lithocolletis*) *millierella* (Stgr.) [9]. In this case non-quantitative information is represented, namely a network of interrelations described by yes/no Boolean functions. The CoDe Model in Fig. 6 provides the relations between predator/parasite and prey at three different stages of development, and the relationships between the various species. A possible visualization is given in Fig. 7.

The enemies are represented by squares on the bottom of the display, while the three rectangles grouped on the top represent the three preimmaginal stages of the prey (*larva 1, larva 2, chrysalis*). Moreover, in order to provide an efficient representation of the various kinds of enemy attack (*endofagus parasite, ectofagus parasite, predator*), the visualization function *PLUS* allows to include a legend providing a suitable graphic encoding of these attacks. In particular, the difference between endofagus and ectofagus is represented by the position of a dot inside or outside, respectively, of the ellipse in the rectangle representing a stage of the prey.

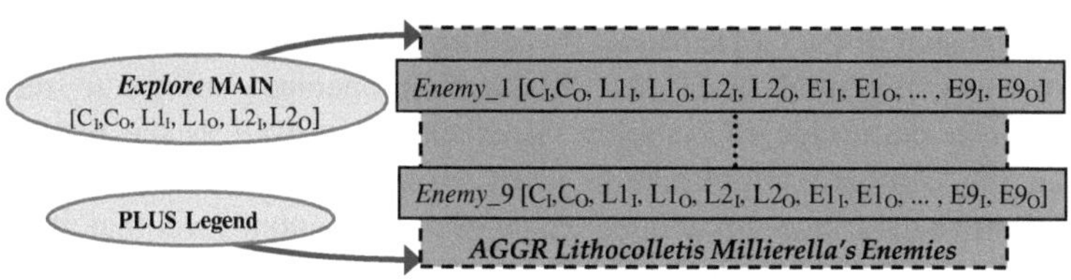

Fig. 6 CoDe Model of *Lithocolletis Millierella's* predator/parasite relations

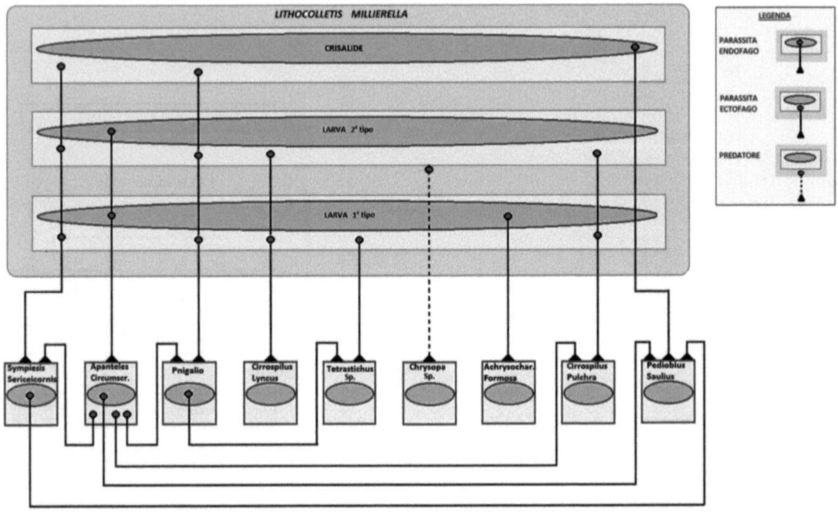

Fig. 7 Visualization of Lithocolletis *Millierella's* predator/parasite relations

The visualization function "Explore" shown in the CoDe Model, allows the application of the "Direct-Walk" interaction technique belonging to this category. Then, when one of the squares on the bottom of the visualization is clicked, the related insect moves to the top of the display and it becomes the reference for the enumeration of the predators/parasites enemies. In the CoDe Model the reference specification is given by the *MAIN* visualization operator. Since the choice of a new reference insect provides a different set of enemies, the information items represented into the CoDe Model are changed. This is a top-level interaction which modify the CoDe Model thus providing non equivalent visualizations.

4 Conclusions and Future Work

The strengthening of tools providing more and more interaction techniques can lead to confused and intricated images, which emphasize aesthetic effects at the expense of information's clarity. Moreover, user's creativity can represent the same semantic contents through visualizations with extremely different graphic impact.

The extension of the CoDe Model by adding the interactive operators based on the taxonomy proposed in [1] as visualization operators allows to represent interaction in the design of complex visualizations as well as the relationships between the considered information items. Thus, two levels of interaction in information visualization are defined: changes at the bottom-level that affect only the aesthetic aspects or the inclusion of cognitive aids (for example, by selecting different types of graphs to represent the information items or by entering "water level" features, etc.). In these cases the CoDe Model structure is not modified and we obtain equivalent visualizations. On the contrary, interactions at the top-level, are changes that modify the relation structure and/or the information items (for example, by selecting a different element with the "Direct-Walk" interaction technique). In these cases the CoDe Model can be modified and semantically different visualizations are obtained.

The CoDe Model based modeling allows to capture a broader spectrum of interaction techniques, by merging the taxonomy proposed in [1] into the descriptive capabilities of the CoDe language. The flexibility of the relationships network of the Code Model allows the user both to experiment different organization of information items and to vary the aesthetic choices. Finally, user's creativity is enhanced thanks to the fact that in the design of complex view, the CoDe Model eliminates the need to choose the graph types for the representation of information items, as well as all the features of aesthetic style, thus leaving the attention focused on the structuring and the significance of the view. In the phase of implementation of the CoDe Model, these choices can be accomplished with great flexibility, and made even more effective thanks to interaction operators that provide a guide to the use of available interactive techniques.

As a future work, we plan to apply the proposed extension of the CoDe Model in the design of interactive visualizations in a GIS project that provides information to support the integrated pest management in precision agriculture.

References

1. Soo Yi J., ah Kang Y., Stasko J. T. (2007). Toward a deeper understanding of the role of interaction in information visualization. *IEEE Transaction on Visualization and Computer Graphics*, *13*(6), 1224–1231.
2. Ciuccarelli, P., Sessa, M. I., Tucci, M. (2010, October, 8–9) *CoDe*: a Graphic language for complex system visualization. In *Proceedings of ITAIS 2010, Naples* (pp. 1–8).
3. Beaudouin-Lafon, M. (2004). Designing interaction, not interfaces. In *Proceedings of AVI'04, Gallipoli (LE), Italy* (pp. 15–22).
4. Thomas, J. J., & Cook, K. A. (2005). *Illuminating the path*. Los Alamitos: IEEE.
5. Risi, M., Sessa, M. I., Tortora, G., Tucci, M. (2011, June, 26–29). Visualizing information in data warehouse reports. In *Proceedings of SEBD 2011* (pp. 246–257). Italy: Maratea.
6. Russel, S., & Norvig, P. (2009). *Artificial intelligence: A modern approach* (3rd ed.). Upper Saddle River: Prentice Hall.
7. Bertin, J. (1983). *Semiology of graphics: Diagrams, networks, maps*. Madison: University of Wisconsin Press.
8. Laudonia, S., & Margiotta, M. (2012). Seasonal phenology of *Glycaspis brimblecombei* Moore (Hemiptera: Psyllidae), the red gum lerp psyllid, in Italy, (technical report 2012).
9. Viggiani, G. (1997). *Lotta biologica ed integrata nelle difesa fitosanitaria* (Vol. 1 pp. 42–43). Napoli: Liguori Editore.

Automatic Usability Evaluation of GUI: A Front-side Approach Using No Source Code Information

Rosanna Cassino and Maurizio Tucci

Abstract The usability of a software system and especially of its user interface now has become crucial and decisive for the success of the application itself. The usability evaluation can be performed by several techniques: classical methods such as tests are performed by experts or end users tester. These approaches require long and expensive testing phases. For this reason, in recent years there has been a rapid spread of automatic tools of evaluation, which allow achieving more objectives in a simple, rapid and economical manner. In this work, we describe an approach to evaluate the usability of a GUI analyzing only its graphical output. The implemented tool allows measuring any usability metrics of usability of the graphical interface of an application using a front-size technique that adopts image processing algorithms to identify and classify the interface components and an automatic interaction system to analyze the dynamic mechanisms. The approach is illustrated using the example of the analysis of a web interface.

Keywords GUI usability · Evaluation tools

1 Introduction

The GUI is a development paradigm that allows the user to interact directly with the computer by manipulating graphical objects. In other words, it is the level of a software application that takes care of the dialogue between the user and the system using a graphical environment. In this perspective, several application

R. Cassino (✉) · M. Tucci
Università di Salerno, Salerno, Italy
e-mail: rcassino@unisa.it

M. Tucci
e-mail: mtucci@unisa.it

P. Spagnoletti (ed.), *Organizational Change and Information Systems*, Lecture Notes in Information Systems and Organisation 2, DOI: 10.1007/978-3-642-37228-5_43,

support sophisticated interfaces often characterized by an ever increasing complexity in terms of functionality, look and feel and behavior. Then, since much of the judgment of a user about an application is determined by the quality of its interface, it follows that the design of the same can be considered one of the most important steps in the development of an entire software system.

The interface design includes at least 29 % of the development software budget; data analysis also showed that the user interface contains 47–60 % of the total lines of a simple application code [1].

The evolution of the various versions of popular operating systems has focused mainly on changing the graphical interface and its interaction mode. Similarly, a web site consists of a set of web pages that represent the interface through the users access to web content. These are just some examples of applications marked by graphical user interfaces. Then, the interest in the design and development of interactive visual applications has increased dramatically in recent years.

In this perspective, the usability of an interface is fundamental to the success of an application. A poor user interface can make the application not useful or not accepted [2].

The most intuitive definition of usability it is the property of the system that defines its degree of simplicity of use in terms of learning, storage and efficiency.

To create a "usable" system, the designer must create a good conceptual model of the system (correct, consistent, simple) and must be able to effectively transmit to the user through the interface that must "accommodate" the expectations of the system mental model of the end user.

It is possible to measure how a GUI is "usable" by several evaluation methods and tools of the same.

Formal techniques support the process of usability engineering. Campos and Harrison [3] describes a technique that explores those features of a specific design that fail to satisfy a set of properties. It also analyzes those aspects of the design where it is possible to quantify the cost of use. The IVY implemented tool is concerned with modeling interactive devices and the analysis of models using model checking tools. The results of the analysis is presented both in terms of animations or prototypes of scenarios and the understanding of the scenarios themselves.

In [4] we have presented a methodology to specify and evaluate interactive visual environments, in particular web interfaces, based on the SR-Action Grammars formalism and we present a bottom-up approach to aid the designer to develop graphical applications that automatically respect a significant number of usability rules before the software is released and tested by standard methods. We show how it is possible to assess the usability metrics of consistency, completeness and user control by means of checks performed at a high level of abstraction.

On the other hand, the evaluation programs typically analyze the underlying interface source code that, obviously, must be available, if the source code is not available is impossible to perform such automatic evaluation. The process described in [5] analyzes the source code of a visual application, the design model of its interface, the graphical aspects and the interaction mechanisms implemented in each frame, panel and/or page of the system, to produce a report of the quantitative evaluation of heuristic factors.

Silva et al. [6] describes the use static analysis techniques to generate models of the user interface behavior from source code. One particular type of model that the tool is able to generate is state machines. Models help in graphical user interface inspection by allowing designers to concentrate on its more important aspects.

The systems AETCC (automatic evaluation tool for consistency checking) base their approach on a essential prerequisite: have access to software source code in question. Of course, this prerequisite is satisfied in the case in which the evaluation is performed, for example, by the developers of the product, or in the case of open source programs, otherwise, it is evident the impossibility of using these instruments.

In this perspective, in this chapter we present a fully automated system that uses an alternative approach for the evaluation of some metrics of usability of GUIs, independent of the source code and based only on the analysis of visual components identified and classified using image processing algorithms. The next section describes the implemented tool. Section 3 presents some conclusions and further refinements.

2 The Implemented Tool

The automated tools previously examined use a back-side approach, which derive from the analysis of the "hidden" elements (source code, logs, etc.) of the system, to evaluate graphical interfaces.

Our idea, on the contrary, is to use a front-side type approach: starting from the visual information of the system or by what the user sees on his monitor and the related objects with which he interacts, in a deductive manner, we deduce the structure and the type of the elements of the interface. In particular, the graphical components of the examined interface are identified and classified by image processing algorithms; an automated mechanisms of interaction is implemented to check the interaction points. In this perspective, we have implemented a tool in Java (named JSherlock, variant of the name of the program written in ANSI C from Mahajan and Shneiderman [1]) using the MVC (Model-View-Control) architectural pattern.

Here we limit ourselves to the description of the implemented tool without showing the details of the methodology underlying the algorithms defined.

The execution flow is divided in the following six modules:

1. Capture and cleaning
2. Segmentation
3. Hierarchy building
4. Automatic interaction
5. Evaluation
6. Result display.

The structure of the several packages reflects, at implementation level, the modules of the system. The it.unibas.jsherlock.view includes the classes relating to the rendering of the model, the controller sends the requests of the user and allows the controller to select a particular view.

The it.unibas.jsherlock.controller defines the flow of execution. It maps the user requests into actions performed on the model and select a view in relation to this requests. For each input event has been written a class that describes the action to be performed on the model and selects the next view. The image segmentation, the hierarchy tree construction, the automatic interaction process and the consistency evaluation of the GUI are delegated to specialized classes defined "engine": "Engine Segmentation", "Engine Hierarchy", "Engine Interaction", "Engine Evaluation".

The it.unibas.jsherlock.model encapsulates the application state.

Figure 1a shows an example of capture of a page of a web site to analyze. At present, the tool has been tested for web interfaces, and then the input data required are the web page URL to be evaluated and the path of the browser. The "Engine Interaction" orders to the browser, by pressing a button, to switch to full screen mode, performs a series of screenshots of the monitor (10) at intervals of 1 s, returns to the main process list of the captured images.

Figure 1b shows the result of the segmentation phase. The implemented segmentation strategy is the split and merge type. At first, the split phase divides the image into many regions as there are pixels in the image, each region will be composed initially of a single pixel. Then, a connection is created for each pair of adjacent regions in one of 4 directions; a connection is an abstraction that encapsulates the following information: a reference to the two connecting regions, the degree of similarity of the regions involved by the connection.

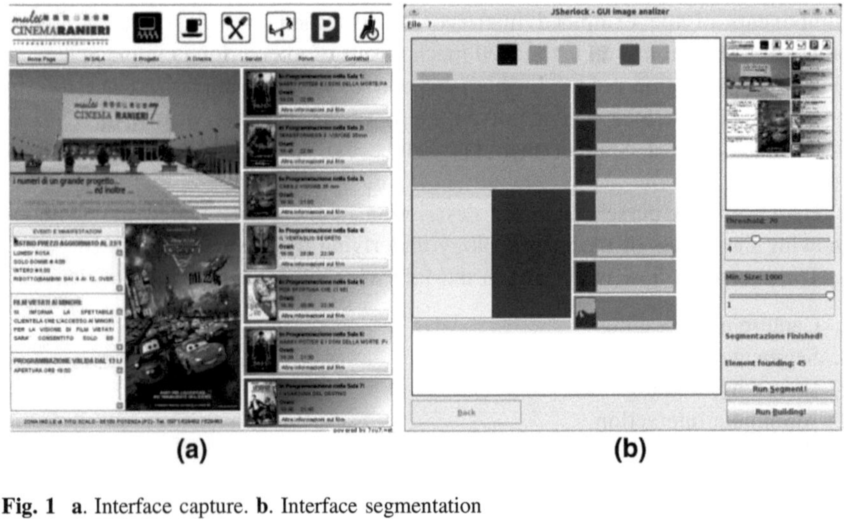

Fig. 1 **a**. Interface capture. **b**. Interface segmentation

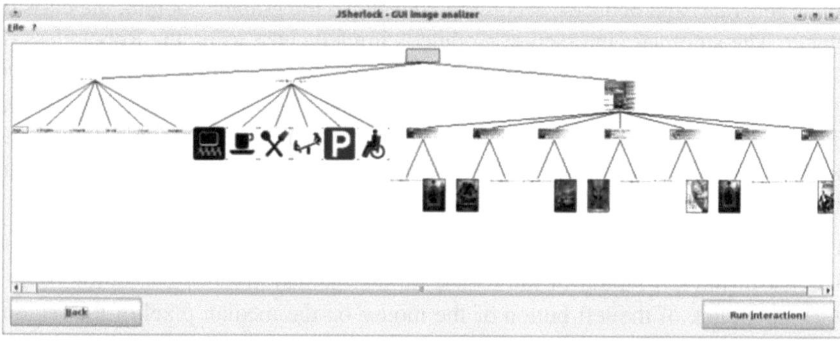

Fig. 2 The hierarchy tree

The third task of our algorithm is to create the hierarchy of elements: the correct taxonomy of the objects on the page is reconstructed through the creation of relationships between them. The tree is the data structure used to describe the relations between the several elements of the GUI and their hierarchical composition.

The father–son type relationship allows us, in fact, to assert that one or more elements (child nodes) are contained in an element "container" (father node) (Fig. 2).

The approach is bottom-up. At first, are inserted all the regions in a list and sorted according to their coverage area (i.e. the area of the minimum rectangle that contains all the pixels of the region). It will always greater than or equal to the number of pixels present in the same. An iterative loop is performed on each region of the list obtained (the region is named "examined region" or "son candidate region"). At each step of the main loop, a nested loop to the first is performed from the smallest region with an area greater than that at issue and iterates until the end of the list (this region is named "compared region" or "father candidate region"). At each step of the nested loop is executed the following check: if the surface of the examined region is fully understood in the surface of the compared region, the iteration stops and the examined region is included in the set of child-nodes of the father candidate region, creating a new type of parent–child hierarchical relationship; otherwise the cycle continues repeating on the next father candidate region. At the end, we will have a certain number of nodes with one or more child nodes without parent node (root), some with one or more child nodes and a single parent node (intermediate nodes) and then some with a single parent node without child nodes (leaves). If there are nodes without a parent node is created a dummy node that will become the new root of the tree and all nodes in the previous step become his children.

To analyze the interaction mechanism of the examined interface, an automatic interaction process is implemented. The task was divided into two modules: an automatic interaction module that simulates the input events generation, a decision algorithm that chooses with which interface element to interact (and what type of input generate) and deduces, according changes to the graphics output, the class of object. The automatic interaction module is implemented using the Robot class of the java.awt package, the related methods allow the generation of system native input events. The decision algorithm is implemented using the "Interaction Engine". Starting from the hierarchy of elements, the program performs a post-order visit of the tree and for each object indicates to the Robot to interact with it through the following events:

- Input/output of the mouse in/out the region;
- Click of the left button of the mouse on the median pixel of the region;
- Double click of the left button of the mouse on the median pixel of the region;
- Enter a character.

For each event you enter will be made a new screenshot of the page. Next, we will examine the results of the XOR logical operator between the screenshot of the captured image and the screenshot before interaction. If the result is true, the robot concludes that the element with which it has interacted is dynamic and its type (button, text area, links). The automatic interaction phase ends with a step of refinement of the results by implosion of buttons, links or defragmentation of introducing a new hierarchy among the elements of the tree.

The "Evaluator Engine" performs the GUI evaluation of the inconsistencies.

Based on Nielsen's heuristics examined [7], were identified 15 usability metrics for the automatic evaluation of the consistency of the interface through the proposed approach:

1. *Aspect ratio*. It is the ratio between the height of a window and its width. The numbers in the range from 0.5 to 0.8 are acceptable. This ratio must be the same if there are more screens of the same system, including dialog boxes.
2. *Widget nesting*. A nesting high imply an incorrect design and excessive use of containers. The widgets such as buttons, labels and text-area should not exceed the third level of nesting.
3. *Relationship between background and widgets*. It is the ratio between the non-widget and the total area of the interface, expressed in percentage. High numbers (>80) interfaces are "thin", low numbers (<30) show interfaces too "heavy".
4. *Widgets density*. It is the number of widgets divided by the total area of the screen (multiplied by 100,000 to carry out normalization). Numbers greater than 100 indicate that in a small area are present a relatively large number of widgets. This number is a measure of the crowding of the widgets on the screen.
5. *Widgets deployment*. It indicates a measure of how equally distributed the widget on the screen. Are measured twice: one to measure the horizontal balance (the ratio of the total area of the widget, in the left half of the screen, with the total area of the widget in the right half) and the vertical equilibrium,

which compares the top with the lower one. Higher values, between 4 and 10, show screens unbalanced. A limit value 10 represents areas empty or nearly empty (for example, a dialog box which has a single button).

6. *Margins between widgets.* The measure of the margin between a widget and another and between a widget and the edge of the screen. Values below a certain level (i.e. 5 pixels, or 1/10 of its size) are considered inappropriate. In addition, children of the same container widget should have the same margins.
7. *Widgets alignment.* All nodes, children of the same node ("brothers" node), must have at least one coordinate in common among those of the 4 possible corners. Otherwise, a mismatch is reported.
8. *Color widgets.* The color distribution (histogram), applied only to the widget is calculated, with the exception of the pictures (if possible). A good deployment must contain 2 or 3 peaks: a greater number of peaks or a flat histogram indicate the use of an excessive number of colors.
9. *Background color.* The color distribution (histogram), applied only to the non-widgets area is calculated. A good deployment must bear only one peak of color: a greater number of peaks or a flat histogram indicate that the interface has an unclear background.
10. *Easily recognizable edges in widgets.* Widget free edge are acceptable only if they have a very high contrast with the background (in the case of the Euclidean distance at least greater than the value 100).
11. *Widgets shape and size.* The widgets that are contained in the same physical or logical container (brother nodes in the tree hierarchy) should have similar values such as size, shape and aspect ratio, (same order of magnitude or ratio close to the value 1).
12. *Clear and recognizable buttons.* Each button interface must know them well in terms of contrast, that there must be a high contrast between a button node and its father node (in the case of the Euclidean distance at least greater than the value 200). In addition, each node button (identified by mouse click) must show a clear change of state on mouse over.
13. *Permitted actions and immediate feedback.* Each input action should not lead in an inconsistent state or system failure. For every action there must be a clear and visible change. In the case of lengthy operations, the processing state of the system must be communicated to the user.
14. *Reversibility.* At any time should be possible to return to the previous state of the system.
15. *Enter text* (input area). The text area should have a single background color. The contrast between the entered text and the background must be very high (in the case of the Euclidean distance for example at least greater than the value 300).

Then, the evaluation process will run for each element or set of elements classified, all the controls listed above. At the end of the evaluation process, each node is assigned a list of the inconsistencies identified and a score (rating between 1 and 10), which should indicate the "quality" of the node. The evaluation result will be shown to the user in a simplified or detailed manner. The "aggregated" first form for each element shows a numerical score between 1 (maximum score) and 0 (minimum score). For the root node, the score is computed using a recursive relationship that links the inconsistencies of the node to the score of its child-nodes. The second form of use of the visualization of the output is to display a list that lists the inconsistencies identified for each node of the hierarchy. For the i-th element, the list presents the following information: the upper-left pixel coordinates, size (width and height), surface, medium color, dynamic nature, listened the event list, inconsistencies list; evaluation degree.

3 Conclusions

In this chapter, we have presented a tool that implement a methodology "front-end" to evaluate the graphical properties of visual user interfaces using image processing algorithms and an automatic interaction technique to analyze the interaction elements of the GUI. Using this system, we have examined any web interfaces and it has proved to be easy to use and objective in the production of the results. However, the efficiency of the tool could be improved through the use of: OCR systems and inference engines.

Obviously subjective aspects of usability as the sense of satisfaction are not measurable characteristics with automated methods. But the metrics evaluated using the proposed methodology is a useful complement to standard techniques of evaluation.

References

1. Shneiderman, B., & Mahajan, R. (1997). Visual and textual consistency checking tools for graphical user interfaces. *IEEE Transactions on Software Engineering archive*, *23*(11) (Nov 1997).
2. Shneiderman, B. Designing the user interface. 4D, Boston: Addison-Wesley.
3. Campos, J. C., & Harrison, M. D. (2009). *Interaction engineering using the IVY Tool,—EICS '09: Proceedings of the 1st ACM SIGCHI Symposium on Engineering Interactive Computing Systems.*
4. Cassino, R., & Tucci, M. (2011). Developing usable web interfaces with the aid of automatic verification of their formal specification. *Journal of Visual Languages & Computing*, *22*(2), 140–149 (Jan 2011).
5. Cassino, R., & Tucci, M. (2007). *Usability evaluation of interactive visual applications: A quantitative approach: DMS'07—Proceedings of the 13th International Conference on Distributed Multimedia Systems—San Francisco Bay, USA* (6–8 Sep 2007).

6. Silva, J. C., Creissac, J. C., & Saraiva, J. A. (2010). GUI inspection from source code analysis. Foundations and techniques for open source software certification (Vol. 33).
7. Nielsen, J. (1994). Heuristic evaluation. In J. Nielsen & R. L. Mack (Eds.), *Usability inspection method* (pp. 25–62). New York: Wiley.

Part VIII
Information and Knowledge Management

The Role of Roles in Eunomos, a Legal Document and Knowledge Management System for Regulatory Compliance

Guido Boella, Llio Humphreys and Leendert van der Torre

Abstract Legal ontology is one of the most researched areas of Artificial Intelligence and Law, but is less applied in the compliance world. In this chapter we discuss the application of a domain-specific ontology building tool used for compliance monitoring with suitable extensions for modelling duties and roles. We first provide a description of the Eunomos package, before describing in detail the extensions with duties and roles applied to the Eunonmos ontology so that compliance officers can research laws and monitor compliance within the same web environment.

1 Motivations and Research Question

The law is getting more and more complex and difficult to understand due to subsidiarity, specialisation and the increasing power of state authorities. In Italy, for example, finance law is one area of the law which is so complex and ever-changing that they employ or sub-contract compliance officers to monitor and check that banking processes remain compliant. This is largely due to a fundamental change in the law on accountability of financial institutions, a change that has resulted in continuous clarification and extension of the law over the last decade.

G. Boella (✉) · L. Humphreys
Università di Torino, Torino, Italy
e-mail: guido@di.unito.it

L. Humphreys
e-mail: humphreys@di.unito.it

L. Humphreys · L. van der Torre
University of Luxembourg, Luxembourg city, Luxembourg
e-mail: leon.vandertorre@uni.lu

P. Spagnoletti (ed.), *Organizational Change and Information Systems*, Lecture Notes in Information Systems and Organisation 2, DOI: 10.1007/978-3-642-37228-5_44,

Until ten years ago *Societas delinquere non potest*[1] was the dominant doctrine in Italian financial law. This meant that if the director of a bank or insurance company committed a crime, he may be tried and punished, but the company would not be liable. Legislative Decree 231/2001 was a radical piece of legislation that changed the nature of legal obligations for banks and insurance companies. Now such organisations can be held responsible for criminal activities carried out by their employees even when such activities were not prescribed or authorised. Legislative Decree 231/2001 and related legislation impose permissions, obligations and constraints on financial professionals in given situations.

Financial institutions have a strong business motivation for ensuring they comply with the law, and demonstrating that they have systems and procedures for compliance monitoring. If a financial organisation has demonstrated that they have a responsible monitoring system in place but an employee still manages to engage in illegal activities under their watch, the organisation can avoid paying out substantial fines and incurring damage to its reputation. Financial institutions manage compliance law by summarizing the legislation in a series of so-called prescriptions and mapping them to processes in the workflow. However, financial institutions do not make the best use of technology. They employ legal researchers who trawl through various sources to manage information about legislative changes and influential cases. For particularly difficult areas, they seek the expensive guidance of lawyers expert in this field. But the information is sought on an ad-hoc basis, is not stored and managed effectively, and not linked to terminology and relevant legislation that are crucial to a true understanding of the law.

Boella et al. [1] provides a general description of Eunomos, a legal document management system developed by the University of Turin for researching legislation and legal terminology. Boella et al. [2] describes the extension of the Eunomos ontology with a prescription data type so that a compliance officer can view related legal requirements, accountable job roles and sanctions in one web view. This bases on the Eunomos system and introduces in it the notion of role. Roles have several uses in a system to support compliance:

- Prescriptions are associated with roles rather than individuals.
- Participation in processes is distributed in terms of roles.
- Permissions to access resources, primarily to information systems, are associated with roles, as in the Role Based Access Control (RBAC) methodology.
- Constraints like separation of duties are expressed in terms of roles, e.g., preventing role combinations such as receiving checks (payment on account) and approving write-offs, depositing cash and reconciling bank statements, approving time cards and having custody of pay checks.
- Risk management is often based on the responsibilities assigned to the different roles.

[1] (Savigny - XIX Century)

However, often all these dimensions are kept separate, leading to problems when they interact. For examples, access permissions are assigned by offices which do not have a complete picture of the evolution of who plays which role. Analogously separation of duties fails when people change role after static verification of the constraints. Finally—the example we will consider in this chapter—roles associated with duties in the law are not always immediately mapped onto processes of an organization. The problem is that there is no common conceptual framework defining the notion of a role. Ontology is the discipline in Computer Science which studies how to provide a formal, explicit specification of a shared conceptualisation. The research question of the chapter is: how to construct an ontologically well founded notion of role that is practical at the same time?

The methodology of this chapter is to start from the foundational work of Boella and van der Torre [3] on roles and adapt it to a practical scenario. In this chapter we will focus on the interplay between roles and duties and processes, while we leave other issues as future work. Moreover, here we do not consider in detail the ontology of processes and we abstract them as concepts with relationships concerning the participants.

The intersection between legal and organisational knowledge is a difficult domain to model in an ontology because many legal and organisational concepts are socially constructed objects that may or may not have a close connection to physical reality. Moreover, relating organisational roles as defined in legislation to other concepts is impossible with classical is-a hierarchies only [4].

2 Eunomos for Compliance

2.1 The Eunomos' Infrastructure

Eunomos is a knowledge management system that enables users to research laws and legal concepts. Eunomos offers a highly structured framework with legislative XML, enabling users to view relevant legislation from various sources from the same web interface, and access a database of duties and prohibitions, annotated with explanations in natural language, as well as an ontology of terms that are relevant for particular domains. Each piece of legislation in the Eunomos database is stored in accordance with the Norme in Rete (NIR) legislative XML standard using the ITTIG CNR parser[2].

The Legal Taxonomy Syllabus ontology [5] integrated in Eunomos was originally modelled on European Consumer Law, where terms can mean different things in different languages, within European versus national jurisdictions, and

[2] The conversion in the current version of the software is done using the XMLeges Marker tool developed by Istituto di Teoria e Tecniche dell' Informazione Giuridica (ITTIG) of Florence (http://www.xmleges.org)

within different domains. As such the main assumptions of the Legal Taxonomy Syllabus ontology come from studies in comparative law and ontologies engineering. Eunomos also contains an extended structure for certain concept types. We discuss the Prescriptions and Roles extensions below.

2.2 Prescriptions

Within Eunomos, a prescription is a legal rule abstracted from legislation and linked to information that is relevant to that particular rule. Each prescription is necessarily connected to other concepts in the ontology by the relations:

Deontic clause: the type of prescription: obligation, prohibition, permission, exception.
Active role: the addressee of the norm (e.g., director, employee).
Passive role: the beneficiary of the norm (e.g., customer).
Crime: the type of crime resulting from violation of the prescription, often defined in other legislation such as the Penal Code.
Sanction: a concept describing the sanction resulting from the violation.

Figure 1 illustrates a prescription together with its links to other concepts.

Each prescription contains links to the articles of legislation in which the prescription is defined. Note that some prescriptions can span several paragraphs and/or articles of a piece of legislation; conversely a single paragraph within one article can include more than one prescription. A macro-prescription can also be stored which specifies a general principle and contains links to specific prescriptions that come under this principle. For each prescription, the relevant text are quoted and then described in natural language.

2.3 Roles

To ensure traceability and accountability, each business process is subject to prescriptions either directly or via the links to roles and the individuals who act in those roles, depending on whether the prescription refers to processes or roles.

Modelling roles is not as easy as it seems—how can ontologies model the fact that roles can be held by more than one person, that roles can be vacant, that individuals can change jobs or hold multiple roles concurrently or switch between different roles at different times, or that roles can take on other roles. The latter is a real issue in compliance—a general manager or managing director assumes the role of a public officer in situations where the bank performs services in the public interest, e.g., collecting taxes on behalf of the state, and is then subject to prescriptions that apply to public officers. The issue of changing jobs can also cause problems such as conflict of interest. For instance, the law states that the same

Fig. 1 The description of a prescription with the related concepts

person cannot approve their own expenses. However it is perfectly conceivable that an employee might submit an expenses claim as a sales representative, move to an expenses administration role, and end up monitoring their own expenses claims.

Even if it is well recognized that roles are a representation primitive which should be described in the meta-ontology, we adopt a pattern based approach which allows roles to be expressed in current ontology formats such as Web Ontology Language (OWL), the de facto standard language for ontology. This not only simplifies the adoption of the notion of roles but also allows roles to be integrated with legacy systems.

In this chapter we use as an example a subtle interaction between roles concerning prescriptions and roles concerning processes.

In art. 318 of the Penal Code "public officers" or persons involved in functions of public service (*pubblica utilità*) are subject to obligations to prevent corruption. This norm would not appear to be relevant for a private institution like a bank.

However, in Italy, there is a relationship, since banks can provide functions of public service, and banks need to know which employees are subject to these obligations. We can make this reasoning only by analysing which roles in the organization participate in processes which can be considered a public service: the reasoning pattern is that the subjects (here called activeRole) of the obligations are not only agents playing the role of public officer, but also further roles (e.g., bank director) when they are considered as public officers, due to the kind of processes they are involved into.

Note that there are several complexities concerning the meanings of the term "role" in this example. First of all, we have the notion of social role, an individual of type agentive entity, which is part of an organization. E.g., the director is a role of a bank and public officer a role of the public administration. The second issue is the notion of a participant in a process, a processual role. There are subtle interplays between these two notions. On the one hand, processual roles connect processes to social roles: e.g., the bank director (a social role) is the activeRole of the process of giving loans or collecting taxes. On the other hand, as agentive entities, social roles such as bank director can play other social roles. Hence, the bank director plays the role of public officer when involved in some process. Due to the anti-rigidity of this property (i.e., it can change over time), the director cannot be considered as a specification of public officer so the former is not connected to the latter in the "is-a" hierarchy but by a playerOf relation. Note that in our model it is the director role instance which is playing the role of public officer and not the directly the person who is acting as director: the rationale is that in the latter case we would lose the intuition that the person is a public officer only *qua* director.

To model these distinctions, we resort to two patterns for modelling roles in ontologies. The first is to model processual roles, with a simplified view of roles. The other is to model social roles in a full fledged mode. To model processual roles we regard them as properties or relations, without introducing a proper role concept to be instantiated. E.g., the active role is represented with an activeRole property. Its domain and range represent the context on which the role depends and the potential players that can play the role, respectively. Therefore, the role makes sense only if individuals of the process and players exist.

We adopt the same solution for roles concerning prescriptions: active and passive roles. Using [6]'s terminology, we call them relational roles.

Meanwhile, social roles, since they are individuals, are modelled using a more complex pattern (see Fig. 2). We introduce role concepts, and specifications of that class, e.g., director. Roles are related to a context, the organization class via a roleOf relation and their possible players are connected via a playerOf relation (a person in the case of a director). On the one hand, role concepts are associated with an organization concept which provides the context of the role. On the other hand, they are also associated with the class of the player, creating a restriction on the possible players. The introduction of role concepts means that the roles are treated as instances separated from the instance of their players. This allows properties to be associated with the role, which are different from that of the player. Moreover, it allows for identity of roles (thereby addressing the so-called counting problem) and the possibility that an individual can play multiple roles: this is represented by connecting the same individual as the player of several role instances. Dynamics of roles (players can stop playing roles) is ensured by changing the playerOf relationship.

Since Eunomos uses a lightweight ontology, in our model we do not consider explicitly restrictions on fillers of relations. However, constraints are ensured at the level of the insertion and modification interfaces and at the level of database, with a system of triggers for ensuring consistency. The reason for this is that roles have been added to a legacy system which started with the Legal Taxonomy Syllabus whose first aim is the acceptability to law scholars and practitioners. For example, a role instance must be always connected to an instance of an organization by a roleOf relation and to an instance of a class connected by the playerOf relation to the role class. Thus, the latter arrow in the figure does not mean that the instances of a player class must be always connected to an instance of the role class, since roles are anti-rigid by definition. Moreover, roles can be played by instances of different classes.

Figure 2 illustrates the example about public officers. On the top left corner we have the role concept associated with its context: an organization related with the roleOf relation. Each role can belong only to one organization, due to definitional dependence, while organizations can have multiple roles. However, as discussed above, we do not have such explicit constraint in the ontology. Each specialization of the role concept is related to a specialization of the organization class. In the figure, the director role is associated with a bank. Instances of director roles can be played only by instances of persons (see the playerOf relation). The director role participates in the process of collecting taxes with the processual role activeRole. Note that this process is also considered a public service besides being a process of a bank (processOf).

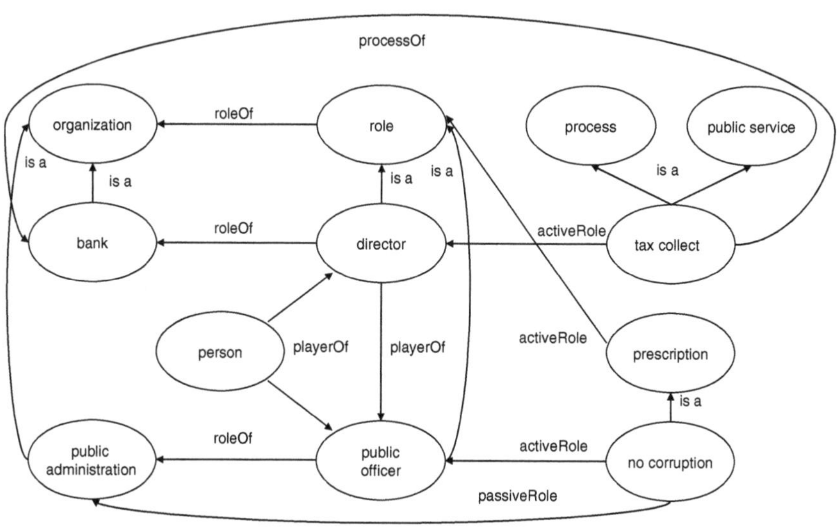

Fig. 2 The ontology of roles.

Analogously, the public officer role is a role of the public administration and can be played only by persons. The public officer is subject to the obligation not to be corrupted. The relation between the prescription and the social role of public officer is similar to the processual roles: the public officer is the active role in the prescription, while the public administration is the passive role (i.e., the beneficiary of the obligation). For simplicity we do not represent in the figure the link between processes and the organizations defining them: e.g., a public service is a process within a public organization. The link with the regulations (Art. 318 of Penal code) is not illustrated in the figure, but it is an essential component of Eunomos' ontology.

Coming to the main question of the example, the bank can understand who is subject in the bank to the prescription against corruption when there is a link playerOf between an instance of the role director and and one of the role public officer, a link which must be set when a director plays the role of public officer in the context of a process which is a public service.

The key to unravelling these problems is to look at the context—namely prescriptions, process universals and process instances. Prescriptions are assigned active and passive role relations to universal role concepts which are defined by the law. Universal processes are assigned active and passive role relations to universal role concepts defined by the organisation. Instance processes are assigned active and passive role relations to instances of roles defined by the organisation.

3 Related Work and Conclusions

There is a wealth of literature about roles [7], and we will focus here on only the most relevant work. The distinction between processual and social roles is inspired by Loebe [6], however we have a simplified view of processual roles in our model. Loebe [6], for the sake of generality proposes a unified model of processual and social roles, in which the former also have instances of role concepts. In our model processual roles are modelled as relations connecting processes (and prescriptions) to the players (which happen to be social roles). The model is very similar to the one of HOZO [8], with the exception that we do not model the aggregation of the role instance and the role player. In particular, we are inspired by the HOZO philosophy of mapping the notion of role onto traditional ontology patterns.

We have described a practical use of an ontological model of roles within a legal monitoring system for regulatory compliance. The basic ontology of prescriptions for compliance as described in [2] is suitable not only for navigating conceptual terms and linking to source legislation in a highly complex area of the law but also for managing structured information about the ever-evolving series of prescriptions that apply to the financial sector. This chapter has discussed a further extension to the ontology to reason about roles so as to enable monitoring of actual processes and ensure accountability on an individual level.

References

1. Boella, G., Humphreys, L., Martin, M., Rossi, P., & van der Torre, L. (2012). Eunomos, a legal document and knowledge management system to build legal services. In Proceedings of AI Approaches to the Complexity of Legal Systems Workshop (AICOL). Berlin: Springer.
2. Boella, G., Martin, M., Rossi, P., van der Torre, L., & Violato, A. (2012). Eunomos a legal document and knowledge management system for regulatory compliance. In Proceedings of Information Systems: a Crossroads for Organization, Management, Accounting and Engineering (ITAIS) Conference. Berlin: Springer.
3. Boella, G., & van der Torre, L. (2007). The ontological properties of social roles in multi-agent systems: definitional dependence, powers and roles playing roles. *Artificial Intelligence Law*, *15*(3), 201–221.
4. Steimann, F. (2000). On the representation of roles in object-oriented and conceptual modelling. *Data and Knowledge Engineering*, *35*(1), 83–106.
5. Ajani, G., Lesmo, L., Boella, G., Mazzei, A., & Rossi, P. (2007). Terminological and ontological analysis of european directives: multilinguism in law. In Proceedings of the 11th International Conference on Artificial Intelligence and Law (ICAIL) (pp. 43–48). ACM.
6. Loebe, F. (2007). Abstract versus social roles: Towards a general theoretical account of roles. *Applied Ontology*, *2*, 127–158.
7. Boella, G., van der Torre, L., & Verhagen, H. (2007). Roles, an interdisciplinary perspective. *Applied Ontology*, *2*(2), 81–88.
8. Mizoguchi, R., Sunagawa, E., Kozaki, K., & Kitamura, Y. (2007). The model of roles within an ontology development tool: Hozo. *Applied Ontology*, *2*(2), 159–179.

References

[illegible]

Modeling Collaboration for Mashup Design

Devis Bianchini, Valeria De Antonellis and Michele Melchiori

Abstract Enterprises often promote internal collaboration to improve performances, in terms of time and quality, of their design and operational processes. Recently, enterprise mashup has been introduced as an approach for quick developing applications which are created to satisfy short term business needs. Mashup development leverages on collaboration to integrate software components, called Web APIs, which can provide access to complex functionalities and rich data sources. To this aim, we propose a collaboration model-based approach that includes description of Web API features based on the ProgrammableWeb.com public repository and social relationships among developers. This model is proposed as part of the Enterprise 2.0 paradigm, that has been recently introduced as application of the Web 2.0 technologies and ideas to the enterprise environment. In the discussed model, a mashup developer is supported in searching for the other developers' assistance and advices according to different perspectives reflecting typical collaboration patterns: (1) experience on the use of specific Web APIs; (2) experiences on specific Web API technologies; (3) competencies in developing specific types of mashups.

1 Introduction

Collaboration is often promoted in enterprises to improve performances of enterprise processes in terms both of time and quality of the outputs. Recently, collaboration in enterprises can take advantage of the specialization of Web 2.0 social-based technologies to enterprise needs and requirements. This specialization is commonly referred as Enterprise 2.0 [1] and provides the knowledge workers

D. Bianchini (✉) · V. De Antonellis · M. Melchiori
Dipartimento di Ingegneria dell'Informazione, Università di Brescia,
via Branze 38, 25123 Brescia, Italy

P. Spagnoletti (ed.), *Organizational Change and Information Systems*, Lecture Notes in Information Systems and Organisation 2, DOI: 10.1007/978-3-642-37228-5_45,

with models and tools to enhance collaboration and content/application joint creation. Currently, a number of collaboration platforms is appearing [2–4] to provide enterprises with tools that allow for social linking and tagging of resources, that support the user feedback/opinions, and user-produced content management platforms (blogs and Wikis). For example, the YAMMER Web platform[1] allows an enterprise to create a private social network implementing collaborative workspaces for project team members and external selected partners. Another recent trend in enterprises is mashup [5] that has been introduced as development style for quick-to-build applications which are created to satisfy situational short term business needs by combining more Web APIs into a single lightweight Web application. A Web API can provide access to complex functionalities and rich data provided by sources either internal or external to the company. Mashup design and implementation typically leverages on collaboration to discover, understand and integrate Web APIs. On the one hand, developers can exploit a large and always growing collection of Web APIs described in public Web registries like ProgrammableWeb[2] or made available inside enterprises by means of searchable catalogs (e.g., IBM Mashup Center Catalog[3]). Beside technical documentation, Web registries provide also information about how APIs are used in mashups and user community feedback. On the other hand, mashup development is hindered by the heterogeneity of Web APIs and related documentation.

Basic steps in mashup development are: (1) searching and identifying the most suitable APIs; (2) understanding functional and nonfunctional features of the selected APIs with the purpose to compose them. Accordingly, research has been done to define search tools based on semantic/functional/non functional characterization of APIs [5], on their social characterization/tagging [6, 7], on past use/ collective knowledge of APIs [8], on techniques that mix social and functional features [9]. Some of these approaches support API composition based on semantic matching of I/O parameters [9, 10]. Mashup development exploiting collaboration in Enterprise 2.0 has been studied in [4] that propose reference architecture for a collaboration platform to provide knowledge workers with a component catalog and tools to simplify composition.

Also our proposal focuses on collaborative development in Enterprise 2.0 contexts. Specifically, with reference to mashup development, the cited search approaches focus on recommending Web APIs to the developer. Our proposal is complementary to these approaches and comes as a successive phase by suggesting to the developer those colleagues inside the enterprise that have useful knowledge about the selected Web APIs. We define the kind of advice that the developer can request on the basis of typical mashup collaboration patterns:

[1] https://www.yammer.com/

[2] www.programmableweb.com

[3] http://www-10.lotus.com/ldd/mashupswiki.nsf/dx/Introduction__Mashup_Center_2.0.0.2

(1) experience on the use of specific Web APIs; (2) experiences on specific Web API technologies; (3) competencies in developing specific types of mashups.

The main contributions of this chapter are: (1) a lightweight model based on largely accepted requirements to support the collaboration; (2) definition of collaboration use cases and patterns based on the model. The chapter is organized as follows. In Sect. 1.1 we present a brief motivating scenario. In Sect. 2, we introduce the collaborative model based on the concepts of: developer, Web API, mashup. In Sect. 3, we define the support given to developers in terms of use cases and collaboration patterns. In Sect. 4 we discuss some architectural issues of the proposal and in Sect. 5 we provide conclusive remarks and future work.

1.1 Motivating Scenario

Let us consider an enterprise with various branches and departments in which operate expert users and developers that need sometime to implement situational applications. For example, consider also a webmaster working for the marketing department of this enterprise that has to build an application to visualize on an interactive map, information about the customers, about sales and demographic data. The webmaster finds the APIs (developed internally, as part of the ERP, and published on the Web) that she/he needs implementing the single functional blocks. However, now she/he can face difficulties in: (1) using a specific API, because of not clear API documentation/semantics or because of the I/O parameters data format; (2) integrating the selected APIs, because of heterogeneity of documentation, languages, technologies.

2 Modeling for Collaborative Mashups Development

In this section we propose a lightweight model for collaborative developing in enterprises including social and usage information on Web APIs. Without losing generality, we can assume that this model maintains at least:

- Web APIs descriptions at the same level of detail of public registries like ProgrammableWeb.
- Social information about developers based on a specialization of FOAF[4].

ProgrammableWeb has been chosen because it is the most complete public registry of Web APIs and mashups. The choice of FOAF is due to the fact that it is a well known and standard proposal of ontology for conceptualization of people and social relationships. The model of social network, shown in Fig. 1, includes

[4] http://www.foaf-project.org/

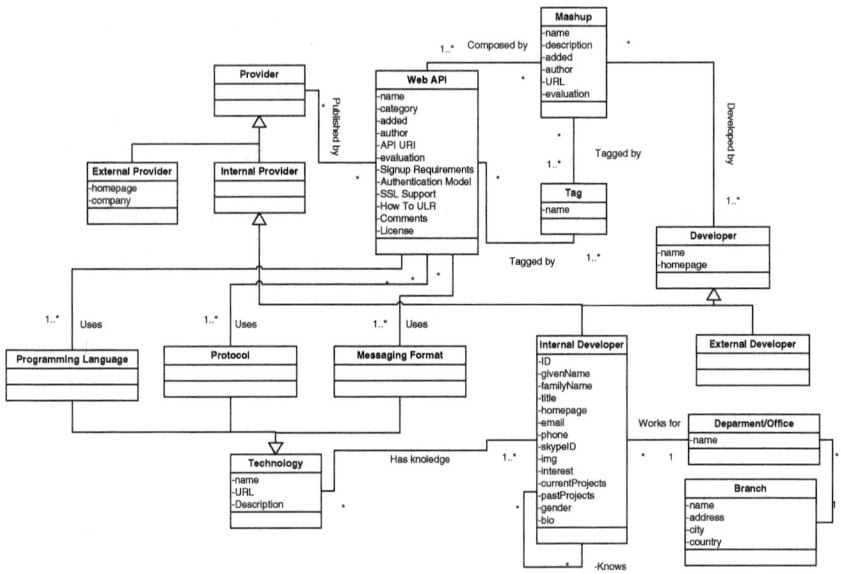

Fig. 1 UML model for the collaborative

that information that satisfies the requirements for the collaboration scenario considered in the following section. Note that the Person class of FOAF has been here specialized in the class Internal Developer. An Internal Developer can have knowledge about technologies used by Web API. The classes External Provider and External Developer allow keeping supplementary information about providers and developer of public Web APIs and mashups.

In the model we focus specifically on the classes Internal Developer, Mashup, Web API. We associate each object of these classes with a set of descriptors. A descriptor $\mathrm{Des_p(o_i)}$ for an object o_i according to a perspective p is defined as:

$$\mathrm{Des_P(o_i)} = \{\mathrm{t_{pi}}\} \tag{1}$$

where $\mathrm{t_{pi}}$ are terms extracted from the object descriptions, specifically from class attribute values and relationships involving the class of $\mathrm{o_i}$. In Table 1 is shown the applicability of perspectives to each considered class.

A developer is described by an organizational perspective (office/department, current projects, past projects), the Web APIs she/he has used/developed, the mashups developed, the technologies on which she/he has expertise and her/his social connections (developers that she/he knows, developers belonging to the same office, that have worked on the same project or on the same mashup). A Web API is described by the mashups in which it has been used, the technologies (programming languages, protocols, messaging formats), the developers that used or provided it. Finally, a mashup is specified by the Web APIs that it includes and the developer/s that developed it.

Table 1 Applicability of perspectives

	Perspectives					
	Organizational	**Web API**	**Mashup**	**Technologies**	**Developer**	**SocialConnectivity**
Developer	X	X	X	X		X
Web API			X	X	X	
Mashup		X			X	

3 Collaboration Patterns

Descriptors associated with developers, mashups and Web APIs enable the definition of collaboration patterns. A collaboration pattern is identified by a type of request. We define in a general way a request R for collaboration submitted by a developer D_R as follows.

$$R = < T_R, D_R, M_R, W_R > \tag{2}$$

where T_R is the type of request, $M_R = \{W^{Ri}\}$ is a set of Web APIs W^{Ri}, possibly empty, selected for implementing a mashup. For simplicity we can refer to this set as the mashup M_R. W_R is a Web API optionally specified.

With reference to the example described in Sect. 1.1, we distinguish three different collaboration use cases that D_R can invoke:

1. **Search for specific Web API collaboration:** the mashup designer is looking for collaboration from developers that have experience with a specific Web API W_R she/he has chosen and needs to use in the mashup. In this case, $R = <\text{wApi}, D_R, \emptyset, W_R>$.
2. **Search for Web API technology collaboration:** the mashup designer is looking for developers that have experience with specific technologies of the Web API W_R. For example, this case is invoked, as second option, if the result of application of the previous case *Search for specific Web API collaboration* is empty. As a consequence, the developer shifts the request to collaboration on the W_R technologies. In this case, $R = <\text{tech}, D_R, \emptyset, W_R>$.
3. **Search for Mashup collaboration:** the mashup designer is looking for collaboration with developers that have experience in mashups built with the same set of Web APIs of M_R or at least with a subset of it. In this case, $R = <\text{mash}, D_R, M_R>$ with M_R not empty.

3.1 Definition of Collaboration Patterns

The illustrated use cases are implemented by the following collaboration patterns that provide the functionalities to satisfy a request. Formally, a *collaboration pattern* is defined as a 4-uple:

$$CP_\pi = <R_\pi, m_\pi, \delta_\pi, \angle_\pi> \tag{3}$$

where π is the goal of the collaboration pattern. The goal π is chosen in the set {wApi, tech, mash} on the basis of the invoked collaboration use case. The purpose of a pattern CP_π is to suggest a ranked list of developers satisfying the request R_π. The metrics m_π are used to evaluate the degree of matching between a developer and the request R, on the basis of the specified goal. The threshold δ_π is used to filter out developers with low relevance with respect to R_π. A developer Dj is proposed to the mashup designer if $m_\pi(R_\pi, D_j) > \delta_\pi$. Finally, $\angle_\pi$ is a ranking function to present the developers relevant for R_π. In particular, $D_i \angle_\pi D_j$, that is D_i precedes D_j in the ranking, if $m_\pi(R_\pi, D_j) \geq m_\pi(R_\pi, D_j)$

Collaboration pattern metrics m_π are based on a notion of similarity between descriptors. The similarity between pairs of descriptors is defined according to the classical Dice's formula for similarity over sets:

$$\mathrm{Sim}(\mathrm{Des_P}(o_{i1}),\ \mathrm{Des_P}(o_{i2})) = \frac{2 \cdot |\mathrm{Des_P}(o_{i1}) \cap \mathrm{Des_P}(o_{i2})|}{|\mathrm{Des_P}(o_{i1})| + |\mathrm{Des_P}(o_{i2})|} \in [0\ldots1] \tag{4}$$

- With reference to the definition (3) of collaboration pattern, let be π = 'wApi' and let be $R = <wApi, D_R, \emptyset, W_R>$ the request (that is, $R_\pi = R$). The metric m_π used to evaluate the degree of matching of a candidate for collaboration D_j with the request R_π is defined as:

$$m_\pi(R_\pi, D_j = \begin{cases} 0 & \text{if } W_R \notin \mathrm{Des_{P1}}(D_j) \\ \alpha\,\mathrm{Sim_{P2}}(D_R), \mathrm{Des_{P2}}(D_j)) & \text{otherwise} \\ \quad + \beta\,\mathrm{Sim}(\mathrm{Des_{P3}}(D_R), \mathrm{Des_{P3}}(D_j)) & \end{cases} \tag{5}$$

with $\alpha + \beta \in [0\ldots1]$ and α, $\beta \geq 0$. The perspective P1 is 'Web API', P2 is 'Organizational' and P3 is 'SocialConnectivity'. That is, if the developer D_j has experience with W_R then her/his evaluation is not zero and is based on a weighted sum of two terms: (1) similarity of D_j and D_R with respect the Organizational perspective, (2) similarity of D_j and D_R with respect to the SocialConnectivity perspective. So, developers that have a higher number of social/organizational connections with D_R receive a higher degree because it is supposed to be easier to contact and involve them.

- Let be $\pi =$ 'tech' and R = <tech, D_R, $\varnothing$, W_R> the request. The metric m_π is defined for this case as:

$$m_\pi(R_\pi, D_j) = \begin{cases} 0 & \text{if } \mathrm{Sim}(\mathrm{Des}_{P1}(D_j), \mathrm{Des}_{P1}(W_R)) = 0 \\ \alpha\, \mathrm{Sim}(\mathrm{Des}_{P1}(D_j), \mathrm{Des}_{P1}(W_R)) & \\ \quad + \beta\, \mathrm{Sim}(\mathrm{Des}_{P2}(D_R), \mathrm{Des}_{P2}(D_j)) & \text{otherwise} \\ \quad + \gamma\, \mathrm{Sim}(\mathrm{Des}_{P3}(D_R), \mathrm{Des}_{P3}(D_j)) & \end{cases} \tag{6}$$

with $\alpha + \beta + \gamma \in [0\ldots1]$ and $\alpha, \beta, \gamma \geq 0$. The perspective P1 is 'Technologies', P2 is 'Organizational' and P3 is 'SocialConnectivity'. That is, if the developer D_j has used (at least partially) the technologies of W_R then her/his evaluation is not zero and is based on a weighted sum of three terms: (1) similarity between technologies on which D_j has expertise and the technologies used by W_R, (2) similarity of D_j and D_R with respect the Organizational perspective, (3) similarity of D_j and D_R with respect to the SocialConnectivity perspective.

- Let be $\pi =$ 'mash' and R = <mash, D_R, M_R > the request. The metric m_π is defined for this case as:

$$m_\pi(R_\pi, D_j) = \begin{cases} 0 & \text{if } \mathrm{Sim}(\mathrm{Des}_{P1}(D_j), M_R) = 0 \\ \alpha\, \mathrm{Sim}(\mathrm{Des}_{P1}(D_j), M_R) & \\ \quad + \beta\, \mathrm{Sim}(\mathrm{Des}_{P2}(D_R), \mathrm{Des}_{P2}(D_j)) & \text{otherwise} \\ \quad + \gamma\, \mathrm{Sim}(\mathrm{Des}_{P3}(D_R), \mathrm{Des}_{P3}(D_j)) & \end{cases} \tag{7}$$

with $\alpha + \beta + \gamma \in [0\ldots1]$ and $\alpha, \beta, \gamma \geq 0$. The perspective P1 is'Web API, P2 is 'Organizational' and P3 is'SocialConnectivity'. $\mathrm{Des}_{P1}(D_j)$ includes the Web APIs used in the mashups developed by D_j. That is, if the developer D_j has used (at least one of) the Web APIs in M_R then her/his evaluation is not zero and is based on a weighted sum of three terms: (1) her/his similarity with M_R with respect the Web API perspective, that is high similarity if D_j has developed mashups using the APIs in M_R, (2) similarity of D_j and D_R with respect the Organizational perspective, (3) similarity of D_j and D_R with respect to the SocialConnectivity perspective. Note that $\mathrm{Des}_{P1}(D_j)$ and M_R are both sets of Web APIs so it is meaningful to evaluate their similarity.

For each of these patterns, the parameters α, β, γ are initially set to default values. During a training phase with the involvement of developers, the values are adjusted to obtain the expected ranking.

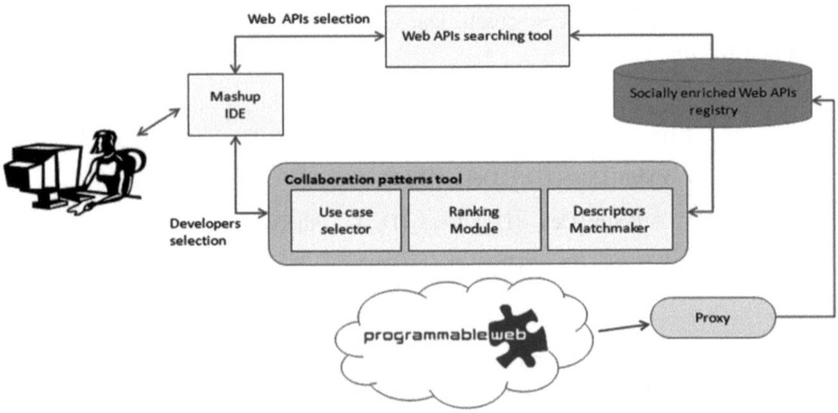

Fig. 2 Reference architecture for collaborative mashup development

4 Architectural Issues

In this section we briefly discuss some architectural points of our proposal. The architecture in Fig. 2 shows how developers can receive support by the joint use of a Web APIs searching tool and the collaboration patterns tool based on our proposal. In particular, the API searching tool allows the developer to explore and select the APIs described in a socially enriched registry based on the model presented in Sect. 2. The registry includes information also about public APIs whose description is obtained by accessing the programmableWeb content through a proxy that uses the programmableWeb API.[5] A prototype of the registry is under development based on the Neo4J NoSQL DBMS (http://neo4j.org/). The graph data model made available by Neo4J is suitable to represent social networks in a natural schema-less way as graphs. The selected APIs can be integrated by the developer inside an IDE mashup tool. The collaboration pattern tool allows the developer to select and invoke a collaboration use case. The matchmaker selects developer's descriptions from the registry and evaluates them with respect to the request. Finally, the ranking module orders the list of results to be returned to the developer.

5 Conclusions

In this chapter, we have proposed a collaboration model-based approach for mashup development in the context of Enterprise 2.0. Specifically, we introduce collaboration use cases to support the developer in automatically discovering

[5] http://api.programmableweb.com/

potential collaboration with other developers in the enterprise. Future work includes the extension of the model by considering additional information, like tags, Web APIs categories and user's feedbacks. Moreover, completing the development of the collaboration patterns tool and testing it on real case scenarios.

References

1. Mcafee, A. P. (2006). Of emergent collaboration enterprise 2.0: The dawn of emergent collaboration. *MIT Sloan Management Review, 47*(3), 21–28.
2. IBM, IBM connections. http://www-01.ibm.com/software/lotus/products/connections.
3. TELLIGENT, TELLIGENT enterprise. http://telligent.com/social-enterprise-software.
4. Soriano, J., Lizcano, D., Cañas, M. A., Reyes, M., & Hierro, J. J. (2007). Fostering innovation in a mashup-oriented enterprise 2.0 collaboration environment. *Business, 24*(1), 62–68.
5. Gomadam, K., Ranabahu, A., Nagarajan, M., Sheth, A. P., & Verma, K. (2008). *A faceted classification based approach to search and rank web APIs, 6th IEEE International Conference on Web Services (ICWS08)*.
6. Goarany, K., Kulczycki, G., & Blake, M. B. (2010). Mining social tags to predict mashup patterns. *Information Systems Journal*, 10(Smuc), 71–77.
7. Bianchini, D., De Antonellis, V., & Melchiori, M. (2012). Semantic collaborative tagging for web APIs sharing and reuse. In *Proceedings of the 12th International Conference on Web Engineering (ICWE'12)*, pp. 76–90. (LNCS No. 7387).
8. Greenshpan, O., Milo, T., & Polyzotis, N. (2009). Autocompletion for mashups. In *Proceedings of the 35th International Conference on Very Large DataBases (VLD B'09)*, pp. 538–549.
9. Tapia, B., Torres, R., & Astudillo, H. (2011). Simplifying mashup component selection with a combined similarity- and social-based technique. In A. Koschmider., E. Wilde & C. Zirpins (Eds.), *Proceedings of the 5th International Workshop on Web APIs and Service Mashups (Mashups '11)*. New York: ACM.
10. Bianchini, D., De Antonellis, V., & Melchiori. M. (2011). Semantics-enabled web APIs selection patterns. In *Proceedings of the ACM 15th Symposium on International Database Engineering & Applications (IDEAS '11)*. Lisbon, pp. 204–208.

Tabularizing the Business Knowledge: Modeling, Maintenance and Validation

Nicola Boffoli, Daniela Castelluccia and Giuseppe Visaggio

Abstract Achieving business flexibility implies to explicitly represent business knowledge and make it easy to understand for decision-makers. There is a renewed interest for decision tables as knowledge modeling formalism able to provide representation of the relationships among business conditions, actions and decisions with completeness and consistency. We explore the benefits of decision tables applied to modeling and management of business rules and constraints, finding the major advantages in their compact formalization, safe maintenance and automated validation.

Keywords Business knowledge · Business rules · Decision tables

1 Introduction

Today, companies operate in an ever-changing business environment, where web applications and web services are required to react quick and flexible in order to adapt to new business strategies and new products.

N. Boffoli (✉) · D. Castelluccia · G. Visaggio
Department of Informatics, University of Bari, Bari, Italy
e-mail: nicola.boffoli@uniba.it

D. Castelluccia
e-mail: daniela.castelluccia@uniba.it

G. Visaggio
e-mail: giuseppe.visaggio@uniba.it

N. Boffoli · G. Visaggio
SER&Practices, Software Engineering Research and Practices,
Spin-Off of the University of Bari, Bari, Italy

P. Spagnoletti (ed.), *Organizational Change and Information Systems*, Lecture Notes in Information Systems and Organisation 2, DOI: 10.1007/978-3-642-37228-5_46,

However, when a significant amount of business knowledge is contained only in the source code of applications or represented in the database tables, the communication between ICT professionals and business managers is difficult. Achieving flexibility implies to explicitly represent business knowledge and make it easy to understand for decision makers.

In particular, companies operate according to business rules and constraints that are not explicitly documented, but they are hidden inside the ICT system. The design document explains the ICT system in terms of business operations to be executed, business functions to be performed, data structure to be used, but often design doesn't model business rules and constraints. Modeling explicitly the business knowledge is the main challenge today.

In this context, there is a renewed interest for decision tables as knowledge modeling formalism. Though originally used as a technique to support programming, decision tables have proven an useful aid in modeling complex decision situations of various sorts [1–5], so that they are now spreading as an accepted approach focused on understanding business logic.

The reasons lie in a representation of the relationships among business conditions, constraints and rules in a complete manner, without inconsistencies. Decision tables assure a compact overview of a large number of information, modular knowledge organization, effective evaluation of consistency, completeness and redundancy.

In summary, the focal point of this chapter is decision tables as a modeling formalism for expressing the business knowledge.

We explore the benefits of decision tables searching for the following major advantages:

- they formalize knowledge and provide a compact and customizable view;
- they maintain knowledge as the business rules evolve and can be easily updated by decision makers;
- they validate knowledge by automated verification and validation checkers for preventing and detecting anomalies in decision points.

The chapter is structured as follows: the Sect. 2 introduces the decision table approach in order to represent the business knowledge; the Sect. 3 focuses on the decision table modeling and maintenance; the Sect. 4 explains the technique of knowledge verification and validation and the use of the decision table checkers; finally, the conclusions are drawn.

2 Business Rules and Decision Tables

Nowadays decision tables are continuously being used in representing and validating the complex business knowledge, so that business rules and constraints have to be modeled and managed. The essence of the business rules approach is to describe and automate aspects of the business function in a declarative instead of a procedural way. Odell defines business rules as "declarations of policy or conditions that must be satisfied" [6]. Decision tables seem to be particularly appropriate for eliciting, modeling and maintaining business rules.

A decision table is a tabular representation used to describe and analyze decision situations, where the state of a number of conditions determines the execution of a set of actions. Not just any combinations, however, but one in which all distinct situations are shown as columns in a table, such that every possible case is included in one and only one column (completeness and exclusivity).

Moreover, it is clear that the quality of the set of business rules is essential: that rules should not duplicate or conflict other rules, and they are correct, complete and simple. We give more details in the following (Sects. 3 and 4).

3 Business Knowledge Modeling and Maintenance

One of the main problems in modeling business knowledge is eliciting all the business rules and constraints in a complete and coherent manner. A list of business rules expressed in a formal language usually inherits a lot of contradictions and insufficiencies that have to be detected and solved. So business managers have to look inside the rule list for incomplete specifications, ambiguities, redundancies in order to direct and improve the elicitation process.

Otherwise, modeling with decision tables strategically supports the knowledge elicitation because they are able to address the complexity of the business domain and drive managers for thinking about all possible values of business conditions that imply several set of rules. Therefore, the number of conditions is only limited by human capabilities during the knowledge modeling using decision tables, that don't limit the size of decision space (Fig. 1).

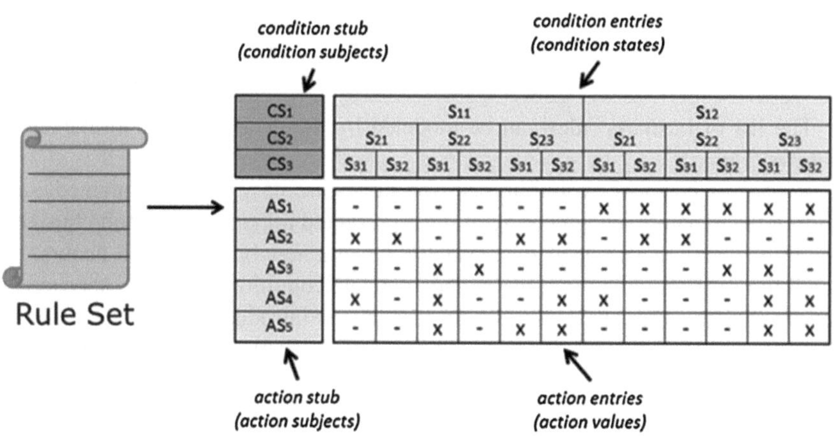

CS1	S11						S12					
CS2	S21		S22		S23		S21		S22		S23	
CS3	S31	S32	S31	S32	S31	S32	S31	S32	S31	S32	S31	S32
AS1	-	-	-	-	-	-	x	x	x	x	x	x
AS2	x	x	-	-	x	x	-	x	x	-	-	-
AS3	-	-	x	x	-	-	-	-	-	x	x	-
AS4	x	-	x	-	-	x	x	-	-	-	x	x
AS5	-	-	x	-	x	x	-	-	-	-	x	x

Fig. 1 A decision-table schema

A decision-making task can be tabularized by a decision table, where the state of a set of conditions determines the execution of a set of actions [7, 8]. A decision table has four quadrants: condition subjects, condition states, action subjects and action values. In details:

- the *condition subjects* quadrant contains all the possible decision points that may affect the set of actions to be performed;
- the *condition states* quadrant contains all the alternative values that are meaningful for the condition subjects;
- the *action subjects* quadrant contains all the possible actions to be performed;
- the *action values* quadrant identifies the relationship between each condition state and the corresponding actions.

The table is defined so that each combination of condition values corresponds to a set of actions to be performed.

Concerning the business rule formalism, it is based on *premises* that lead to *conclusions* by means of *inferences*. A mapping between business rule formalism and decision table formalism is in the following:

- each premise is represented by a combination of *condition states*;
- each conclusion is represented by a set of *action subjects*;
- each inference is represented by a column containing the *action values* entries.

In order to explain the application of decision table formalism, we provide the following illustrative example. A sales company offers special shipping fees, according to the number of items and the type of delivery. Basically, the business rules are the following ones:

1. *if the delivery is by* 1 *day then the basic cost is* € 35;
2. *if the delivery is by* 2 *days then the basic cost is* € 15;
3. *if the delivery is ordinary then the basic cost is* € 10;
4. *if the number of items is up to* 3 *then the cost has no extra else the cost depends from the delivery type;*
5. *if the number of items is more* 3 *then, for each extra item, add* € 7 *if* "1 *day" delivery, add* € 3 *if* "2 *days" delivery and add* € 2 *if ordinary one.*

The list of business rules can be modeled by the decision table formalism as follows (Fig. 2):

In case of business evolution, decision tables are easy to be maintained, supporting the dynamic reengineering of the represented relationships among business conditions, actions and decisions. Usually, when a new business need occurs, the condition set is modified (i.e. insert/update/delete conditions), a set of appropriate actions is defined, finally a new set of decisions is introduced in order to execute such actions according to the selected conditions. Exploiting the decision table formalism:

- if we need to formalize a new premise, we have to insert a new condition in the *condition stub* and enter new columns as many as its possible condition states;

C1. number of items	<=3			>3		
C2. delivery	1 day	2 days	ordinary	1 day	2 days	ordinary
A1. € 35,00	X	-	-	X	-	-
A2. € 15,00	-	X	-	-	X	-
A3. € 10,00	-	-	X	-	-	X
A4. add € 7,00 per extra item	-	-	-	X	-	-
A5. add € 3,00 per extra item	-	-	-	-	X	-
A6. add € 2,00 per extra item	-	-	-	-	-	X

Fig. 2 First modeling of the "Shipping" decision-table

- if we need to formalize a new conclusion, we have to insert new rows in the *action stub* as many as the actions needed for implementing the conclusion;
- if we need to formalize a new inference, we have to relate conditions state to actions through new decisions in the *action values* quadrant.

In this way, decision tables are able to track and manage all the emerging business needs with the purpose of maintaining their relationships with conditions and rules.

Even in more complex scenarios, decision tables are able to dominate the scalability issue. In fact, whenever domain requires decision table to grow quickly, decision table is able to minimize the size of decision space by means of columns contraction (excluding irrelevant combinations) and assures a compact and customizable view.

Resuming the illustrative example, the company needs to introduce a new shipping criterion, which provides the following business rule:

6. *if the purchase amount is more than* € 300 *then the ordinary delivery is free* (Fig. 3).

C1. number of items	<=3						>3					
C2. delivery	1 day		2 days		ordinary		1 day		2 days		ordinary	
C3. purchase amount	<=300	>300	<=300	>300	<=300	>300	<=300	>300	<=300	>300	<=300	>300
A1. € 35,00	X	X	-	-	-	-	X	X	-	-	-	-
A2. € 15,00	-	-	X	X	-	-	-	-	X	X	-	-
A3. € 10,00	-	-	-	-	X	X	-	-	-	-	X	X
A4. add € 7,00 per extra item	-	-	-	-	-	-	X	X	-	-	-	-
A5. add € 3,00 per extra item	-	-	-	-	-	-	-	-	X	X	-	-
A6. add € 2,00 per extra item	-	-	-	-	-	-	-	-	-	-	X	X
A7. FREE	-	-	-	-	-	X	-	-	-	-	-	X

Fig. 3 Maintenance of the "Shipping" decision-table

Table 1 Definitions of types of anomaly

Redundancy	
Redundant rule	1 rule is the combination of 2 other rules
Subsumed rule	2 rules with the same conclusion:
	the rule having the more specific premise appears before the rule having the less specific one
Duplicate rule	2 rules with the same premises and same conclusion
Unfirable rule	There is a combination of the condition values that is inconsistent and therefore the rule is unfirable
Unusable consequent	1 consequence not linked to any of the possible premises of the rules
Unnecessary condition	2 ore more rules whose combination makes irrelevant all (or part) the inputs of the premises
Inconsistency	
Ambivalent rules	2 rules (having the same or subsumed premises) lead to different conclusions. It is an anomaly if the problem domain requires one and only one conclusion
Conflicting rules	2 rules (having same or subsumed premises) lead to different AND conflicting conclusions
Deficiency	
Missing rules	There is a combination of allowable inputs for which it produces no conclusion

The new business rule can be easily embedded in the decision table by adding a new condition (C3 in bold-italic font), a new action subject (A7 in bold-italic font), and two appropriate action values ("x" in bold-italic font). New columns have been generated and added in the table (yellow columns).

4 Business Knowledge Verification and Validation

It is important that knowledge in specifications is correct, consistent, complete and non-redundant. However, validating a set of business rules is not a trivial task and often introduces unnoticed inconsistencies, contradictions or other anomalies.

The strength of decision table formalism is the prevention of a large number of anomaly types in decision points by means of an automated verification, that guarantees consistency of the business knowledge model and makes possible to integrate an incremental validation step into the modeling phase itself.

Starting from the classification by Preece et al. [9] it was investigated how these types of anomalies can be detected by decision table approach [10].

(a) **Non redundancy of decisions**. Redundancy usually does not lead to errors although it may harm efficiency. Redundancy affects maintenance and consistencies when changing the specifications. Some common forms of redundancy are the following: *subsumption, duplication, unfirable rule, unusable consequent, unnecessary condition.*

Table 2 Decision table-based prevention of anomalies

Redundancy	
Redundant rule Subsumed rule Duplicate rule	Anomalies prevention at table building time: the definition of a decision table only allows for tables where every possible case is included in one (completeness criterion) and only one (exclusivity criterion) column. The exclusivity criterion enables the prevention of duplicate and subsumed column pairs
Unfirable rule	Check on a column level: removal of the column that has inconsistent condition
Unusable consequent	Check on a row level: removal of the blank row
Unnecessary condition	Anomaly prevention at table construction time: the contracted decision table, which is obtained by merging neighboring columns with identical action values, will show a "-" entry for all condition entries associated with an irrelevant condition subject. If necessary the irrelevant condition subject can be removed
Inconsistency	
Ambivalent rules	Check on a column level: searching for columns which have more than "x" - removal of all the ambivalent "x" automated check: max 1 "x" per column
Conflicting rules	Check on a column level: Searching for columns which have more than "x" - removal of all the conflicting "x" - automated check: - max 1 "x" per column - rule constraint that avoid conflicting "x"
Deficiency	
Missing rules	Check on a column level: fill the blank column

(b) **Consistency of decisions**. Splitting the knowledge over a large number of rules, designed independently, may lead to problems of inconsistency, such as: ambivalent rules, conflicting rules.
(c) **Completeness of decisions**. Within a specific domain area, omissions often occur (missing rules)

In details, Table 1 contains the definitions of the main types of anomaly and Table 2 explains who decision table approach solves the different types of anomaly.

In the example (Fig. 4) a "conflicting rule" anomaly has been detected. The yellow columns highlight the inconsistency between the action A7 "FREE" and other actions (A3 and A6) that charge extra shipping cost. Such inconsistency can be easily removed by fixing the appropriate action values (changing each circled "X" in "-").

C1. number of items	<=3						>3					
C2. delivery	1 day		2 days		ordinary		1 day		2 days		ordinary	
C3. purchase amount	<=300	>300	<=300	>300	<=300	>300	<=300	>300	<=300	>300	<=300	>300
A1. € 35,00	X	X	-	-	-	-	X	X	-	-	-	-
A2. € 15,00	-	-	X	X	-	-	-	-	X	X	-	-
A3. € 10,00	-	-	-	-	X	X	-	-	-	-	X	X
A4. add € 7,00 per extra item	-	-	-	-	-	-	X	X	-	-	-	-
A5. add € 3,00 per extra item	-	-	-	-	-	-	-	-	X	X	-	-
A6. add € 2,00 per extra item	-	-	-	-	-	-	-	-	-	-	X	X
A7. FREE	-	-	-	-	-	X	-	-	-	-	-	X

Fig. 4 Conflicting rule anomaly detection in "Shipping" decision-table

5 Conclusion

Achieving business flexibility implies to explicitly represent business knowledge and make it easy to understand for decision-makers. There is a renewed interest for decision tables as knowledge modeling formalism. We explore the benefits of decision tables applied to modeling and management of business rules and constraints, finding the major advantages in their compact formalization, safe maintenance and automated validation.

By deepening the application of decision tables to modeling and maintenance of business knowledge, we find that decision tables strategically support knowledge elicitation and update with a compact and intuitive representation of the relationships among business conditions, actions and rules with completeness and consistency. Also in case of business evolution, our illustrative example proves that decision tables are easy to be maintained, supporting the dynamic reengineering of the represented relationships.

By analyzing the application of decision tables to knowledge verification and validation, we find that decision tables help preventing and detecting several types of anomalies in decision points by means of automated verification, that guarantees consistency of the business knowledge formalization and makes possible to integrate an incremental validation step into the modeling phase itself. The illustrative example shows how easy the detection of a "conflicting rule" anomaly is.

The study is encouraging and opens to further application of decision tables in different knowledge domains.

References

1. Boffoli, N., Caivano, D.,Castelluccia, D., and Visaggio, G. (2012) Business process lines and decision tables driving flexibility by selection. In: LNCS: Software composition (pp. 178–193). Heidelberg: Springer.

2. Ardimento, P., Boffoli, N., Caivano, D.,Castelluccia, D., & Visaggio, G. (2012) Innovation in business processes: Pattern-driven process modeling. In: Information systems: Crossroads for organization, management, accounting and engineering. ISBN: 978-3-7908-2788-0.
3. Boffoli, N., Caivano, D.,Castelluccia, D., Maggi, F. M., and Visaggio, G. (2008) Business process lines to develop service-oriented architectures through the software product lines paradigm. In: SPLC'08: 12th International Software Product Line Conference (pp. 143–147). IEEE Press.
4. Boffoli, N., Castelluccia, D., Maggi, F.M., Rutilo, R. (2008) Flexible process modeling through decision tables. In: IASTED Software Engineering.
5. Baesens, B., Mues, C., De Backer, M., Vanthienen, J., Setiono, R. (2003) Building intelligent credit scoring systems using decision tables. In: ICEIS No 2. pp. 19–25.
6. Odell, J. (1995) Business rules. In: Object Magazine pp. 53–56.
7. Maes, R., & Van Dijk, J. E. M. (1988). On the role of ambiguity and incompleteness in the design of decision tables and rule-based systems. *The Computer Journal, 31*(6), 481–489.
8. Vanthienen, J., Mues, C., Wets, G., & Delaere, K. (1998). A tool-supported approach to inter-tabular verification. *Expert Systems with Applications, 15*, 277–285.
9. Preece, A., & Shinghal, R. (1994). Foundation and application of knowledge base verification. *International Journal of Intelligent Systems, 9*(8), 683–701.
10. Vanthienen, J., Mues, C., & Aerts, A. (1998). An illustration of verification and validation in the modelling phase of KBS development. *Data Knowledge Engineering, 27*(3), 337–352.

MIX
Papier aus verantwortungsvollen Quellen
Paper from responsible sources
FSC® C105338
www.fsc.org

If you have any concerns about our products,
you can contact us on
ProductSafety@springernature.com

In case Publisher is established outside the EU,
the EU authorized representative is:
Springer Nature Customer Service Center GmbH
Europaplatz 3, 69115 Heidelberg, Germany

Printed by Libri Plureos GmbH
in Hamburg, Germany